PERFORMERS' RIGHTS

AUSTRALIA
LBC Information Services
Sydney

CANADA and USA
Carswell
Toronto

NEW ZEALAND
Brooker's
Auckland

SINGAPORE and MALAYSIA
Thomson Information (S.E. Asia)
Singapore

PERFORMERS' RIGHTS

by

Richard Arnold
Barrister
Gray's Inn, London

SECOND EDITION

LONDON • SWEET & MAXWELL • 1997

First edition 1990
Second edition 1997

First edition published in 1990 as *Performers' Rights and Recording Rights*

Published in 1997 by
Sweet & Maxwell Limited
of 100 Avenue Road, London NW3 3PF
Typeset by Tradespools Ltd, Frome, Somerset
Printed and bound in Great Britain
by Butler & Tanner Ltd, Frome and London

No natural forests were destroyed
to make this product only farmed
timber was used and replanted.

A CIP catalogue record for this book
is available from the British Library

ISBN 0 421 54140 7

Preface to the Second Edition

In the Preface to the first edition of this book, the enactment of Part II of the Copyright, Designs and Patents Act 1988 was somewhat rashly hailed as heralding a new era in the protection of performers from the unauthorised exploitation of their performances. In the event, the actual impact of the 1988 Act was muted. While it did give performers new legal rights and remedies, which were found to be of some use in combating bootlegging and piracy, the 1988 Act made surprisingly little difference to the economic position of performers. In the end it was significant that the legislature had stopped just short of granting performers a copyright.

At about the same time that the 1988 Act finally reached the statute book, however, developments were starting in Europe which have finally resulted in a material improvement of performers' economic status. The European Commission's Green Paper on *Copyright and the Challenge of Technology* led to the adoption of five Council Directives to harmonise aspects of the law of copyright and neighbouring rights. One of these, the Rental and Lending Rights Directive, which was eventually implemented in the United Kingdom on December 1, 1996, has brought performers a significantly higher level of protection throughout the European Union. Not only do performers now have half a copyright, but the United Kingdom has at long last given performers a legal right to equitable remuneration from the public performance and broadcasting of sound recordings so as to comply with its obligations under Article 12 of the Rome Convention. This improvement in their bargaining position should result in a significant increase in the revenues received by performers from this source.

Nor is this the end of the matter so far as the evolution of performers' rights is concerned. At the time of writing of this preface, a Diplomatic Conference in Geneva has just concluded a new WIPO Performances and Phonograms Treaty. Although a disappointment in some ways, this Treaty does break new ground in one respect, which is that it requires contracting parties to grant performers moral rights albeit only in respect of their live aural performances and performances fixed in phonograms. In addition the Commission of the European Communities has recently announced a further programme of action to harmonise aspects of copyright and neighbouring rights.

Part I of the first edition of the book is now of historical interest only and so has not been reproduced. All the historical material from the old Chapter 1 and Appendices 1 and 2 of the First edition has been brought together in an extended and revised Chapter 1. As result of the legislative changes since the first edition, every chapter of what was Part II of the book has been substantially rewritten. Old Chapter 4 has been divided into two: Chapter 2, dealing with subsistence and duration, and Chapter 3, much of which is new, dealing with ownership, licensing, equitable remuneration and the Copyright Tribunal. In addition, two entirely new chapters have been included: Chapter 8, dealing with other legal remedies for performers, and Chapter 9, dealing with performers' rights in other countries. Even where the statute has remained unamended, the treatment in the first edition has been reconsidered and a number of errors corrected.

I am grateful to Michael Flint of Denton Hall, Anne Rawcliff-King of PAMRA, Hugh Stubbs and Jean Hughes of Freshfields and Horace Trubridge of the Musicians' Union for their assistance in supplying information. Any errors that remain are entirely mine. I would be pleased to be notified of these. The law is stated as at January 1, 1997, although some subsequent developments have been included.

This edition is dedicated to Judith, whose gestation was rather shorter than that of the book, and so arrived first.

Richard Arnold
11 South Square
Gray's Inn
London WC1R 5EU

Contents

Appendices

CONTENTS

Table of Cases

Table of United Kingdom Statutes

Table of United Kingdom Statutory Instruments

Table of E.C. Legislation

Table of International Conventions

1. The Evolution of Performers' Rights in the United Kingdom

Introduction

This book is primarily concerned with the law of performers' rights and   **1.01**
recording rights under Part II of the Copyright, Designs and Patents Act 1988
(as amended). Before this is considered in detail, this chapter examines why
the law exists at all and how it has arrived at its present form. First the
rationale for giving performers rights at all will be briefly debated. Then, after
a short discussion of the concepts of copyright and neighbouring rights, the
history of the development of performers' rights will be described. The reason
for this exposition is that, as is so often the case with United Kingdom
intellectual property legislation, an appreciation of the history is necessary
for a full understanding of the present statutory provisions. Readers will also
find that it illustrates some of the points made in the section on the rationale
for protection. Finally, some proposals for reform are made.

Why Should Performers Have Rights?

The sighted reader of a book such as the present can read it without needing it   **1.02**
to be performed by another. Similarly a painting or sculpture speaks (or
should speak) for itself (however fashionable it may be to surround it with
large volumes of exegesis). A play or a piece of music, however, must be
performed to be fully appreciated. Indeed, many people are unable to read
music and so cannot appreciate it otherwise than through performance.
Going further, a film cannot really exist without performances (a screenplay
bearing an even remoter relation to the finished film than a script to a play
production). Thus the skill and labour of the performer is as essential to the
public enjoyment of such art works as is the inspiration and effort of the
author. Even where performance is not necessary, for example in the
recitation of a poem, the performer adds to the pre-existing work by the
process of interpretation, a process which requires a similar degree of artistic
creativity to that of authorship.[1] Moreover, a recording of a performance by

---

[1] The work of a performer may compared with that of a translator or arranger. Both take a
pre-existing text or score and translate it into a different form with, supposedly, no addition. Yet
translators and arrangers were recognised as authors and granted proprietary rights long before
performers. Although this equivalence was explicitly recognised at an early date by German law
(see note 50, below), it has not been widely accepted until recent years.

an actor or a musician can be reproduced and sold to millions round the world. Accordingly it might be thought obvious that a performer should be entitled to protection against the unauthorised exploitation of his or her performance in the same way as an author, namely by means of a proprietary right in the nature of copyright. The historical review below shows, however, that at least until recently this has usually been thought far from obvious. It is therefore necessary to consider the arguments for and against performers' rights. Before doing so, it is worth putting the question in context by briefly surveying the way in which the position of performers more generally has changed in history.

1.03   In traditional societies authors and performers were usually the same person, a poet, singer and/or storyteller. The development of religious choral hymns (dithyrambs) into drama in classical Greece led to an increasing separation between the functions of authorship and performance. Thus the Attic poet Thespis is usually considered to have founded drama in the sixth century B.C. by being the first to employ an actor (the Protagonist) in addition to the chorus and its leader to perform his works. Later authors such as Aeschylus and Sophocles added a second actor (the Deuteragonist) and then a third (the Tritagonist). As Athenian tragedy declined and comedy began to predominate in the fourth century B.C., the actors became more prominent and the names of a number have survived. These actors were, probably due to the association between Greek drama and religious festivals (particularly that of Dionysus), men of repute and members of guilds such as the Artists of Dionysus. Even in Greece, however, the social standing, if not the economic power, of the actors was lower than that of the authors. For example, Sophocles held important civic and military offices and appears to have been a man of considerable distinction among his contemporaries.

1.04   This difference between the respectability of authors and performers became more pronounced in Roman theatre. Although it does not appear that the theatrical profession was regarded as degrading in itself, so that Rome's most famous actor, Roscius Gallus, could be raised to equestrian rank by the dictator Sulla, the actors included people of little respectability such as courtesans and even slaves. From the end of the second century B.C. onwards, the distinction became acute as light entertainment such as mime, pantomime and farce predominated in the theatres while the writing of plays became the preserve of literary men such as Seneca, who wrote for private readings rather than public performance.

1.05   The rise of Christianity resulted in real hostility to theatre. No devout Christian would attend a performance, and to be an actor was forbidden on pain of excommunication. Ultimately, in the sixth century A.D. the theatres in Europe closed. For the next four hundred years the only providers of drama were itinerant minstrels and jongleurs. In the tenth century, however, the Church changed direction and began to act out the liturgy to communicate its message to its congregations. Initially, liturgical drama was simply an extension of the service, but gradually separate Easter and Christmas plays evolved. The performers were priests and choirboys, and so, once again, theatre gained some respectability. This led to the development of vernacular mystery plays performed by the laity outside the churches. Although no longer strictly liturgical, these plays escaped censure by being based on scripture and performed primarily by amateurs.

In the sixteenth century secular drama re-established itself throughout Europe. In Italy the *commedia dell'arte* emerged towards mid-century. In France, the Confrerie de la Passion, an association of Parisian burghers which performed religious plays, started presenting secular plays and comedies at the Theatre de l'Hotel de Bourgogne in 1548. In England Burbage built the first theatre in London in 1576 and gave a variety of secular entertainments there. These developments and similar ones in other countries gave rise to the first professional actors and later actresses. The social position of these performers remained very low, however. In Catholic countries actors were refused the sacrament, while actors in Shakespeare's England were regarded as rogues and vagabonds unless they were under royal or noble protection. **1.06**

For the next three centuries performers and particularly actors continued to be regarded as virtual outcasts, whereas authors increasingly came to be recognised as having a high cultural status. Among performers, the first to achieve recognition were musicians, who had already begun to receive significant royal and aristocratic patronage by the end of the sixteenth century. Theatrical performers, however, continued to be regarded with great suspicion into the twentieth century. Thus the first English actor to achieve social prominence was Henry Irving, knighted in 1895. During the course of the twentieth century, however, the position of performers has changed radically. **1.07**

Although the great Victorian and Edwardian actors and actresses achieved a degree of social credit that was then unprecedented, it was the advent of the film and music industries which really transformed the position. In the first quarter of this century performers such as Charlie Chaplin achieved the first mass audiences for their performances. In the second quarter of the century this led to the "star" system, mainly in cinema but also to some extent in popular music. In the third quarter the stars achieved social, though not economic, dominance in the music industry, although in the cinema they began to decline. The extent of the social transformation is shown by, for example, the marriage of an actress, Grace Kelly, to a monarch, Prince Rainier of Monaco. By contrast, the prominence of authors during this period declined, and in particular declined relative to that of performers. **1.08**

Starting in the third quarter and continuing in the fourth, performers have begun to achieve great economic power as well as social position. It is still the case that those performers who achieved greatest economic power have done so through combining performance with authorship. Thus a relatively new phenomenon in this period was that the performers started to become authors of the works they performed, particularly in popular music. This trend has continued in the fourth quarter, so that, for example, the term "singer-songwriter", which became current in the mid-1960s, is now largely obsolete since in most cases it is a tautology. **1.09**

Nevertheless, the rise in the economic power of performers as performers has begun to be increasingly felt. In the music industry the most obvious effect has been an increase in the number of contractual disputes between performers and record companies as performers struggle to break free of **1.10** lengthy contracts.[2] In the film industry, where performers (at least, star performers) have already achieved much greater contractual freedom,[3] performers are achieving greater artistic and economic control by producing their own films. Even where this is not the case, production of a film in Hollywood often depends upon the agreement of a "bankable" star to appear in it.

1.11   The changes in the social and economic standing of performers have been reflected in changes to their legal rights, and in particular the legal protection afforded to performers against unauthorised exploitation of their performances. As noted above, at the end of the twentieth century it may seem self-evident that performers should be protected in this way, but it is clear from the history discussed below that for most of the century this has not been the case. On the contrary, legal protection of performers, and in particular the according of proprietary rights to performers, has been widely resisted.

1.12   In the case of authors' rights, the principal reasons for affording protection have been economic and moral. In the common law tradition economic reasons have been paramount. It was recognised at a comparatively early date that an author who was not supported by patronage required legal protection to ensure that he profited from the exploitation of his works and that it was just that he should receive it. More cynically, perhaps, it was found that the economics of the publishing industry depended upon protection from piracy. In the civil law tradition, on the other hand, *droits d'auteur* or *Urheberrechte* were conceived of as an aspect of an individual's natural rights. Thus, an author had a moral right to control the dissemination of his intellectual creations. These two traditions came together in the Berne Convention,[4] although there has continued to be tension between them (for example, common law countries largely ignored moral rights for a century after Berne).

1.13   In the case of performers' rights, economic factors did not become relevant until the technical means to fix performances emerged. Once it became possible to exploit performances by means of the phonogram and the cinematographic film, however, the economic arguments in favour of authors' rights, and particularly those in favour of copyright-style protection for phonograms and films, became equally applicable to performers' rights. In particular, only copyright-style protection can ensure that performers are remunerated as exploitation occurs, including payment for new forms of exploitation; otherwise, performers are forced to bargain for the right to exploit their performances in advance, at a time when the potential market, and perhaps even the technical means of exploitation, are unknown. So far as the moral case is concerned, a performance is as much of an intellectual creation as a copyright works. Thus performers easily satisfy any test of originality which may be required for copyright protection. Indeed, it could be said that the moral case is stronger in the case of performers, since the performance is so intimately connected with the performer's own personality.

---

[2] See Chap. 8, para. 8.24.
[3] Whereas actors used to be contracted to studios for long periods—often seven years—they are now usually hired for each film or perhaps for a "package" of two or three.
[4] Convention for the Protection of Literary and Artistic Works (1886).

In England at least, there was some recognition of the need to protect **1.14** performers at an early stage. As described below,[5] this led to the passage of the Dramatic and Musical Performers' Act 1925, which criminalised the exploitation of dramatic and musical performances without the performers' consent. Yet the logical consequence, that performers should be given civil rights and remedies, was resisted by the legislature for 60 years and even then it baulked at giving performers proprietary rights.[6] Similar resistance has subsequently been encountered in other countries.[7]

Given that the arguments in favour of performers' rights seem so strong, at **1.15** least to this author, it is worth considering some of the arguments that have been advanced against protecting performers:

(1) Performers are less deserving of protection since their contribution is subsidiary to that of authors. (This view led to the classification of performers' rights as "neighbouring rights" or "related rights".[8]) It is far from clear, however, why the fact that a performance is dependent upon an act of authorship should mean that it is either economically or morally less deserving of protection. And what about performers who do not perform pre-existing works?

(2) Granting rights to performers may prejudice the rights of authors.[9] Legally speaking, it is fairly obvious that this is not the case. Accordingly, the only prejudice that could be suffered by authors is an economic one. This depends on whether the "cake" to be divided up is of fixed size so that giving some to performers inevitably means that authors must receive less. It is undoubtedly the case that authors' organisations have often voiced the fear that this will be the consequence, and thus have been instrumental in resisting the grant of performers' rights.[10] It may be that one of the reasons why this resistance is now falling away is the rise of the performer-author already described. More generally, the argument assumes an inelastic market. In practice it seems likely that the market is more elastic than this, for no evidence has ever been found that authors' remuneration has fallen as a result of the granting of rights to performers.

(3) Performers' rights are an industrial relations issue, that is to say, they are a matter for collective bargaining between unions and employers.[11] This may be true in part, but it is beside the point, since any collective bargaining has to take place in a legal context. The

---

[5] paras. 1.40–1.45.
[6] See para. 1.83, below.
[7] For example, the Report on Performers' Protection by the Australian Copyright Law Review Committee in 1987 recommended by a majority that performers should not be granted proprietary rights: para. 1.
[8] See para. 1.23, below.
[9] The Gregory Committee (as to which see para. 1.48, below) were evidently concerned about this: Cmnd. 8662 at para. 176.
[10] See para. 1.52, below.
[11] See, for example, the ACLRC Report (note 7, above) at para. 118. This argument underlies part of the reasoning of the Gregory Committee, although it is not very clearly articulated: note 9 above, at para. 175.

question is, what shall that legal context be?[12] Furthermore, it is not a complete answer, for although collective bargaining may enable performers to obtain adequate remuneration from those they contract with, it has little or no bearing on those they are not in contract with, such as "bootleggers".[13]

(4) Granting rights to performers is impracticable. For example, it is impracticable for all 100 members of a symphony orchestra performing a symphony to have a proprietary right.[14] Again, there is no doubt that this factor has been influential in the resistance to performers' rights.[15] It is suggested that this concern was always exaggerated, since it was always likely that potential difficulties could be resolved by collective agreements and collective licensing. After all, copyright in contemporary popular music would be close to unworkable in the absence of collective licensing.[16] Experience has shown that this is indeed the case. It is telling that in the six-year period between the commencement of Part II of the Copyright, Designs and Patents Act 1988, which contained a provision for the Copyright Tribunal granting consent to exploitation where a performer had unreasonably refused to do so,[17] and the repeal of that provision,[18] there was no instance of this provision being invoked.[19]

(5) Performances do not merit (or perhaps need) protection because they are transitory, whereas by contrast copyright works have permanent form.[20] This argument has been fallacious ever since it become technically possible to record and reproduce performances. A rider to the argument is that it is only the contribution of the phonogram producer or film producer which enables the performance to be recorded and thus only the latter merits protection.[21] This is a non-sequitur. Moreover, the converse is equally true—there could be no phonograms and few films without performers—yet copyright-style protection has long been accorded to producers of phonograms and films.

---

[12] Granting performers proprietary rights may, but will not necessarily, increase their individual and collective bargaining power.

[13] That is to say, those who record live performances and reproduce and sell the resulting recording without the consent of the performers. Bootlegging is to be distinguished from "piracy", which is the unauthorised reproduction and sale of commercially published recordings.

[14] See, *e.g.* McCardie J. in the *Blackmail* case, discussed in para. 1.47, below.

[15] It also led some countries to legislate for the collective exercise of performers' rights, particularly secondary use rights.

[16] See Chap. 3, paras. 3.59–3.60.

[17] Copyright, Designs and Patents Act 1988, s. 190(1)(b). See first edition, Chap. 6, paras. 6.53–6.69.

[18] By the Copyright and Related Rights Regulations 1996 (S.I. 1996 No. 2967). See Chap. 3, para. 3.25.

[19] Information supplied by the Copyright Tribunal.

[20] This argument seems to have weighed with the Gregory Committee which described performances as being "elusive in substance": Cmnd. 8662 at paras. 172, 175.

[21] *ibid.*

(6) Performers benefit from free copying, for example because it increases their reputations.[22] It is difficult to see why this argument does not apply equally to authors, in which case it is also an argument against copyright. It is submitted that this argument is clearly fallacious as a matter of economics. Moreover, many performers would strongly disagree that unrestricted bootlegging increases their reputations, preferring to be able to exercise control over which of their performances is disseminated to a wider public and which not.[23]

(7) Granting performers rights is anti-competitive. This is undeniably so, but the question is whether unauthorised exploitation of performances is fair competition. All civilised legal systems distinguish between competition that is fair and competition that is unfair. The same argument applies to copyright, which is equally if not more anti-competitive. Of course, copyright may be used or abused in such a way that its anti-competitive effect outweighs its benefits, but this can be remedied, for example by appropriate compulsory licensing provisions.[24]

(8) A variation of the bald anti-competitive argument is the concern that to require consent from performers may inhibit exploitation of, say, records, particularly given that performers' rights would be additional to those of others such as authors and phonogram producers.[25] There are two answers to this. The first is that this argument assumes that authors (and even phonogram producers) are entitled to protection in priority to performers, a point which has already been discussed. The second is that it is in performers' economic interest to ensure the widest possible dissemination of their performances consistent with obtaining remuneration for that dissemination and with preserving their reputations. Accordingly, it is inherently unlikely that performers will arbitrarily stifle recordings. As has already been noted,[26] experience has shown that collective agreements and collective licensing work efficiently and there is little tendency for individual performers or groups of performers to block exploitation of performances. (This is not to say that disputes do not sometimes arise, such as where a particular performer wishes to suppress a performance for artistic reasons, but it is submitted that this raises no issue of principle).

(9) The floodgates argument: if you grant rights to performers, others may start demanding rights, such as sportsmen.[27] Experience to date has been that, although performers' rights are increasingly being conceded, so far there has been relatively little agitation for their extension to other persons. Nevertheless, it may be asked whether it

---

[22] See, for example, the ACLRC Report (note 7, above) at para. 115.

[23] Although a fashion has recently developed in the wake of the Beatles' *Anthology* for releasing formerly suppressed recordings.

[24] See Chap. 3, paras. 3.23–3.42.

[25] The Gregory Committee seem to have been particularly concerned by this argument: Cmnd 8662 at paras. 176–177.

[26] Sub-paragraph (4), above.

[27] *cf.* the ACLRC Report (note 7, above) at para. 116.

would be such a bad thing if sportsmen were to be protected in the same way. As will be submitted below, the economic arguments are very similar and the moral arguments nearly as compelling.[28]

(10) It is not necessary to comply with a state's international obligations.[29] This, of course, is no reason. Furthermore, the extent of a state's obligations are a matter of choice. Thus since 1961 states have had the option of joining the Rome Convention on the protection of (*inter alia*) performers, but for many years most states chose not to do so.[30] It may be true, however, that some states felt that while there was not a sufficient international consensus in favour of granting performers' rights they risked disadvantaging their entertainment industries by doing so.[31] Recent harmonisation moves, both within the European Union and globally,[32] have changed this position.

1.16 It is suggested that none of the reasons discussed above, whether individually or collectively, justifies denying performers the right, and indeed the proprietary right, to prevent the unauthorised exploitation of their performances. The economic and moral arguments are compelling.[33]

COPYRIGHT AND NEIGHBOURING RIGHTS

1.17 Performers' rights and recording rights are species of the genus *copyright*[34] or, more strictly, *neighbouring right*. It may therefore be of assistance to some readers briefly to explain what copyright and neighbouring rights are.

What is copyright?

1.18 Copyright is first and foremost the right to control copying of a work. The owner of copyright has the right to copy the copyright work, while others do not. By extension, the copyright owner can control the way in which copies are dealt with. As new ways have been found to exploit copyright works by reproduction and dissemination, so the scope of copyright has progressively been enlarged. Copyright may thus conveniently be viewed as a bundle of rights in a work: the right to copy it, the right to adapt it, the right to perform it in public, the right to sell copies, the right to rent out copies and so on. These rights are *proprietary* rights, that is to say they can be transferred and dealt

---

[28] para. 1.105, below and Chap. 2, paras. 2.18–2.19.

[29] See, for example, the ACLRC Report (note 7, above) at para. 60.

[30] See para. 1.56, below.

[31] See, for example, the ACLRC Report (note 7, above) at paras. 82, 101, 119.

[32] See paras. 1.85–1.94 below.

[33] For a particularly clear and eloquent exposition of the case in favour of a performer's copyright, see the view of the minority in Part IV of the ACLRC Report (note 7, above) at paras. 120–181.

[34] It should be made clear that this is an assertion, not an unequivocal statement of legal fact. Part II of the Copyright, Designs and Patents Act 1988 deliberately eschews the word "copyright". Nevertheless, it is argued below, the effect is to create two new copyrights (or, more strictly, neighbouring rights, since they are not full copyrights): see paras. 1.83–1.84, below.

with like other forms of property. They may also be enforced by civil remedies including an injunction and damages.

Copyright is a member of the family *intellectual property*. This family, which also includes patents, registered designs and trade marks, is so called because it consists of rights of property in intellectual creations. All of these rights are intangible, but it is fundamental that they are regarded as property just as much as tangible property. Thus copyright is capable of being owned by one or more persons and of being bought and sold or otherwise dealt in. **1.19**

It is a truism that, unlike some other intellectual property rights such as patents, copyright is not a monopoly. Copyright does not inhibit independent creation. The owner of the copyright in a photograph of St Paul's Cathedral cannot complain if another person independently takes an identical photograph of St Paul's Cathedral. It will be appreciated, however, that in many contexts a right to prevent copying is as good as a true monopoly. The high degree of improbability that two persons will independently write the same song means that having copyright in a song is virtually the same as having a monopoly in that song. Nevertheless, there is a difference. **1.20**

It is an interesting question whether this is true of performances, with which this book is concerned. The *Oxford English Dictionary* definition is suggestive: **1.21**

> performance ... 3. *spec*. a. The action of performing a ceremony, play, part in a play, piece of music, etc.; formal or set execution.... c. The performing of a play, of music, of gymnastic or conjuring feats, or the like, as a definite act or series of acts done at an appointed place and time; a public exhibition or entertainment.[35]

What this omits, however, is that the act or series of acts is done by an appointed individual or individuals. Thus a performance is a something done by a particular individual at a particular place and at a particular time.[36]

It follows from this that it is impossible to create the same performance twice. Even if the same individual were to give a subsequent performance that was indistinguishable from the first, it would still be a different performance merely by virtue of taking place at a different time. Still less is it possible for a different performer to produce the same performance. In short, it is inherent in the concept of performance that each performance is unique. This is the distinction between creative artistry and interpretative artistry: the creative artist produces an artefact, an object separate from himself, whereas the interpretative artist produces a performance that is inseparable from himself. It is therefore this author's view that copyright in a performance (meaning at least the exclusive right to record, broadcast and exploit recordings of that performance) is, contrary to the general rule, a genuine monopoly. It is not, of course, a monopoly so far as performances of any particular work are concerned. **1.22**

---

[35] 2nd ed.
[36] See Chap. 2, para. 2.03 for the present statutory definition.

P. 41

What are neighbouring rights?[37]

1.23   The term "neighbouring rights" is used in a narrow sense (meaning rights of performers, phonogram producers and broadcasters) and in a broad sense (meaning rights similar to but less than full copyright). The latter sense derives from the traditional reluctance of civil law systems based on the concept of *droit d'auteur* or *Urheberrecht* to accord full copyright where the object to be protected is derivative from a literary or musical work and particularly where "author" is a corporation, as with record companies and broadcasting organisations. In such cases rights which are "neighbours" to true "authors' rights" are conferred. The expression originates from the phrase *droits voisins* contained in a *voeu* adopted by the Brussels Conference for the Revision of the Berne Convention in 1948. The terms "connected rights" (from the Italian, *diritti conessi*) and "related rights" (from the German, *verwandte Schutzrechte*) are also used. None of these terms are used in any of the U.K. copyright statutes, and therefore they are likely to be unfamiliar to English readers. Nevertheless, they are useful in the context of performers' rights since even the rights conferred by the Copyright, Designs and Patents Act 1988 are less than full copyrights.[38] Moreover, familiarity with these terms, particularly "related rights", is likely to increase as a result of the three recent E.C. Directives discussed below.[39] Thus the term "related rights" has been used in the title of the regulations which implement the Rental and Lending Rights Directive.

HISTORICAL REVIEW

A brief history of copyright[40]

1.24   Although it is sometimes said that the first copyright case was that of St Columba,[41] it is generally accepted that there was no copyright or anything similar prior to the invention of printing. Printing in itself may not have led to any demand for copyright, but it seems that over the following three centuries, a combination of commercial pressure by booksellers and a desire for censorship by Church and State led to rigorous controls on printing.

1.25   The first form of copyright consisted of the prerogative claim by the Crown to the exclusive right to print books such as the Bible, statutes and, in due

---

[37] See Stewart, *International Copyright and Neighbouring Rights*, (2nd ed., Butterworths, 1989), Chap. 7 and Chap. 8, paras. 8.01–8.02 and Sterling, "Harmonisation of Usage of the Terms 'Copyright', 'Author's Right' and 'Neighbouring Right'" [1989] 1 EIPR 14.

[38] See para. 1.80.

[39] paras. 1.82–1.87. The Commission's intention in using the term "related rights" in the E.C. Rental and Lending Rights Directive was to use a neutral term which did not distinguish between copyrights and and neighbouring rights in the narrow sense: Reinbothe and von Lewinski, *The E.C. Directive on Rental and Lending Rights and on Piracy* (Sweet & Maxwell, 1993), pp. 9, 84.

[40] See generally Birrell, *The Law and History of Copyright in Books* (1899); Scrutton, *Law of Copyright* (4th ed., 1903); Feather, "Authors, Publishers and Politicians: The History of Copyright and the Book Trade" [1988] 12 EIPR 377.

[41] St Columba is supposed to have copied Abbot Fenian's Psalter. The Abbot complained to King Diarmed, who gave judgment for the Abbot, saying "to every cow her calf, and accordingly to every book its copy".

course, common law books. This privilege was naturally exercised by the King's Printer. Other printers, however, were able to petition the Crown for the grant of letters patent giving them a monopoly over the printing of particular books, in some cases for a period of years. These rights could be enforced by injunction in the Court of Chancery.[42]

Needless to say, a system that depended on petitions to the Crown was rather haphazard. Much more effective was the control that came to be exercised over the printing of books by the printers' and stationers' guilds. This was formalised by the grant of a charter to the Stationers' Company in 1556. The charter created a system with three main elements. Lawfully printed books were those entered on the Stationers' Register; only Company members could enter a book on the Register; and the Company was empowered to search for and destroy unlawfully printed books. The significance of the second element was that Company members could be expected not to copy each others' books for fear of expulsion or other penalty.[43] In other words, the system was based on restrictive practice.   **1.26**

Originally, the Stationers' Register was a record of who owned the manuscript which had been approved by censors such as the Archbishop of Canterbury. State control over the printing of subversive or heretical material was enforced by the Court of the Star Chamber. Decrees issued by the Star Chamber in 1586 and 1637 codifying the law as to printing may be regarded as the first attempts at a copyright statute (the 1637 decree later formed the basis for the Licensing Act of 1662).   **1.27**

Under this system, control over printing was vested in the stationer, and not the author. The author's only property was in his manuscript: he could not even print it himself, but had to contract with a member of the Stationer's Company. As registration came to be regarded as giving an exclusive right, the stationers got into the habit of purchasing from authors the right to print a book "for ever". Ownership of "copies" came to be treated as property, being inherited by sons or widows and also bought and sold. This became commercially very significant in the book trade, and gave rise to the argument that there was at common law a perpetual copyright.   **1.28**

After the abolition of the Star Chamber, this system was preserved first by orders of Parliament and then by statute, with a brief lapse from 1679 to 1685, until Parliament refused to renew it in 1694. After this, piracy (that is to say, unauthorised copying of published editions) of books, particularly by Scottish publishers after the Act of Union,[44] became so common that authors and booksellers were moved to agitate for a statutory copyright. Legend has it that the resulting Copyright Act of 1709, known as the Statute of Anne, was originally drafted by Swift.[45]   **1.29**

This Act for the first time conferred rights on authors and through them their assigns. Under it the author and his assigns had the sole right of printing   **1.30**

---

[42] See, *e.g. Stationer's Company v. Lee* (1681) 2 Show. 258 and *Stationer's Company v. Partridge* (1709) 11 Ann B.R. Lucas, both cited in *Millar v. Taylor* (1769) 4 Burr 2303, 2328.
[43] A byelaw of the Company made in 1681 imposed a fine of 12 pence per copy for copying another member's book.
[44] See Prescott, "The Origins of Copyright: A Debunking View" [1989] 12 EIPR 453.
[45] Birrell, note 40 above, pp. 20, 93.

books for a term of 14 years from the date of publication, and if the author was still alive at the expiry of this period there was a second term of 14 years. Books published before the Act were protected for 21 years from the date of commencement. The titles of books still had to be registered at Stationers' Hall, but it was no longer a stationers' monopoly.

1.31   Nevertheless, the book trade seems to have regarded the Act as little more than providing statutory penalties for infringement of their property rights. After the expiry of the 21-year transitional period a number of cases were brought, particularly against Scots and country booksellers, in which it was argued that, notwithstanding the expiry of the statutory protection, booksellers had property rights in copies which were perpetual like any other form of property. This question was not settled until 1774, when the House of Lords in *Donaldson v. Becket*[46] held that the Statute of Anne had abolished common law copyright in published works.

1.32   After the Statute of Anne, copyright developed in four ways. First, the term of protection was successively extended by amending Acts of 1802 and 1814 and by the Copyright Act 1842 (Talfourd's Act), which repealed the Statute of Anne. Under the 1842 Act, copyright in published works lasted for the life of the author plus seven years or 42 years, whichever was the longer.

1.33   Secondly, the protection afforded by copyright was enlarged to include "use rights". Thus the Dramatic Copyright Act 1833 (Bulwer Lytton's Act) created the performing right for dramatic works, and this was extended by the 1842 Act to musical works.

1.34   Thirdly, copyright was accorded to other classes of work. Engravings were first protected by the Prints Copyright Act of 1734 (succeeded by statutes of 1766, 1777 and 1836). Sculptures followed in the Copyright Act of 1798 (and 1814), and drawings, paintings and photographs were brought into the fold by the Fine Arts Copyright Act 1862.

1.35   Fourthly, copyright became international. The Statute of Anne only protected books by British authors. In 1838 the first International Copyright Act was passed which enabled copyright to be conferred on foreign authors by Order in Council; a wider Act was passed in 1844. In 1851 Britain entered into the first bilateral copyright convention. This was succeeded by a number of others until in 1886 a multilateral convention was agreed at Berne. This provided for reciprocal protection to be accorded by Contracting States to each others' authors. It was given effect to by the International Copyright Act 1886. At the Berlin revision of the Berne Convention in 1908, two important matters were agreed: that copyright should arise automatically on making the work, without any need for registration or other formality; and that the minimum term should be the author's life plus 50 years.

1.36   All these developments were brought together in the Copyright Act 1911, the first modern copyright statute. This brought all the different copyrights under one piece of legislation, including giving statutory protection to

---

[46] (1774) 4 Burr. 2408.

unpublished works for the first time.[47] In addition, the first "neighbouring right"[48] was established, namely the copyright in sound recordings.

The 1911 Act was succeeded by the Copyright Act 1956. This again 1.37 established a number of new rights, in this case copyright in cinematograph films, broadcasts and the typographical format of published editions. Technological change meant that the 1956 Act was out of date very soon after it arrived on the statute book: it made little or no allowance for either new subject matter for copyright, such as computer programs,[49] or for new means of copying, such as photocopiers and cassette recorders. Nevertheless, a new statute had to wait until 1988 and the creation of yet further new rights by the Copyright, Designs and Patents Act 1988. It is with two of these new rights that this book is concerned.

Performers' rights before 1925

To begin with, copyright was concerned with artefacts, with books and then 1.38 engravings. Bulwer Lytton's Act arose from a recognition that certain classes of work were principally exploited through performance, and accordingly rights in performances were required. At this time no thought was given to the performers involved, merely to the author of the work performed. The reason for this was obvious enough, namely that performers did not need protection, for the only way in which their performance could be exploited was by the public paying for admission to a performance. Performers might be unfairly exploited by impresarios, but that was simply a matter of contract between the performer and the impresario.

As ever with copyright, it was technology which changed the position. 1.39 Once performances could be fixed, it was possible to exploit them other than by simply charging the public admission to a show. A new artefact came into being which could be reproduced and disseminated. As is often the case, however, the legislature was slow to react to this development. Although both sound recordings and cinematograph films were both well-established technologies by 1911 (indeed, the 1911 Act accorded copyright to producers of sound recordings), the position of performers was neglected. Not until 1925 was any attempt made in the United Kingdom[50] to protect performers from the unauthorised exploitation of their performances that the new technologies made possible.

---

[47] s. 31 abolished common law copyright in unpublished works.
[48] See para. 1.23, above.
[49] These were not specifically provided for by statute until the passing of the Copyright (Computer Software) Amendment Act 1985.
[50] Although the United Kingdom was one of the first countries to protect performers against unauthorised exploitation of their performances, it was not the first. Art. 2 of the German Author's Rights Law of 1901 as amended by the Law of 1910 equated a performance of a literary or musical work for the purposes of sound recording with an arrangement and gave the performer the same rights as an arranger.

The Dramatic and Musical Performers' Protection Act 1925

1.40   On February 13, 1925 the Dramatic and Musical Performers' Protection Bill was introduced into the House of Commons by Sir Martin Conway M.P.[51] It was a Private Member's Bill, but received the support of the Baldwin Government. Conway's primary sponsor appears to have been The Gramophone Company Limited (now EMI Records Limited).[52] The Bill received its second reading on May 1 and was reported from standing committee with amendments on June 25.

1.41   Moving that the Bill be read for the third time, Conway stated that he had introduced it "in order to make it possible to improve broadcast programmes". He explained that at that moment it was inadvisable for artists to perform for broadcasts since records could be made illicitly from the broadcast and sold. The performer had no protection against this, and it had the effect of breaking contracts between the artists and the gramophone companies.[53]

1.42   The only objection the Bill met with in the Commons came from Sir Henry Slesser, who had been Solicitor-General in the 1924 Labour administration.[54] He argued that the mischief at which the Bill was directed should be remedied by an amendment to the Copyright Act 1911, and protested at the creation of new crimes when the civil law was quite adequate to deal with the situation.[55] Later in the debate, he added that the appropriate remedies were an injunction and damages.[56] The House appears to have regarded this as a technical point of little merit, however, and the Bill was carried to a third reading on June 26.[57]

1.43   The Bill received its first reading in the House of Lords shortly thereafter, on June 29. Moving that the Bill be read a second time on July 13, the Earl of Shaftesbury stated that it had the support of the Broadcasting Company (that is, the BBC) and of the gramophone companies as well as of artists.[58] When the question was raised whether it was not more appropriate to make it a matter of civil rather than criminal liability, Viscount Haldane, who had piloted the 1911 Act through the Lords, said that that was "a gigantic Act" as it was without amending it, and it was simpler to proceed by way of the

---

[51] Later Lord Conway of Allington. Conway represented the Combined English Universities as a Conservative member of the Coalition Government, having previously been a Liberal. He was a distinguished art historian, critic and collector who had been Slade Professor of Fine Art at Cambridge and the first Director-General of the Imperial War Museum. He was also a noted mountaineer and explorer.

[52] Conway's diary entry for February 13 includes the note "H. of C. & put in the Grammo/phone [sic] Co's Bill.", while the entry for May 25 includes the note "Got my Grammo-/phone [sic] Bill thro' Com^{ee}C.': Conway Papers, Cambridge University Library, Add. 7676/Y 58. According to Conway's biographer, he was rewarded by the presentation to him of a "magnificent" gramophone: Joan Evans, The Conways: A History of Three Generations (1966), p. 245.

[53] H.C. Deb., Vol. 185, ser. 5, cols. 1970–1971 (1925).

[54] Later Slesser L.J. Slesser had the unusual distinction of being appointed directly to the Court of Appeal at the age of 46 without having first sat as a judge of first instance. He resigned in 1940 at the age of 57 owing to ill-health, but lived on until 1970.

[55] H.C. Deb., note 46, above, cols. 1971–1972.

[56] ibid., col. 1975.

[57] ibid., col. 1979.

[58] H.L. Deb., Vol. 62, ser. 5, cols. 18–21 (1925).

criminal law[59] (thereby, as Shaftesbury put it, overruling his colleague Slesser[60]).

The Bill was reported without amendments from the House in committee **1.44** on July 16, was given its third reading on July 20 and received the Royal Assent on July 31, 1925.

On its face, the 1925 Act merely created criminal offences and did not **1.45** confer any civil right of action. As we have seen, this was not accidental. Nevertheless, there was soon an attempt to enforce the Act by civil proceedings. This was to be the first of many such attempts under the 1925 Act and its successors. The principal reason for this, of course, was the availability of an injunction through the civil process, a remedy not available from the criminal courts. In addition, the fines were small and did not benefit either the performer or those he contracted with.

The *Blackmail* case

The first and only case under the 1925 Act on the question was *Musical* **1.46** *Performers' Protection Association Ltd v. British International Pictures Ltd.*[61] The case arose out of the making of the Alfred Hitchcock film *Blackmail*. The defendant was the production company. It hired musicians to provide incidental music for the film. Although the musicians were paid, they were not asked to nor did they consent in writing to the use of their performances in the film. Five of the musicians later assigned their rights under the 1925 Act to the plaintiff association which brought proceedings.

McCardie J. began with the proposition that the Court would not grant an **1.47** injunction to restrain the commission of a criminal offence in the absence of actual or prospective injury to property.[62] He then considered whether the 1925 Act conferred any right of property:

A consideration of the Act shows that there are no words providing it is to be read as one with the Copyright Acts. Nay, more, as I have already pointed out, the Copyright Acts are not mentioned in any way. The Act does not provide for "penalties"; it provides for a "fine" on summary conviction for an offence. The fine does not go to the performers; it goes to the Crown, and the performers get no share. Nowhere in the Act is there any indication of an intention to give the performers any "right of property" in the performance of works. The prohibitions of the Act apply as much to non-copyright works as to copyright works. Any member of the public may commence a prosecution.

Upon considering the Act, I come to the conclusion that the Legislature did not, by any inadvertence, omit to give a right of property to the performers, but that they deliberately so worded the Act as to preclude any notion that a right of property was conferred. Nothing would have been easier than to confer a right of property if

---

[59] *ibid.*, col. 21.
[60] *ibid.*, cols. 22–23. Haldane had been a member of the Liberal Government in 1911, but was Lord Chancellor to Slesser's Solicitor-General in 1924.
[61] (1930) 46 T.L.R. 485.
[62] Relying upon Turner L.J. in *Emperor of Austria v. Day* (1861) 3 De G.F. & J. 217, 253.

such was the wish of Parliament. The Act, however, is most significant alike in its wording and in its omissions.[63]

He was fortified in this view by the consideration that otherwise there would be 100 separate rights of property in a performance by an orchestra of 100 performers. Accordingly McCardie J. held that the 1925 Act did not confer a civil right of action. It does not appear to have been argued that the plaintiff could sue for breach of statutory duty imposed by the Act, although the concept was well known by that time.[64]

The Gregory Report and the Copyright Act 1956

1.48 In 1952 the Gregory Committee in its Report on the reform of copyright stated (although without referring to the *Blackmail* case) that the 1925 Act did not give civil rights to performers.[65] The Committee rejected a proposal by the Musicians' Union, Equity and the Variety Artistes' Federation[66] that performers should be given a "performers' right" in the nature of copyright.[67] The Committee reasoned that it would be impossible to extend copyright to performers and undesirable to confer a more limited right.[68] Although the Committee was concerned by a number of the arguments rehearsed in paragraph 1.15 above, the consideration which seems to have proved decisive was simply that it hadn't been done before.[69] Accordingly, the Copyright Act 1956, which was passed following the Gregory Committee's Report, did not provide for any such right. On the contrary, section 45 and Schedule 6 to the 1956 Act amended the 1925 Act by extending it to films but without changing the principle that breach was only a matter for the criminal courts.

The Dramatic and Musical Performers' Protection Act 1958

1.49 The Dramatic and Musical Performers' Protection Act 1958 was, as its long title said, an Act to consolidate the 1925 Act and the amendments made by the 1956 Act. No substantive changes to the law were made. This remained the principal statute until the passing of the Copyright, Designs and Patents Act 1988.

The Rome Convention[70]

1.50 Internationally, the first move towards granting rights to performers was made by the Rome Conference to revise the Berne Convention in 1928. Although the Conference refused to confer copyright on performers, it expressed a *"voeu"* that member states should consider measures to

---

[63] (1930) 46 T.L.R. 485, 488.

[64] The classic decision in favour of an apparently criminal statute imposing a civil duty being *Groves v. Lord Wimborne* [1898] 2 Q.B. 402.

[65] Cmnd. 8662 at para. 172.

[66] Although it is not entirely clear who this body represented, it appears that the term "variety artiste" is intended to refer to performers such as magicians, clowns, jugglers, acrobats, etc.: see Chap. 2, paras 2.15–2.17.

[67] Note 65, above, at para. 180.

[68] *ibid.*, at para. 176.

[69] More precisely, that copyright had never been extended to performers before.

[70] See generally Stewart, note 37, above, Chap. 8 and Masouyé and Wallace, *WIPO Guide to the Rome Convention* (WIPO, 1981).

safeguard performers' rights. Little progress was made until 1948, when the Brussels Conference expressed further *"voeux"* on the subject. The International Labour Organisation then took up the matter. In conjunction with the Berne Union Secretariat it convened a meeting in Rome in 1951 which produced a draft convention for the protection of performers, phonogram producers and broadcasters. In 1952 UNESCO, as the Secretariat for the Universal Copyright Convention, also became a participant in the preparation of the new convention. The draft convention was revised during meetings in Geneva in 1956, Monaco in 1957 and The Hague in 1960 before being finalised at a Diplomatic Conference in Rome. The International Convention for the Protection of Performers, Producers of Phonograms and Broadcasting Organisations was signed on October 26, 1961 and came into force on May 18, 1964.[71]

Like the Berne Convention, the Rome Convention lays down minimum standards of protection for certain persons—authors in the case of the Berne Convention, performers, phonogram producers and broadcasting organisations in the case of the Rome Convention. The new right owners were those whose involvement was derivative from that of the author in that by their contribution (performance, recording, broadcast) they converted the original work into a new form.[72] Unlike the Berne Convention, however, the Rome Convention was not drawn up solely to harmonise national laws and encourage reciprocity: its purpose was in large measure to provide for rights to be granted to persons who under many national laws had not previously enjoyed rights. Most countries therefore had to legislate to create the minimum rights stipulated before they could ratify the Convention—including the United Kingdom. The rights thus pioneered were the "neighbouring rights".[73]

1.51

Because performing, recording and broadcasting are so interconnected, it was decided that a single convention should deal with the creation of these rights and that it should strike a balance between the three different right owners. This balancing process seems to have worked to the relative disadvantage of performers. The reason for this were mainly political. Authors' representatives feared that an absolute performers' right would compete with authors' rights; broadcasters feared that it would give performers' unions too powerful a weapon; and an absolute right was opposed by countries like the United Kingdom which already had legislation protecting performers by way of criminal penalties.[74] The result was that performers were given a different right to phonogram producers and broadcasters.

1.52

This can be seen by comparing Article 7(1) with Articles 10 and 13:

1.53

---

[71] Cmnd. 2425.

[72] The nearest right owners under the Berne Convention were translators and arrangers, the rationale for whose protection was essentially the same: see notes 1 and 50, above.

[73] See para. 1.23, above.

[74] Stewart, note 70, above, para. 8.16 (at the time of the Rome Diplomatic Conference which led to the Convention, Stewart was Director General of the International Federation of the Phonographic Industry (IFPI) and a leading participant at the Conference) and Sterling, *Intellectual Property Rights in Sound Recordings, Film and Video* (Sweet & Maxwell, 1992), para. 7B.07.

> 7(1) The protection provided for performers by this Convention shall include *the possibility of preventing* [broadcasting, fixation and the reproduction of fixations without consent].
>
> 10 Producers of phonograms shall enjoy *the right to authorise or prohibit* the direct or indirect reproduction of their phonograms.
>
> 13 Broadcasting organisations shall enjoy *the right to authorise or prohibit* [rebroadcasting, fixation and the reproduction of fixations of their broadcasts]. [emphases added]

Although the wording is notably unhappy, it is clear that the "possibility of preventing" accorded to performers was different to, and lesser than, the absolute "right to authorise or prohibit" granted to phonogram producers and broadcasters. This was entirely deliberate, as the *WIPO Guide to the Rome Convention*[75] explains:

> 7.3 Note that the words "possibility of preventing" differ from those in the articles dealing with protection for producers of phonograms and broadcasting organisations. The latter have the right "to authorise or prohibit". Some think this paradoxical, regrettable and unfair. But it is of course only a minimum and national laws can go further.
>
> 7.4 The reason for the wording in this paragraph is to leave complete freedom of choice as to the means to implement the Convention, and to choose those which member countries think most appropriate and best. They may be based on any one or more of a number of legal theories: laws of employment, of personality, of unfair competition or unjust enrichment, etc.—and, of course, if they wish, an exclusive right. The important thing is that those means achieve the purpose of this Article, namely that the performer has the possibility of preventing the acts enumerated.
>
> 7.5 The wording used also allows countries like the United Kingdom to retain their method of protection which is by criminal law, punishing those who make and/or use performances without consent. These countries think this solution best and refuse the grant of a property right in the nature of copyright.

This is confirmed by the records of the Rome Diplomatic Conference.[76]

1.54   The position may be contrasted with that under the Model Law Concerning Protection of Performers, Producers of Phonograms and Broadcasting Organisations promulgated by WIPO, ILO and UNESCO in 1974 which provides in section 2(1) that "without the authorisation of the performers, no person shall do any of the following acts ...", the form of words being the same as that in section 4 relating to producers and in section 6 relating to broadcasters. Similarly, Chapter II of the E.C. Rental and Lending Rights Directive[77] consistently refers to performers having "the exclusive right to

---

[75] Note 70, above. The authors of the Guide both attended the Diplomatic Conference, Masouyé as Deputy Director General of the Berne Union and Wallace as a U.K. delegate.

[76] Records of the Diplomatic Conference on the International Protection of Performers, Producers of Phonograms and Broadcasting Organisations, Rome, 1961 (ILO/UNESCO/BIRPI, 1968), pp. 43, 136–137.

[77] Council Directive 92/100, November 19, 1992 on rental and lending rights and on certain rights related to copyright in the field of intellectual property. See para. 1.86, below.

authorise or prohibit" the various acts.[78] (Article 14 of TRIPs, on the other hand, follows the wording of the Rome Convention.) Thus, although to an English reader the use of the word "prevent" in Article 7 of the Rome Convention suggests a right to an injunction, it is clear that the intention was that the provision by national laws of something less than a performers' copyright—such as protection through the criminal law—should be permissible.[79] The significance of this point is that it appears to be have been misunderstood in the judgment of the Court of Appeal in the *Peter Sellers* case.[80]

Performers were disadvantaged under the Convention[81] in at least four other significant respects. The first is that the Convention provides that Article 7 shall have no application once the performer has consented to the incorporation of his performance in a visual or audiovisual fixation.[82] Thus performers have no rights at all in respect of secondary uses so far as films are concerned. The second is that performers' rights in respect of secondary uses of phonograms are limited to sharing in a single equitable remuneration.[83] The third is that, unlike the Berne Convention,[84] the Rome Convention contains no protection for the moral rights of performers (although such a provision was originally included in the draft Convention). The fourth is that the Convention permits Contracting States to enact quite extensive derogations from its provisions, and in particular not to apply Article 12 (which confers the right to equitable remuneration) at all.[85]   **1.55**

For many years after it was signed, the Rome Convention was very slow to gain adherents. Recently, however, the number of contracting states has risen considerably. Thus in 1992 a (non-binding) E.C. Council Resolution was passed recording undertakings by the Member States to become parties to *inter alia* the Rome Convention by January 1, 1995.[86] In addition, the Member States of the European Economic Area agreed to accede to Rome by the same date[87] and states party to the Strasbourg Convention on satellite broadcasting agreed to give neighbouring right holders at least the protection conferred by Rome.[88] Since then a number of the European countries which   **1.56**

---

[78] *ibid.*, Arts. 6(1), 7(1), 8(1), 9(1). See also Arts. 1(1) and 2(1).

[79] This was recognised by the Australian Copyright Law Review Committee in its Report on Performers' Protection: para. 24.

[80] See para. 1.76, below.

[81] Even where the Convention did make provision it was not always implemented in a manner consistent with the interests of performers. An example of this is the way in which the United Kingdom discharged—or failed to discharge—its obligations under Article 12, as to which see Chap. 3, para 3.44.

[82] Art. 19.

[83] Art. 12.

[84] Art. 6*bis*.

[85] Art. 16(1)(a)(i).

[86] Council Resolution of May 14, 1992 on increased protection for copyright and related rights, [1992] O.J. C138/1. In addition Chapter II of the E.C. Rental and Lending Rights Directive required Member States to grant performers, phonogram producers and broadcasters rights such that implementation of the Directive would substantially enable Member States which had not already ratified the Convention to do so.

[87] Agreement on the European Economic Area signed at Oporto on May 2, 1992 as adjusted by the Protocol signed at Brussels on March 17, 1993, Protocol 28, Art. 5(c).

[88] European Convention relating to questions on copyright law and neighbouring rights in the

had not previously ratified the Convention have done so. Worldwide, further accessions have occurred as a by-product of the Agreement on Trade-Related Aspects of Intellectual Property (TRIPs), which requires member states to provide performers with protection close to that required under Rome for an extended period of 50 years from the end of the calendar year in which the performance was given.[89]

The Performers' Protection Acts 1963 and 1972

1.57 In the United Kingdom the Rome Convention was given effect to by the Performers' Protection Act 1963 which amended the 1958 Act. The principal change effected by this statute was to enlarge the categories of performers able to claim protection under the 1958 Act, the basic structure being left unchanged. On the face of it, the remedies provided were still only criminal. This was intentional.

1.58 Moving that the Bill be read a second time in the House of Lords, its sponsor Lord Mancroft[90] explained that the purpose of the Bill was to make "the small changes required in our law to ratify this Convention of Rome". He continued:

> The rights of record producers and broadcasting organisation are contained in our Copyright Act 1956, which I had the honour of piloting through your Lordships' House, so it is a certain amount of personal satisfaction to me to be able to ratify by my Bill this Convention without in any way having to change our own Act of 1956. That is about the record producers and broadcasting organisations.
>
> Now the performer—the band or the pianist—is in a different position. He is protected in this country not by the grant of a property right, not by copyright, but by an Act known as the Dramatic and Musical Performers' Protection Act 1958. This makes it a criminal offence to record or broadcast his performance without his written consent.[91]

Lord Mancroft went on to say that "the only changes necessary in our legislation are in the criminal statute which protects performers" and explained that these changes were to the definition of performers, to make it clear that the place of performance was immaterial, to extend the Act to records made abroad without the consent required by local law and to extend the Act to the relaying of performances by wire.[92] He concluded:

> Little has been done to alter the balance between the three categories most concerned: the performers, the record producers and the broadcasting authorities; or to alter the relationship between any of those three and the public. Our

---

framework of transfrontier broadcasting by satellite signed at Strasbourg on May 11, 1994, Art. 5(1). The Commission has proposed a Council Decision for the Convention to be approved by the Community: [1996] O.J. C164/10.

[89] Art. 14. See para. 1.91, below.

[90] The Bill was a Private Members' Bill with Government support.

[91] H.L. Deb., Vol. 246, ser. 5, cols. 513–514 (1963). S. 4 of the Act was added by amendment during the Third Reading.

[92] ibid., cols 514–515.

protection system works satisfactorily and there have been very few prosecutions under the 1958 Act.[93]

Similarly in the Commons, the Bill's sponsor there, Ronald Bell M.P., stated, when moving that the Bill be read a third time, that the Bill was to make "a very few marginal adjustments" to the 1958 Act to enable the United Kingdom to ratify the Rome Convention. He explained that the reason why the United Kingdom could fulfil its obligations under the Bill with "so short and modest a Bill" was that the Convention very largely reflected existing English law on the subject, the English participants having played a large part in drawing it up.[94] He went on: **1.59**

> We mainly rely on the Copyright Act, 1956, for the regulation of copyright, a system under which we give to the author or producer of a work of art a kind of industrial property in his production. Performers, as distinct from authors, are not protected in that way by the grant of a property right or copyright but by an Act known as the Dramatic and Musical Performers' Protection Act, 1958, which makes it a criminal offence to record or broadcast a performance of a performer without his written consent.
>
> The performer does not have a copyright, but it is made a criminal offence to pirate his performance...[95]

The Performers' Protection Act 1972 merely increased the penalties for offences under the 1958 Act as amended by the 1963 Act. **1.60**

✴ Civil claims under the Performer's Protection Acts 1958–1972

Between 1977 and 1983 there were a series of cases in which performers and those with whom they had exclusive contracts (particularly record companies) argued that they had civil rights of action under the Performers' Protection Acts. Some temporary successes were achieved, notably in the *Island Records* case,[96] but these were effectively reversed by the decision of the Court of Appeal in *RCA v. Pollard*.[97] The state of the authorities remained uncertain, however, until another decision of the Court of Appeal in the *Peter Sellers* case[98] in 1987, in which it was held that performers did have a civil right of action after all (though not record companies and the like). **1.61**

The Beatles *case*

The first attempt to bring civil proceedings under the Performers' Protection Acts 1958–1972 was *Apple Corps Ltd v. Lingasong Ltd.*[99] This case concerned a tape recording of a concert by the Beatles at the Star Club in Hamburg in 1961 or 1962. The Beatles and their record company sought to restrain the making of records from the tape without their written consent. It was argued on behalf of the plaintiffs that a breach of the Performers' **1.62**

---

[93] *ibid.*, col. 516.
[94] H.C. Deb., Vol. 679, ser. 5, cols. 895–897, 900 (1963).
[95] *ibid.*, col. 897.
[96] *Ex p. Island Records Ltd* [1978] Ch. 122.
[97] [1983] Ch. 135.
[98] *Rickless v. United Artists Corp.* [1988] Q.B. 40.
[99] [1977] F.S.R. 345

Protection Acts was actionable on the basis of breach of statutory duty, and it was pointed out that this argument had not been advanced in the *Blackmail* case. Sir Robert Megarry V.-C. applied the earlier decision, however, observing:

> Whatever might have been the position under the Acts of 1925 and 1958 if they had stood alone, I think that it would be quite wrong to construe them as if no Copyright Acts had ever existed. The concept of copyright has been with us for a very long time, and when Parliament came to enact the Act of 1925 it cannot have failed to know that there was such a thing as copyright. The Copyright Act 1956, indeed, amended the Act of 1925 (see section 45 of and Schedule 6 to the Act of 1956); and the Act of 1958 consolidated the Act of 1925 as amended. Side by side with the individual rights of property given by the Copyright Act 1956 and its predecessors, Parliament enacted the limited remedies laid down by the Acts of 1925 and 1958, and abstained from conferring any copyright in a performance. What I think [counsel for the plaintiffs] is seeking to do is to bring into being a right of action in tort for breach of statutory duty which will confer something of the effect of a copyright on something that Parliament has refrained from making the subject of copyright.[1]

1.63 The Vice-Chancellor also rejected an argument that the position had been altered by the giving of effect to the Rome Convention by the 1963 Act:

> [Counsel for the plaintiffs] emphasised the words "protection of performers" in the long title of the Act of 1963, and the words "the protection provided for performers" in Article 7 of the Convention. Such expressions, he said, made it plain that the purpose of this legislation was to protect performers, and this protection could not be provided to the requisite extent unless there was a right of civil action.[2] In my judgment the inference to be drawn is the opposite. Let the protection of performers be duly emphasised; yet what does Parliament do? It carries out the Convention by making certain changes in the Act of 1958, but leaves its structure and operation just as they were; in particular, the only remedy provided still remains a prosecution.[3]

The Island Records *case*

1.64 The next case was *Ex p. Island Records Ltd*[4] in which various performers and their record companies applied for an Anton Piller[5] order against a bootlegger. Walton J. held that there was no jurisdiction to make the order. The plaintiffs appealed, arguing first that a civil action lay for breach of statutory duty under the Performers' Protection Acts, and secondly that where a business or trade or interest in the nature of property was caused damage by criminal acts over and above that suffered by the public at large a

---

[1] *ibid.*, at 349.
[2] This was before the decision in *Pepper v. Hart* [1993] A.C. 593 permitted reference to be made to the Parliamentary materials.
[3] [1977] F.S.R. 345, 350.
[4] [1978] Ch. 122.
[5] *Anton Piller KG v. Manufacturing Processes Ltd* [1976] Ch. 55.

civil action could be brought without requiring the relation of the Attorney-General.[6]

Shaw and Waller L.JJ. rejected the first argument, Shaw L.J. expressly   **1.65**
approving the *MPPA v. BIP* and *Apple v. Lingasong* cases, while Lord
Denning M.R. declined to decide the point. The reasoning of both Shaw and
Waller L.JJ. was that, while the statute was arguably for the benefit of a
particular class of persons, it did not impose any defined duty. Waller L.J.
observed:

> The words "if a person knowingly ... makes a record ... or sells ... he shall be guilty
> of an offence" do not impose a duty. All the cases in which it has been held that
> there is a duty imposed which can be made the subject of a private action are cases
> where a clear duty is stated. For example, the "roof and sides of every ... working
> place shall be made secure": section 49 of the Coal Mines Act 1911. Dangerous
> parts of machinery "shall be securely fenced": see *Groves v. Lord Wimborne*
> [1898] 2 Q.B. 402 ... We were referred to a number of other cases, but there is no
> case so far as counsel could discover where phraseology similar to that in the
> section we are considering has been held to impose a duty on which an action can be
> framed.[7]

The appeal was allowed, however, by a majority (Lord Denning M.R. and   **1.66**
Waller L.J., Shaw L.J. dissenting) on the second ground. Both Lord Denning
M.R. and Waller L.J. held that the rights of the performers and the record
companies under the contracts between them were rights in the nature of
rights of property[8] damage to which by criminal acts gave rise to a civil cause
of action.

The Lonrho *case*

The correctness of the decision in *Island Records* came under scrutiny in   **1.67**
Lonrho Ltd v. Shell Petroleum Co. Ltd (No. 2)[9] in which Lonrho were
claiming damages for alleged breaches by Shell and BP of sanctions orders
against Rhodesia after UDI.

Lord Diplock (with whom the other members of the House of Lords   **1.68**
agreed) began with the presumption laid down by Lord Tenterden CJ. in *Doe
d. Murray v. Bridges*[10] that:

> ... where an Act creates an obligation, and enforces the performance in a specified
> manner ... that performance cannot be enforced in any other manner.

Where the only manner of enforcing performance provided by the Act was
criminal prosecution for failure to perform the statutory obligation or for
contravening the statutory prohibition, said Lord Diplock, there were two
classes of exception:

---

[6] [1978] Ch. 122, 126G, 127G–H and 128A. It was stated that an attempt had previously been
made to bring a relator action, but the Attorney-General had refused consent: at 125H, 136H.
[7] *ibid.*, at 142F–H.
[8] *ibid.*, at 137C–D and 144C–E respectively.
[9] [1982] A.C. 173.
[10] (1831) 1 B. & Ad. 847, 859.

The first is where upon the true construction of the Act it is apparent that the obligation or prohibition was imposed for the benefit or protection of a particular class of individuals, as in the case of the Factories Acts and similar legislation ...

The second exception is where the statute creates a public right (that is, a right to be enjoyed by all those of Her Majesty's subjects who wish to avail themselves of it) and a particular member of the public suffers what Brett J. in *Benjamin v. Storr* (1874) L.R. 9 C.P. 400, 406 described as "particular, direct and substantial" damage "other and different from that which was common to all the rest of the public".[11]

1.69   Lord Diplock rejected any wider basis of liability:

... I should mention two cases, one in the Court of Appeal of England, *Ex parte Island Records Ltd* [1978] Ch. 122, and in the High Court of Australia, *Beaudesert Shire Council v. Smith* (1966) 120 C.L.R. 145, which counsel for Lonrho, as a last resort, relied upon as showing that some broader principle has of recent years replaced these long-established principles that I have just stated for determining whether a contravention of a particular statutory prohibition by one private individual makes him liable in tort to another private individual who can prove that he has suffered damage as a result of the contravention.

Ex parte Island Records Ltd was an unopposed application for an Anton Piller order ... against a defendant who, without the consent of the performers, had made records of musical performances for the purposes of trade. This was an offence, punishable by a relatively small penalty under the Dramatic and Musical Performers' Protection Act 1958. The application for the Anton Piller order was made by performers whose performances had been "bootlegged" by the defendant without their consent and also by record companies with whom the performers had entered into exclusive contracts. *So far as the application by performers was concerned, it could have been granted for entirely orthodox reasons. The Act was passed for the protection of a particular class of individuals, dramatic and musical performers; even the short title said so.*[12] Whether the record companies would have been entitled to obtain the order in a civil action to which the performers whose performances had been bootlegged were not parties is a matter which for present purposes it is not necessary to decide. Lord Denning M.R., however, with whom Waller L.J. agreed (Shaw L.J. dissenting) appears to enunciate a wider general rule, which does not depend upon the scope and language of the statute by which a criminal offence is committed, that whenever a lawful business carried on by one individual in fact suffers damage as a consequence of a contravention by another individual of any statutory prohibition the former has a civil right of action against the latter for such damage.

My Lords, with respect, I am unable to accept that this is the law...[13] [emphasis added]

---

[11] [1982] A.C. 173, 185D, G.
[12] This was still before *Pepper v. Hart*, note 2, above.
[13] [1982] A.C. 173, 187B–F.

*The Post-*Lonrho *cases*

It is clear that Lord Diplock was disapproving the ruling of Lord Denning   **1.70**
M.R. and Waller L.J. on the second argument.[14] Whether he was also, in the
sentences italicised above, disapproving the ruling of Shaw and Waller L.JJ.
on the first argument so far as performers were concerned gave rise to a
difference of judicial opinion in a series of cases which followed. The first was
Warner Bros Records Inc. v. Parr,[15] in which Julian Jeffs Q.C. held that he
was bound by the judgments of Shaw and Waller L.JJ. on the issue of breach
of statutory duty under the Performers' Protection Acts not only with respect
to record companies,[16] but also with respect to performers.[17] Two months
later Vinelott J. in *RCA Corp. v. Pollard*[18] took the view that, as regards
performers, *Lonrho v. Shell* had effectively overruled *Island Records.*[19]
Shortly after that, Peter Gibson J. in *Ekland v. Scripglow Ltd*[20] agreed with
Vinelott J. Meanwhile, in the Scottish case of *Silly Wizard Ltd v. Shaugh-
nessy*[21] Lord Kincraig expressed the provisional view that performers did
have a civil right of action. When the *RCA* case came to the Court of Appeal
later the same year,[22] Oliver L.J. held that as regards performers the decision
of Shaw and Waller L.JJ. had *not* been overruled by *Lonrho v. Shell* and so
was binding,[23] while Lawton and Slade L.JJ.[24] expressed no view on this
point.[25] Finally, Harman J. in *Shelley v. Cunane*[26] declined to follow Vinelott
and Peter Gibson JJ. and applied the decision of Shaw and Waller L.JJ. in
Island Records.

The Peter Sellers *Case*

The Judgment of Hobhouse J.—The score at this stage, then, was that in   **1.71**
the space of 12 months three judges had said that performers could sue
for breach of statutory duty, three had said they could not and two had
refrained from expressing an opinion. This was still the state of the

---

[14] It having been argued on behalf of Lonrho that *Ex parte Island Records Ltd* was directly
applicable since in both cases the only rights which had been damaged were contractual rights:
ibid., at 180A–C. See also the judgment of Lawton L.J. in *RCA Corp. v. Pollard* [1983] Ch. 135,
146C–147B and 147B–148C.
[15] [1982] F.S.R. 383.
[16] *ibid.,* at 394. He nevertheless granted the plaintiff record companies relief on the same ground
as Lord Denning M.R. and Waller L.J., taking the view that Lord Diplock had not intended to
disapprove their ruling but merely some of Lord Denning's wider dicta.
[17] *ibid.,* at 395.
[18] [1982] F.S.R. 369.
[19] As regards record companies, he held that it was arguable that they had a cause of action for
unlawful interference with contractual relations apart from the Performers' Protection Acts.
[20] [1982] F.S.R. 431.
[21] [1984] F.S.R. 163, 174.
[22] [1983] Ch. 135.
[23] *ibid.,* at 150D–G.
[24] Hobhouse J. suggested in the *Peter Sellers* case that Slade L.J. used language which was open to
the inference that he disagreed with Oliver L.J.: [1986] F.S.R. 502, 516 referring to [1983] Ch.
135, 157. It is submitted, however, that the single sentence relied upon for this is too fragile to
[25] So far as recording companies were concerned, all three members of the Court of Appeal
agreed that the decision of Shaw and Waller L.JJ. in *Island Records* was binding on the issue of
breach of statutory duty, but that the decision of Lord Denning M.R. and Waller L.J. on the issue
of damage to contractual rights had been overruled by *Lonrho v. Shell.*
[26] [1983] F.S.R. 390.

authorities at the time of the *Peter Sellers* case. This concerned the making by Blake Edwards and United Artists of a sixth Pink Panther film after the death of Peter Sellers using clips and out-takes from previous films in the series. Sellers' personal representatives brought proceedings relying on a number of causes of action including breach of statutory duty under the Performers' Protection Acts.

1.72   At first instance, Hobhouse J. held that the relevant law to be applied was contained in the speech of Lord Diplock in the *Lonrho* case. As to the principles enunciated by Lord Diplock, Hobhouse J. made four points:

> The first is that Lord Diplock does not treat any particular statutory formulation of the criminal offence as being conclusive. Secondly, he expressly refers not only to the performance of a statutory obligation but also to the contravention of a statutory prohibition. Thus he rejects any argument that there must be an obligation stated in the statute and specifically recognises that statutory prohibitions can give rise to civil remedies as well. The third point is that Lord Diplock specifically recognises two classes of exception to the rule, the first of which he identifies as being "where upon the true construction of the Act it is apparent that the obligation or prohibition was imposed for the benefit or protection of a particular class of individuals".
>
> This exception then depends upon examining the purpose of the legislation. If it is legislation for the protection of a particular class ... then *prima facie* the statute should be construed as giving a right to a civil remedy to the members of that class. This is a *prima facie* position because, of course, the construction of any statute has to take into account all the terms of the statute and all the relevant aids to construction. (See for example the *McCall* case.[27]) Lastly the second exception stated by Lord Diplock contains two aspects, the first of which involves a consideration of when a private individual can sue without the intervention of the Attorney General; this aspect really turns upon considerations of the *locus standi* of a plaintiff in a particular situation. In contrast the second aspect clearly depends upon a specific question of statutory interpretation because Lord Diplock says: "It has first to be shown that the statute having regard to its scope and language does fall within that class of statutes which creates a legal right to be enjoyed by all ... A mere prohibition upon members of the public generally from doing what it would otherwise be lawful for them to do is not enough." In this connection therefore one can see that Lord Diplock draws a distinction between language which creates a legal right and language which creates a mere prohibition. It is at this point in his formulation and at this point alone that the type of criterion to which Shaw L.J. referred in the *McCall* case[28] enters the analysis. It does not enter the analysis under the first class of exception which Lord Diplock formulated.[29]

1.73   The significance of all this, as the judge pointed out, was that Lord Diplock

---

[27] *McCall v. Abelesz* [1976] 1 Q.B. 585. Following *Pepper v. Hart*, note 2, above, these aids may include the Parliamentary debates and other materials.
[28] *ibid.*, at 600.
[29] *Rickless v. United Artists Corp.* [1986] F.S.R. 502, 513.

had effectively disapproved the reasoning of Shaw and Waller L.JJ. in *Island Records*:

> In the *Island Records* case two members of the Court of Appeal, Waller L.J. and Shaw L.J., specifically rejected an argument that performers ... were entitled to relief on the basis that the 1958 Act fell within the equivalent of the first class of exception formulated by Lord Diplock ... With regard to the 1958 Act, their reasoning was in essence that formulated by Shaw L.J. in the *McCall* case. Thus Shaw L.J. himself ... looked for a defined duty for the benefit of a particular class and said that the 1958 Act contained no "definition in terms of a such duty". He refused to "distil from the language of the section a specific duty to performers"... Lord Denning was not willing to agree with that approach either in the *Island Records* case itself nor in the Court of Appeal in the *Lonrho* case. It is clear that Lord Diplock did not agree with it either and formulated his statement of the law in terms which are inconsistent with the reasoning of Shaw L.J. and Waller L.J.[30]

Not only had Lord Diplock disapproved the reasoning of Shaw and Waller L.JJ., but in the view of Hobhouse J. he had also disapproved their conclusion. Having quoted the passage italicised above, Hobhouse J. said this:

> There can be no doubt that in *Lonrho*, Lord Diplock was intending to hold that as regards the 1958 Act, it fell within his first class of exception and he was leaving it open whether or not it could also be construed as an Act passed for the protection of record companies.[31]

Considering for himself whether there were any reasons why the 1958 Act should not be construed as implicitly conferring a right to civil remedies, Hobhouse J. thought not. On the contrary, he was of the view that "a coherent scheme of protection" would be established.[32]   **1.74**

The Judgment of the Court of Appeal—On appeal, Sir Nicolas Browne-Wilkinson V.-C. (with whom the other members of the Court of Appeal agreed) began by considering the matter apart from authority. In the Vice-Chancellor's view, the fact that the Performers' Protection Acts were passed for the protection of performers was "a very strong pointer" in favour of civil liability under Lord Diplock's first class of exception, but not decisive. Against civil liability were four "formidable" arguments: the wording of sections 1 and 2 of the 1958 Act, which simply created offences; the decision in *MPPA v. BIP*, which Parliament had to be presumed to have known of when it enacted the Copyright Act 1956 and the 1958 Act; the contents of the Gregory Report, which formed the basis for the 1956 Act; and that the result would be to give performers a right of perpetual duration and without any of the limitations on copyright, for example as to fair dealing. Nevertheless, the Vice-Chancellor found himself unable to get   **1.75**

---

[30] *ibid.*, at 514–5.
[31] *ibid.*, at 514.
[32] *ibid.*, at 517.

away from the fact that the Act was in terms one for the protection of performers.[33]

1.76   As to Parliament's intention,[34] the Vice-Chancellor found assistance in the manner in which the 1963 Act implemented the Rome Convention:

> [Under the Rome Convention] the contracting states (of which the United Kingdom was one) undertook to protect, *inter alia*, "the rights of performers" on records. Article 7(1) of the Convention provides that "the protection provided for performers by this Convention shall include the possibility of preventing" the broadcasting, fixation or reproduction of the fixation of the performance without the consent of the performers. Two things seem to be clear. First, under the Convention the performer himself was to have "rights". Secondly, the performer's rights were to include something which, in some circumstances, would make it possible to *prevent* unauthorised reproduction, *i.e.* a *quia timet* injunction. Therefore, compliance with the Rome Convention required that there should be an English Act of Parliament which enabled the performer to obtain an injunction to prevent unauthorised reproduction on records. The Performers' Protection Act 1963 was passed expressly "to enable effect to be given to" the Rome Convention. The Act of 1963 merely altered the class of acts which infringe sections 1 and 2 of the Act, *i.e.* the Act continued on its face as one imposing criminal sanctions only. In my judgment Parliament must have considered that the Performers' Protection Act 1963 gave rise to civil rights to obtain an injunction, since otherwise Parliament would not have been carrying out its declared intention of giving effect to the Convention.[35]

1.77   It does not appear from the report that this point was argued before the Court of Appeal; nor was *Apple v. Lingasong*, in which the Vice-Chancellor's predecessor had rejected the same argument,[36] cited. Moreover, the Vice-Chancellor's interpretation of the Rome Convention is rather less convincing than it appears at first sight, for the reasons discussed in paragraphs 1.52–1.54, above. In short, it is respectfully submitted that the Vice-Chancellor's interpretation of Parliament's intention when enacting the 1963 Act is mistaken,[37] and that his predecessor's view is to be preferred.

1.78   Having given his view apart from authority, the Vice-Chancellor turned to the authorities. Here he was faced with the argument that the Court of Appeal was bound by its previous decision in *Island Records* to hold that the 1958 Act did not confer any right to civil remedies. The problem was that this could not have been overruled by *Lonrho*, since Lord Diplock's dicta concerning the position of performers under the 1958 Act were plainly *obiter*. The Vice-Chancellor's elegant solution to this dilemma was to point out that the Court was only bound by the *ratio decidendi* of the previous case, and that the *ratio decidendi* was the reason given by the Court for making the order actually made. Thus the Court was not bound by reasons given, on an

---

[33] *Rickless v. United Artists Corp.* [1988] Q.B. 40, 51E–52E.
[34] This was still before *Pepper v. Hart*, note 2, above.
[35] [1988] Q.B. 40, 52F–53A.
[36] See paras. 1.62–1.63, above.
[37] That is, even without reference to the Parliamentary materials discussed in paras. 1.40–1.45 and 1.57–1.59. Reference to those materials, of course, makes the position clearer still.

independent issue, for *not* making the order. Thus the reasons of Shaw and Waller L.JJ. were *obiter*. That being the case, the Court of Appeal was free to apply the higher source of persuasive authority, namely the dicta of Lord Diplock in *Lonrho*.[38]

The author's view is that the argument based upon breach of statutory **1.79** duty, if it had been run in *MPPA v. BIP*, ought to have succeeded (although the plaintiff might well have failed on other grounds) for the reasons given later by Lord Diplock in *Lonrho* and applied by Hobhouse J. and the Court of Appeal in *Rickless*. After the passing of the 1958 Act, however, it was too late. Sir Robert Megarry V.-C.'s analysis of the statutory history of the Performers' Protection Acts and the conclusions he drew from that history cannot be faulted. It is, in the end, significant that Lord Diplock's remarks in *Lonrho* were *obiter*. The House of Lords had not had a full argument on the Performers' Protection Acts addressed to it. If Lord Diplock had had the benefit of reading *Apple v. Lingasong*, he might well have expressed himself differently. In short, it is submitted that the Court of Appeal's decision was wrong.

That the Court of Appeal was somewhat uncertain about the conclusion it **1.80** had reached is suggested by the fact that the defendants were granted leave to appeal to the House of Lords limited to the Performers' Protection Acts point. The defendants did not pursue the matter, however, presumably because it was thought that they would not succeed in the House of Lords on the other issue.

If the matter were to be argued now that *Pepper v. Hart*[39] has permitted **1.81** reference to be made to the Parliamentary materials in appropriate cases, it is submitted that it is clear from the discussion in paragraphs 1.40–1.45 above that Parliament did not intend to provide civil remedies when it passed the 1925 Dramatic and Musical Performers' Protection Act, and from that in paragraphs 1.57–1.59 that it did not intend to change the position when it passed the 1963 Act to give effect to the Rome Convention. In other words, the Parliamentary materials reveal that the Court of Appeal's deductions as to Parliament's intentions were simply incorrect.[40] Furthermore, as discussed in paragraphs 1.52–1.54 above, the Records of the Diplomatic Conference show that the Court of Appeal misinterpreted Article 7 of the Rome Convention.

The Whitford Report and the Copyright, Designs and Patents Act 1988

In the meantime, the process of legislative reform was underway. The **1.82** Whitford Committee was appointed in 1972 to review the law of copyright and reported in 1977. The Committee, rather oddly,[41] recommended against

---

[38] [1988] Q.B. 40, 55F–56B.

[39] [1993] A.C. 593.

[40] This is nearly as good a demonstration of the virtue of the decision in *Pepper v. Hart* as the facts of that case.

[41] The Report notes that the Committee was not asked to consider the grant of new rights as such but only new remedies: Cmnd. 6723 at para. 409. Nevertheless the Whitford Committee stated that they agreed with the Gregory Committee that no copyright or similar right should be conferred. If they had disagreed, it does not appear that there would have been any obstacle to their making an appropriate recommendation.

giving performers a copyright in their performances, but in favour of making civil remedies such as an injunction and damages available.[42] The Committee felt that giving a performer a copyright in his performance could lead to considerable practical difficulties, but did not explain why. It was this compromise recommendation that ultimately led to Part II of the Copyright, Designs and Patents Act 1988.

1.83   The Whitford Report was followed by Green Papers in 1981[43] and 1983,[44] a White Paper in 1986[45] and finally by legislation in the shape of the Copyright, Designs and Patents Act 1988. In short, Part II of the 1988 Act respectively endorsed and reversed the decisions of the Court of Appeal under the Performers' Protection Acts in *Rickless v. United Artists Corp.*[46] and *RCA Corp. v. Pollard.*[47] Thus for the first time both performers and those with whom they enter into exclusive recording contracts had statutory civil rights of action to prevent the unauthorised exploitation of performances. Although Part II was studiously (and, in places, cumbersomely[48]) drafted so as to avoid use of the word "copyright",[49] the effect was to confer on performers and recording companies two new copyrights. The new rights were not full copyrights[50] (they were not assignable,[51] and imitation of a performance was not an infringement[52]), but they were bundles of rights subject to very similar provisions as to subsistence, infringement, remedies for infringement and to a lesser extent ownership as those applicable under Part I of the 1988 Act. Indeed, much of the drafting (for example, the provisions as to permitted acts, infringement and remedies) was identical.

1.84   The result is that application of copyright concepts and copyright case law is essential to understanding the new provisions. In this book, therefore, Part II is treated as having created two new species of copyright which are referred to as "performers" rights'[53] and "recording rights" respectively. These are the terms by which the draughtsman describes the new rights conferred: the terms are merely used in a slightly different way. It is hoped that this enables the reader more easily to appreciate the effect of the Act without introducing non-statutory terminology.

---

[42] Cmnd. 6723 at para. 412. Interestingly a majority of the Australian Copyright Law Review Committee in its Report on Performers' Protection made a similar recommendation, the minority favouring a proprietary right: paras. 1–2.

[43] Cmnd. 8302.

[44] Cmnd. 9445.

[45] Cmnd. 9712.

[46] [1988] Q.B. 40.

[47] [1983] Ch. 135.

[48] See, for example, Chap. 4, para. 4.03.

[49] Although the draughtsman had to admit defeat in one or two places. Thus the Copyright Tribunal was given jurisdiction over rights under Part II, a jurisdiction which has been considerably expanded by the amendments made by Copyright and Related Rights Regulations 1996: see Chap. 3.

[50] They are "neighbouring rights" in both the narrow and wide senses of the phrase: see para 1.23, above.

[51] See Chap. 3, para. 3.01.

[52] See Chap. 4, para. 4.08.

[53] Not, of course, to be confused with perform*ing* rights (sometimes referred to in older sources as perform*ance* rights , a term which is now used to refer to Part II rights), which are among the bundle of rights comprising copyright.

Three recent E.C. Directives

Legislative reform has not been confined to domestic legislation. The E.C. **1.85**
Commission has been proceeding with a programme first outlined in a 1988
Green Paper on *Copyright and the Challenge of Technology*[54] to create
uniform and improved Community-wide protection for copyright and
related right owners. There has also been a separate but complementary
effort to create a single market in broadcasting. These initiatives have led to
the passage of five Council Directives to harmonise various aspects of the law
of copyright and related rights throughout what is now the European Union,
of which two[55] are irrelevant for present purposes. Two of the remaining
three Directives in particular have necessitated amendment of Part II of the
1988 Act in order for them to be implemented and have resulted in increased
rights for performers.

The first was the Rental and Lending Rights Directive.[56] This had two main **1.86**
objectives: first to harmonise (and for many Member States to introduce for
the first time) rental and lending rights for all categories of work and
subject-matter; and secondly, to harmonise laws concerning a range of
neighbouring rights or related rights.[57] These two aspects of the Directive had
their origins in Chapters 2 and 4 of the Green Paper, dealing with rental rights
and piracy respectively, but went rather further than the original proposals,
to the benefit of performers in particular. The Directive requires Member
States to provide performers with fixation,[58] reproduction,[59] broadcasting
and communication to the public[60] and distribution rights[61] as well as rental
and lending rights.[62] Of these rights, the reproduction, distribution, rental
and lending rights are to be proprietary rights.[63] In addition, it was provided
that performers should share in a single equitable remuneration paid for
public performance or broadcasting of recordings of their performances[64]
and that performers should have an unwaivable right to equitable remuneration in circumstances where they had assigned or were to be deemed to have
assigned rental rights to phonogram or film producers.[65] The Directive was

---

[54] Document COM (88) 172 final, [1988] O.J. C71/89.
[55] Council Directive 91/250, May 14, 1991 on the legal protection of computer programs,
[1991] O.J. L122/42, and Council Directive 96/9 March 11, 1996 on the legal protection of
databases, [1996] O.J. L77.
[56] Council Directive 92/100, November 19, 1992 on rental right and lending right and on certain
rights related to copyright in the field of intellectual property, [1992] O.J. L346/61. See generally
Reinbothe and von Lewinski, note 39 to para. 1.23, above, which describes the legislative history
of the Directive and gives a detailed commentary on its provisions. The authors of the book, a
member of and a consultant to the Commission, were closely involved in the preparation,
drafting and adoption of the Directive.
[57] Chapter II of the Directive closely follows the main provisions of the Rome Convention
although it goes further in certain respects.
[58] E.C. Rental and Lending Rights Directive, note 56, above, Art. 6(1).
[59] *ibid.*, Art. 7(1), (2).
[60] *ibid.*, Art. 8(1).
[61] *ibid.*, Art. 9(1).
[62] *ibid.*, Art. 1(1), 2(1), 2(4).
[63] *ibid.*, Art. 2(4), 7(2), 9(4).
[64] *ibid.*, Art. 8(2).
[65] *ibid.*, Art. 4.

due to be implemented by July 1, 1994.[66] In the event was not implemented by the United Kingdom until December 1, 1996[67] after the circulation of a draft statutory instrument in March 1995 and extensive lobbying by interested parties.

1.87   The second was the Satellite Broadcasting Directive.[68] The main effect of this so far as performers are concerned was to provide that performers' rights under Chapter II of the Rental and Lending Rights Directive applied to satellite broadcasting.[69]

1.88   The third and most controversial (at least so far as copyright is concerned) was the Term Directive.[70] This was primarily designed to overcome the difficulties caused by the differing periods of protection among Member States.[71] It provided that the duration of performers' rights should be a 50-year term starting from the end of the calendar year in which the performance was given or, if a fixation was lawfully published or communicated to the public within that period, from the date of first publication or first communication.[72] More importantly, perhaps, the Term Directive introduced the principle of "reciprocal treatment" for protection of performers of non-E.U. nationals in place of the principle of "national treatment" previously applied in U.K. law. This means that non-E.U. nationals are given the same protection as under their own law, rather than the same protection as domestic and other E.U. nationals. This Directive was due to be implemented by July 1, 1995,[73] but in the event was not implemented by the United Kingdom until January 1, 1996.

1.89   The implementation of these Directives in the United Kingdom, and in particular the requirement of the Rental and Lending Rights Directive that certain performers' rights be proprietary, has resulted in performers' rights being further assimilated with copyright. Thus a subset of performers' rights (referred to as "performers' property rights") are now full property rights. As well as being assignable, such rights may be exclusively licensed such that the exclusive licensee acquires a concurrent right of action. They are also subject to provisions corresponding to those in Part I relating to remedies and to the regulation by the Copyright Tribunal of collective licensing bodies.

---

[66] *ibid.*, Art. 15(1)

[67] Thus potentially exposing the U.K. to liability under the principle in case C-479/93, *Francovich v. Italy* [1991] I E.C.R. 5357; [1993] 2 C.M.L.R. 66; and case C-46/93, *Brasserie du Pecheur SA v. Germany* [1996] All E.R. (E.C.) 301; [1996] 1 C.M.L.R. 889.

[68] Council Directive 93/83, September 27, 1993 on the co-ordination of certain rules concerning copyright and rights related to copyright applicable to satellite broadcasting and cable transmission, [1993] O.J. L248/15. (In addition the Commission has proposed a Council Decision that the Community approve the European Convention relating to questions on copyright law and neighbouring rights in the framework of transfrontier broadcasting by satellite (the Strasbourg Convention): [1996] O.J. L164/10.)

[69] *ibid.*, Art. 4.

[70] Council Directive 93/98, October 29, 1993 harmonising the term of protection of copyright and certain related rights, [1993] O.J. L290/9.

[71] Highlighted by Case 341/87, *EMI Electrola GmbH v. Patricia Im- und- Export Verwaltungs GmbH* [1989] E.C.R. 79; [1989] 2 C.M.L.R. 235 in which the European Court of Justice held that the owner of the German copyright in certain sound recordings of performances by Cliff Richard was entitled to enforce that copyright against imports from Denmark where the corresponding copyright had already expired.

[72] Term Directive, note 70, above, Art. 3(1).

[73] *ibid.*, Art. 13(1).

When implementing these Directives, the Government also gave effect to **1.90**
the European Economic Area Act 1993[74] by making reference to "EEA
nationals" and "EEA States" rather than "E.C. (or E.U.) nationals" and
"EEC (or Member) States". The main effects of this are to extend national
treatment to EEA nationals as well as E.U. nationals and to extend the free
circulation rule to EEA states.

TRIPs

Probably the most significant step in the international development of **1.91**
performers' rights since the Rome Convention was the Agreement on
Trade-Related Aspects of Intellectual Property Rights (TRIPs) which is
annexed to and forms part of the Marrakesh Agreement Establishing the
World Trade Organisation signed by 124 nations on April 15, 1994.[75] Article
14(1) of TRIPs requires performers to be granted "the possibility of
preventing" the following acts without their authorisation: the fixation of
their performance on a phonogram; the reproduction of such fixation; and
the broadcasting by wireless means and the communication to the public of
their live performance. Furthermore the term of protection for performers
shall last at least until the end of a period of 50 years computed from the end
of the calendar year in which the fixation was made or the performance took
place (presumably, if unfixed).[76] The implementation of these provisions will
result in a massive worldwide extension of performers' rights.[77]

The WIPO Performances and Phonograms Treaty

In 1993 WIPO started work on a Possible Instrument (Treaty) for the **1.92**
Protection of Rights of Performers and Producers of Phonograms as an
offshoot of its work on a Possible Protocol to the Berne Convention. This
work involved discussion of various proposals to strengthen performers'
rights, including extension of the definition of performers to variety artists
and performers of folklore, granting performers moral rights, providing
performers with a right in respect of the broadcasting of recordings of their
performances and extending the term of protection to 50 years.[78] The
resulting WIPO Performances and Phonograms Treaty was finalised at a

---

[74] Which itself implemented the EEA Agreement, note 87, above.
[75] The WTO Agreement is often referred to as "GATT [General Agreement on Tariffs and
Trade]" but in fact GATT 1994 is another annexe to the WTO Agreement. The WTO Agreement
together with a bundle of Ministerial Declarations and Decisions form the Final Act of the
Uruguay Round of Multilateral Trade Negotiations.
[76] Art. 14(5).
[77] It has been suggested that TRIPs may have direct effect in European Union law, but in *R. v.
Comptroller of Patents, Designs and Trade Marks, ex p. Lenzing AG* [1997] R.P.C. 245 it was
held that this was not so. It would not appear that it makes any difference either way so far as
performers' rights in the United Kingdom are concerned, however, since the protection provided
exceeds that laid down by Art. 14.
[78] See the Memorandum prepared for the Third Session of the Committee of Experts in
December 1994, [1994] *Copyright* 241 and the Memorandum prepared for the Fourth Session in
September 1995, [1995] *Industrial Property and Copyright* 363. The Fifth Session was held in
February 1996 ([1996] *Industrial Property and Copyright* 118) and the Sixth Session in May
1996 ([1996] *Industrial Property and Copyright* 236). The draft treaties prepared by the
Chairman of the Committee of Experts for discussion at the Geneva Conference were published
as a supplement to [1996] 11 EIPR.

Diplomatic Conference in Geneva in December 1996 attended by 762 representatives of 127 states, 7 inter-governmental organisations and 76 non-governmental organisations.[79]

1.93 The principal advance made by the Treaty so far as performers are concerned is that at long last a performer must be accorded inalienable moral rights, namely "the right to claim to be identified as the performer of his performances, except where omission is dictated by the manner of the use of the performance, and to object to any distortion or mutilation or other modification of his performances that would be prejudicial to his reputation", albeit only in respect of live aural performances and performances fixed in phonograms.[80] These rights are to last at least until the expiry of performers' economic rights, except that Contracting Parties whose existing legislation does not provide for protection after death may provide that the rights cease on death.[81] In addition, performers are to have the "exclusive right of authorizing" (rather than the mere "possibility of preventing") broadcasting (except rebroadcasting), communication to the public (except where the performance is a broadcast performance) and fixation of live performances,[82] direct or indirect reproduction of performances fixed in phonograms,[83] distribution of performances fixed in phonograms,[84] commercial rental of performances fixed in phonograms[85] and making available on demand (*e.g.* on-line) performances fixed in phonograms.[86] As under the Rome Convention, performers and phonogram producers have a right to a single equitable remuneration for the use of phonograms published for commercial purposes for broadcasting or communication to the public,[87] but Contracting Parties may enter reservations with respect to this provision.[88] The definition of performers has been extended to include performers of folklore, but not variety artists.[89] The term of protection for performers is 50 years computed from the end of the year in which the performance was fixed in a phonogram.[90] There also provisions concerning copy protection measures, rights management information and enforcement.[91] The Treaty shall enter into force three months after 30 instruments of ratification or accession have been deposited with WIPO.[92]

1.94 Otherwise the Treaty is something of a disappointment. The major

---

[79] See Reinbothe, Martin-Prat and von Lewinski, "The New WIPO Treaties: A First Resumé" [1997] 4 EIPR 171.

[80] Art. 5(1).

[81] Art. 5(2).

[82] Art. 6.

[83] Art. 7.

[84] Art. 8(1). Contracting Parties are free to determine whether and if so in what circumstances this right is exhausted by first sale with the performer's consent: Art. 8(2).

[85] Art. 9(1). This is subject to the proviso that Contracting Parties which on April 15, 1994 had in force a system of equitable remuneration for such rental may maintain that systems provided that it does not materially impair performers' rights of reproduction: Art. 9(2).

[86] Art. 10.

[87] Art. 15(1).

[88] Art. 15(3).

[89] Art. 2(a).

[90] Art. 17(1).

[91] Arts. 18, 19 and 23.

[92] Art. 29.

omission, as under the Rome Convention, is the absence of any rights for performers in respect of performances fixed in films. This was at the insistence of the United States. In return for the European Union's agreement to this, however, a resolution was passed that an extraordinary session of competent WIPO Governing Bodies should take place in the first quarter of 1997 to start preparatory work on a Protocol to the Treaty concerning audiovisual performances with a view to the adoption of such a Protocol not later than 1998. This meeting was held on March 20–21, 1997 and will be followed by further discussion.

Future European developments

The three Directives discussed in paragraphs 1.85–1.90 above are not the end of the story so far as European legislation is concerned. On July 19, 1995 the European Commission published a Green Paper on *Copyright and Related Rights in the Information Society*.[93] This paper was primarily a discussion document, addressing in particular issues raised by digitalisation, rather than a policy statement, but a number of proposals for extensions of intellectual property rights were aired. In the context of performers' rights the most significant proposals were for an exclusive broadcasting right instead of a mere right to equitable remuneration[94] and for extension of the rental and lending rights to digital transmission over networks.[95] In addition it was suggested that it may be desirable to harmonise national definitions of "communication to the public"[96] and national provisions relating to private copying[97] and that protection of moral rights should be improved,[98] both of which could affect performers. Interested parties made more than 350 submissions in response to the Green Paper and a hearing was held in Brussels in January 1996. A conference on *Copyright and Related Rights on the Threshold of the 21st Century* held at Florence in June 1996 concluded the consultation process.

1.95

A follow-up communication was adopted by the Commission on November 20, 1996.[99] This proposes a programme of legislative action to harmonise further aspects of copyright and neighbouring rights. In particular the Commission proposes to harmonise the scope of the following rights with respect to all categories of work and subject matter: the reproduction right, including the limitations and exceptions to it[1]; the right of communication to the public, including the limitations and exceptions to it[2]; and the distribution right.[3] So far as the reproduction right is concerned, it is

1.96

---

[93] COM (5) 382 final.
[94] *ibid.*, pp. 61–64.
[95] *ibid.*, pp. 56–60. It may be noted that the Commission considers that the definition of "rental" in the Rental and Lending Rights Directive "clearly includes activities such as video on demand and other electronic forms based on point-to-point transmission" (*cf.* Chap. 4, para 4.34), but suggests that the position should be clarified by express provision.
[96] *ibid.*, pp. 53–55.
[97] *ibid.*, pp. 49–52.
[98] *ibid.*, pp. 65–68. See also Commission Press Release IP/93/1 of January 4, 1993.
[99] IP/96/1042.
[1] *ibid.*, pp. 9–12.
[2] *ibid.*, pp. 12–14.
[3] *ibid.*, pp. 17–19.

envisaged that this will be extended to cover acts such as uploading and downloading of digitised material as well as transient acts of reproduction. In addition the communication emphasises the importance of harmonising the limitations and exceptions to the right, and in particular private copying. This raises the hotly contested issue of a levy: at present 11 of the 15 Member States impose a levy on blank tape and/or recording equipment to compensate copyright owners for private copying, but these systems vary widely in their scope and operation, and the other Member States (in particular the United Kingdom) oppose such a levy.[4] The communication proposes that in some situations private copying may be made a restricted act while in others it may be permitted with or without remuneration. As to communication to the public, it is proposed that this be extended so as to cover digital on-demand transmission, with limitations and exceptions harmonised along the same lines as for the reproduction right. With respect to the distribution right, the main proposal is to stipulate that this may only be exhausted by the first sale in the Community by or with the consent of the rightholder. In addition to these proposals the Commission is continuing to study questions concerning the broadcasting right, moral rights, applicable law and law enforcement and management of rights.[5]

PROPOSALS FOR REFORM

1.97   As we have seen, the 1988 Act had not been on the statute book long before it was being amended, particularly in consequence of the three E.C. Directives. Although these have strengthened the position of performers considerably, the developments have been piecemeal. There remain a number of respects in which Part II is still not everything it could be and would benefit from reappraisal as a whole. These proposals are solely concerned with the position in the United Kingdom, but some are of more general relevance.

1.98   The first task is to bring performers into the copyright fold proper, rather than to continue to pretend that performers' rights are in some way different to other copyrights. This should be done by bringing performers' rights under what is now Part I of the Act, rather than in a separate Part, and by using the term copyright. This would have the advantages of dispensing with some rather cumbersome terminology, eliminating unnecessary duplication in drafting (in particular, Schedules 2 and 2A to the Act), avoiding complicated cross-referencing between Parts (for example the provisions concerning permitted acts) and ensuring consistency of interpretation. In short, the law could be more briefly, simply and straightforwardly expressed. It may be

---

[4] On September 22, 1992 the Commission informally submitted a draft directive to the Internal Market Council proposing a levy on blank tapes and recording equipment. Although this was opposed by the U.K., Italy, Ireland and Luxembourg, the Commission announced that a formal proposal for a directive would be released in the near future: Communication from the European Commission entitled *Europe's Way to the Information Society: An Action Plan*, COM (94) 347 final, July 19, 1994. After this, continued opposition by Member States and lobbying by tape and hardware manufacturers led to this proposal being temporarily shelved.

[5] Note 99, above, pp. 20–28.

objected that performers' rights *are* different to copyright at least[6] to the extent that they are not infringed by copying or reproduction of the performance itself.[7] This is a point that in itself deserves consideration (see paragraph 1.104, below), but even if this limitation were retained, it is not on its own a sufficient reason to treat performers' rights as so different to other copyrights that they need to be exiled to a separate Part. This argument has become even stronger with the advent of performers' property rights.

While this redrafting was carried out the opportunity could also be taken to **1.99** remove certain minor anomalies in the current scheme. For example, not all of the permitted acts laid down in Chapter 3 of Part I of the 1988 Act are reproduced in Schedule 2. A glaring example is that Schedule 2 contains no exception for fair dealing for research or private study.[8] It is difficult to see why researchers and students should be permitted to copy copyright works but not recordings of performances, particularly when such an exception is provided for by both the Rome Convention[9] and the E.C. Rental and Lending Rights Directive.[10]

Turning to more substantial matters, performers' exclusive rights should **1.100** be upgraded to full property rights so as to be assignable and otherwise transmissible to the same extent as other copyrights, rather than to the limited extent provided at present.[11] It is hard to see why performers and their heirs should be prejudiced by comparison with other copyright owners in this way. The present position whereby some performers' rights have the status of a property right and others do not is irrational. (Requiring that performers' rights to equitable remuneration from secondary uses be unwaivable is a different matter.) Although the Rental and Lending Rights Directive does not provide for performers' fixation, broadcasting and public communication rights (as opposed to their rental, lending, reproduction and distribution rights[12]) to be proprietary, it does not appear that it prohibits Member States making these rights property rights.[13] In most other Member States performers' rights other than moral rights are assignable.[14] Moreover, the division of performers' rights into those which are proprietary and those which are not makes the law unnecessarily complicated.

In addition, performers should be given rights which are of equivalent **1.101** breadth to those of authors, and especially producers of sound recordings and films. At present, performers, unlike producers of sound recordings and films, do not have exclusive rights to authorise the public performance and broadcasting of recordings of their performances. Instead they merely have

---

[6] Purists may also protest at the erosion of the distinction between a "neighbouring right" and a copyright, but the true distinction, which is between a "neighbouring right" and an "author's right" (see para. 1.23, above), is not one recognised by the Copyright, Designs and Patents Act 1988: Part I contains common provisions for copyrights which are "authors' rights" and for those which are not.

[7] See Chap. 4, para. 4.08.

[8] See Chap. 5, para. 5.03.

[9] Art. 15(1).

[10] Art. 10(1).

[11] See Chap. 3, paras. 3.05–3.07, 3.11–3.15.

[12] See para. 1.86, above.

[13] Reinbothe and von Lewinski, note 39 to para. 1.23, above, pp. 53–54, 94.

[14] See Chap. 9.

secondary rights to prevent the public performance or broadcasting of recordings made without their consent and to receive equitable remuneration from the public performance and broadcasting of sound recordings of performances made with their consent.[15] Recital (20) of the Rental and Lending Rights Directive expressly permits Member States to grant performers greater rights than those conferred by Article 8, but so far the United Kingdom has not availed itself of this option. It is submitted that there is no justification for the unequal treatment of performers by comparison with producers of sound recordings and films. It appears likely that the granting to performers of exclusive rights will in any event be required by a future E.U. directive.[16] At the very least, performers should be entitled to equitable remuneration for the public performance and broadcasting of films and videos of their performances as well as sound recordings.[17]

1.102   Another area where performers are, at least in theory, treated less advantageously in the United Kingdom than copyright owners is that of private copying. Private copying is an infringement of copyright but not of performers' rights. In practice the consequence is that neither group of right owners is compensated for this activity, since it is impossible to enforce copyright to stop it. It now seems likely that the European Union will introduce legislation to deal with the problem. As noted above, most Member States now impose levies to compensate right owners for private copying and in many countries performers share in the payments made from the levies. Plainly it is not possible to consider performers in isolation from other right owners, however.

1.103   Next, there is the question of moral rights. At present, performers' rights are exclusively economic, and they do not have the moral rights accorded to authors by Chapter IV of Part I of the 1988 Act.[18] While it is possible that granting performers a paternity right (*i.e.* the right to be identified when the performance is reproduced) might cause some difficulties (although not, it is submitted, insuperable ones),[19] it is submitted that there is a strong case for granting performers an integrity right (*i.e.* the right not to have their performances subjected to derogatory treatment; that is, distortion or mutilation or treatment which is otherwise prejudicial to the honour or reputation of the performer).[20] Technology has now made it possible by means of digital manipulation to alter recordings of performances in ways which could easily be very damaging to a performer. There is no good reason why performers should not be protected against this being done without their consent. Most Member States of the European Union already grant performers moral rights, and again it appears likely that there will be an E.U. Directive to harmonise moral rights as some point in the future. In any event, the United Kingdom will have to grant performers moral rights in respect of

---

[15] See Chap. 4., paras. 4.40–4.44 and Chap. 3, paras. 3.44–3.47.
[16] See para. 1.95, above.
[17] *cf.* Chap. 3, paras. 3.44–3.47.
[18] Which itself probably does not comply with Art. 6*bis* of the Berne Convention.
[19] After all, many other countries have granted performers a paternity right as well as an integrity right: see Chap. 9.
[20] *cf.* Copyright, Rights and Designs Act 1988, s. 80(2).

their aural performances and performances fixed on phonograms if it is to ratify the new WIPO Treaty.

Then there is the difficult question of copying of performances themselves **1.104** (as opposed to recordings or broadcasts of them). If the protection afforded to a playwright includes preventing another person from copying the whole or a substantial part of his play, is there any reason of principle why an actor should not be accorded the same right? Identical copying is, of course, an impossibility in the case of performances.[21] Copying of a substantial part is quite possible, however. The difficulty then lies in deciding where to draw the line between the permissible and the impermissible. Most people, one suspects, would say that impersonators should be permitted to continue their acts. But what about less frivolous copying of performances? An example of this is "sound alike" advertising.[22] Another is "sound alike music", music intended primarily for public performance (particularly as background music in shops and the like) in which the performers deliberately strive to imitate an existing performance as closely as possible. Since activities of this nature are economically damaging to the original performers and would seem to have little "artistic" justification, it would appear reasonable to give performers the right to prevent them.[23] Again few countries presently provide such protection,[24] but the trend toward giving performers equal rights with authors suggests that it may begin to happen soon.

Finally, performers' rights should be extended to sportsmen and women. **1.105** As is argued elsewhere in this book,[25] no theoretical distinction can be drawn between sportsmen and other performers. Nor is there any economic justification for so doing. On the contrary, the economic arguments for granting performers' rights to sportsmen have becoming compelling, for example with the introduction of satellite television channels devoted solely to sport. Similarly with the moral argument for protection: a sportsman's sporting prowess is as much an aspect of his personality as is a musician's artistry.[26] It is only snobbery that says that an opera singer should be accorded rights in his or her performance and not a boxer or tennis player.[27] As matters stand a sportsman's commentary on another's performance is protected,[28] but not his own performance. As yet, few if any countries have

---

[21] See paras. 1.21–1.22, above.

[22] See Chap. 4, para. 4.08 and Chap. 8, para. 8.19.

[23] It appears that the Nigerian Copyright Act (Cap 68, 1990 Laws of the Federation of Nigeria), s. 23 does give performers the right to restrain imitations of a performance: see Sodipo, "Nigeria Accedes to the Rome Convention: Is Rome Satisfactory for Nigerian Performers?" [1994] 1 ENT. LR 20.

[24] Where there is protection, it is usually by other means such as the rights of personality and publicity in the USA and Canada or a general unfair competition provision. Thus in the Spanish case *Rocio Jurado* (High Court, June 9, 1990, Aranzadi 5251) [1991] 7 EIPR D-131 it was held that slavish imitation of the style of a performer constituted plagiarism punishable under article 534 of the Criminal Code.

[25] Chap. 2, paras. 2.18–2.19.

[26] In common parlance sportsmen and women are now "personalities" just as much as other entertainers.

[27] On this question see Pasek, "Performers' Rights in Sports: Where Does Copyright Stand?" (1990) 8 *Copyright World* 13 and "Performers' Rights in Sports—The Experts Comment" (1990) 9 *Copyright World* 12.

[28] See Chap. 2, paras. 2.10–2.14.

granted sportsmen performers' rights, but the trend of protection is clearly in that direction.

1.106   In the first edition of this book, it was tentatively suggested that performers' rights merited a more extended duration than the fixed 50-year term originally adopted in the 1988 Act.[29] With the advent of the Term Directive this is now a dead issue for the foreseeable future. Nevertheless, it may reasonably be questioned why a playwright should be entitled to life plus 70 years,[30] but an actor or director only to 50 years (from whichever starting point).[31] The principal reason why copyright in films and sound recordings has traditionally had a fixed term is that the "author" for the purpose of these species of copyright is likely to be a corporation, and so it is not possible to set a term *post mortem auctoris*. The Term Directive has abandoned this approach in the case of films, however, by linking the duration to the lives of the principal creative contributors.[32] In any event, this difficulty does not apply to performers.

---

[29] First edition, Chap. 1, para. 1.30(4).
[30] In Peru performers are protected for life plus 70 years: see Chap. 9, para. 9.182.
[31] One answer, of course, is that the term of authors' rights is now excessive, but the political reality is that the lobbies for greater protection have greater influence than the public interest lobbies.
[32] Art. 2(2) implemented by Copyright, Designs and Patents Act 1988, ss. 12(1A), (1B).

2. Subsistence and Duration

Not all performances qualify for protection under Part II of the Copyright, Designs and Patents Act 1988. As with copyright under Part I of the 1988 Act, various conditions must be satisfied in order for performers' rights or recording rights to subsist.[1] In summary, the conditions for subsistence of performers' rights are that: (1) the performance must be of a type in which performers' rights are capable of subsisting (2) which is a live performance (3) given by one or more individuals in circumstances such that (4) the statutory qualification requirements are satisfied. For recording rights to subsist, there is an additional condition, namely that (5) the performance is the subject of an exclusive recording contract.

2.01

Unlike copyright in literary, dramatic, musical and artistic works, there is no requirement of originality. Thus an actor, for example, may have performers' rights in each and every performance he gives in a particular play. Nor is there any requirement that the performance be a professional one, and so amateur performances are also protected. Performances given before Part II of the 1988 Act came into force on August 1, 1989[2] are protected[3] provided that the rights have not expired.[4]

2.02

SUBSISTENCE OF PERFORMERS' RIGHTS ✳

Protected types of performance

Section 180(2) of the 1988 Act defines "performance" for the purposes of Part II[5] as meaning

2.03

  (a) a dramatic performance (which includes dance and mime),

  (b) a musical performance,

  (c) a reading or recitation of a literary work, or

---

[1] Unlike Part I of the 1988 Act (see s. 1), Part II does not expressly refer to performers' rights or recording rights "subsisting" in a performance (except, curiously, in s. 191), but the effect is the same.

[2] Copyright, Designs and Patents Act 1988 (Commencement No. 1) Order 1989, S.I. (1989 No. 816).

[3] Copyright, Designs and Patents Act 1988, s. 180(3).

[4] As to which see paras. 2.55–2.75, below.

[5] Note that the different definition of "performance" contained in s. 19(2) of the 1988 Act only applies to Part I.

ʎ (d) a performance of a variety act or any similar presentation, which is, or so far
        as it is, a live performance given by one or more individuals.

Categories (a)–(d) are therefore the types of performance in which performers' rights are capable of subsisting.

2.04 The definition of "performance" is something of a hybrid, in that the first
two categories are not on their face defined in terms of any work or type of
work performed, but the second two categories are. Furthermore, it is
expressly provided in Part II that the expression "literary work" is to have the
same meaning as in Part I,[6] but there is no provision relating the meanings of
"dramatic" and "musical" to their meanings in Part I. Although it is tempting
to assume that these terms are to be construed in accordance with the
meaning that they have in Part I, this suggests that there may be some
difference. An important question which bears upon this is whether the four
categories are mutually exclusive.

Dramatic performances

2.05 Just as "dramatic work" in Part I of the 1988 Act includes a work of dance or
mime,[7] so too "dramatic performance" includes dance and mime. The
definitions are not necessarily co-extensive, however, for it would seem that a
dramatic performance need not be a performance of a "work". It is submitted
that this makes it clear that performers' rights may subsist in an improvised
dramatic performance (that is, even if a purely improvised dramatic piece is
not a work[8]).

2.06 Other than this, "dramatic performance" is not defined. It is arguable,
however, that "dramatic performance" excludes the other three categories of
performance. This argument depends partly upon the structure of the
subsection, which is comparable to that of section 3(1) in Part I, and partly
upon a consideration of the definitions of the other categories.[9] If it is right, it
is submitted that "dramatic performance" is to be understood as comprising
one or both of two aspects[10]: (a) *speech*, that is to say, the use of the human
voice to convey dramatic meaning to an audience (but excluding singing,
which is a musical performance); and (b) *movement*, that is to say, the use of
facial and bodily gesture and movement to convey dramatic meaning to an
audience. Although *design* (scenery, costumes, props and lighting) and *sound*
(music and sound effects) are important elements of drama,[11] it seems
probable that these are not dramatic performances within the meaning of
section 180(2)(a).[12]

---

[6] Copyright, Designs and Patents Act 1988, s. 211(1).
[7] Copyright, Designs and Patents Act 1988, s. 3(1).
[8] Compare the discussion of improvised literary works in paras. 2.10–2.12.
[9] See in particular paras. 2.07–2.08.
[10] See para. 2.24, however.
[11] See, *e.g.* Raymond Williams, *Drama in Performance* (Open University Press), pp. 161–162.
[12] See further para. 2.24, below.

Musical performances

"Musical performance" is not defined in Part II. In Part I of the 1988 Act   **2.07**
"musical work" is defined as:

> a work consisting of music, exclusive of any words or action intended to be sung,
> spoken or performed with the music.[13]

Again, it is submitted that a musical performance need not be a performance
of a "work", so that an improvised musical performance will suffice.[14]

On the other hand, it is submitted that "musical performance" should be   **2.08**
understood as excluding performances in other categories; in particular, that
"musical performance" should exclude any dramatic performance that
accompanies it. Such an interpretation may be supported both by analogy
with the definition of musical work ("exclusive of ... any action ...
performed with the music") and by reference to the structure of section
180(2).

The point is not an idle one, for the significance of the definition of musical   **2.09**
work is that separate copyrights subsist in, say, the music and words of a
song. Similarly, separate performers' rights should subsist in, for example,
the musical performance and the dramatic performance of an opera. A rough
and ready distinction in this example is between what the audience hears
(musical performances) and what the audience sees (dramatic performances).
The two categories of performances may involve different performers; for
example, orchestral musicians who give musical performances but do not
appear on stage or dancers who give dramatic performances but neither sing
nor play an instrument. The two categories of performances may also involve
different recording rights: for example, a record company may have
recording rights in the orchestral musicians' musical performances while a
film or television company may have recording rights in the dancers' dramatic
performances. Then the two categories of performance may be exploitable in
different ways: for example, the musical performances alone by the
publication of records, etc.; the dramatic performances alone by the
publication of still photographs; and the musical and dramatic performances
together by the publication of films or videos.

Readings and recitals

"Literary work" is defined in section 3(1) of the Act to mean: **2.10**

> any work, other than a dramatic or musical work, which is written, spoken or sung,
> and accordingly includes:
> (a) a table or compilation, and
> (b) a computer program.

A performance which consists of reading or reciting will therefore not be one
in which performers' rights subsist unless what is read or recited is a "work".

---

[13] Copyright, Designs and Patents Act 1988, s. 3(1).
[14] *cf.* para. 2.05.

This raises the question of fixation, that is, whether an improvised reading or recital is within the definition. This question can be approached in two stages.

2.11   First, suppose that what is read or recited (a poem or a legal judgment, for example) existed in the author's mind but had not been reduced to writing or other material form prior to the performance. In this case, it is submitted that it is clear that under the 1988 Act[15] a literary work may exist before it is recorded. This follows from the inclusion of the words "any work ... which is ... spoken" in the definition just quoted. It is confirmed by subsections 3(2) and (3) of the 1988 Act, which provide that copyright does not subsist in a literary, dramatic or musical work unless and until it is recorded and that, where it is recorded by someone other than the author, the question whether copyright subsists in the record is distinct from the question whether it subsists in the work.

2.12   Secondly, suppose that the piece is composed and performed entirely extempore. Again, it is submitted that under the 1988 Act the position is clear.[16] "Any work ... which is spoken" must include works spoken extempore. An example may help. A prominent contemporary instance of the extempore literary work is the diary dictated into a tape recorder. It is submitted that there can be no doubt that this is a "literary work" so as to qualify for copyright protection. It is an interesting question how far this may be taken: is all speech a literary work?[17] It is tentatively suggested that this is not so, for there must be an identifiable "work". The "work" may be a work in progress or unfinished or improvised, but it must be in some way a distinct and identifiable creation. A mere snippet of speech is not a literary work.[18] An alternative view might be that all speech is a literary work, but that copyright protection is reserved for those speeches upon which the author has expended a significant degree of skill or labour and which are recorded.

2.13   It may be objected that, whatever the position is under Part I of the Act, a work that is composed extempore is not read or recited, for these words imply that the work existed prior to the performance. It is submitted that this construction is too narrow. If it were adopted, it would lead to an arbitrary distinction between works composed but not recorded prior to performance and works truly extempore. The *Oxford English Dictionary* definition suggests that the word "recite" is capable of bearing the wider construction even if it is not the most natural:

> recite ... 1. a. *trans.* To repeat or utter aloud (something previously composed, heard, or learned by heart); now *spec.* to repeat to an audience (a piece of verse or other composition) from memory and in an appropriate manner. Also, to read out

---

[15] The position was less clear under the Copyright Act 1956. Interested readers are referred to the discussion in the first edition, Chap. 2, paras. 2.05–2.06.

[16] Again it was more doubtful under the 1956 Act. See Chap. 2, para. 2.07 of the first edition.

[17] *cf.* Moliere, *Le Bourgeois Gentilhomme*, Act II, scene iv: M. Jourdain: *Par ma foi! il y a plus de quarante ans que je dis de la prose sans que j'en suisse rien* (Good heavens! For more than 40 years I have been speaking prose without knowing it). But did M. Jourdain speak literary works without knowing it?

[18] *cf. Exxon Corp. v. Exxon Insurance Consultants International Ltd* [1982] R.P.C. 69, in which the Court of Appeal held that the invented word "Exxon" was not a literary work. See also paras. 2.21–2.22, in which interviews are considered.

or aloud (now *rare*) ... 2. a. To relate, rehearse, narrate, tell, declare; to give an account of; to describe in detail. ? *Obs* ... 3. To compose; to write *down*. *Obs. rare....* 6. a. *intr.* (or without direct object) To relate, rehearse, etc. *Obs.* (cf. sense 2).[19]

Similarly, it is submitted that there is a performance within the meaning of **2.14** section 180(2) even if only part of a literary work (for example, a novel) is read or recited. Such a performance is a reading or recitation from the work, and in that sense is a reading or recitation of the work even though not of the whole work.

Performances of variety acts—circus performers

"Variety act" is nowhere defined in the 1988 Act. Furthermore, the term has **2.15** no previous statutory history, having appeared neither in the Copyright Act 1956[20] nor in the Performers' Protection Acts 1958–1972. On the face of section 180(2), it would appear that sub-subsection (d) is intended to cover performances of a nature not within categories (a) to (c). *The Oxford English Dictionary*, however, gives the following:

> **variety** ... 9b. Used to designate music-hall or theatrical entertainments of a mixed character (songs, dances, impersonations, etc.). Also applied to things or persons connected with such entertainments.

Everything within this definition falls within one of categories (a) to (c). Thus an impersonation is a dramatic performance. If "variety act" is given its dictionary definition, sub-subsection (d) will be mere surplusage.

The use of the term "variety act" appears to stem from the Report of the **2.16** Whitford Committee which used the term "variety artistes" compendiously to describe performers such as magicians, clowns, jugglers, acrobats and the like.[21] This usage may derive from the name of the Variety Artistes' Federation.[22] While some performances given by circus performers could be regarded as dramatic performances (clowning, for example), others do not fit into this category so easily. Interpreting "variety act" in this way will therefore serve a useful purpose. It is submitted that it is legitimate to have regard to the legislative history for this purpose.[23]

On normal principles, the words "or any similar presentation" would be **2.17**

---

[19] 2nd ed.

[20] A proposal was made to made to amend what became s. 45 and Schedule 6 to the 1956 Act with the intention of extending the protection under the 1925 Act to variety artists, but the amendment was withdrawn: H.C. Deb., Vol. 195, ser. 5, cols. 316–317, 1186–1188 (1955–1956); Vol. 196, cols. 762, 765 (1956).

[21] Cmnd. 6732 at para. 407. The expression was also used in the 1986 White Paper: Cmnd. 9712 at para. 14.5. The same usage appears in the *WIPO Guide to the Rome Convention* (WIPO, 1981) in the commentary on Art. 9, but the term is not used in the Convention itself.

[22] The Report of the Gregory Committee refers to a submission made by the Variety Artistes' Federation, even though this is not one of the organisations listed in the relevant appendix: Cmnd. 8662 at para. 165. The Variety Artistes' Federation is now incorporated within Equity. The Variety & Allied Entertainments' Council, however, is a confederation of unions representing performers who appear in clubs, cabarets and "variety venues".

[23] Either under the mischief rule (see *Halsbury's Laws*, 4th ed., Vol. 44, para. 901) or under the rule in *Pepper v. Hart* [1993] A.C. 593.

—of the same kind.

construed *ejusdem generis* with "variety act". The words may allow some latitude, however, for covering borderline cases. Thus a puppet show, for example, would probably be covered by these words even if it is not regarded as a variety act (or dramatic performance). Either way, it would seem clear that an improvised performance will be within subsection (d).

departure

Sporting performances

2.18   In general, sporting performances are outside the categories of performance listed in section 180(2). Certain sports are arguably exceptions to this, however. Thus it is submitted that performances of ballroom dancing, ice dancing and possibly figure skating are forms of dance and therefore within category (a); the mere fact of competition should not alter this. In addition, if "variety act" is interpreted as referring to circus performances, it may be possible to include certain forms of sport, such as gymnastics, within the ambit of the words "or any similar presentation" in category (d). It would be difficult, after all, to distinguish between gymnastics and circus performances such as high-wire or trapeze acts.

2.19   An interesting theoretical question is whether a general distinction between sportsmen and women and other performers can be justified. Given the possible latitude in interpretation of section 180(2), this question has practical relevance also, for the answer to it may (if only subconsciously) influence courts in how widely they are prepared to extend the ambit of the definition. The author's view is that, if improvised performances are regarded as worthy of the protection given by Part II of the Act, no such general distinction can be drawn, for sportsmen and women are simply performers whose performances are always improvised within the constraints imposed by the rules of the particular sport. This is true even of athletes who are judged merely on the criterion of speed. Although the presence of competition in sport might be cited as a distinction, it is surely not relevant to whether or not protection should be granted.[24] Certainly it must be accepted that sporting performances are equally susceptible of commercial exploitation by diffusion and/or fixation as other performances. To put it more succinctly, sportsmen are entertainers too. Thus the economic considerations are the same. Prior to the enactment of the Copyright Act 1956 the Gregory Committee was urged to extend copyright to sportsmen but rejected the proposal, essentially on the ground that it had never been done before.[25] The question does not seem to have been reconsidered by the Whitford Committee, or in any of the Green Papers leading up to the 1988 Act.

Improvised performances

2.20   Although the point is not explicitly addressed by the 1988 Act, it is submitted that the width of the definitions in section 180(2) is sufficient to embrace improvised performances of every description. Only in the case of literary performances is there is any reference to performance of a "work"; and, as

---

[24] Particularly since it could be said that the arts are becoming increasingly competitive as more and more prizes are instituted.
[25] Cmnd. 8662 at para. 180. See Chap. 1, para. 1.48.

discussed in paragraphs 2.10–2.14 above, even in that case the requirement for a work does not necessarily mean that the work must be pre-existing. In this respect section 180(2) may go further than Article 3(a) of the Rome Convention. Moreover, unlike copyright,[26] there is no general requirement of fixation as a condition precedent to protection of performers' rights. For further details, see the commentary on each sub-subsection.

Interviews

It is submitted that performers' rights may subsist in an interview as being an improvised performance of two or more individuals within category (c) of section 180(2). At first sight the words "reading or recitation" may appear to militate against this. If, however, it is accepted that a monologue composed extempore as it is performed is "read or recited" just as much as one that has been written prior to performance,[27] it is difficult to see why the same principle should not apply to an interview. An interview can be regarded as a collective literary improvisation in the same way that a jazz performance is a collective musical improvisation.   **2.21**

It may be objected (on the assumption that not all speech is a literary work) that an interview is no different from any conversation and that therefore there is no "work". It is submitted that a distinction (albeit a somewhat precarious one) can be drawn between an interview and a conversation so as to make the former and not the latter a "work". This is that an interview is distinct, identifiable and takes place for a particular purpose.[28] The provisions of paragraph 13 of Schedule 2 to the 1988 Act, which in the words of the rubric permit "use of recordings of spoken works in certain cases", suggest that the draughtsman of the Act envisaged that performers' rights would subsist in an interview.[29]   **2.22**

Aleatoric works

An aleatoric (or aleatory) work is a work which is "dependent on uncertain contingencies",[30] for example one in which the author gives the performer (or even the audience) a number of options to choose between or one in which options are selected by some random means. Works of this character have recently become quite common in music and drama.[31] Performances of such works are clearly musical or dramatic performances and within section 180(2).   **2.23**

---

[26] Copyright, Designs and Patents Act 1988, s. 3(2).

[27] See paras. 2.11–2.12.

[28] *cf. Donoghue v. Allied Newspapers Ltd* [1938] 1 Ch. 106 in which Farwell J. held that on the facts an interviewee was neither the author nor the joint author of articles derived from the interview, and so not the owner of any copyright in them. It was not suggested that no copyright subsisted in the articles, and the judgment implies that if the articles had consisted of a transcript of the interview, the interviewee would have been a joint author of the work and therefore a co-owner of the copyright. See also para. 2.12.

[29] Similarly with s. 58 (the rubric to which reads "use of notes or recordings or spoken words in certain cases") and copyright if the interview is recorded. See Chap. 5, paras. 5.31–5.33.

[30] *Oxford English Dictionary* (2nd ed.). The word is derived from *aleator*, a dice player, from *alea*, a die.

[31] For example, certain plays by the dramatist Alan Ayckbourn.

Artistic works

2.24 Unlike section 8(1) of the Dramatic and Musical Performers' Protection Act 1958 as amended,[32] section 180(2) of the 1988 Act does not extend to performances of artistic works. Although artistic works in the shape of designs for sets and costumes play an important role in theatre and film, they are not usually considered to require performance. Accordingly, the omission of artistic works from section 180(2) probably does not reduce the scope of protection. The only artistic works that are performable are almost certainly within one of categories (a) to (d): for example, so-called "performance art" is probably more accurately categorised as a species of dramatic performance than as an artistic work. The only performances that might be excluded from protection are those of persons such as lighting technicians. It was possible that section 8(1) of the 1958 Act protected such performances, since the lighting design for a play or opera was a part literary and part artistic work which was in a real sense "performed" by a technician each night.[33] Under the 1988 Act such a performance might be considered to be a dramatic performance on the basis that it helps to convey dramatic meaning to an audience. It does not fit into either of the two subdivisions of dramatic performance advanced in paragraph 2.06 above, however.

The requirement for live performance

2.25 "Live" is not defined in the Act, and has no previous statutory history. There would appear to be two possible meanings: first, a performance that is not pre-recorded; and, secondly, a performance given in the presence of an audience. Curiously, the *Oxford English Dictionary* definition gives only the first meaning, although the illustrative quotations contain both:

> **live** ... 2. *trans.* and *fig.* in various applications ... d. Of a performance, heard or watched at the time of its occurrence, as distinguished from one recorded on film, tape, etc. Also quasi-*adv.*

> **1934** *B.B.C. Year-Bk.* 248 Listeners have ... complained of the fact that recorded material was too liberally used ... but ... transmitting hours to the Canadian and Australasian zones are inconvenient for broadcasting "live" material ... **1944** *Ann. Reg. 1943* 348 It was still felt ... that attendance at concerts and listening to "live" performances belonged to a better order of things.[34]

Thus a performance by an orchestra in a broadcasting studio may be broadcast "live" in the first sense although no audience is present in the studio; conversely, a recording of a performance by an orchestra when an audience is present may be described as a "live" recording in the second sense even though the recording is broadcast or sold some time after the event.

2.26 It is submitted that the first meaning is to be preferred in the context of

---

[32] This odd provision appears to have originated from a misunderstanding of Art. 3(a) of the Rome Convention: see para. 2.27, below.
[33] Although nowadays lighting desks are usually computerised. To the extent that the performance is computer-generated it will fall outside the definition in s. 180(2): see para. 2.26.
[34] 2nd ed.

section 180(2), for a number of reasons. The simplest is that this seems to be the sense in which the word is used elsewhere in Part II, notably in section 182(1)(a)–(c).[35] Then, to apply the second meaning might have the effect of denying performers' rights to many performers. For example, a film actor's only immediate audience (other than the film crew) is the camera. It would be surprising if by introducing the word "live" the legislature had reversed the decision in the _Peter Sellers_ case,[36] where the performances in question were film performances. Similarly, it would be surprising if a stage actor's performance in rehearsal was not protected.[37] Next, it is submitted that the first, but not the second, interpretation is in accordance with the Rome Convention. If a performance was unprotected simply because it did not take place in front of an audience, the performers could not prevent their performance being fixed without their consent as required by Article 7. On the other hand, the Convention only provides for protection of fixed performances against reproduction for purposes other than those for which the fixation was made.[38] Finally, to interpret "live" in the first way does not render it surplusage, for it ensures that the duration of performers' rights cannot be indefinitely extended by including an old recording in a new performance.[39] It may also mean that performances, or parts of perform-ances, which are computer-generated are excluded from protection, at least where the computer is effectively being used as a substitute for a recording.[40]

Performances must be given by one or more individuals

Section 180(1) of the 1988 Act states that Part II of the Act "confers rights on a performer, by requiring his consent to the exploitation of his perform-ances". "Performer" is not defined in the Act, but it would appear from the definition of "performance" in section 180(2) that any individual who gives a live performance is a "performer" for the purposes of Part II. This may be compared with the Rome Convention, Article 3(a) of which defines "performers" as

2.27

> actors, singers, musicians, dancers, and other persons who act, sing, declaim, play in, or otherwise perform literary or artistic[41] works.

Article 9 expressly states, however, that Contracting States may extend the protection provided for in the Convention to persons who do not perform

---

[35] See Chap. 4, para. 4.12. See also para. 2.48, below.
[36] [1988] Q.B. 40.
[37] This approach is also consistent with regarding a stage director as a performer.
[38] Compare Art. 7, paras. (a) and (b) with para. (c).
[39] The use of recordings during otherwise live performances has recently become common in pop music. It may become more common in theatre: in 1987 Laurence Olivier appeared in the musical _Time_ in London by way of a hologram.
[40] Computers are increasingly being used in performances of both avant-garde and popular music. The computer may be used simply as an instrument or part of an instrument, for example by generating a variety of pitches and tones that are then played in performance through conventional control means (typically a keyboard, but guitars, wind instruments and percussion have been used). Alternatively, the computer may be used instead of a recording, for example, to produce a pre-programmed rhythm track.
[41] "Artistic" in this context has the same meaning as in s. 2(1) of the Berne Convention, _i.e._ it includes dramatic and musical works.

literary or artistic works. The use of the general word "individual" in the 1988 Act, together with the absence of any requirement that the performance be professional, suggests that no particular skill on the part of the performer is required. Thus, to take a fairly extreme example, it is at least arguable that a contestant on a television game show is a performer of a dramatic performance.

Individuals

2.28 "Individual" means natural person. Thus bodies corporate are excluded. It might be argued that computer-generated performances are also excluded in this way, but it is submitted that this is not so, for an individual must at least give the computer the instruction to start at a particular time. The real distinction is between using the computer as an instrument and using it as a form of recording, and this distinction is provided by the word "live".[42]

One performance or many?

2.29 The definition of "performance" as a performance given by "one *or more* individuals" (emphasis added) might be thought to suggest that, for example, a concert given by an orchestra is *one* performance given by a number of individuals in respect which there is *one* performers' right shared among the participants. Reading Part II as a whole, however, it seems clear that the intention is that *each* individual performer has his *own* performers' right in any particular collective performance.[43]

Interpreters and executants

2.30 The absence of any definition of "performer" raises a question as to whether interpretative (as opposed to executive) artists such as conductors and directors are performers who can have rights under Part II. At first blush, a theatre director does not "give a performance" of a play, for he merely directs the rehearsals beforehand. On the other hand, much of a conductor's work is done in rehearsal too. Is a distinction to be drawn between a conductor who rehearses an orchestra but does not appear in the concert hall[44] and one who does appear in the concert hall? It is submitted that "performer" should be construed broadly so as to avoid such distinctions.[45] Support for such a broad construction can be gained from the Rome Convention. Although the English text of the Rome Convention only refers to "performers", the French text uses the expression "*artistes interprètes ou executants*".[46] This makes it clear that both *artistes interprètes* and *artistes executants* should be protected.[47] The 1988 Act should therefore be construed so as to comply with the Convention.

---

[42] See note 40, above.

[43] For example, this is the rationale for the powers given to the Copyright Tribunal to give consent on behalf of a performer: see Chap. 3, paras. 3.24–3.33.

[44] For example, a choir master.

[45] On the other hand, collaborative artists such as set and costume designers are presumably not included: see para. 2.24, above.

[46] The English, French and Spanish texts of the Convention are equally authentic: Art. 33(1).

[47] See "Preparatory Document for and Report of the WIPO/UNESCO Committee of Governmental Experts on Dramatic, Choreographic and Musical Works", para. 62 in [1987] *Copyright* 185, 199.

Even if this is right, however, it still leaves the question whether a film **2.31**
director qualifies as a performer, particularly now that film directors have the
status of authors.[48] The corresponding Spanish legislation, for example,
defines "performer" so as to include a director of a stage performance, which
would seem to exclude film directors.[49] It is submitted, however, that there is
no distinction between the work of a stage director and the work of a film
director which would justify protecting the former and not the latter.

It has been suggested[50] that, in the context of circus performances,[51] a **2.32**
performance by animals should nevertheless be regarded as a performance
given by an individual, namely the trainer, notwithstanding that the animals
are not individuals. This is to stretch the concept of an interpretative
performer nearly to breaking point, but it may be justifiable on grounds of
policy.[52]

Performance or adaptation

Some performers alter the works they perform to such an extent that it is **2.33**
arguable that their contribution should be categorised as adaptation rather
than "mere" performance. The consequence would be that the artist acquired
a separate copyright in the adaptation. This question is discussed in Chapter
8.[53] For present purposes it is only necessary to observe that even if there is an
adaptation of the underlying work, and the consequent creation of a new
copyright, it does not mean that the performance ceases to attract performers'
rights.

Qualification requirements for performers' rights

Performers' rights subsist in a performance if it is a "qualifying perform- **2.34**
ance",[54] that is, if it given by a qualifying individual or takes place in a
qualifying country.[55] Although, in contrast with Part I of the 1988 Act,[56] there
is no express definition of the "material time" at which the qualification
requirements must be satisfied, it is clear that the relevant time is when the
performance is given. Thus a performance does not become a qualifying
performance merely because the performer subsequently becomes resident in
a qualifying country; but the position may be different if a country he was
connected with at the time of the performance subsequently becomes a
qualifying one.[57]

---

[48] Copyright, Designs and Patents Act 1988, s. 9(2)(ab) as amended by the Copyright and
Related Rights Regulations 1996 to implement Art. 2(1) of the E.C. Term Directive.
[49] See Chap. 9, para. 9.215.
[50] Lester and Mitchell, *Joynson-Hicks on U.K. Copyright Law* (Sweet & Maxwell, 1989), para.
12.12.
[51] See paras. 2.15–2.17.
[52] The corresponding Indian legislation expressly applies to snake charmers: see Chap. 9, para.
9.107.
[53] paras. 8.02–8.07.
[54] The Act does not express it in this way, but this is the effect since only rights in qualifying
performances may be infringed: Copyright, Designs and Patents Act 1988, ss. 182, 183 and 184.
See also Chap. 4, para. 4.03.
[55] Copyright, Designs and Patents Act 1988, s. 181.
[56] *ibid.*, s. 154(4), (5).
[57] See paras. 2.42–2.44 below.

Qualifying individuals

2.35 A qualifying individual is an individual who is either (a) a citizen or subject of a qualifying country or (b) resident in a qualifying country.[58]

Citizen or subject

2.36 In the case of the United Kingdom, a person is a citizen or subject if he is a British citizen.[59] In the case of a colony of a United Kingdom, a person is a citizen or subject if he is a British Dependent Territories' citizen by connection with that colony.[60] Whether a person is a citizen or subject of another country must be decided according to the law of the country concerned.[61] This will be a question of fact to be proven by expert evidence in English proceedings.

Resident

2.37 Whether a person is resident in a particular country must be decided according to the appropriate United Kingdom law—in other words, the *lex fori* rather than the law of the country in question.[62] Unfortunately, "residence" is a word that has different meanings in different branches of the law, at least so far as the law of England and Wales is concerned.[63] Taxation and voter registration cases would seem to provide a suitable guide, however. These indicate that a person is resident in a particular country if he is present there other than casually or as a visitor, or if he has a home that is (in substance) constantly available to him for his own use and which he occupies from time to time.[64] Residence implies a degree of permanence and continuity, a genuine and substantial connection.[65] Even prolonged absence does not cause a person to cease to be resident.[66] It is possible to be resident in more than one country at once.[67]

---

[58] Copyright, Designs and Patents Act 1988, s. 206(1).

[59] *ibid.*, s. 206(2)(a). For the definition of British citizen, see the Nationality Act 1981.

[60] *ibid.*, s. 206(2)(b). For the definition of British Dependent Territories' citizen, see the Nationality Act 1981.

[61] *Stoeck v. Public Trustee* [1921] 2 Ch. 67, *Re Chamberlain's Settlement* [1921] 2 Ch. 553.

[62] Dicey and Morris, *The Conflict of Laws* (12th ed., Sweet & Maxwell, 1993), Rule 8 and *Re Annesley* [1926] Ch. 692. Both the Rule and the case are concerned with domicile, but it seems clear that the same principle must apply to residence.

[63] Dicey and Morris, *op cit.*, p. 158.

[64] *Re Young* (1875) 1 T.C. 59; *Cooper v. Cadwallader* (1904) 5 T.C. 101; *Levene v. Inland Revenue Commissioners* [1928] A.C. 217.

[65] *Fox v. Stirk* [1970] 2 Q.B. 463; *Brokelman v. Barr* [1971] 2 Q.B. 602. This accords with the requirement for "habitual residence" in Art. 3(2) of the Berne Convention (Paris Revision, 1971), but the latter provision is not necessarily a guide to interpretation since it is open to the United Kingdom to be more generous in conferring protection than the Convention requires.

[66] *Re Young*, note 64, above; *Levene v. Inland Revenue Commissioners*, Note 64, above; *Brokelman v. Barr*, note 65, above.

[67] *Inland Revenue Commissioners v. Lysaght* [1928] A.C. 234; *Sinclair v. Sinclair* [1968] P. 189.

Qualifying countries

The following are qualifying countries[68]:

    (a)   the United Kingdom[69];

    (b)   other Member States of the European Economic Community[70]; and

    (c)   countries designated by Order in Council as enjoying reciprocal protection.[71]

2.38

Countries enjoying reciprocal protection

A country may be designated by Order in Council as enjoying reciprocal protection if it is either:

    (a)   a country which is party to a convention relating to performers' rights to which the United Kingdom is a party[72]; or

    (b)   a country which the Crown is satisfied has given or will give adequate protection to British performances, that is, performances either given by individuals who are British citizens or resident in the United Kingdom or taking place in the United Kingdom.[73] If a country provides adequate protection only for certain descriptions of British performances, the Order designating it may be limited to a corresponding extent.[74]

2.39

Convention countries—There are two relevant conventions, namely the Rome Convention and TRIPs. At the time of writing, the convention countries which have been designated are listed in the Schedule to the Performances (Reciprocal Protection)(Convention Countries) Order 1995.[75] The Schedule is divided in two parts. Part 1 lists countries which are party to the Rome Convention. Performances connected with those countries are granted full protection under Part II of the 1988 Act.[76] Part 2 lists countries which have signed TRIPs but are not party to the Rome Convention. Performances connected with those countries are only granted partial protection: Part II only applies to the extent that it confers rights on a performer in respect of (a) the making of a sound recording directly from a live performance or of a copy of such a sound recording and (b) the broadcasting or cable transmission of a live performance.[77] Thus performers from countries listed in part 2 of the Schedule have no rights in respect of films of their performances.[78]

2.40

---

[68] Copyright, Designs and Patents Act 1988, s. 206(1).
[69] See Chap. 4, para. 4.79.
[70] Presently Norway, Iceland and Liechtenstein in addition to the members of the European Union (France, the German Federal Republic, the Netherlands, Italy, Belgium, Luxembourg, the Republic of Ireland, Denmark, Greece, Spain, Portugal, Austria, Sweden and Finland). Although Switzerland is a member of EFTA it chose not to participate in the EEA.
[71] Copyright, Designs and Patents Act 1988, s. 206(1).
[72] *ibid.*, s. 208(1)(a), (2).
[73] *ibid.*, s. 208(1)(b), (3).
[74] *ibid.*, s. 208(4).
[75] S.I. 1995 No. 2990. See Appendix 3C.
[76] *ibid.*, Art. 2(a).
[77] *ibid.*, Arts. 2(b), 3.
[78] Unless, that is, the country in question qualifies by another route: thus Belgium, for example, is listed in part 2, yet its performers received full protection by virtue of the fact that it is a Member State of the EEA.

2.41 **Countries giving adequate protection**—The Channel Islands, the Isle of Man and colonies of the United Kingdom (such as Bermuda, the Falkland Islands and Gibraltar) may be designated in this category in addition to any foreign country.[79] At the time of writing no countries have been designated.

Springing performers' rights

2.42 The first Order in Council made under section 208,[80] which came into force on the same day as the 1988 Act, designated all the then signatories to the Rome Convention.[81] Since then additional countries have joined,[82] and further Orders have been made designating those countries. The current Order came into force with regard to those countries on December 15, 1995.[83] In addition, the current Order designates countries which have signed TRIPs but which are not parties to the Rome Convention, with effect from January 1, 1996.[84] Since the 1995 Order contains no transitional provisions, a question arises as to whether performances given before December 15, 1995 or January 1, 1996 in countries which are designated under the 1995 Order, but not under the 1989 Order, are protected. On the face of it, such performances are protected. Moreover, this interpretation is in accordance with Article 14(6) of TRIPs which provides that the provisions of Article 18 of the Berne Convention shall apply *mutatis mutandis* to performers' rights. The combined effect of paragraphs (1) and (4) of Article 18 of Berne is that the Convention shall apply to all works which at the time of accession of a country to the Union have not yet fallen into the public domain through expiry of the term of protection. Thus to comply with Article 14(6) any performance that would be within the 50-year rule on December 15, 1995 or January 1, 1996 must be protected.

2.43 The difficulty with this is that not only does the 1995 Order not contain transitional provisions, but also it does not contain any saving for vested rights.[85] This means that acts carried out between August 1, 1989 and December 15, 1995 or January 1, 1996 could become unlawful retrospectively, which is contrary to principle. It has been suggested[86] that in order to

---

[79] Copyright, Designs and Patents Act 1988, s. 208(5).

[80] Performances (Reciprocal Protection)(Convention Countries)(No. 2) Order 1989 (S.I. 1989 No. 1296) [the No. 1 Order was replaced by the No 2. before it came into force because it was defective].

[81] Austria, Barbados, Brazil, Burkina Faso, Chile, Columbia, People's Republic of Congo, Costa Rica, Czechoslovakia, Denmark, Dominican Republic, Ecuador, El Salvador, Fiji, Finland, France, Federal Republic of Germany, Guatemala, Republic of Ireland, Italy, Luxembourg, Mexico, Monaco, Niger, Norway, Panama, Paraguay, Peru, Philippines, Sweden, Uruguay.

[82] Argentina, Australia, Bolivia, Bulgaria, Czech Republic, Denmark (including Greenland and the Faroe Islands), Greece, Honduras, Hungary, Iceland, Jamaica, Japan, Lesotho, Moldova, The Netherlands, Nigeria, Slovak Republic, Spain and Switzerland. Venezuela became party to the Convention on January 30, 1996, Saint Lucia on August 17, 1996 and Slovenia on October 9, 1996, but at the time of writing none of these three have yet been designated.

[83] Performances (Reciprocal Protection)(Convention Countries) Order 1995, note 75, above, Art. 1.

[84] *ibid.*

[85] Unlike the Orders which confer copyright on works of foreign origin such as the Copyright (Application to Other Countries) Order 1993 (S.I. 1993 No. 942).

[86] Laddie, Prescott & Vitoria, *Modern Law of Copyright and Designs* (2nd ed., Butterworths, 1995), para. 26.6.

avoid this result, section 16(1)(c) of the Interpretation Act 1978 should be invoked. This provides that, where an enactment is repealed, the repeal does not, unless a contrary intention appears, affect any right, privilege, obligation or liability acquired, accrued or incurred under that enactment.[87] Accordingly it may be argued that the repeal of the 1989 Order (and the intervening Orders) and its replacement by the 1995 Order does not affect accrued rights under the former, but only acts committed after the latter came into force.

This problem does not arise with the Copyright and Related Rights Regulations 1996, which expressly provide that they apply to performances given before commencement[88] but that no act done before commencement[89] or pursuant to an agreement entered into before November 19, 1992[90] is an infringement of any new right (*i.e.* a right arising by virtue of the Regulations[91]). In addition, there are specific transitional provisions which apply to the right to equitable remuneration in lieu of rental right.[92]   **2.44**

No formalities

No formalities are required for the subsistence of performers' rights. Thus there is no need for any registration, deposit or marking of recordings: the rights arise automatically if the performance qualifies.   **2.45**

Performers' rights independent of copyright

Performers' rights are independent of any copyright that may subsist in any work performed or any film or sound recording of, or broadcast or cable programme including, the performance.[93]   **2.46**

SUBSISTENCE OF RECORDING RIGHTS

Exclusive recording contracts

In addition to performers, Part II of the Copyright, Designs and Patents Act 1988 confers rights on persons who have the benefit of exclusive recording contracts with performers or their licensees. An "exclusive recording contract" is defined as: **2.47**

> a contract between a performer and another person under which that person is entitled to the exclusion of all other persons (including the performer) to make recordings of one or more of his performances with a view to their commercial exploitation.[94]

Performances which are subject to such a contract are those in which recording rights are capable of subsisting.

---

[87] By s. 23(1), s. 16 applies equally to subordinate legislation.
[88] Regs. 26(1) and 30(1).
[89] Reg. 26(2).
[90] Reg. 27(2).
[91] Reg. 25(3).
[92] Reg. 33. See Chap. 3, para. 3.58.
[93] Copyright, Designs and Patents Act 1988, s. 180(4)(a).
[94] *ibid.*, s. 185(1).

Recordings

2.48 "Recording" is defined as meaning

> a film or sound recording
> - (a) made directly from the live performance,
> - (b) made from a broadcast of or cable programme including the performance, or
> - (c) made, directly or indirectly, from another recording of the performance.[95]

"Film" and "sound recording" bear the same meanings as in Part I.[96] Thus a film is a recording on any medium from which a moving image may by any means be produced.[97] This definition is broad enough to encompass conventional films, videotapes and videodisks or, indeed, moving pictures stored in any other medium (but not a still photograph). A sound recording is either a recording of sounds from which the sounds may be reproduced, or a recording of the whole or part of a literary, dramatic or musical work, from which sounds reproducing the work or part of it may be produced, in either case regardless of medium or method of reproduction.[98] The soundtrack of a film is to be treated as part of the film, but only for the purposes of Part I[99]; for the purposes of Part II, a soundtrack is merely a sound recording. Assuming that "live" means "not pre-recorded",[1] the word "live" in (a) would appear to be surplusage.

Protected performances

2.49 The definition of "performance" is the same for the purpose of recording rights as for the purpose of performers' rights,[2] so that recording rights are capable of subsisting in all performances in which performers' rights may subsist.

With a view to commercial exploitation

2.50 This is defined to mean "with a view to the recordings being sold or let for hire, or shown or played in public".[3] This does not advance matters greatly. It is not clear whether a mere test of intention is intended, or whether something more will be required. Equally, if it is merely a test of intention, is it subjective or objective? It is submitted that the definition should be read as imposing an objective test, so that the question to be asked is whether the contract on its true construction gives the other person the exclusive right to make recordings for any commercial purpose. Thus the performer may have the right to make recordings of his own performances for his private and

---

[95] *ibid.*, s. 180(2).
[96] *ibid.*, s. 211(1).
[97] *ibid.*, s. 5B(1) (substituted by the Duration of Copyright and Rights in Performances Regulations 1995).
[98] *ibid.*, s. 5A(1) (ditto).
[99] *ibid.*, s. 5A(2) (ditto).
[1] See paras. 2.25–2.26 and Chap. 4, para. 4.12.
[2] See paras. 2.03–2.04.
[3] Copyright, Designs and Patents Act 1988, s. 185(4).

domestic use[4] without preventing the contract from being an exclusive recording contract within the meaning of section 185(1).

Qualification requirements for recording rights

Recording rights may subsist in a performance in either of two ways:　　　**2.51**

(i)　where the person who has the benefit of an exclusive recording contract to which the performance is subject (either by virtue of that person being a party to the contract or by virtue of an assignment of the benefit of the contract) is a qualifying person[5]; or

(ii)　(if the person referred to in (i) is not a qualifying person) where another person who is licensed to make recordings of the performance with a view to their commercial exploitation (either by virtue of an agreement with the person who has the benefit of an exclusive recording contract to which the performance is subject or by virtue of an assignment of the benefit of such an agreement) is a qualifying person.[6]

The difference between the two situations is that in (i) a licence from the person having the benefit of the recording contract permitting another to make recordings of a particular performance will operate as a licence of the first person's recording rights as well as of his contractual rights, whereas in (ii) there will only be a licence of the first person's contractual rights, and the recording rights will belong to the second person, the licensee. Interestingly, the licensee in (ii) need not be exclusive.

Qualifying persons

A qualifying person is either (i) a qualifying individual[7] or (ii) a body　**2.52** corporate or other body having legal personality which (a) is formed under the law of a qualifying country and (b) has in any qualifying country a place of business at which substantial business activity is carried on.[8] There appears to be no requirement that the qualifying country in which business is carried on be the same as that under the law of which the body is formed. In determining whether substantial business is carried on, however, no account is to be taken of dealings in goods which are at all material times outside the country in question.[9] Thus mere brokerage businesses are excluded.

Contracts with service companies

A complication arises where the performer contracts with a record or film　**2.53** company via a service company (sometimes known as a management company or a loan-out company). A service company is a corporate vehicle for the performer, in that the performer owns the company.[10] The performer

---

[4] *cf.* the definitions of category (1) infringements of performers' rights and recording rights. See Chap. 4, paras. 4.10 and 4.63.
[5] Copyright, Designs and Patents Act 1988, s. 185(2).
[6] *ibid.*, s. 185(3).
[7] See para. 2.35.
[8] Copyright, Designs and Patents Act 1988, s. 206(1).
[9] *ibid.*, s. 206(3).
[10] Needless to say, the objective is to obtain tax advantages.

is employed by the company, and the company then hires out his or her services to the record or film company. Usually the performer's contract of employment with the service company provides for the service company to be exclusively entitled to make recordings of the performer's services. Thus the contract of employment is an exclusive recording contract within the meaning of section 185(1). If the service company is not a qualifying person (*e.g.* because it is incorporated in the United States), there is no difficulty, since it can licence a record company which is a qualifying person to make recordings and the record company will have recording rights by virtue of section 185(3). The problem arises where the service company is a qualifying person (*e.g.* because it is incorporated in England). In that case prima facie the service company will own the recording rights and not the record company. This may of course be desirable from the performers' point of view, but record companies find that it handicaps anti-piracy operations. A possible way round this difficulty is to argue that the contract between the service company and the record company (under which the service company agrees to provide the performer's services exclusively to the record company) amounts to an assignment of the benefit of the exclusive recording contract to the record company within the meaning of section 185(2)(b). Whether this is so depends on the true construction of the contract between the service company and the record company, but it is submitted that this is not correct interpretation of most such agreeements.

No formalities, rights independent of copyright

2.54   As with performers' rights, there are no formalities to be observed, and the rights are independent of any copyright.

DURATION OF PERFORMERS' RIGHTS AND RECORDING RIGHTS

The 1988 Provisions

2.55   As originally enacted, Part II of the 1988 Act simply provided that performers' rights and recording rights which subsisted in a performance continued to subsist until the expiration of 50 years from the end of the calendar year in which the performance took place.[11] This applied to all performances in which such rights subsisted, regardless of the nationality of the performer or the place of the performance.

The New Provisions under the Term Directive

2.56   The implementation of the E.C. Term Directive[12] by the Duration of Copyright and Rights in Performances Regulations 1995[13] has changed the law in two significant respects:

---

[11] Copyright, Designs and Patents Act 1988, s. 191 (unamended).
[12] Council Directive 93/98, October 29, 1993 harmonising the term of protection of copyright and certain related rights, [1993] O.J. L290/9.
[13] S.I. 1995 No. 3297 in force from January 1, 1996.

(1)   If within the initial period of 50 years from the end of the year in which the performance took place a recording of the performance is released, the rights continue to subsist for 50 years from the end of the calendar year in which the recording is released.[14] Thus performers' rights may subsist for up to 101 years (less two days).

(2)   Where the performer is not a national of an EEA state, the principle of "reciprocal treatment" of duration[15] has been introduced. This means that the duration of the rights shall be that period to which the performance is entitled in the country of which the performer is a national (but may not exceed the period which would apply if the performer were an EEA national).[16]

50 years from first release

"Released" for this purpose is defined to mean when a recording is first   **2.57** published, played or shown in public, broadcast or included in a cable programme service.[17] For this purpose unauthorised acts are to be discounted.[18] "Published" has the same meaning as in Part I of the 1988 Act,[19] namely the issue of copies to the public[20] but excluding any publication which is merely colourable and not intended to satisfy the reasonable requirements of the public.[21]

National treatment for EEA Nationals

The amendments to Part II of the 1988 Act made by the 1995 Regulations do   **2.58** not change the position with regard to "national treatment" for nationals of European Union (and now also European Economic Area) states. "National treatment" means that nationals of those countries are given precisely the same protection as domestic nationals. Thus a French performer, for example, continues to have the same rights for the same period in respect of his performances as an English performer.[22]

Reciprocal treatment for non-EEA nationals

For non-EEA nationals, however, the effect of the amendments to the 1988   **2.59** Act necessitated by Article 7(2) of the Term Directive is to introduce reciprocal treatment of duration (subject to the uncertain ambit of the derogation discussed below[23]). This is a regrettable departure from the

---

[14] Copyright, Designs and Patents Act 1988, s. 191(2) (as amended).

[15] Also known as "comparison of terms".

[16] Copyright, Designs and Patents Act 1988, s. 191(3).

[17] *ibid.*, s. 191(3).

[18] *ibid.*

[19] *ibid.*, s. 211(1).

[20] *ibid.*, s. 175(1)(a). The meaning of this expression is discussed in Chap. 4, paras. 4.25–4.32.

[21] *ibid.*, s. 175(5).

[22] Thus no amendment of English law was necessary to comply with the ruling of the European Court of Justice in C–92/92 *Collins v. Imtrat Handelsgesellschaft mbH* [1993] 3 C.M.L.R. 773: [1994] EMLR 108. In that case it was held that German laws which meant that a non-German (British) performer was not protected in respect of his performances given outside Germany whereas a German performer was protected contravened Art. 7(1) of the Treaty of Rome (now Art. 6(1)).

[23] See paras. 2.61–2.64, below.

principle of national treatment previously applied by English law to nationals of countries which adhered to the relevant international convention.[24] The effect on performers is that, if the performer is a national of country X which is not an EEA state and whose law only gives its own nationals a right of (say) 20 years' duration, then the duration of that performer's rights under Part II is 20 years and not 50 years. This of course means that in order to determine whether rights still subsist in a performance given, for example, by an United States citizen 30 years ago, it is necessary to investigate the relevant foreign provisions. Those of the more frequently encountered countries are summarised in Chapter 9, but this should not be regarded as a substitute for professional advice from an advisor qualified in the relevant law.

2.60   In relation to performances given before July 1, 1995, the performer is to be treated as an EEA national if he was on July 1, 1995 regarded under the law of the United Kingdom or under the law of another EEA state relating to performers' rights as a national of that state.[25]

Derogation from reciprocal treatment: international obligations

2.61   Section 191(5) of the 1988 Act as amended contains a derogation from the reciprocal treatment provision contained in section 194(4) in the following terms:

> If or to the extent that the application of subsection (4) would be at variance with an international obligation to which the United Kingdom became subject prior to 29 October 1993, the duration of the rights conferred by this Part shall be as specified in subsections (2) and (3).

This subsection is lamentably opaque. It is intended to give effect to Article 7(3) of the Term Directive, which permits Member States that at the date of adoption of the Directive granted a longer term of protection pursuant to their international obligations than would result from application of the reciprocal treatment requirement of Article 7(1) to continue to do so.[26] But instead of spelling out the cases to which this derogation shall apply, Parliament has left it to parties and their advisors (and ultimately the courts)

---

[24] In accordance with the United Kingdom's obligations under Art. 5 of the Berne Convention and Arts. 4–6 of the Rome Convention. (Strictly speaking, the Berne Convention is not based on the nationality of the author but on the country of origin of the work, this being the Berne State where the work is first published or, if first published outside the Union, the country of the Union of which the author is a national: Art. 5(4).) In fact, the reciprocal treatment requirement of the Term Directive does not contravene the Berne Convention since Art. 7(8) of the latter permits reciprocal treatment so far as the term of protection is concerned. In the case of the Rome Convention, it appears that this is not permissible, but Art. 7(3) of the Term Directive allows Member States to maintain longer periods of protection which at the date of adoption of the Directive they granted pursuant to their obligations under the Rome Convention: see paras. 2.61–2.64 below.

[25] Duration of Copyright and Rights in Performances Regulations 1995, note 13, above, Reg. 36(2).

[26] See also recital (23), which states that where a rightholder who is not a Community national qualifies for protection under an international agreement the term of protection of related rights should be the same as that laid down in the Directive, except that it should not exceed that fixed in the country of which the rightholder is a national.

to try and work it out for themselves. Moreover, this legislative technique is a particularly odd one to adopt given that it is an axiom of English constitutional law that international treaties entered into by the Crown have no effect in domestic law unless and until legislation is passed to give effect to them.[27] Almost uniquely,[28] section 191(5) makes rights under domestic legislation directly dependent upon the interpretation and effect of an international convention without making that convention part of English law (as in the case of the Civil Jurisdiction and Judgments Act 1982, for example, which makes the Brussels Convention part of domestic law).

It appears that this derogation will apply in cases where the performance is **2.62** not given by a national of an EEA State but is connected with a Contracting State of the Rome Convention.[29] Article 4 of the Rome Convention (which the United Kingdom ratified on October 30, 1963) requires each Contracting State to grant "national treatment"[30] to performers where certain connecting factors are present. Although the Rome Convention stipulates a minimum duration of 20 years,[31] it does not otherwise specify the duration of performers' rights. Accordingly, where the performance is not given by an EEA national but is connected with country X which is a Rome Contracting State and which confers a right of 20 years' duration (so that application of reciprocal treatment would lead to 20 years' protection in the United Kingdom), the derogation contained in subsection (5) will come into effect (so that national treatment must be applied leading to at least 50 years' protection in the United Kingdom).

The connecting factors specified in Article 4 of the Rome Convention are as **2.63** follows:

(a) the performance took place in a Contracting State;
(b) the performance has been incorporated in a phonogram which is protected under Article 5 of the Convention; or
(c) the performance, not being fixed in a phonogram, has been carried by a broadcast protected under Article 6 of the Convention.

Phonograms are protected under Article 5 if either:

(a) the producer of the phonogram is a national of a Contracting State; or
(b) the sounds were first fixed in a contracting state; or

---

[27] *Attorney-General for Canada v. Attorney-General for Ontario* [1937] A.C. 326, 347 and *J.H. Rayner Ltd v. Department of Trade* [1990] 2 A.C. 418, 476 (Lord Templeman), 500 (Lord Oliver of Aylmerton).

[28] The nearest comparable measure of which the author is aware is s.45(3) of the Patents Act 1949, as to which see *Parke Davis & Co. v. Comptroller of Patents, Designs and Trade Marks* [1954] A.C. 321 and *Allen & Hanburys Ltd v. Controller of Patents, Designs and Trade Marks* [1997] F.S.R. 1.

[29] It does not apply where the connection is with a member state of TRIPs, since this was signed after October 29, 1993.

[30] Defined in Art. 2(1)(a) to mean the treatment accorded by the domestic law of the Contracting State in which protection is claimed to performers who are its nationals as regards performances taking place, broadcast or first fixed on its territory. It has been suggested by some that the effect of Art. 2(2) is that national treatment is not required insofar as a state's laws extend beyond the minima laid down by the Convention (which would not prevent the U.K. from applying reciprocal treatment to non-EEA nationals of Contracting States), but this does not appear to be correct.

[31] Art. 14.

(c) the phonogram was first published[32] in a Contracting State.[33]

Broadcasts are protected under Article 6 if the headquarters of the broadcasting organisation is situated in a Contracting State and the broadcast was transmitted from a transmitter situated in the same Contracting State.[34]

2.64   Accordingly, to return to the example of country X, national treatment (*i.e.* 50 years plus protection) will apply if the performance took place in X or the performance was recorded in a phonogram by a national of X or it was broadcast by a broadcaster headquartered in X from a transmitter situated in X. If the only connection with X is that the performer is a national of X, however, reciprocal treatment will apply (*i.e.* 20 years' protection).

Application of the new provisions

2.65   The new provisions as to duration contained in section 191 as amended apply to the following:

(1)   performances which take place after January 1, 1996[35];
(2)   performances which were given before January 1, 1996 ("existing performances"[36]) but which first qualify for protection under Part II of the Act after January 1, 1996[37]; and
(3)   existing performances in which rights under Part II of the Act had expired before January 1, 1996 (either because Part II rights expired between August 1, 1989 and December 31, 1995 or because no rights subsisted under Part II, although the performance was protected under the Performers' Protection Acts, by reason only that the performance was given more than 50 years before August 1, 1989) but which were on July 1, 1995 protected in another EEA state under legislation relating to copyright or related rights.[38]

2.66   The last of these provisions implements Article 10(2) of the Term Directive. The effect of it is to revive United Kingdom rights in any performance which was protected in any EEA State on July 1, 1995. Since some European Union Member States had already implemented the Term Directive by that date and since no EEA state provided a longer period of protection for performers than that provided by the Term Directive, to a rough approximation this means that rights are revived in any performance which would have been protected by virtue of the new provisions if they had been in force on July 1, 1995. This is only a rough approximation, however, because the date of release of a recording may vary from State to State.

---

[32] First publication for this purpose includes first publication in a non-Contracting State and publication within 30 days thereafter in a Contracting State: Art. 5(2).
[33] When the U.K. ratified the Convention it declared pursuant to Art. 5(3) that it would not apply the third alternative criterion for protection contained in Art. 5(1)(b).
[34] Again, when the U.K. ratified the Convention it declared pursuant to Art. 6(2) that it would not apply these criteria as alternatives.
[35] Duration of Copyright and Rights in Performances Regulations 1995, note 13, above, Reg. 29(a).
[36] *ibid.*, Reg. 27(1)(a).
[37] *ibid.*, Reg. 29(b).
[38] *ibid.*, Reg. 29(d).

In addition to the three categories of performances listed above, the new provisions apply to existing performances in which rights under Part II subsisted immediately before January 1, 1996 ("existing protected performances"[39]), except that the rights shall continue to subsist until the date on which they would have expired under the 1988 provisions if that date is later than the date on which the rights would expire under the new provisions.[40]

2.67

Transitional provisions

The 1995 Regulations contain extensive transitional provisions relating to rights which are extended or revived by virtue of the new duration provisions. "Extended performance rights" are rights under Part II of the Act which subsist by virtue of the new provisions after the date on which they would have expired under the 1988 provisions.[41] "Revived performance rights" are rights under Part II which subsist by virtue of the new provisions and which either (a) arose and then expired under the 1988 provisions ("revived 1988 rights") or (b) only did not arise under the 1988 Act (although the performance was protected under the Performers' Protection Acts) by reason that the performance was given more than 50 years before August 1, 1989 ("revived pre-1988 rights").[42]

2.68

Ownership of extended and revived rights—Extended performance rights vest in the person who was entitled to exercise those rights immediately before January 1, 1996, *i.e.* (in the case of performers' rights) the performer or his successor under section 192(2) or (in the case of recording rights) the owner of the recording rights under section 185.[43]

2.69

Revived performance rights vest as follows[44]:

2.70

(a) in the case of rights which expired after August 1, 1989, in the person who was entitled to the rights immediately before expiry;

(b) in the case of revived pre-1988 performers rights, in the performer or his personal representatives;

(c) in the case of revived pre-1988 recording rights,[45] in the person who would have been the person having those rights immediately before August 1, 1989 or, if earlier, immediately before the death of the performer, applying section 185 to the circumstances then obtaining.

Any remuneration or damages received by a person's personal representatives by virtue of extended or revived performance rights devolve as part of that person's estate as if the rights had vested in him immediately before death.[46]

2.71

---

[39] *ibid.*, Reg. 27(1)(b).
[40] *ibid.*, Regs. 29(c), 28.
[41] *ibid.*, Reg. 30.
[42] *ibid.*
[43] *ibid.*, Reg. 31(1).
[44] *ibid.*, Reg. 31(2).
[45] In actual fact, there never were any pre-1988 recording rights to revive, since the Court of Appeal in *RCA Corp. v. Pollard* held that the Performers' Protection Acts did not protect persons with whom performers contracted: see Chap. 1, para 1.70. It seems clear, however, that the effect of this provision is retrospectively to create such rights albeit only with effect for the future.
[46] Duration of Copyright and Rights in Performances Regulations 1995, note 13 above, Reg. 31(3).

2.72 **Licences under extended rights**—Any licence relating to the exploitation of an existing protected performance which subsists immediately before January 1, 1996 and is not to expire before the end of the period for which Part II rights subsist in relation to that performance is automatically extended for the period of extended performance rights subject to any agreement to the contrary.[47]

2.73 **Defences to infringement of revived rights**—There are a number of defences to infringement of revived performance rights, as follows:

(1) No act done before January 1, 1996 is an infringement of revived performance rights.[48]

(2) No act done after January 1, 1996 pursuant to arrangements for the exploitation of the performance in question made before January 1, 1995 at a time when the performance was not protected either under Part II or under the Performers' Protection Acts is an infringement of revived performance rights.[49]

(3) It is not an infringement of revived performance rights to issue to the public after January 1, 1996 a recording of a performance made before July 1, 1995 at a time when the performance was not protected.[50]

(4) It is not an infringement of revived performance rights to do anything after January 1, 1996 in relation to a sound recording or film made before January 1, 1996, or made pursuant to arrangements made before that date, which contains a recording of a performance if the recording was either made before July 1, 1995 at a time when the performance was not protected or made pursuant to arrangements made before July 1, 1995 at a time when the performance was not protected.[51]

2.74 **Licence of right under revived rights**—Licences are available as of right in respect of revived performance rights subject only to the payment of reasonable remuneration.[52] In order to exercise the compulsory licence the prospective licensee must give reasonable notice of his intention to the owner of the rights, stating when he intends to commence the acts in question.[53] If he does not give notice his acts will not be licensed.[54] If he does give notice, his acts will be licensed and reasonable remuneration will be payable in respect of them even if its amount is not agreed or determined until later.[55] It is not clear what the consequence is if the licensee fails to pay the sum determined, *i.e.*

---

[47] *ibid.*, Reg. 32.
[48] *ibid.*, Reg. 33(1).
[49] *ibid.*, Reg. 33(2)(a).
[50] *ibid.*, Reg. 33(2)(b).
[51] *ibid.*, Reg. 33(3).
[52] *ibid.*, Reg. 34(1).
[53] *ibid.*, Reg. 34(2).
[54] *ibid.*, Reg. 34(3).
[55] *ibid.*, Reg. 34(4).

whether his acts then become infringements or whether he merely owes the rights owner a debt. On balance it would appear that the intention is that the only consequence is a debt, but the contrary is arguable.[56]

In default of agreement, the amount of the remuneration shall be   **2.75** determined by the Copyright Tribunal.[57] Applications to settle the remuneration payable may be made by either the owner of the rights or the licensee.[58] Once the Tribunal has made an order, either party may apply to the Tribunal for the order to be varied subsequently,[59] but except with the leave of the Tribunal no such application may be made within 12 months of the date of the previous order.[60] A variation order has effect from the date on which it is made or such later date as the Tribunal may specify.[61] This implies that the Tribunal has no power to backdate a variation order.

---

[56] *cf.* Chap. 5, para. 5.55.
[57] Duration of Copyright and Rights in Performances Regulations 1995, note 13 above, Regs. 34(1), 35(2).
[58] *ibid.*, Reg. 35(1).
[59] *ibid.*, Reg. 35(3).
[60] *ibid.*, Reg. 35(4).
[61] *ibid.*, Reg. 34(5).

3. Ownership, Licensing, Equitable Remuneration and the Copyright Tribunal

INTRODUCTION

3.01 The Whitford Committee's compromise recommendation that performers should not have a copyright in their performances but should have civil remedies for the unauthorised exploitation of those performances[1] was enacted by expressly making infringement of performers' rights actionable as breach of statutory duty. The effect of this was to confer on performers and recording companies two new rights which were very similar to, but not so extensive as, full copyrights. One of the main differences between these new rights and copyright was that they were not assignable (although performers' rights could be transmitted on death).[2] With the amendments made by the Copyright and Related Rights Regulations 1996[3] this has now changed. Performers' rights (but not recording rights) have been partially upgraded to the status of a property right. Accordingly questions of ownership will now assume greater importance than was the case under the original legislation. The same is true of licensing, particularly collective licensing. In addition, performers have been given rights to equitable remuneration in certain circumstances. The Copyright Tribunal's jurisdiction has been further widened to embrace both equitable remuneration and collective licensing of performer's property rights.

FIRST OWNERSHIP

First ownership of performers' rights

3.02 Performers' rights are first owned by the performer. Unlike copyright,[4] there is no provision for first ownership by an employer. (Performers' property rights may, however, be assigned prospectively in the same way as copyrights.[5])

3.03 The only exception to this is that created by a transitional provision in the

---

[1] Cmnd. 6723 at para. 412. See Chap. 1, paras. 1.82–1.83.
[2] Copyright, Designs and Patents Act 1988 (unamended), s. 192(1).
[3] S.I. 1996 No. 2967.
[4] Copyright, Designs and Patents Act 1988, s. 11(2).
[5] See para. 3.08, below.

Copyright and Related Rights Regulations 1996.[6] Where the owner or prospective owner of performers' rights in a performance has authorised a person to make a copy of a recording of that performance before commencement of the Regulations (December 1, 1996), any new right (*i.e.* a right arising by virtue of the 1996 Regulations[7]) in relation to that copy vests in that person on commencement.[8]

First ownership of recording rights

Recording rights are first owned either (i) by the person having the benefit (including the benefit by assignment) of the recording contract to which the performance is subject if that person is qualified[9] or (ii) if not, by that person's licensee (including the assignee of the licensee) if the licensee is qualified.[10]   **3.04**

TRANSMISSION OF PERFORMERS' RIGHTS

The Copyright and Related Rights Regulations 1996 divide performers' rights in those which may be assigned and those which may not. The former are referred to as "performers' property rights".[11] Although the latter may not be assigned, they are transmissible on death.   **3.05**

Performers' property rights

A performer's property rights are the rights conferred on him by sections 182A (reproduction right), 182B (distribution right) and 182C (rental right and lending right).[12] These rights are transmissible by assignment, by testamentary disposition or by operation of law as personal or moveable property.[13] Where the performance is included in a film by agreement, however, there is a presumed transfer of the rental right to the film producer unless the agreement provides to the contrary.[14]   **3.06**

Assignment of performers' property rights

Assignments (or other transmissions) of performers' property rights may be partial, *i.e.* limited to certain acts or in time.[15] An assignment is not effective unless it is in writing signed by or on behalf of the assignor.[16] Where there is an agreement to assign, but no executed assignment, then it is submitted that equitable title to performers' property rights will pass in the same way as copyright.[17] An assignment does not include the right to bring proceedings   **3.07**

---

[6] Note 3, above.
[7] Copyright and Related Rights Regulations 1996, note 3, above, Reg. 25(3).
[8] *ibid.*, Reg. 31.
[9] Copyright, Designs and Patents Act 1988, s. 185(2).
[10] *ibid.*, s. 185(3).
[11] *ibid.*, s. 191A(1).
[12] *ibid.*
[13] *ibid.*, s. 191B(1).
[14] See paras. 3.09–3.10.
[15] Copyright, Designs and Patents Act 1988, s. 191B(2). *cf.* s. 90(2) (Part I).
[16] *ibid.*, s. 191A(3). *cf.* s. 90(3) (Part I).
[17] See Laddie, Prescott & Vitoria, *The Modern Law of Copyright and Designs* (2nd ed., Butterworths, 1995), para. 13.8.

and claims damages for past infringements unless it is expressed to do so.[18]

3.08　　Where a performer or his agent purports wholly or partially to assign his performers' property rights in relation to a future recording of a performance, then if when the rights come into existence the assignee or his successor in title would be entitled as against all other persons to require the rights to be vested in him, they shall vest in the assignee or successor in title.[19] The effect of this is that, if the assignee would be entitled to specific performance of the agreement, he becomes the legal owner of the rights as soon as the recording is made without the need for any further document. If the assignee would not be entitled to specific performance, then the purported assignment is ineffective. Circumstances in which the assignee would not be so entitled might include: a prior assignment; where there was no consideration; where there was a condition precedent which remained unfulfilled; or where the purported assignment formed part of a contract which had been held to be unenforceable as being in restraint of trade.[20]

Presumed transfer of rental rights in films

3.09　　Where there is an agreement between a film producer[21] and a performer concerning the production of a film, the performer is presumed, unless the agreement provides to the contrary, to have transferred to the film producer any rental right in relation to the film arising from the inclusion of a recording of his performance in the film.[22] In place of the rental right the performer receives a right to equitable remuneration.[23] There is no such presumption of transfer in relation to agreements for the making of sound recordings.[24]

3.10　　For this purpose an agreement between a film producer and a performer includes any agreement having effect between them, whether made directly or through intermediaries.[25] It would appear that this is intended to cover the situation where the performer contracts with the film producer via his service company.[26] The absence of signature by or behalf of the performer does not prevent the agreement taking effect as a future assignment of performers' property rights.[27]

Performers' non-property rights

3.11　　Performers' non-property rights, namely the rights conferred by sections 182 (fixation and live broadcasting of performance), 183 (public performance and broadcasting by means of recording made without consent) and section

---

[18] *Wilden Pump Engineering Co. v. Fusfeld* (1985–1987) 8 I.P.R. 250 and *Taypar Ltd v. Santic* (1990) 17 I.P.R. 146.
[19] Copyright, Designs and Patents Act 1988, s. 191C(2). *cf.* s. 91(1) (Part I).
[20] See Laddie, Prescott & Vitoria, note 17, above, paras. 13.5 and 13.53.
[21] See para. 3.48, below, for the meaning of this term.
[22] Copyright, Designs and Patents Act 1988, s. 192F(1).
[23] *ibid.*, s. 191F(4).
[24] This distinction originates in the E.C. Rental and Lending Rights Directive: Art. 2(5) provides for a presumption in the absence of any agreement to the contrary that performers have transferred their rental rights to film producers (subject to the unwaivable right to equitable remuneration) but there is no corresponding provision concerning sound recordings.
[25] Copyright, Designs and Patents Act 1988, s. 191F(3).
[26] See Chap. 2, para. 2.53.
[27] Copyright, Designs and Patents Act 1988, s. 191F(2).

184 (dealing in illicit recording), are not assignable.[28] They are, however, transmissible on death.

Disposition of performers' non-property rights

Any performers' non-property right may be passed on death to "such person as [the performer] may by testamentary disposition specifically direct".[29] This might be taken to suggest that each right can only be transmitted to *one* person.[30] Section 192A(4), however, makes it clear that each right may be transmitted to more than one person, in which case the recipients will be able to exercise the rights independently of each other.[31] **3.12**

A disposition of a performer's property rights can be partial in the same way as an assignment.[32] There is no equivalent provision in respect of a performer's non-property rights, however, which seems to suggest that partial disposition of those rights is not permissible. On the other hand, it is arguable that the reference to "any such right" in section 192A(2) implicitly recognises that different rights may be assigned to different persons. **3.13**

Transmission of performers' non-property rights on death in absence of disposition

If or to the extent that there is no express provision in the will, performers' non-property rights are exercisable after death by the deceased's personal representatives.[33] Damages recovered by the personal representatives in respect of an infringement occurring after the deceased's death devolve as part of the deceased's estate as if the right of action had subsisted and been vested in the deceased immediately before death.[34] In either case, any consent which was binding upon the deceased will bind the person or persons to whom the rights pass.[35] **3.14**

Bequests of unpublished recordings

Where a person becomes entitled by virtue of a bequest (whether specific or general) to any material thing containing a recording of a performance which was not published before the testator's death, the bequest is to be construed as including any performers' rights in relation to the recording which the testator owned immediately before his death unless a contrary intention is indicated in his will or a codicil to it.[36] On its face this provision applies to *all* performers' rights in the recording, but the rubric to the section refers to "performer's *property* right" [emphasis added] and the section is contained in the bundle of sections dealing with performers' property rights. It would **3.15**

---

[28] *ibid.*, s. 192A(1).
[29] *ibid.*, s. 192A(2)(a).
[30] Although in general the single includes the plural unless the contrary intention appears: Interpretation Act 1978, s. 6(c).
[31] See para. 3.18, below.
[32] Copyright, Designs and Patents Act 1988, s. 191B(2).
[33] *ibid.*, s. 192A(2)(b). *cf. Rickless v. United Artists Corp.* [1988] Q.B. 40.
[34] Copyright, Designs and Patents Act 1988, s. 192A(5).
[35] *ibid.*, s. 193(3).
[36] *ibid.*, s. 191E.

therefore seem that it should be interpreted as applying only to performers' property rights.[37]

TRANSMISSION OF RECORDING RIGHTS

3.16 Recording rights may not be assigned or otherwise transmitted.[38] The restriction on assignment of recording rights does not matter greatly, however, since the contractual rights upon which they depend are assignable and it is expressly provided that sections 185(2)(b) or (3)(b), under which assignees of such rights may acquire recording rights, are not affected.[39] Thus if A has recording rights in a performance by virtue of an exclusive recording contract with the performer to which the performance is subject, he cannot assign those rights to B. He can, however, assign the benefit of the contract to B who will, if he is a qualified person, automatically acquire the recording rights thenceforward. Such an assignment would probably not carry with it any accrued rights of action (unlike an assignment of copyright), but these could be assigned to B together with the benefit of the contract. If B is not a qualified person, he will be able to license someone, who is a qualified person, to make recordings (including recordings made from a recording) of the performance with a view to commercial exploitation. Any consent which was binding upon the assignor or licensor of such contractual rights will bind the assignee or licensee.[40]

JOINT OWNERSHIP

Performers' rights

3.17 Now that performers' property rights are assignable, the possibility arises that they may be assigned to joint owners.[41] Joint ownership of performers' rights (both property and other rights) may also arise by virtue of testamentary disposition. Although the point has not been conclusively decided, the weight of authority is that joint owners of copyright hold as tenants in common who, in the absence of any agreement to the contrary, hold in equal shares.[42] The same rule will apply to performers' property rights.

3.18 Where a performer's property rights are owned by more than one person jointly, references to the rights owner are to all the owners, so that any licence

---

[37] The corresponding provision contained in the March 1995 draft of the Copyright and Related Rights Regulations 1996 (s. 191A(5)(a) applying s. 93) was explicit as to this.
[38] Copyright, Designs and Patents Act 1988, s. 192B(1).
[39] ibid., s. 192B(2).
[40] ibid., s. 193(2).
[41] Unlike copyright, joint ownership cannot arise by virtue of joint authorship or employment of the author by joint employers.
[42] *Lauri v. Renad* [1892] 3 Ch. 402; *Prior v. Lansdowne Press Pty Ltd* [1977] R.P.C. 511; *Redwood Music Ltd v. B. Feldman & Co. Ltd* [1979] R.P.C. 385; *Acorn Computers Ltd v. MCS Microcomputer Systems Pty Ltd* (1983–1985) 4 I.P.R. 214. The only modern case to the contrary is *Mail Newspapers plc v. Express Newspapers plc* [1987] F.S.R. 90, an interlocutory decision in which none of the preceding authorities are cited.

must be granted by all of them.[43] There is no equivalent provision for performers' non-property rights. Instead, where performers' rights other than performers' property rights enter joint ownership by virtue of a testamentary disposition, section 192A(4) provides that the rights are exercisable "by each of them independently of the other or others". It is not entirely clear what this means. It is submitted that this must mean that each owner may sue for infringement without the presence of the others (although possibly he may have to account to the others for their share of the damages). It may also mean that (a) each owner can himself do acts within the scope of the performers' rights without committing an infringement even if he does not have the permission of the others; and/or (b) he may grant a licence to a third party without the consent of the others. It would be surprising, however, if joint owners of performers' non-property rights were able to act in a way possibly detrimental to each others' interest without the others' consent when this is clearly not permitted in the case of performers' property rights. This may suggest that section 192A(4) should be given a narrow construction.

Recording rights

Assuming that recording rights are neither assignable nor otherwise transmissible, it is not possible for multiple ownership of them to arise in the same way as for performers' rights. What would appear to be possible, however, is for the benefit of the underlying recording contract to be jointly owned by two or more persons and hence for the recording rights arising out of it to be jointly owned. It is submitted that in such circumstances each owner should be able to take proceedings for infringement without the presence of the other owners, but should not be able to exploit or license the exploitation of the rights without the consent of the others.

3.19

LICENCES

It is expressly provided that an owner of performers' non-property rights or recording rights may grant licences in relation to a specific performance, a specific description of performances or performances generally, whether past or future.[44] There is no such provision in relation to performers' property rights, but the position must be the same. On the other hand, it seems clear that in the case of performers' property rights, licences may be granted in relation to specific acts concerning specific performances, so that, for example, the rights owner may license one person to record the performance and another to broadcast it.[45] The same principle should apply to non-property rights and recording rights.

3.20

Licences will be subject to normal contractual principles, so that, for example, they may be express or implied and may be revocable at will if bare

3.21

---

[43] Copyright, Designs and Patents Act 1988, s. 191A(4). *cf*. s. 173(2) (Part I).
[44] *ibid*., s. 193(1).
[45] *ibid*., s. 191A(3).

or in accordance with the contract if supported by consideration.[46] It is expressly provided that a licence of a performer's property rights is binding on every successor in title to the licensor's interest (or prospective interest) except a purchaser in good faith for valuable consideration without actual or constructive notice of the licence.[47]

Exclusive licences of performers' property rights

3.22 Where an exclusive licence is granted in respect of a performer's property rights the exclusive licensee is given the same rights and remedies (except against the licensor) as if it were an assignment.[48] An exclusive licence for this purpose is defined as:

> a licence in writing signed by or on behalf of the owner of a performer's property rights authorising the licensee to the exclusion of all other persons, including the person granting the licence, to do anything requiring the consent of the rights owner.[49]

While there is nothing to prevent the owner of a performer's non-property rights granting an exclusive licence, it will not have the same consequence.

COMPULSORY LICENSING

3.23 Part II of the 1988 Act as amended contains a number of provisions for what amounts to compulsory licensing of performers' rights in particular circumstances. These are as follows:

(1) The Copyright Tribunal has power to consent on behalf of the owner of a performer's rights where the identity or whereabouts of the owner cannot be ascertained by reasonable inquiry.

(2) Where a performance or recording is included in a cable programme service pursuant to a requirement imposed under the Broadcast Act 1990 but the inclusion is not within the exception provided by Schedule 2, paragraph 19(2) of the 1988 Act, the inclusion is covered by a statutory licence upon payment of a reasonable royalty or other payment.

(3) Where the Monopolies and Mergers Commission has reported that performers' rights are being exercised contrary to the public interest, the Secretary of State has power to provide that licences of performers' rights shall be available as of right.

(4) The Secretary of State has power to make an order providing that in particular cases the lending to the public of copies of films or sound recordings shall be treated as licensed by the owner of relevant performers' rights subject only to the payment of a reasonable royalty or other payment.

---

[46] See Chap. 5, para. 5.55.
[47] Copyright, Designs and Patents Act 1988, ss. 191B(4), 191C(3).
[48] *ibid.*, s. 191L(1). See Chap. 6, para. 6.05.
[49] Copyright, Designs and Patents Act 1988, s. 191D(1).

(5) Licences are available as of right in respect of rights under Part II which had expired but are revived by the implementation of the E.C. Term Directive subject only to the payment of reasonable remuneration. This topic is dealt with in Chapter 2.[50]

The Copyright Tribunal's power to give consent

The powers of the Copyright Tribunal established under the 1988 Act[51] include a power to give consent on behalf of a performer in certain cases, in effect a form of compulsory licensing.

3.24

Extent of the Tribunal's jurisdiction to give consent

Until the 1988 Act was amended by the Copyright and Related Rights Regulations 1996, the Copyright Tribunal had jurisdiction on an application by a person who wished to make a copy of a recording of a performance to give consent in place of a performer in either of two cases[52]:

3.25

(a) where the identity or whereabouts of the performer could not be ascertained by reasonable inquiry; or
(b) where the performer had unreasonably withheld his consent.

The primary effect of the amendments is to remove the Tribunal's jurisdiction in situation (b).[53]

The Tribunal has no jurisdiction to give consent to either the making of a recording from a performance or the broadcasting or inclusion in a cable programme service of a live performance.[54] As the Act has now been amended, the rationale for these omissions is presumably that in these circumstances there can be no question of the identity or whereabouts of the performer being unascertainable by reasonable inquiry.

3.26

In addition, the Tribunal has no jurisdiction to give consent for the purposes of the provisions of Part II of the 1988 Act relating to recording rights.[55] It is not clear why these should have been excluded from the Tribunal's jurisdiction.

3.27

Identity or whereabouts of the owner of the reproduction right cannot be ascertained by reasonable inquiry

Even if the identity and whereabouts of the performer is known, it may not be possible to ascertain the identity or whereabouts of the present owner(s) of his reproduction right. Thus in *Ex parte Sianel Pedwar Cymru*[56] the Tribunal gave consent on behalf of the unknown personal representatives of a known deceased performer. It is implicit in the Tribunal's decision that the Tribunal

3.28

---

[50] paras. 2.74–2.75.
[51] See para. 3.62, below, for a brief description of this body and its history.
[52] Copyright, Designs and Patents Act 1988, s. 190(1) (before amendment).
[53] Copyright and Rights in Performances Regulations 1996 (S.I. 1996 No. 2967), Regulation 23(2) deleting s. 190(1)(b). This change was required by the E.C. Rental and Lending Rights Directive which did not allow for such compulsory licensing.
[54] Where the performance has already been recorded with the performer's consent, it can be broadcast or included in a cable programme service without further ado.
[55] Copyright, Designs and Patents Act 1988, s. 190(2); *cf.* s. 198(3)(b).
[56] [1993] EMLR 251.

construed the expression "the performer", which appeared in section 190 before it was amended, as meaning "the owner(s) for the time being of the relevant performers' rights", although it gave no reasons. The amendments have dealt with the transmissibility of performers' reproduction rights by substituting references to "the person entitled to the reproduction right" for references to "the performer".

3.29   "Reasonable inquiry" will doubtless include taking such steps as writing to Equity or the Musicians' Union and writing to the appropriate collecting society (if any). The Tribunal may not give consent in this case until after 28 days after the service on such persons as it considers are likely to have relevant information and/or the publication in such publications as it considers appropriate of a notice setting out brief particulars of the application and requesting information as to the identity or whereabouts of the performer.[57]

Factors to be taken into account

3.30   Two particular factors are laid down by the Act for the Tribunal to take into account in deciding whether to give consent[58]:

(a) whether the original recording was made with the performer's consent and is lawfully in the possession of the person proposing to make the further recording; and

(b) whether the making of the further recording is consistent with the purposes for which the original recording was made.

The implication is that if either is not complied with then the Tribunal will not give consent or will only do so on appropriate terms as to remuneration. Certainly, that is how this provision should be interpreted so as to comply with Article 7 of the Rome Convention. In *Ex parte Sianel Pedwar Cymru*[59] the Tribunal's order contained an express provision that persons on whose behalf consent was given were at liberty to apply to the Tribunal for an order as to payment or other terms.

Ambit of consent given by the Tribunal

3.31   It should be noted that there is no provision that the Tribunal's consent to the making of copies of a recording of performance also operates as consent to the issuing to the public or rental and lending of those copies. This would appear to be deliberate, for section 190 as amended is carefully drafted so as to refer to the reproduction right and not to the distribution or rental and lending rights. Since few, if any, people will wish to go to the trouble of obtaining consent to the making of a copy purely for private use, it appears that the primary use of the provision will be to enable copies of old recordings to be publicly performed and broadcast.

---

[57] Copyright, Designs and Patents Act 1988, s. 190(3); Copyright Tribunal Rules 1989, Rule 35.
[58] Copyright, Designs and Patents Act 1988, s. 190(5).
[59] Note 56, above.

Terms

The Tribunal may give consent subject to any conditions it thinks fit,[60] including terms as to the payment to be made to the owner of the reproduction right (if and when identified or located).[61]   **3.32**

Mode of application

An application to the Tribunal for consent is made by service by the applicant on the Secretary to the Tribunal of a notice in Form 14 to the Copyright Tribunal Rules 1989[62] stating the inquiries made by the applicant to ascertain the identity or whereabouts of the performer and the result of those inquiries.[63]   **3.33**

Inclusion in a cable programme service pursuant to a relevant requirement

Where a broadcast is included in a cable programme service pursuant to a "relevant requirement", but the area covered by the cable programme falls outside the area for reception in which the broadcast is made so that the exception provided by Schedule 2, paragraph 19(2) does not apply, then the inclusion of the performance or recording is subject to a statutory licence upon payment of a reasonable royalty or other payment.[64] In default of agreement the amount of the payment is to be determined by the Copyright Tribunal.[65]   **3.34**

Relevant requirement

A "relevant requirement" for this purpose is a requirement for certain services to be included in local delivery services provided by digital means imposed under section 78A of the Broadcasting Act 1990 or a requirement for certain services to be included in cable services originally licensed under the Cable and Broadcasting Act 1984 imposed under Schedule 12, Part III, paragraph 4 of the 1990 Act.[66]   **3.35**

Applications to settle the royalty or other payment

Applications to settle the royalty or other payment may be made either by the owner of the rights or by the person making the broadcast.[67] Once the Tribunal has made an order, either party may apply to the Tribunal for the order to be varied subsequently,[68] but except with the leave of the Tribunal no such application may be made within 12 months of the date of the previous order.[69] An order made by the Tribunal on a application for variation has effect from the date on which is made or on such later date as the Tribunal   **3.36**

---

[60] Copyright, Designs and Patents Act 1988, s. 190(2).
[61] *ibid.*, s. 190(6).
[62] S.I. 1989 No. 1129. (See Appendix 3A.)
[63] Copyright Tribunal Rules 1989, *ibid.*, Rule 34.
[64] Copyright, Patents and Designs Act 1988, Sched. 2, para. 19(3) (corresponding to s. 73(4) of Part I).
[65] *ibid.*, Sched. 2, paras. 19(3) and 19A(2).
[66] *ibid.*, s. 73 (7).
[67] *ibid.*, Sched. 2A, para. 19A(1).
[68] *ibid.*, Sched. 2A, para. 19A(3).
[69] *ibid.*, Sched. 2A, para. 19A(4).

may specify.[70] Thus the Tribunal has no power to backdate its orders in such cases.

Powers exercisable in consequence of a Monopolies and Mergers Commission report

3.37   More explicit compulsory licensing powers are available where the Monopolies and Mergers Commission reports that certain practices have operated or may be expected to operate against the public interest. The practices in question are as follows:

(a) the inclusion of conditions in licences granted by the owner of a performer's property rights which restrict the use to which a recording or copy of a recording may be put by the licensee or which restrict the right of the owner to grant other licences; and

(b) the refusal of an owner of a performer's property rights to grant licences on reasonable terms.[71]

3.38   In these circumstances the appropriate Minister in the Department of Trade and Industry has powers (i) to cancel or modify the conditions and/or (ii) to provide that licences in respect of the performer's property rights shall be available as of right.[72] The Minister shall only exercise those powers, however, if he is satisfied that to do so would not contravene any convention relating to performers' rights to which the United Kingdom is a party.[73]

Licences of right

3.39   Where a licence is available as of right by virtue of the exercise of these powers, the terms of the licence shall in default of agreement be settled by the Copyright Tribunal on an application by the person requiring the licence.[74] Where the Tribunal settles the terms of the licence, the licence has effect from the date on which the application was made.[75]

Lending to the public of copies of films and sound recordings

3.40   The Secretary of State is empowered to make an order providing that, in such cases as the order may specify, the lending[76] to the public of copies of films or sound recordings shall be treated as licensed by the performer subject only to the payment of a reasonable royalty or other payment.[77] In default of agreement the amount of the payment is to be determined by the Copyright Tribunal.[78] Such an order is to be made by statutory instrument, a draft of which has been laid before and approved by a resolution of each House of Parliament.[79] The order may make different provision for different cases and

---

[70] *ibid.*, Sched. 2A, para. 19A(5).
[71] *ibid.*, Sched. 2A, para. 17(1).
[72] *ibid.*
[73] *ibid.*, Sched. 2A, para. 17(3).
[74] *ibid.*, Sched. 2A, para. 17(4).
[75] *ibid.*, Sched. 2A, para. 17(5).
[76] See Chap. 4, para. 4.35 for the meaning of "lending".
[77] Copyright, Designs and Patents Act 1988, Sched. 2, para. 14A(1) (corresponding to s. 66 of Part I).
[78] *ibid.*
[79] *ibid.*, Sched. 2, para. 14A(4).

may specify cases by reference to any factor relating to the work, the copies lent, the lender or the circumstances of the lending.[80]

Applications to settle the royalty or other payment

Applications to settle the royalty or other payment may be made either by the owner of the performer's property rights or by the person claiming the benefit of the compulsory licence.[81] Once the Tribunal has made an order, either party may apply to the Tribunal for the order to be varied subsequently,[82] but except with the leave of the Tribunal no such application may be made within 12 months of the date of the previous order.[83] An order made by the Tribunal on a application for variation has effect from the date on which is made or on such later date as the Tribunal may specify.[84] Thus the Tribunal has no power to backdate its orders in such cases.

3.41

Certification of licensing schemes

Orders made under paragraph 14A of Schedule 2 do not apply where there is a licensing scheme providing for the grant of licences which has been certified by the Secretary of State under paragraph 16 of Schedule 2A.[85] Applications for certification may be made by persons who operate or propose to operate such a scheme.[86] The Secretary of State is to certify the scheme by statutory instrument if he is satisfied that it enables the works to which it relates to be identified with sufficient certainty by persons likely to require licences and that it sets out clearly any charges payable and the other terms on which the licences will be granted.[87] The certification comes into effect on the date specified which must be not less eight weeks after the order is made, or, if there is a pending reference to the Copyright Tribunal under paragraph 3 of Schedule 2A, the date when the Tribunal's order comes into force or the reference is withdrawn.[88] Variations of the scheme are not effective unless a corresponding amendment of the order is made.[89] Where the Tribunal orders a variation under paragraphs 3, 4 or 5 of Schedule 2A the Secretary of State is required to make an order; otherwise he has a discretion.[90] The order must be revoked if the scheme ceases to be operated, and the Secretary of State may revoke the order if it appears to him that the scheme is not being operated according to its terms.[91]

3.42

---

[80] *ibid.*, Sched. 2, para. 14A(3).
[81] *ibid.*, Sched. 2A, para. 15(1).
[82] *ibid.*, Sched. 2A, para. 15(3).
[83] *ibid.*, Sched. 2A, para. 15(4).
[84] *ibid.*, Sched. 2A, para. 15(5).
[85] *ibid.*, Sched. 2, para. 14A(2).
[86] *ibid.*, Sched. 2A, para. 16(1).
[87] *ibid.*, Sched. 2A, para. 16(2).
[88] *ibid.*, Sched. 2A, para. 16(3).
[89] *ibid.*, Sched. 2A, para. 16(4).
[90] *ibid.*
[91] *ibid.*, Sched. 2A, para. 16(5).

RIGHTS TO EQUITABLE REMUNERATION

3.43　The amendments to Part II of the 1988 Act made by the Copyright and Related Rights Regulations 1996[92] to implement the E.C. Rental and Lending Rights Directive[93] introduced two rights to equitable remuneration for performers. The first is a right to equitable remuneration from public performances and broadcasts of sound recordings (but not films). The second is a right to equitable remuneration where the performer transfers (or is deemed to transfer) his rental right in a film or sound recording to its producer. These provisions, particularly the latter, bear certain similarities to compulsory licences and so it is convenient to deal with them here. In addition they have a number of features in common.

Right to equitable remuneration from public performance and broadcast of sound recordings

Background

3.44　Traditionally, performers in the music industry contracted with record companies on the basis that the consideration for the provision of the performers' services for the making of sound recordings was the payment of royalties on sales of copies of the recordings (often with an advance payment). The record companies, as the owners of the copyrights in the sound recordings, were entitled to all the income derived from other means of exploitation of the recordings.[94] In particular, the record companies were exclusively entitled to the income from public performance and broadcasting of the recordings collected on their behalf by collecting societies, such as Phonographic Performance Limited (PPL) in the United Kingdom.[95] From the outset performers regarded it as unfair that they should not be entitled to income generated at least in part by their performances, and sought a share of the public performance and broadcasting revenues. In response to this demand, PPL agreed in 1934 to pay 20 per cent of its net revenues to named artists on an *ex gratia* basis.[96] In 1946, it agreed to pay a further 12.5 per cent to the Musicians' Union in recognition of the services of unnamed session musicians. When the United Kingdom ratified the Rome Convention, Article 12 of which provided that users should pay a "single equitable remuneration" to be shared between record producers and performers according to domestic law, it regarded these arrangements as sufficiently discharging its obligations under Article 12. An investigation by the Monopolies and Mergers Commission into collective licensing found, however, that in practice the arrangements did not operate satisfactorily.[97] Owing to PPL's

---

[92] S.I. 1996 No. 2967.

[93] Council Directive 92/100, November 19, 1992 on rental right and lending right and on certain rights related to copyright in the field of intellectual property, [1992] O.J. L346/61.

[94] Typically the contract would contain a blanket consent by the performer to exploitation of recordings of his performance.

[95] See paras 3.59–3.60, below.

[96] Originally these payments were made to artists signed to PPL members in the U.K., but later this was extended to artists signed to PPL members in any E.C. Member State.

[97] Cm. 530 at para. 7.36.

sampling methods, the way in which the 20 per cent was distributed bore little relationship with the frequency with which named performers' recordings were played (although these methods have since been improved). Moreover, not all named artists actually received their PPL payments.[98] As for the 12.5 per cent, this was paid by the Musicians' Union into a "Special Fund" and was not distributed to the session musicians who had generated the income (although following the MMC Report the Musicians' Union did start to distribute these monies to session musicians). The MMC doubted that these arrangements did properly discharge the United Kingdom's obligations under Article 12 and recommended that all performers should received equitable remuneration paid directly by PPL according to the usage of each recording.[99] By contrast, Denmark, France, Germany, Greece, Italy, the Netherlands, Portugal and Spain had all enacted legislation stipulating that a minimum of 50 per cent (in Germany 64 per cent) of the public performance and broadcasting revenues was to be paid to performers.[1]

The new provisions under the Rental and Lending Rights Directive

Following the belated implementation of the Rental and Lending Directive by the 1996 Regulations, the position of performers in the United Kingdom has been considerably improved. Where a commercially published sound recording of the whole or any substantial part of a performance in which performers' rights subsist is either (a) played in public or (b) included in a broadcast or cable programme service, the performer is entitled to equitable remuneration from the owner of the copyright in the sound recording.[2] This applies whether or not the performer consented to the making of the recording in question.   **3.45**

Commercially published—"Commercially published" is not defined for this purpose, but presumably has the same meaning as in Part I.[3] There "publication" is defined as the issue of copies of public,[4] but not including publication which is merely colourable and not intended to satisfy the reasonable requirements of the public[5] or unauthorised acts.[6] "Commercial publication" is not further defined in the case of films and sound   **3.46**

---

[98] In a significant number of cases PPL does not have a current address for the artist. This is because there is no contract between the artist and PPL and it is PPL's member's responsibility to notify PPL of the artist's address. Even if the record company discharges this responsibility on signing the artist, changes of address are not always notified to PPL and it is not uncommon for record companies to lose contact with artists at the end of their contract. Where it does not have an address for an artist, PPL's practice is to accumulate the payments for seven years (three years prior to 1982), after which the oldest year's payment is reallocated so as to maintain a rolling seven-year total.

[99] Note 97, above, para. 7.38.

[1] See Robinson, "U.K. Copyright and the Communication of Sound Recordings to the Public", [1995] 8 ENT. LR 312.

[2] Copyright, Designs and Patents Act 1988, s. 182D(1) implementing Art. 8(2) of the E.C. Directive on Rental and Lending Rights which itself follows Art. 12 of the Rome Convention.

[3] The corresponding expression in the Directive is "published for commercial purposes" (Art. 8(2)), which does not take matters any further.

[4] Copyright, Designs and Patents Act 1988, s. 175(1)(a).

[5] *ibid.*, s. 174(5).

[6] *ibid.*, s. 174(6).

recordings (unlike literary, dramatic, musical and artistic works[7]), but it is provided that in this case "publication", and hence "commercial publication", does not include being shown to played in public or broadcasting or inclusion in a cable programme service.[8]

3.47 **Owner of the copyright in the sound recording**—It would appear that the "owner of the copyright in the sound recording" for this purpose is the primary owner of copyright (*i.e.* the original producer of the sound recording or his assignee) rather than the owner of the public performance and broadcasting rights, namely PPL.[9] If this is correct, it means that performers now have a right exercisable directly against their record companies which is independent of the record companies' right to receive royalties from PPL. While this is to performers' advantage, it is not clear that this correctly implements Article 8(2) of the Directive, which requires a *single* equitable remuneration paid by the user to be shared between performers and phonogram producers.[10] The net result, however, is much the same: the user pays a single fee to PPL which pays a royalty to the producer who pays equitable remuneration to the performers. Moreover, there appears to be nothing to stop performers and record companies agreeing that the equitable remuneration be paid by a suitable division of the PPL revenues. In practice, most performers will be covered by an agreement reached between the International Managers Forum and the Association of United Recording Artists on the one hand and PPL and the British Phonographic Industry on the other hand which provides for performers to receive 50 per cent of the net distributable income received by PPL.[11]

Right to equitable remuneration on transfer of rental right

3.48 Where there is either a presumed transfer of a performer's rental right in copies of a film or an actual transfer of his rental right in copies of a film or of a sound recording to the producer, the performer retains a right to equitable remuneration.[12] This includes any arrangement having the effect of transferring the rental right, whether made directly between the producer and the performer or through intermediaries.[13] It would appear that this is intended to cover the situation where the performer contracts with the producer via his service company, although the wording is more general than this. "Producer" is not defined for the purposes of Part II, but presumably it has the same meaning as in Part I where it is defined as the person by whom the

---

[7] *ibid.*, s. 174(2).
[8] *ibid.*, s. 174(4)(c).
[9] See para. 3.60, below. By contrast, the March 1995 draft of the Copyright and Related Rights Regulations 1996 provided (s. 184A) that the performer was entitled to a reasonable proportion of the royalties paid for a public performance or broadcasting licence, *i.e.* the royalties paid to PPL.
[10] See Reinbothe and von Lewinski, *The E.C. Directive on Rental and Lending Rights and on Piracy* (Sweet & Maxwell, 1993), p. 98.
[11] In accordance with the WIPO Model Law Concerning the Protection of Performers, Producers of Phonograms and Broadcasting Organisations, Art. 5(2). At the time of writing, the division between named artists and unidentified performers such as session musicians has yet to be settled.
[12] Copyright, Designs and Patents Act 1988, ss. 191F(4) and 191G(1).
[13] *ibid.*, ss. 191F(3) and 191G(1).

arrangements for making the film or sound recording are undertaken.[14] Equitable remuneration is payable by the person who is entitled to the rental right for the time being.[15] Thus if the producer assigns the rental right to a third party, the third party is liable to pay the equitable remuneration. There is no equivalent right upon a transfer of a performer's lending right.[16]

Rights to equitable remuneration are unwaivable

Agreements which purport to exclude or restrict the rights to equitable remuneration are of no effect,[17] as are agreements which purport to prevent anyone from questioning the amount of equitable remuneration or to restrict the powers of the Copyright Tribunal (as to which, see below).[18] Thus the rights are unwaivable, and copyright owners and producers cannot force performers to contract out of them.[19]

3.49

Transmission of rights to equitable remuneration

The rights to equitable remuneration may not be assigned by the performer except to a collecting society for the purpose of enabling it to enforce the right on his behalf.[20] The rights are, however, transmissible by testamentary disposition or by operation of law as personal or moveable property.[21] A person who inherits such a right in this way may assign or otherwise transmit it.[22]

3.50

Applications to determine the amount payable

In default of agreement as to the amount payable by way of equitable remuneration, an application to determine the amount payable may be made to the Copyright Tribunal.[23] Applications to determine the amount payable may be made by either the person to whom or the person by whom the equitable remuneration is payable.[24] On such an application the Tribunal shall make such order as to the method of calculating and paying equitable remuneration as it may determine to be reasonable in the circumstances.[25] The Tribunal is specifically directed to take into account the importance of the contribution of the performer to the film or sound recording.[26] This implies that, in general, featured artists or leading actors should receive more than backing musicians or extras. Although the Tribunal has no express

3.51

---

[14] *ibid.*, s. 178.
[15] *ibid.*, s. 191G(3).
[16] A distinction that originates in the E.C. Rental and Lending Rights Directive, Art. 4 of which is restricted to assignments of rental rights.
[17] Copyright, Designs and Patents Act 1988, ss. 182D(7)(a) and 191G(5).
[18] *ibid.*, ss. 182D(7)(b) and 191H(5).
[19] In this respect the Regulations arguably go further than the Directive, which expressly provides that the right to equitable remuneration in lieu of rental right is unwaivable (Art. 4(2)), but does not provide that the right to equitable remuneration for broadcasting and communication to the public is unwaivable.
[20] Copyright, Designs and Patents Act 1988, ss. 182D(2) and 191G(2).
[21] *ibid.*
[22] *ibid.*
[23] *ibid.*, ss. 182D(4) and 191H(1).
[24] *ibid.*
[25] *ibid.*, ss. 182D(6) and 191H(3).
[26] *ibid. cf.* Recital (17) of the E.C. Rental and Lending Rights Directive.

power to backdate such orders, this would appear to be implicit.

3.52   In addition, either party may apply to the Tribunal either to vary any agreement as to the amount payable or to vary any previous determination by the Tribunal.[27] In the latter case, no such application may be made except with the leave of the Tribunal within 12 months from the date of the previous determination.[28] An order made by the Tribunal on a application for variation has effect from the date on which it is made or on such later date as the Tribunal may specify.[29] Thus the Tribunal has no power to backdate its orders in such cases. It follows that performers may be better advised to make no agreement as to equitable remuneration pending a reference to the Tribunal.

What is equitable remuneration?

3.53   In the case of equitable remuneration in lieu of rental right, it is provided that remuneration shall not be considered inequitable merely because it was paid by way of a single payment or at the time of the transfer of the rental right.[30] There is no corresponding provision in the case of equitable remuneration for exploitation of sound recordings. Otherwise, the Act contains no guidance as to what amounts to "equitable" remuneration.

3.54   In particular, it is not clear whether equitable remuneration is to be judged in the light of the actual extent of exploitation: if, for example, a lump sum is agreed in advance but the film or record becomes a surprise success, is the performer entitled to increased remuneration? In the case of equitable remuneration for exploitation of sound recordings, it appears to be intended that the remuneration shall be commensurate with the degree of exploitation. There is no express provision to this effect, however, although it is arguable that section 182D(1) requires the payment of equitable remuneration each time that a sound recording is played. An agreement to a suitable division of the PPL revenues will achieve this. On the other hand, in the case of equitable remuneration in lieu of rental right, it appears to be intended that a lump sum paid in advance may be equitable even though this means that the remuneration is unlikely to be commensurate with the degree of exploitation. It is difficult to see any rational basis for this distinction. It is therefore submitted that at least where the producer has gained a disproportionate benefit from the transfer (as in the case where a small lump sum was agreed but the film or record is a surprise success), the performer should be entitled to claim further remuneration.

3.55   Ultimately the question of what constitutes "equitable remuneration" in the context of rental right depends on the interpretation of the E.C. Rental and Lending Rights Directive. This would appear to support the view that the remuneration should be commensurate with the extent of exploitation. Article 4(1) requires the payment of "equitable remuneration *for the rental*" [emphasis added], which seems to imply that the remuneration must relate to the actual rental that occurs. Although recital (16) of the Directive states that

---

[27] *ibid.*, Copyright, Designs and Patents Act 1988, ss. 182D(5) and 191H(2).
[28] *ibid.*
[29] *ibid.*
[30] *ibid.*, s. 191H(4).

equitable remuneration "may be paid on the basis of one or several payments at any time on or after the conclusion of the contract", this only deals with the method and time of payment, not the amount.[31]

Administration by collecting societies[32]

As noted above, the rights to equitable remuneration may be assigned by a performer to a collecting society. In the case of equitable remuneration in lieu of rental right, the collecting society must be an organisation which has as its main object, or one of its main objects, the exercise of the right to equitable remuneration on behalf of more than one performer.[33] There is no such restriction in the case of equitable remuneration for exploitation of sound recordings.   **3.56**

Transitional provisions

The right to equitable remuneration for exploitation of sound recordings is not subject to any special transitional provisions. It is, however, subject to the general transitional provision under the Copyright and Related Rights Regulations 1996 that no act done before commencement (December 1, 1996) gives rise to any right to remuneration.[34] On the other hand, the provision that acts done pursuant to an agreement made before November 19, 1992 do not infringe any new right[35] does not apply to the rights to equitable remuneration.[36]   **3.57**

The right to equitable remuneration in lieu of rental right is also subject to the following special transitional provisions: **3.58**

(1)   There is no right to equitable remuneration in respect of any rental of a film or sound recording before April 1, 1997.[37]

(2)   There is no right to equitable remuneration in respect of any rental after April 1, 1997 of a film or sound recording made pursuant to an agreement entered into prior to July 1, 1994 *unless* the performer (or his successor in title) has before January 1, 1997 notified the person by whom the remuneration would be payable of the former's intention of exercising the right.[38] In practice this provision will prevent many performers from exercising the right, since it requires the performer to have identified the current owner of the rental right and to have notified him of the performer's intention to exercise his right to remuneration, all before January 1, 1997. The ability of performers to comply with this requirement will not have been assisted by the fact that the March 1995 draft of the Regulations was differently worded and the final draft of the Regulations was not published until August 1996.

---

[31] See the discussion in Reinbothe and von Lewinksi, note 10, above, pp. 68–71.
[32] See para. 3.59, below, for an explanation of the role of collecting societies.
[33] Copyright, Designs and Patents Act 1988, s. 191G(6).
[34] Copyright and Related Rights Regulations 1996 (S.I. 1996 No. 2967), Reg. 26(2).
[35] *ibid.*, Reg. 27(2).
[36] *ibid.*, Reg. 25(3)(b).
[37] *ibid.*, Reg. 33(a).
[38] *ibid.*, Reg. 40(b).

COLLECTIVE LICENSING AND THE COPYRIGHT TRIBUNAL

3.59 Collective licensing bodies (also known as collecting societies) are organis- ations which license the use of copyright works, monitor the extent of use by licensees, enforce the conditions of use by licensees, take action against infringers and collect and distribute royalties.[39] The system of collective licensing, under which users normally pay a fee in return for a blanket licence of the society's entire repertoire, is convenient both for users, who are saved the necessity of seeking individual licences from copyright owners, and owners, who are saved the burden of identifying users of their works and enforcing their rights against those users.[40] The fee is usually calculated from a standard formula (known as a tariff) based on the extent of use. Different tariffs exist for different types of use.[41] The tariffs are usually negotiated with bodies representative of each of class of users. Returns are made by each user indicating the extent of use of works within the repertoire. These returns are used by the licensors to calculate the sums to be distributed to their members. In addition to these blanket licences, specific one-off licences may be negotiated in appropriate cases.

3.60 The main collecting societies in the United Kingdom are PPL, which administers the performing, broadcasting and cable diffusion rights in sound recordings[42]; Mechanical-Copyright Protection Society Limited (MCPS), which licences the "mechanical rights" in music and lyrics (*i.e.* the rights to reproduce them on records, cassettes and compact discs); Performing Right Society Limited (PRS) administers the performing, broadcasting and cable diffusion rights in music and lyrics[43]; and Video Performance Limited (VPL) carries out the same functions as PPL in relation to videos. PPL and PRS take assignments of copyright from the owners,[44] while MCPS and VPL act as the owners' agent. The advantage of taking an assignment is that it makes enforcement easier, for the collecting society can thus bring proceedings in its own name.

3.61 Prior to the coming into force of the Copyright, Designs and Patents Act 1988, there was no collecting society for the collection of monies due to performers.[45] The gap was filled to some extent by Equity and by the

---

[39] Monopolies and Mergers Commission, *Collective Licensing: A Report on Certain Practices in the Collective Licensing of Public Performance and Broadcasting Rights in Sound Records*, Cm. 530, glossary and para. 3.4. See generally *Collective Administration of Copyright and Neighbouring Rights* (WIPO, Geneva, 1990).

[40] Taking PRS as an example: PRS has some 28,000 members (writers and publishers), about 260,000 licensed premises and well over 2 million works in its repertoire.

[41] Thus PRS has 41 tariffs ranging from AC (aircraft) to YC (youth clubs). Within each tariff there may be different rates for different classes of use which may vary according to the user, the premises, the type of performance or a combination of these.

[42] PPL's work was scrutinised in the MMC Report on *Collective Licensing*, note 39, above.

[43] PRS was the subject of a further Monopolies and Mergers Commission investigation: *Performing Rights: A Report on the Supply in the U.K. of the Services of Administering Performing Rights and Film Synchronisation Rights*, Cm. 3147.

[44] That is, of the performing, broadcasting and dubbing (copying for the purpose of performance or broadcasting) rights. PPL also optionally acts as agent for administering rights for controlled choice interactive services and multichannel digital diffusion (residential) services.

[45] Although Musical Performers' Protection Association Limited was apparently such a body while it existed.

Musicians' Union, each of which collected and distributed certain payments on behalf of its members. For example, Equity collected and distributed "residuals", that is, payments to actors for repeats and foreign sales of British television programmes. Surprisingly, this position did not change following the passage of the 1988 Act. The E.C. Rental and Lending Rights Directive did, however, lead to the setting up of two new collecting societies. The Performing Artists' Media Rights Association Limited (PAMRA) was instigated by the Musicians' Union, which was joined by Equity, REPRO (the Guild of Recording Producers, Directors and Engineers), the Incorporated Society of Musicians, the Northern Ireland Musicians' Association and the International Artist Managers' Association, but is independent of these bodies. Its mandate is to represent and be accountable to all performers. The International Managers' Forum (IMF) and the British Academy of Songwriters, Composers and Authors (BASCA) have formed the Association of United Recording Artists (AURA) primarily to represent named performers (mainly musicians). PAMRA acts as agent for its members and hopes to begin distibuting remuneration collected on their behalf in 1998.

The monopoly power exercised by collective licensing bodies is capable of   **3.62**
being abused. In order to prevent this, the Copyright Act 1956 created the Performing Right Tribunal to regulate the activities of PPL and PRS. The 1988 Act renamed the PRT as the Copyright Tribunal and gave it a considerably expanded jurisdiction. Originally Part II of the 1988 Act did not originally contain any provision dealing with collective licensing of performers' rights. Such provisions have now been introduced in relation to performers' property rights by the Copyright and Related Rights Regulations 1996. These inserted Schedule 2A to the 1988 Act which regulates the operation of "licensing schemes" and "licensing bodies".

Licensing schemes

A licensing scheme is a scheme which set out (i) the classes of case in which the   **3.63**
operator of the scheme, or the person on whose behalf he acts, is willing to grant performers' property right licences and (ii) the terms on which licences will be granted in those classes of case.[46]

Licensing bodies

A licensing body is an organisation which has as its main object, or one of its   **3.64**
main objects, the negotiation or granting, either as owner or prospective owner or as agent for the owners of performers' property rights, of licences of performers' property rights and whose objects include the granting of licences covering the performances of more than one performer.[47] Licences and schemes covering the performances of more than one performer do not include licences or schemes covering only performances recorded in a single recording or performances recorded in more than one recording where the performers giving the performances are the same or where the recordings are

---

[46] Copyright, Designs and Patents Act 1988, Sched. 2A, para. 1(1).
[47] *ibid.*, Sched. 2A, para. 1(2).

made by, or by employees of, or commissioned by, a single individual, firm, company or group of companies.[48]

Scope of the Tribunal's jurisdiction

3.65 Licensing schemes operated by licensing bodies may be referred to the Copyright Tribunal, and applications for licences under such schemes made, insofar as they relate to licences for copying a recording of the whole or any substantial part of a performance in which performers' rights subsist or for renting or lending such copies to the public.[49] On the face of it, the Tribunal has no jurisdiction to entertain references which relate to licences for issuing such copies to the public otherwise than by rental or lending, in particular by sale. When this point came up in relation to the corresponding provision in Part I,[50] however, the Tribunal held that it could consider as a whole a scheme which licensed both manufacture and sale on the footing that it had jurisdiction to consider the former, and for commercial purposes the two aspects of the licence were inseparable.[51] While this makes perfect sense, it may be questioned whether it is correct given the manner in which Parliament expressly limited the Tribunal's jurisdiction.

References of licensing schemes to the Tribunal

3.66 A licensing scheme which is proposed to be operated by a licensing body may be referred to the Tribunal by an organisation which claims to be representative of persons claiming that they require licences in cases of a description to which the scheme would apply,[52] but not by a single such person. The Tribunal may decline to entertain the reference on the ground that it is premature.[53] The Tribunal must decline to entertain the reference unless it is satisfied that the organisation is reasonably representative of the class of persons it claims to represent.[54] If it entertains the reference, it may make such order as it considers reasonable in the circumstances, either confirming or varying the scheme as a whole or in relation to cases of the description to which the reference relates.[55] The order may be for a fixed period or indefinite.[56] There is nothing to prevent the scheme coming into operation while the reference is pending, but the Tribunal can backdate the operation of the order, so far as any charges payable are concerned, to the date on which the scheme came into operation.[57]

3.67 Where a licensing scheme is already in operation, a reference can be made either by a person claiming that he requires a licence in a case of a description to which the scheme applies or by an organisation claiming to be representative

---

[48] *ibid.*, Sched. 2A, para. 1(4).
[49] *ibid.*, Sched. 2A, para. 2.
[50] *ibid.*, s. 117(a).
[51] *The British Phonographic Industry Ltd v. Mechanical-Copyright Protection Society Ltd, Composers' Joint Council Intervening (No. 2)* [1993] EMLR 86, 98–99.
[52] Copyright, Designs and Patents Act 1988, Sched. 2A, para. 3(1).
[53] *ibid.*, Sched. 2A, para. 3(2).
[54] *ibid.*, s. 205B(3).
[55] *ibid.*, Sched. 2A, para. 3(3).
[56] *ibid.*, Sched. 2A, para. 3(4).
[57] *ibid.*, Sched. 2A, para. 8(3).

of such persons.[58] Where the reference is made by an organisation, the Tribunal must decline to entertain the reference unless it is satisfied that the organisation is reasonably representative of the class of persons it claims to represent.[59] Again, the Tribunal may make whatever order it considers reasonable either for a fixed period or indefinitely.[60] While the reference is pending the scheme remains in operation,[61] but the Tribunal can backdate the operation of the order with respect to any charges payable to the date when the reference was made.[62]

Where the Tribunal has previously made an order in respect of a licensing   **3.68** scheme under paragraphs 3 or 4 of Schedule 2A, then any of the operator of the scheme, a person claiming that he requires a licence or an organisation claiming to be representative of such persons may refer the scheme to the Tribunal again[63]; but except with the leave of the Tribunal such a reference may not be made in respect of the same description of case within 12 months of the previous order or (if the order was to be in force for less than 15 months) until the last three months before expiry of the order.[64] Once again the Tribunal must decline to entertain the reference unless it is satisfied that the organisation is reasonably representative of the class of persons it claims to represent.[65]

Applications to the Tribunal for the grant of licences under licensing schemes

A person who claims that the operator of a licensing scheme has refused or   **3.69** failed within a reasonable time to grant or procure the grant of a licence to him in a case covered by the scheme can apply to the Tribunal for a declaration that he is entitled to a licence.[66] An application for a declaration may also be made in cases which are excluded from the scheme either because they fall within an exception to the scheme or because they fall outside the scheme altogether, provided in the latter instance that the case is so similar to those in which licences are granted under the scheme that it is unreasonable that it should not be dealt with in the same way.[67] In either of these cases an application may be made not only where the operator has refused or failed to grant a licence but also where the operator has proposed unreasonable terms.[68] The Tribunal may make a declaration that the applicant is entitled to a licence on the terms of the scheme or on such terms as it considers reasonable.[69] The order may be for a fixed period or indefinite.[70]

Where the Tribunal has previously made an order in respect of a licensing   **3.70**

---

[58] *ibid.*, Sched. 2A, para. 4(1).
[59] *ibid.*, s. 205B(3).
[60] *ibid.*, Sched. 2A, para. 4(3),(4).
[61] *ibid.*, Sched. 2A, para. 4(2).
[62] *ibid.*, Sched. 2A, para. 8(3).
[63] *ibid.*, Sched. 2A, para. 5(1).
[64] *ibid.*, Sched. 2A, para. 5(2).
[65] *ibid.*, s. 205B(3).
[66] *ibid.*, Sched. 2A, para. 6(1).
[67] *ibid.*, Sched. 2A, para. 6(2),(3).
[68] *ibid.*, Sched. 2A, para. 6(2).
[69] *ibid.*, Sched. 2A, para. 6(4).
[70] *ibid.*, Sched. 2A, para. 6(5).

scheme under paragraph 6 of Schedule 2A, then either the operator of the scheme or the original applicant may refer the scheme to the Tribunal again[71]; but except with the leave of the Tribunal such a reference may not be made within 12 months of the previous order or (if the order was to be in force for less than 15 months) until the last three months before expiry of the order.[72]

Licences granted by licensing bodies otherwise than under licensing schemes

3.71 The Copyright Tribunal has a parallel jurisdiction to entertain references and applications in relation to licences covering the performances of more than one performer granted by licensing bodies otherwise than under a licensing scheme, namely in relation to licences for copying recordings and renting or lending copies to the public.[73]

3.72 The terms on which a licensing body proposes to grant a licence otherwise than pursuant to a licensing scheme may be referred to the Tribunal by the prospective licensee.[74] The Tribunal may decline to entertain the reference on the ground that it is premature.[75] If it entertains the reference, it may make such order as it considers reasonable in the circumstances, either confirming or varying the terms.[76] The order may be for a fixed period or indefinite.[77] There is nothing to prevent the licence coming into effect while the reference is pending, but the Tribunal can backdate the operation of the order so far as any charges payable are concerned to the date on which the licence came into effect.[78]

3.73 A licensee whose licence is about to expire, whether by effluxion of time or on notice given by the licensing body, may where it is unreasonable that the licence should expire apply to the Tribunal for a declaration that he should continue to be entitled to the benefit of the licence on such terms as the Tribunal considers reasonable in the circumstances.[79] The application may not be made until three months before the licence expires,[80] but while the reference is pending the licence remains in operation.[81] As usual, the Tribunal's order may be indefinite or for a fixed period.[82]

3.74 Where the Tribunal has previously made an order in respect of a licence under paragraphs 10 or 11 of Schedule 2A, then either the licensing body or the person entitled to the benefit of the order may refer the licence to the Tribunal again[83]; but except with the leave of the Tribunal such a reference may not be made within 12 months of the previous order or (if the order was

---

[71] *ibid.*, Sched. 2A, para. 7(1).
[72] *ibid.*, Sched. 2A, para. 7(2).
[73] *ibid.*, Sched. 2A, para. 9.
[74] *ibid.*, Sched. 2A, para. 10(1).
[75] *ibid.*, Sched. 2A, para. 10(2).
[76] *ibid.*, Sched. 2A, para. 10(3).
[77] *ibid.*, Sched. 2A, para. 10(4).
[78] *ibid.*, Sched. 2A, para. 13(3).
[79] *ibid.*, Sched. 2A, para. 11(1),(4).
[80] *ibid.*, Sched. 2A, para. 11(2).
[81] *ibid.*, Sched. 2A, para. 11(3).
[82] *ibid.*, Sched. 2A, para. 11(5).
[83] *ibid.*, Sched. 2A, para. 12(1).

to be in force for less than 15 months) until the last three months before expiry of the order.[84]

Factors to be taken into account

In considering what is reasonable the statute specifically directs the Tribunal to have regard to (a) the availability of other schemes, or the granting of other licences, to other persons in similar circumstances and (b) the terms of those schemes and licences and to exercise its powers so as to secure that there is no unreasonable discrimination between licences or prospective licensees under the scheme or licence in question and licensees under those other schemes and licences.[85] Otherwise, the Tribunal is to have regard to all relevant circumstances[86] and has an unfettered discretion.[87]

3.75

Effect of the Tribunal's order on reference or application

Where the Tribunal has made an order on a reference or an application relating to a licensing scheme, persons who in a class of case to which the order applies pay the appropriate charges or (if they cannot be ascertained) give an undertaking to the operator to pay the appropriate charges and comply with any other applicable terms are deemed to be licensed under the relevant performers' property rights.[88] The same applies to the person entitled to the benefit of the order where the Tribunal has made an order on a reference or application relating to a licence not under a licensing scheme.[89]

3.76

---

[84] *ibid.*, Sched. 2A, para. 12(2).

[85] *ibid.*, Sched. 2A, para. 14(1).

[86] *ibid.*, Sched. 2A, para. 14(2).

[87] See *The British Phonographic Industry Ltd v. Mechanical-Copyright Protection Society Ltd, Composers' Joint Council Intervening (No. 2)* [1993] EMLR 86, 97, 99 and *The Association of Independent Radio Companies Ltd v. Phonographic Performance Ltd, British Broadcasting Corporation Intervening* [1993] EMLR 181, 226–227.

[88] Copyright, Designs and Patents Act 1988, Sched. 2A, para. 8(2),(5).

[89] *ibid.*, Sched. 2A, para. 13(1).

4. Infringement

INTRODUCTION

4.01 When originally enacted, Part II of the Copyright, Designs and Patents Act 1988, following the Whitford Committee's recommendation,[1] expressly made infringements of performers' rights and recording rights in performances actionable as breaches of statutory duty.[2] With the amendments made by the Copyright and Related Rights Regulations 1996[3] to implement the E.C. Rental and Lending Rights Directive[4] it is now provided that infringements of performers' property rights are actionable in the same way as infringements of other property rights, and in particular copyright,[5] while infringements of performers' non-property rights and recording rights remain actionable as breaches of statutory duty.[6] In practice the distinction makes little difference, however, except that certain remedies are available for infringements of performers' property rights which are not available for other infringements, notably additional damages and accounts of profits.[7] In either case the owner of the rights has a right enforceable by civil action to prevent future unauthorised exploitation of the performance and to obtain compensation for such acts in the past. The substantive amendments made by the 1996 Regulations are the introduction of new rights for performers in respect of distribution (issuing to the public), rental and lending.[8]

INFRINGEMENT OF PERFORMERS' RIGHTS

4.02 Like other forms of copyright, performers' rights and recording rights are bundles of rights. They may thus be infringed in a number of different ways. Performers' rights which subsist[9] in a performance are infringed by the doing of any of the following acts without the consent of the performer[10]:

---

[1] Cmnd. 6723 at para. 412. See Chap. 1, paras. 1.82–1.83.
[2] Copyright, Designs and Patents Act 1988 (unamended), s. 194.
[3] S.I. 1996 No. 2967.
[4] Council Directive 92/100 on rental right and lending right and on certain rights related to copyright in the field of intellectual property, [1992] O.J. L346/61.
[5] Copyright, Designs and Patents Act 1988, s. 191L. *cf.* s. 96 (Part I).
[6] *ibid.*, s. 194 (as amended).
[7] See Chap. 6, paras. 6.21–6.22 and 6.29–6.30.
[8] See paras. 4.25–4.39 below.
[9] See para. 4.03, below.
[10] In all six of ss. 182–182C and 183–184 of the Copyright, Designs and Patents Act 1988, the word "his" in "without his consent" has two possible antecedents: "a performer" and "a person". The former is clearly correct. Matters are not helped, however, by the reappearance of

(1) making (otherwise than for the maker's private and domestic use) a recording of the whole or any substantial part of the performance directly from the live performance[11];

(2) broadcasting live, or including live in a cable programme service, the whole or any substantial part of the performance[12];

(3) making (otherwise than for the maker's private and domestic use) a recording of the whole or any substantial part of the performance directly from a broadcast of, or cable programme including, the live performance[13];

(4) copying (otherwise than for the copier's private or domestic use) a recording of the whole or any substantial part of the performance[14];

(5) issuing to the public copies of a recording of the whole or any substantial part of the performance[15];

(6) renting or lending to the public copies of a recording of the whole or any substantial part of the performance[16];

(7) showing or playing in public the whole or any substantial part of the performance by means of a recording or a copy of a recording which, as the exhibitor knows or has reason to believe, was made without the performer's consent[17];

(8) broadcasting or including in a cable programme service the whole or any substantial part of the performance by means of a recording or a copy of a recording which, as the broadcaster knows or has reason to believe, was made without the performer's consent[18];

(9) importing into the United Kingdom otherwise than for the private and domestic use of the importer a recording or a copy of a recording which is, and the importer knows or has reason to believe is, an "illicit recording"[19];

(10) in the course of a business possessing, selling, letting for hire, offering or exposing for sale or hire or distributing a recording or a copy of a recording which is, and the dealer knows or has reason to believe, is an "illicit recording".[20]

In addition, performers have rights to equitable remuneration which are discussed in Chapter 3.[21]

---

the word "his" in the phrase "for his private and domestic use" in ss. 182(2), 182A(1) and 184(1)(a), where it has the same possible antecedents but the latter must be intended.

[11] Copyright, Designs and Patents Act 1988, s. 182(1)(a), (2). See paras. 4.10–4.14.

[12] *ibid.*, s. 182(1)(b). See paras. 4.15–4.19.

[13] *ibid.*, s. 182(1)(c), (2). See para. 4.20.

[14] *ibid.*, s. 182A. See paras. 4.21–4.24.

[15] *ibid.*, s. 182B. See paras. 4.25–4.32.

[16] *ibid.*, s. 182C. See paras. 4.33–4.39.

[17] *ibid.*, s. 183(a). See paras. 4.40–4.43.

[18] *ibid.*, s. 183(b). See para. 4.44.

[19] *ibid.*, s. 184(1)(a). See paras. 4.45–4.50.

[20] *ibid.*, s. 184(1)(b). See paras. 4.51–4.62.

[21] paras. 3.48–3.58.

Subsistence of rights

4.03 It should be noted that (as a consequence of the original avoidance of copyright-style drafting) the infringement-defining provisions in Part II in fact refer to a "qualifying performance". There is no explicit limitation to performances in which performers' rights subsist at the time of the infringement. This must be the intention, however, for otherwise section 191 (duration of rights)[22] would be of no effect. The various sections must be read together. For the sake of clarity, therefore, reference is made in this chapter to performances in which performers' rights subsist rather than to qualifying performances.

Primary and secondary infringement

4.04 Infringements in categories (1) to (6) and those in categories (7) to (10) will be referred to as primary and secondary infringements respectively, by analogy with the customary usage that grew up under the Copyright Act 1956 and is (partially) recognised in Part I of the 1988 Act.[23] It should be noted, however, that this description is incorrect in one respect. Secondary infringements are so called because they are dealings in an article the making of which was (or is deemed to have been) a primary infringement. Conversely, a primary infringement consists of making an article which may be dealt in in the ways that constitute a secondary infringement. Category (2) infringement is not true primary infringement in this sense, for the broadcast or cable programme that is made cannot be dealt in in any way that constitutes an infringement of categories (7) to (10), unlike a recording made in category (1) or category (3) infringement. Category (2) infringement does, however, share with category (1) and (3) infringement another characteristic of primary infringement, namely that both are torts of strict liability, since no particular mental state is required to accompany the overt act. The opposite is true of infringements in categories (7) to (10), for which knowledge or reason to believe is an ingredient of the tort. For this reason it is useful to classify category (2) infringement as primary infringement, provided that it is remembered that in this case it cannot lead to any secondary infringement.

Substantial part

4.05 Part II of the 1988 Act contains no guidance as to what might constitute a substantial part of a performance. A question which presents itself is whether or not substantiality is to be measured by reference to any works performed. "A performance" might be either the performance of a single work or the performance of all works performed on one occasion. Thus a concert in which 20 songs are sung might be one performance or 20. The definition of "performance" in section 180(2) provides little assistance in answering this question. On the one hand, paragraph (c) could be taken to indicate that the reading of each literary work is a performance; but, on the other hand, paragraphs (a) and (b) could be taken as indicating the opposite.

---

[22] See Chap. 2, paras. 2.55–2.67.
[23] The rubric to ss. 22–26 refers to "secondary infringement", but the term "primary infringement" is not used.

It is submitted that the question whether infringement has taken place **4.06** should not depend on the correct resolution of this question. Instead, the traditional approach of the courts when faced with deciding questions of substantiality in connection with copyright should be adopted. This approach may be expressed in two ways. The first is in the rule of thumb or maxim, "what is worth copying is prima facie worth protecting".[24] The second is in the series of dicta which support the proposition that substantiality is a matter of impression, taking into account the quality of what has been taken as well as the quantity.[25] In short, if what is taken is substantial, the courts will not concern themselves with whether many works or only part of a work is involved.

Nevertheless, modern technology may give rise to some difficult questions **4.07** on substantiality. A particular example is provided by the use of digital electronic sampling, which permits a musician using a computer to "sample" any pre-existing sound and then manipulate it. If the pre-existing sound is a performance, say by an opera singer, and a very short phrase is taken and then manipulated in various ways, has a substantial part been taken? It is submitted that no clear answers can be given to such hypothetical cases in advance, but that each case will be decided on its facts in accordance with the approach just described.

This does not mean that it is an infringement of performers' rights to take a **4.08** substantial part by *imitating* a performance. The reason is that (by contrast with infringement of copyright under Part I[26]) copying or reproduction of the performance is not a primary infringement, only making a recording from or broadcasting a performance or copying a recording or issuing copies to the public. Performers' rights will therefore be of little assistance to those seeking legal protection for personality merchandising, that is to say, the exploitation of a person's name, likeness and performance characteristics. Thus in the United States of America "sound alikes", persons who can imitate a performer's manner of speaking, have become a popular form of advertising. A performer who sought to restrain such activities in the United Kingdom could not rely on performers' rights for this purpose, but would have to rely on such rights in passing off as he or she might have.[27]

Without consent

Although absence of consent is an element of the tort, it is convenient to deal **4.09** with this topic when dealing with defences.[28]

---

[24] *Per* Petersen J. in *University of London Press Ltd v. University Tutorial Press Ltd* [1916] 2 Ch. 601, 610. This dictum was approved by the House of Lords in *Ladbroke (Football) Ltd v. William Hill (Football) Ltd* [1964] 1 W.L.R. 273, 279, 288, 294. It must be applied with caution, however, since the whole point of the requirement of substantiality is to ensure that a small degree of copying does not infringe.

[25] See in particular *Ladbroke v. William Hill*, note 24, above.

[26] Copyright, Designs and Patents Act 1988, s. 17(1).

[27] See Chap. 8, paras. 8.10–8.21.

[28] See Chap. 5, paras. 5.48–5.59. See also para. 4.43, below.

1. Making a recording directly from the live performance

4.10   Section 182(1)(a) of the 1988 Act makes it an infringement without the consent of the performer to make, otherwise than for the maker's[29] private and domestic use, a recording of the whole or any substantial part of a performance in which performers' rights subsist directly from the live performance.

Recording

4.11   "Recording" is defined as meaning:

> a film or sound recording
>   (a) made directly from the live performance,
>   (b) made from a broadcast of or cable programme including the performance
>   (c) made, directly or indirectly, from another recording of the performance.[30]

This definition is discussed in Chapter 2.[31]

Live

4.12   "Live" is not defined in the Act. It would seem, however, that the only possible meaning here is the obvious one, that is, not prerecorded: compare section 182(1)(b) with section 183(b). [32]

Otherwise than for private and domestic use

4.13   Under the Performers' Protection Acts 1958–1972 it was a defence to charges under sections 1(a) and 2(a) of the 1958 Act to show that the record or film was made for the defendant's private and domestic use only. Thus the burden of proof that the use intended was private and domestic was clearly upon the defendant. It is not quite so clear upon whom the burden of proof falls under the new Act. It would appear, however, that by shifting the exception from a separate proviso to the substantive definition of the tort, the draughtsman has made "otherwise than for his private and domestic use" an element of the tort that the burden is upon the plaintiff to prove. It may well be, on the other hand, that if the legal burden is upon the plaintiff, there will nevertheless be an evidential burden upon the defendant: if no evidence is adduced to show what use was intended, it will be inferred that the use intended was not private and domestic.

4.14   Although it is clear that the essential thrust of the phrase is that the use must be non-commercial, it is not clear whether "private" is intended to add anything to "domestic". There are copyright cases which decide that a "public" performance is one for which the audience is not a "domestic or quasi-domestic" one, and that a "domestic or quasi-domestic" audience is one that lives under one roof.[33] It is submitted that a similar test should be applied, so use will be private and domestic if it is by persons living under one

---

[29] See note 10, above.
[30] Copyright, Designs and Patents Act 1988, s. 180(2).
[31] See para. 2.48.
[32] See also Chap. 2, paras. 2.25–2.26.
[33] *Jennings v. Stephens* [1936] 1 Ch. 49 explaining *Duck v. Bates* (1884) 13 Q.B.D. 843. See also para. 4.41, below.

roof. Too much stress should not be laid on the word "his" in this context, for it is unlikely that the draughtsman intended to restrict the exception to the *personal* private use of the maker of the recording: if he had so intended, it would have been easy enough to say so, and in that case the word "domestic" would surely have been omitted. It may be noted, however, that the wording in the E.C. Rental and Lending Rights Directive refers only to "private use".[34]

2. Broadcasting live or including live in a cable programme

Section 182(1)(b) makes it an infringement without the consent of the performer to broadcast live or include live in a cable programme the whole or any substantial part of a performance in which performers' rights subsist.

4.15

Broadcast

"Broadcast" has the same meaning as in Part I.[35] Thus a broadcast is a transmission by wireless telegraphy of visual images, sounds or other information which is either (a) capable of being lawfully received by the public or (b) transmitted for presentation to members of the public.[36] The definition includes satellite television broadcasts, but does not include microwave transmission between terrestrial fixed points.[37] Encrypted transmissions are to be regarded as capable of being lawfully received by members of the public only if decoding equipment has been made available to the public by or with the authority of the person making the transmission or the person providing the contents of the transmission.[38]

4.16

Cable programme service

"Cable programme service" has the same meaning as in Part I.[39] Thus a cable programme service is a service which consists wholly or mainly in sending visual images, sounds or other information by means of a telecommunications system, otherwise than by wireless telegraphy, for reception (a) at two or more places (whether simultaneously or at different times in response to requests by different users) or (b) for presentation to members of the public.[40] The following are excepted[41]:

4.17

(i) interactive services[42];

(ii) services run for the internal purposes of businesses rather than to render a service or provide amenities for others, the apparatuses of which are under the sole control of the business and which are not connected to any other telecommunications system[43];

---

[34] Art. 10(1)(a).

[35] Copyright, Designs and Patents Act 1988, s. 211(1).

[36] *ibid.*, s. 6(1).

[37] *ibid.*, s. 178 (definition of "wireless telegraphy" as amended by Copyright and Related Rights Regulations 1996, Reg. 8).

[38] *ibid.*, s. 6(2). See *BBC Enterprises Ltd v. Hi-Tech Xtravision Ltd* [1990] F.S.R. 217 and *British Sky Broadcasting Group Ltd v. Lyons* [1995] F.S.R. 357.

[39] *ibid.*, s. 211(1).

[40] *ibid.*, s. 7(1).

[41] Subject to any amendment by the Secretary of State by order under s. 7(3).

[42] Copyright, Designs and Patents Act 1988, s. 7(2)(a).

[43] *ibid.*, s. 7(2)(b).

(iii) services run by individuals solely for domestic purposes of the individuals, the apparatuses of which are under the control of the individuals and which are not connected to any other telecommunications system[44];

(iv) services where all the apparatus is situated in or connects premises under single occupation which are not operated as part of the amenities provided for residents or inmates of premises run as a business and which are not connected to any other telecommunications system[45]; and

(v) services run for broadcasters or cable programme transmitters or persons providing programmes.[46]

It has been held in a Scottish case to be at least arguable that material displayed on an Internet web site is a "cable programme service" and does not fall within the exception for interactive services.[47]

Person broadcasting a performance

4.18 By virtue of section 6(3) of the Act, which it is expressly provided applies to infringements of performers' rights,[48] the following persons are to be regarded as broadcasting a performance (subject to special rules under section 6A in the case of certain satellite broadcasts):

(i) the person transmitting the programme in question if he has responsibility to any extent for its contents; and/or

(ii) any person providing the programme who makes the arrangements necessary for its transmission with the person transmitting it.

Thus more than one person may be liable for any infringement. It is not clear, however, in what circumstances the person transmitting the programme will be held to be responsible for its contents. The use of the words "to any extent" would seem to cast the net very wide.

Person including a performance in a cable programme service

4.19 By virtue of section 7(5) of the Act, which it is expressly provided applies to infringements of performers' rights,[49] the person who includes a performance in a cable programme service is the person providing the service. In contrast with the position in respect of broadcasting, the person providing the programme is not liable.

3. Making a recording from a broadcast or cable programme

4.20 Section 182(1)(c) makes it an infringement without the consent of the performer to make, otherwise than for the maker's[50] private and domestic use, a recording of the whole or any substantial part of a performance in

---

[44] *ibid.*, s. 7(2)(c).
[45] *ibid.*, s. 7(2)(d).
[46] *ibid.*, s. 7(2)(e).
[47] *The Shetland Times Ltd v. Wills* [1997] EMLR 277.
[48] Copyright, Designs and Patents Act 1988, s. 211(2).
[49] *ibid.*, s. 211(2).
[50] See note 10 above.

which performers' rights subsist directly from a broadcast of, or cable programme including, the live performance.

4. Copying a recording

Section 182A of the 1988 Act makes it an infringement without the consent of the performer to make, otherwise than for the maker's[51] private and domestic use, a copy of a recording of the whole or any substantial part of a performance in which performers' rights subsist. The right to authorise or prohibit the making of such copies is referred to as the "reproduction right".[52]   **4.21**

Copy

"Copy" is not defined for this purpose. It is tempting to assume it is intended to have the same meaning as in Part I of the 1988 Act,[53] but if so it may be asked why this has not been expressly provided. If it does have the same meaning as in Part I, two consequences follow. First, where the recording is a film, copying includes making a photograph of the whole or any substantial part of any image which forms part of the film.[54] It is not clear whether this overrides the requirement for a substantial part of the performance to be taken, but presumably it does. Secondly, copying includes making copies which are transient or are incidental to some other use of the recording.[55] This means that loading part of a recording of a performance into the memory of computer may infringe. The Rental and Lending Rights Directive does not assist on this question, for it simply refers to "reproduction".   **4.22**

Directly or indirectly

What is expressly provided is that it is immaterial whether the copy is made directly or indirectly.[56] This is by way of belt-and-braces. Prior to the amendments made by the Copyright and Related Rights Regulations 1996, section 182(1)(a) made it an infringement to make a recording of a performance without the performer's consent otherwise than for private and domestic use. The definition of 'recording' quoted in paragraph 4.11 above meant that this included a recording made directly or indirectly from another recording of the performance. Thus a person who copied, say, a compact disc made a recording directly from the recording of the performance(s) embodied in the disc and indirectly from the original recording of the performance(s) from which the disc was made. If this was done without consent and for commercial purposes it was an infringement. Similarly, the use of out-takes and clips from previous films to make a new film such as was made by the defendants in the *Peter Sellers*[57] case would be an infringement. To avoid   **4.23**

---

[51] See note 10 above.
[52] Copyright, Designs and Patents Act 1988, s. 182A(3). *cf.* E.C. Rental and Lending Rights Directive, note 4, above, Art. 7(1).
[53] The index of defined expressions contained in s. 179 of Part I has an entry for "copy" which refers to s. 17.
[54] Copyright, Designs and Patents Act 1988, s. 17(4).
[55] *ibid.*, s. 17(6).
[56] *ibid.*, s. 182A(3).
[57] [1988] Q.B. 40.

infringement, consent would be needed to the making of the recording or recordings in question; consent to the making of the original recording would not be enough.

4.24   In *Mad Hat Music Ltd v. Pulse 8 Records Ltd,*[58] however, Mervyn Davies J. doubted this conclusion and held that it was arguable that where the performer consented to the making of the original recording no further consent was needed to the making of records from that recording. The learned judge's reasoning was that section 182(1) referred to the making of a recording and not of a record.[59] With respect, it is submitted that this was clearly wrong in view of paragraph (c) of the definition of "recording".[60] In *Bassey v. Icon Entertainment plc*[61] Sir John Vinelott declined to follow *Mad Hat Music* and held that consent was needed for the making of records from the recording. It is submitted that section 182A now makes it clear that this is the correct position.

5. Issuing copies of a recording to the public

4.25   Section 182B of the 1988 Act makes it an infringement without the consent of the performer to issue to the public copies of a recording of the whole or any substantial part of a performance in which performers' rights subsist. The right to authorise or prohibit such issue to the public is referred to as the "distribution right".[62]

Issue to the public

4.26   "Issue to the public" is defined as:

(a) the act of putting into circulation in the EEA copies not previously put into circulation in the EEA by or with the consent of the performer, or

(b) the act of putting into circulation outside the EEA copies not previously put into circulation in the EEA or elsewhere.[63]

It does not include:

(a) any subsequent distribution, sale, hiring or loan of copies previously put into circulation (but see section 182C: consent required for rental or lending), or

(b) any subsequent importation of such copies into the United Kingdom or another EEA state;

except so far as paragraph (a) of subsection (2) applies to putting into circulation in the EEA copies previously put into circulation outside the EEA.[64]

This parallels the corresponding provision contained in Part I of the Act,

---

[58] [1993] EMLR 172.

[59] *ibid.* at 179.

[60] See also the definition of "sound recording" in s. 5 of the 1988 Act discussed in Chap. 2, para. 2.48.

[61] [1995] EMLR 596, 604–606.

[62] Copyright, Designs and Patents Act 1988, s. 182B(5). *cf.* E.C. Rental and Lending Rights Directive, note 4 above, Art. 9(1).

[63] *ibid.,* s. 182B(2).

[64] *ibid.,* s. 182B(3).

section 18 (as amended), which was originally introduced to overrule the decision of the House of Lords in *Infabrics Ltd v. Jaytex Ltd*[65] that section 5 of the Copyright Act 1956 was restricted to first publication of a work. It is immaterial whether or not the copies in question are illicit recordings.

For there to be an issue to the public, specific copies which have not **4.27** previously been in circulation in the relevant area must be put into circulation. Once a particular copy has been put into circulation in the EEA then no subsequent importation, distribution or sale of that copy can be an infringement except where the copy is rented or lent to the public in the United Kingdom. Distribution of a copy imported from outside the EEA can be an infringement, however, even if the copies were in circulation in the state of origin with the consent of the performer.[66]

Putting copies into circulation—It is not entirely clear what does and what **4.28** does not constitute putting copies into circulation. One possible reading of the section is that any act of distribution, sale, hiring or lending will put the copies in circulation. Another possible reading is that an act of distribution, sale, hiring or lending only puts the copies into circulation if it amounts to distribution etc. *to the public.* Suppose, for example, that the copies are manufactured by A in France exclusively for sale to B with the consent of the performer and that B imports them into the United Kingdom and sells them to the general public there without the consent of the performer. Does the sale of the copies by A to B put them into circulation? If it puts them into circulation, B does not infringe under section 182B. If it does not put them into circulation, B does infringe. This depends on whether the expression "putting into circulation" carries with it the notion of availability to the general public or at least more than one exclusive customer. There is no clear answer to this question. Since the provision is new, reference to earlier legislation in which similar wording appeared[67] is unhelpful. It is submitted, however, that distribution etc. to one exclusive customer is not sufficient to put copies into circulation since it is not an issue "to the public".

Circulation in the EEA by or with the consent of the performer—The **4.29** reference to "copies not previously put into circulation in the EEA by or with the consent of the performer" is a statutory extension to the European Economic Area[68] of the "free circulation" rule of European Community law.[69] This states that the proprietor of an industrial or commercial property right protected by the law of a Member State cannot rely on that law to prevent the importation of a product which has lawfully been marketed in

---

[65] [1982] A.C. 1.
[66] This follows from the fact that Art. (3) of the E.C. Rental and Lending Rights Directive, note 4, above, only permits intra-Community free circulation and not international free circulation. See Reinbothe and von Lewinksi, *The E.C. Directive on Rental and Lending Rights and on Piracy* (Sweet & Maxwell, 1993), p. 105.
[67] In particular, the expression "the issue of copies of the work to the public" was used to define "publication" in s. 1(3) of the Copyright Act 1911, but this was in the context of a qualification requirement; and there was no reference to "putting into circulation".
[68] Pursuant to the European Economic Area Act 1993 giving effect to the Agreement on the European Economic Area, Art. 1(2)(a) and Protocol 28, Art. 2(1).
[69] See generally Bellamy and Child, *Common Market Law of Competition* (4th ed., Sweet & Maxwell, 1993), paras. 8–009 to 8–063.

another Member State by the proprietor himself or with his consent.[70] The rule has been elaborated by the European Court of Justice in a series of cases concerning the interpretation of Articles 30, 34 and 36 of the Treaty of Rome. Articles 30 and 34 state the basic rule, namely that quantitative restrictions on imports and exports, and all measures having equivalent effect (which includes the enforcement of industrial property rights), are prohibited as between Member States. Article 36 provides a number of exceptions to this, including restrictions justified on grounds of protection of industrial and commercial property. Whether a particular restriction is justified depends on the "specific subject-matter" of the right. Thus in the case of patents, "the substance of a patent right lies essentially in according the inventor an exclusive right of first placing the product on the market".[71] In cases where copyright is for practical purposes a monopoly right,[72] the same is true of copyright.[73]

4.30   The rule is widely but inaccurately referred to as the "exhaustion of rights" doctrine. Inaccurately, since the rule applies even if there were no right to be exhausted in the Member State of first marketing. Thus Merck could not enforce its Dutch patent against parallel imports of a drug marketed by it in Italy, where it could not obtain a patent (under a law subsequently ruled unconstitutional by the Italian Supreme Court).[74] Nevertheless, the phrase "exhaustion of rights" is a useful reminder that a proprietor of industrial property rights is not to be taken to have consented to that which he cannot lawfully prevent. Thus a performer is not prohibited from exercising his performers' rights to prevent importation into the United Kingdom of illicit recordings merely by reason of his performers' rights in another Member State having expired[75] (as could well happen until the implementation of the Term Directive, given that the 50-year term of protection originally provided under the 1988 Act was considerably in excess of the 20-year minimum stipulated by the Rome Convention[76]). Nor would a performer be prevented from exercising his rental right in a Member State due to having marketed recordings in a Member State where no such right existed.[77] Similarly,

---

[70] Case 119/75, *Terrapin (Overseas) Ltd v. Terranova Industrie CA Kapferer & Co.* [1976] E.C.R. 1039; [1976] 2 C.M.L.R. 482.
[71] Case 187/80, *Merck & Co. Inc. v. Stephar BV* [1981] E.C.R. 2063; [1981] 3 C.M.L.R. 463.
[72] See Chap. 1, para. 1.20.
[73] Case 78/70. *Deutsche Grammophon GmbH v. Metro-SB-Grossmarkte* [1971] E.C.R. 487; [1971] C.M.L.R. 631, and Case 55/80, *Musik Vertrieb Membran v. GEMA* [1981] E.C.R. 147. Contrast Case 262/81, *Coditel SA v. Ciné-Vog Films SA* [1982] E.C.R. 3381; [1983] 1 C.M.L.R. 49, and Case 402/85, *Bassett v. SACEM* [1987] E.C.R. 1747. See also the Opinion of Darmon A.G. in Case 341/87, *EMI Electrola GmbH v. Patricia Im- und Export Verwaltungsgesellschaft GmbH* [1989] E.C.R. 79; [1989] 2 C.M.L.R. 413.
[74] *Merck v. Stephar*, note 71, above. In contrast Parke Davis was able to enforce its rights against products marketed by a third party in Italy: Case 24/67, *Parke Davis & Co. v. Probel* [1968] E.C.R. 55; [1968] C.M.L.R. 47. In Cases C-267/95 and C-268/95 *Merck & Co. Inc. v. Primecrown Ltd* [1997] F.S.R. 237 the ECJ held that *Merck v. Stephar* was still good law.
[75] *EMI Electrola GmbH v. Patricia Im-und Export Verwaltungsgesellschaft GmbH*, note 73, above. In that case the ECJ held that EMI was not prevented from exercising its German copyright in sound recordings against parallel imports from Denmark, where the sound recording copyright had already expired.
[76] See Chap. 2, paras. 2.55–2.67.
[77] Case 158/86, *Warner Bros Inc. v. Christiansen* [1988] E.C.R. 2605; [1990] 3 C.M.L.R 268.

recordings marketed under a compulsory licence are not in free circulation.[78] It has been suggested in a copyright case that products made under licence outside the EEC and imported into a Member State where there is no right corresponding to the licensed right should thereafter be treated as in free circulation[79]; but it is submitted that this is wrong.[80] Finally it should be noted the rule does not apply to the provision of services as opposed to the circulation of goods.[81]

Putting copies into circulation outside the EEA —It is not entirely clear what the effect is of the extension of issuing to the public to putting copies into circulation outside the EEA, which necessarily means outside the United Kingdom. At first sight this may be thought to make the doing of an act outside the United Kingdom an infringement of U.K. performers' rights. This is contrary to the principle that copyright and related rights are territorial in nature, however.[82] It is therefore submitted that this provision should be interpreted as applying to acts done in the United Kingdom which have the effect of putting copies into circulation outside the EEA. An example might be the exportation of copies from the United Kingdom to members of the public in the United States.

4.31

Copies

"Copies" for this purposes includes the original (first-generation) recording of the live performance.[83] By extension, it would seem that an infringement may also be committed by the issuing of a single second-generation recording.[84]

4.32

6. Renting or lending copies of a recording to the public

Section 182C of the 1988 Act makes it an infringement without the consent of the performer to rent or lend to the public copies of a recording of the whole or any substantial part of a performance in which performers' rights subsist. The rights to authorise or prohibit such rental and lending to the public are referred to as the "rental right" and "lending right".[85]

4.33

---

[78] Case 19/84, *Pharmon BV v. Hoechst AG* [1985] E.C.R. 2281; [1985] 3 C.M.L.R. 775 (a patent case).
[79] *The Who Group Ltd v. Stage One (Records) Ltd* [1980] F.S.R. 268, 276.
[80] *cf.* Case 270/80, *Polydor Ltd v. Harlequin Record Shops* [1982] E.C.R. 329; [1982] 1 C.M.L.R. 677.
[81] *Coditel v. Ciné-Vog Films* [1980] E.C.R. 881; Case 262/81, *Coditel v. Ciné-Vog Films* [1982] E.C.R. 3381; [1983] 1 C.M.L.R. 49; *Warner Bros Inc v. Christiansen*, note 77, above.
[82] *ABKCO Music & Records Inc. v. Music Collection International Ltd* [1995] EMLR 449. See also paras. 4.79–4.83, below.
[83] Copyright, Designs and Patents Act 1988, s. 182B(4).
[84] Since the plural includes the singular unless a contrary intention appears: Interpretation Act 1978, s. 6(c). Although a contrary intention might have appeared from the use of the word "copies", it is submitted that it does not where it is clear that in at least one case a single recording suffices.
[85] Copyright, Designs and Patents Act 1988, s. 182C(7).

Rental

4.34 "Rental" is defined as:

> making a copy of a recording available for use, on terms that it will or may be returned, for direct or indirect economic or commercial advantage.[86]

It does not include:

> (a) making available for the purpose of public performance, playing or showing in public, broadcasting or inclusion in a cable programme service;
> (b) making available for the purpose of exhibition in public; or
> (c) making available for on-the-spot reference use. [87]

This is a very broad definition. In particular, it does not require money to change hands if there is some other direct or indirect economic or commercial advantage. Nor does it require actual economic or commercial advantage if the purpose is to obtain such an advantage. Nevertheless, it appears that the definition is narrower than the corresponding definition in the E.C. Rental and Lending Rights Directive[88] in at least one respect, namely the inclusion of the words "on terms that it will or may be returned" instead of the words "for a limited period of time" which appear in the Directive.[89] The significance of this is that, whereas it is just arguable that the definition of "rental" in the Directive extends to activities such as video-on-demand[90] services, these are clearly excluded by the above definition. On the other hand, the retention of these words from the original 1988 Act may also extend beyond the Directive to catch sales of videos in circumstances where the vendor operates a policy that persons dissatisfied with the film can return it within a specified period. The exclusions in paragraphs (a), (b) and (c) do not derive from the main text of the Directive but from recital (13).[91]

Lending

4.35 "Lending" is defined as:

> making a copy of a recording available for use, on terms that it will or may be returned, otherwise than for direct or indirect economic or commercial advantage, through an establishment that is accessible to the public.[92]

---

[86] *ibid.*, s. 182C(2)(a).

[87] *ibid.*, s. 182C(3).

[88] Note 4 above, Art. 1(2). See also recital (13).

[89] Note 4, above, Art. 1(2).

[90] *i.e.* services in which the viewer selects a film from a library and pays to view it, whereupon the film is electronically transmitted to the household, *e.g.* via the Internet. This is to be distinguished from pay-per-view which is a form of cable diffusion service and thus outside the definition of rental even in the Directive. See Reinbothe and von Lewinski, note 66, above, pp. 41–42.

[91] It appears that the reason why these matters are dealt with in the recital and not in the body of the Directives is that the exact scope of the exclusion could not be agreed, and so it was fudged by leaving it as a recital which is open-ended: Reinbothe and von Lewinski, note 66 above, at pp. 36–38. In consequence it is possible that the ECJ will say that other activities are also excluded from "rental" or "lending".

[92] Copyright, Designs and Patents Act 1988, s. 182C(2)(b).

It does not include:

(a) making available for the purpose of public performance, playing or showing in public, broadcasting or inclusion in a cable programme service;

(b) making available for the purpose of exhibition in public; or

(c) making available for on-the-spot reference use.[93]

Nor does it include making available between establishments that are accessible to the public.[94] Again this is a very broad definition. In essence, though, it encompasses lending by libraries and similar institutions. For this purpose there is no direct or indirect economic or commercial advantage if the amount of any payment does not go beyond what is necessary to cover the operating costs of the establishment.[95] This means that an activity does not cease to be lending because a fee is charged, provided that lender is not engaged in making a profit. Again, it may be noted that the words "on terms that it will or may be returned" do not appear in the corresponding definition in the Directive.[96]

On-the-spot reference use

While it is fairly clear what is meant by "on-the-spot reference use" in the case of literary, dramatic, musical and artistic works, it is not quite so clear what is meant by it in the case of recordings of performances. Suppose, for example, that a video library has on its premises individual booths for viewing films. Watching a film in these circumstances is plainly "on-the-spot", but is it "reference"? It might be argued that "reference" does not extend to complete viewing. It seems probable, however, that this exception will be broadly interpreted provided that the service is for research or study purposes and not commercial ones.

4.36

Copies

Again, "copies" is defined to include the original recording of the live performance.[97]

4.37

Presumed transfer of rental right in copies of films

Unless otherwise provided, agreements between performers and film producers are presumed to include a transfer of the performers' rental right in copies of the film with the substitution of a right to equitable remuneration. This subject is discussed in Chapter 3.[98]

4.38

---

[93] *ibid.*, s. 182C(3).
[94] *ibid.*, s. 182C(4). *cf.* E.C. Rental and Lending Rights Directive, note 4, above, recital (13).
[95] *ibid.*, s. 182C(5). *cf.* E.C. Rental and Lending Rights Directive, note 4 above, recital (14).
[96] Note 4, above, Art. 1(3).
[97] Copyright, Designs and Patents Act 1988, s. 182C(6).
[98] paras. 3.09–3.10.

Transitional provision in relation to rental and lending rights[99]

4.39 Section 182C does not apply to any copy of a recording acquired by a person before commencement of the Copyright and Related Rights Regulations 1996 (December 1, 1996) for the purpose of renting it or lending it to the public.[1]

7. Showing or playing a recording in public

4.40 Section 183(a) makes it an infringement without the performer's consent to show or play in public the whole or any substantial part of a performance in which performers' rights subsist by means of a recording or a copy of a recording which was, and which the exhibitor knows or has reason to believe was, made without the performer's consent.

In public

4.41 "In public" is not defined in either Part I or Part II of the 1988 Act. Although it is not expressly provided that the expression should have the same meaning in Part II as in Part I, this must be the intention. The meaning of "in public" was considered in a number of cases under earlier Copyright Acts.[2] It would appear that these authorities are still good law in relation to Part I,[3] and therefore applicable to Part II.[4] They indicate that the decisive factor is the *nature* of the audience, rather than its size or whether it paid for the pleasure or the nature of the venue. A public performance or exhibition is one for which the audience is not a "domestic or quasi-domestic one". It seems that a "domestic or quasi-domestic" audience is one that lives under one roof.[5] Thus a performance of a play by members of the Women's Institute of one village to an audience of members of the Institute of another village was held to have been "in public" even though non-members had not been admitted and no charge had been made.[6]

Knowledge or reason to believe

4.42 This topic is dealt with separately.[7]

Without consent[8]

4.43 It should be noted that in all forms of secondary infringement under Part II, it is a requirement that the performer's consent be absent at two stages. First, the performer must not have consented to the making of the recording in question. Secondly, the performer must not have consented to the particular dealing in question. Thus if the performer consented to the making of the recording there can be no secondary infringement. It would appear that this is

---

[99] See also Chap. 3, paras. 3.57–3.58.
[1] Copyright and Related Rights Regulations 1996, Reg. 34(2).
[2] See Laddie, Prescott & Vitoria, *The Modern Law of Copyright and Designs*, (2nd ed., Butterworths, 1995), paras. 2.126, 4.38 and 5.70.
[3] Copyright, Designs and Patents Act 1988, s. 172(2), (3).
[4] See also para. 4.14, above.
[5] *Jennings v. Stephens* [1936] 1 Ch. 469 explaining *Duck v. Bates* (1884) 13 Q.B.D. 843.
[6] *Jennings v. Stephens, ibid.*
[7] See paras. 4.70–4.78, below.
[8] See also Chap. 5, paras. 5.48–5.59.

the case even if the performer gave his consent to the making of the recording only on condition that the recording be used for a specific, limited purpose but the recording is subsequently used for a different purpose.

8. Broadcasting or including a recording in a cable programme service

Section 183(b) makes it an infringement without the performer's consent to **4.44** broadcast or include in a cable programme service the whole or any substantial part of a performance in which performers' rights subsist by means of a recording or a copy of a recording which was, and which the broadcaster knows or has reason to believe was, made without the performer's consent.

9. Importing illicit recordings into the United Kingdom

Section 184(1)(a) makes it an infringement without the performer's consent **4.45** to import into the United Kingdom otherwise than for the importer's private and domestic use a recording or a copy of a recording in which performers' rights subsist which is, and which the importer knows or has reason to believe is, an illicit recording.

Import

Under the Performers' Protection Acts 1958–1972 importation *per se* was **4.46** not a prohibited dealing in contraband recordings, although dealing in the United Kingdom in records made abroad might be prohibited.[9] Under Part II of the new Act, the position has been brought into line with the position in respect of copyright under Part I.[10] It seems that "import" means simply to bring into the country.[11] Importation occurs when the goods are physically received in the United Kingdom.[12] It is not clear whether goods are imported if they are merely brought into the territorial waters of the United Kingdom. If the goods are brought into the territorial waters for landing at a U.K. port then it is arguable that they have been imported,[13] but it would be surprising if goods in transit from say Ireland to France were held to have been imported into the United Kingdom merely because the ship passed through U.K. waters. Nor is it clear whether goods are imported if they are brought into a U.K. port in transit for somewhere else.[14]

Illicit recording

An "illicit recording" is a recording of the whole or any substantial part of a **4.47** performance made otherwise than for private purposes without the performer's consent.[15] It is immaterial where the recording was made.[16] On the face of it, the omission of the word "qualifying" means that a recording

---

[9] Interested readers are referred to the first edition, Chap. 2, paras. 2,42 and 2.76–2.79.
[10] Copyright, Designs and Patents Act 1988, s. 22.
[11] *Infabrics Ltd v. Jaytex Ltd* [1982] A.C. 1. *cf. R. v. Smith (Donald)* [1973] Q.B. 924.
[12] *LA Gear Inc. v. Hi-Tec Sports Ltd* [1992] F.S.R. 121, 130.
[13] Although *R. v. Bull* (1974) 131 C.L.R. 203 would suggest the opposite.
[14] Contrast *Mattel Inc. v. Tonka Corp.* (1992) 23 I.P.R. 91 with *Wilson v. Chambers & Co. Pty Ltd* (1926) 38 C.L.R. 131 and *R. v. Bull*, note 13, above.
[15] Copyright, Designs and Patents Act 1988, s. 197(2).
[16] *ibid.*, s. 197(6).

can be an illicit recording even if no performer's rights subsist in the performance. It is difficult to believe that this is intended, however.

4.48   The private purposes are presumably those of the person making the recording. It is not clear whether the omission of the words "and domestic" in the phrase "for private purposes" (by comparison with sections 182(2) and 182A(1)[17]) is intended to have any effect, or if so what effect. A possible interpretation is that in this context a recording made without consent is only not illicit if made for the maker's *personal* private use, but is illicit if made for his domestic use, that is that of his household. It is difficult to see why this distinction should be drawn here and not elsewhere in the Act, however.

4.49   A recording may also become illicit under the provisions of Schedule 2 to the Act,[18] as to which see Chapter 5.[19]

Parallel imports[20]

4.50   What if the performer consented to the making of the recording in question but he did so for the purposes of sale in another country and not for the purposes of sale in the United Kingdom? As noted above,[21] the Act does not appear to distinguish for this purpose between general and limited consent. It therefore appears that in such a case the recording is not an "illicit recording". Accordingly it may be imported without committing a secondary infringement. If the recording was not in circulation in the EEA by or with the consent of the performer, however, any subsequent issue of it to the public will be an infringement.[22]

10. Dealing in illicit recordings

4.51   Section 184(1)(b) makes it an infringement without the consent of the performer in the course of a business to possess, sell or let for hire, offer or expose for sale or hire, or distribute a recording or a copy of a recording in which performers' rights subsist which is, and which the dealer knows or has reason to believe is, an illicit recording.

In the course of a business

4.52   There are two possible interpretations of sub-subsection (b). The first is that it is only an infringement to possess an illicit recording without consent if the possession is in the course of a business, but that it is an infringement to sell etc. an illicit recording without consent even if this is not done in the course of a business. The second is that all the acts listed must be done in the course of a business in order to amount to infringement.

4.53   Comparison with section 23 in Part I of the Act suggests that the latter construction is the correct one, for in that case the wording is unambiguous:

---

[17] See paras. 4.13–4.14, above.
[18] Copyright, Designs and Patents Act 1988, s. 197(5) referring to paras. 4(3), 6(2), 12(2) and 16(3) of Schedule 2.
[19] paras. 5.11, 5.15, 5.27, 5.41.
[20] For a general treatment of this subject see Rothnie, *Parallel Imports* (Sweet & Maxwell, 1993).
[21] See para. 4.43, above.
[22] See para 4.27, above.

The copyright in a work is infringed by a person who, without the licence of the copyright owner:

(a) possesses in the course of a business

(b) sells or lets for hire, or offers or exposes for sale or hire,

(c) in the course of a business exhibits in public or distributes, or

(d) distributes otherwise than in the course of a business to such an extent as to affect prejudicially the owner of the copyright,

an article which is, and which he knows or has reason to believe is, an infringing copy of the work.

Comparison with the definition of the corresponding offence[23] is inconclu- **4.54** sive. The offence is defined so as to make it absolutely clear that the acts of selling, etc., must be committed in the course of a business. One may conclude from this that the same must be true of the tort; or one may conclude that the legislature has deliberately drawn the offence more narrowly.

The phrase "in the course of a business" in itself gives rise to two questions **4.55** of construction. The first is what is meant by "business". This "includes a trade or profession",[24] but is otherwise undefined. The word is not a term of art, and its meaning depends on its context[25]; thus decisions on its meaning in other contexts are unhelpful. It would seem that two main elements must be present, namely that transactions are carried out for money or money's worth (though not necessarily for profit) and with a degree of regularity. Thus it is submitted that a person who engages in home taping, even if regularly, will not be held to be conducting a business in this activity, while a person who makes a one-off sale for profit will not either.

The second is what is meant by "in the course of". In the leading case on **4.56** this point under section 1 of the Trade Descriptions Act 1968, *Davies v. Summer*,[26] the House of Lords held that the sale by a self-employed courier of his car was not in the course of a trade or business. Although the courier was in business, he was not in the business of selling cars. To be in the course of business there had to be transactions which had some degree of regularity so that they formed part of the normal practice of the business.[27] It is submitted that Part II should be construed in the same way.

Possession

Making mere possession of recordings tortious is new to both Part I and Part **4.57** II of the Copyright, Designs and Patents Act 1988. On the face of the Act, persons who had recordings made otherwise than for private purposes without consent in their possession and who had the requisite knowledge or reason for belief prior to commencement suddenly, after midnight on the day of commencement, became secondary infringers. This is because the Act is

---

[23] Copyright, Designs and Patents Act 1988, s. 198(1)(d). See Chap. 7, para. 7.09.

[24] *ibid.*, s. 178.

[25] *Per* Lord Diplock in *Town Investments Ltd v. Department of the Environment* [1978] A.C. 359, 383.

[26] [1984] 1 W.L.R. 1301.

[27] Although Lord Keith was careful to say that this did not mean that a one-off sale could not be a trade! See also *R&B Customs Brokers Ltd v. UDT Ltd* [1988] 1 W.L.R. 321.

partially retrospective, yet has only the crudest transitional provision.[28] It is difficult to imagine, however, that the courts will interpret the Act strictly in this respect. Presumably some positive act of reducing a recording to possession after commencement will be required.[29] Note that "possession" may be wider than actual physical possession: control over goods in the custody of a servant, agent or bailee may be enough.[30] On the other hand, physical custody without any control may not constitute "possession".[31]

Sale or return

4.58   It was suggested by Neville J. in *E.W. Savory Ltd v. The World of Golf Ltd*[32] that a person who supplied goods to another on sale or return and subsequently received notice that the goods infringed a third party's copyright would be liable for secondary infringement if he failed to demand the return of the goods. This was later doubted by Clauson J.,[33] who relied on *Moss v. Sweet*[34] as authority for the proposition that the buyer of goods on sale or return had an option to return the goods within the time specified or within a reasonable time, but that the seller could not demand their return, his only remedy for failure to return being an action for the price. That being the case, the seller had no control over the buyer's acts and should not be liable.

4.59   Both courts seem to have overlooked the fact that the common law had been substantially codified by the Sale of Goods Act 1893.[35] What is now the fourth rule set out in section 18 of the Sale of Goods Act 1979 provides that, unless a different intention appears:

> when goods are delivered to the buyer on approval or on sale or return or other similar terms the property in the goods passes to the buyer: (a) when he signifies his approval or acceptance to the seller or does any other act adopting the transaction; (b) if he does not signify his approval or acceptance to the seller but retains the goods without giving notice of rejection, then, if a time has been fixed for return of the goods, on the expiration of that time, and, if no time has been fixed, on the expiration of a reasonable time.

Thus the buyer may prevent the passing of property by giving notice of rejection without returning the goods as was required under *Moss v. Sweet*. Nevertheless it is submitted that the Act makes it clear that Clauson J.'s view is the correct one.

---

[28] See para. 4.01, above.

[29] *cf.* the corresponding offence: see Chap. 7, paras. 7.07–7.08.

[30] See *Towers & Co. Ltd v. Gray* [1961] 2 Q.B. 351 and *Morton-Norwich Products Inc. v. Intercen Ltd* [1978] R.P.C. 501.

[31] See *Bellerby v. Carle* [1983] 2 A.C. 101. The position is otherwise if the person has control but he is not aware of the true nature of the article: *Warner v. Metropolitan Police Commissioner* [1969] 2 A.C. 256.

[32] [1914] 2 Ch. 566.

[33] In *Schofield & Sims Ltd v. Robert Gibson & Sons Ltd* [1928–1935] M.C.C. 64.

[34] (1851) 16 Q.B. 493.

[35] See *Benjamin's Sale of Goods*, (4th ed., Sweet & Maxwell, 1992), paras. 5–039 *et seq.*

Exposure for sale

"Exposure for sale" covers cases where there is no offer for sale but merely an   **4.60**
invitation to treat, such as displaying goods in a shop window. It is
immaterial that the goods cannot be properly inspected due to their
packaging.[36] It appears that the goods displayed must be available for sale
there and then,[37] so that showing a sample to a potential customer and asking
for orders to be delivered later is apparently not an exposure for sale.[38]

Distribution for the purposes of trade

It is possible for a trader to handle goods without distributing them. For   **4.61**
example, a bookbinder who bound infringing copies of trade lists did not
distribute them because his only intention was to return them to the printer
after binding.[39] It is not clear, however, whether a carrier or warehouseman
who does no more than carry or store goods for a consignor or consignee
could be said to be distributing the goods so as to be liable if given the
requisite knowledge. It is submitted that a person who merely holds goods to
someone else's order in this way should not be regarded as a distributor[40]
(though he may possess them in the course of a business).

Dealing outside the United Kingdom

This is dealt with elsewhere.[41]   **4.62**

INFRINGEMENT OF RECORDING RIGHTS

Recording rights which subsist[42] in a performance are infringed by the doing   **4.63**
of any of the following acts without the consent of the owner of the recording
rights or (in category (1), in any event, and in categories (2) to (5), if
performer's rights subsist in the performance) the performer:

(1)   making a recording of the whole or any substantial part of the
performance otherwise than for the maker's private and domestic
use[43];

(2)   showing or playing in public the whole or any substantial part of the
performance by means of a recording which was, and the exhibitor
knows or has reason to believe was, made without the consent of

---

[36] *Wheat v. Brown* [1892] 1 Q.B. 418.
[37] See, for example, *Newman v. Lipman* [1951] 1 K.B. 333.
[38] *Britain v. Kennedy* (1903) 19 T.L.R. 122.
[39] *J. Whitaker & Sons Ltd v. Publishers Circular Ltd* [1946–1949] M.C.C. 10.
[40] *cf. Smith Kline & French Laboratories Ltd v. R.D. Harbottle (Mercantile) Ltd* [1979] F.S.R. 555.
[41] See paras. 4.79–4.90, below.
[42] Again, the draftsman avoids use of the word "subsist", referring instead to "the rights of a person having recording rights in relation to a performance". For the sake of clarity, reference is made to performances in which recording rights subsist in this chapter. *cf.* para. 4.03, above.
[43] Copyright, Designs and Patents Act 1988, s. 186(1). *cf.* paras. 4.10–4.14.

either the performer or the owner of the recording rights at the time that the recording was made[44];

(3) broadcasting or including in a cable programme service the whole or any substantial part of the performance by means of a recording which was, and the broadcaster knows or has reason to believe was, made without the consent of either the performer or the owner of the recording rights at the time that the recording was made[45];

(4) importing into the United Kingdom otherwise than for the importer's private and domestic use a recording of the performance which is, and the importer knows or has reason to believe is, an "illicit recording"[46];

(5) in the course of business, possessing, selling, letting for hire, offering or exposing for sale or hire, or distributing a recording of the performance which is, and the dealer knows or has reason to believe is, an "illicit recording".[47]

4.64 As can be seen, these are parallel to category (1), (3) and (4) and (7) to (10) infringements of performers' rights. Again, they divide into primary infringements (category (1)) and secondary infringements (categories (2) to (5)). The comments made in relation to infringements of performers' rights are equally applicable here,[48] except that it should be noted that the definition of "illicit recording" is different for the purposes of infringement of recording rights[49] to that for the purposes of infringement of performers' rights.[50] The principal difference is that, whereas the latter refers to a recording made "without his consent", the former refers to one made "without his consent or that of the performer". This reflects the drafting of the infringement-defining sections.

Without his consent or that of the performer

4.65 Section 186(1) reads in full as follows:

> A person infringes the rights of a person having recording rights in relation to a performance who, without his consent or that of the performer, makes a recording of the whole or any substantial part of the performance, otherwise than for his private and domestic use.

This presents two problems of construction. The first is the usual problem of multiple antecedents.[51] The second is less straightforward. This is that there are two possible interpretations of "without his consent or that of the

---

[44] *ibid.*, s. 187(1)(a). *cf.* paras. 4.40–43.
[45] *ibid.*, s. 187(1)(b). *cf.* para. 4.44.
[46] *ibid.*, s. 188(1)(a). *cf.* paras. 4.45–4.50.
[47] *ibid.*, s. 188(1)(b). *cf.* paras. 4.51–4.62.
[48] See the paras. noted below each category.
[49] Copyright, Designs and Patents Act 1988, s. 197(3).
[50] *ibid.*, s. 197(2).
[51] The word "his" in the phrase "without his consent" has two possible antecedents, "a person" and "a person having recording rights"; while in the phrase "his private and domestic use" it has three—"a person", "a person having recording rights" and "the performer". It is reasonably clear that in the former case the owner of the recording rights is meant and in the latter case the infringer. *cf.* note 10 to para. 4.02, above.

performer". First, that the consent of *both* the performer and the owner of the recording rights is required if infringement is to be avoided ("without his consent or without that of the performer"). Secondly, that the consent of *either* will suffice ("without either his consent or that of the performer"). Either reading is possible, and both lead to odd results. The former reading would have the odd result that the maker of the recording would have to obtain consent from the performer in addition to any consent from the owner of the recording rights even if performers' rights did *not* subsist in the performance. The latter reading would have the odd result of making the performer an alternative source of consent to the owner of the recording rights—even if the owner has specifically refused consent.[52]

Support for both readings can be found in the definition of the other **4.66** categories of infringement. Section 187(1) reads as follows:

A person infringes the rights of a person having recording rights in relation to a performance who, without his consent or, in the case of a qualifying performance, that of the performer, [(a) or (b)] by means of a recording which was, and which that person knows or has reason to believe was, made without the appropriate consent.

The "appropriate consent" is:

the consent of:
(a) the performer, or
(b) the person who at the time the consent was given had recording rights in relation to the performance (or, if there was more than one such person, of all of them).[53]

(It would seem that "at the time the consent was given" means "at the time the consent was required"). It is reasonably clear that the recording "by means of" which this category of secondary infringement is committed must be one the making of which constituted a primary infringement contrary to section 186(1). Thus paragraph (a) of the definition of "appropriate consent" is not restricted to where the performance is a qualifying performance. Now the use of the singular "consent" rather than the plural "consents" in "appropriate consent" suggests that the consent of one of the two alternatives rather than both is what is required. If this construction of section 187(1) is correct, the same should apply to section 186(1).

On the other hand, both section 187(1) and section 188(1) substitute **4.67** "without his consent or, in the case of a qualifying performance, that of the performer" for "without his consent or that of the performer" in section 186(1). It would seem to make more sense only to *require* consent of the

---

[52] It is true that the owner of the recording rights will in all probability have recourse against the performer under the contract between them if the performer improperly gives consent; but this may be of small comfort to the owner of the recording rights if the performer has improperly consented to a valuable transaction yet is himself a man of straw. The owner may have a cause of action against the "infringer" for inducing breach of contract, but only it can be shown that the "infringer" had notice of the relevant term of the contract.
[53] Copyright, Designs and Patents Act 1988, s. 187(2).

performer to secondary acts in addition to consent of the owner of the recording rights if the performance is one in which performers' rights subsist than only to *permit* the performer to be an alternative source of consent in those circumstances. To put it another way, if the performance is non-qualifying, it would seem to make more sense, nevertheless, to require the performer's consent to avoid primary infringement of recording rights but not to require it to avoid secondary infringement than it would to permit the performer to consent to primary acts in the alternative to the owner of the recording rights but to permit him to consent to secondary acts. Interpretation is not assisted by the fact that it is hard to see what object the draughtsman had in mind when drafting these sections. Why was it thought that the performer should be either required or permitted to give consent to interference with another's rights?

4.68   A final possible source of assistance in dealing with the problem is the definition of "sufficient consent" in the offence-creating provision, section 198.[54] Although this is not the simplest of definitions either, it seems reasonably clear that a person obtains "sufficient consent" to avoid committing an offence if he obtains consent *either* from the performer *or* from the owner of the recording rights. Of course, this is not conclusive, for it would not be unreasonable that the legislature should require only one consent to prevent the commission of a criminal offence, yet provide for a civil tort to be committed if less than two were obtained. Nevertheless, the general parallels that can be drawn between the offences created by section 198 and the infringements defined by sections 182–184 and 186–188 suggests that one consent is sufficient.

4.69   On balance, therefore, it is submitted that the better view is to construe "or" in section 186(1) as disjunctive rather than conjunctive. It must be recognised, however, that it is not a foregone conclusion that the courts will adopt this construction.

KNOWLEDGE OR REASON FOR BELIEF

4.70   It is a requirement for all forms of secondary infringement of performers' rights and recording rights that the infringer knows or has reason to believe that the recording he is using or dealing in was made without consent. The same words are used in sections 22, 23, 24 and 26 of Part I of the 1988 Act to define forms of secondary infringement of copyright. This represents a change from both the Performers' Protection Acts 1958–1972 and the Copyright Act 1956, in each of which there was a requirement of knowledge. The courts approached those statutory provisions somewhat differently, however.

4.71   In the only case on the mental element of the offence under the Performers' Protection Acts, *Gaumont British Distributors Ltd v. Henry*,[55] it was held

---

[54] See Chap. 7, para. 7.03.
[55] [1939] 2 K.B. 711.

that the word "knowingly" imported a requirement that the defendant had actual knowledge of all the relevant matters.[56]

The cases under the Copyright Acts 1911 and 1956 proceeded somewhat differently. In *Van Dusen v. Kritz*[57] the facts were as follows. On 16 October the plaintiff wrote a letter before action complaining about posters and show-cards being displayed by the defendant. The defendant consulted his solicitors forthwith and took down the show-cards. On 18 October the defendant's solicitors received copies of the copyright works relied upon. On 23 October the defendant's solicitors wrote to the plaintiff's solicitors denying the allegation of infringement but offering to withdraw the posters and show-cards and to undertake not to issue any more. A writ was issued on the same day. The action was dismissed on the ground that there was no cause of action at the date of writ since the defendant did not have the requisite knowledge.

4.72

That decision (which was approved by the House of Lords in *Infabrics Ltd v. Jaytex Ltd*[58]) was subsequently interpreted[59] as establishing the following propositions:

4.73

(i) "knowledge" for the purposes of secondary copyright infringement might be actual or imputed;

(ii) if a dealer in articles did not have actual knowledge that the articles were infringing copies, he could be fixed with knowledge by giving him notice;

(iii) knowledge would not be imputed to the dealer unless:

(a) the notice contained sufficient particulars of the claim to copyright to enable it to be investigated; and

(b) the dealer was given a reasonable period in which to investigate the claim to copyright.

Thus if notice was duly given, and the dealer continued the acts complained of after the expiry of a reasonable period, he would be taken to have the requisite knowledge. It should be noted, however, in those circumstances he would not have actual knowledge of the facts which meant that the articles were infringing copies, still less that they were infringing copies (which could not be known for certain until the court gave judgment).

Has the position been altered by the 1988 Act? It is clear that the intention was to make it easier to prove secondary infringement.[60] In particular, the introduction of "reason to believe" was intended to catch someone who turns a blind eye to the facts; but it was not intended to catch someone who has

4.74

---

[56] Note, however, that the decision in the *Peter Sellers* case (discussed in para. 4.77, below) is not easy to reconcile with this authority.

[57] [1936] 2 K.B. 176.

[58] [1982] A.C. 1, 20.

[59] See *Hoover plc v. George Hulme (Stockport) Ltd* [1982] F.S.R. 565, *Sillitoe v. McGraw-Hill Book Co. (U.K.) Ltd* [1983] F.S.R. 545, *Monsoon v. India Imports of Rhode Island Ltd* [1993] F.S.R. 486.

[60] See the 1986 White Paper which preceded the Act, Cmnd. 9712 at Chap. 12 (copyright) and para. 14.3(b) (performers' rights).

"grounds to suspect" but fails to appreciate the significance of the facts.[61] Whether this has actually made a material difference to the law is debatable.

4.75   Section 172(2) of Part I provides that:

> A provision of this Part which corresponds to a provision of the previous law shall not be construed as departing from the previous law merely because of a change of expression.

The change from knowledge to knowledge or reason to believe would appear to be more than a mere change of expression, but, nevertheless, it is submitted that the law has not been changed. The natural interpretation of "knows or has reason to believe" is the same as the way "knows" was actually interpreted by the courts: it imports an objective test which means that the defendant cannot say that though he had all the relevant information, he did not *know*. In effect, Parliament has endorsed the existing approach of the courts under the Copyright Acts.

4.76   This view has received some confirmation from the decision of the Court of Appeal in *LA Gear Inc. v. Hi-Tech Sports plc.*[62] At first instance Morritt J. held that because the phrase "reason to believe" was new in the 1988 Act it should be construed in accordance with its natural meaning and not by reference to the authorities under the 1956 Act and that a person had "reason to believe" if he knew facts from which a reasonable man would arrive at the belief given time to evaluate the facts. The Court of Appeal endorsed this,. The effect of this is practically indistinguishable from the test applied under the 1956 Act. Moreover, in *Linpac Mouldings Ltd v. Eagleton Direct Export Ltd*[63] the Court of Appeal relied upon the earlier authorities as showing that, where the defendant had been given sufficient time to evaluate the facts but failed to give an undertaking, the plaintiff was entitled to a *quia timet* injunction. Although it has been suggested that the better view is that the test is a subjective one, *i.e.* it must be shown that the defendant did in fact believe that the copy was infringing,[64] this does not seem to accord with the wording of the statute: it does not say "which he knows or believes" but "which he knows or has reason to believe". In *LA Gear* it was stated that the test was an objective one.

4.77   So far as performers' rights are concerned, Parliament again appears to have been anticipated by the decisions of the courts in the *Peter Sellers* case.[65] What Hobhouse J. found in that case was not that the defendants had actual knowledge that Peter Sellers had not consented, but in effect that they had reason to believe that he had not. The defendants' case was that Sellers had given his consent in the contracts under which the earlier films were made. Having taken legal advice, they believed that this case was fully arguable and decided to take the risk of proceeding; but it followed that they had reason to believe that Sellers had not consented.

---

[61] H.L. Deb., Vol. 490, ser. 5, cols. 1213, 1218 (1987) (Lord Beaverbook).

[62] [1992] F.S.R. 121.

[63] [1994] F.S.R. 545.

[64] See Laddie, Prescott & Vitoria, note 2 to para. 4.41, above, paras. 10.5–10.6.

[65] *Rickless v. United Artists Corp.* [1988] Q.B. 40.

Companies

On normal tortious principles a company will be vicariously liable for   **4.78**
infringements of performers' rights and recording rights committed by its
employees during the course of their employment.[66] In the case of secondary
infringements, it is the employee who commits the act in question whose state
of mind will usually be material. If he has the requisite knowledge or reason
for belief, it is irrelevant that the company's directors do not have it. (If, on the
other hand, the directors had the knowledge or reason for belief and
instructed an innocent employee to do the act there would be primary rather
than vicarious liability.)

TERRITORIALITY ✳

Part II of the Copyright, Designs and Patents Act 1988 'extends to' England   **4.79**
and Wales, Scotland and Northern Ireland[67] (but not to the Channel Islands,
the Isle of Man or any colony[68]). Things done in the following places are to be
treated as done in the United Kingdom[69]:

(a) the territorial waters of the United Kingdom[70];
(b) on a structure or vessel which is present in the United Kingdom sector
of the continental shelf[71] for purposes directly connected with the
exploration of the sea bed or subsoil or the exploitation of their natural
resources[72];
(c) on a British ship,[73] aircraft or hovercraft.[74]

It is clear from this that acts done in any of these places are actionable in the   **4.80**
United Kingdom without further ado. What is less clear is whether acts
committed in other places are actionable in the United Kingdom. This
question can only be answered in a number of stages.

Are performers' rights territorial?

The first stems from the fact that (perhaps due to the avoidance by the   **4.81**
draughtsman of copyright-style definitions) most of the rights conferred by
Part II, unlike those conferred by Part I, are not specifically expressed to be
territorially limited. Thus whereas section 16(1) of the Act states that the
owner of the copyright in a work has the exclusive right to do certain acts *in
the United Kingdom*, section 182(1) of the Act merely states that a

---

[66] See *Clerk & Lindsell on Torts* (17th ed., Sweet & Maxwell, 1995), paras. 5–20 to 5–45.
[67] Copyright, Designs and Patents Act 1988, s. 207.
[68] *ibid.*, s. 208(5).
[69] *ibid.*, s. 210(1).
[70] *ibid.*, s. 209(1).
[71] That is, the areas designed by order under s. 1(7) of the Continental Shelf Act 1964: Copyright,
Designs and Patents Act 1988, s. 209(3).
[72] Copyright, Designs and Patents Act 1988, s. 209(2).
[73] That is, a ship which is British for the purposes of the Merchant Shipping Acts (see s. 2 of the
Merchant Shipping Act 1988) otherwise than by virtue of registration in a country outside the
United Kingdom: Copyright, Designs and Patents Act 1988, s. 210(2).
[74] That is, an aircraft or hovercraft registered in the United Kingdom: Copyright, Designs and
Patents Act 1988, s. 210(2).

performer's rights are infringed by the doing of certain acts without his consent. The question therefore arises whether, on the true construction of Part II of the 1988 Act, the rights granted are territorially limited.[75]

4.82   The main argument against territoriality is the omission from most of the infringement-defining sections of the words "in the United Kingdom". It is arguable that this omission must be given effect, particularly when comparison is made with the corresponding sections in Part I of the Act. Against this are the following points:

(1)   It is difficult to see what is the effect of section 207, which provides that Part II "extends to" the United Kingdom, if not to make the operation of Part II territorial.

(2)   Section 194 of the Act provides that infringement of performers' rights and recording rights is actionable as breach of statutory duty. Although there does not appear to be any direct authority on the point,[76] it is submitted that a statutory duty does not extend outside the United Kingdom unless the statute in question expressly so provides.[77] Thus, it can be said, section 194 explains the omission from most of the infringement-defining sections of the words "in the United Kingdom".

(3)   It is significant that importation of illicit recordings into the United Kingdom is made an infringement.[78] This would seem clearly to imply a territorial scheme: if making recordings abroad was an infringement, it would not be necessary to make importation an infringement.

(4)   Similarly, if making recordings abroad were in itself an infringement, it would be unnecessary to stipulate in defining "illicit recording" for the purposes of Part II that it is immaterial where the record was made.[79]

(5)   Interpreting Part II as territorial in operation is consistent with the provisions for protection of nationals of other countries which by their law provide adequate protection for British performances.[80]

---

[75] cf. ABKCO Music & Records Inc. v. Music Collection International Ltd [1995] EMLR 449.

[76] Perhaps the nearest is Coupland v. Arabian Gulf Oil Co. [1983] 1 W.L.R. 1136, a case concerning an accident to a British citizen in the course of employment in Libya, in which Robert Goff L.J. said:

"The pleaded case of the plaintiff, as one would expect, puts forward the claim on three grounds: first on the basis of negligence; second on the basis of breach of contract; and third on the basis of breach of statutory duty, which I understand to mean breach of Libyan statutory duty.

It is not clear from the report, however, precisely what statutory duty was being alleged; nor was the question addressed how breach of Libyan statutory duty could be actionable in England."

[77] This is an application of the well-established presumption in construing offence-creating statutes that, in the absence of clear and specific words to the contrary, such statutes are not intended to make conduct taking place outside the jurisdiction an offence triable in England: Cox v. Army Council (1962) 46 Cr. App. R. 258; Air India v. Wiggins (1980) 71 Cr. App. R. 213.

[78] Copyright, Designs and Patents Act 1988, ss. 184(1)(a) and 188(1)(a).

[79] ibid., s. 197(6).

[80] ibid., ss. 181, 206 and 208. See Chap. 2, paras. 2.38.

It is therefore submitted that the better view is that Part II rights are territorial in the same way as Part I rights.

Jurisdiction: the *Moçambique* rule[81]

The next stage is to consider whether the English courts have jurisdiction to entertain an action for an alleged infringement of performers' rights committed outside the United Kingdom; or whether such an action is barred by the *Moçambique* rule[82] as modified by section 30(1) of the Civil Jurisdiction and Judgments Acts 1982, namely that (subject to certain exceptions) the English courts do not have jurisdiction over actions principally concerned with title to, or right to possession of, immovable property situated outside England.[83] If the action is framed in terms of local rights, this will depend on whether performers' rights are regarded as immovable property by the law of the country in question. If no evidence of that law is before the court, however, the court will apply the English rule. Thus in *Tyburn Productions Ltd v. Conan Doyle*,[84] Vinelott J. held that intellectual property rights in general and copyrights in particular are immovables,[85] and so an action concerning United States copyrights was struck out. If it is correct that rights under Part II of the 1988 Act are territorial in the same way as rights under Part I, this decision also applies to performers' rights, particularly now that performers' rights are partially assignable.[86] In *Pearce v. Ove Arup Partnership Ltd*[87] and *Coin Controls Ltd v. Suzo Investments (UK) Ltd*,[88] however, it was held that, where the defendant is domiciled in a Contracting State of the Brussels (or Lugano) Convention, Articles 2–6 of the Convention override the *Moçambique* rule and require the court to accept jurisdiction over the subject-matter of the action if it has jurisdiction over the defendant.

4.83

Actionability at common law: the double actionability rule[89]

Assuming that the *Moçambique* rule as modified by section 30(1) of the 1982 Act is inapplicable, the third stage is to consider whether an action for an alleged infringement of performers' rights committed outside the United Kingdom is actionable under English private international law. At common law this depended on the "double actionability" rule. The double actionability rule was a rule for choice of law in tort actions which permitted the

4.84

---

[81] See Arnold, "Can One Sue in England for Infringement of Foreign Intellectual Property Rights?" [1990] 7 EIPR 254.

[82] *British South Africa Co. v. Companhia de Moçambique* [1893] A.C. 602; *Hesperides Hotels Ltd v. Muftizade* [1979] A.C. 508. See Dicey and Morris, *The Conflict of Laws* (12th ed., Sweet & Maxwell, 1993), Rule 116(3) and p. 1517.

[83] In addition, where the country in question is a Contracting State of the Brussels Convention 1968 or of the Lugano Convention 1988, Art. 16(1)(a) of the Conventions grant exclusive jurisdiction over such actions to the courts of the country in question. See Dicey & Morris, above, note 82, Rule 115(1).

[84] [1990] 1 All E.R. 909.

[85] Following a decision of the High Court of Australia, *Potter v. The Broken Hill Pty Co. Ltd* (1906) 3 C.L.R. 479.

[86] See Chap. 3, paras. 3.05–3.15.

[87] [1997] 2 W.L.R. 779.

[88] Unreported, Laddie J., March 26, 1997.

[89] See Arnold, note 81, above, and Floyd and Purvis, "Can an English Court Restrain Infringement of a Foreign Patent?" [1995] 3 EIPR 110.

application of English law (the *lex fori*) to foreign torts subject to the condition that the tort in question was actionable according to the local law (the *lex loci delicti commissi*) as well as according to English law.[90] It was stated in Rule 203(1) of Dicey and Morris, *The Conflict of Laws*,[91] as follows:

> As a general rule, an act done in a foreign country is a tort and actionable as such in England, only if it is both
>
> (a) actionable as a tort according to English law, or in other words is an act which, if done in England, would be a tort; and
>
> (b) actionable according to the law of the foreign country where it was done.

4.85 In *Def Lepp Music v. Stuart-Brown*[92] the plaintiffs, who claimed to be the owners of United Kingdom copyrights, attempted to sue two defendants in England for acts committed in Luxembourg and Holland. The action was struck out on the basis that the plaintiffs could not bring themselves within what is now Rule 203(1) since the acts complained of, being committed outside the United Kingdom, were not an infringement of any U.K. copyright and so were not actionable in accordance with requirement (a). Sir Nicolas Browne-Wilkinson V.-C. observed that it could not be right to determine actionability (as suggested by the concluding words of Rule 205(1)(a)) by asking what the position would be if the acts had been done in England when the statute only made acts *in fact* done in England actionable.[93] If it is correct that rights under Part II are territorial in the same way as rights under Part I, as submitted in paragraph 4.82, above, this decision is on its face directly applicable to the question whether "infringements" of performers' rights committed abroad are actionable in the United Kingdom.[94]

4.86 In *Red Sea Insurance Co. Ltd v. Bouygues SA*,[95] however, the Privy Council, as well as confirming Rule 203(1), approved the exception to the rule formulated in Dicey and Morris in the following terms:

> But a particular issue between the parties may be governed by the law of the country which, with respect to that issue, has the most significant relationship with the occurrence and the parties.

Furthermore, Lord Slynn of Hadley who delivered the opinion of the Board said this:

> Can the exception be relied upon to enable a plaintiff to rely on the *lex loci delicti* if his claim would not be actionable under the *lex fori*? ... Their Lordships do not consider that the element of flexibility which exists is so limited [to exclusion of the *lex loci delicti* in favour of the *lex fori*]. Whilst recognising that to do so is a

---

[90] *Boys v. Chaplin* [1971] A.C. 356, 389 (*per* Lord Wilberforce), *Coupland v. Arabian Gulf Oil Co.*, note 75, above.
[91] Note 82, above.
[92] [1986] R.P.C. 273.
[93] *ibid.*, at 276.
[94] It was followed in *James Burroughs Distillers plc v. Speymalt Whisky Distributors Ltd* 1989 S.L.T. 561 and *Tyburn Productions Ltd v. Conan Doyle*, note 84, above.
[95] [1995] A.C. 190.

departure from the strict rule in *The Halley*, L.R. 2 P.C. 193, they consider that in principle the exception can be applied in an appropriate case to enable a plaintiff to rely exclusively on the *lex loci delicti*.[96]

Accordingly, this opened up the possibility that even at common law an English court could be persuaded to distinguish the *Def Lepp* case by applying the exception in Rule 203(2) so as to permit the plaintiff to rely upon the *lex loci delicti*. If so, it would become possible to bring an action in England in respect of acts committed in, say, France upon proof that they were actionable under the French law of performers' rights. The harmonisation of the relevant laws under the E.C. Directives would be an argument in favour of this. The reluctance of the courts to entertain such an action, even in a case involving a European patent,[97] was shown by the *obiter dicta* of Aldous J. in *Plastus Kreativ AB v. Minnesota Mining & Manufacturing Co.*[98] Nevertheless, in *Pearce v. Ove Arup Partnership Ltd*[99] Lloyd J. held that, where the defendant is domiciled in a Contracting State of the Brussels Convention, Articles 2–6 of the Convention override the double actionability rule and require the court to entertain the action if it has jurisdiction over the defendant. Apparently this entitles the plaintiff to rely upon the *lex loci delicti*. It is submitted that this is wrong, since it is clear that the Convention does not affect the substantive law of Contracting States.

Another more limited possibility was that the English court could be persuaded to grant interim relief under Article 24 of the Brussels Convention where substantive proceedings have been or are about to be commenced in another Contracting State. Again, however, there might have been a judicial reluctance to do so for the reasons outlined by Aldous J. (now L.J.). **4.87**

Actionability: the new law

Whatever the position may have been under the common law, the law as to actionability has now been radically changed by the Private International Law (Miscellaneous Provisions) Act 1995 which came into force on May 1, 1996.[1] Section 10 of the Act abolishes the double actionability rule. Section 11(1) replaces it with a general rule that the applicable law is the law of the country in which the events constituting the tort or delict in question occur. This general rule may be displaced if it is substantially more appropriate to apply the law of another country connected with the tort: section 12. The applicable law is then used to determine whether an actionable tort has occurred: section 9(4). **4.88**

Prima facie, therefore, it is now possible to bring an action in England in respect of an alleged infringement of performer's rights committed in France. By virtue of section 11(1) the applicable law is French law and by virtue of section 9(4) liability is to be determined according to that law. While it would **4.89**

---

[96] *ibid.*, at 206E–H.
[97] Where the law is, in theory, the same being governed by the European Patent Convention.
[98] [1995] R.P.C. 438, 447.
[99] Note 87, above. This point did not arise in *Coin Controls Ltd v. Suzo Investments (UK) Ltd* (note 88, above), since the 1995 Act applied.
[1] S.I. 1996 No. 995.

theoretically be possible to argue that another law should be applied under section 12, there is no obvious reason why in such a case it should be appropriate to apply anything other than French law. Presumably in such a case it will be necessary for the plaintiff specifically to plead and prove by expert evidence the relevant provisions of French law relied upon.

Jurisdiction and forum

4.90 A final point to be borne in mind is that, even if a claim in respect of acts committed abroad is actionable in England, it will be necessary to establish jurisdiction of the English court over the particular defendant involved. This will depend on the application of the usual rules as to jurisdiction[2] which are outside the scope of this book. It will also depend on the question of *forum conveniens* where this is applicable. Thus even if the claim is actionable it may not be possible to establish jurisdiction; and even if it is possible to establish jurisdiction the action will be stayed if there is a more appropriate forum, unless there are special circumstances which militate a trial in the United Kingdom.[3]

---

[2] Under the Brussels or Locarno Conventions or under R.S.C. Order 11.
[3] *Spiliada Maritime Corp. v. Cansulex Ltd* [1987] A.C. 460.

5. Permitted Acts and Defences

INTRODUCTION

Copyright and rights in the nature of copyright such as performers' rights **5.01** can, if rigidly enforced, prove oppressive in that they inhibit activities of other persons that do not cause damage to the right owner or they inhibit them to a degree that is disproportionate to the potential damage to the right owner or are simply contrary to the public interest. For this reason, it is necessary to provide statutory defences to potential infringers in a number of situations. These limitations upon performers' rights are referred to in the 1988 Act as "permitted acts" (and in this book are also sometimes referred to as "exceptions"). They are discussed in this chapter together with five more fundamental defences: consent, free circulation within the EEA, "innocence" (that is, lack of knowledge), private and domestic use, and arrangements made before commencement. Other limitations upon performers' rights are the various types of compulsory licensing and the Copyright Tribunal's jurisdiction over collective licensing. These are discussed in Chapter 3.

PERMITTED ACTS

The Performers' Protection Acts 1958–1972 provided for a number of what **5.02** were essentially fair dealing defences or permitted acts.[1] These have been considerably supplemented in the Copyright, Designs and Patents Act and are now contained in Schedule 2 to the Act. The exceptions run closely parallel to those in Chapter 3 of Part I of the Act. Furthermore, most of the expressions used are expressly stated to have the same meaning as in the corresponding provisions in Part I.[2] Decisions under Part I will therefore be applicable to Schedule 2.

It should be noted, however, that not all the exceptions contained in Part I **5.03** are reproduced in Schedule 2. Some, of course, are not reproduced since they are only applicable to copyright. Others, however, are potentially applicable but nevertheless have still not been reproduced. Two in particular should be noticed. First, there is no equivalent in Schedule 2 to the Part I exception for fair dealing for research or private study.[3] It may be that this is because

---

[1] Interested readers are referred to the first edition, Chap. 2, paras. 2.88–2.93.
[2] Copyright, Designs and Patents Act 1988, Sched. 2, paras. 2(2), 3(4), 4(4), 5(3), 6(3), 6A(2), 6B(2), 7(2), 8(2), 9(2), 10(2), 11(4), 12(6), 13(3), 14(4), 14A(6), 15(3), 16(4), 17(4), 18(5), 19(9), 20(2) and 21(2).
[3] *ibid.*, s. 29.

showing or playing a recording is only an infringement if done "in public": if a student views or listens to a recording privately,[4] there will probably be no infringement. Nevertheless, the absence of such an exception prevents copying even where it would qualify as fair dealing for these purposes. Secondly, there is no equivalent in Schedule 2 to the Part I exception for time-shifting.[5] It may be that this is for a similar reason: because a recording made for the purposes of time-shifting will almost invariably be made for private and domestic purposes, and so not an infringement.

5.04   Some of the current exceptions appear to be contrary to Chapter II of the E.C. Rental and Lending Rights Directive.[6] In accordance with the Rome Convention,[7] this only provides for the following limitations on the related rights harmonised by that Chapter:

(a) private use;
(b) use of short excerpts in connection with the reporting of current events;
(c) ephemeral fixation by a broadcasting organisation by means of its own facilities and for its own broadcasts;
(d) use solely for the purposes of teaching or scientific research.[8]

Although the Directive, again following the Convention,[9] also permits Member States to impose the same limitations on these rights as they do upon copyrights in literary and artistic works,[10] the present exceptions go further than this since there are a number of permitted acts that apply to performances (and sound recordings and broadcasts) that do not apply to literary and artistic works, in particular those in Schedule 2, paragraphs 15 and 18 (corresponding to sections 67 and 72 of Part I).[11] (The reason why the United Kingdom is not in breach of the Convention for the same reason is that when it ratified the Convention it made reservations in respect of these acts.[12])

1. Criticism, reviews and news reporting

5.05   Fair dealing with a performance or recording for the purpose of either (a) criticism or review (whether of that or of another performance or recording or of a work) or (b) reporting current events, does not infringe performers' rights or recording rights.[13] It should be noted that (by contrast to section 30) there is no requirement for any acknowledgment. The corresponding provisions under the Copyright Act 1956[14] were somewhat narrowly

---

[4] For example, in a video library which provides individual booths for viewing films—assuming that this qualifies as "on-the-spot reference" so as not to infringe the lending right, as to which see Chap. 4, para. 4.36.
[5] Copyright, Designs and Patents Act 1988, s. 70.
[6] Council Directive 92/100, November 19, 1992 on rental right and lending right and on certain rights related to copyright in the field of intellectual property, [1992] O.J. L346/61.
[7] Art. 15(1).
[8] Rental and Lending Rights Directive, note 6, above, Art. 10(1).
[9] Art. 15(2).
[10] Rental and Lending Rights Directive, note 6, above, Art. 10(2).
[11] See paras. 5.37–5.40 and 5.43, below.
[12] See the reservation (a) in respect of Art. 12 in Appendix 5a.
[13] Copyright, Designs and Patents Act 1988, Sched. 2, para. 2(1) (corresponding to s. 30(2), (3) of Part I). See also paras. 5.31–5.33, below.
[14] ss. 6(2),(3).

interpreted,[15] but since the passage of the 1988 Act the courts have adopted a slightly more generous approach.[16]

Criticism or review

"Criticism or review" is not limited to comment on the quality of the performance, but extends to such matters as the ideas or doctrines embodied in the performance[17] and its suitability for public exhibition.[18] The criticism may be hostile, and possibly even defamatory, yet still be fair dealing.[19]

5.06

Reporting current events

"Current events" are not restricted to news and current affairs. Thus the inclusion of excerpts from football matches in sports news bulletins was held to be reporting current events.[20] On the other hand, such authority as there is suggests a rather narrow view of what is "current".[21] It is submitted, however, that in the light of Article 10 of the European Convention on Human Rights a broad interpretation is appropriate so as to preserve freedom of expression.[22]

5.07

Fair dealing

What constitutes fair dealing is a matter of fact and degree in all the circumstances of the particular case.[23] Among the factors that may be relevant, however, are the following:

5.08

(a) Whether what is sought to be justified as a fair dealing in fact amounts to competition with the performance.[24] If so, it is unlikely to be held to be fair.

(b) The motive for the dealing.[25] Thus if the motive is to gain a commercial advantage from the performer's work even if there no competition with the performer, the courts will be slow to recognise the dealing as fair.[26]

---

[15] See, in particular, *Sillitoe v. McGraw-Hill Book Co. (U.K.) Ltd* [1983] F.S.R. 545 and *Independent Television Publications Ltd v. Time Out Ltd* [1984] F.S.R. 64.

[16] See *British Broadcasting Corp. v. British Satellite Broadcasting Ltd* [1992] Ch. 141 and *Time Warner Entertainments Co. LP v. Channel Four Television Corp. plc* [1994] EMLR 1.

[17] *Hubbard v. Vosper* [1972] 2 Q.B. 84, 94, 98 and *Distillers Co. (Biochemicals) Ltd v. Times Newspapers Ltd* [1975] Q.B. 613, 625.

[18] *Time Warner Entertainments Co. LP v. Channel Four Television Corp plc*, note 16, above.

[19] *Fraser v. Evans* [1969] 1 Q.B. 349, *Hubbard v. Vosper*, note 17, above, and *Kennard v. Lewis* [1983] F.S.R. 346.

[20] *British Broadcasting Corp. v. British Satellite Broadcasting Ltd*, note 16, above.

[21] *Distillers Co. (Biochemicals) Ltd v. Times Newspapers Ltd*, note 17, above, at 626.

[22] See the dicta in *R. v. Advertising Standards Authority Ltd, ex p. Vernons Organisation Ltd* [1992] 1 W.L.R. 1289; *Secretary of State for the Home Department v. Central Broadcasting Ltd* [1993] EMLR 253, 274; *Tsikata v. Newspaper Publishing plc* [1995] EMLR 8, 16; and *R. v. Broadcasting Complaints Commission, ex p. British Broadcasting Corp.* [1995] EMLR 241, 255–257 (not cases on fair dealing).

[23] *Hubbard v. Vosper*, note 17, above.

[24] *Hubbard v. Vosper*, note 17, above, at 93–94; *Associated Newspapers Group plc v. News Group Newspapers Ltd* [1986] F.S.R. 515.

[25] *Johnstone v. Bernard Jones Publications Ltd* [1938] Ch. 599, 607, *Associated Newspaper Group plc v. News Group Newspapers Ltd*, note 24, above.

[26] *Time Warner Entertainments Co. LP v. Channel Four Television Corp. plc*, note 16, above.

(c) Whether the performance or recording was published or not. If it was not, it will be more difficult to establish fair dealing.[27] Where the material was unpublished the method by which the defendant obtained it may be relevant.[28]

(d) The amount and importance of what has been taken.[29] In certain circumstances it may be proper to take the whole of a performance, especially if it is short. In general, however, the greater and the more important the part that is taken, the more difficult it will be to establish that the dealing is fair.

(e) The nature of the accompanying material and the relation it bears to what has been taken. This may, for example, show that the taking is not for the purpose of criticism or review but for exposition.[30]

(f) Whether it was necessary to use the performance or whether the use was gratuitous. It is not incumbent on the defendant to show that the use was necessary, but if it was gratuitous, it will be harder to justify as fair dealing.[31]

2. Incidental inclusion

5.09 The incidental inclusion of a performance or recording in a sound recording, film, broadcast or cable programme does not infringe performers' rights or recording rights.[32] The exception extends to subsequent dealings in anything the making of which was not an infringement by virtue of paragraph 3(1) and in copies of any such thing.[33]

Deliberate inclusion

5.10 It is expressly provided that music and any accompanying words (whether spoken or sung)[34] that are deliberately included are not incidentally included.[35] It is not clear whether this means that any other class of performance must be included non-deliberately in order to be incidental or whether there may be deliberate incidental inclusion. Where music and any accompanying words are deliberately included, it is irrelevant whether or not they are in copyright.

---

[27] *British Oxygen Co. Ltd v. Liquid Air Ltd* [1925] Ch. 383; *Beloff v. Pressdram Ltd* [1973] R.P.C. 765.

[28] *Time Warner Entertainments Co. LP v. Channel Four Television Corp. plc*, note 16, above.

[29] *Hubbard v. Vosper*, note 17, above, at 94, 98.

[30] *Sillitoe v. McGraw-Hill Book Co.*, note 15, above.

[31] *Associated Newspaper Group plc v. News Group Newspapers Ltd*, note 24, above.

[32] Copyright, Designs and Patents Act 1988, Sched. 2 para. 3(1) (corresponding to s. 31(1) of Part I).

[33] *ibid.*, Sched. 2, para. 3(2).

[34] In this respect the drafting of para. 3(3) is somewhat clearer than that of s. 31(3). In s. 31(3) it is not at all clear whether the words must be accompanied by music for the subsection to bite or whether it is sufficient that the words were written for use with music. In para. 3(3) it seems clear that the words must be accompanied by music.

[35] Copyright, Design and Patents Act 1988, Sched. 2, para. 3(3).

3. Instruction or examination

Copying of a recording of a performance in the course either of instruction or **5.11**
of preparation for instruction in the making of films or film soundtracks does
not infringe performers' rights or recording rights provided it is done by a
person either giving or receiving instruction.[36] Similarly, copying of a
recording of a performance for the purposes of setting or answering questions
in an examination does not infringe performers' rights or recording rights,
nor does anything done by way of communicating the questions[37] to the
candidates.[38] The exception does not extend to any subsequent dealing in
such recordings if they would otherwise be illicit recordings.[39] The apparent
oddity of limiting the exception for instruction to film-making but not the
exception for examinations is accounted for by the fact that instruction in
other subjects is sufficiently allowed for by the following exception.[40] It is
submitted that "instruction" does not include self-instruction. It may be
noted that (unlike section 32) there is no exclusion for copying by
reprographic processes.

4. Playing or showing at educational establishments

A sound recording, film, broadcast or cable programme played or shown at **5.12**
an educational establishment for the purposes of instruction before an
audience consisting of teachers, pupils and persons directly connected with
the activities of the establishment[41] is not played or shown "in public" so as to
infringe performers' rights or recording rights.[42]

Educational establishment

"Educational establishment" means any school[43] or any other description of **5.13**
educational establishment specified by order of the Secretary of State under
section 174(1)(b) of the Act.[44] These are[45]:

    (a) any university empowered by Royal Charter or Act of Parliament to
        award degrees and any college, or institution in the nature of a college,
        in such a university;

    (b) any institution providing further education within the meaning of
        section 1(5)(b) of the Education (Scotland) Act 1980 and any
        educational establishment (other than a school) within the meaning of
        section 135(1) of that Act;

---

[36] *ibid.*, Sched. 2, para. 4(1) (corresponding to s. 32(2) of Part I).
[37] *e.g.* issuing copies of recordings of performances to candidates.
[38] Copyright, Designs and Patents Act 1988, Sched. 2 para. 4(2).
[39] *ibid.*, Sched. 2, para. 4(3).
[40] What is not allowed by either provision is instruction in subjects other than film-making
otherwise than at an educational establishment
[41] Presumably it is not a requirement that all three categories of persons be present, only that no
one falling outside those categories be present.
[42] Copyright, Designs and Patents Act 1988, Sched. 2 para. 5(1) (corresponding to s. 34(2) of
Part I).
[43] As defined in the Education Act 1944, the Education (Scotland) Act 1962 (but including an
approved school as defined in the Social Work (Scotland) Act 1968) and the Education and
Libraries (Northern Ireland) Order 1986).
[44] Copyright, Designs and Patents Act 1988, Sched. 2, para. 5(3); s. 34; s. 174(1).
[45] Copyright (Educational Establishments) (No. 2) Order 1989 (S.I. 1989 No. 1068).

(c) any institution providing further education within the meaning of Article 5(c) of the Education and Libraries (Northern Ireland) Order 1986 and any college of education within the meaning of that Order;

(d) any institution the sole or main purpose of which is to provide further education within the meaning of section 41 of the Education Act 1944 or higher education within the meaning of section 120 of the Education Reform Act 1988; and

(e) any theological college.

Persons directly connected with the activities of the establishment

5.14   A person is not directly connected with the activities of an establishment merely because he or she is the parent of a pupil.[46] Otherwise, it is somewhat unclear who is covered by this phrase. Presumably it means ancillary staff, governors and the like; but what about a parents' representative on a Parent-Teacher Association?

5. Recording by educational establishments

5.15   A recording of a broadcast or cable programme, or a copy of such a recording, may be made by or on behalf of an educational establishment for educational purposes without thereby infringing performers' rights or recording rights in any performance or recording included in it.[47] The exception does not extend to subsequent dealings.[48] The exception also applies in relation to teachers who are employed by local education authorities to give instruction elsewhere to pupils who are unable to attend an educational establishment.[49] Curiously, this does not appear to be the case for the preceding exception.[50]

5.16   Unlike the corresponding provision in Part I,[51] this exception is not excluded if or to the extent that a licensing scheme is certified under section 143 of the Act. It would therefore appear that the licensing schemes[52] which have been certified for the purposes of Part I rights do not apply to Part II rights.

6. Lending of copies of recordings by educational establishments

5.17   Performers' rights and recording rights are not infringed by the lending of copies of a recording of a performance by an educational establishment.[53]

---

[46] Copyright, Designs and Patents Act 1988, Sched. 2 para. 5(2).

[47] *ibid.*, Sched. 2, para. 6(1) (corresponding to s. 35(1) of Part I).

[48] *ibid.*, Sched. 2, para. 6(2).

[49] *ibid.*, Sched. 2, para. 6(3); s. 35; s. 174(2); Copyright (Application of Provisions Relating to Educational Establishments to Teachers) (No. 2) Order 1989 (S.I. 1989 No. 1067).

[50] The statutory instrument does not apply to s. 34 and hence does not apply to Sched. 2, para. 5(3)

[51] Copyright, Designs and Patents Act 1988, s. 35(2).

[52] Namely that operated by Educational Recording Agency Ltd and Open University Educational Enterprises Ltd: Copyright (Certification of Licensing Scheme for Educational Recording of Broadcasts and Cable Programmes) (Educational Recording Agency Limited) Order 1990 (S.I. 1990 No. 879) (as amended by S.I. 1992 No. 211, S.I. 1993 No. 193, S.I. 1994 No. 247 and S.I. 1996 No. 191) and Copyright (Certification of Licensing Scheme for Educational Recording of Broadcasts) (Open University Educational Enterprises Ltd) 1993 (S.I. 1993 No. 2755) (as amended by S.I. 1996 No. 190).

[53] Copyright, Designs and Patents Act 1988, Sched. 2, para. 6A(1) (corresponding to s. 36A of Part I).

7. Lending of copies of recordings by libraries and archives

Performers' rights and recording rights are not infringed by the lending of copies of a recording by a prescribed library or archive (other than a public library) which is not conducted for profit.[54]

5.18

Prescribed libraries and archives

The prescribed libraries and archives are those prescribed by regulations made under section 37 of the 1988 Act for the purposes of section 40A(2). Until such regulations are made, these are the libraries and archives prescribed by paragraphs 2 to 6 of Part A of Schedule 1 to the Copyright (Librarians and Archivists)(Copying of Copyright Material) Regulations 1989.[55]

5.19

8. Copies of works made as a condition of export

It is not an infringement of performers' rights or recording rights to make a copy of a work of an article of cultural or historical importance for deposit in an appropriate library or archive where this is a condition of export.[56] "Appropriate" is not defined; it seems likely that it will be broadly construed.

5.20

9. Parliamentary and judicial proceedings

Performers' rights and recording rights are not infringed by anything done for the purposes of parliamentary or judicial proceedings or for the purpose of reporting such proceedings.[57] It is not clear exactly how widely this exception extends: for example, whether it extends to things done by way of preparation for such proceedings as well as things done during the proceedings. It is submitted that the exception should be broadly construed.

5.21

Proceedings

"Parliamentary proceedings" include proceedings of the Northern Ireland Assembly and of the European Parliament.[58] "Judicial proceedings" include proceedings before any court, tribunal or person having authority to decide a person's legal rights or liabilities.[59] This is wide enough to include arbitration proceedings. It is not clear whether proceedings before foreign courts or tribunals are covered.

5.22

10. Royal Commissions and statutory inquiries

Performers' rights and recording rights are not infringed by anything done for the purposes of the proceedings of Royal Commissions and statutory inquiries or for reporting such proceedings held in public.[60] Unlike the

5.23

---

[54] *ibid.*, Sched. 2, para. 6B(1) (corresponding to s. 40A(2) of Part I).
[55] S.I. 1989 No. 1212.
[56] Copyright, Designs and Patents Act 1988, Sched. 2, para. 7(1) (corresponding to s. 44 of Part I).
[57] *ibid.*, Sched. 2, para. 8(1) (corresponding to s. 45(1),(2) of Part I).
[58] *ibid.*, s. 178.
[59] *ibid.*
[60] *ibid.*, Sched. 2, para. 9(1) (corresponding to s. 46(1),(2) of Part I).

preceding exception, therefore, this provision does not extend to reporting proceedings held in private.

Statutory inquiries

5.24 A statutory inquiry is an inquiry held or investigation conducted pursuant to a duty imposed or power conferred by or under any statute.[61]

11. Public records

5.25 Material in public records[62] which are open to public inspection may be copied, and a copy supplied to any person, by or with the authority of any officer appointed under the Public Records Act without infringing performers' rights or recording rights.[63]

12. Statutory authority

5.26 To do any act which is specifically authorised by an Act of Parliament is not an infringement of performers' rights or recording rights unless the Act so provides.[64] This applies no matter when the Act was passed.

13. Recordings in electronic form

5.27 Where a recording of a performance in electronic form has been purchased on terms which allow the purchaser to make further recordings from it, a person to whom the recording is transferred may do anything which the purchaser was allowed to do without infringement of performers' rights or recording rights.[65] This is provided that there are no express terms which either (a) prohibit transfer of the recording by the purchaser, impose obligations[66] which continue after a transfer, prohibit the assignment of any consent or terminate any consent on transfer or (b) stipulate the terms on which a transferee may do the things that the purchaser was permitted to do. The exception applies whether what is transferred is the original purchased recording or (if this is no longer usable) a copy of it.[67] Otherwise, a recording made by the purchaser which is not transferred together with the original recording will be treated as an illicit recording.

5.28 It therefore appears that the purpose of the exception is to permit transferees from purchasers who are allowed to make back-up copies[68] also to make back-up copies, but to ensure that any back-up copies are transferred together with the original. Thus a purchaser cannot buy a recording, make a back-up copy and sell on so as to get free use of the back-up copy.

---

[61] *ibid.*, Sched. 2, para. 9(2); s. 46(4).

[62] As defined in the Public Records Act 1958, the Public Records (Scotland) Act 1937 or the Public Records (Northern Ireland) Act 1923.

[63] Copyright, Designs and Patents Act 1988, Sched. 2, para. 10(1) (corresponding to s. 49 of Part I).

[64] *ibid.*, Sched. 2, para. 11(1) (corresponding to s. 50(1) of Part I).

[65] *ibid.*, Sched. 2, para. 12(2) (corresponding to s. 56(2) of Part I).

[66] Presumably this means obligations which are inconsistent with the transferee having the same rights as the transferor.

[67] Copyright, Designs and Patents Act 1988, Sched. 2, para. 12(3).

[68] A back-up copy is a copy made in case the original becomes corrupt.

In electronic form

"In electronic form" is defined in section 178 of Part I as follows: **5.29**

> "electronic" means actuated by electric, magnetic, electro-magnetic, electro-chemical or electro-mechanical energy and "in electronic form" means in a form usable only by electronic means.

The definition would appear to be broad enough to cover most software media. The following in particular would seem to be within the definition: floppy disks and diskettes, cassettes, videotapes and compact discs (these are only usable when read by a laser, that is, by electro-magnetic energy). LPs, however, would not seem to be within the definition, as these are read mechanically (although the mechanical movement of the needle is then translated into an electrical signal). Needless to say, this is an odd result, for there does not seem to be any reason to distinguish between LPs and other media—save, perhaps, that LPs are not subject to corruption in the same way as electronic forms of information storage and so it is not so necessary to make back-up copies.

Subsequent transfers

This provision applies to subsequent transfers.[69] It appears, however, that **5.30** there is an unintended loophole. Suppose A, the original purchaser, makes a back-up copy and transfers both original recording and back-up copy to B. If B transfers the original recording to C but retains the back-up copy himself, then the back-up copy does not become an illicit recording. This is because it is only back-up copies "made by the subsequent transferor", in this case B, that are caught. Similarly if B retains the original recording but sells the back-up copy to C. In either of these situations B may escape without infringing performers' rights, since there may be no primary infringement if the transfer to C is not an issue to the public[70] and there can be no secondary infringement since there is no illicit recording.

14. Spoken works

It is not an infringement of performers' rights or recording rights to use a **5.31** recording (or to copy it and use the copy) of the reading or recitation of a literary work for the purposes of either (a) reporting current events or (b) broadcasting or including in a cable programme service the whole or part of the reading or recitation if the recording was made for that purpose.[71] The following conditions must be met, however[72]:

    (a) the recording must be a direct recording of the reading or recital and not taken from a previous recording or from a broadcast or cable programme;

---

[69] Copyright, Designs and Patents Act 1988, Sched. 2, para. 12(4).
[70] As to which see Chap. 4, paras. 4.26–4.32.
[71] Copyright, Designs and Patents Act 1988, Sched. 2, para. 13(1) (corresponding to s. 58(1) of Part I).
[72] *ibid.*, Sched. 2, para. 13(2).

(b) the making of the recording must not have been prohibited by or on behalf of the person giving the reading or recitation;

(c) the use made of the recording must not be of kind prohibited by or on behalf of the person giving the reading or recitation before the recording was made; and

(d) the use must be by or with the authority of a person who is lawfully in possession of the recording.

5.32   Although it is nowhere made explicit, it appears that this exception is directed to the use of public statements and interviews.[73] Comparison may be made with the corresponding Part I provision, section 58, which is directed to the use of records of spoken words. Subparagraph (b) of the exception appears to have been included to ensure that the broadcasting of a public statement or interview for its own sake[74] is permitted, and not just if the interview is included in a news programme.

5.33   The effect of the first condition is that a broadcaster who wants to use a statement or interview must make his own recording rather than use another's. The second and third conditions presuppose that the person giving the reading or recitation knows that he is being recorded. Thus there is a loophole if he was clandestinely recorded. The only solution to this would appear to be for persons who do not wish to be recorded to issue a prohibition even if the prohibition appears unnecessary.

15. Recordings of folksongs

5.34   A recording may be made of a performance of a song for the purpose of including it in an archive maintained by a designated body without infringing performers' rights or recording rights.[75] A designated body is one designated by order of the Secretary of State under section 61 of the Act[76]; he must be satisfied that it is not established or conducted for profit.[77] The following conditions must be met, however[78]:

(a) the words must be unpublished and of unknown authorship at the time the recording is made[79];

(b) the making of the recording must not infringe any copyright; and

---

[73] See Chap. 2, paras. 2.21–2.22.

[74] For example, as in the television programme *Face to Face*.

[75] Copyright, Designs and Patents Act 1988, Sched. 2, para. 14(1) (corresponding to s. 61(1) of Part I).

[76] *ibid.*, Sched. 2, para. 14(4). The following are designated bodies: The Archive of Traditional Welsh Music, University College of North Wales; The Centre for English Cultural Tradition and Language; The Charles Parker Archive Trust (1982); The European Centre for Traditional and Religious Cultures; the Folklore Society; the Institute of Folklore Studies in Britain and Canada; the National Museum of Wales, Welsh Folk Museum; the National Sound Archive, the British Library; the North West Sound Archive; the Sound Archives, British Broadcasting Corporation; Ulster Folk and Transport Museum; the Vaughan Williams Memorial Library, English Folk Dance and Song Society: Copyright (Recordings of Folksongs for Archives) (Designated Bodies) Order 1989, S.I. 1989 No. 1012.

[77] Copyright, Designs and patents Act, 1988, s. 61(5)(a).

[78] *ibid.*, Sched. 2, para. 14(2).

[79] Any song which fulfils these criteria may be recorded, not just folksongs, although few other songs are likely to qualify.

(c) the making of the recording must not have been prohibited by any performer.[80]

Copies of a recording so made may be made and supplied by the archivist if conditions prescribed by the Secretary of State are met.[81] The prescribed conditions are[82]:   **5.35**

(a) that the person requiring a copy satisfies the archivist that he requires it for the purposes of research or private study and will not use it for any other purpose; and

(b) that no person is furnished with more than one copy of the same recording.

16. Lending to the public of copies of films or sound recordings

Where the Secretary of State has made an appropriate order, it is not an infringement of performers' rights to lend to the public copies of films or sound recordings provided that a reasonable royalty or other payment is made.[83] This provision is discussed in Chapter 3.[84]   **5.36**

17. Playing sound recordings for clubs, etc.

It is not an infringement of performers' rights or recording rights to play a sound recording[85] as part of the activities of, or for the benefit of, a club, society or other organisation.[86] The following conditions must be met, however[87]:   **5.37**

(a) the organisation (i) must not be established or conducted for profit and (ii) its main objects must be charitable or otherwise concerned with the advancement of religion, education or social welfare; and

(b) the proceeds of any charge for admission to the place where the recording is to be heard must be applied solely for the purposes of the organisation.

Organisation

It would seem that "organisation" is to be construed *ejusdem generis* with "club" and "society". The essence of a club (proprietary and investment clubs apart) is that it is an association of persons for purposes other than those of trade: for social reasons, for the promotion of politics, sport, art, science and so on.[88] Trading activities which are incidental to the club's   **5.38**

---

[80] As with the preceding section there is the problem of clandestine recording.
[81] Copyright, Designs and Patents Act 1988, Sched. 2, para. 14(3), (4) and s. 61(5)(a).
[82] Copyright (Recordings of Folksongs for Archives) (Designated Bodies) Order 1989, note 76, above, Art. 3.
[83] Copyright, Designs and Patents Act 1988, Sched. 2, para. 14A(1).
[84] paras. 3.40–3.42.
[85] See Chap. 2, para. 2.48 for the definition of "sound recording".
[86] Copyright, Designs and Patents Act 1988, Sched. 2, para. 15(1) (corresponding to s. 67(1) in Part I).
[87] *ibid.*, Sched. 2, para. 15(2).
[88] See *Halsbury's Laws* (4th ed.), Vol. 6, para. 201.

purposes will not prevent it from being a club, however. A club may be incorporated or unincorporated.

Not established or conducted for profit

5.39   This requirement does not mean that profits cannot be made but rather that they cannot be made with the object of distributing them in a normal commercial way. If profits are made in order to achieve charitable purposes, so that they are incidental and subsidiary to those purposes and not an end in themselves, the organisation is not established or conducted for profit.[89]

Charitable, etc., objects

5.40   The inclusion of the words "or otherwise concerned with the advancement of religion, education or social welfare" means that this provision is not restricted to charities[90] *per se*. This does not make it any easier to decide which organisations are within its scope and which are not. The same words were contained in section 8(1) of the Rating and Valuation (Miscellaneous Provisions) Act 1955 (now repealed), but it is difficult to extract any coherent principle out of the decided cases under that Act.[91] In any event, it does not follow that, because a phrase has been interpreted in one way in one statutory context, it should be interpreted in the same way in a different statutory context.

18. Incidental recordings for broadcasts or cable programmes

5.41   A person who is able to broadcast or include in a cable programme service a recording of a performance without infringing performers' rights or recording rights is deemed to have consent to the making of a further recording for the purposes of the broadcast or cable programme.[92] The following conditions must be met, however[93]:

(a) the further recording must not be used for any other purpose; and
(b) the further recording must be destroyed within 28 days of being first used for broadcasting the performance or including it in a cable programme service.

If either condition is breached the further recording becomes an illicit recording.[94] In short, this provision enables broadcasters to make ephemeral recordings in circumstances where there might otherwise be a technical infringement because they are licensed to broadcast but not to copy the recording.

---

[89] *Guinness Trust v. West Ham Corp.* [1959] 1 W.L.R. 233; *National Deposit Friendly Society Trustees v. Skegness Urban District Council* [1959] 1 W.L.R. 1197; and *North of England Zoo v. Chester Urban District Council* [1959] 3 All E.R. 116.
[90] See *Halsbury's Laws* (4th ed.), Vol. 5(2) (reissue), paras. 2–13 for the meaning of "charitable" purposes.
[91] Discussed in Laddie, Prescott & Vitoria, *The Modern Law of Copyright* (2nd ed., Butterworths, 1995), paras 6.39–6.40.
[92] Copyright, Designs and Patents Act 1988, Sched. 2 para. 16(1) (corresponding to s. 68(2) of Part I).
[93] *ibid.*, Sched. 2, para. 16(2).
[94] *ibid.*, Sched. 2, para. 16(3).

19. Recordings for supervision of broadcasts and cable programmes

There are various exceptions which permit regulatory bodies to do various acts without infringing performers' rights or recording rights[95]:

5.42

(1) The BBC may make or use recordings for the purposes of maintaining supervision and control over programmes broadcast by it.

(2) Rights under Part II are not infringed by anything done pursuant to sections 11(1), 95(1) or 167(1) of the Broadcasting Act 1990 or sections 115(4) or (6), 116(5) or 117 of the Broadcasting Act 1996.

(3) Rights under Part II are not infringed by anything done pursuant to a condition included under sections 11(2) or 95(2) of the 1990 Act in any licence granted under Part I or Part III of that Act or Part I or Part II of the 1996 Act.

(4) The Radio Authority may require recordings to be produced under section 109(2) of the 1990 Act.

(5) The Independent Television Commission and the Radio Authority may use for the performance of any of their functions under the Broadcasting Acts 1990 and 1996 any recording which is provided to them under any provision of those Acts.

(6) The Broadcasting Standards Commission may use in connection with any complaint made to it under the Broadcasting Act 1996 any recording provided under sections 115(4) or (6) or 116(5) of that Act.

20. Free public shows

Performers' rights and recording rights are not infringed by the showing or playing in public of a broadcast or cable programme to an audience which has not paid for admission.[96] The audience is be treated as having paid for admission if either[97]:

5.43

(a) they have paid for admission to a place of which the place where the broadcast or programme is to be seen or heard forms part; or

(b) goods or services are supplied at prices which either (i) are substantially attributable to the facilities for seeing or hearing the broadcast or programme or (ii) exceed those usually charged at the place in question and are partly attributable to those facilities.

On the other hand, the following are to be treated as not having paid for admission[98]:

(a) residents or inmates of the place in question; and

(b) members of a club or society where the payment is only for membership of the club or society and the provision of facilities for seeing or hearing broadcasts or programmes is only incidental to the main purposes of the club or society.

---

[95] *ibid.*, Sched. 2, para. 17(1),(2),(3) (corresponding to s. 69(1),(2),(3) of Part I).
[96] *ibid.*, Sched. 2, para. 18(1) (corresponding to s. 72(1) of Part I).
[97] *ibid.*, Sched. 2, para. 18(2).
[98] *ibid.*, Sched. 2, para. 18(3).

21. Reception and retransmission of broadcasts in cable programme services

5.44   A broadcast made from a place in the United Kingdom may be included in a cable programme service by reception and immediate retransmission without infringing performers' rights or recording rights if and to the extent that the broadcast is made for reception in the area in which the cable programme service is provided.[99] The Secretary of State has powers to extend or exclude this power by order[1] but to date no order has been made. Where the broadcast is included in the service pursuant to a requirement imposed under the Broadcasting Act 1990, but the area covered by the cable programme falls outside the area for reception in which the broadcast is made, then the inclusion of the performance or recording is subject to a statutory licence upon payment of a reasonable royalty or other payment.[2]

22. Subtitled copies of broadcasts and cable programmes

5.45   Recordings of television broadcasts or cable programmes may be made by a designated body for the purpose of providing people who are deaf or hard of hearing or physically or mentally handicapped with copies which are subtitled or otherwise modified for their special needs without infringing performers' rights or recording rights.[3] A designated body is one designated by order of the Secretary of State under section 74 of the Act[4]; he must be satisfied that it is not established or conducted for profit.[5]

23. Recordings of broadcasts or cable programmes for archival purposes

5.46   A recording or copy of a recording of a broadcast or cable programme of a designated class may be made for placing in an archive maintained by a designated body without infringing performers' rights or recording rights.[6] A designated body is one designated by order of the Secretary of State under section 75 of the Act[7]; he must be satisfied that it is not established or conducted for profit.[8]

---

[99] *ibid.*, Sched. 2, para. 19(2) (corresponding to s. 73(3) of Part I).

[1] *ibid.*, Sched. 2, paras. 19(5)–(8) (corresponding to ss. 73(9)–(12) of Part I).

[2] *ibid.*, Sched. 2, para. 19(3) (corresponding to s. 73(4) of Part I). See Chap. 3, paras. 3.34–3.36

[3] *ibid.*, Sched. 2, para. 20(1) (corresponding to s. 74(1) of Part I).

[4] *ibid.*, Sched. 2, para. 20(2). The National Subtitling Library for Deaf People is a designated body: Copyright (Subtitling of Broadcasts and Cable Programmes) (Designated Body) Order 1989 (S.I. 1989 No. 1013).

[5] Copyright, Designs and Patents Act 1988, s. 74(2).

[6] *ibid.*, Sched. 2, para. 21(1) (corresponding to s. 75(1) of Part I).

[7] *ibid.*, Sched. 2, para. 21(2). The British Film Institute, the British Library, the British Medical Association, the British Music Information Centre, the Imperial War Museum, the Music Performance Research Centre, the National Library of Wales and the Scottish Film Council are all designated in respect of all broadcasts other than encrypted transmissions and all cable programmes: Copyright (Recording for Archives of Designated Class of Broadcasts and Cable Programmes) (Designated Bodies) Order 1993 (S.I. 1993 No. 74).

[8] *ibid.*, s. 75(2).

DEFENCES

Other than the permitted acts contained in Schedule 2 (which are dealt with   **5.47**
above) the following defences are available under Part II: consent, free
circulation within the European Economic Area, "innocence" (that is, lack of
knowledge), private and domestic use and arrangements made before
commencement. In addition, general defences to torts may be relied upon, in
particular acquiescence and expiry of the limitation period. The latter is six
years, for section 2 of the Limitation Act 1980 applies to both to
infringements of property rights and to breaches of statutory duty.[9] Other
so-called "Euro-defences" relying on Articles 85 and 86 of the Treaty of
Rome may be available in appropriate fact situations.[10] There must be a
sufficient nexus between the infringement and the conduct complained of,
however, and a number of attempts to plead such defences have been struck
out.[11]

1. Consent

Consent may be given in relation to a specific performance, to a specified   **5.48**
description of performances or to performances generally; the performances
may be past or future.[12] Consent may be oral: in contrast to the Performers'
Protection Acts,[13] there is no requirement of writing.

(a) Performers' rights

By the performer—Consent by the performer is a defence to an allegation of   **5.49**
infringement of performers' rights other than performers' property rights
(reproduction and issuing to the public). In relation to secondary infringement, consent of the performer may be a defence in either of two ways:
consent to the making of the recording or consent to the dealing in question.[14]
In relation to performers' property rights, consent of the performer is not a
defence if the performer was not the owner of the rights having assigned them
to another.

By the performer's agent—Part II of the 1988 Act does not contain any   **5.50**
provision corresponding to section 7 of the Dramatic and Musical Performers' Protection Act 1958.[15] It is not entirely clear what the effect of this

---

[9] *Clarkson v. Modern Foundries Ltd* [1957] 1 W.L.R. 1210.
[10] See Laddie, Prescott & Vitoria, note 91, above, paras. 17.17, 17.28–17.41.
[11] *Imperial Chemical Industries Ltd v. Berk Pharmaceuticals Ltd* [1981] F.S.R. 1; *Lansing Bagnall Ltd v. Buccaneer Lift Parts Ltd* [1984] F.S.R. 241; *British Leyland Motor Corp. Ltd v. Armstrong Patents Co. Ltd* [1986] R.P.C. 279; *Ransberg-Gema AG v. Electrostatic Plant Systems Ltd* [1990] F.S.R. 287; *Yale Security Products Ltd v. Newman* [1990] F.S.R. 320; *Pitney Bowes Inc. v. Francotyp-Postalia GmbH* [1990] 3 C.M.L.R. 466; *Chiron Corp v. Murex Diagnostics Ltd (No. 2)* [1994] F.S.R. 187.
[12] Copyright, Designs and Patents Act 1988, s. 193(1). Although this subsection is now excluded from application to performers' property rights by Reg. 21(3)(a) of the Copyright and Related Rights Regulations 1996 it is submitted that the same principles must nevertheless apply. See Chap. 3, para. 3.20.
[13] Dramatic and Musical Performers' Protection Act 1958, ss. 1–3; Performers' Protection Act 1963, s. 3.
[14] See Chap. 4, para. 4.43.
[15] Discussed in the first edition, Chap. 2, para. 2.82.

omission is. It continues to be an offence falsely to represent that one is authorised to give consent by a performer.[16] This would seem to imply that the representation may be true, that a performer can authorise another to give consent. Otherwise, the offence would one of purporting to give consent on behalf of a performer rather than of falsely representing. Moreover, in general the act of an agent is the act of his principal, and there is no reason why this should not be true here.

5.51 **By the performer's assignee**—Where a performer has assigned his property rights, consent of the assignee is a defence.[17]

5.52 **By the performer's estate**—After a performer's death, consent may be given by his legatee or (if there is no legatee) his personal representatives except insofar as the performers' property rights have been assigned to third parties.[18]

5.53 **By a person falsely representing himself as authorised to consent on behalf of the performer**—The omission of any provision corresponding to section 7 of the 1958 Act also raises the question whether a person who commits what would otherwise be a primary infringement[19] on the strength of consent purportedly given by another who falsely represents himself as authorised to consent on behalf of the performer (whether as the performer's agent, assignee or personal representative) has a defence. It appears that, at best, such a person merely has a defence to an award of damages,[20] rather than a complete defence.

5.54 **By the Copyright Tribunal**—The Copyright Tribunal can give consent in place of the owner of the reproduction right to what would otherwise be an infringement of performers' rights where the identity or whereabouts of the owner cannot be ascertained by reasonable inquiry. This is discussed in Chapter 3.[21]

5.55 **Consent upon terms**—Consent may be given upon terms, for example as to payment. This raises the question of what the result is if the terms are not complied with: is it infringement or merely breach of contract? There were conflicting authorities under the Copyright Act 1956 as to the problem of "conditional licences". In *Macaulay v. Screenkarn Ltd*,[22] it was held[23] that the licence was bound up with the observance of its conditions so that if the conditions were not complied with there was no licence. In *Hunter v. Fitzroy Robinson & Partners*,[24] on the other hand, it was held that that non-

---

[16] Copyright, Designs and Patents Act 1988, s. 201(1).
[17] *ibid.*, s. 191A(1).
[18] *ibid.*, s. 192(2).
[19] In the case of secondary infringement, such a person would doubtless have a defence on the basis that he lacked the requisite knowledge or reason for belief, having instead reason to believe that the recording was made *with* the performer's consent.
[20] Where it is a category (1), (2) or (3) infringement. See Chap. 6, paras. 6.24–6.25.
[21] paras. 3.24–3.33.
[22] [1987] F.S.R. 257 but not reported on this point.
[23] Following Kennedy J. in *The Incandescent Gas Light Co. Ltd v. Brogden* (1899) 16 R.P.C. 179, 183 (a patent case).
[24] [1978] F.S.R. 167.

compliance with the conditions was merely a breach of contract. It is submitted that the answer to this question should depend upon the application of normal contractual principles. Thus if the breach is either of a condition or is of an innominate term and is sufficiently serious to constitute repudiation, the performer may treat the agreement to give consent as at an end, so that any acts committed thereafter are infringements. If, on the other hand, the breach either is of a warranty or is of an innominate term but is not serious, the performer is restricted to his right to damages for breach of contract.

(b) Recording rights

By the performer—It is not clear from sections 186–188 of the Act whether consent by the performer without consent by the owner of the recording rights is a defence to an allegation of infringement. For the reasons discussed elsewhere,[25] however, it is submitted that it is. **5.56**

By the owner of the recording rights—By the same token, it is not clear whether consent by the owner of the recording rights without consent by the performer is a defence to an allegation of infringement. Again, it is submitted that it is. **5.57**

By the owner's agent—Since it is equally an offence under the 1988 Act falsely to represent that one is authorised to give consent on behalf of an owner of recording rights as it is in relation to a performer, it would seem that owners of recording rights may also authorise agents to consent.[26] **5.58**

By the Copyright Tribunal—The Copyright Tribunal is *not* empowered to consent to what would otherwise be an infringement of recording rights.[27] However, it would seem that the giving of consent by the Tribunal on behalf of a performer would prevent there being any infringement of recording rights. **5.59**

2. Free circulation within the European Economic Area

A recording which has been sold in any other EEA State by or with the consent of the owner of a performer's property rights is in free circulation, and accordingly it may be imported into the United Kingdom and dealt with here (other than by rental or lending) without infringing performers' rights. This topic is dealt with in Chapter 4.[28] **5.60**

3. "Innocence"

Part II of the 1988 Act contains no explicit defence of innocence.[29] It will, however, be a defence to allegations of secondary infringement (not of **5.61**

---

[25] See Chap. 4, paras. 4.65–4.69.
[26] *cf.* para. 5.50, above.
[27] See Chap. 3, para. 3.27.
[28] paras. 4.29–4.30; see also para. 4.50.
[29] Although certain innocence-type defences to damages are provided. See Chap. 6, paras. 6.23–6.28.

primary infringement) that the alleged infringer did not have the required knowledge or reason for belief.[30]

4. Private and domestic use/private or domestic use

(a) Of the maker of the recording

5.62 **Primary infringement**—It is a defence to allegations of category (1), (3) and (4)[31] infringement that the recording was made for private and domestic use only. The defence is inapplicable to category (2) infringement, since the infringing act is committed without use of a recording. It is not a defence to category (5) infringement that either the recording was or the copies were made for private and domestic use.

5.63 **Secondary infringement**—Curiously, that the recording was made for private and domestic use only is *not* a defence to category (7) and category (8) secondary infringement, but *is* a defence to category (9) and category (10) secondary infringement. That a recording made without consent was not a primary infringement since it was originally made for private and domestic use is no defence to an allegation of secondary infringement if the recording is subsequently shown in public or broadcast or included in a cable programme without consent.[32] A recording made without consent for private purposes is not an "illicit recording",[33] however, and so importation of and dealing in the recording cannot amount to secondary infringement.[34] It is difficult to see the rationale for this distinction.

(b) Of the importer

5.64 It is a defence to an allegation of category (9) secondary infringement (importation) that the recording was imported for the private and domestic use only of the importer.[35] This is so whether or not the recording was made for private purposes.

5. Arrangements made before commencement

5.65 Although Part II of the Copyright, Designs and Patents Act 1988 came into force on August 1, 1989,[36] so that it was possible for performers' rights and recording rights to be infringed from that day, the Act provides that no act done in pursuance of arrangements made before August 1, 1989 is to be regarded as infringing.[37] Since the Performers' Protection Acts 1958–1972 were repealed in their entirety on August 1, 1989,[38] acts done after that day,

---

[30] See Chap. 4, paras. 4.70–4.78.
[31] See Chap. 4, paras. 4.02 and 4.63 for summaries of the categories of infringing acts.
[32] See Chap. 4, paras. 4.40–4.43.
[33] See Chap. 4, paras. 4.47–4.49.
[34] See Chap. 4, paras. 4.45–4.62. By contrast, recordings made for certain permitted purposes (as to which see paras. 5.11, 5.15, 5.27, 5.41 above) are "illicit" if subsequently dealt in: Copyright, Designs and Patents Act 1988, s. 197(5).
[35] See Chap. 4, paras. 4.45–4.48.
[36] Copyright, Designs and Patents Act 1988 (Commencement No. 1) Order 1989 (S.I. 1989 No. 816).
[37] Copyright, Designs and Patents Act 1988, s. 180(3).
[38] *ibid.*, s. 303(2) and Sched. 8; Copyright, Designs and Patents Act 1988 (Commencement No. 1) Order 1989, note 36, above.

but pursuant to "arrangements made" before it, are not caught by either the Performers' Protection Acts or by Part II of the new Act. This suggests that "arrangements" should be narrowly interpreted.[39]

Section 180(3) of the 1988 Act provides that no act done "in pursuance of arrangements made" before August 1, 1989 is to be regarded as an infringement. It is uncertain precisely what is meant by this. It seems clear that it is meant to protect a person who, for example, enters into a contract to sell 10,000 records, sells 5,000 before 1 August and sells 5,000 after 1 August. The rationale for this is unclear, however, for if the records sold after 1 August would otherwise be infringements, it is likely that the sales before 1 August would be actionable under the Performers' Protection Act as interpreted in the *Peter Sellers* case.[40] The explanation may lie in the absence of a requirement of knowledge with respect to certain categories of infringement under the 1988 Act.[41] Whatever the explanation, the lacuna that is created by section 180(3) suggests that "arrangements" should be construed narrowly. The word is wide enough, however, to cover situations other than direct contractual relationships. Thus a person who makes records pursuant to a sub-contract made after August 1, 1989 but under a main contract made before 1 August is arguably protected. **5.66**

By contrast, Regulation 27(2) of the Copyright and Related Rights Regulations 1996 provides that no act done pursuant to an agreement (not arrangement) made before November 19, 1992 infringes any new right (*i.e.* a right arising by virtue of the Regulations). **5.67**

---

[39] In *Grower v. BBC* [1990] F.S.R. 595 it was conceded that the plaintiffs had no cause of action under the 1988 Act in relation to acts done pursuant to a copyright licence granted in July 1988.
[40] [1988] Q.B. 40.
[41] An alternative, if unlikely, explanation is that Parliament considers the decision in the *Peter Sellers* case to be wrong and liable to be overruled by the House of Lords.

6. Proceedings

INTRODUCTION

6.01 As with copyright in Part I, Part II of the Copyright, Designs and Patents Act 1988 provides three different procedures for enforcing performers' rights and recording rights, namely (1) a full-blown action for infringement, (2) stand-alone applications for delivery-up and forfeiture and (3) a self-help remedy consisting of a right of seizure. The amendments introduced by the Copyright and Related Rights Regulations 1996 have complicated the position in relation to performers' property rights by introducing provisions modelled on the corresponding copyright infringement provisions. The main changes of substance as a result of this are that exclusive licensees have a concurrent right of action and an account of profits is now available as a remedy.

WHO MAY SUE?

1. Performers' property rights

6.02 Proceedings may be commenced by the owner of performers' property rights for the time being (who may well not be the performer)[1] or by an exclusive licensee (whether or not the exclusive licensee has recording rights).[2]

Legal owner

6.03 The legal owner (who if he is not the performer must have acquired his title by an assignment in writing signed by the assignor, by testamentary disposition or by operation of law) has an unfettered power to bring proceedings. Where there are joint owners, each owner may sue without joining the others and without their consent.[3] In an appropriate case a plaintiff may sue in a representative capacity.[4] This is frequently done in anti-piracy copyright actions.

---

[1] Copyright, Designs and Patents Act 1988, s. 191I(1).
[2] *ibid.*, s. 191L.
[3] *Powell v. Head* (1879) 12 Ch. D. 686; *Trade Auxiliary Co v. Middlesborough and District Tradesman's Protection Association* (1889) 40 Ch. D. 425, 434; *Prior v. Lansdowne Press Pty Ltd* [1977] R.P.C. 511.
[4] *EMI Records Ltd v. Riley* [1981] 1 All E.R. 293; *CBS Songs Ltd v. Amstrad Consumer Electronics plc* [1987] R.P.C. 429, 445, 465–466.

Beneficial owner

The owner of equitable title to performers' property rights (for example, an **6.04** assignee whose assignment does not fulfil the statutory requirements) may commence proceedings in his own name and obtain interlocutory relief.[5] He cannot, however, obtain relief at trial unless he either joins the legal owner or acquires the legal title before judgment.[6] Nevertheless, it is safest to obtain an assignment of the legal title before issuing the writ.[7]

Exclusive licensee

An exclusive licensee has, except against the owner of the rights, the same **6.05** rights and remedies in respect of matters occurring after the grant of the licence as if the licence were an assignment.[8] An exclusive licence for this purpose is defined as:

> a licence in writing signed by or on behalf of the owner of a performer's property rights authorising the licensee to the exclusion of all other persons, including the person granting the licence, to do anything requiring the consent of the rights owner.[9]

Since the exclusive licensee's rights and remedies are concurrent with those of the owner, either may bring proceedings. Whichever one commences proceedings, he cannot proceed with the action beyond an application for interlocutory relief[10] without joining the other one (either as plaintiff or as defendant) without the leave of the court.[11] Where the other is added as defendant, he is not liable for any costs unless he takes part in the proceedings.[12] Where the exclusive licensee sues, the defendant may avail himself of any defence which would have been available to him if the action had been brought by the copyright owner.[13] It appears that the effect of conferring concurrent rights of action on an exclusive licensee is that the exclusive licensee will have rights and remedies even if he does not have recording rights (*e.g.* because he is not a qualifying person).

Mere licensee

A non-exclusive licensee has no right of action. **6.06**

---

[5] *Merchant Adventurers Ltd v. M. Grew & Co.* [1971] 1 Ch. 242.
[6] *Batjac Productions Inc. v. Simitar Entertainment (U.K.) Ltd* [1996] F.S.R. 139 applying *Performing Right Society Ltd v London Theatre of Varieties* [1924] A.C. 1.
[7] The problems that can be encountered are illustrated by the cases of *Nicol v. Barranger* [1917–1923] M.C.C. 219 and *Roban Jig & Tool Co. Ltd v. Taylor* [1979] F.S.R. 130 in both of which it was held that the plaintiffs had no title to sue despite attempts to secure their title.
[8] Copyright, Designs and Patents Act 1988, s. 191L(1).
[9] *ibid.*, s. 191D(1).
[10] *ibid.*, s. 191M(3).
[11] *ibid.*, s. 191M(1).
[12] *ibid.*, s. 191M(2).
[13] *ibid.*, s. 191L(3).

2. Performers' non-property rights and recording rights

6.07 The owner for the time being of performers' non-property rights (*i.e.* the performer or his heirs or personal representatives) or of recording rights may commence proceedings. Since there does not appear to be any scope for separate beneficial ownership of performers' rights other than property rights or of recording rights, this means the legal owner. Where there are joint owners, one may commence proceedings without joining the other owners and without their consent.[14] There is no right of action for an exclusive licensee of performers' non-property rights (though a beneficiary of an exclusive recording contract may have his own separate recording rights).

WHO MAY BE SUED?

6.08 Any infringer may be sued, that is to say any person who commits one of the acts restricted by performers' rights or recording rights without the appropriate consent.[15] Persons who procure the commission of such acts or participate in a common design to commit such acts may be sued as joint tortfeasors on normal principles.[16] There is no specific tort of authorisation, as with copyright,[17] however. In an appropriate case a defendant may be sued in a representative capacity.[18]

VENUE

6.09 It seems clear that actions for infringement of performers' rights and recording rights may be brought in the county court[19] as well as in the High Court. Such an action would appear to be within the general jurisdiction of the county court to hear actions in tort, and not to be excluded by the bar on actions concerning title to a franchise.[20] It is expressly provided, however, that applications for the "stand-alone" remedies of delivery up and forfeiture may be made in the county court,[21] which might be thought to suggest that the county court would not otherwise have jurisdiction. It is submitted that the explanation for this is that section 15 of the County Courts Act 1984 only gives the county court jurisdiction to hear "any action", and that such applications would not fall within this.

---

[14] See note 3, above.
[15] A person who is holding illicit recordings but has not infringed may be made the respondent to an application for delivery up and forfeiture, see paras. 6.31–6.38, below.
[16] See *Grower v. BBC* [1990] F.S.R. 595, *C. Evans & Sons Ltd v. Spritebrand Ltd* [1985] 1 W.L.R. 317; *CBS Songs Ltd v. Amstrad Consumer Electronics plc* [1988] A.C. 1013 and *Unilever plc v. Gillette U.K. Ltd* [1989] R.P.C. 583.
[17] Copyright, Designs and Patents Act 1988, s. 16(2).
[18] *EMI Records Ltd v. Kudhail* [1985] F.S.R. 36.
[19] Subject to the usual rules on venue, as to which see the *County Court Practice*.
[20] County Courts Act 1984, s. 15.
[21] Copyright, Designs and Patents Act 1988, s. 205(1). See para. 6.36, below.

REMEDIES

Performers' property rights

For the purposes of remedies for infringement, performers' property rights **6.10** are assimilated to copyright. Thus is it is expressly provided that the following remedies are available: injunctions, damages or accounts or profits, delivery up, seizure and forfeiture.[22]

Performers' non-property rights and recording rights

Sections 194 to 197 (inclusive) of Part II of the 1988 Act are headed by the **6.11** rubric "Remedies for infringement". It is curious, however, that the only remedies expressly provided are delivery up, seizure and forfeiture of illicit recordings.[23] Furthermore, it appears that these three remedies are available independently of an action for infringement (although the Act is not as explicit as it might be about this). Otherwise, it is merely stated that infringement is actionable as breach of statutory duty.[24] Presumably it is to be inferred that the normal remedies for breach of statutory duty are available. The remedies available therefore appear to be as follows: injunctions, damages, delivery up, seizure and forfeiture.

1. Injunctions

An injunction will issue to restrain further infringements on normal **6.12** principles. It should be remembered that injunctions are an equitable remedy, and so may be refused on equitable grounds such as delay or unclean hands.

Innocence

In addition, the 1988 Act provides two "innocence" defences which prevent **6.13** the grant of an injunction against an infringer. In both cases the burden of proof is upon the defendant.

(a) Secondary infringements of performers' rights—In actions for category **6.14** (9) and (10)[25] infringements of performers' rights, the only remedy available against a defendant who shows that the illicit recording was innocently acquired by him or by a predecessor in title of his is damages not exceeding a reasonable payment in respect of the act complained of.[26] "Innocently acquired" means that the person acquiring the recording did not know and had no reason to believe that it was an illicit recording.[27] Curiously, this defence is not available in respect of category (7) and (8) infringements. What is a "reasonable payment" will naturally depend on the circumstances of each case, but a possible method of assessment would be to award a reasonable royalty, that is, whatever is the going rate for acts of the kind in question.

(b) Secondary infringements of recording rights—In actions for category **6.15**

---

[22] *ibid.*, s. 191L(2).
[23] *ibid.*, ss. 195 and 196. See paras. 6.31–6.59, below.
[24] *ibid.*, s. 194. *cf.* s. 96(2) in Part I and s. 229(2) of Part III.
[25] See Chap. 4, para. 4.02 for the categories of infringement.
[26] Copyright, Designs and Patents Act 1988, s. 184(2).
[27] *ibid.*, s. 184(3).

(4) and (5)[28] infringements of recording rights, the only remedy available against a defendant who shows that the illicit recording was innocently acquired by him or by a predecessor in title of his is damages not exceeding a reasonable payment in respect of the act complained of.[29] "Innocently acquired" means that the person acquiring the recording did not know and had no reason to believe that it was an illicit recording.[30] Again, this defence is not available in respect of category (2) and (3) infringements.

Undertaking to take licence of right

6.16 Where there is a licence of right under paragraph 17 of Schedule 2A[31] and the defendant gives an undertaking to take such a licence on such terms as may be agreed or settled by the Copyright Tribunal, then no injunction may be granted against him.[32] The undertaking may be given at any time before final order in the proceedings without any admission of liability.[33]

2. Damages

6.17 Since performers' property rights are a property right, infringement is actionable without proof of damage.[34] The position is different for other performers' rights and recording, however, since these are actionable as breach of statutory duty.[35] It is a requirement for any action for breach of statutory duty that the plaintiff establish damage of a kind against which the statute was designed to give protection.[36] In the present case, it is clear that the statute is designed to give protection against the damage caused by unauthorised exploitation of performances, which will primarily be economic loss. It will be rare for a plaintiff to have difficulty in establishing that he has suffered or will suffer damage of this kind. More problematic will be the question of quantification.

Measure of damages

6.18 (a) **Performers' property rights**—In the case of performers' property rights, as with copyright, the measure of damages is assessed on the basis that the defendant has invaded the plaintiff's property.[37] Accordingly, the measure of damages for infringement of these rights depends on whether the owner of the rights exploits his property and, if so, how. If the owner exploits his property by making and selling copies of recordings of the performance, then the invasion of his property will cause damage to this business and he will be compensated for the loss subject to the normal principles of causation and remoteness.[38] If the owner exploits his property by licensing it, then prima facie the owner has merely lost an opportunity to grant a licence and the

---

[28] See Chap. 4, para. 4.63 for the categories of infringement.
[29] Copyright, Designs and Patents Act 1988, s. 184(2).
[30] *ibid.*, s. 184(3).
[31] See Chap. 3, paras. 3.37–3.39.
[32] Copyright, Designs and Patents Act 1988, s. 191K(1)(a).
[33] *ibid.*, s. 191K(2).
[34] *ibid.*, s. 191I(2).
[35] *ibid.*, s. 194.
[36] *Halsbury's Laws* (4th ed.), Vol. 45, para. 1279.
[37] Note 34, above.
[38] *Gerber Garment Technology Ltd v. Lectra Systems Ltd* (*The Times*, January 17, 1997).

damages will be assessed at his normal royalty rate[39] although an increase may be awarded.[40] If the owner does not exploit his property, a reasonable royalty for the use made of the property by the infringer will be awarded.[41] Where some of the infringer's sales represent lost sales to the plaintiff but others do not, lost profits may be awarded for the former and a royalty for the latter.[42]

(b) Performers' non-property rights and recording rights—Performers' non-property rights and recording rights, however, are clearly not property rights although they are otherwise very similar. This poses a difficulty: should the measure of damages for infringement of these rights be assessed as if they are property rights or not? It is submitted that the just and convenient course is to proceed on this basis. It is just because it will ensure that performers are properly compensated for infringements of their rights. It is convenient because it will mean that the courts have ready to hand a set of principles established by copyright case law for the assessment of damages (that is, those outlined in the preceding paragraph). Any other approach would be fraught with uncertainty. **6.19**

Matters to be taken into account

The Act does, however, contain four provisions as to the quantification of damages in particular circumstances: **6.20**

(1)   Where the owner of performers' property rights and an exclusive licensee have concurrent rights of action, the court must, when assessing damages, take into account the terms of the licence and any damages or profits already awarded or available to them in respect of the infringement.[43]

(2)   Although it is not an infringement to show or play in public a broadcast or cable programme to an audience who have not paid for admission to the place where the broadcast or programme is played or shown,[44] if the making of the broadcast or the inclusion of the programme in the service was an infringement, then the fact that it was seen or heard in public by reception of the broadcast or programme is to be taken into account in assessing the damages for that infringement.[45]

(3)   Similarly, although it is not an infringement to retransmit a broadcast as part of a cable programme service in certain circumstances,[46] where the making of the broadcast was infringement, then the fact that it was retransmitted is also to be taken into account.[47]

---

[39] *General Tire & Rubber Co. v. Firestone Tyre & Rubber Co.* [1976] R.P.C. 197.
[40] *Chabot v. Davies* [1936] 3 All E.R. 221.
[41] See *Meikle v. Maufe* [1941] 3 All E.R. 144; *Stovin-Bradford v. Volpoint Properties Ltd* [1971] Ch. 1007 and *General Tire & Rubber Co. v. Firestone Tyre & Rubber Co.*, note 39, above.
[42] *Gerber Garment Technology Ltd v. Lectra Systems Ltd* [1995] R.P.C. 383.
[43] Copyright, Designs and Patents Act 1988, s. 191M(4)(a).
[44] See Chap. 5, para. 5.43.
[45] Copyright, Designs and Patents Act 1988, Sched. 2, para. 18(4).
[46] See Chap. 5, para. 5.44.
[47] Copyright, Designs and Patents Act 1988, Sched. 2, para. 19(2).

(4) Where there is a licence of right under paragraph 17 of Schedule 2A and the defendant undertakes to take a licence, the damages awarded against him shall not exceed double the amount which would have been payable by him as licensee if such a licence had been granted before the earliest infringement.[48] Thus although the licence will not be retrospective,[49] the cap on damages will be. This does not apply to any infringement committed before the licence of right became available, however.[50]

Additional, aggravated and exemplary damages

6.21 For infringements of performers' property rights, additional damages may be awarded, that is to say, damages which are additional to the damages required to compensate the plaintiff for his loss.[51] It has been held in an English copyright case that additional damages may also be awarded where the successful plaintiff elects for an account of profits rather than damages,[52] but this has been disapproved by the Inner House of the Court of Session.[52a] The court has a general discretion as to whether to award additional damages and if so in what amount,[53] but it is to have particular regard to (a) the flagrancy of the infringement and (b) any benefit accruing to the defendant by reason of the infringement.[54] Flagrancy includes scandalous conduct, deceit and deliberate and calculated infringement.[55] The reference to benefit to the defendant shows that the section may be used to prevent unjust enrichment of the defendant, and so to some extent this provision creates an overlap with the remedy of an account of profits. Additional damages may be awarded for non-financial injury to the plaintiff or benefit to the defendant.[56] It is common for the issue of whether or not to award additional damages to be decided at trial, leaving the quantum to be decided on the inquiry,[57] but the issue of principle can be left over to the inquiry as well.

6.22 Additional damages are not available for infringements of performers' non-property rights or recording rights. It appears, however, that additional damages are merely a statutory form of aggravated damages.[58] Aggravated damages are damages awarded where the defendant has invaded a property right in such a way as to injure the plaintiff's feelings and dignity.[59] If the

---

[48] *ibid.*, s. 191K(1)(c).
[49] *Allen & Hanburys Ltd v. Generics (U.K.) Ltd* [1986] R.P.C. 203.
[50] Copyright, Designs and Patents Act 1988, s. 191K(3).
[51] *ibid.*, s. 191J(2).
[52] *Cala Homes (South) Ltd v. Alfred McAlpine Homes East Ltd (No. 2)* [1996] F.S.R. 36.
[52a] *Redrow Homes Ltd v. Bett Brothers plc* (*The Times*, May 2, 1997).
[53] *Concrete Systems Pty Ltd v. Devon Symonds Holdings Ltd* (1978) 20 A.L.R. 677, 683 (commenting on corresponding Australian provision).
[54] Copyright, Designs and Patents Act 1988, s. 191J(2).
[55] *Ravenscroft v. Herbert* [1980] R.P.C. 193; *Nichol Advanced Vehicle Systems Inc. v. Rees* [1979] R.P.C. 127; *ZYX Music GmbH v. King* [1995] EMLR 281.
[56] *Nichols Advanced Vehicle Systems Inc. v. Rees*, note 55, above.
[57] See *Nichols Advanced Vehicle Systems Inc. v. Rees* and *ZYX Music GmbH v. King*, both note 55, above.
[58] *Rookes v. Barnard* [1964] A.C. 1129, 1225; *Broome v. Cassell & Co. Ltd* [1972] A.C. 1027, 1134; *Beloff v. Pressdram Ltd* [1973] 1 All E.R. 241, 265–266.
[59] See *McGregor on Damages* (15th ed., Sweet & Maxwell, 1988), para. 409.

courts are prepared to assess damages for infringements of performers' non-property rights and recording rights on the basis that they are to be treated as property rights, it is arguably open to the courts to award aggravated damages if the circumstances warrant it.

Exemplary damages are not available whether for infringements of performers' property rights or of the other rights under Part II.[60]   **6.23**

Innocence

The 1988 Act provides a number of "innocence" defences which either prevent or limit awards of damages. In all cases the burden of proof is upon the defendant.   **6.23**

(a) Primary infringements of performers' rights—In actions for category (1), (2) and (3)[61] infringements of performers' rights, damages may not be awarded against a defendant who shows that at the time of the infringement he believed on reasonable grounds that consent had been given.[62] It appears that the principal beneficiaries of this provision will be persons who are the victims of false representations of authority to give consent.   **6.24**

In actions for infringement of any performers' property rights, damages may not be awarded against a defendant who shows that at the time of infringement he did not know, and had no reason to believe, that the rights subsisted in the recording to which the action relates.[63] This is not a question of not knowing the law, but of not knowing and having no reason to believe the facts relevant to subsistence. Thus the defence is of narrow scope, and does not protect victims of false representations of authority to grant a licence.[64] Furthermore, it has been held that the defence is not available to a defendant who copies material without making inquiries as to the source of what he is copying.[65]   **6.25**

(b) Secondary infringements of performers' rights—In actions for category (9) and (10) infringements of performers' rights, the only remedy available against a defendant who shows that the illicit recording was innocently acquired by him or by a predecessor in title of his is damages not exceeding a reasonable payment in respect of the act complained of.[66] "Innocently acquired" means that the person acquiring the recording did not know and had no reason to believe that it was an illicit recording.[67] Curiously, this defence is not available in respect of category (7) and (8) infringements.   **6.26**

(c) Primary infringements of recording rights—In actions for category (1)[68] infringements of recording rights, damages may not be awarded against   **6.27**

---

[60] *A.B. v. South West Water Services Ltd* [1993] Q.B. 507 explaining *Rookes v. Barnard* [1964] A.C. 1129 and *Cassell & Co. Ltd v. Broome* [1972] A.C. 1027.
[61] See Chap. 4, para. 4.02 for the categories of infringement.
[62] Copyright, Designs and Patents Act 1988, s. 182(3).
[63] *ibid.*, s. 191J(1).
[64] *Byrne v. Statist Co.* [1914] 1 K.B. 622.
[65] *Cramp v. Smythson* [1943] 1 Ch. 133.
[66] Copyright, Designs and Patents Act 1988, s. 184(2).
[67] *ibid.*, s. 184(3).
[68] See Chap. 4, para. 4.63 for the categories of infringement.

a defendant who shows that at the time of the infringement he believed on reasonable grounds that consent had been given.[69]

6.28 **(d) Secondary infringements of recording rights**—In actions for category (4) and (5) infringements of recording rights, the only remedy available against a defendant who shows that the illicit recording was innocently acquired by him or by a predecessor in title of his is damages not exceeding a reasonable payment in respect of the act complained of.[70] "Innocently acquired" means that the person acquiring the recording did not know and had no reason to believe that it was an illicit recording.[71] Again, this defence is not available in respect of category (2) and (3) infringements.

Account of profits

6.29 Where performers' property rights have been infringed, the successful plaintiff may elect[72] for an account of profits instead of an award of damages.[73] Unlike an award of damages, however, an account of profits is an equitable remedy and so the court has a discretion whether or not to order it. For example, an account may be refused if the plaintiff has delayed[74] or the infringement is trivial. The basis of an account is the prevention of unjust enrichment, in that the infringer is required to hand over to the plaintiff the net profits he has made from the infringement. The infringer is usually permitted an allowance for his skill and labour.[75] The difficulty and complexity of accounts mean that they are rarely opted for except in situations where the plaintiff has suffered no loss and a notional royalty would be likely to be small. In addition, an account of profits may be elected where damages may not be awarded because the defendant has made out an "innocence" defence.

6.30 Where the owner of performers' property rights and an exclusive licensee have concurrent rights of action, no account of profits may be directed in favour of one if an award of damages has been made, or an account of profits directed, in favour of the other in respect of the same infringement.[76] If an account of profits is directed, the court shall apportion the profits between the rights owner and the licensee as its considers just, subject to any agreement between them.[77]

---

[69] Copyright, Designs and Patents Act 1988, s. 186(2).

[70] *ibid.*, s. 184(2).

[71] *ibid.*, s. 184(3).

[72] The election is to be made once the plaintiff has sufficient information to make an informed choice and for this purpose the defendant may ordered to give discovery or an affidavit: *Island Records Ltd v. Tring International plc* [1995] F.S.R. 560 and *Brugger v. Medic-Aid Ltd* [1996] F.S.R. 362.

[73] Copyright, Designs and Patents Act 1988, s. 191I(2).

[74] *Edward Young & Co. Ltd v. Stanley S. Holt* (1947) 65 R.P.C. 25; *Electrolux Ltd v. Electrix Ltd* (1953) 70 R.P.C. 158.

[75] *Redwood Music Ltd v. Chappell & Co. Ltd* [1982] R.P.C. 109; *Potton Ltd v. Yorkclose Ltd* [1990] F.S.R. 11.

[76] Copyright, Designs and Patents Act 1988, s. 191M(4)(b).

[77] *ibid.*, s. 191M(4)(c).

3. Statutory delivery up

Section 195 of the 1988 Act enables the owner of performers' rights or recording rights in a performance (and an exclusive licensee of performers' property rights[78]) to apply to the court for an order for delivery up of illicit recordings of that performance. The remedy is subject to certain restrictions and conditions, however. These may be tabulated as follows: **6.31**

(i) The remedy only applies to "illicit" recordings.

(ii) Only illicit recordings that are in the possession, custody or control of the respondent (to the application for an order) in the course of a business may be ordered to be delivered up.[79]

(iii) Applications may not be made after the expiry of the limitation period imposed by section 203 of the Act.[80]

(iv) No order for delivery up may be made unless the court also makes, or it appears to the court that there are grounds for making, an order under section 204 of the Act for forfeiture or destruction of the illicit recording.[81]

(v) The person to whom a recording is delivered up must, if an order under section 204 has not been made, retain it pending a decision of the court whether or not to make such an order.[82]

(vi) Where an exclusive licensee of performer's property rights has concurrent rights, the owner must notify him before applying for an order,[83] and the exclusive licensee can oppose the granting of the order.[84]

Illicit recording

'Illicit recording" is defined in section 197 of the Act.[85] It is submitted that the recording must actually be an illicit recording and not only arguably so,[86] for delivery up to be ordered under the statutory provisions (as opposed to an interim delivery up order under the court's inherent jurisdiction, which is not affected by the statutory provisions[87]). This, of course, raises the question of how the court is to know this if the application is made otherwise than at the conclusion of a trial or summary judgment application.[88] The answer would appear to be that, if there is a dispute as to whether the recordings are illicit or **6.32**

---

[78] *ibid.,* s. 191L(1).
[79] *ibid.,* s. 195(1).
[80] *ibid.,* s. 195(2).
[81] *ibid.*
[82] *ibid.,* s. 195(3).
[83] Strangely, the converse does not apply.
[84] Copyright, Designs and Patents Act 1988, s. 19M(5).
[85] See Chap. 4, paras. 4.47–4.49.
[86] Although *Lagenes Ltd v. It's At (U.K.) Ltd* [1991] F.S.R. 492 might appear at first sight to be authority to the contrary, the actual order under consideration in that case was a *Norwich Pharmacal*-type order for the disclosure of the identities of customers to whom allegedly infringing goods had been supplied. Ferris J. observed at 505 that the issue whether the goods were infringing would not decided as between the plaintiff and the persons in possession of the goods until proceedings under section 99 were brought against those parties, which would seem to be correct.
[87] Copyright, Designs and Patents Act 1988, s. 195(4).
[88] See para 6.36 below.

not which has yet to be resolved by a judicial determination, the statutory remedy is not available and the plaintiff must obtain such relief as he can under the court's inherent jurisdiction. This view of the matter is consistent with the fact that the statutory remedy was introduced mainly as a partial substitute for conversion damages.[89]

Possession in the course of a business

6.33　This restriction reflects the corresponding definition of secondary infringement in sections 184(1)(b) and 188(1)(b) of the Act, and is subject to the same difficulties of construction.[90]

Limitation period

6.34　No application for an order for delivery up may be made after the end of six years from date on which the illicit recording (or article) was made,[91] unless

(a) the applicant is under a disability within the meaning of the Limitation Act 1980, or
(b) is prevented by fraud or concealment from discovering the facts entitling him to apply,

in which case an application may be made up to six years from when the applicant ceases to be under a disability or could with reasonable diligence have discovered the facts.[92]

No order unless grounds for order under section 204

6.35　No order may be made for delivery up unless one is also made for forfeiture or destruction under section 204 or there are grounds for making such an order.[93] For this reason it would seem sensible to combine applications under sections 195 and 204 where this is feasible.[94]

Mode of application

6.36　Applications for delivery up may be made in England, Wales and Northern Ireland in the county court, but in Northern Ireland the county court can only entertain the application where the value of the illicit recordings in question does not exceed the county court limit for actions in tort.[95] In Scotland such applications may be made in the sheriff court.[96] The jurisdiction of the High Court and Court of Session is stated to be unaffected,[97] and so presumably applications may also be made in these courts. It is not entirely clear what

---

[89] H. L. Deb., Vol. 491, ser. 5, col. 410 (Earl of Dundee) (1987).
[90] See Chap. 4, paras. 4.52–4.57.
[91] Copyright, Designs and Patents Act 1988, s. 203(1).
[92] *ibid.*, s. 203(2).
[93] See paras. 6.50–6.59.
[94] See paras. 6.57–6.58 for further discussion.
[95] Copyright, Designs and Patents Act 1988, s. 205(1) (as amended by the High Court and County Courts Jurisdiction Order 1991 (S.I. 1991 No. 724)).
[96] Copyright, Designs and Patents Act 1988, s. 205(2). Application is by motion or incidental application where proceedings have been commenced and by summary application where no proceedings have been commenced: Act of Sederunt (Copyright, Designs and Patents) 1990 (S.I. 1990 No. 380) (S. 37), para. 2(2).
[97] Copyright, Designs and Patents Act, 1988, s. 205(3).

procedure should be followed if the application is made outside an action for infringement. In the High Court the most appropriate procedure would seem to be by way of an originating motion under Order 8 of the Rules of the Supreme Court; applications under section 204, however, are to be made by originating summons under Order 7,[98] and so it may be advisable to adopt this procedure for applications under section 195 as well. If the application is made in a pending action, the appropriate procedure would be a summons or motion; but if relief is only sought at trial there does not appear to be any reason why it should not simply be claimed in the writ and prayer in the normal way.[99]

Whether application is made in the county court or in the High Court, an important question the answer to which is unclear from the Act is whether or not an application may be made *ex parte*. The requirement for service of notice of applications under section 204[1] suggests that applications under section 204 must be made *inter partes*; conversely, the absence of such a requirement under section 195 may indicate that an application under this section can be made *ex parte*.

Interlocutory or final?

It should be noted that a combined order under sections 195 and 204 is final, regardless of what stage the action (if any) has reached; whereas an order under section 195 alone is in a sense "interlocutory", in that it is subject to the making or refusal of an order under section 204, although not to judgment in the action (if any). Either way, however, it would seem that there is no requirement for the applicant to give a cross-undertaking in damages pending an order under section 204 or judgment in any action, as is normally the case where interlocutory relief is sought.

4. Seizure of illicit recordings

Section 196 of the 1988 Act provides for what has been described as a "do-it-yourself Anton Piller order", namely a right for owners of performers' rights and recording rights (and exclusive licensees of performers' property rights[2]) and persons authorised by them to seize illicit recordings without first obtaining a court order. A more accurate, if less catchy, description would be "do-it-yourself *ex parte* delivery up order", since the section only applies to premises to which the public have access; there is nothing to require a person to permit access to private premises so that they may be searched, as in a true Anton Piller order. Furthermore, the right is only available in limited circumstances and subject to stringent conditions. These may be tabulated as follows:

   (i)   The right only applies to "illicit" recordings.

6.37

6.38

6.39

---

[98] See para. 6.53.
[99] But see para. 6.59.
[1] See para. 6.54.
[2] Copyright, Designs and Patents Act 1988, s. 191L(1).

(ii) The right only applies to an illicit recording in respect of which the person by or on whose behalf the right of seizure is exercised would be entitled to apply for an order for delivery up under section 195.[3]

(iii) Only illicit recordings which are found exposed or otherwise immediately available for sale or hire may be seized.[4]

(iv) Before anything is seized notice of the time and place of the proposed seizure must be given to a local police station.[5]

(v) Premises to which the public have access may be entered for the purpose of exercising the right, but nothing in the possession, custody or control of a person at a permanent or regular place of business of that person may be seized.[6]

(vi) The person exercising the right of seizure may not use any force.[7]

(vii) At the time when anything is seized, notice must be left at the place where it is seized in prescribed form containing prescribed particulars as to the person by whom or on whose authority the seizure is made and the grounds upon which it is made.[8]

(viii)The right is subject to any decision of the court under section 204.[9]

(ix) Where an exclusive licensee of performer's property rights has concurrent rights the owner must notify him before exercising the right,[10] and the exclusive licensee can apply to the court for an order prohibiting the owner from exercising the right.[11]

Entitled to apply for an order under section 195

6.40   This appears to be an indirect way of importing into section 196 the limitations:

(a) that an illicit recording can only be seized from a person who has it in his possession, custody or control in the course of a business[12] and

(b) that an illicit recording cannot be seized after the expiry of the limitation period imposed by section 203.[13]

6.41   It is not, however, a requirement that the right owner would succeed in obtaining an order under section 195. Therefore it would seem that this does *not* import the limitation that the court be satisfied that there are grounds for making an order under section 204.[14] This is important, because otherwise a person exercising the right of seizure would be subject to the notional comparison with other remedies in an action for infringement.[15]

6.42   It is not quite clear what the position is if an illicit recording is seized by or

---

[3] *ibid.*, s. 196(1).
[4] *ibid.*
[5] *ibid.*, s. 196(2).
[6] *ibid.*, s. 196(3).
[7] *ibid.*
[8] *ibid.*, s. 191A(5)(b), applying s. 100(4) and s. 196(4).
[9] *ibid.*, s. 196(1).
[10] Again the converse does not apply.
[11] Copyright, Designs and Patents Act 1988, s. 191M(5).
[12] See para. 6.33.
[13] See para. 6.34.
[14] See para. 6.35.
[15] See paras. 6.51–6.53.

on behalf of a person who is not entitled to apply for such an order. Presumably, though, he would be liable to an action for wrongful interference for goods. (The same is true if it turns out that the recording is not illicit.)

Exposed or otherwise immediately available for sale

This formulation appears to be apt to cover goods that are either (a) on **6.43** display or (b) for sale from stock, both of which situations are as a matter of contract law regarded as merely invitations to treat.

Notice of the time and place of the proposed seizure

It would appear that the requirement of notice to a police station is intended **6.44** to ensure that exercise of the right of seizure does not cause a breach of the peace.[16] There is no duty upon the police to take any action upon receipt of the notice, however. It will, therefore, be a matter for the discretion of the duty officer whether any action is taken. Many may take the view that their resources are already overstretched without intervening in what is essentially a civil dispute. Curiously, no minimum period of advance notice is required: one minute's notice would appear to comply. Furthermore, the requirement is merely to notify *a* local police station, not *the* local police station, raising the question of how local is "local" for the purposes of the section. Finally, no set form of notice is prescribed. A notice modelled on that prescribed under section 196(4)[17] would appear to be satisfactory. It would seem, on the other hand, that a general notice to the police that any illicit recordings found (for example, any Michael Jackson bootlegs at a Michael Jackson concert) will be seized is insufficient: notice must be given of *the* proposed seizure.

Premises

"Premises" are defined as including land, buildings, fixed or moveable **6.45** structures, vehicles, aircraft and hovercraft.[18]

Permanent or regular place of business

"Regular place of business" covers any place where business is conducted **6.46** with any regularity. "Place" is not confined to "premises" (though "premises" is itself widely defined for the purposes of section 196[19]). This provision would appear to place considerable limits on the applicability of the remedy, for even a market trader has a regular stall. It would seem that the only persons who are not protected by this provision are unlicensed street traders, in particular those who sell goods from temporary stalls at car boot sales and the like.[20] The remedy is still useful against those selling infringing merchandise at pop concerts and the like, however.

---

[16] See also para. 6.47.
[17] See para. 6.48.
[18] Copyright, Designs and Patents Act 1988, s. 196(5).
[19] See para. 6.45.
[20] This was the legislative intention: H.L. Deb., Vol. 501, ser. 5, col. 247 (Lord Strathclyde) (1988).

May not use any force

6.47   The prohibition on the use of force goes to the heart of the difficulty with this remedy. The stipulation is necessary, for otherwise the existence of the remedy would be tantamount to an invitation to use violence. Two problems arise, however. The first is that even if the person seeking to exercise the right does not use force, the person from whom the illicit recording is sought to be seized may respond with violence.[21] Secondly, it is unclear what sanction, if any, exists if the person from whom the illicit recording is sought to be seized declines to permit it to be seized (*e.g.* by clutching onto it so that the person seeking to seize cannot do so without using force). In the case of a true Anton Piller order, the sanction is proceedings for contempt of court. No corresponding sanction is provided by section 196. It is perhaps arguable that a person who declined to deliver up an illicit recording could be sued for breach of statutory duty, but this removes the whole point of the provision, which is to avoid cumbersome and lengthy legal proceedings.

Prescribed form and particulars

6.48   The prescribed form and particulars are set out in the Schedule to the Copyright and Rights in Performances (Notice of Seizure Order) 1989.[22]

Subject to decision under section 204

6.49   The provision that the right to seize illicit recordings is subject to any decision of the court under section 204 means that a person from whom recordings are seized may apply for a decision that no order shall be made under that section, in which case the recordings must be returned to him—although it appears that such a person would not be entitled to damages for the period of detention if the recordings were validly seized. In a sense, therefore, seizure under section 196 is an "interlocutory" form of relief, as is an order under section 195. Both forms of relief become final when an order under section 204 is made. Section 196 differs from section 195, however, in that under the latter the onus is on the right owner to apply for an order under section 204, while under the former the onus is on the person from whom the recordings are seized. Thus if a seizure is made under section 196, and the person seized from makes no application, the right owner need do nothing further.[23] In neither case is there is any requirement for the person claiming performers' or recording rights to give a cross-undertaking in damages pending any order under section 204 (still less pending judgment in any action).

5. Forfeiture or destruction

6.50   Section 204 of the 1988 Act provides that an application may be made to the court for an order that an illicit recording shall either be forfeited to the owner of the performers' or recording rights or destroyed or otherwise dealt with,[24]

---

[21] No doubt the person making the seizure would have the ordinary right of self-defence, but this does not prevent trouble occurring.
[22] S.I. 1989 No. 1006. (See Appendix 2A.)
[23] This was the legislative intention: H.L. Deb., Vol. 491, ser. 5, col. 412 (Earl of Dundee) (1987).
[24] For example, forfeited to the exclusive licensee where there is one.

or for a decision that no such order shall be made. Once again, the remedy is subject to certain restrictions and conditions:

(i)   It only applies to "illicit" recordings.[25]

(ii)   It only applies to illicit recordings delivered up pursuant to an order under section 195[26] or section 199[27] or seized pursuant to section 196[28] of the Act.[29]

(iii) In deciding whether to grant such an order the court must consider what other remedies available in an action for infringement would be adequate to compensate the right owner and to protect his interests.[30]

(iv) Notice may be required to be served on persons having an interest in the recording.[31]

(v)   Persons having an interest in the recording may appear (whether or not served with notice) and may appeal against any order (whether or not they appeared).[32]

(vi) Where more than one person has an interest in a recording, the court may direct that the recording be sold and the proceeds divided.[33]

Whether other remedies adequate

In considering what order, if, any, to make on an application under section 204, the court must consider what other remedies available in an action for infringement of performers' rights or recording rights would be adequate to compensate the right owner and to protect his interests.[34]   **6.51**

This is a strange provision, the purpose of which is not entirely clear. It might perhaps be argued that it implies that an order under section 204 can only be made in the context of an action for infringement, but it is submitted that this is not right. Like applications under section 195,[35] it is provided that the county court may entertain applications under section 204. This, together with the fact that the subject-matter of an application under section 204 may be recordings seized pursuant to section 196, suggests that applications under section 204 do not have to be made in the context of an action for infringement.   **6.52**

If this is correct, section 204(2) is asking the court notionally to compare the right owner's actual position on a stand-alone application for forfeiture and his hypothetical position if he were to bring an action for infringement. In effect, this amounts to asking whether an injunction and damages which the right owner has chosen not to ask for would be sufficient protection of his interests. Presumably the purpose of this is to discourage right owners from making applications for forfeiture when damages would be an adequate   **6.53**

---

[25] See para. 6.31(i).
[26] See paras. 6.31–6.38.
[27] The counterpart to s. 195 in criminal proceedings: see Chap. 7, paras. 7.30–7.32.
[28] See paras. 6.39–6.49.
[29] Copyright, Designs and Patents Act 1988, s. 204(1).
[30] *ibid.*, s. 204(2).
[31] *ibid.*, s. 204(3).
[32] *ibid.*
[33] *ibid.*, s. 204(4).
[34] *ibid.*, s. 204(2).
[35] And under ss. 99 and 114 of Part I.

remedy, but it is not easy to see how the courts will apply this in practice. (There appears to be no reason why an application under section 204 should not if so desired be made in the context of an action for infringement, in which case the test will be easier to apply.)

Service of notice

6.54　Where an application is made under section 204,[36] the applicant must serve notice of the application on all persons so far as reasonably ascertainable having an interest[37] in the recording which is the subject of the application.[38]

Persons having an interest in the recording

6.55　Any person having an interest in the recording is entitled to appear in proceedings for an order for forfeiture or destruction, whether or not he has been served with notice of them, and to appeal against any order made, whether or not he has appeared.[39] Persons having an interest in the recording include[40]:

(a) persons in whose favour an order for forfeiture could be made (that is, other owners of performers' or recording rights in the performance in question);

(b) persons in whose favour an order for forfeiture of infringing copies under section 114 could be made (that is, copyright owners, where the illicit recording is also an infringing copy);

(c) persons in whose favour an order for forfeiture of infringing articles[41] under section 231 of the 1988 Act could be made (that is, design right owners, where the illicit recording is also an infringing article);

(d) persons in whose favour an order for forfeiture of goods under section 19 of the Trade Marks Act 1994 could be made (that is, trade mark owners, where the illicit recording bears infringing trade marks).

More than one person interested in the recording

6.56　Where more than one person has an interest in a recording, the court has a wide discretion to make whatever order it thinks just. In particular, it has power to order that the recording be sold or otherwise dealt with and the proceeds divided.[42]

---

[36] If no application is made, for example because recordings have been seized under s. 196 and the person from whom they were seized does not make any application, there is no requirement of notice. This is unfortunate, for it may deprive other persons with interests in the recordings from doing anything to protect them.

[37] See paras. 6.55–6.56, below.

[38] Ord. 93, Rule 24 of the Rules of the Supreme Court, added by R.S.C. (Amendment No. 3) Order 1989 (S.I. 1989 No. 1307), made under s. 204(3) of the Act. This is applied to county courts by Ord. 49 Rule 4A of the County Court Rules.

[39] Copyright, Designs and Patents Act 1988, s. 204(3).

[40] *ibid.*, s. 204(6).

[41] That is, articles made in infringement of design right.

[42] Copyright, Designs and Patents Act 1988, s. 204(4).

Timing of application

The wording of section 204(1) suggests that applications for orders for **6.57** forfeiture can only be made *after* delivery up or seizure. Section 195(2), however, expressly contemplates that an order for forfeiture may be made *at the same time* as an order for delivery up or subsequently. It seems clear that the latter must prevail, and that therefore an application for an order for forfeiture can be made at the same time as an application for an order for delivery up.

If no order for forfeiture is made at the time of the application for delivery **6.58** up (and *a fortiori* if no application is made), the court must nevertheless consider whether there are grounds for making a forfeiture order. Furthermore, delivery up under section 195 merely gives the deliveree custody of the illicit recordings pending a decision under section 204. In addition, it would appear that the respondent to an application for delivery up could counter with a cross-application for a decision that no order for forfeiture should be made (or, perhaps, a declaration that there were no grounds for making such an order): if no order is made, the person in whose possession the illicit recording was before being delivered up or seized is entitled to its return.[43] It would therefore seem sensible to combine applications under sections 196 and 204 rather than to make them separately. Whether this is feasible may depend on whether others are interested in the illicit recording in question.

Mode of application

Applications for forfeiture or destruction may be made in the county court in **6.59** England and Wales and also in Northern Ireland where the value of the illicit recordings in question does not exceed the county court limit for actions in tort.[44] In Scotland, such applications may be made in the sheriff court.[45] In the High Court, applications must be made by originating summons[46] if there is no pending action for infringement or by summons or motion in that action if there is.[47] Whatever procedure is adopted, it seems clear that interlocutory applications can only be made *inter partes*. If relief under section 204 is sought only at trial, there does not appear to be any reason why it should not be claimed in the writ and prayer in the normal way, but this will not obviate the necessity to serve a summons or notice of motion returnable at the trial on all persons having an interest in the recording.

---

[43] *ibid.*, s. 204(5).
[44] *ibid.*, s. 205(1). Applications in pending actions should be made under Ord. 13 of the County Court Rules and originating applications under Ord. 3, Rule 4.
[45] Copyright, Designs and Patents Act 1988, s. 205(2). Application is by motion or by incidental application where proceedings have been commenced and by summary application where no proceedings have been commenced: Act of Sederunt (Copyright, Designs and Patents Act) 1990 (S.I. 1990 No. 380) (S.37), para. 2(2).
[46] Ord. 7 of the Rules of the Supreme Court.
[47] Ord. 93, Rule 24(2) of the Rules of the Supreme Court, added by R.S.C. (Amendment No. 3) Ord. 1989 (S.I. 1989 No. 1307), made under s. 204(3) of the Act.

INTERLOCUTORY PROCEEDINGS

6.60 There appears to be no reason why all the usual forms of interlocutory relief (including injunctions, delivery up, discovery and inspection) should not be available in actions for infringement under Part II. Two forms of relief are worthy of brief notice here, namely interlocutory injunctions and Anton Piller orders. An appropriate text on civil procedure should be consulted for a full treatment of these and other forms of interlocutory relief.

Interlocutory injunction

6.61 An interlocutory injunction is a temporary order to restrain the infringement complained of pending the trial of the action. Given that it may take one or two years to bring an action to trial, the remedy is a valuable one for plaintiffs. The essence of the jurisdiction, however, is that the court does not know and should not attempt to predict which party will succeed at trial.[48] The task of the court hearing an application for interlocutory injunction is therefore to decide which course will cause the least risk of ultimate injustice: to grant or to refuse an injunction.[49]

6.62 The principles to be applied by the court on an application for an interlocutory injunction were laid down by the House of Lords in *American Cyanamid Co. v. Ethicon Ltd.*[50] They may be summarised as follows:

(i)   Has the plaintiff established that there is a serious question to be tried, that he has a real prospect of succeeding at trial? If not, no injunction will be granted.

(ii) Assuming that the plaintiff will succeed at trial, would an award of damages at trial adequately compensate the plaintiff for the damage that he would suffer by reason of the defendant continuing to infringe until then? If it would, no injunction will be granted.

(iii) Assuming that the defendant will succeed at trial, would an award of damages under the plaintiff's cross-undertaking adequately compensate the defendant for the damage that he would suffer through being injuncted until then? If the plaintiff would suffer uncompensatable or irreparable harm and the defendant would not on these respective assumptions, an injunction will be granted.

(iv) If both parties would suffer uncompensatable or irreparable harm, which party will suffer most if the court decides against it?

(v)   If the balance of irreparable harm is roughly even, are there other factors which make it more just to grant or to refuse an injunction (what is the "balance of convenience")? For example, has the plaintiff acted promptly or has he delayed unduly in making his application?

(vi) If the balance of convenience is fairly even, the court may consider it prudent to preserve the status quo. In a very close case on balance, the

---

[48] See, however, *Series 5 Software Ltd v. Clarke* [1996] F.S.R. 273.
[49] *Cayne v. Global Natural Resources* [1984] 1 All E.R. 225; *Films Rover International Ltd v. Cannon Film Sales Ltd* [1986] 3 All E.R. 722; *Factortame Ltd v. Secretary of State (No. 2)* [1991] 1 All E.R. 70.
[50] [1975] A.C. 396.

court may be justified in taking into account the respective strengths of the parties' cases.

Anton Piller orders

In certain cases the plaintiff may have evidence that, if the defendant is given notice of any proceedings, he will destroy or conceal documents or other evidence, perhaps including any illicit recordings. The Anton Piller order[51] is designed to meet this difficulty. The order requires the defendant to permit the plaintiff to enter and search the defendant's premises and to seize categories of documents and other material. The order is made *ex parte* so as to enable the plaintiff to take the defendant by surprise: the first that the defendant will know of the proceedings is when the plaintiff's solicitors arrive at his premises to serve and execute the order. The principles applied by the courts in considering whether to grant such orders may be summarised as follows:

6.63

(i) The plaintiff must establish that he has a strong prima facie case.
(ii) The plaintiff must adduce evidence tending to show that there is a likelihood that the defendant, if given notice of the proceedings, would destroy or conceal documents or other materials.
(iii) As with all *ex parte* applications, the plaintiff must disclose to the court all relevant facts within his knowledge.
(iv) The order must contain appropriate safeguards for the defendant, including limitations on the time of day when it may be executed, on the number and identity of the persons executing it, undertakings by the plaintiff's solicitors to serve the defendant with copies of the evidence in support, to explain the order in everyday language and to make a record of all material seized which must be agreed with the defendant.[52] It is now usual for the safeguards to include the appointment of an independent solicitor to supervise the execution of the order.[53] There is a standard form of order which must be used unless good reason not to do so is shown.[54]

---

[51] *Anton Piller KG v. Manufacturing Processes Ltd* [1976] Ch. 55.
[52] See *Columbia Picture Industries Inc. v. Robinson* [1987] Ch. 38 for a discussion of the need for safeguards.
[53] See *Universal Thermosensors Ltd v. Hibben* [1992] 1 W.L.R. 840.
[54] *Practice Direction (Anton Piller and Mareva Orders)* [1996] 1 W.L.R. 1552.

7. Criminal Law

INTRODUCTION

7.01 The Performers' Protection Acts on their face provided performers with exclusively criminal remedies. By contrast, the Copyright Acts of 1911 and 1956 were primarily concerned with civil remedies, although criminal penalties for copyright infringement had existed since at least the Copyright Act 1842. Since 1956, however, the legislature has enlarged the criminal aspect of copyright law, first by increasing the penalties for the offences under the 1956 Act[1] and now by creating a wider scheme of offences with further increased penalties.[2] The criminal side of performers' rights has been brought into line with this. In both cases the criminal offences created are virtually co-extensive with civil infringements: there is nothing in the statute which limits the offences to bootleggers or pirates.[3] In relation to performers' rights this has involved the creation of two new offences,[4] when compared with the Performers' Protection Acts, but the decriminalisation of one old one.[5] In addition some penalties have been reduced.[6]

PRINCIPAL OFFENCES

7.02 Section 198 of the Copyright, Designs and Patents Act 1988 makes it an offence for a person to do any of the following acts (subject[7] to the exceptions contained in Schedule 2[8]):

    (1)   make for sale or hire without "sufficient consent" a recording or a copy of a recording which is, and which that person knows or has reason to believe is, an "illicit recording"[9];

    (2)   import into the United Kingdom otherwise than for his private or domestic use without "sufficient consent" a recording or a copy of a

---

[1] Copyright (Amendment) Act 1983.
[2] Copyright, Designs and Patents Act 1988, ss. 107–110.
[3] *Thames & Hudson Ltd v. Designs & Artists Copyright Society Ltd* [1995] F.S.R. 153.
[4] Categories (2) and (3) in para. 7.02, below.
[5] Live broadcasting of performances without consent: Dramatic and Musical Performers' Protection Act 1958, s. 3.
[6] *e.g.* the maximum penalty for selling or letting for hire illicit recordings has been reduced from 2 years (Performers' Protection Act 1972, s. 2) to 6 months' imprisonment (Copyright, Designs and Patents Act 1988, s. 198(6)).
[7] Copyright, Designs and Patents Act 1988, s. 198(4).
[8] As to which, see Chap. 5, paras. 5.02–5.46.
[9] Copyright, Designs and Patents Act 1988, s. 198(1)(a). See para. 7.05.

recording which is, and which that person knows or has reason to believe is, an "illicit recording"[10];

(3) in the course of a business possess with a view to committing an infringement of performers' rights or recording rights without "sufficient consent" a recording or a copy of a recording which is, and which that person knows or has reason to believe is, an "illicit recording"[11];

(4) in the course of a business sell, let for hire, offer or expose for sale or hire or distribute without "sufficient consent" a recording or a copy of a recording which is, and which that person knows or has reason to believe is, an "illicit recording"[12];

(5) cause a recording of a performance made without "sufficient consent" to be shown or played in public so that, and so that person knows or has reason to believe that, performers' rights or recording rights are infringed[13];

(6) cause a recording of a performance made without "sufficient consent" to be shown or played in public so that, and so that person knows or has reason to believe that, performers' rights or recording rights are infringed.[14]

Sufficient consent

"Sufficient consent" for the purposes of section 198(1) and (2) is defined as follows[15]:   **7.03**

(a) where performers' rights subsist,[16] the consent of the performer (in relation to recordings) or of the owner of the performers' rights (in relation to copies of recordings);

(b) where performers' rights do not subsist but recording rights do subsist[17]:

   (i) for category (1) above, the consent of the performer or the owner of the recording rights;

   (ii) for categories (2) to (6) above, the consent of the owner(s) of the recording rights.

Thus if performers' rights subsist, consent of the performer is always sufficient to prevent the commission of an offence in relation to a first-generation recording of a performance. In relation to second- and subsequent generation recordings, the consent of the owner of the performers' rights is

---

[10] ibid., s. 198(1)(b). See para. 7.06.
[11] ibid., s. 198(1)(c). See paras. 7.07–7.08.
[12] ibid., s. 198(1)(d). See paras. 7.09–7.10.
[13] ibid., s. 198(2)(a). See para. 7.11
[14] ibid., s. 198(2)(b). See para. 7.12
[15] ibid., s. 198(3).
[16] See Chap. 4, para. 4.03.
[17] The words used are "in the case of a non-qualifying performance subject to an exclusive recording contract", but it is clear from the context that it must be a performance in which recording rights subsist rather than simply *any* performance subject to an exclusive recording contract.

required. If recording rights also subsist, it is not necessary also to obtain the consent of the owner of those.

Illicit recording

7.04 "Illicit recording" has the same meaning as for civil infringement[18] except that for the purpose of the criminal offences it does not include recordings which fall to be treated as illicit under Schedule 2.[19]

1. Making for sale or hire

7.05 This offence corresponds approximately to categories (1), (3) and (4) of infringements of performers' rights and to category (1) infringement of recording rights. The correspondence is not exact, however. Whereas it is an infringement to make a recording without consent for any purpose save private and domestic use, it is only an offence to make it for sale or hire. Thus it is not an offence to make a recording without consent for the purpose of broadcasting it (although it may be an offence then to broadcast it).

2. Importation

7.06 This offence corresponds to category (9) infringement of performers' rights and to category (4) infringement of recording rights. It does not appear that there is any difference between the scope of the offence and the scope of the tort.

3. Possession in the course of a business

7.07 This offence (together with the succeeding offence) corresponds approximately to category (10) infringement of performers' rights and category (5) infringement of recording rights. The correspondence is not exact, however. Whereas it is an infringement to possess in the course of a business an "illicit recording" for any purpose, it is only an offence to possess it "with a view to committing any act infringing" performers' rights or recording rights. Presumably mere possession is not a sufficient "act" for this purpose.

With a view to committing any act

7.08 It is not clear whether the words "with a view to committing any act" import a test purely of intention or whether they import something more than that. On the one hand, if what was meant was "with intent to commit any act", it would have been easy enough for the draughtsman to say so. On the other hand, if what was meant was "while taking steps to commit any act", the words chosen do not seem very apt for the purpose. Since it is undesirable to criminalise mere states of mind, it is submitted that the words should be construed as importing more than a simple test of intention. For the offence to be committed, the defendant should have taken steps towards committing an act of infringement.

---

[18] See Chap. 4, paras. 4.47–4.49.
[19] Copyright, Designs and Patents Act 1988, s. 197(4).

4. Sale, etc., in the course of a business

This offence (together with the preceding offence) corresponds to category **7.09** (10) infringement of performers' rights and category (5) infringement of recording rights. It does not appear that there is any difference between the scope of the offence and the scope of the torts. It is worth noting, however, that the offence is defined in such a manner as to make it absolutely clear that the acts must be committed in the course of a business, whereas this is not so for the torts.[20]

Distribution

A distinction must be drawn between sale, letting for hire and offering or **7.10** exposing for sale or hire on the one hand, and distributing on the other hand. The reason for this is that the penalties for the latter act are heavier than those for the former acts.[21] This would seem to imply that, say, offer for sale does not, without more, constitute distribution.

5. Causing to be shown or played in public

This offence, though similar to category (7) infringement of performers' **7.11** rights and to category (2) infringement of recording rights, differs in two respects. First, it is sufficient for the offence to be committed if the putative offender causes a recording to be shown or played; he does not have to do the act himself.[22] Secondly, and more importantly, the offence is not committed unless the tort is committed; but an additional element has to be present for the offence to be committed. The additional element is the satisfaction of a second, and different, knowledge requirement. For an offence to be committed, the putative offender must know or have reason to believe:

(i) that the recording was made without the appropriate consent; and
(ii) that the playing or showing of the recording is an infringement of performers' rights or recording rights.

It is possible, however, that the courts will take the view that (ii) adds nothing to (i).

6. Causing to be broadcast or included in a cable programme service

This offence bears the same relationship to category (8) infringement of **7.12** performers' rights and category (3) infringement of recording rights as the preceding offence does to categories (7) and (2) respectively. The same comments therefore apply.

---

[20] See Chap. 4, paras. 4.52–4.56.
[21] See paras. 7.28–7.30, below.
[22] A person who causes a recording to be shown or played may be a joint tortfeasor; but this depends upon the operation of normal common law principles rather than upon any statutory definition.

ADDITIONAL OFFENCES

1. False representation of authority to consent

7.13 By section 201(1) of the 1988 Act, it is an offence for a person falsely to represent that he is authorised by another to give consent for the purposes of Part II in relation to a performance unless he believes on reasonable grounds that he is so authorised. The anomaly of section 4 of the Performers' Protection Act 1963—that the representor was only guilty of an offence if the representation afforded the representee a defence under section 7 of the Dramatic and Musical Performers' Protection Act 1958[23]—has therefore been removed.

Authorised

7.14 It is arguable (by analogy with the Court of Appeal's construction of section 7 of the 1958 Act in the *Peter Sellers* case[24]) that a person who represents, contrary to the fact, that he is a deceased person's personal representative and as such purports to give consent does not commit an offence under this provision. The argument would be that such a person does not represent that he is "authorised *by any person*" to give consent (emphasis added), which would require a representation of agency, but that he is authorised *by law* to give it on his own behalf standing in the deceased's shoes. It is submitted, however, that this is to adopt too legalistic an approach. Assuming that both representor and representee are ignorant of the niceties of the law as to executors, it is likely that the representor will represent—and, more importantly, be understood by the representee to represent—that he is authorised to consent on the performer's behalf, notwithstanding that it is as a matter of law impossible for the representation to be true. It is consistent with the purposes of the subsection for the representor in those circumstances to be guilty of an offence.

Reasonable grounds

7.15 It is unclear what the effect of the proviso to the subsection is. One possibility is that the prosecution has to prove, as an element of the *actus reus*, that the defendant did not have reasonable grounds. A second possibility is that the proviso provides a defence but does not otherwise affect the scope of the offence. A third possibility is that the existence of the proviso, in addition to providing a defence, indicates that the offence is to be a treated as one of strict liability. Of these possibilities, the third appears to be the most likely.

7.16 If this is correct, a defendant will be guilty of the offence once it is established that he made the false representation unless he proves (i) that he believed that the representation was true and (ii) that he had reasonable grounds for doing so. In effect, the proviso is an enactment of the former *Tolson* rule[25] that an "an honest and reasonable belief" in the existence of

---

[23] See first edition, Chap. 2, para. 2.57.

[24] [1988] Q.B. 40. See first edition, Chap. 2, paras. 2.22 and 2.58.

[25] *R. v. Tolson* (1889) 23 Q.B.D. 168 and *Bank of New South Wales v. Piper* [1897] A.C. 383. Nowadays the usual approach adopted by the courts is that the reasonableness or

circumstances which, if true, would make an act with which a person has been charged innocent is a good defence.

2. Connivance of director, etc., of body corporate

Section 202(1) of the 1988 Act provides that where an offence under Part II committed by a body corporate is proved to have been committed with the consent or connivance of a director, manager,[26] secretary or other similar officer of the body, or a person purporting to act in any such capacity, that person too is guilty of the offence. Directors and others are no longer guilty if the commission of the offence by the body corporate is merely attributable to neglect on their part, however, as under section 4A of the Performers' Protection Act 1963.[27] "Connivance" would seem to imply knowledge of, and acquiescence in, the commission of the offence but not necessarily any active participation.[28]

7.17

Director

In the case of a body corporate whose affairs are managed by its members, "director" means a member of the body corporate.[29] Presumably if only some members take part in the management, it means a managing member.

7.18

MENS REA[30]

Corresponding to the common law maxim *actus non facit reum nisi mens sit rea*[31] is the rebuttable presumption that statutory offences require proof of *mens rea*.[32] Under the Performers' Protection Acts 1958–1972, it was necessary for the prosecution to prove knowledge on the part of the defendant of all elements of the offence charged.[33] It is submitted that on general principles the same ought to apply under Part II of the 1988 Act. The drafting of section 198 indicates, however, that it is merely necessary for the prosecution to prove the defendant did in fact do the acts charged and that he knew or had reason to believe that the recording was an "illicit recording". In other words, the effect is that the test of *mens rea* in criminal cases is the same as the test of knowledge or reason for belief in civil proceedings under the Act,[34] only the standard of proof is higher. Thus even though copyright

7.19

---

unreasonableness of the defendant's belief is material only to the question of whether he actually held the belief at all: *R. v. Kimber* (1983) 77 Cr. App. R. 225, *R. v. Williams (G)* (1984) 78 Cr. App. R. 276 and *Beckford v. R.* [1987] 3 All E.R. 425. See Archbold, *Pleading, Evidence and Practice in Criminal Cases* (1996 ed., Sweet & Maxwell), vol. 2, chap. 17, paras. 17–10 to 17–24.

[26] In the sense of a manager who manages the company rather than a branch manager: *cf. Tesco Supermarkets Ltd v. Nattrass* [1972] A.C. 153.

[27] See first edition, Chap. 2, para. 2.59.

[28] See *Huckerby v. Elliott* [1970] 1 All E.R. 189.

[29] Copyright, Designs and Patents Act 1988, s. 202(2).

[30] See generally Archbold, note 25, above, vol. 2, chap. 17.

[31] The deed does not make the man guilty unless his mind be guilty.

[32] See, for example, *Sweet v. Parsley* [1970] A.C. 132 and *Gammon (Hong Kong) Ltd v. Attorney-General of Hong Kong* [1984] 2 All E.R. 503.

[33] *Gaumont British Distributors Ltd v. Henry* [1939] 2 K.B. 711. See first edition, Chap. 2, paras. 2.60–2.63.

[34] See Chap. 4, paras. 4.70–4.78.

infringement is treated as an offence akin to theft when it comes to sentencing,[35] unlike theft[36] it is not necessary for the prosecutor to prove dishonesty.

Companies

7.20   It is clear from section 202(1) of the 1988 Act that a body corporate may be guilty of an offence under Part II. In the case of a company, however, it is not entirely clear which individuals' knowledge or reason for belief will be attributed to the company. One possibility is that if the employee who committed the *actus reus* had the relevant knowledge or reason for belief, then his state of mind will be attributed to the company. The alternative possibility is that the company will only be liable if at least one of the directors or managers of the company (the "directing minds") had the requisite knowledge or reason for belief. This is a question of statutory construction[37] as to which there is presently no clear authority. The *Gaumont* case[38] does not really assist, firstly because the individual in question was the defendants' general manager rather than a more lowly employee, and secondly because it was decided before the modern developments in this branch of the law. It is submitted that the better view is that the first answer identified above is the correct one. Considering the purpose of the legislation, it would seem surprising that, if an employee who is authorised by his employer to deal in certain recordings knows that those recordings were illicit, then the company should only liable for his dealings if a director shares that knowledge.[39]

DEFENCES

7.21   The following defences to a prosecution under Part II of the 1988 Act are available: the act was one permitted under Schedule 2[40]; sufficient consent; "innocence" (that is, lack of knowledge); private and domestic use; and arrangements made before commencement. See Chapter 5, paragraphs 5.02–5.66 for discussion of these. So far as the last defence is concerned, although section 180(3), unlike Schedule 2, is not expressly provided to apply to offences under section 198, it is arguably implicit that it does.

Delay

7.22   Informations alleging offences under Part II of the 1988 Act which are only triable summarily[41] must be laid within six months of the commission of the offence if the justices are to have jurisdiction to try the case.[42] Offences which

---

[35] See para. 7.28, below.
[36] *R. v. Ghosh* [1982] 3 W.L.R. 110.
[37] See *Meridian Global Funds Management Asia Ltd v. Securities Commission* [1995] 2 A.C. 500, 511H–512B (*per* Lord Hoffmann).
[38] Note 33, above.
[39] Compare *Meridian v. Securities Commission*, note 37, above, and *Tesco Stores Ltd v. Brent London Borough Council* [1993] 1 W.L.R. 1037 with *Tesco Supermarkets Ltd v. Nattrass*, note 26, above, and *Textron Inc's Patent* [1989] R.P.C. 441.
[40] Copyright, Designs and Patents Act 1988, s. 198(4).
[41] That is, those under s. 198(1)(c), (d)(i) and (ii) and (2).
[42] Magistrates Court Act 1980, s. 127(1).

are triable either way,[43] however, are not subject to any statutory limitation period[44] and at common law there is no time-limit on criminal prosecutions.[45] Nevertheless, delay in bringing a prosecution may in exceptional cases give rise to prejudice and unfairness which by itself amounts to an abuse of process such that the tribunal may decline to entertain the proceedings.[46]

ENFORCEMENT

Section 198A(1) of the 1988 Act[47] will, when it is brought into force, make it the duty of every local weights and measures authority in England and Wales to enforce section 198 within its area. For this purpose the authorities may use their powers under the Trade Descriptions Act 1968 to make test purchases[48] and enter premises and inspect and seize goods and documents.[49] In Northern Ireland, enforcement will be the responsibility of the Department of Economic Development.[50]

7.23

Private prosecutions

The right of any citizen to bring a private prosecution for a criminal offence is a well-established constitutional principle[51] which was expressly preserved when the Crown Prosecution Service was set up.[52] This means that performers and bodies representing performers may bring prosecutions. Such prosecutions must be handled carefully, however. In *R. v. Ealing Justices, ex p. Dixon*[53] the defendant had been charged by police at a police station with an offence of copyright infringement following the execution by the police accompanied by two FACT (Federation Against Copyright Theft) officers of search warrants obtained under section 21A(1) of the Copyright Act 1956. A subsequent prosecution brought by FACT was dismissed by the magistrates. The Divisional Court dismissed an application by FACT for judicial review of this decision, holding that under section 3(2) of the Prosecutions of Offences Act 1985, all prosecutions of offences charged by the police had to be conducted by the Director of Public Prosecutions or the Crown Prosecution Service. The police had no power to permit FACT to bring the prosecution. The correct course was for FACT to lay an information. The disadvantage of this for a body such as FACT is that it cannot obtain a search warrant itself,

7.24

---

[43] That is, those under s. 198(1)(a), (b) and (d)(iii).

[44] See *Kemp v. Liebherr-GB Ltd* [1987] 1 All E.R. 885.

[45] *Halsbury's Laws* (4th ed. (reissue)), Vol. 11(1), para. 786.

[46] *R. v. Bow Street Stipendiary Magistrate, ex p. Director of Public Prosecutions* (1990) Cr. App. R. 283 as explained in *Attorney-General's Reference (No. 1 of 1990)* [1992] Q.B. 630 and *Tan v. Cameron* [1992] 2 A.C. 205.

[47] Inserted by the Criminal Justice and Public Order Act 1994, s. 165(1),(3).

[48] Trade Descriptions Act 1968, s. 27 applied by Copyright, Designs and Patents Act 1988, s. 198A(2).

[49] Trade Descriptions Act 1968, s. 28 applied by Copyright, Designs and Patents Act 1988, s. 198A(2).

[50] Copyright, Designs and Patents Act 1988, s. 198A(3).

[51] See *Gouriet v. Union of Post Office Workers* [1978] A.C. 435, 477 (Lord Wilberforce), 497 (Lord Diplock).

[52] Prosecution of Offences Act 1985, s. 6(1).

[53] [1989] 2 All E.R. 1050.

and the deterrent value of the defendant being charged by the police is lost.[54] On the other hand, there may be a reluctance to leave prosecution to the overburdened and unspecialised CPS. It is presumably for these reasons that it is intended to make enforcement the responsibility of local weights and measures authorities.

Parallel civil proceedings

7.25   It is quite possible for a criminal prosecution to be brought in parallel with civil proceedings. Where this occurs the court will not generally order a stay of the criminal proceedings unless they are vexatious.[55] If a prosecution is brought in parallel with civil proceedings, however, it is an abuse of process for the civil plaintiff to be in effective control of the criminal proceedings so that the prosecutor is not in a position independently to exercise its duties.[56] This means that care be must taken in the institution and conduct of such a prosecution, particularly if it is a private prosecution or a trading standards prosecution brought on the instigation of a complainant who is also a civil plaintiff.

SEARCH WARRANTS

7.26   Section 200 of the 1988 Act gives a justice of the peace power to issue a warrant authorising a constable to enter and search premises if certain conditions are satisfied. These are that the justice must be satisfied by information given on oath by a constable that there are reasonable grounds for believing[57]:

(a) that an offence under section 198(1)(a),(b) or (d)(iii) (making, importing or distributing illicit recordings) has been or is about to be committed in any premises; and

(b) that evidence that such an offence has been or is about to be committed is in those premises.

7.27   The "premises" that may be searched include land, buildings, fixed or moveable structures, vehicles, vessels, aircraft and hovercraft.[58] The warrant may authorise persons to accompany any constable executing the warrant,[59] for example a representative of the record company concerned and/or their solicitor. It may not authorise a search for material covered by section 9(2) of the Police and Criminal Act 1984,[60] namely items subject to legal privilege, "excluded material" (which includes confidential personal records acquired

---

[54] Other advantages and disadvantages of private prosecutions are described in Harbottle, "Criminal Remedies for Copyright and Performers' Rights Infringement under the Copyright, Designs and Patents Act 1988" [1994] 1 ENT. LR 12.

[55] *Thames & Hudson Ltd v. Design & Artists Copyright Society Ltd* [1995] F.S.R. 153.

[56] *R. v. Leominster Magistrates Court, ex p. Aston Manor Brewery Co.* (*The Times*, January 8, 1997).

[57] Copyright, Designs and Patents Act 1988, s. 200(1).

[58] *ibid.*, s. 200(4).

[59] *ibid.*, s. 200(3)(a).

[60] *ibid.*, s. 200(2).

in the course of a trade, business, profession, occupation or office and confidential journalistic material) and "special procedure material" (which includes other material acquired during the course of a trade, business, profession, occupation or office which is subject to an obligation of confidence).[61]

PENALTIES

Imprisonment and/or fine

The penalty on summary conviction under sub-subsections (a), (b) and (d)(iii) **7.28**
of section 198 (making, importing and distributing illicit recordings) is imprisonment for up to six months or a fine not exceeding the statutory maximum (presently £5,000[62]) or both.[63] The penalty on conviction on indictment is imprisonment for up to two years or a fine or both.[64] There is no limit to the fine that may be imposed by a Crown Court, but it should be within the offender's means.[65] In R. v. Carter[66] the Court of Appeal upheld a sentence of nine months' imprisonment suspended for two years concurrent on each of two counts of making for sale or hire and hiring out pirate videos contrary to section 107 of Part I of the 1988, emphasising that the offence was a serious one and one really of dishonesty.

The penalty on summary conviction under sub-subsections (c) and (d)(i) **7.29**
and (ii) of section 198 (possession, sale or hire and offer for sale or hire) and under section 201(1) (false representation of authority) is imprisonment for up to six months or a fine not exceeding level 5 on the standard scale[67] (presently £5,000[68]) or both.[69] These offences are only triable summarily.

It may be noted that the penalties for distributing illicit recordings are **7.30**
heavier than those for selling, letting for hire, offering or exposing for sale or hire. It is not quite clear why this should be. A possible explanation is that it is thought that distribution is more likely to involve organised crime.

Delivery up

Section 199 of the 1988 Act gives a court seized of proceedings for an offence **7.31**
under section 198[70] power, if satisfied that the defendant at the time of his arrest or charge[71] had in his possession, custody or control in the course of a

---

[61] Police and Criminal Evidence Act 1984, ss. 10–14.
[62] Magistrates' Courts Act 1980, s. 32(9) as amended by the Criminal Justice Act 1991, s. 17(2)(c).
[63] Copyright, Designs and Patents Act 1988, s. 198(5)(a).
[64] ibid., s. 198(5)(b).
[65] R. v. Churchill (No. 2) [1967] 1 Q.B. 190 (reversed on other grounds sub nom. Churchill v. Walton [1967] 2 A.C. 224).
[66] [1993] F.S.R. 303.
[67] Defined by the Criminal Justice Act 1982, s. 75 as the scale set out in the Criminal Justice Act 1982, s. 37(2).
[68] Criminal Justice Act 1982, s. 37(2) as amended by the Criminal Justice Act 1991, s. 17(1).
[69] Copyright Tribunal Rules 1989, s. 198(6) and s. 201(2).
[70] See paras. 7.02–7.12, above.
[71] That is, when he is orally charged or is served with a summons or indictment or (in Scotland) when he is cautioned, charged or served with a complaint or indictment: Copyright, Designs and Patents Act 1988, s. 199(2).

business[72] an illicit recording[73] of a performance, to order that it be delivered up to an owner of performers' rights or recording rights in the performance or to any other person that the court directs. Unlike the power to order destruction of records and films under section 5 of the 1958 Act,[74] this power may be exercised whether or not the defendant is convicted.[75] The power may also be exercised of the court's own motion.[76]

7.32   No order may be made after the expiry of six years from the date on which the recording in question was made[77]; nor may any order for delivery up be made if it appears to the court unlikely that any order for forfeiture[78] will be made.[79] A person to whom a recording is delivered up must retain it pending a decision on whether to make an order for forfeiture.[80]

7.33   Where an order for delivery up is made by a Magistrate's Court, an appeal lies against the order to the Crown Court.[81] Since an order may be made in the absence of a conviction, such an appeal may be made even if there is no appeal against conviction.

Compensation

7.34   The court has power when dealing with an offender for any offence to order him to pay compensation for any loss or damage resulting from the offence.[82] In a Magistrates' Court compensation is limited to £5,000,[83] while there is no such limit in the Crown Court. Compensation is only appropriate, however, when there no doubt not only about the offender's liability but also the amount of the liability.[84]

Confiscation order

7.35   In respect of offences committed on or after January 1, 1996, Magistrates' Courts have power to make a confiscation order under Part VI of the Criminal Justice Act 1988.[85] By virtue of the amendments to the 1988 Act made by the Proceeds of Crime Act 1995, the court has a duty to make a confiscation order in certain circumstances and to do so with a view to confiscating the offender's benefit from a course of criminal conduct.

---

[72] See para. 7.07, above.
[73] See Chap. 4, paras. 4.47–7.49.
[74] See first edition, Chap. 2, para. 2.95.
[75] Copyright, Designs and Patents Act 1988, s. 199(3).
[76] *ibid.*
[77] *ibid.*, s. 203(4). *cf.* the period during which orders for delivery up may be made in civil proceedings: see Chap. 6, para. 6.34.
[78] Under s. 204: see Chap. 6, paras. 6.50–6.59.
[79] Copyright, Designs and Patents Act 1988, s. 199(3)(b).
[80] *ibid.*, s. 199(5).
[81] *ibid.*, s. 199(4). In Northern Ireland the appeal is to the county court, and in Scotland the appeal is in the same manner as against sentence: *ibid.*
[82] Powers of Criminal Courts Act 1973, s. 35.
[83] Magistrates' Courts Act 1980, s. 40(1).
[84] *R. v. Vivian* [1979] 1 W.L.R. 291.
[85] Criminal Justice Act 1988, Sched. 4, Part I as amended by the Criminal Justice Act 1988 (Confiscation Orders) Order 1995, S.I. 1995 No. 3415.

8. Other Forms of Protection for Performers

Introduction

Although Part II of the Copyright, Designs and Patents Act 1988 as amended now grants performers fairly extensive rights, there are still situations in which performers are not protected. The most notable of these is where the performance has been imitated rather than exploited without the performer's consent. As has been pointed out,[1] imitation of the performance is not an infringement of performers' rights under Part II. In these circumstances performers must look to other legal remedies. The remedies that are likely to be of most use for this purpose are those for infringement of copyright and passing off. In addition, the topics of moral rights, breach of confidence and contractual protection will be briefly addressed.

8.01

Copyright

Performance or adaptation

In certain fields, such as contemporary popular music, it is commonplace for performers also to be authors of copyright works. In these circumstances it is clear that the performer can rely upon copyright in the work indirectly to prevent imitation of the performance of that work. There are other fields, however, where performers are usually considered merely to perform works written by authors and where therefore copyright is thought to be of no assistance in preventing imitations of the performance. It is submitted, however, that this is an unduly conservative view and that upon examination it may often be found that performers can be afforded some protection by copyright.

8.02

The basis for this contention is that many performers alter the work performed to such an extent that it is arguable that their contribution should be categorised as adaptation or arrangement rather than "mere" performance, or even as a new work. This has the consequence that the artist may acquire a separate copyright in the adaptation or new work. A number of examples may be considered:

8.03

---

[1] Chap. 4, para. 4.08.

(1) A classical pianist writes a new cadenza for an existing piano concerto. Obviously he is entitled to copyright in the new cadenza (subject, of course, to satisfying the usual requirements of fixation and qualification).

(2) A popular musician makes a "disco" version of an existing song, changing the harmonies, tempi, dynamics and phrasing as well as the instrumentation. He is entitled to the copyright in the new arrangement or adaptation: *ZYX Music GmbH v. King.*[2]

(3) A classically trained musician joins a pop group and embellishes their existing songs by means ranging from writing a full-blown orchestral arrangement to adding new instrumental passages. He is entitled (jointly with the original authors) to copyright in the songs as thus arranged or adapted: *Godfrey v. Lees.*[3]

(4) The members of a pop group collectively develop and arrange the music of songs although the lyrics and the main melodic ideas for the songs are contributed by just one member. All the members are jointly entitled to copyright in the music as thus developed and arranged: *Stuart v. Barrett.*[4]

(5) A recording engineer "remixes" an existing recording of a song. If he simply makes a different combination of existing "tracks" (recordings of a single instrument or voice), he may create a new copyright sound recording but no more. If he uses electronic devices such as digital samplers to manipulate the existing tracks, he may create a new arrangement or adaptation which is sufficiently original to qualify as a copyright musical work. If he goes still further and (say) replaces the existing instrumental tracks with new ones (*e.g.* replacing guitar, bass and drums with a synthesiser), this is more likely still.

(6) A musician specialising in early music makes a "performing edition" of an old choral work from an obscure manuscript for the purpose of making a recording. Assuming, as may well be the case, that this involves considerable skill and labour in deciphering the manuscript, assigning modern note values and pitches, distributing parts and deciding on dynamics and phrasing, then the performing edition will qualify as a copyright musical work.

(7) A theatre director stages a new production of a Shakespeare play in which he has made a number of cuts and transpositions in the text, has chosen to set the play in a particular modern historical period (say, 1914) and has cast a woman in a part usually played by a man. It is submitted that he is entitled to copyright in this adaptation.

8.04 If the last example is thought doubtful, it may be instructive to compare the work of a theatre director with that of a film director. Few would question that a film is a separate copyright work from any antecedent work such as a

---

[2] [1995] EMLR 281. Note that it was held on the facts that his co-performers were not co-authors of the arrangement and thus were not joint copyright owners, but it is implicit in the decision that had the facts been otherwise they would have been.
[3] [1995] EMLR 307.
[4] [1994] EMLR 448.

play; that, even if there is a detailed screenplay, there can be no question of "mere" interpretation such that there would be no copyright in the film separate from that in the screenplay. This might be explained[5] in one of two ways. First, that "translating" a work from one medium to another, namely paper to celluloid, and so creating a new object for consumption, must give rise to a fresh copyright. Secondly, that, no matter how detailed a screenplay is, it must necessarily give the director considerable latitude in selecting the images that will constitute the film. But if these explanations are tested against the work of a theatre director, their cogency may be doubted. For a theatre director also "translates" a work from one medium to another, namely from paper to speech and action, so as to create a new object for consumption. It might be objected that speech and action do not constitute a material form, but since they are capable of fixation there is no reason why copyright should not subsist once fixed.[6] Then again, a play gives a director considerable latitude in how he directs his actors.[7] Why then should copyright not subsist in a production of a play?[8]

It could be argued by extension of this that every performer interprets the work he or she performs and in doing so adapts it to some extent—a musician, for example, may vary tempi or dynamics or phrasing. Thus, it might be said, every performer is protected by copyright in any event. This is almost certainly not the law (though the argument does not seem ever to have been put in this way). It is not easy, however, to explain why not. The difficulty—the fineness of the distinction that needs to be drawn—may perhaps best be seen by comparing the work of a performer with the work of an editor of a musical score such as that in example (6) above. There seems little doubt that the latter but not the former attracts copyright for his labours.[9]

8.05

This raises the question of where to draw the line—or rather, of what test to apply in drawing it. It might be thought that in deciding whether there has been an adaptation rather than merely an interpretation, the ordinary test of originality for copyright purposes should be applied. In current English (and Commonwealth) jurisprudence this can be summarised by saying that a work is original if it is the author's own work rather than copied from a previous source. Another test that is often used, particularly in compilation cases, is whether sufficient skill and labour (other than skill and labour in mere copying) has been expended. Almost all performances, however, are the performer's own work and require considerable skill and labour. Nor it is possible, it is submitted, to make a clear distinction between the skill and

8.06

---

[5] As a matter of principle, rather than simply of what the Copyright Act provides.

[6] As it may in an improvised dramatic performance: see Chap. 2, paras. 2.05, 2.10–2.12.

[7] Although the degree of latitude varies from play to play, and in particular between plays from different historical periods (see Raymond Williams, *Drama in Performance*, Open University Press), the modern approach to directing is such that even productions of a Greek tragedy may vary considerably.

[8] Particularly if the director has cut or reordered the text.

[9] The fineness of the distinction is emphasised by the fact that, with the rise of the early music movement, it has become increasingly common for one person—the musicologist-performer—to do both tasks. Where this happens, it is inevitable that "interpretative" considerations will influence the "musicological" task of editing, and "musicological" considerations will influence the "interpretative" task of performing.

labour expended merely in performing or interpreting from that expended in adapting. Some objective test is required. The Copyright, Designs and Patents Act 1988 gives no guidance on this, however, and it remains to be to seen what attitude the courts will take. This may depend on whether, as a result of the various European harmonisation measures,[10] English courts start to adopt a more civil law-type approach to originality. The traditional approach of civil law jurisdictions to originality has been to ask to whether the work is the author's "intellectual creation" within the meaning of Article 2(5) of the Berne Convention. On a practical level it seems likely that moving in this direction will make it more difficult for performers to claim copyright in their performances as arrangements or adaptations, but drawing the line will be no easier.

8.07　　It is worth pointing out, finally, that this question is not an entirely academic one. There are two main reasons for this, one technical and one more general. The technical reason is that the period of copyright protection is longer than that of performers' rights: 70 years from the end of the year of the author's death as opposed to 50 years from the end of the year in which a recording of the performance is first released. This may make a substantial difference. The more general reason is that artists such as film directors and theatre directors are becoming more concerned to protect their work through copyright. Two recent results of this are the according of limited *droits morals* to film directors under Chapter IV of Part I of the 1988 Act[11] and redefinition of the "author" of a film to include the director as a result of the E.C. Term Directive.[12] It is to be expected that pressure to give such artists further protection will increase.

Sets, costumes and props

8.08　　Even if it is not possible to contend that a performance that has been imitated was such as to amount to a new copyright work as an adaptation or arrangement, there may be cases where copyright can be relied upon in other ways. The most obvious examples are sets, costumes and props. Thus in *Shelley Films Ltd v. Rex Features Ltd*,[13] it was held to be arguable that copyright subsisted in (1) costumes as works of artistic craftsmanship, (2) latex prosthetic make-up as a sculpture or work of artistic craftsmanship and (3) a film set as a work of artistic craftsmanship. It may also be possible to rely upon more conventional artistic works. Suppose, for instance, that a particular mime-artist, A, has a well-known act in which he creates certain drawings and that for the purposes of a television advertisement another mime-artist, B, performs an act which is not an infringement of any dramatic copyright of A's, having a different plot, but utilising similar drawings. In these circumstances it may be possible to say that B has infringed A's

---

[10] In particular the Computer Program and Database Directives, both of which stipulate that the criterion for copyright protection is whether the work is the author's own intellectual creation.
[11] Copyright, Designs and Patents Act 1988, ss. 76, 80.
[12] s. 9(2)(ab) of the Copyright, Designs and Patents Act 1988 as amended by regulation 18(1) of the Copyright and Related Rights Regulations 1996, implementing Art. 2(1) of the Directive.
[13] [1994] EMLR 134.

copyright in his drawings. Of course, none of these examples involve direct protection for the performance, but indirectly a measure of protection may be obtained.

Basic requirements

The basic requirements for a cause of action for infringement of copyright are similar to those in relation to performers' rights, namely that (1) copyright subsists in a work, (2) the plaintiff owns that copyright, and (3) the defendant has committed or threatened to commit an infringing act. In order for copyright to subsist, the work must be of a kind that copyright is capable of subsisting in, it must have been recorded in some material form, it must be original (or in the case of films and sound recordings not a mere copy) and the qualification requirements must be met (usually by virtue of either the author being a qualifying national or the work having been first published in a qualifying country). In order for copyright to have been infringed, the defendant must have committed or threatened to commit a restricted act or to deal in an infringing copy with the requisite knowledge or reason for belief. The alleged infringement must have been derived from the copyright work and it must reproduce a substantial part of it. For further details the reader should consult an appropriate text.[14]

8.09

PASSING OFF

In situations where a performance has been imitated so that there is no infringement of performers' rights, and no copyright can be relied upon to afford protection, the only means of redress in English law is likely to be under the doctrine of passing off. This is most likely to be relevant in cases of personality merchandising, that is to say, the exploitation of a person's name, likeness and performance characteristics, in particular in connection with sales of clothing, games, memorabilia, etc. This field has obvious similarities with that of character merchandising in which fictional characters, particularly cartoon or puppet characters, are exploited. English passing-off law and practice has now evolved to the point where licensors of character merchandise can obtain a substantial degree of protection against producers and suppliers of unauthorised merchandise. The question is whether the same is true of personality merchandising featuring real persons such as performers.

8.10

Until relatively recently, it was not possible to obtain protection in either field. Thus in *McCulloch v. Lewis A. May (Produce Distributors) Ltd*[15] a well-known radio broadcaster failed to prevent the use of his performing name ("Uncle Mac") for a breakfast cereal. The plaintiffs were similarly unsuccessful in cases such as *Wombles Ltd v. Wombles Skips Ltd*[16] (use of name of television cartoon characters), *Lyngstad v. Annabas Products Ltd*[17]

8.11

---

[14] *e.g.* Laddie, Prescott & Vitoria, *The Modern Law of Copyright and Designs* (2nd ed., Butterworths, 1995).
[15] (1947) 65 R.P.C. 58.
[16] [1975] F.S.R. 488.
[17] [1977] F.S.R. 62.

(merchandise bearing the name and photographs of the pop group Abba), *Merchandising Corp. of America v. Harpbond*[18] (photograph of pop star) and *Stringfellow v. McCain Foods (G.B.) Ltd*[19] (name of nightclub proprietor used for oven chips advertised on television using theme of kitchen turned into a discotheque), while in *Tavener Rutledge Ltd v. Trexapalm Ltd*[20] an injunction was granted against the licensed user of *Kojak* for lollipops in favour of an unlicensed business which started first. In most of these cases the reason given for the plaintiff failing was that he or she did not have a reputation and goodwill in connection with the products in question (there was no "common field of activity"), and thus there was no likelihood of misrepresentation because members of the public would not think that the plaintiff had licensed or endorsed the products, although in the *Stringfellow* case it was held that there was some likelihood of misrepresentation but not such as to cause the plaintiff damage.

8.12   It is widely thought that the decision of Sir Nicolas Browne-Wilkinson V.-C. in favour of the plaintiffs in *Mirage Studios v. Counter-Feat Clothing Co. Ltd*[21] (the *Teenage Mutant Ninja Turtles* case) marked a turning-point in English law. In that case the first plaintiff was the owner of the copyright in the drawings for the hugely successful Ninja Turtles cartoon characters and through the second and third plaintiffs had licensed some 150 U.K. licensees to produce a wide range of merchandise featuring the Turtles. One of the licensees was the fourth plaintiff, which was licensed in respect of clothing. The defendants had commissioned artwork for similar, although not identical, turtle characters which they were licensing third parties to reproduce, in particular on T-shirts. On a motion for an interlocutory injunction the Vice-Chancellor held that the balance of convenience was so finely balanced that it was legitimate to take into account that the strength of the parties' cases and that the plaintiffs would succeed in passing off, although it was uncertain whether or not they would succeed in copyright.

8.13   So far as passing off is concerned, the Vice-Chancellor's reasoning appears from the following passages in the judgment:

> . . .first, has there been a misrepresentation? The critical evidence in this case is that a substantial number of the buying public now expect and know that where a famous cartoon or television character is reproduced on goods, that reproduction is the result of a licence granted by the owner of the copyright or the owner of other rights in that character. . .If, as the evidence shows here, the public mistake the defendants' turtles for those which might be called genuine plaintiffs' Turtles, once they have made that mistake they will assume that the product in question has been licensed to use the Turtles on it. That is to say, they will connect what they mistakenly think to be the plaintiffs' Turtles with the plaintiffs. To put on the market goods which the public mistake for the genuine article necessarily involves a misrepresentation to the public that they are genuine. On the evidence in this case,

---

[18] [1983] F.S.R. 32.
[19] [1984] R.P.C. 501.
[20] [1975] F.S.R. 479.
[21] [1991] F.S.R. 145.

the belief that the goods are genuine involves a further misrepresentation, namely that they are licensed.[22]

In my judgment the law as developed in Australia[23] is sound. There is no reason why a remedy in passing off should be limited to those who market or sell the goods themselves. If the public is misled in a relevant way as to a feature or quality of the goods sold, that is sufficient to found a cause of action in passing off brought by those people with whom the public associate that feature or that quality which has been misrepresented.[24]

In my judgment the three English cases [*Wombles, Kojak* and *Abba*] do not touch on a case such as the present where the plaintiff clearly has copyright in the drawings and is in business on a large scale in this country in licensing the use of the copyright in those drawings. The defendant is misrepresenting to the public that his drawings are the drawings of the plaintiffs or are licensed by the plaintiffs. I can see no reason why, in those circumstances, the defendants should be allowed to misrepresent his goods in that way. I therefore consider that if the case went to trial, the plaintiffs' case in passing off would succeed.[25]

In so holding the Vice-Chancellor professed to be applying orthodox **8.14** passing-off principles under English law,[26] although as can be seen he approved the two Australian cases cited. It is therefore worth examining the bases on which he distinguished the three earlier English cases.[27] So far as the *Wombles* case was concerned, he pointed out that Walton J. had been mistaken in thinking that it was a requirement of passing off that there be a common field of activity in which the parties were operating but stated that the decision "may still be good law" on the ground that the defendants were only using the name "Wombles" and there was no copyright in a name. The same points applied to the *Kojak* case. In addition, it had not been established on the evidence before Walton J. in that case that the system of character merchandising was known to the man in the street, whereas the evidence before the Vice-Chancellor 13 years later was to the contrary. As to the *Abba* case, this again was said by the Vice-Chancellor to be a case of taking the name alone, although this seems to overlook the fact that photographs of the group were being used by the defendants. Moreover, there had been no evidence of substantial exploitation by Abba of any licensing rights in the United Kingdom.

It is probably true to say that the *Ninja Turtles* case marks the final *quietus* **8.15** in English law of the supposed requirement of a "common field of activity"

---

[22] *ibid.* at 155.
[23] Referring to the cases of *Children's Television Workshop Inc. v. Woolworths (New South Wales) Ltd* [1981] R.P.C. 1987 (the *Muppets* case) and *Fido Dido Inc. v. Venture Stores (Retailers) Pty Ltd* (1988) 16 I.P.R. 365, both of which concerned the merchandising of fictional characters (puppets and cartoons respectively).
[24] [1991] F.S.R. 145, 157.
[25] *ibid.* at 159.
[26] In particular the well-known passage from the speech of Lord Diplock in *Erven Warnink BV v. J. Townend & Sons (Hull) Ltd* [1980] R.P.C. 31, 93.
[27] [1991] F.S.R. 145, 157–158.

(although it should be noted that on the facts of the case there was a common field of activity[28]). This doctrine had, however, already been discredited by then anyway. Apart from that, it does not represent any substantial change in the law. Its real significance therefore probably lies in the fact that it demonstrates judicial acceptance of the reality that, because character merchandising has now become so pervasive, members of the public do now expect merchandise to be licensed or endorsed by those with whom it appears to be connected at least where copyright material is involved. This does not mean that the law of passing off as such has changed, but rather that it is now possible to obtain evidence which will persuade the court of the merits of the complaint whereas previously this was not so.

8.16   Because the Vice-Chancellor was careful to restrict his judgment to situations involving the merchandising of copyright material, and stressed that there is no copyright in a name,[29] the *Ninja Turtles* case may itself be distinguished from cases of personality merchandising featuring the name and/or likeness of a real person such as a performer. In principle, however, there is no reason why the same approach should not extend to such cases, provided that the appropriate evidence can be put before the court. It is common for celebrities to endorse products, and sometimes whole ranges of merchandise, in return for a fee. It is submitted that this practice is now well known to members of the public in the United Kingdom, and it ought to be possible to produce evidence of this. If a particular celebrity has endorsed certain products in this way, then it is likely that, if his or her name and/or likeness are used without authority in relation to other products, members of the public will be misled into believing that the celebrity has endorsed those products contrary to the fact. In the words of the Vice-Chancellor in the second passage quoted above, the public will be misled as to a relevant quality of the goods. Given how widespread the practice is, the same may occur even if the particular celebrity in question has not previously endorsed or licensed any goods. In *Elvis Presley Enterprises Inc.'s Applications*,[29a] however, Laddie J. held that on the evidence in that case it had not been established that the public were interested in the source of the goods as opposed to the name (and appearance) of Elvis Presley on them. Moreover, the learned judge cast doubt on the validity, or at least the general applicability, of the reasoning in *Ninja Turtles*.

8.17   Assuming that in an appropriate case credible evidence of deception could be produced, the practical effect will be to bring English passing-off law and practice close to that in Australia although not identical to it. In the leading Australian case of *Henderson v. Radio Corporation Pty Ltd*[30] the plaintiffs were well-known professional ballroom dancers. The defendant released a record of music for ballroom dancing featuring a photograph of the plaintiffs

---

[28] Both because the defendants were licensing their characters in direct competition with the third plaintiff and because the defendants' licensees included manufacturers of T-shirts in direct competition with the fourth plaintiff.

[29] [1991] F.S.R. 145, 157–158.

[29a] *The Times*, March 25, 1997.

[30] [1969] R.P.C. 218. Approved obiter by the High Court of Australia in *Moorgate Tobacco Co. Ltd v. Philip Morris Ltd* (1984) 3 I.P.R. 545, 566.

on the sleeve, albeit not very prominently. The plaintiffs had appeared in some advertisements or promotions but had not endorsed any records. The Full Court of New South Wales held that the defendant had wrongfully appropriated the plaintiffs' professional reputation so as to cause them damage by depriving them of the fee they could have charged for endorsing the record. This decision was followed in cases such as *10th Cantanae Pty v. Shoshana Pty Ltd*[31] and *Honey v. Australian Airlines.*[32] In *Hogan v. Koala Dundee Pty Ltd*[33] Pincus J. held that the plaintiffs could succeed even in the absence of any cogent evidence of misrepresentation because in Australia there was an extended form of passing off which protected images of characters from appropriation even in the absence of any misrepresentation. In *Hogan v. Pacific Dunlop Ltd*,[34] however, the Full Court of the Federal Court of Australia held that misrepresentation such that a significant proportion of the public was misled into believing that there was a commercial arrangement between the plaintiff and the defendant was required. Assuming that the last case and not the earlier *Hogan* case correctly represents the law of Australia, there is little difference of principle between English and Australian law. Such difference as remains lies rather in the greater readiness of the Australian courts to accept what may often be less than compelling evidence of misrepresentation and in the greater readiness of the Australian courts to accept that loss of a licensing or endorsement fee is in itself sufficient damage to support an action.

On this analysis a performer whose name and/or likeness is used in merchandising, advertising or other commercial activities in such a manner as to suggest that he or she has licensed or endorsed those activities is likely to have a remedy in passing off in England as well as in Australia, although this is more certain in Australia. It remains the case, however, that the performer does not have any remedy if his or her name or likeness is used in manner which does not mislead members of the public into believing that he or she has licensed or endorsed the use contrary to the fact. As yet neither the English courts nor (on the evidence of the second *Hogan* case) the Australian courts have been prepared to go as far as the Canadian[35] and Jamaican[36] courts have gone, to adopt a new tort of misappropriation of personality which is actionable without proof of misrepresentation.[37] Nor has either jurisdiction adopted privacy legislation such as that which enabled the plaintiff violinist

8.18

---

[31] (1987) 10 I.P.R. 289.

[32] (1990) 18 I.P.R. 185.

[33] (1988) 12 I.P.R. 508.

[34] (1989) 14 I.P.R. 398.

[35] The leading case is *Athans v. Canadian Adventure Camps Ltd* (1977) 80 D.L.R. (3d) 583 where an alternative claim in passing off failed on the ground that there was insufficient likelihood of deception. See also *Krouse v. Chrysler Canada Ltd* (1977) 40 D.L.R. (3d) 15, *Racine v. CJRC Radio Capitale Ltee* (1977) 35 C.P.R. (2d) 236, *Heath v. Weist-Barron School of TV Ltd* (1981) 34 O.R. (2d) 126, *Dowell v. Mengen Institute* (1983) 72 C.P.R. (2d) 238, *Joseph v. Daniels* (1986) 11 C.P.R. (3d) 544 and *Baron Philippe de Rothschild SA v. Casa de Habana Inc.* (1988) 19 C.P.R. (3d) 114.

[36] See *The Robert Marley Foundation Ltd v. Dino Michelle Ltd* (unreported, Clarke J., May 12, 1994) discussed in Hylton and Goldson, "The New Tort of Appropriation of Personality: Protecting Bob Marley's Face" (1996) 55 C.L.J. 56.

[37] See Frazer, "Appropriation of Personality—A New Tort?" (1983) 99 L.Q.R. 281 and Howell, "The Common Law Appropriation of Personality Tort" (1986) 2 I.P.J. 150.

in *Bogajewicz v. Sony of Canada Ltd*[38] successfully to complain that the use of a photograph of himself in a promotional brochure without his consent was an infringement of his rights to dignity and privacy under Sections 4 and 5 of the Quebec Charter.

8.19   This leads to the question of imitation of performance characteristics, particularly where this does not involve use of the performer's name or likeness. In the United States of America "sound alikes", persons who can imitate a particular performer's manner of singing or speaking, were at one time a popular form of advertising. In *Midler v. Ford Motor Co.*[39] and *Waits v. Frito-Lay Inc.*[40] the U.S. Ninth Circuit Court of Appeals held[41] that the deliberate imitation of the distinctive voice of a well-known professional singer for advertising purposes was actionable by the performer as an infringement of a proprietary right of publicity.[42] In *White v. Samsung Electronics America Inc.*[43] the same court made it clear that this cause of action applied to any imitation of a well-known performer's identity including, in that case, the use in an advertisement of a robot wearing a costume and using a prop similar to those used by the plaintiff game show hostess. While few other circuits or states have gone quite as far as the Ninth Circuit, many now recognise a right of publicity which prevents use or imitation of a performer's name, likeness and other characteristics[44] either at common law or by virtue of statute including privacy statutes.[45]

8.20   Since no proprietary right of personality or publicity nor any right of privacy is recognised in English law, a performer who sought to restrain such activities in England could only rely on such rights in passing off as he or she might have. In principle, it would appear that an action for passing off should succeed if members of the public were led to think that, for example, a particular singer had sung a song for an advertisement contrary to the fact, although in practice there might be evidential difficulties. In *Sim v. H.J. Heinz*

---

[38] (1995) 63 C.P.R. (3d) 458.

[39] 849 F. 2d 460 (9th Cir., 1988) *cert. den* 112 S.C. 1513 (1992). See Frazer, "Vox-Pop: U.S. Law Finds a Voice on Sound-Alikes" [1990] 1 ENT. LR 26.

[40] 23 U.S.P.Q. 2d 1721 (9th Cir., 1992).

[41] Contrary to earlier authorities such as *Sinatra v. Goodyear Tire & Rubber Co.* 435 F. 2d 711 (9th Cir., 1970) *cert. den.* 402 U.S. 906 (1971), *Davis v. Transworld Airlines* 297 F. Supp. 1145 (C.D. Calif., 1969) and *Booth v. Colgate-Palmolive Corp.* 362 F. Supp. 343 (S.D.N.Y., 1973).

[42] In *Waits* the court also held that there had been infringement of the plaintiff's rights under s. 43(a) of the Lanham Act.

[43] 23 U.S.P.Q. 2d 1583 (9th Cir., 1992). See Borchard, "The Common Law Right of Publicity is Going Wrong in the United States" [1992] 6 ENT. LR 208.

[44] See, *e.g. Haelen Laboratories Inc. v. Topps Chewing Gum Inc.* 202 F. 2d 866 (2nd Cir., 1953) *cert. den* 346 U.S. 816 (1953), *Motschenbacher v. R.J. Reynolds Tobacco Co.* 498 F. 2d 821 (9th Cir., 1974), *Zacchini v. Scripps-Howard Broadcasting Co.* 453 U.S. 562 (1977), *Carson v. Here's Johnny Portable Toilets Inc.* 698 F. 2d 831 (6th Cir., 1983).

[45] This stems from Prosser's classification of invasion of privacy into four torts, the fourth being the appropriation for the defendant's advantage of the plaintiff's name or likeness, in his seminal article "Privacy" (1960) 48 Calif. L.R. 383 and in his book *Handbook of the Law of Torts* (see 4th ed. (West, 1971), chap. 20, para. 117, pp. 804–805). This approach was adopted in the Second Restatement of the Law of Torts (1977), para. 652 for which Prosser was the Reporter. Many jurisdictions now distinguish between appropriation of a private person's personality and that of a celebrity: the former is treated as an invasion of privacy attracting compensation for injured feelings, while the latter is treated as an infringement of the right of publicity attracting compensation for loss of goodwill and endorsement fees. The distinction is not uniformly observed, however.

Co. Ltd[46] the plaintiff was an actor whose voice was imitated in an advertisement. An application for an interlocutory injunction was refused, but the judge and the Court of Appeal declined to express an opinion as to whether the action could succeed at trial. It appears that the major reason why the plaintiff was unsuccessful in obtaining an injunction was that he also sued for libel, and the courts applied the rule that no interlocutory injunction will be granted to restrain an alleged defamatory publication.[47] If appropriate evidence could be adduced, however, it is difficult to see why the plaintiff in a case such as *Sim v. Heinz* should not succeed at trial.

Basic requirements

The basic requirements for a cause of action in passing off are that (1) the plaintiff has a goodwill in connection with some distinctive indication (such as a trade mark, name, get-up, etc.) which he uses in relation to the supply of goods of services, (2) the defendant is supplying goods or services using an indication which by virtue of its similarity to that used by the plaintiff leads to a misrepresentation to consumers of those goods or services that they are the goods or services of or connected or associated with the plaintiff and (3) the plaintiff suffers damage as a result. Again, readers should consult a specialist text.[48]

8.21

MORAL RIGHTS

Part I of the Copyright, Designs and Patents Act grants limited moral rights to the authors of copyright literary, dramatic, musical and artistic works and also to directors of copyright films. These are the rights to be identified as the author or director of the work or film (the "paternity" right)[49] and the right to object to derogatory treatment of the work or film (the "integrity" right).[50] In addition, a person has a right not to have a work or film falsely attributed to him.[51] Under Part II of the 1988 Act, however, there are no moral rights in performances at present.[52] Accordingly, moral rights may only be relied upon where there is a copyright work or film in question. Nevertheless, moral rights may be still of assistance to performer-authors in circumstances where economic rights are not. Thus in *Morrison Leahy Music Ltd v. Lightbond Ltd*[53] the defendants had produced a sound recording which was a melody of words and music from five compositions of which the second plaintiff was the author and the first plaintiff the copyright owner. The excerpts from the five compositions were interspersed with fill-in music composed by others. The defendants claimed to be entitled to do this pursuant to a clearance which

8.22

---

[46] [1959] 1 W.L.R. 313.
[47] *Bonnard v. Perryman* [1891] 2 Ch. 269.
[48] *e.g.* Wadlow, *The Law of Passing-Off* (2nd ed., Sweet & Maxwell, 1995) or Drysdale and Silverleaf, *Passing Off: Law and Practice*, (2nd ed., Butterworths, 1995).
[49] Copyright, Designs and Patents Act 1988, s. 77.
[50] *ibid.*, s. 80.
[51] *ibid.*, s. 84.
[52] This will change when the WIPO Treaty is ratified: see Chap. 1, para. 1.93.
[53] [1993] EMLR 144.

they had obtained from Mechanical-Copyright Protection Society Limited. In the alternative to the first plaintiff's claim for copyright infringement (based on the argument that MCPS did not have the right to licence the defendant to modify the works in such a way as to alter their character) the second plaintiff claimed for infringement of his moral rights. It was held to be arguable that what the defendants had done amounted to distortion or mutilation of the works contrary to section 80(2)(b) of the 1988 Act. Generally, however, the restrictions upon moral rights contained in Chapter IV of the 1988 Act mean that they are not of great practical assistance.[54]

BREACH OF CONFIDENCE

8.23 In the celebrated case of *Fraser v. Thames Television Ltd*,[55] three actresses who were also singers devised an idea for a television series featuring the professional and private lives of three female singers which would be partly autobiographical. Their main purpose in devising the idea was to secure employment for themselves by being cast as the three singers. They disclosed the idea in confidence to the defendant television company which proceeded to make and broadcast a series (*Rock Follies*) without their consent and with different actresses as the three singers. It was held that the defendant was liable for breach of confidence. Save in exceptional circumstances such as these, however, confidence is unlikely to be of much relevance to the protection of performers.

CONTRACT

8.24 For many performers, contractual protection is the most important form of protection of all, since the provisions of, say, a musician's recording contract are likely to have a much greater effect on him or her both financially and artistically than any success in an action for infringement of performer's rights. In recent years there has been a considerable amount of litigation concerning the contracts between performers and record companies, in particular the *Holly Johnson*,[56] *Stone Roses*[57] and *George Michael*[58] cases. These cases have mainly centred around allegations by the performers that their recording and publishing contracts are unenforceable as being in undue restraint of trade.[59] In the *Holly Johnson* and *Stone Roses* cases the performers were successful in this allegation while in the *George Michael* case he was not. In addition, there have been several cases, notably the *Gilbert*

---

[54] *e.g.* the requirement that the paternity right be "asserted": Copyright, Designs and Patents Act 1988, s. 80.

[55] [1984] Q.B. 44.

[56] *Zang Tumb Tuum Records Ltd v. Johnson* [1993] EMLR 61.

[57] *Silvertone Records Ltd v. Mountfield* [1993] EMLR 152.

[58] *Panayiotou v. Sony Music Entertainment (U.K.) Ltd* [1994] EMLR 229. Michael also alleged breach of Art. 85 of the Treaty of Rome.

[59] Applying *A. Schroeder Music Publishing Co. Ltd v. Macaulay* [1974] 1 W.L.R. 1308 and *Clifford Davis Management Ltd v. WEA Records Ltd* [1975] 1 W.L.R. 61.

O'Sullivan[60] and *Elton John*[61] cases, in which performers have successfully alleged that their contracts are voidable on the ground of undue influence.[62] Discussion of the doctrines of restraint of trade and undue influence is outside the scope of this book,[63] as is consideration of the terms typically to be found in such agreements.[64] Attention is, however, drawn to two points concerning the drafting of such agreements.

The first point is that now that performers' property rights are assignable it **8.25** is to be anticipated that record companies (and others with whom performers contract, such as film and broadcasting companies) may seek to include assignments of these rights in the same way that at present they habitually seek assignments of copyright in the sound recordings (and films) embodying the performers' performances. In the *George Michael* case Jonathan Parker J. held that the doctrine of restraint of trade had essentially no application to the outright sale of property such as copyright.[65] If this is right, then the fact that the record company insists upon an assignment will not without more amount to an undue restraint of trade. Moreover, even if the contract is held to be in restraint of trade for other reasons, this will not lead to an order for reassignment of the rights.[66] It is therefore suggested that it behoves performers not to agree to assign their proprietary rights, but instead to grant a licence which if necessary may be exclusive.

The second point is conveniently illustrated by *Stansfield v. Sovereign* **8.26** *Music Ltd.*[67] The plaintiff was a singer who had entered into a recording agreement with D. Clause 2 of the agreement provided that the plaintiff gave all requisite consents for the purposes of the Performers' Protection Acts (equivalent to a blanket licence under Part II of the 1988 Act). Clause 13 provided that D was entitled to assign its rights, liabilities and obligations under the agreement on certain conditions. After the termination of the main provisions of the agreement, D had assigned the benefit of the agreement to C which had licensed the defendant to make records from the recordings made by the plaintiff under the agreement. There was a factual dispute as to whether the conditions for assignment had been complied with. The defendant argued that on the true construction of the agreement the conditions for assignment only applied before termination and not after, so that it was immaterial whether or not they had in fact been complied with. In the result it was held that the point was arguable either way.

The moral of this case is that it behoves performers and their advisors to **8.27** ensure that, if a wide-ranging licence of performers' rights is to be granted, it

---

[60] *O'Sullivan v. Management Agency and Music Ltd* [1985] Q.B. 428.
[61] *John v. James* [1991] F.S.R. 397.
[62] Applying *Lloyds Bank v. Bundy* [1975] Q.B. 326 and *National Westminster Bank v. Morgan* [1985] A.C. 686 respectively. Now see also *Barclays Bank v. O'Brien* [1994] 1 A.C. 180.
[63] See *Chitty on Contracts* (27th ed., Sweet & Maxwell, 1994), Chaps. 16 and 7.
[64] See Bagehot, *Music Business Agreements* (Sweet & Maxwell, 1989).
[65] [1994] EMLR 229, 373–374.
[66] The only case in which this has been ordered is the *O'Sullivan* case, where the basis for the order was the finding of undue influence: [1985] Q.B. 428, 449A–460C (Dunn L.J.), 464H–469D (Fox L.J.), 470F–473E (Waller L.J.). In the *Elton John* case a similar order was refused on the ground of delay.
[67] [1994] EMLR 224.

is counterbalanced by some appropriate restriction on assignment. If this is not done, the performer runs the risk that the benefit of the agreement will be assigned to a third party which will exploit the performances leaving the performer with a royalty claim against the original contracting party which by this time may be insolvent. Moreover there may be a series of such assignments to fourth and fifth parties and these parties may grant licences to yet further parties. Thus the potential consequence of a failure to restrict assignment is that it may lead to exploitation of the performer's performances on a substantial scale without the performer receiving compensation and for which the performer has no remedy under Part II of the 1988 Act.

9. Performers' Rights in Other Countries

INTRODUCTION

At the time that the first edition of this book was published, international 9.01
provision for performers' rights was patchy and, where it existed, highly
variable.[1] Of the present Members of the European Union, for example, only
Austria, Denmark, France, Germany, Ireland, Italy, Luxembourg, Sweden
and the United Kingdom had then ratified the Rome Convention; while
Belgium, Greece and the Netherlands did not confer performers' rights at all.
The United States, Australia, Canada and New Zealand had not joined the
Convention either. Among states that did adhere to the Convention the term
of protection varied from the minimum specified under the Convention, 20
years from the date of performance or its fixation (*e.g.* Luxembourg[2]) to up to
50 years from performance (Germany[3]).

Seven years later there has been a substantial shift. Not only do many more 9.02
states provide for at least the level of protection specified by the Rome
Convention, but in addition there has been a substantial degree of harmonisation at a higher level of protection. In Europe this has mainly been due to the
adoption and transposition into national laws of the E.C. Rental and Lending
Rights Directive. The Directive itself, however, is a symptom of a wider trend
towards treating holders of related rights, and in particular performers, more
equally with owners of authors' rights. For example, Member States of the
European Economic Area agreed to accede to the Rome Convention as part
of the EEA Agreement[4]; and further accessions either have occurred or are
likely as result of the association agreements signed by Poland, Hungary,
former Czechoslovakia, the Ukraine, Romania and Bulgaria with the
European Union. Another important catalyst for change has been TRIPs,
adherence to which requires member nations to give performers protection
close to that required under the Rome Convention and for a period of at least
50 years.[5] (Although the North American Free Trade Agreement contains a
chapter dealing with intellectual property rights,[6] it makes little provision for
performers' rights.)

---

[1] See Stewart, *International Copyright and Neighbouring Rights* (2nd ed., Butterworths, 1989
and 1993) and Sterling, *Intellectual Property Rights in Sound Recordings, Film and Video*
(Sweet & Maxwell, 1992).
[2] Law of September 23, 1975, s. 12.
[3] That is, 25 years from the performance or 25 years from publication of a recording of the
performance if published within that period: Copyright Act 1965, s. 82.
[4] See Chap. 1, para 1.56.
[5] See paras. 9.10–9.14, below.
[6] Chapter 17.

9.03   The purpose of this chapter is to give a brief survey of the current state of performers' rights around the world. First, the rights respectively accorded to performers under the Rome Convention and under TRIPs are summarised. Secondly, an alphabetical list of countries is provided which attempts to summarise the level of protection provided by each country. The scheme of this listing is to indicate first whether the country is a party to the Rome Convention, and if so to give details, and secondly whether the country is a signatory to TRIPs. If a country is neither party to the Rome Convention nor a signatory to TRIPs, then it is probable that it accords no rights to performers; exceptions to this of which the author is aware are noted, however. In addition, a potted summary of the relevant law is given for the more significant jurisdictions. This is restricted to outlining the nature of the rights provided and their duration, so as to give readers an initial guide, for example when considering questions of reciprocal treatment.[8] It should be emphasised that it is not a substitute for proper professional advice from an adviser qualified in the relevant jurisdiction, particularly since many national laws have recently undergone and continue to undergo considerable amendments. In particular, no attempt has been made to describe the extent to which, or the conditions on which, protection is conferred on foreign (*e.g.* British) performers since this would double the length of this chapter and would be very difficult to make accurate for even a short period of time following publication. In general, however, parties to the Rome Convention and signatories to TRIPs *should* provide foreign performers with at least the levels of protection laid down in the respective treaties.[7]

SUMMARY OF PERFORMERS' RIGHTS UNDER THE ROME CONVENTION

9.04   For the purposes of the Rome Convention, Article 3 defines performers as actors, singers, musicians, dancers and other persons who act, sing, deliver, declaim, play in or otherwise perform literary or artistic works; although Article 9 expressly provides that Contracting States may extend the protection to artistes who do not perform literary or artistic works.[9]

9.05   Article 4 of the Rome Convention provides that each Contracting State shall grant "national treatment" to performers if any of the following conditions are met:

(a) the performance takes place in another Contracting State;
(b) the performance is incorporated in a phonogram which is protected under Article 5 of the Convention;

---

[7] Unfortunately it is not possible to state which developing countries are taking advantage of the extra 4-year period allowed for implementing TRIPs under Art. 65(2): see para 9.14, below. This means that until January 1, 2000 there will be considerable uncertainty as to which developing countries have and which have not yet implemented TRIPs. The same is true of the least developed countries, which have a further six years to implement TRIPs.

[8] See Chap. 2, para. 2.59.

[9] See Chap. 2, paras. 2.27, 2.30–2.32 and 2.15–2.17.

(c) the performance, not being fixed on a phonogram, is carried by a broadcast which is protected by Article 6 of the Convention.

"National treatment" means the treatment accorded by the domestic law of that Contracting State to performers who are its nationals and to performances taking place, broadcast or first fixed on its territory, subject to the protection guaranteed and the limitations provided for by the Convention. Thus each Contracting State must give the same treatment to performances connected with other Contracting States as to those connected with itself, and must provide at least the level of protection provided under the Convention.[10]

Article 7(1) provides that the protection provided for performers shall **9.06** include "the possibility of preventing":

(a) the broadcasting and communication to the public of their performance without their consent, except where the performance used for this purpose is itself already a broadcast performance or is made from a fixation;

(b) the fixation of their unfixed performance without their consent;

(c) the reproduction without their consent of a fixation of their performance if:

    (i)   the original fixation was made without their consent;

    (ii) the reproduction is made for purposes different from those for which the performers gave their consent;

    (iii) the original fixation was made in accordance with Article 15 of the Convention (private use, etc.), and the reproduction is made for different purposes.[11]

Article 19 provides, however, that once a performer has consented to the incorporation of his performance in a visual or audiovisual fixation, Article 7 shall have no further application.[12]

Article 12 provides that where a phonogram published for commercial **9.07** purposes, or a reproduction of such a phonogram, is used directly for broadcasting or for any communication to the public, a "single equitable remuneration" shall be paid by the user to the performers, or to the producer of the phonogram, or to both. It goes on to provide that domestic law may, in the absence of agreement between these parties, lay down the terms for the sharing of this remuneration.[13] Article 16 enables Contracting States to enter reservations with respect to the operation of Article 12, however.[14]

Article 14 provides that the term of protection under the Convention shall **9.08** last at least until the end of a period of 20 years calculated from the end of the year in which the fixation was made, for performances incorporated in phonograms, or in which the performance took place, for performances not incorporated in phonograms.

Article 15(1) provides for exceptions to the protection under the Conven- **9.09**

---

[10] See Chap. 2, para. 2.40.
[11] See Chap. 1, paras. 1.51–1.54.
[12] See Chap. 1, para. 1.55.
[13] See Chap. 3, paras. 3.44–3.47.
[14] See Chap. 1, para. 1.55.

tion in the cases of (a) private use; (b) use of short excerpts in connection with the reporting of current events; (c) ephemeral fixation by a broadcasting organisation by means of its own facilities and for its own broadcasts; and (d) use solely for the purposes of teaching or scientific research. In addition, Article 15(2) provides that Contracting States may enact the same limitations with respect to performers' rights as they do with respect to copyrights in literary and artistic works.[15]

Summary of Performers' Rights under TRIPs

9.10   TRIPs contains certain general provisions which are relevant to performers' rights. Article 3 provides that each Member shall accord to the nationals of other Members treatment no less favourable than it accords to its own national with regard to the protection of intellectual property ("national treatment"), subject to the exceptions provided in the Rome Convention. This obligation only applies in respect of the rights provided under TRIPs, however. Article 4 provides that any advantage, favour, privilege or immunity granted by a Member to the nationals of any other country shall be accorded immediately and unconditionally to the nationals of all other Members ("most-favoured-nation treatment"). This is subject, however, to exceptions in the case of advantages etc. granted pursuant to provisions of the Rome Convention authorising treatment according to the treatment accorded in another country and in the case of performers' rights not provided under TRIPs.

9.11   Performers' rights specifically are dealt with in Article 14 of TRIPs. Article 14(1) provides that performers shall have the "possibility of preventing" the fixation of their unfixed performance on a phonogram and the reproduction of such a fixation without their consent. Performers shall also have the "possibility of preventing" broadcast by wireless means and the communication to the public of their live performances without their consent.

9.12   Article 14(5) provides that the term of protection available to performers shall last at least until the end of a period of 50 years calculated from the end of the calendar year in which the fixation was made or the performance took place.

9.13   Article 14(6) provides that Members may provide for conditions, limitations, exceptions and reservations to the rights of performers to the extent permitted by the Rome Convention. In addition, the provisions of Article 18 of the Berne Convention (Paris Act, 1971) shall apply *mutatis mutandis* to the rights of performers.

9.14   Article 65(1) provides that no Member shall be obliged to apply the provisions of TRIPs before the expiry of one year from the date of entry into force of the WTO Agreement (*i.e.* before January 1, 1996) but Article 65(2) provides that a "developing country Member" is entitled to delay the application of TRIPs other than Articles 3–5 for a period of four years (*i.e.* until January 1, 2000) and Article 66(1) provides that "least-developed

---

[15] See Chap. 5, in particular para. 5.04.

country Members" may delay for ten years (*i.e.* until January 1, 2006). Since WIPO does not have any central register of which developing countries are taking advantage of these provisions, it is difficult to be certain whether developing countries have yet implemented Article 14 of TRIPs or not. This should be borne in mind when consulting the survey below.

LIST OF COUNTRIES

Afghanistan

At the time of writing Afghanistan is neither a party to the Rome Convention nor a signatory to TRIPs. **9.15**

Albania

At the time of writing Albania is neither a party to the Rome Convention nor a signatory to TRIPs, but has applied to join the WTO. **9.16**

It is understood that the Law on Author's Rights, No. 7564 of May 19, 1993, provides protection for performers. **9.17**

Algeria

At the time of writing Algeria is neither a party to the Rome Convention nor a signatory to TRIPs, but has applied to join the WTO. **9.18**

Andorra

At the time of writing Andorra is neither a party to the Rome Convention nor a signatory to TRIPs. **9.19**

Angola

Angola became a signatory to TRIPs with effect from November 23, 1996. **9.20**

Antigua and Barbuda

Antigua and Barbuda became signatories to TRIPs with effect from January 1, 1995. **9.21**

Argentina

Argentina became party to the Rome Convention on March 2, 1992, with no reservations. It became a signatory to TRIPs with effect from January 1, 1995. **9.22**

Argentina's Intellectual Property Act of 1933[16] was one of the first to grant performers rights in respect of their live or recorded performances. It has since been amended. Performers have the right to authorise or prohibit the recording of their performances; the reproduction of such recordings; the communication of live performances to the public; the communication to the public of recordings not commercially published. Performers also have the right to equitable remuneration for the use of recordings for broadcasting or other communication to the public. In addition performers have moral rights, **9.23**

---

[16] No. 11.723.

namely a paternity right and an integrity right. The term of protection is 50 years.

Armenia

9.24   At the time of writing Armenia is neither party to the Rome Convention nor a signatory to TRIPs, but it has applied to join the WTO. On April 22, 1996 Armenia signed a Partnership Co-operation Agreement with the European Union under which it agreed to make efforts to attain a level protection of intellectual property rights similar to that of the European Union within five years of entry into force of the Agreement.

Australia

9.25   Australia became party to the Rome Convention on September 30, 1992, with reservations under Article 5(3) (concerning Article 5(1)(c)), 6(2), 16(1)(a)(i) and 16(1)(b).[17] It became a signatory to TRIPs with effect from January 1, 1995.

9.26   The Copyright Act 1968 was amended by the Copyright Amendment Act 1989 to confer rights on performers for the first time. The 1968 Act was further amended by the Copyright (World Trade Organisation Amendments) Act 1994[18] *inter alia* so as to extend performers' rights.[19] The 1994 Act came into force on July 1, 1995. Performers have a non-assignable right to authorise (i) the first fixation of their performance, (ii) the broadcast of their performance and (iii) the transmission of their performance to subscribers to a diffusion service. In addition, performers have rights to prohibit dealings in unauthorised recordings of their performance and to authorise the inclusion of their performance in the soundtrack of a film. Otherwise, performers do not have the right to control copying of an authorised recording of their performance. The term of protection against unauthorised recording is 50 years from the date of the performance while the term of protection against unauthorised broadcasting and diffusion is 20 years.

9.27   In August 1994 the Music Industry Advisory Council published a discussion paper canvassing the arguments for and against the introduction of a performers' copyright.[20] Following this the Government agreed in principle to investigate the introduction of a performers' copyright which was assignable and corresponded with the rights in sound recordings and audiovisual productions. The Government referred the question to an interdepartmental committee consisting of representatives from the Departments of Industry, Science and Technology, Communications and the Arts and the Attorney-General, to report by September 1995. In addition, the Minister for Justice initiated a major review of the Copyright Act 1968 by the Copyright Law Review Committee. While this review is not particularly concerned with related rights issues, one of the specific questions to be addressed is the desirability of maintaining existing distinctions between

---

[17] [1992] *Copyright* 301.
[18] Act 149/94.
[19] See Peach and Gilchrist, "Recent Developments in Australian Copyright Law" [1996] 7 EIPR 409.
[20] Music Industry Advisory Council, *Performers' Copyright* (August 1994).

different categories of works and other subject matters. In February 1996 the CLRC published a discussion paper.[21] A further report is due by November 30, 1997.

Austria

Austria became party to the Rome Convention on June 9, 1973, with reservations under Article 16(1)(a)(iii) and (iv) and 1(b).[22] It became a signatory to TRIPs with effect from January 1, 1995.

    9.28

The Copyright Law of 1936[23] was probably the first to create a structured system of civil rights for performers. Since then it has been amended a number of times, the latest amendment[24] being to introduce rental and lending rights in accordance with the E.C. Directive with effect from January 1, 1994. The performer of a work of literature or music has an exclusive right to record the performance and to reproduce and distribute the recording.[25] Performers have the right to authorise the broadcasting of their performances unless a recording to which they have consented is used in which case they are entitled to a proper share of fair remuneration paid to the producer of the recording; in the absence of agreement this share is 50 per cent.[26] Performers have a paternity right consisting of a right to be identified on recordings.[27] The term of protection is 50 years from publication.[28] The Copyright Amendment Act 1996 came into force on April 1, 1996.[29]

    9.29

Azerbaijan

At the time of writing Azerbaijan is neither party to the Rome Convention nor a signatory to TRIPs, but on April 22, 1996 Azerbaijan signed a Partnership Co-Operation Agreement with the European Union under which it agreed to make efforts to attain a level protection of intellectual property rights similar to that of the European Union within five years of entry into force of the Agreement.

    9.30

Bahamas

At the time of writing the Bahamas are neither a party to the Rome Convention nor a signatory to TRIPs.

    9.31

Bahrain

Bahrain became a signatory to TRIPs with effect from January 1, 1995.

    9.32

Bangladesh

Bangladesh became a signatory to TRIPs with effect from January 1, 1995.

    9.33

---

[21] "Copyright Reform: A Consideration of Rationales, Interests and Objectives".
[22] [1973] *Copyright* 67.
[23] Law of April 9, 1936, BGBl 1936/111.
[24] Of November 1993.
[25] Art. 66(1).
[26] Art. 76(3).
[27] Art. 68.
[28] S. 67(1).
[29] See Kucsko and Windish, "The 1996 Austrian Copyright Amendment Act" (1996) 62 *Copyright World* 38.

Barbados

9.34 Barbados became party to the Rome Convention on September 18, 1983, with no reservations. It became a signatory to TRIPs with effect from January 1, 1995.

Belarus

9.35 At the time of writing Belarus is neither a party to the Rome Convention nor a signatory to TRIPs, but it has applied to join the WTO.

Belgium

9.36 At the time of writing Belgium is a signatory to TRIPs with effect from January 1, 1995, but is not party to the Rome Convention.

9.37 On June 30, 1994 Belgium passed a new Law on Copyright and Neighbouring Rights[30] to replace the previous (1886) law. The new law, which came into force on August 1, 1994, granted neighbouring rights to performers and others for the first time.[31] The law conforms to the three E.C. Directives and will enable Belgium to ratify the Rome Convention, although at the time of writing it has not done so. Minor amendments were made by the law of April 3, 1995 which came into force on May 9, 1995.[32] Performers have the exclusive right to reproduce a performance or authorise its reproduction in any manner and in any form, which includes rental, lending and communicating the performance to the public by any method.[33] In addition, performers have the exclusive right of distribution of reproductions of their performances which is only exhausted by sale within the European Union by or with the consent of the performer.[34] Performers also have inalienable moral rights, namely a paternity right to be credited according to the fair practice of the relevant profession, a right to prohibit false attribution and an integrity right.[35] When a performance is lawfully reproduced or broadcast, performers may not prohibit broadcasting or other communication to the public, provided that the performance is not used in an entertainment and no entrance or other fee is charged to the public,[36] but the performer and producers have a right to equitable remuneration[37] to be shared equally between them.[38] Unless otherwise agreed, performers are deemed to assign their exploitation rights to the producers of an audiovisual work.[39] Performers who transfer their rental rights in respect of phonograms and films have an unwaivable right to equitable remuneration.[40] There are

---

[30] Official Journal of July 27, 1994 corrected in Official Journal of November 22, 1994.
[31] See van Luchem and Glas, "The 1994 Belgian Act on Copyright and Neighbouring Rights" [1995] 2 ENT. LR 63.
[32] A translation of the amended Act was published in the Copyright and Neighbouring Rights Laws and Treaties supplement to *Industrial Property and Copyright*, December 1996.
[33] Article 35(1).
[34] *ibid.*
[35] Art. 34.
[36] Art. 41.
[37] Art. 42.
[38] Art. 43.
[39] Art. 36.
[40] Art. 40.

permitted acts which are mainly parallel to those permitted under copyright.[41] Performer's economic rights are assignable, but subject to certain restrictions.[42] Variety and circus artists are protected but not "ancillary performers".[43] In the case of live performances by groups of performers, authorisation is to be given by soloists, conductors, directors and (for other performers) the manager of the group.[44] The period of protection is 50 years from the end of the calendar year in which the performance was given or 50 years from publication if a recording is published within that period.[45]

Belize

Belize became a signatory to TRIPs with effect from January 1, 1995.　　9.38

Benin

Benin became a signatory to TRIPs with effect from February 22, 1996.　　9.39

Bolivia

Bolivia became party to the Rome Convention on November 24, 1993, with　9.40
no reservations. It became a signatory to TRIPs with effect from September
13, 1995.

　　Under Law No. 1322 of April 13, 1992, performers have the right to　9.41
authorise or prohibit the fixation, reproduction, communication to the
public, transmission or other uses of their performances. Performers and
phonogram producers have the right to receive equitable remuneration for
broadcasting and public performance of phonograms, to be shared equally in
the absence of agreement to the contrary. The term of these rights is 50 years.
Interpretative artists such as stage directors and conductors have moral rights
consisting of a paternity right, an integrity right and preservation of their
reputation for life plus 20 years.[46]

Bosnia and Herzogovina

At the time of writing Bosnia and Herzogovina are neither parties to the　9.42
Rome Convention nor signatories to TRIPs.

Botswana

Botswana became a signatory to TRIPs with effect from May 31, 1995.　　9.43

Brazil

Brazil became party to the Rome Convention on September 29, 1965, with no　9.44
reservations. It became a signatory to TRIPs with effect from January 1995.

---

[41] Arts. 46, 47.
[42] Arts. 33, 35(2).
[43] Art. 35(1).
[44] Art. 37.
[45] Art. 38.
[46] Art. 53.

Brunei Darussalam

9.45 Brunei Darussalam became a signatory to TRIPs with effect from January 1, 1995.

Bulgaria

9.46 Bulgaria became party to the Rome Convention on August 31, 1995, with no reservations. It became a signatory to TRIPs with effect from December 1, 1996.

9.47 A new Law on Author's Right and Neighbouring Rights[47] came into force on August 1, 1993. Performers are granted the exclusive right to authorise broadcasting, cable transmission or recording of their performances[48] and to authorise the distribution, broadcasting, cable transmission and public performance of such recordings.[49] Unless otherwise agreed, the producer of a sound recording or film is deemed to have been granted exploitation rights by the performer.[50] Performers also have moral rights, namely a paternity right and an integrity right.[51] The term of protection is 50 years.

Burkina Faso

9.48 Burkina Faso became party to the Rome Convention on January 14, 1988, with no reservations. It became a signatory to TRIPs with effect from June 3, 1995.

Burundi

9.49 Burundi became a signatory to TRIPs with from July 23, 1995.

Cameroon

9.50 Cameroon became a signatory to TRIPs with effect from December 13, 1995.

Canada

9.51 Canada became a signatory to TRIPs with effect from January 1, 1995.

9.52 The World Trade Organisation Implementing Act 1994, which came into force on January 1, 1996, amended the Copyright Act so as to confer rights on performers in respect of their performances. A performer's performance is a live performance of a pre-existing artistic, dramatic or musical work or a live recitation or reading of a pre-existing literary work, whether or not the work was previously fixed in any material form, and a live improvisation of an artistic, dramatic, musical or literary work, whether or not based on a pre-existing work.[52] Where a performer's performance takes place in a country that is a WTO Member, on or after the later of January 1, 1996 and the day on which that country becomes a WTO Member, the performer has the sole right to do and to authorise the following acts: (a) to fix the

---

[47] Of June 16, 1993.
[48] Art. 76(1).
[49] Art. 76(2).
[50] Arts. 76(3), 78.
[51] Art. 75.
[52] s. 2.

performer's performance (or any substantial part thereof) by means of a record, perforated roll or other contrivance by means of which sounds may be mechanically reproduced; (b) to reproduce the fixation (or any substantial part thereof) or any reproduction of that fixation (or any substantial part thereof) where that fixation was made without the performer's consent; and (c) to communicate the performance (or any substantial part thereof) to the public by telecommunication at the time of the performer's performance.[53] Where a performer's performance took place in a country that is a WTO member before this date, the performer only has right (b).[54] In addition, it is an infringement of performers' rights to (a) sell or let for hire, or by way of trade expose or offer for sale or hire, (b) distribute either for the purposes of trade or to such an extent as to affect prejudicially the owner of the performer's right, (c) by way of trade exhibit in public or (d) import for sale or hire into Canada any fixation of the performer's performance, or any reproduction of such a fixation, that to the knowledge of the person doing the act infringes the performer's right.[55] Performers' rights subsist for 50 years from the end of the calendar year in which they were given.[56] Performers' rights are not infringed by fair dealing with the performance, a fixation thereof or a reproduction of the fixation for the purpose of private study, research, criticism, review or newspaper summary; in addition there are certain other permitted acts.[57] Remedies for infringement include injunctions, damages, accounts of profits and delivery up.[58] Interestingly, infringing fixations and infringing reproductions of a fixation, together with plates used or intended to be used for making infringing reproductions, are deemed to be the property of the owner of the performers' rights.[59] This means that conversion damages are available. There are also criminal offences in respect of certain infringements of performers' rights.[60]

Central African Republic

The Central African Republic became a signatory to TRIPs with effect from May 31, 1995.

9.53

Chad

Chad became a signatory to TRIPs with effect from October 19, 1996.

9.54

Chile

Chile became party to the Rome Convention on September 5, 1974, with no reservations. It became a signatory to TRIPs with effect from January 1, 1995.

9.55

---

[53] s. 14.01(1).
[54] s. 14.01(4).
[55] s. 28.02(3).
[56] s. 14.01(5).
[57] s. 28.02(2).
[58] s. 34(1.01).
[59] s. 38(2).
[60] s. 43.1.

People's Republic of China

9.56 At the time of writing China is neither party to the Rome Convention nor a signatory to TRIPs, but it has applied to join the WTO.

9.57 The Copyright Act 1990[61] and Implementing Regulations 1991 which came into force on June 1, 1991 confer related rights on performers. Performers have in relation to their performances a paternity right, an integrity right, the right to authorise others to make live broadcasts and the right to authorise others to make recordings for commercial purposes and to receive remuneration therefrom.[62] The moral rights are perpetual.[63] The right to remuneration for use of a performance in a broadcast or recording lasts for as long as the corresponding right of the record producer or broadcaster,[64] namely 50 years from first publication or first broadcast. The limitations which apply to copyright also apply to performers' rights.[65] Performances by foreign performers given in China are protected.[66]

Colombia

9.58 Colombia became party to the Rome Convention on September 17, 1976, with no reservations. It became a signatory to TRIPs with effect from April 30, 1995.

9.59 The Law on Copyright of 1982[67] was amended in 1993.[68] Performers or their representatives have the right to authorise or prohibit the fixation, recording communication to the public, transmission or any other form of use of their performances.[69] Consequently, no one may do any of the following acts without the authorisation of the performers: (a) broadcasting and communication to the public, except where it is made from a previously authorised fixation or where the transmission is authorised by the broadcasting organisation, (b) fixation or (c) reproduction of a fixation where the performance was fixed without authority or where the reproduction is made for different purposes to those for which authorisation was given or which are lawful.[70] Once performers have consented to the incorporation of their performance in visual or audiovisual fixation, their rights are exhausted.[71]

---

[61] Law Adopted at the 15th Session of the Standing Committee of the 7th National People's Congress on September 7, 1990. An English translation of the Act and of the Implementing Regulations of May 24, 1991 is in Appendix A to Stewart, in Stewart, in vol. 2, note 1, above; see also Gou Shoukang in the same volume. Further Implementing Regulations of September 25, 1992 implemented the Berne and Universal Copyright Conventions, but not the Rome Convention. An English translation was published in [1992] 11 EIPR D-231.

[62] Art. 36.

[63] Implementing Regulations, Art. 44, para. 1.

[64] Implementing Regulations, Art. 44, para. 2.

[65] Art. 22.

[66] Implementing Regulations, Art. 46.

[67] Law No. 23 of January 28, 1982. A translation was published in *Copyright Laws and Treaties of the World*, 1981–1983 Supplement.

[68] By Law No. 44 of February 5, 1993. A translation was published in the Copyright and Neighbouring Rights Laws and Treaties supplement to *Industrial Property and Copyright*, December 1995.

[69] Art. 166.

8.

Performers also have moral rights which parallel those of authors.[72] Where a phonogram published for commercial purposes or a reproduction thereof is used for broadcasting or other communication to the public, the user must pay a single equitable royalty to the performers and the phonogram producer through the collective administration organisations for distribution in equal shares.[73] Performers' rights are transferable apart from moral rights.[74] The duration of the rights is life plus 80 years.[75] Authors' rights take precedence over those of performers, phonogram producers and broadcasting organisations and prevail in the case of conflict.[76]

Congo

Congo became party to the Rome Convention on May 18, 1964, with reservations under Article 5(3) (concerning Article 5(1)(c)) and 16(1)(a)(i).[77] It is not a signatory to TRIPs, however.

9.60

Costa Rica

Costa Rica became party to the Rome Convention on September 9, 1971, with no reservations. It became a signatory to TRIPs with effect from January 1, 1995.

9.61

Côte d'Ivoire

Côte d'Ivoire became a signatory to TRIPs with effect from January 1, 1995.

9.62

Croatia

At the time of writing Croatia is neither party to the Rome Convention nor a signatory to TRIPs, but it has applied to join the WTO.

9.63

Croatia adopted the Federal Authors' Rights Act 1990 of former Yugoslavia on declaring independence in October 1991.[78] This included some amendments passed by the last Yugoslavian Government[79] to protect performers for the first time, Yugoslavia never having joined the Rome Convention. In June 1993 Croatia enacted amendments to the Authors' Rights Act.[80] Under the Act as amended, performers have rights to prevent unauthorised broadcasting of their performances; to prevent unauthorised direct communication to the public of their performances (*e.g.* by a loudspeaker outside the room where the performance is given); to prevent unauthorised recording of their performances; to prevent copying of such recordings; and to prevent distribution of such copies. The duration of such rights is 20 years from the date of broadcasting, recording or performance. Broadcasters are given a blank compulsory licence to broadcast recording of

9.64

---

[72] Art. 171.
[73] Art. 173 as amended.
[74] Art. 182.
[75] Art. 29 as amended.
[76] Art. 2 as amended.
[77] [1964] *Le Droit d'auteur* 127.
[78] Official Gazette 53/91.
[79] An English translation of the Act as amended is included in *Copyright and Neighbouring Rights Laws and Treaties* (WIPO).
[80] Official Gazette 58/93. See Singer and Vukmir, "A Review of Croatian Law on Authors' Rights" [1995] 2 ENT. LR 48.

performances. It is anticipated that Croatia will enact a new Act in conformity with the E.C. Directives and will join the Rome Convention shortly.

Cuba

9.65   Cuba became a signatory to TRIPs with effect from April 20, 1995.

Cyprus

9.66   Cyprus became a signatory to TRIPs with effect from July 30, 1995.

Czech Republic

9.67   The Czech Republic became party to the Rome Convention on January 1, 1993, with reservations under Article 16(1)(a)(iii) and (iv). It became a signatory to TRIPs with effect from January 1, 1995.

9.68   The Czechoslovakian Copyright Act 1965[81] as amended by the Copyright Act Amendment 1990[82] remains in force in the Czech Republic which came into existence on January 1, 1993.[83] Performers are those who interpret in a creative way literary or artistic works. Performances may not be used without the consent of the performer for a recording made for the production of reproductions designed for public sale or for the production of films designed for public projection; or for making films designed for public sale; or for use of recordings other than those to which the performer has consented; or for broadcasts; or for public projection or other distribution if the performance was given for someone other than the person who wishes to use it.[84] In addition, performers are entitled to remuneration for the use of their performance.[85] There are various exceptions to the requirement for consent, in particular for recordings made by broadcasting organisations for their own broadcasts and for broadcasting and public presentation of performances by means of a recording or film produced with the consent of the performer.[86] Performers also have moral rights. The rights cannot be assigned as a whole, but they can be inherited and licences can be granted. The rights in a collective performance can only be exercised by the whole collective. The rights apply to foreign nationals protected under the Rome Convention.[87] The duration of the rights is 50 years from the end of the year in which the performance was first recorded.

Denmark

9.69   Denmark became party to the Rome Convention on September 23, 1965, with reservations under Articles 6(2), 16(1)(ii) and (iv) and 17.[88] It became a signatory to TRIPs with effect from January 1, 1995.

9.70   A new Copyright Act 1995 came into force in Denmark on July 1, 1995

---

[81] No. 35/65 Coll.
[82] No. 89/90 Coll.
[83] See Loebl, Bohacek and Slanina in Stewart, vol. 2, note 1, above, chap. 5.
[84] s. 36(2).
[85] s. 36(3).
[86] s. 37.
[87] s. 50.
[88] [1965] Copyright 214.

which constituted a major overhaul of the previous (1961) Act and implemented the E.C. Rental and Lending Rights, Satellite Broadcasting and Term Directives.[89] Under the new Act the performance of a literary or artistic work by a performing artist may not without his consent be (i) recorded on tape, film or any other device by means of which it can be reproduced or (ii) made available to the public.[89a] In addition, a recording of a performance must not be transferred to any other device by means of which it can be reproduced or made available to the public without the consent of the artist.[89b] An agreement between a performing artist and a film producer to take part in a recording of a film implies that the artist has assigned his right to the rental of the film to the producer in the absence of agreement to the contrary.[89c] Published sound recordings may be used in broadcasts on radio and television and for other public performances, in which case the performing artists and producers are entitled to remuneration which may only be claimed by a joint organisation approved by the Ministry of Culture.[89d] There is a special exception which permits the Royal Theatre to allow gala performances or performances in connection with official visits to be broadcast by Danmarks Radio or TV2 on radio or television.[89e] Various provisions of copyright law apply *mutatis mutandis* to performers' rights.[89f] In accordance with the Term Directive, the period of protection is 50 years from the end of the year in which the performace was given or 50 years from publication if a recording is published within that period.[89g]

Djibouti

Djibouti became a signatory to TRIPs with effect from May 31, 1995.   9.71

Dominica

Dominica became a signatory to TRIPs with effect from January 1, 1995.   9.72

Dominican Republic

The Dominican Republic became party to the Rome Convention on January 27, 1987, with no reservations. It became a signatory to TRIPs with effect from March 9, 1995.   9.73

Ecuador

Ecuador became party to the Rome Convention on May 18, 1964, with no reservations. It became a signatory to TRIPs with effect from January 21, 1996.   9.74

---

[89] A translation was published in the Copyright and Neighbouring Rights Laws and Treaties Supplement to *Industrial Property and Copyright*, January 1997. See Neumann, "New Copyright Act Passed in Denmark Offering Increased Protection for Photographers, Performers and Producers" [1995] 8 ENT. LR 337.
[89a] s.65(1).
[89b] s.65(2).
[89c] s.65(3).
[89d] s.68.
[89e] s.65(5).
[89f] s.65(4).
[89g] s.65(2).

Egypt

9.75 Egypt became a signatory to TRIPs with effect from June 30, 1995.

El Salvador

9.76 El Salvador became party to the Rome Convention on April 11, 1979, with no reservations. It became a signatory to TRIPs with effect from May 7, 1995.

9.77   The Law on the Promotion and Protection of Intellectual Property, Decree No. 604 of July 15, 1993,[90] which came into force on October 15, 1993, confers neighbouring rights on performers. A performer is any actor, singer, musician, dancer or other person who interprets a role, sings, declaims or in any way performs a literary or artistic work.[91] Performers have the right to authorise or prohibit the fixation, reproduction or communication to the public of their performances by any means or process, except that they may not object to communication by means of commercially published recordings made with their consent.[92] In addition, performers have a paternity right and an integrity right.[93] Orchestras, vocal ensembles and other groups of performers must appoint a representative to exercise their rights, failing which the director or leader is responsible.[94] The term of protection is 50 years from the end of the calendar year in which the performance was given if unrecorded or in which the recording was published if recorded.[95]

Estonia

9.78 At the time of writing Estonia is neither party to the Rome Convention nor a signatory to TRIPs, but it has applied to join the WTO.

9.79   Under the Copyright Law of November 11, 1992,[96] which came into force on December 12, 1992, performers have neighbouring rights.[97] Performers have a general right regarding the use of their performances and a right to remuneration for such use.[98] The term of protection is 50 years.[99] Performers also have extensive moral rights of "performership", use of their name, integrity and protection of honour and reputation.[1] There are limitations upon performers' rights.[2]

Ethiopia

9.80 At the time of writing Ethiopia is neither party to the Rome Convention nor a signatory to TRIPs.

---

[90] A translation was published in the Copyright and Neighbouring Rights Laws and Treaties supplement to *Industrial Property and Copyright*, February 1995.
[91] Art. 80.
[92] Art. 81.
[93] *ibid.*
[94] Art. 82.
[95] Art. 86(f).
[96] A translation was published in the Copyright and Neighbouring Rights Laws and Treaties supplement to *Industrial Property and Copyright*, January 1995.
[97] See Pisuke, "Estonia Again on the World Copyright Map" (1993) 28 *Copyright World* 24.
[98] Art. 67(1).
[99] Art. 74.
[1] Art. 66.
[2] Art. 75.

Fiji

Fiji became party to the Rome Convention on April 11, 1972, with   **9.81**
reservations under Article 5(3) concerning Articles 5(1)(b), 6(2) and 16(1)(a)
(i).[3] It became a signatory to TRIPs with effect from January 14, 1996.

Finland

Finland became party to the Rome Convention on October 21, 1983, with   **9.82**
reservations under Articles 16(1)(a)(i), (ii) and (iv) and 17.[4] It became a
signatory to TRIPs with effect from January 1, 1995.

The basic Law on Author's Right of 1961[5] has been followed by a number   **9.83**
of other acts including an amending act of 1991.[6] The E.C. Rental and
Lending Rights Directive was implemented as of May 1, 1995 and the Term
Directive was implemented as of July 1, 1995.

France

France became party to the Rome Convention on July 3, 1987, with   **9.84**
reservations under Articles 5(3) (concerning Article 5(1)(c)) and 16(1)(a)(iii)
and (iv).[7] It became a signatory to TRIPs with effect from January 1, 1995.

The Law on the Intellectual Property Code (Legislative Part)[8] as last   **9.85**
amended[9] came into force on January 5, 1995.[10] Performers are those persons
who act, sing, deliver, declaim, play in or otherwise perform literary or
artistic works, variety, circus or puppet acts, except ancillary performers
considered as such by professional practices.[11] Performers have a moral right,
namely an inalienable right to respect for their name, capacity and
performance.[12] Written authority is required for the fixation of performances, reproduction and communication to the public.[13] The making of
contract between a performer and the producer of an audiovisual work
implies authorisation by the former to fix, reproduce and communicate to the
public his performance.[14] Such a contract must lay down separate remuneration for each mode of exploitation.[15] Where the remuneration is not stated it
shall be determined by reference to schedules agreed between employers' and
employees' organisations.[16] Where a phonogram has been commercially
published, neither the performer nor the producer may prohibit either its
communication to the public where it is not used as an entertainment nor its
broadcasting or cable diffusion, but these uses entitle the performer and the

---

[3] [1972] *Copyright* 88, 178.
[4] [1983] *Copyright* 287; [1994] *Copyright* 152.
[5] No. 404 of July 8, 1961.
[6] No. 34 of January 11, 1991.
[7] [1987] *Copyright* 184.
[8] No. 92–597 of July 1, 1992.
[9] By Law No. 94–361 of May 10, 1994 and Law No. 95–4 of January 3, 1995.
[10] A translation of the Law as amended was published in the Copyright and Neighbouring Rights
Laws and Treaties supplement to *Industrial Property and Copyright*, September 1995.
[11] Art. L212–1.
[12] Art. L212–2.
[13] Art. L212–3.
[14] Art. L212–4.
[15] *ibid.*
[16] Art. L212–5.

producer to remuneration which is to be shared 50/50.[17] The duration of performer's economic rights is 50 years from the end of the calendar year in which the performance or its reproduction is first communicated.[18] The moral right appears to be indefinite duration. There are exceptions for (1) private and gratuitous performances within the family circle, (2) reproductions for private use, (3) criticism and review and (4) parody and caricature.[19] Private copying of phonograms and videograms is subject to a right of remuneration, however.[20] The remuneration is a share of a levy paid by the manufacturers and importers of blank tapes.[21] The performers' share is one quarter in the case of phonograms and one third in the case of videograms.[22] In addition to the exceptions listed above, performers may not prohibit reproduction or public communication of their performance if it is accessory to an event which constitutes the main subject of a sequence within a work or an audiovisual document.[23] Infringement may also be criminal offence punishable by a two-year prison term and a fine of 1,000,000 FF.[24]

Gabon

9.86   Gabon became a signatory to TRIPs with effect from January 1, 1995.

The Gambia

9.87   The Gambia became a signatory to TRIPs with effect from October 23, 1996.

Georgia

9.88   At the time of writing Georgia is neither party to the Rome Convention nor a signatory to TRIPs, but it has applied to join the WTO. On April 22, 1996 Georgia signed a Partnership Co-operation Agreement with the European Union under which it agreed to make efforts to attain a level protection of intellectual property rights similar to that of the European Union within five years of entry into force of the Agreement.

Germany

9.89   Germany became party to the Rome Convention on October 21, 1966, with reservations under Articles 5(3) (concerning Article 5(1)(b)) and 16(1)(a) (iv).[25] It became a signatory to TRIPs with effect from January 1, 1995.

9.90   The Author's Rights and Related Rights Act of September 9, 1965[26] was amended on June 23, 1995[27] with effect from July 1, 1995 to implement both

---

[17] Art. L214–1.
[18] Art. L211–4.
[19] Art. L211–3.
[20] Art. L311–1.
[21] Art. L311–3, 4.
[22] Art. L311–7.
[23] Art. L210–10.
[24] Art. L335–4.
[25] [1966] Copyright 237.
[26] BGBl. I. 1273. A translation of the Act as previously amended on July 9, 1993 was published in the Copyright and Neighbouring Rights Laws and Treaties supplement to Copyright, June 1994.
[27] BGBl. I. 842. A translation of the Amending Law was published in the Copyright and Neighbouring Rights Laws and Treaties supplement to Industrial Property and Copyright, March 1996.

the E.C. Rental and Lending Rights Directive and the Term Directive.[28] Performers have the right to authorise the transmission of their performances (*e.g.* by a loudspeaker outside the place where the performance is given)[29]; the recording of their performances[30]; the reproduction of such recordings[31]; the distribution of their performances[32]; and the live broadcasting of their performances.[33] In addition, performers are entitled to fair remuneration if a recording of a performance is broadcast or publicly performed.[34] Performers also have an integrity right.[35] The rights are assignable.[36] There are limitations which parallel those for author's rights.[37] In accordance with the Term Directive, the period of protection is 50 years from the end of the year in which the performance was given or 50 years from publication if a recording is published within that period.[38]

Ghana

Ghana became a signatory to TRIPs with effect from January 1, 1995.   **9.91**

Greece

Greece became party to the Rome Convention on January 6, 1993, with no reservations. It became a signatory to TRIPs with effect from January 1, 1995.   **9.92**

A new law on Intellectual Property, Related Rights and Cultural Themes[39] came into force on March 4, 1993 which implemented the E.C. Rental and Lending Rights Directive.[40] Performers are persons who in any way act or perform works, such as actors, musicians, singers, chorus singers, dancers, puppeteers, shadow theatre artists, variety performers or circus artists.[41] Performers have the right to authorise or prohibit: (a) fixations of their live performances on a visual or sound or audiovisual recording; (b) the direct or indirect reproduction of fixations of their performances as well as the distribution of the recording via a transfer of ownership, a rental arrangement or public lending; (c) the radio or television broadcasting by any means such as wireless waves, satellite or cable, as well as the public performance of a recording with an illegal fixation of their performances; (d) the radio or television broadcasting by any means such as wireless waves, satellite or cable of their live performances, except where the said broadcasting is a rebroadcasting of a lawful broadcasting; and (e) the communication to the public of   **9.93**

---

[28] See von Lewinski, "The Implementation of the E.C. Rental and Duration Directives in Germany" (1995) 55 *Copyright World* 30.
[29] Art. 74.
[30] Art. 75(1).
[31] *ibid.*
[32] Art. 75(2).
[33] Art. 76(1).
[34] Art. 76(2), 77.
[35] Art. 83.
[36] Art. 78.
[37] Art. 84.
[38] Art. 82.
[39] Law No. 2121/1993.
[40] A translation was published in the Copyright and Neighbouring Rights Laws and Treaties supplement to *Industrial Property and Copyright*, September 1996.
[41] Art. 46(1).

their live performances by any means other than radio or television transmission.[42] Where a performance is made by an ensemble, these rights must be exercised by an elected representative except for conductors, soloists, principal actors and principal directors.[43] Unless otherwise agreed, where a performer is employed the employer is granted a licence to use the performance for the purpose of the employment contract but the performer has an unwaivable right to remuneration; in particular, the performer retains an unwaivable right to remuneration where he or she has authorised a producer of sound, visual or audiovisual recordings to rent out recordings carrying fixations of his performance.[44] Where sound, visual or audiovisual recordings are used for a radio or television broadcast by any means, such as wireless waves, satellite or cable, or for communication to the public, a single equitable remuneration is to be paid to the performers and the producer.[45] The remuneration, which is to be administered collectively, is shared 50/50 between the performers and the producer.[46] Performers also have a right to equitable remuneration for the radio or television rebroadcasting of their performances.[47] Performers have moral rights consisting a right to full acknowledgment and credit for their performances and a right to prohibit any form of alteration of their performances.[48] The limitations which apply to copyright apply *mutatis mutandis*.[49] Performers' economic rights last for 50 years from the end of the year in which the performance took place or until the death of the performer if later.[50]

Grenada

9.94　Grenada became a signatory to TRIPs with effect from February 22, 1996.

Guatemala

9.95　Guatemala became party to the Rome Convention on January 14, 1977, with no reservations. It became a signatory to TRIPs with effect from July 21, 1995.

Republic of Guinea

9.96　Guinea became a signatory to TRIPs with effect from October 25, 1995.

Guinea-Bissau

9.97　Guinea-Bissau became a signatory to TRIPs with effect from May 31, 1995.

Guyana

9.98　Guyana became a signatory to TRIPs with effect from January 1, 1995.

---

[42] Art. 46(2).
[43] Art. 46(4).
[44] Art. 46(3).
[45] Art. 49(1).
[46] Art. 49(3).
[47] Art. 49(4).
[48] Art. 50(1).
[49] Art. 52(b)
[50] Art. 52(c).

Haiti

Haiti became a signatory to TRIPs with effect from January 30, 1996. **9.99**

Honduras

Honduras became party to the Rome Convention on February 16, 1990, with   **9.100**
no reservations. It became a signatory to TRIPs with effect from January 1,
1995.

Hong Kong

Hong Kong became a signatory to TRIPs with effect from January 1, 1995.   **9.101**
    The Intellectual Property (World Trade Organisation Amendments)   **9.102**
Ordinance 1996[51] was passed on April 24, 1996 to implement TRIPs. Among
other things this amends the Copyright Ordinance to add a new Part IV which
confers performers' rights. The provisions are modelled on the Copyright,
Designs and Patents Act 1988 as originally enacted. Performers of literary,
dramatic and musical works[52] enjoy the right to prevent their live performances from being recorded or broadcast without their consent and to prevent
the reproduction of unauthorised recordings of their live performances.[53] In
addition it is an infringement to play in public, broadcast or include in a cable
programme service a performance by means of a record or a copy of a record
that was, and which the defendant knows or has reason to believe was, made
without the performer's consent.[54] The term of protection is 50 years from the
end of the calendar year in which the performance took place.[55] The rights are
not transmissible save on death.[56] There are exceptions for fair dealing, etc.[57]
Civil remedies for infringement such as injunctions, damages, accounts of
profits and orders for delivery up are available.[58]

Hungary

Hungary became party to the Rome Convention on February 10, 1995, with   **9.103**
no reservations. It became a signatory to TRIPs with effect from January 1,
1995.
    Act III of 1969 on Authors Rights and the Rights of Performers and   **9.104**
Broadcasting Organisations was amended by Acts VII and LXXII of 1994
with effect from July 1, 1994 and January 1, 1995 respectively.[59] Performers
have the rights provided by Article 7 of the Rome Convention[60] subject to the
limitation provided by Article 19.[61] Performers and producers of phono-

---

[51] Ordinance No. 11 of 1996.
[52] Copyright Ordinance, s. 23.
[53] *ibid.*, s. 25.
[54] *ibid.*, s. 26.
[55] *ibid.*, s. 27.
[56] *ibid.*, s. 28.
[57] *ibid.*, s. 30.
[58] *ibid.*, ss. 31–32.
[59] A translation was published in the Copyright and Neighbouring Rights Laws and Treaties
supplement to *Industrial Property and Copyright*, July/August 1996.
[60] Art. 49(1).
[61] Art. 49(3).

grams have a right to remuneration in respect of the use of commercially published phonograms for broadcasting or communication to the public; this remuneration is due to the performer and producer on an equal basis unless otherwise agreed.[62] The same applies to the rental and lending of published phonograms.[63] Performers also have a paternity right and an integrity right.[64] The term of protection is 50 years from the end of the year in which the performance was given (if unrecorded) or 50 years from the end of the year in which the phonogram was made or (if put into circulation within that period) from the end of the year in which the phonogram was first put into circulation (for performances fixed on phonograms).[65] There is a levy on blank audio and video tape for home copying which is shared among performers and other right owners.[66]

Iceland

9.105 Iceland became party to the Rome Convention on June 15, 1994, with reservations under Article 5(3) concerning Article 5(1)(b), 6(2) and 16(1)(a) (ii).[67] It became a signatory to TRIPs with effect from January 1, 1995.

India

9.106 India became a signatory to TRIPs with effect from January 1, 1995.

9.107 The Copyright (Amendment) Act 1994,[68] which came into force on May 10, 1995, amended the Copyright Act 1954 to introduce performers' rights.[69] A performer includes an actor, singer, musician, dancer, acrobat, juggler, conjurer, snake charmer, a person delivering a lecture or any other person who makes a performance[70]; and performance means any visual or acoustic presentation made live by one or more performers.[71] A performer's rights are infringed by any of the following acts without the consent of the performer: (a) making a sound or visual recording of the performance; (b) reproducing a sound or visual recording made without the performer's consent or for purposes different from those to which the performer consented or from a sound or visual recording the making of which was excepted from infringement; (c) broadcasting the performance except by means of a sound or visual recording; or (d) communicating the performance to the public otherwise than by broadcast except by means of a sound or visual recording or a broadcast.[72] The performer has no rights where he consents to the

---

[62] Art. 50C.
[63] Art. 50D.
[64] Art. 50A.
[65] Art. 50K.
[66] Art. 50J.
[67] [1994] *Copyright* 152.
[68] No. 38 of 1994.
[69] The text of the Act as amended was published in the Copyright and Neighbouring Rights Laws and Treaties supplement to *Industrial Property and Copyright*, November 1996.
[70] s. 2(qq).
[71] s. 2(q).
[72] s. 38(3).

incorporation of his performance in a film.[73] The rights subsist for 25 years from the end of the calendar year in which the performance was given.[74] There are limitations similar to those for copyright.[75]

Indonesia

Indonesia became a signatory to TRIPs with effect from January 1, 1995. **9.108**

Iran

At the time of writing Iran is neither party to the Rome Convention nor a **9.109** signatory to TRIPs.

Iraq

At the time of writing Iraq is neither party to the Rome Convention nor a **9.110** signatory to TRIPs.

It appears that the Author's Right Law of January 21, 1971 grants **9.111** performers the same rights as authors.[76]

Ireland

Ireland became party to the Rome Convention on September 19, 1979, with **9.112** reservations under Article 5(3) concerning Articles 5(1)(b), 6(2) and 16(1)(a) (ii).[77] It became a signatory to TRIPs with effect from January 1, 1995.

The Performers' Protection Act 1968 protected performers by criminal **9.113** sanctions in the same way as the U.K. Performers' Protection Acts. At the time of writing new Irish legislation to replace the Copyright Act 1963 and the Performers' Protection Act was in preparation.

Israel

Israel became a signatory to TRIPs with effect from April 21, 1995. **9.114**

Under the Performers' Rights Law 5744–1984 performers have exclusive **9.115** rights of recording, reproduction, sale or other commercial disposition of such recordings or reproductions and public broadcast of their performances. The law only applies to performances given in Israel. Performers do not have rights in respect of the public performance of authorised recordings other than by way of broadcasting where they are entitled to a royalty.[78] The term of protection is 25 years. The Performers' Rights Law was recently amended by the Copyright (Blank Tapes) and Performers' Law 5756–1996 to give performers a rental right and moral rights, namely a right of attribution and an integrity right.[79]

---

[73] s. 38(4).
[74] s. 38(2).
[75] ss. 39 and 39A.
[76] Art. 5.
[77] [1979] *Copyright* 218.
[78] See note by Wilkof in [1996] 6 ENT. LR E-120.
[79] See note by Wilkof in [1996] 8 ENT. LR E-166.

Italy

9.116 Italy became a party to the Rome Convention on April 8, 1975, with reservations under Articles 6(2), 16(1)(a)(ii), (iii) and (iv) and 17.[80] It became a signatory to TRIPs with effect from January 1, 1995.

9.117 The basic Copyright Law of 1941[81] has been amended on a number of occasions, most recently by a law of 1992.[82] Performers have economic rights and moral rights. The E.C. Rental and Lending Rights Directive was implemented by Law No. 685 of November 16, 1994. Legislative Decree 198 of March 18, 1996[83] made pursuant to Article 3 of Law 747 of December 29, 1994, which entered into force on April 16, 1996, amends and supplements Italian intellectual property legislation so as to give effect to TRIPs.

Jamaica

9.118 Jamaica became party to the Rome Convention on January 27, 1994, with no reservations. It became a signatory to TRIPs with effect from March 9, 1995.

Japan

9.119 Japan became party to the Rome Convention on October 26, 1989, with reservations under Articles 5(3) (concerning Article 5(1)(c)), 16(1)(a)(ii), and (iv).[84] It became a signatory to TRIPs with effect from January 1, 1995.

9.120 The Copyright Law[85] as last amended[86] confers neighbouring rights on performers. Performers are actors, dancers, musicians, singers and other persons who give a performance as well as those who conduct or direct a performance.[87] Performance means the acting on stage, dancing, musical playing, singing, delivering, declaiming or performing in other ways of a work, and includes similar acts not involving the performance of a work which have the nature of public entertainment.[88] Performers have the exclusive right to make sound or visual recordings of their performances, except where the performance is incorporated in a film with their authority.[89] Performers also have the exclusive right to broadcast and transmit by cable their performances,[90] except where the performance is incorporated in a recording made with their authority or where a broadcast performance is transmitted.[91] Where a recording made for broadcasting purposes is

---

[80] [1975] *Copyright* 44.

[81] No. 663 of April 22, 1941.

[82] No. 93 of February 5, 1992.

[83] Ordinary Supplement 64 of the Official Journal of the Italian Republic, No. 88, April 15, 1996.

[84] [1989] *Copyright* 288.

[85] Law No. 48 of May 6, 1970.

[86] By Law No. 91 of May 12, 1995. A translation was published in the Copyright and Neighbouring Rights Laws and Treaties supplement to *Industrial Property and Copyright*, September 1996. Further proposed amendments have been announced, in particular to grant retroactive protection to performances given before January 1, 1971: see note by Doi in [1996] 9 EIPR D-261.

[87] Art. 2(iv).

[88] Art. 2(iii).

[89] Art. 91(1).

[90] Art. 92(1).

[91] Art. 92(2).

broadcast, the broadcaster must pay the performer reasonable remuneration.[92] Where a commercial phonogram is broadcast or transmitted, a secondary use fee must be paid to the performer[93] unless the producer of the phonogram is a national of a country of a Rome Convention country that does not apply Article 12.[94] If the producer of the phonogram is a national of a country which provides a shorter period of protection, that period applies.[95] Performers also have an exclusive right to communicate their performances to the public by lending commercial phonograms, a right limited to a period of 1–12 months from first sale, after which reasonable remuneration must be paid by the lender.[96] There provision for limitations on the rights.[97] The duration of the rights is 50 years from the end of the year in which the performance took place.[98]

Jordan

At the time of writing Jordan is neither party to the Rome Convention nor a signatory to TRIPs, but it has applied to join the WTO.

    The Law on Author's Right, No. 22 of 1992, appears to provide that the performers of a work performed in public are deemed to be authors and to have rights accordingly.[99] The term of protection is life plus 30 years.

9.121

9.122

Kampuchea (Cambodia)

At the time of writing Kampuchea is neither party to the Rome Convention nor a signatory to TRIPs, but it has applied to join the WTO.

9.123

Kazakhstan

At the time of writing Kazakhstan is neither party to the Rome Convention nor a signatory to TRIPs, but it has applied to join the WTO.

9.124

Kenya

Kenya became a signatory to TRIPs with effect from January 1, 1995.

    The Copyright Act 1966[1] as amended by the Copyright (Amendment) Acts of 1975,[2] 1982[3] and 1989[4] confers rights on performers. A performer is an actor, singer, declaimer, musician or other person who performs a literary or musical work and includes the conductor or director of the performance of any such work, while performance means the presentation of a work by such action as dancing, playing, reciting, singing, declaiming or projecting to listeners by any means whatsoever.[5] Without

9.125

9.126

---

[92] Art. 94(2).
[93] Art. 95(1).
[94] Art. 95(2).
[95] Art. 95(3)
[96] Art. 95*bis*.
[97] Art. 102.
[98] Art. 101.
[99] Art. 5.
[1] No. 3 of 1966.
[2] No. 5 of 1975.
[3] No. 5 of 1982.
[4] No. 14 of 1989.
[5] s. 10B(5).

the authorisation of the performer no person shall do any of the following acts: (a) broadcast his performance except where the broadcast is made from a fixation authorised by the performer; (b) communicate to the public his performance except where the communication is made from fixation or from a broadcast authorised by the performer; (c) make a fixation of the unfixed performance; (d) reproduce a fixation where either the performance was initially fixed without the authorisation of the performer or the reproduction is made for purposes different from those authorised by the performer.[6] In addition, performers' rights are infringed by a person who without the consent of the performer imports or causes to be imported, otherwise than for his own private or domestic use, an article which he knows would have been made contrary to section 10B had it been made in Kenya by the importer.[7] The rights last for 50 years from the end of the calendar year in which the performance took place.[8]

Kirgyz Republic (Kyrgyzstan)

9.127   At the time of writing the Kirgyz Republic is neither party to the Rome Convention nor a signatory to TRIPs, but it has applied to join the WTO.

Kiribati

9.128   At the time of writing Kiribati is neither party to the Rome Convention nor a signatory to TRIPs.

Democratic People's Republic of Korea (North Korea)

9.129   At the time of writing the Democratic People's Republic of Korea is neither party to the Rome Convention nor a signatory to TRIPs.

Republic of Korea (South Korea)

9.130   The Republic of Korea became a signatory to TRIPs with effect from January 1, 1995.

9.131   The Copyright Act was amended with effect from July 1, 1994 so as to increase the term of performers' rights from 20 years to 50 years.

Kuwait

9.132   Kuwait became a signatory to TRIPs with effect from January 1, 1995.

Laos

9.133   At the time of writing Laos is neither party to the Rome Convention nor a signatory to TRIPs.

Latvia

9.134   At the time of writing Latvia is neither party to the Rome Convention nor a signatory to TRIPs, but it has applied to join the WTO.

9.135   The Law on Author's Right and Neighbouring Rights of May 11, 1993 confers neighbouring rights on performers including moral rights. A

---

[6] s. 10B(1).
[7] s. 13(1).
[8] s. 10B(4).

performer is an artist-performer, that is an actor, singer, musician, dancer or other person who publicly plays a role, sings, reads, declaims, plays a musical instrument or in some other way performs literary or artistic works, concerts, circus or puppet acts, as well as a conductor, director or producer of an audiovisual work or sound recording.[9] Performers have exclusive rights: (1) to acknowledgment of their name; (2) to protection from distortion or change or other alteration in a performance or production that may cause damage to the honour or reputation of the performer; (3) to permit or prohibit the live broadcast, transmission by wire or other communication to the public except where the performance has previously been broadcast, transmitted or lawfully fixed; (4) to permit or prohibit the fixation of a previously unfixed performance or production; (5) to permit or prohibit the reproduction of fixations of the performance where the initial fixation was made without the consent of the performer or where the fixation is reproduced for purposes other than those for which the performer granted permission or are permitted by law; (6) to permit or prohibit the live broadcast, transmission by wire or communication to the public of a fixation of a performance, except where the fixation was made for non-commercial purposes; (7) to permit or prohibit rental or lending of published sound recordings.[10] When a contract is signed for the fixation of a performance or production, the rental and lending rights are transferred to the producer but the performer retains a right to compensation.[11] If sound recordings published for commercial purposes, or reproductions thereof, are used for broadcasting or transmission by wire, the user must pay equitable compensation to the performers and the producer.[12] There are limitations for (1) personal use, (2) reporting current events, (3) teaching or scientific research, (4) quotation for informational purposes and (5) in other cases by analogy with the limitations on copyright.[13] The term of protection is 50 years from the first performance or production except for moral rights which are unlimited in time.[14]

Lebanon

At the time of writing Lebanon is neither party to the Rome Convention nor a signatory to TRIPs. **9.136**

Lesotho

Lesotho became party to the Rome Convention on January 26, 1990, with reservations under Articles 16(1)(a)(ii) and (1)(b).[15] It became a signatory to TRIPs with effect from May 31, 1995. **9.137**

Liberia

At the time of writing Liberia is neither a party to the Rome Convention nor a signatory to TRIPs. **9.138**

---

[9] Art. 1(12).
[10] Art. 40(1).
[11] *ibid.*
[12] Art. 44.
[13] Art. 47(1).
[14] Art. 48(1).
[15] [1990] *Copyright* 95.

Libya

9.139   At the time of writing Libya is neither a party to the Rome Convention nor a signatory to TRIPs.

Liechtenstein

9.140   Liechtenstein became a signatory to TRIPs with effect from September 1, 1995.

Lithuania

9.141   At the time of writing Lithuania is neither party to the Rome Convention nor a signatory to TRIPs, but it has applied to join the WTO.

Luxembourg

9.142   Luxembourg became party to the Rome Convention on February 24, 1976, with reservations under Articles 5(3) (concerning Article 5(1)(c)), 16(1)(a)(i) and 16(1)(b).[16] It became a signatory to TRIPs with effect from January 1, 1995.

9.143   The Law on Author's Right of 1972[17] as last amended[18] came into force on March 3, 1995. It is assumed that the other E.U. Directives are in the process of being implemented.

Macau

9.144   Macau became a signatory to TRIPs with effect from January 1, 1995.

Republic of Macedonia (Skopje)

9.145   At the time of writing Macedonia is neither party to the Rome Convention nor a signatory to TRIPs, but it has applied to join the WTO.

Madagascar

9.146   Madagascar became a signatory to TRIPs with effect from November 17, 1995.

Malawi

9.147   Malawi became a signatory to TRIPs with effect from May 31, 1995.

Malaysia

9.148   Malaysia became a signatory to TRIPs with effect from January 1, 1995.

Maldives

9.149   The Maldives became signatories to TRIPs with effect from May 31, 1995.

Mali

9.150   Mali became a signatory to TRIPs with effect from May 31, 1995.

---

[16] [1976] *Copyright* 24.
[17] Law of March 29, 1972.
[18] By the Law of April 24, 1995 to give effect to the Software Directive.

Malta

Malta became a signatory to TRIPs with effect from January 1, 1995. **9.151**

Mauritania

Mauritania became a signatory to TRIPs with effect from May 31, 1995. **9.152**

Mauritius

Mauritius became a signatory to TRIPs with effect from January 1, 1995. **9.153**

Mexico

Mexico became party to the Rome Convention on May 18, 1964, with no **9.154**
reservations. It became a signatory to TRIPs with effect from January 1,
1995.

Republic of Moldova

The Republic of Moldova became party to the Rome Convention on **9.155**
December 5, 1995, with reservations under Articles 5(3) (concerning Article
5(1)(b)), 6(2) and 16(1)(a)(ii), (iii) and (iv).[19] It is not a signatory to TRIPs, but
it has applied to join the WTO.

The Law on Copyright and Neighbouring Rights, No. 293-XII of **9.156**
November 23, 1994, which came into force on March 2, 1995, confers
neighbouring rights on performers.[20] Performers have exclusive rights to
authorise or prohibit: (a) recording of unrecorded performances; (b)
reproduction of recordings of performances except where the reproduction is
made for the same purpose for which the performer gave his consent when
authorising the recording; (c) broadcasting the performance over the air or by
cable, or making any other communication of it to the public, except where a
recording to which the performer consented is used; and (d) renting of a
published phonogram incorporating the performance.[21] In addition,
performers have a right to remuneration for each form of use, a right to be
named and an integrity right.[22] Commercially published phonograms may be
publicly performed or broadcast over the air or by cable without the consent
of performer (or producer) if remuneration is paid.[23] This remuneration is to
be collectively administered and unless otherwise agreed shall be distributed
as follows: 40 per cent to the authors, 30 per cent to the performers and 30 per
cent to the producers.[24] The term of performers' exclusive rights is 50 years
from the end of the calendar year in which the performance took place, while
their moral rights are unlimited in time.[25]

---

[19] [1996] *Industrial Property and Copyright* 40.
[20] A translation was published in the Copyright and Neighbouring Rights Laws and Treaties supplement to *Industrial Property and Copyright,* June 1996.
[21] Art. 27(2).
[22] Art. 27(1).
[23] Art. 31(1).
[24] Art. 31(2).
[25] Art. 33(1).

Monaco

9.157 Monaco became party to the Rome Convention on December 6, 1985, with reservations under Articles 5(3) (concerning Article 5(1)(c)), 16(1)(a)(i) and 16(1)(b).[26] It is not a signatory to TRIPs, however.

Mongolia

9.158 Mongolia became a signatory to TRIPs with effect from January 29, 1997.

Montenegro

9.159 At the time of writing Montenegro is neither party to the Rome Convention nor a signatory to TRIPs.

Morocco

9.160 Morocco became a signatory to TRIPs with effect from January 1, 1995.

Mozambique

9.161 Mozambique became a signatory to TRIPs with effect from August 26, 1995.

Myanmar (formerly Burma)

9.162 Myanmar became a signatory to TRIPs with effect from January 1, 1995.

Namibia

9.163 Namibia became a signatory to TRIPs with effect from January 1, 1995.

Nepal

9.164 At the time of writing Nepal is neither party to the Rome Convention nor a signatory to TRIPs, but it has applied to join the WTO.

The Netherlands[27]

9.165 The Netherlands became party to the Rome Convention on October 7, 1993, with reservations under 16(1)(a)(iii) and (iv).[28] It became a signatory to TRIPs with effect from January 1, 1995.

9.166 Ratification of the Convention was achieved by the passage of the Law on Neighbouring Rights, which came into force on July 1, 1993.[29] Performers are actors, singers, musicians, dancers and other persons who act, sing, deliver or otherwise perform a literary or artistic work, together with artists who perform variety or circus acts or puppet shows.[30] Performers have the exclusive right to authorise (a) the recording of a performance, (b) the

---

[26] [1985] *Copyright* 422.
[27] Including Netherlands Antilles.
[28] [1993] *Copyright* 253.
[29] Law of March 18, 1993, S. 179 (1993). A translation was published in the Copyright and Neighbouring Rights Laws and Treaties supplement to *Industrial Property and Copyright*, December 1995.
[30] Art. 1(a).

reproduction of a recording of performance, (c) the sale, supply, offer for sale or supply, importation or other distribution of a recording of a performance or a reproduction thereof and (d) the broadcasting, rebroadcasting or other communication to the public of a performance or a recording of a performance or a reproduction thereof.[31] The distribution right is exhausted where a reproduction of a recording of performance has been put into circulation by or with the consent of the right owner.[32] Communication to the public does not include a performance in the family circle[33] or for teaching and the like.[34] Except where otherwise agreed or where equity demands it, an employer is entitled to exploit the rights of a performer but must pay equitable remuneration for each form of exploitation.[35] Contracts with producers of cinematographic works are deemed to include consent but the producer is required to pay equitable remuneration for each form of exploitation.[36] Commercially published phonograms or reproductions thereof may be broadcast or communicated to the public without the consent of the performer on condition that equitable remuneration is paid.[37] Performers also have moral rights, namely (a) to oppose communication to the public of a performance without acknowledgment of their name or other designation as performer, unless such opposition would be unreasonable, (b) to oppose communication to the public of a performance under a name other than their own or the making of any alteration in the way they are designated insofar as such name or designation is given or communicated to the public in connection with the performance, (c) to oppose any other alteration to the performance, unless the alteration is of such nature that opposition would be unreasonable and (d) to oppose any distortion, mutilation or other impairment of the performance that may prejudice the reputation or the name of the performer or his value in that capacity.[38] The moral rights last for the same period as the economic rights.[39] Performers' rights are assignable except for moral rights and are transmissible on death.[40] There are exceptions to the economic rights for (a) personal study and use, (b) reporting current affairs, (c) recordings made by broadcasting organisations for the purposes of their own programs and (d) criticism and review.[41] There are also exceptions for use in teaching.[42] The rights subsist for 50 years from the end of the calendar year in which the performance took place or in the which the phonogram was made in the case of performances recorded thereon.[43] In the case of a joint performance of six or more persons, the economic rights may only be exercised by a representative chosen by a majority of the performers, but this

---

[31] Art. 2(1).
[32] Art. 2(2).
[33] Art. 2(3).
[34] Art. 2(4).
[35] Art. 3.
[36] Arts. 45a–45g of the Copyright Law of 1912 (as amended) applied by Art. 4.
[37] Art. 7(1).
[38] Art. 5(1).
[39] Art. 5(2).
[40] Art. 9.
[41] Art. 10.
[42] Art. 11.
[43] Art. 12.

does not apply to a soloist, director or conductor participating in the performance.[44] Intentional infringement of performers' rights is an offence punishable by up to six months' imprisonment or a fine[45] except where the offence is an infringement of economic rights committed by way of habitual trade or by way of business in which case the penalty is up to four years' imprisonment.[46]

New Zealand

9.167   New Zealand became a signatory to TRIPs with effect from January 1, 1995.
9.168   The New Zealand Copyright Act 1994, which is largely based on the U.K. Copyright, Designs and Patents Act 1988 before it was amended to implement the recent E.C. Directives, came into force on January 1, 1995.[47] Performers' rights are granted in respect of live dramatic performances (including dance, mime and puppet shows), musical performances, readings or recitations of literary works and performances of variety acts or similar presentations.[48] Reading, recital or delivery of any item of news or information, performances of a sporting activity and participation in a performance as a member of the audience are specifically excluded.[49] Performers' rights are infringed by the unauthorised recording (other than for private and domestic purposes) or live broadcasting of a performance[50]; by the unauthorised showing or playing in public or broadcasting of an illicit recording of a performance[51]; by the copying of an illicit recording (other than for private and domestic use)[52]; and by the importation of or dealing in an illicit recording.[53] Permitted acts correspond closely with those under Schedule 2 of the 1988 Act.[54] The period of protection is 50 years from the end of the calendar year in which the performance takes place.[55] There are provisions concerning qualification, consent by the Copyright Tribunal, proceedings and criminal offences which largely follow those under the 1988 Act.

Nicaragua

9.169   Nicaragua became a signatory to TRIPs with effect from September 3, 1995.

Niger

9.170   Niger became party to the Rome Convention on May 18, 1964, with reservations under Articles 5(3) (concerning Article 5(1)(c)) and 16(1)(a)(i).[56] It became a signatory to TRIPs with effect from December 13, 1996.

---

[44] Art. 13.
[45] Arts. 21, 22, 25.
[46] Art. 23
[47] See Sullivan, "The New Zealand Copyright Act 1994" [1995] 2 ENT. LR 69.
[48] s. 169.
[49] *ibid.*
[50] s. 171.
[51] s. 172.
[52] s. 173.
[53] s. 174.
[54] ss. 175–191.
[55] s. 193.
[56] [1963] *Le Droit d'auteur* 155.

Nigeria

Nigeria became party to the Rome Convention on October 29, 1993,[57] with reservations under Articles 5(3) (concerning Article 5(1)(c)), 6(2) and 16(1)(a)(ii), (iii) and (iv).[58] It became a signatory to TRIPs with effect from January 1, 1995.

9.171

The Copyright Act 1988[59] (which was amended by the Copyright (Amendment) Decree No. 96 of 1992 wth effect from December 28, 1992) is partly based on the U.K. Copyright, Designs and Patents Act 1988. The following performances are protected: dramatic performances (including dance and mime), musical performances and readings or recitations of literary works or similar presentations.[60] There is no qualification requirement, from which it appears that all performances are protected regardless of the nationality of the performer or the place of the performance. Performers have the exclusive right to control the following acts in relation to their performances: performing, recording, live broadcasting, reproducing in a material form and adaptation.[61] In addition, performers' rights are infringed by public performance for commercial purposes and by broadcasting, importation (other than for private and domestic use) and distribution (including rental) of infringing recording of performances.[62] Performers' rights subsist for 50 years from the end of the year in which the performance took place.[62a] Infringement is actionable as breach of statutory duty and the performer is entitled to an injunction and damages or an account of profits.[62b]

9.172

Norway

Norway became party to the Rome Convention on July 10, 1978, with reservations under Articles 6(2), 16(1)(a)(ii), (iii) and (iv).[63] It became a signatory to TRIPs with effect from January 1, 1995.

9.173

Act No. 2 of May 12, 1961 Relating to Copyright in Literary, Scientific and Artistic Works, etc., as last amended by Law No. 27 of June 2, 1995 came into force on June 30, 1995.[64] A performing artist's performance of a work may not without the consent of the artist be: (a) fixed on film or on a device which can reproduce the performance, (b) broadcast or (c) made publicly available to persons other than the immediate audience through simultaneous transmission by any technical means.[65] No copies of a fixation shall be made or distributed to the public without the artist's consent.[66] When a copy of a fixation has been sold with the artist's consent within the EEA, the copy may

9.174

---

[57] See Sodipo, "Nigeria Accedes to the Rome Convention: Is Rome Satisfactory for Nigerian Performers?" [1994] 1 ENT. LR 20.
[58] [1993] *Copyright* 253.
[59] Cap 68, 1990 Laws of the Federation of Nigeria.
[60] s. 23(2).
[61] s. 23(1).
[62] s. 25.
[62a] s. 24.
[62b] s. 26(1)
[63] [1978] *Copyright* 133, [1989] *Copyright* 288.
[64] A translation was published in the Copyright and Neighbouring Rights Laws and Treaties supplement to *Industrial Property and Copyright*, April 1996.
[65] s. 42.
[66] *ibid.*

be further distributed by means other than rental.[67] Film production agreements include the right to rent out copies of the film unless otherwise agreed.[68] The rights in respect of fixations last until 50 years from the end of the calendar year in which the performance took place unless the fixation is issued within this period, in which case the period is 50 years from the end of the calendar year in which it was first issued.[69] Where sound fixations are communicated to the public by means of a broadcast or retransmission of a broadcast, the performing artists and the producer are entitled to remuneration which must be claimed through a collecting society.[70] Numerous provision of the Act relating to copyright apply *mutatis mutandis*, in particular moral rights of paternity and integrity,[71] some of the limitations,[72] compulsory licensing and collective licensing[73] and transfer of rights.[74] There are also criminal sanctions.[75]

Oman

9.175   At the time of writing Oman is neither a party to the Rome Convention nor a signatory to TRIPs, but it has applied to join the WTO.

Pakistan

9.176   Pakistan became a signatory to TRIPs with effect from January 1, 1995.

Panama

9.177   Panama became party to the Rome Convention on September 2, 1983, with no reservations. It is not a signatory to TRIPs, but it has applied to join the WTO.

9.178   The Law on Copyright and Neighbouring Rights and Enacting Other Provisions[76] confers neighbouring rights on performers. A performer is one who performs, sings, reads, recites, interprets or otherwise executes a work.[77] Performers have the exclusive right to authorise or prohibit the fixation, reproduction or communication to the public, by any means or process, of their performances.[78] They may not, however, object to communication by a fixation made with their consent and commercially published.[79] Performers also have paternity and integrity rights.[80] Orchestras,

---

[67] *ibid.*
[68] *ibid.*
[69] *ibid.*
[70] s. 45b.
[71] s. 3.
[72] ss. 15 (use by health institutions), 16 (copying by archives, libraries and museums), 17 (copies for the disabled), 18 (collective works for use in education and religious services), 21 (performances in educational contexts and religious services), 22 (quotations), 25 (news reports in broadcasts and films), 27 (public administration and freedom of information), 28 (proceedings) and 33–34 (fixations for the purposes of broadcasting and retransmission).
[73] ss. 35–38.
[74] ss. 39–39c.
[75] s. 54.
[76] No. 15 of August 8, 1994. A translation was published in the Copyright and Neighbouring Rights Laws and Treaties supplement to *Industrial Property and Copyright*, June 1995.
[77] Art. 2.
[78] Art. 87.
[79] *ibid.*
[80] *ibid.*

vocal ensembles and other groups must designate a representative for the exercise of their rights.[81] The duration of the rights is 50 years from the end of the calendar year in which an unfixed performance was given or in which a recording was published.[82]

Papua New Guinea

Papua New Guinea became a signatory to TRIPs with effect from June 9, 1996.

9.179

Paraguay

Paraguay became party to the Rome Convention on February 26, 1970, with no reservations. It became a signatory to TRIPs with effect from January 1, 1995.

9.180

Peru

Peru became party to the Rome Convention on August 7, 1985, with no reservations. It became a signatory to TRIPs with effect from January 1, 1995.

9.181

A new Copyright Law[83] came into force on May 24, 1996 which confers neighbouring rights on performers. Performers have the exclusive right to carry out, authorise or prohibit (a) communication of their performances to the public in any form, (b) fixation and reproduction of their performances by any means or process and (c) reproduction of an authorised fixation for purposes other than those for which the authorisation was given.[84] Performers may not object to the communication of their performances to the public if made with their prior consent and published for commercial purposes,[85] but in the case of phonograms they have the right to equitable remuneration which in the absence of agreement is to be shared equally between the performers and the phonogram producer.[86] Performers also have paternity and integrity rights.[87] Orchestras, vocal ensembles and other groups of performers must designate a representative to exercise their rights and in the absence of such designation the leader or conductor shall exercise the rights.[88] Performers' rights are subject to the same limitations and exceptions as copyright.[89] It appears that performers' rights are assignable to the same extent as copyright.[90] The term of protection is 70 years from the death of the performer.[91]

9.182

---

[81] Art. 88.
[82] Art. 89.
[83] Legislative Decree No. 822, *El Peruano* of April 24, 1996, pp. 139104 *et seq*. A translation was published in the Copyright and Neighbouring Rights Laws and Treaties supplement to *Industrial Property and Copyright*, November 1996.
[84] Art. 132.
[85] *ibid*.
[86] Art. 133.
[87] Art. 131.
[88] Art. 134.
[89] Art. 129.
[90] Art. 130.
[91] Art. 135.

Philippines

9.183　The Philippines became party to the Rome Convention on September 25, 1984, with no reservations. It became a signatory to TRIPs with effect from January 1, 1995.

Poland

9.184　Poland became party to the Rome Convention on June 13, 1997, with reservations in respect of Articles 5(3), 6(2) and 16(a)(i), (iii), (iv).[91a] It became a signatory to TRIPs with effect from July 1, 1995.

9.185　The Law of February 4, 1994 on Copyright and Neighbouring Rights came into force on May 23, 1994.[92] It protects any performance of an artistic character made of a work regardless of the value, intended purpose or form of expression, in particular performances of actors, reciters, orchestra conductors, instrumentalists, dancers and singers and the persons who contribute creatively to the performance.[93] Performers have the exclusive right to protection for the personal attributes of the performance, to make use of the performance and exploit it in particular fields and to receive remuneration for use of the performance.[94] The right to exploit extends to fixation, reproduction, distribution, communication to the public except by means of a distributed copy, rental, lending and broadcasting except by means of a distributed copy.[95] In the case of broadcasting or communication to the public by means of a distributed copy the performer is entitled to appropriate remuneration.[96] A contract between a performer and the producer of an audiovisual work is deemed to transfer the right to use the performance contained in the work in all areas of exploitation known at that time.[97] The leader of a group of performers is presumed to be competent to represent the rights of the group.[98] The duration of the rights is 50 years from the end of the calendar year in which the performance took place.[99] There are limitations by analogy with those applying to copyright.[1]

Portugal

9.186　Portugal became a signatory to TRIPs with effect from January 1, 1995.

9.187　The Code on Author's Right and Related Right[2] was amended in 1991.[3] It is understood that the E.C. Rental and Lending Rights and Term Directives have since been implemented.

[91a] [1997] *Industrial Property and Copyright* 170.
[92] A translation was published in the Copyright and Neighbouring Rights Laws and Treaties supplement to *Industrial Property and Copyright*, March 1995.
[93] Art. 85.
[94] Art. 86(1).
[95] Art. 86(2).
[96] Art. 86(3).
[97] Art. 87.
[98] Art. 91.
[99] Art. 89.
[1] Art. 100.
[2] No. 45/85 of September 17, 1985.
[3] By Law No. 114/91 of September 3, 1991. A translation was published in the Laws and Treaties supplement to *Copyright*, September/October 1992.

Qatar

Qatar became a signatory to TRIPs with effect from January 13, 1996.   9.188

Romania

Romania became a signatory to TRIPs with effect from January 1, 1995.   9.189
   Copyright Law No. 9/1996 in force March 26, 1996 is understood to bring   9.190
Romanian law into line with E.U. standards.

Russian Federation[4]

At the time of writing the Russian Federation is neither party to the Rome   9.191
Convention nor a signatory to TRIPs, but has applied to join the WTO. It is
also expected that Russia will join the Rome Convention.

   Under the Law of the Russian Federation on Author's Right and   9.192
Neighbouring Rights,[5] performers are granted neighbouring rights. A
performer is an actor, singer, musician, dancer or any other person who
performs, recites, declaims, sings, plays an instrument or in any other manner
presents a literary or artistic work (including a variety turn, circus act or
puppet show); and also a director or conductor.[6] Performers have the
exclusive right to exploit a performance in any form, including the right to
receive remuneration for each form of use.[7] The right to exploit means the
right to do or authorise the doing of any of the following acts: live
broadcasting or cable transmission of the performance; recording the
performance; reproducing such a recording, unless the original recording was
made with the consent of the performer and the reproduction is made for the
same purposes as the performer consented to; renting a sound recording
containing the performance, unless a contract for the recording of the
performance for commercial purposes has been concluded; broadcasting or
cable transmission of a recording of the performance made for non-
commercial purposes; rental of sound recordings.[8] The rental right is
transferred on the making of a contract between the performer and the
producer of the sound recording, but the performer retains a right to
remuneration.[9] There are exceptions which parallel those for authors'
rights.[10] Performers also have moral rights, namely a paternity right and an
integrity right.[11] The economic rights are assignable[12] while the moral rights
are inalienable. The duration of the economic rights is 50 years from the end
of the calendar year in which the performance was given while the moral
rights are perpetual.[13]

---

[4] See Savelyeva in Stewart, note 1 to para. 9.01, above, chap. 2 and Pozhitkov, "Author's Right
and Neighbouring Right Protection in the Russian Federation" [1994] 4 ENT. LR 124.
[5] No. 5351-I of July 9, 1993, published on August 3, 1993. A translation was published in the
Laws and Treaties supplement to *Copyright*, January 1994.
[6] Art. 4.
[7] Art. 137(1).
[8] Art. 37(2).
[9] Art. 37(5).
[10] Art. 42.
[11] Art. 37(1).
[12] Art. 37(7).
[13] Art. 43(1).

Rwanda

9.193   Rwanda became a signatory to TRIPs with effect from May 22, 1996.

Saint Kitts and Nevis

9.194   Saint Kitts and Nevis became signatories to TRIPs with effect from February 21, 1996.

Saint Lucia

9.195   Saint Lucia became a party to the Rome Conversion on August 17, 1996 with reservations under Articles 5(3) (concerning Article 5(1)(c)) and 16(1)(a)(iii). It became a signatory to TRIPs with effect from January 1, 1995.

Saint Vincent and the Grenadines

9.196   Saint Vincent and the Grenadines became signatories to TRIPs with effect from January 1, 1995.

Samoa

9.197   At the time of writing Samoa is neither a party to the Rome Convention nor a signatory to TRIPs.

San Marino

9.198   At the time of writing San Marino is neither a party to the Rome Convention nor a signatory to TRIPs.

9.199   Under Law No. 8 of January 25, 1991 on authors' and performers' rights, performers of dramatic, literary and musical works whose performances are used for making a sound or audiovisual recording or a broadcast are entitled to equitable remuneration.[14] Performers also have an integrity right.[15] These rights do not apply where the performers have been specifically remunerated in respect of the production.[16] Performers have a paternity right to which the last provision does not apply.[17] The term of protection is unclear.

Saudi Arabia

9.200   At the time of writing Saudi Arabia is neither party to the Rome Convention nor a signatory to TRIPs, but it has applied to join the WTO.

Senegal

9.201   Senegal became a signatory to TRIPs with effect from January 1, 1995.

Serbia

9.202   At the time of writing Serbia is neither party to the Rome Convention nor a signatory to TRIPs.

Seychelles

9.203   At the time of writing the Seychelles are neither party to the Rome Convention nor a signatory to TRIPs, but they have applied to join the WTO.

---

[14] Art. 93.
[15] Art. 94.
[16] Art. 95.
[17] Art. 97.

Sierra Leone

Sierra Leone became a signatory to TRIPs with effect from July 23, 1995. **9.204**

Singapore

Singapore became a signatory to TRIPs with effect from January 1, 1995. **9.205**

Slovak Republic

The Slovak Republic became party to the Rome Convention on January 1, **9.206**
1993, with reservations under Article 16(1)(a)(iii) and (iv).[18] It became a
signatory to TRIPs with effect from January 1, 1995.

The Czechoslovakian legislation remains in force in the Slovak Republic in **9.207**
the same way as in the Czech Republic.[19]

Slovenia

Slovenia became party to the Rome Convention on October 9, 1996, with **9.208**
reservations under Articles 5(3) (in respect of Article 5(1)(c)) and 16(1)(a)(i)
(in respect of Article 12 until January 1, 1998).[20] It became a signatory to
TRIPs with effect from July 30, 1995.

The Law on Copyright and Related Rights,[21] in force from April 29, 1995, **9.209**
is intended to harmonise Slovenian copyright and related rights law with
those of the European Union. Performers are actors, singers, musicians,
dancers and other persons who by acting, singing, dancing, reciting or in
some other way artistically perform copyright works or works of folklore.[22]
Theatre directors, orchestra conductors, choir directors, sound editors and
variety and circus artists are deemed to be performers.[23] Performers who take
part in a performance collectively, such as members of an orchestra, choir,
dance troupe, theatrical group or similar ensemble, must designate one of
their number to be their representative for the purpose of granting
authorisations.[24] Performers have the exclusive right: (i) to broadcast or
otherwise publicly communicate their performance to the public, except
where such performance is in itself a broadcast or it is broadcast from a
fixation; (ii) to fix their live performance; (iii) to reproduce the fixation of
their performance on phonograms or videograms; (iv) to distribute phonograms or videograms containing their performance and (v) to rent
phonograms or videograms containing their performance.[25] Performers also
have the right to share in the remuneration received by the producer of a
phonogram for communication to the public of a phonogram in which his
performance is fixed[26] and a right to remuneration for home copying.[27] By

---

[18] [1994] *Copyright* 110.
[19] See para. 9.68, above.
[20] [1996] *Industrial Property and Copyright* 318.
[21] No. 21 of March 30, 1995. A translation was published in the Copyright and Neighbouring
Rights Laws and Treaties supplement to *Industrial Property and Copyright*, May 1996.
[22] Art. 118(1).
[23] Art. 118(2).
[24] Art. 119(1).
[25] Art. 121.
[26] Art. 122.
[27] Art. 123.

entering into a film production agreement, the performer is presumed to have assigned all his economic rights to the film producer unless the contract otherwise provides, but retains an unwaivable right to equitable remuneration from the film producer.[28] Performers have a paternity right (in the case of ensembles, enjoyed by the ensemble as a whole) and an integrity right.[29] The term of protection for performers' rights is 50 years from the date of the performance, unless a fixation is lawfully published or communicated during that period in which case the term runs from the date of first publication or communication.[30]

Solomon Islands

9.210   The Solomon Islands became a signatory to TRIPs with effect from July 26, 1996.

Somalia

9.211   At the time of writing Somalia is neither party to the Rome Convention nor a signatory to TRIPs.

South Africa

9.212   South Africa became a signatory to TRIPs with effect from January 1, 1995.

9.213   The Performers' Protection Act 1967 protects performers in the same way as did the U.K. Performers' Protection Acts 1958–1972. In the recent case of *South African Broadcasting Corp. v. Pollecutt*,[31] the Appellate Division of the Supreme Court of South Africa held that, where a performer had consented to the fixation of his performance for the purposes of a television broadcast, the performer's consent was required by the Act for the reproduction of the fixation for the purpose of the sale of records, etc. It is assumed that the Act will be replaced or amended in the light of TRIPs, but at the time of writing no details are available.

Spain

9.214   Spain became party to the Rome Convention on November 14, 1991, with reservations under Articles 5(3) (concerning Article 5(1)(c)), 16(1)(a)(iii) and (iv).[32] It became a signatory to TRIPs with effect from January 1, 1995.

9.215   The Revised Law on Intellectual Property[33] came into force on April 23, 1996.[34] A performer is a person who presents, sings, reads, recites, interprets or executes a work in any form, including a director of a stage performance

---

[28] Art. 124.

[29] Art. 120.

[30] Art. 127.

[31] [1996] 1 S.A. 546 (A).

[32] [1991] *Copyright* 221.

[33] Approved by Royal Legislative Decree 1/1996 of April 12, 1996 (*Boletin Oficial del Estado*, no. 97, April 22, 1996) making minor amendments to Act 22/1987 of November 11, 1987 as last amended by Act 43/1994 which came into force on January 1, 1995. See Garcia and Pina, "Rental Rights in Spain: Act 43/94 of December 30, 1994" [1995] 7 ENT. LR 292 and note by Lozano in [1996] 5 ENT. LR E-97.

[34] A translation was published in the Copyright and Neighbouring Rights Laws and Treaties supplement to *Industrial Property and Copyright*, December 1996.

and an orchestra conductor.[35] Performers have exclusive rights to authorise the fixing of their performances,[36] the direct or indirect reproduction of fixations,[37] the communication to the public of their performances (except a performance transmitted by broadcasting or made from a previously authorised fixation),[38] and the distribution of fixations of their performances.[39] The distribution right is exhausted in respect of subsequent sales by the first sale within the European Union by the performer or with his consent.[40] Where a commercially published phonogram or a reproduction thereof is used to communicate a performance to the public, the user is obliged to pay a single equitable remuneration to the performers and phonogram producer; in the absence of agreement the remuneration shall be shared equally.[41] The same applies to the use of audiovisual recordings.[42] The rights to equitable remuneration are to be exercised through collecting societies.[43] By entering into a contract with a producer of an audiovisual recording a performer is presumed in the absence of agreement to the contrary to transfer his rental rights to the producer.[44] Performers who transfer their rental rights to producers of phonograms or audiovisual recordings retain an unwaivable right to equitable remuneration.[45] Where a performance is given pursuant to an employment or commission contract, the employer or commissioner acquires the exclusive rights to authorise reproduction and communication to the public unless the contrary is specified.[46] Performers other than soloists, conductors and directors who take part in a collective performance must designate a representative to grant authorisations.[47] Performers' economic rights have a term of 50 years from the end of the calendar year the performance was given or, if a fixation is lawfully published within that period, from the end of the year in which it was published.[48] Performers also enjoy moral rights, namely a paternity right and an integrity right, which last for 20 years after death.[49] Aspects of the law on copyright apply *mutatis mutandis* to performers' rights.[50]

Sri Lanka

Sri Lanka became a signatory to TRIPs with effect from January 1, 1995. **9.216**

---

[35] Art. 105.
[36] Art. 106(1).
[37] Art. 107(1).
[38] Art. 108(1).
[39] Art. 109(1).
[40] Art. 109(2).
[41] Art. 108(2).
[42] Art. 108(3).
[43] Art. 108(4).
[44] Art. 109(3)(1).
[45] Art. 109(3)(2).
[46] Art. 110.
[47] Art. 111.
[48] Art. 112.
[49] Art. 113.
[50] Art. 132.

Sudan

9.217 At the time of writing Sudan is neither party to the Rome Convention nor a signatory to TRIPs, but it has applied to join the WTO.

Surinam

9.218 Surinam became a signatory to TRIPs with effect from January 1, 1995.

Swaziland

9.219 Swaziland became a signatory to TRIPs with effect from January 1, 1995.

Sweden

9.220 Sweden became party to the Rome Convention on May 18, 1964, with current reservations under Article 16(1)(a)(iv).[51] It became a signatory to TRIPs with effect from January 1, 1995.

9.221   The Act on Copyright in Literary and Artistic Works[52] has been amended[53] with effect from January 1, 1996. A performing artist's performance of a literary or artistic work may not without his consent be recorded on a phonographic record, film or other material support from which it may be reproduced, broadcast over radio or television or made available to the public by direct communication.[54] There is exhaustion of rights within the EEA except for rental and lending.[55] There are limitations as for copyright. The duration of the rights is 50 years from the end of the calendar year in which the performance took place or, if the recording is published or made public in that period, from the end of the calendar year when the performance was first published or made public.[56] Sound recordings may be used in a radio or television broadcast or in a public performance or are retransmitted without the consent of the performer but the producer and the performers have a right to remuneration.[57]

Switzerland

9.222 Switzerland become party to the Rome Convention on September 24, 1993, with reservations under Articles 5(3) (concerning Article 5(1)(b)), 16(1)(a) (iii) and (iv).[58] It became a signatory to TRIPs with effect from July 1, 1995.

9.223   Under the Federal Law of October 9, 1992 on author's right and neighbouring rights as amended by the law of December 16, 1994,[59] which came into force on July 1, 1995, performers are granted neighbouring rights. Performers are natural persons who perform a work or who participate

---

[51] [1962] *Le Droit d'auteur* 211; [1986] *Copyright* 382; [1996] *Industrial Property and Copyright* 80.
[52] Law No. 729 of December 30, 1960.
[53] By Law No. 1274 of November 7, 1995. A translation of the amended statute was published in the Copyright and Neighbouring Rights Laws and Treaties supplement to *Industrial Property and Copyright*, September 1996.
[54] Art. 45.
[55] *ibid.*
[56] *ibid.*
[57] Art. 47.
[58] [1993] *Copyright* 254.
[59] A translation was published in the Copyright and Neighbouring Rights Laws and Treaties supplement to *Industrial Property and Copyright*, January 1996.

artistically in the performance of a work.[60] Performers have the exclusive right: (a) to make their performances perceivable in places other than those in which they were performed; (b) to broadcast their works by radio, television or similar process using electromagnetic waves, cable or other means of conduction, and to rebroadcast the broadcast performance by means of technical installations not operated by the original broadcaster; (c) to record their performances on phonograms, videograms or data carriers and to reproduce such recordings; (d) to offer for sale, sell or otherwise distribute reproduced copies of the material on which their performances are recorded; and (e) to make their performances perceivable when they are broadcast or rebroadcast.[61] Where two or more performers have participated in a performance, the rights belong to them jointly.[62] In the case of a choral, orchestral or stage performance, use of the performance requires the consent of the soloists, conductor, producer and a representative of the participating group of performers (or leader if there is no representative).[63] Performers also have a right to remuneration when commercially available phonograms or videograms are used for broadcasting, rebroadcasting and public reception or presentation.[64] The phonogram or videogram producer has a right to an equitable share in this remuneration.[65] Claims for remuneration can only be made through an approved collecting society.[66] The provisions of the law on copyright relating to transfer of rights, enforcement and limitations on protection apply *mutatis mutandis* to performers' rights.[67] The term of protection is 50 years from the end of the calendar year in which the work was performed.[68]

Syria

At the time of writing Syria is neither party to the Rome Convention nor a signatory to TRIPs.

9.224

Tajikistan

At the time of writing Tajikistan is neither party to the Rome Convention nor a signatory to TRIPs.

9.225

Taiwan

At the time of writing Taiwan is neither party to the Rome Convention nor a signatory to TRIPs, but it has applied to join the WTO.

9.226

Tanzania

Tanzania became a signatory to TRIPs with effect from January 1, 1995.

9.227

---

[60] Art. 33(1).
[61] Art. 33(2).
[62] Art. 34(1).
[63] Art. 34(2).
[64] Art. 35(1).
[65] Art. 35(2).
[66] Art. 35(3).
[67] Art. 38.
[68] Art. 39.

Thailand

9.228   Thailand became a signatory to TRIPs with effect from January 1, 1995.

9.229   The Copyright Act BE 2537 (1994),[69] which came into force on March 21, 1995, gave performers rights for the first time. A performer is a performer, musician, vocalist, choreographer, dancer or a person who acts, sings, speaks, dubs a translation or narrates, or gives commentary or performs in accordance with a script, or performs in any other manner.[70] Performers have the following exclusive rights with respect of acts concerning their perform-ances: (1) sound and video broadcasting or communication to the public of a performance, except from a recording medium which has been recorded; (2) recording a performance which has not been recorded; and (3) reproducing a recording of a performance which has been recorded without the consent of the performer or with the consent of the performer but for another purpose or a recording which falls within the exceptions to infringement of performers' rights.[71] Performers also have a right to equitable remuneration from persons who effect the sound broadcasting or direct communication to the public of an audio recording of a performance which has already been distributed for commercial purposes, or copies thereof.[72] Performers' exclusive rights last for 50 years from the end of the calendar year in which the performance took place or, if recorded, 50 years from the end of the calendar year in which the recording took place.[73] Performers' right to equitable remuneration lasts for 50 years from the end of the calendar year in which the audio recording took place.[74] Performers rights are assignable in whole or in part by an assignment in writing signed by both parties.[75] Exceptions to protection under copyright apply *mutatis mutandis* to performers' rights.[76]

Togo

9.230   Togo became a signatory to TRIPs with effect from May 31, 1995.

Tonga

9.231   At the time of writing Tonga is neither party to the Rome Convention nor a signatory to TRIPs, but it has applied to join the WTO.

Trinidad and Tobago

9.232   Trinidad and Tobago became signatories to TRIPs with effect from March 1, 1995.

Tunisia

9.233   Tunisia became a signatory to TRIPs with effect from March 29, 1995.

---

[69] A translation was published in the Copyright and Neighbouring Rights Laws and Treaties supplement to *Industrial Property and Copyright*, June 1996.
[70] s. 4.
[71] s. 44.
[72] s. 45.
[73] s. 49.
[74] s. 50.
[75] s. 51.
[76] s. 53.

Turkey

Turkey became a signatory to TRIPs with effect from March 26, 1995.   **9.234**

Under the Law on Artistic and Intellectual Works, No. 5846 of December   **9.235**
5, 1951 as last amended in 1995 with effect from June 12, 1995,[77] artists who
perform intellectual and artistic works in an original manner enjoy neighbouring rights.[78] Such performers have the exclusive right to make a fixation
of their performances, to reproduce and hire out the fixations thereof, to use
their performances by broadcasting, by wire or over the air or by live
performances. Written consent is required for the performers to do these acts.
Performers may transfer these rights to the producer by contract in return for
equitable remuneration. In the case of a performance by an orchestra, chorus
or a theatrical company, the consent of the manager suffices unless an
individual performer or a group has been engaged under contract to give a
performance, in which case the consent of the promoter is also required.
There are limitations on performers' rights for non-profit making and other
purposes.

Turkmenistan

At the time of writing Turkmenistan is neither party to the Rome Convention   **9.236**
nor a signatory to TRIPs.

Uganda

Uganda became a signatory to TRIPs with effect from January 1, 1995.   **9.237**

Ukraine

At the time of writing Ukraine is neither a party to the Rome Convention nor   **9.238**
a signatory to TRIPs, but it has applied to join the WTO.

The Ukrainian Law on Copyright and Related Rights of December 23,   **9.239**
1993, which came into force on February 23, 1994,[79] substantially follows
that of the Russian Federation.[80] Again it is anticipated that Ukraine will join
the Rome Convention.

United Arab Emirates

The United Arab Emirates became a signatory to TRIPs with effect from April   **9.240**
10, 1996.

United States of America

The United States became a signatory to TRIPs with effect from January 1,   **9.241**
1995.

An Act to Implement the Results of the Uruguay Round of Multilateral   **9.242**
Trade Negotiations, Public Law 103–465 of December 8, 1994, came into

---

[77] A translation was published in the Copyright and Neighbouring Rights Law and Treaties
supplement to *Industrial Property and Copyright*, May 1996.
[78] Art. 80.
[79] A translation was published in the Copyright and Neighbouring Rights Laws and Treaties
supplement to *Industrial Property and Copyright*, January 1996.
[80] See Pozhitkov, "Author's Right and Neighbouring Right Protection in Ukraine" [1994] 5
ENT. LR 171.

force on January 1, 1996. Title V Subtitle A, which deals with copyright, amends Titles 17 and 18 of the United States Code to create civil and criminal penalties for unauthorised fixation of and trafficking in sound recordings and music videos of live musical performances. So far as civil law is concerned, a person who, without consent of the performer: (1) fixes the sounds and images of a live musical performance in a copy or phonorecord or reproduces copies or phonorecords of such a performance from an unauthorised fixation; (2) transmits or otherwise communicates to the public the sound or sounds and images of a live musical performance, or (3) distributes or offers to distribute, sells or offer to sell, rents or offer to rent, or traffics in any copy or phonorecord so fixed, is subject to the same remedies as an infringer of copyright.[81] Other than to this limited extent, the United States does not yet confer performers' rights.

Uruguay

9.243   Uruguay became party to the Rome Convention on July 4, 1977, with no reservations. It became a signatory to TRIPs with effect from January 1, 1995.

Uzbekistan

9.244   At the time of writing Uzbekistan is neither a party to the Rome Convention nor a signatory to TRIPs, but it has applied to join the WTO.

Vanuatu

9.245   At the time of writing Vanuatu is neither a party to the Rome Convention nor a signatory to TRIPs, but it has applied to join the WTO.

Venezuela

9.246   Venezuela became a party to the Rome Convention on January 30, 1996, with no reservations. It became a signatory to TRIPs with effect from January 1, 1995.

9.247   The Law on Copyright of August 14, 1993 came into force on October 15, 1993.[82] Performers and their successors in title have the exclusive right to authorise or prohibit the fixing, reproduction or communication to the public, by whatever means or process, of their performances except where communication is effected using a commercially published recording made with their consent.[83] Performers also have moral rights, namely a paternity right and an integrity right.[84] Orchestras, vocal ensembles and other groups of performers must appoint a representative for the purpose of exercising these rights; in the absence of appointment, the leader of the group is the representative.[85] The term of protection is 60 years from the end of the calendar year in which the performance was given if live or in which it was

---

[81] s. 1101.
[82] A translation was published in the Law and Treaties supplement to *Copyright*, December 1994.
[83] Art. 92.
[84] *ibid.*
[85] Art. 93.

published if recorded.[86] Performers also have the right to receive 50 per cent of the net proceeds received by producers of sound recordings in respect of the communication of phonograms to the public.[87]

Vietnam

At the time of writing Vietnam is neither a party to the Rome Convention nor a signatory to TRIPs, but it has applied to join the WTO.   **9.248**

Yemen

At the time of writing Yemen is neither a party to the Rome Convention nor a signatory to TRIPs.   **9.249**

Zaire

Zaire became a signatory to TRIPs with effect from January 1, 1997.   **9.250**

Zambia

Zambia became a signatory to TRIPs with effect from January 1, 1995.   **9.251**

   The Copyright and Performance Rights Act 1994, No. 44 of 1994, came into force on December 31, 1994.[88] Part V, which confers performers' rights and recording rights, is loosely modelled on the U.K. Copyright, Patents and Designs Act 1988 before its amendment to implement the recent E.C. Directives.   **9.252**

Zimbabwe

Zimbabwe became a signatory to TRIPs with effect from March 3, 1995.   **9.253**

---

[86] Art. 94.
[87] Art. 97.
[88] A copy of the Act was published in the Copyright and Neighbouring Rights Law and Treaties supplement to *Industrial Property and Copyright*, February 1996.

Appendices

APPENDIX 1

Copyright, Designs and Patents Act 1988 (as amended) (c. 48)

PART II RIGHTS IN PERFORMANCES

Introductory

180. Rights conferred on performers and persons having recording rights

Performers' rights

181. Qualifying performances
182. *Consent required for recording or live transmission of performance.* Consent required for recording, etc., of live performance
182A. Consent required for copying of recording
182B. Consent required for issue of copies to the public
182C. Consent required for rental or lending of copies to the public
182D. Right to equitable remuneration for exploitation of sound recording
183. Infringement of performer's rights by use of recording made without consent
184. Infringement of performers' rights by importing, possessing or dealing with illicit recording

Rights of person having recording rights

185. Exclusive recording contracts and persons having recording rights
186. Consent required for recording of performance subject to exclusive contract
187. Infringement of recording rights by use of recording made without consent
188. Infringement of recording rights by importing, possessing or dealing with illicit recording

Exceptions to rights conferred

189. Acts permitted notwithstanding rights conferred by this Part
190. Power of tribunal to give consent on behalf of performer in certain cases

Duration of rights

191. Duration of rights

Performers' property rights

191A. Performer's property rights
191B. Assignments and licences
191C. Prospective ownership of a performer's property rights
191D. Exclusive licences
191E. Performer's property right to part under will with unpublished original recording
191F. Presumption of transfer to rental right in case of film production agreement
191G. Right to equitable remuneration where rental right transferred
191H. Equitable remuneration: reference of amount to Copyright Tribunal
191I. Infringement actionable by rights owner
191J. Provisions as to damages in infringement action
191K. Undertaking to take licence of right in infringement proceedings
191L. Rights and remedies for executive

191M. Exercise of concurrent rights
192. Transmission of rights

Non-property rights

192A. Performers' non-property rights
192B. Transmissibility of rights of person having recording rights.
193. Consent
194. Infringement actionable as breach of statutory duty

Delivery up on seizure of illicit recordings

195. Order for delivery up
196. Right to seize illicit recordings
197. Meaning of "illicit recording"

Offences

198. Criminal liability for making, dealing with or using illicit recordings
198A. Enforcement by local weights and measures authority
199. Order for delivery up in criminal proceedings
200. Search warrants
201. False representation of authority to give consent
202. Offence by body corporate: liability of officers

Supplementary provisions with respect to delivery up and seizure

203. Period after which remedy of delivery up not available
204. Order as to disposal of illicit recording
205. Jurisdiction of county court and sheriff court
205A. Licensing of performers' property rights
205B. Jurisdiction of Copyright Tribunal

Qualification for protection and extent

206. Qualifying countries, individuals and persons
207. Countries to which this Part extends
208. Countries enjoying reciprocal protection
209. Territorial waters and the continental shelf
210. British ships, aircraft and hovercraft

Interpretation

211. Expressions having same meaning as in copyright provisions
212. Index of defined expressions

SCHEDULE 2: PERMITTED ACTS

1. Introductory
2. Criticism, reviews and news reporting
3. Incidental inclusion of performance of recording
4. Things done for purposes of instruction or examination
5. Playing or showing sound recording, film, broadcast or cable programme at educational establishment
6. Recording of broadcasts and cable programmes by educational establishments
6A. Lending of copies by educational establishments
6B. Lending of copies by libraries or archives
7. Copy of work required to be made as a condition of export

SCHEDULE 2A: LICENSING OF PERFORMERS' PROPERTY RIGHTS

PART II: RIGHTS IN PERFORMANCES

Introductory

180. Rights conferred on performers and persons having recording rights   A1.00

(1) This Part confers rights:

  (a) on a performer, by requiring his consent to the exploitation of his performances (see sections 181 to 184), and
  (b) on a person having recording rights in relation to a performance, in relation to recordings made without his consent or that of the performer (see sections 185 to 188),

and creates offences in relation to dealing with or using illicit recordings and certain other related acts (see sections 198 and 201).
(2) In this Part "performance" means:

  (a) a dramatic performance (which includes dance and mime),
  (b) a musical performance,
  (c) a reading or recitation of a literary work, or

(d) a performance of a variety act or any similar presentation,

which is, or so far as it is, a live performance given by one or more individuals; and "recording", in relation to a performance, means a film or sound recording:

(a) made directly from the live performance,
(b) made from a broadcast of, or cable programme including, the performance, or
(c) made, directly or indirectly, from another recording of the performance.

(3) The rights conferred by this Part apply in relation to performances taking place before the commencement of this Part; but no act done before commencement, or in pursuance of arrangements made before commencement, shall be regarded as infringing those rights.

(4) The rights conferred by this Part are independent of:

(a) any copyright in, or moral rights relating to, any work performed or any film or sound recording of, or broadcast or cable programme including, the performance, and
(b) any other right or obligation arising otherwise than under this Part.

Performers' rights

A1.01   **181. Qualifying performances**

A performance is a qualifying performance for the purposes of the provisions of this Part relating to performers' rights if it is given by a qualifying individual (as defined in section 206) or takes place in a qualifying country (as so defined).

A1.02   *182. Consent required for recording or live transmission of performance*

(1) A performer's rights are infringed by a person who, without his consent:

(a) makes, otherwise than for his private and domestic use, a recording of the whole or any substantial part of a qualifying performance, or
(b) broadcasts live, or includes live in a cable programme service, the whole or any substantial part of a qualifying performance.

(2) In an action for infringement of a performer's rights brought by virtue of this section damages shall not be awarded against a defendant who shows that at the time of the infringement he believed on reasonable grounds that consent had been given.

182. Consent required for recording, etc., of live performance

(1) A performer's right are infringed by a person who, without his consent:

(a) makes a recording of the whole or any substantial part of a qualifying performance directly from the live performance,
(b) broadcasts live, or includes live in a cable programme service, the whole or any substantial part of a qualifying performance,
(c) makes a recording of the whole or any substantial part of a qualifying performance directly from a broadcast of, or cable programme including, the live performance.

(2) A performer's rights are not infringed by the making of any such recording by a person for his private and domestic use.

(3) In an action for infringement of a performer's rights brought by virtue of this section damages shall not be awarded against a defendant who shows that at the time of the infringement he believed on reasonable grounds that consent had been given.[1]

---

[1] Substituted by Copyright and Related Regulations 1996, S.I. 1996 No. 2967, Reg. 20(1). In force December 1, 1996.

182A. Consent required for copying of recording   A1.03

(1) A performer's rights are infringed by a person who, without his consent, makes, otherwise than for his private and domestic use, a copy of a recording of the whole or any substantial part of a qualifying performance.
(2) It is immaterial whether the copy is made directly or indirectly.
(3) The right of a performer under this section to authorise or prohibit the making of such copies is referred to in this Part as "reproduction right".

182B. Consent required for issue of copies to the public   A1.04

(1) A performer's rights are infringed by a person who, without his consent, issues to the public copies of a recording of the whole or any substantial part of a qualifying performance.
(2) References in this Part to the issue to the public of copies of recording are to:

  (a) the act of putting into circulation in the EEA copies not previously put into circulation in the EEA by or with the consent of the performer, or
  (b) the act of putting into circulation outside the EEA copies not previously put into circulation in the EEA or elsewhere.

(3) References in this Part to the issue to the public of copies of a recording do not include:

  (a) any subsequent distribution, sale, hiring or loan of copies previously put into circulation (but see section 182C: consent required for rental or lending), or
  (b) any subsequent importation of such copies into the United Kingdom or another EEA state,

except so far as paragraph (a) of subsection (2) applies to putting into circulation in the EEA copies previously put into circulation outside the EEA.
(4) References in this Part to the issue of copies of a recording of a performance include the issue of the original recording of the live performance.
(5) The right of a performer under this section to authorise or prohibit the issue of copies to the public is referred to in this Part as "distribution right".

182C. Consent required for rental or lending of copies to the public   A1.05

(1) A performer's rights are infringed by a person who, without his consent, rents or lends to the public copies of a recording of the whole or any substantial part of a qualifying performance.
(2) In this Part, subject to the following provisions of this section:

  (a) "rental" means making a copy of a recording available for use, on terms that it will or may be returned, for direct or indirect economic or commercial advantage, and
  (b) "lending" means making a copy of a recording available for use, on terms that it will or may be returned, otherwise than for direct or indirect economic or commercial advantage, through an establishment which is accessible to the public.

(3) The expressions "rental" and "lending" do not include:

  (a) making available for the purpose of public performance, playing or showing in public, broadcasting or inclusion in a cable programme service;
  (b) making available for the purpose of exhibition in public; or
  (c) making available for on-the-spot reference use.

(4) The expression "lending" does not include making available between establishments which are accessible to the public.
(5) Where lending by an establishment accessible to the public gives rise to a payment the amount of which does not go beyond what is necessary to cover the operating costs

of the establishment, there is no direct or indirect economic or commercial advantage for the purposes of this section.

(6) References in this Part to the rental or lending of copies of a recording of a performance include the rental or lending of the original recording of the live performance.

(7) In this Part:

— "rental right" means the right of a performer under this section to authorise or prohibit the rental of copies to the public, and

— "lending right" means the right of a performer under this section to authorise or prohibit the lending of copies to the public.

A1.06   **182D. Right to equitable remuneration for exploitation of sound recording**

(1)Where a commercially published sound recording of the whole or any substantial part of a qualifying performance:

(a) is played in public, or

(b) is included in a broadcast or cable programme service,

the performance is entitled to equitable remuneration from the owner of the copyright in the sound recording.

(2) The right to equitable remuneration under this section may not be assigned by the performer except to a collecting society for the purpose of enabling it to enforce the right on his behalf.

The right is, however, transmissible by testamentary disposition or by operation of law as personal or moveable property; and it may be assigned or further transmitted by any person into whose hands it passes.

(3) The amount payable by way of equitable remuneration is as agreed by or on behalf of the persons by and to whom it is payable, subject to the following provisions.

(4) In default of agreement as to the amount payable by way of equitable remuneration, the person by or to whom it is payable may apply to the Copyright Tribunal to determine the amount payable.

(5) A person to or by whom equitable remuneration is payable may also apply to the Copyright Tribunal:

(a) to vary any agreement as to the amount payable, or

(b) to vary any previous determination of the Tribunal as to that matter;

but except with the special leave of the Tribunal no such application may be made within twelve months from the date of a previous determination.

An order made on an application under this subsection has effect from the date on which it is made or such later date as may be specified by the Tribunal.

(6) On an application under this section the Tribunal shall consider the matter and make such order as to the method of calculating and paying equitable remuneration as it may determine to be reasonable in the circumstances, taking into account the importance of the contribution of the performer to the sound recording.

(7) An agreement is of no effect in so far as it purports:

(a) to exclude or restrict the right to equitable remuneration under this section, or

(b) to prevent a person questioning the amount of equitable remuneration or to restrict the powers of the Copyright Tribunal under this section.[2]

A1.07   **183. Infringement of performer's rights by use of recording made without consent**

A performer's rights are infringed by a person who, without his consent:

(a) shows or plays in public the whole or any substantial part of a qualifying performance, or

---

[2] Inserted by C.R.R. 1996, Reg. 20(2). In force December 1, 1996.

(b) broadcasts or includes in a cable programme service the whole or any substantial part of a qualifying performance,

by means of a recording which was, and which that person knows or has reason to believe was, made without the performer's consent.

184. Infringement of performer's rights by importing, possesing or dealing with illicit recording   A1.08

(1) A performer's rights are infringed by a person who, without his consent:

(a) imports into the United Kingdom otherwise than for his private and domestic use, or
(b) in the course of a business possesses, sells or lets for hire, offers or exposes for sale or hire, or distributes,

a recording of a qualifying performance which is, and which that person knows or has reason to believe is, an illicit recording.

(2) Where in an action for infringement of a performer's rights brought by virtue of this section a defendant shows that the illicit recording was innocently acquired by him or a predecessor in title of his, the only remedy avaialable against him in respect of the infringement is damages not exceeding a reasonable payment in respect of the act complained of.

(3) In subsection (2) "innocently acquired" means that the person acquiring the recording did not know and had no reason to believe that it was an illicit recording.

Rights of person having recording rights

185. Exclusive recording contracts and persons having recording rights   A1.09

(1) In this Part an "exclusive recording contract" means a contract between a performer and another person under which that person is entitled to the exclusion of all other persons (including the performer) to make recordings of one or more of his performances with a view to their commercial exploitation.

(2) References in this Part to a "person having recording rights", in relation to a performance, are (subject to subsection (3)) to a person:

(a) who is party to and has the benefit of an exclusive recording contract to which the performance is subject, or
(b) to whom the benefit of such a contract has been assigned,

and who is a qualifying person.

(3) If a performance is subject to an exclusive recording contract but the person mentioned in subsection (2) is not a qualifying person, references in this Part to a "person having recording rights" in relation to the performance are to any person:

(a) who is licensed by such a person to make recordings of the performance with a view to their commercial exploitation, or
(b) to whom the benefit of such a licence has been assigned,

and who is a qualifying person.

(4) In this section "with a view to commercial exploitation" means with a view to the recordings being sold or let for hire, or shown or played in public.

186. Consent required for recording of performance subject to exclusive contract   A1.10

(1) A person infringes the rights of a person having recording rights in relation to a performance who, without his consent or that of the performer, makes a recording of the whole or any substantial part of the performance, otherwise than for his private and domestic use.

(2) In an action for infringement of those rights brought by virtue of this section

damages shall not be awarded against a defendant who shows that at the time of the infringement he believed on reasonable grounds that consent had been given.

A1.11 **187. Infringement of recording rights by use of recording made without consent**

(1) A person infringes the rights of a person having recording rights in relation to a performance who, without his consent or, in the case of a qualifying performance, that of the performer:

    (a) shows or plays in public the whole or any substantial part of the performance, or

    (b) broadcasts or includes in a cable programme service the whole or any substantial part of the performance,

by means of a recording which was, and which that person knows or has reason to believe was, made without the appropriate consent.

(2) The reference in subsection (1) to "the appropriate consent" is to the consent of:

    (a) the performer, or

    (b) the person who at the time the consent was given had recording rights in relation to the performance (or, if there was more than one such person, of all of them).

A1.12 **188. Infringement of recording rights by importing, possessing or dealing with illicit recording**

(1) A person infringes the rights of a person having recording rights in relation to a performance who, without his consent or, in the case of a qualifying performance, that of the performer:

    (a) imports into the United Kingdom otherwise than for his private and domestic use, or

    (b) in the course of a business possesses, sells or lets for hire, offers or exposes for sale or hire, or distributes,

a recording of the performance which is, and which that person knows or has reason to believe is, an illicit recording.

(2) Where in an action for infringement of those rights brought by virtue of this section a defendant shows that the illicit recording was innocently acquired by him or a predecessor in title of his, the only remedy available against him in respect of the infringement is damages not exceeding a reasonable payment in respect of the act complained of.

(3) In subsection (2) "innocently acquired" means that the person acquiring the recording did not know and had no reason to believe that it was an illicit recording.

Exceptions to rights conferred

A1.13 **189. Acts permitted notwithstanding rights conferred by this Part**

The provisions of Schedule 2 specify acts which may be done notwithstanding the rights conferred by this Part, being acts which correspond broadly to certain of those specified in Chapter III of Part I (acts permitted notwithstanding copyright).

A1.14 **190. Power of Tribunal to give consent on behalf of performer in certain cases**

(1) The Copyright Tribunal may, on the application of a person wishing to make a recording from a previous recording of a performance, give consent in a case where:

    (a) the identity or whereabouts of a performer cannot be ascertained by reasonable inquiry, or

(b) a performer unreasonably withholds his consent.

(1) The Copyright Tribunal may, on the application of a person wishing to make a copy of a recording of a performance, give consent in a case where the identity or whereabouts of the person entitled to the reproduction right cannot be ascertained by reasonable inquiry.[3]

(2) Consent given by the Tribunal has effect as consent of the *performer* **person entitled to the reproduction right**[4] for the purposes of:

- (a) the provisions of this Part relating to performers' rights, and
- (b) section 198(3)(a) (criminal liability: sufficient consent in relation to qualifying performances),

and may be given subject to any conditions specified in the Tribunal's order.

(3) The Tribunal shall not give consent under subsection (1)(a) except after the service or publication of such notices as may be required by rules made under section 150 (general procedural rules) or as the Tribunal may in any particular case direct.

(4) The Tribunal shall not give consent under subsection (1)(b) unless satisfied that the performer's reasons for withholding consent do not include the protection of any legitimate interest of his; but it shall be for the performer to show what his reasons are for withholding consent, and in default of evidence as to his reasons the Tribunal may draw such inferences as it thinks fit.[5]

(5) In any case the Tribunal shall take into account the following factors:

- (a) whether the original recording was made with the performer's consent and is lawfully in the possession or control of the person proposing to make the further recording;
- (b) whether the making of the further recording is consistent with the obligations of the parties to the arrangements under which, or is otherwise consistent with the purposes for which, the original recording was made.

(6) Where the Tribunal gives consent under this section it shall, in default of agreement between the applicant and the *performer,* **person entitled to the reproduction right**[6], make such order as it thinks fit as to the payment to be made to *the performer* **that person**[7] in consideration of consent being given.

Duration of rights[8]

191. Duration of rights   A1.15

The rights conferred by this Part continue to subsist in relation to a performance until the end of the period of 50 years from the end of the calendar year in which the performance takes place.

(1) The following provisions have effect with respect to the duration of the rights conferred by this Part.

(2) The rights conferred by this Part in relation to a performance expire:

- (a) at the end of the period of 50 years from the end of the calendar year in which the performance takes place, or
- (b) if during that period a recording of the performance is released, 50 years from the end of the calendar year in which it is released,

subject as follows.

(3) For the purposes of subsection (2) a recording is "released" when it is first published, played or shown in public, broadcast or included in a cable programme

---

[3] Substituted by C.R.R. 1996, Reg. 23(2). In force December 1, 1996.
[4] Substituted by C.R.R. 1996, Reg. 23(3). In force December 1, 1996.
[5] Deleted by C.R.R. 1996, Reg. 23(4) with effect from December 1, 1996.
[6] Substituted by C.R.R. 1996, Reg. 23(5). In force December 1, 1996.
[7] Substituted by C.R.R. 1996, Reg. 23(5). In force December 1, 1996.
[8] Substituted by C.R.R. 1996, Reg. 21(5). In force December 1, 1996.

service; but in determining whether a recording has been released no account shall be taken of any unauthorised act.

(4) Where a performer is not a national of an EEA state, the duration of the rights conferred by this Part in relation to his performance is that to which the performance is entitled in the country of which he is a national, provided that does not exceed the period which would apply under subsections (2) and (3).

(5) If or to the extent that the application of subsection (4) would be at variance with an international obligation to which the United Kingdom became subject prior to 29th October 1993, the duration of the rights conferred by this Part shall be as specified in subsections (2) and (3).[9]

Performers' property rights

A1.16   191A. Performers' property rights

(1) The following rights conferred by this Part on a performer:
— reproduction right (section 182A),
— distribution right (section 182B),
— rental right and lending right (section 182C),

are property rights ("a performer's property rights").

(2) References in this Part to the consent of the performer shall be construed in relation to a performer's property rights as references to the consent of the rights owner.

(3) Where different persons are (whether in consequence of a partial assignment or otherwise) entitled to different aspects of a performer's property rights in relation to a performance, the rights owner for any purpose of this Part is the person who is entitled to the aspect of those rights relevant for that purpose.

(4) Where a performer's property rights (or any aspect of them) is owned by more than one person jointly, references in this Part to the rights owner are to all the owners, so that, in particular, any requirement of the licence of the rights owner requires the licence of all of them.

A1.17   191B. Assignments and licences

(1) A performer's property rights are transmissible by assignment, by testamentary disposition or by operation of law, as personal or moveable property.

(2) An assignment or other transmission of a performer's property rights may be partial, that is, limited so as to apply:
(a) to one or more, but not all, of the things requiring the consent of the rights owner;
(b) to part, but not the whole, of the period for which the rights are to subsist.

(3) An assignment of a performer's property rights is not effective unless it is in writing signed by or on behalf of the assignor.

(4) A licence granted by the owner of a performer's property rights is binding on every successor in title to his interest in the rights, except a purchaser in good faith for valuable consideration and without notice (actual or constructive) of the licence or a person deriving title from such a purchaser; and references in this Part to doing anything with, or without, the licence of the rights owner shall be construed accordingly.

A1.18   191C. Prospective ownership of a performer's property rights

(1) This section applies where by an agreement made in relation to a future recording of a performance, and signed by or on behalf of the performer, the performer purports to assign his performer's property rights (wholly or partially) to another person.

---

[9] Substituted by Duration of Copyright and Rights in Performances Regulations 1995, S.I. 1995 No. 3297, Reg. 10. In force January 1, 1996.

(2) If on the rights coming into existence the assignee or another person claiming under him would be entitled as against all other persons to require the rights to be vested in him, they shall vest in the assignee or his successor in title by virtue of this subsection.

(3) A licence granted by a prospective owner of a performer's property rights is binding on every successor in title to his interest (or prospective interest) in the rights, except a purchaser in good faith for valuable consideration and without notice (actual or constructive) of the licence or a person deriving title from such a purchaser.

References in this Part to doing anything with, or without, the licence of the rights owner shall be construed accordingly.

(4) In subsection (3) "prospective owner" in relation to a performer's property rights means a person who is prospectively entitled to those rights by virtue of such an agreement as is mentioned in subsection (1).

191D. Exclusive licence

A1.19

(1) In this Part an "exclusive licence" means a licence in writing signed by or on behalf of the owner of a performer's property rights authorising the licensee to the exclusion of all other persons, including the person granting the licence, to do anything requiring the consent of the rights owner.

(2) The licensee under an exclusive licence has the same rights against a successor in title who is bound by the licence as he has against the person granting the licence.

191E. Performer's property right to part under will with unpublished original recording

A1.20

Where under a bequest (whether general or specific) a person is entitled beneficially or otherwise to any material thing containing an original recording of a performance which was not published before the death of the testator, the bequest shall, unless a contrary intention is indicated in the testator's will or a codicil to it, be construed as including any performer's rights in relation to the recording to which the testator was entitled immediately before his death.

191F. Presumption of transfer of rental right in case of film production agreement

A1.21

(1) Where an agreement concerning film production is concluded between a performer and a film producer, the performer shall be presumed, unless the agreement provides to the contrary, to have transferred to the film producer any rental right in relation to the film arising from the inclusion of a recording of his performance in the film.

(2) Where this section applies, the absence of signature by or on behalf of the performer does not exclude the operation of section 191C (effect of purported assignment of future rights).

(3) The reference in subsection (1) an agreement concluded between a performer and a film producer includes any agreement having effect between those persons, whether made by them directly or through intermediaries.

(4) Section 191G (right to equitable remuneration on transfer of rental right) applies where there is presumed transfer by virtue of this section in the case of an actual transfer.

191G. Right to equitable remuneration where rental right transferred

A1.22

(1) Where a performer has transferred his rental right concerning a sound recording or a film to the producer of the sound recording or film, he retains the right to equitable remuneration for the rental.

The reference above to the transfer of rental right by one person to another includes any arrangement having that effect, whether made by them directly or through intermediaries.

(2) The right to equitable remuneration under this section may not be assigned by the performer except to a collecting society for the purpose of enabling it to enforce the right on his behalf.

The right is, however, transmissible by testamentary disposition or by operation of law as personal or moveable property; and it may be assigned or further transmitted by any person into whose hands it passes.

(3) Equitable remuneration under this section is payable by the person for the time being entitled to the rental right, that is, the person to whom the right was transferred or any successor in title of his.

(4) The amount payable by way of equitable remuneration is as agreed by or on behalf of the persons by and to whom it is payable, subject to section 191H (reference of amount to Copyright Tribunal).

(5) An agreement is of no effect in so far as it purports to exclude or restrict the right to equitable remuneration under this section.

(6) In this section a "collecting society" means a society or other organisation which has as its main object, or one of its main objects, the exercise of the right to equitable remuneration on behalf of more than one performer.

A1.23   **191H. Equitable remuneration: reference of amount to Copyright Tribunal**

(1) In default of agreement as to the amount payable by way of equitable remuneration under section 191G, the person by or to whom it is payable may apply to the Copyright Tribunal to determine the amount payable.

(2) A person to or by whom equitable remuneration is payable may also apply to the Copyright Tribunal:

    (a) to vary any agreement as to the amount payable; or
    (b) to vary any previous determination of the Tribunal as to that matter;

but except with the special leave of the Tribunal no such application may be made within twelve months from the date of a previous determination.

An order made on an application under this subsection has effect from the date on which it is made or such later date as may be specified by the Tribunal.

(3) On an application under this section the Tribunal shall consider the matter and make such order as to the method of calculating any paying equitable remuneration as it may determine to be reasonable in the circumstances, taking into account the importance of the contribution of the performer to the film or sound recording.

(4) Remuneration shall not be considered inequitable merely because it was paid by way of a single payment or at the time of the transfer of the rental right.

(5) An agreement is of no effect in so far as it purports to prevent a person questioning the amount of equitable remuneration or to restrict the powers of the Copyright Tribunal under this section.

A1.24   **191I. Infringement actionable by rights owner**

(1) An infringement of a performer's property rights is actionable by the rights owner.

(2) In an action for infringement of a performer's property rights all such relief by way of damages, injunctions, accounts or otherwise is available to the plaintiff as is available in respect of the infringement of any other property right.

(3) This section has effect subject to the following provisions of this Part.

A1.25   **191J. Provisions as to damages in infringement action**

(1) Where in an action for infringement of a performer's property rights it is shown that at the time of the infringement the defendant did not know, and had no reason to believe, that the rights subsisted in the recording to which the action relates, the plaintiff is not entitled to damages against him, but without prejudice to any other remedy.

(2) The court may in an action for infringement of a performer's property rights having regard to all the circumstances, and in particular to:

(a) the flagrancy of the infringement, and

(b) any benefit accruing to the defendant by reason of the infringement, award such additional damages as the justice of the case may require.

191K. Undertaking to take licence of right in infringement proceedings   A1.26

(1) If in proceedings for infringement of a performer's property rights in respect of which a licence is as of right under paragraph 17 of Schedule 2A (powers exercisable in consequence of competition report) the defendant undertakes to take a licence on such terms as may be agreed or, in default of agreement, settled by the Copyright Tribunal under that paragraph:

(a) no injunction shall be granted against him,

(b) no order for delivery up shall be made under section 195, and

(c) the amount recoverable against him by way of damages or on an account of profits shall not exceed double the amount which would have been payable by him as licensee if such a licence on those terms had been granted before the earliest infringement.

(2) An undertaking may be given at any time before final order in the proceedings, without any admission of liability.

(3) Nothing in this section affects the remedies available in respect of an infringement committed before licences of right were available.

191L. Rights and remedies for exclusive licence   A1.27

(1) An exclusive licensee has, except against the owner of a performer's property rights, the same rights and remedies in respect of matters occurring after the grant of the licence as if the licence had been an assignment.

(2) His rights and remedies are concurrent with those of the rights owner; and references in the relevant provisions of this Part to the rights owner shall be construed accordingly.

(3) In an action brought by an exclusive licensee by virtue of this section a defendant may avail himself of any defence which would have been available to him if the action had been brought by the rights owner.

191M. Exercise of concurrent rights   A1.28

(1) Where an action for infringement of a performer's property rights brought by the rights owner or an exclusive licensee relates (wholly or partly) to an infringement in respect of which they have concurrent rights of action, the rights owner or, as the case may be, the exclusive licensee may not, without the leave of the court, proceed with the action unless the other is either joined as plaintiff or added as a defendant.

(2) A rights owner or exclusive licensee who is added as a defendant in pursuance of subsection (1) is not liable for any costs in the action unless he takes part in the proceedings.

(3) The above provisions do not affect the granting of interlocutory relief on the application by the rights owner or exclusive licensee alone.

(4) Where an action for infringement of a performer's property rights is brought which relates (wholly or partly) to an infringement in respect of which the rights owner and an exclusive licensee have or had concurrent rights of action:

(a) the court shall in assessing damages take into account:

(i) the terms of the licence, and

(ii) any pecuniary remedy already awarded or available to either of them in respect of the infringement;

(b) no account of profits shall be directed if an award of damages has been made, or an account of profits has been directed, in favour of the other of them in respect of the infringement; and

(c) the court shall if an account of profits is directed apportion the profits bewteen them as the court considers just, subject to any agreement between them;

and these provisions apply whether or not the rights owner and the exclusive licensee are both parties to the action.

(5) The owner of a performer's property rights shall notify any exclusive licensee having concurrent rights before applying for an order under section 195 (order for delivery up) or exercising the right conferred by section 196 (right of seizure); and the court may on application of the licensee make such order under section 195 or, as the case may be, prohibiting or permitting the exercise by the rights owner of the right conferred by section 196, as it thinks fit having regard to the terms of the licence.[10]

A1.29   192. *Transmission of rights*

(1) The rights conferred by this Part are not assignable or transmissible, except to the extent that performer's rights are transmissible in accordance with the following provisions.

(2) On the death of a person entitled to performer's rights:

  (a) the rights pass to such person as he may by testamentary disposition specifically direct, and

  (b) if or to the extent that there is no such direction, the rights are exercisable by his personal representatives;

and references in this Part to the performer, in the context of the person having performers' rights, shall be construed as references to the person for the time being entitled to exercise those rights.

(3) Where by virtue of subsection (2)(a) a right becomes exercisable by more than one person, it is exercisable by each of them independently of the other or others.

(4) The above provisions do not affect section 185(2)(b) or (3)(b), so far as those provisions confer rights under this Part on a person to whom the benefit of a contract or licence is assigned.

(5) Any damages recovered by personal representatives by virtue of this section in respect of any infringement after a person's death shall devolve as part of his estate as if the right of action had subsisted and been invested in him immediately before his death.

Non-property rights

A1.30   **192A. Performers' non-property rights**

(1) The rights conferred on a performer by:

  — section 182 (consent required for recording, etc. of live performance),
  — section 183 (infringement of performer's rights by use of recording made without consent), and
  — section 184 (infringement of performer's rights importing, possessing or dealing with illicit recording),

are not assignable or transmissible, except to the following extent.

They are referred to in this Part as "a performer's non-property rights".

(2) On the death of a person entitled to any such right:

  (a) the right passes to such person as he may by testamentary disposition specifically direct, and

---

[10] Inserted by C.R.R. 1996, Reg. 21(1). In force December 1, 1996.

(b) if or to the extent that there is no such direction, the right is exercisable by his personal representatives.

(3) References in this Part to the performer, in the context of the person having any such right, shall be construed as references to the person for the time being entitled to exercise those rights.

(4) Where by virtue of subsection (2)(a) a right becomes exercisable by more than one person, it is exercisable by each of them independently of the other or others.

(5) Any damages recovered by personal representatives by virtue of this section in respect of an infringement after a person's death shall devolve as part of his estate as if the right of action had subsisted and been vested in him immediately before his death.

192B. Transmissibility of rights of person having recorded rights

A1.31

(1) The rights conferred by this Part on a person having recording rights are not assignable or transmissible.

(2) This does not affect section 185(2)(b) or (3)(b), so far as those provisions confer rights under this Part on a person to whom the benefit of a contract or licence is assigned.[11]

193. Consent

A1.32

(1) Consent for the purposes of this Part **by a person having a performer's non-property rights, or by a person having recording rights**[12] may be given in relation to a specific performance, a specified decription of performances or performances generally, and may relate to past or future performances.

(2) A person having recording rights in a performance is bound by any consent given by a person through whom he derives his rights under the exclusive recording contract or licence in question, in the same way as if the consent had been given by him.

(3) Where a *right* **performer's non-property right**[13] conferred by this Part passes to another person, any consent binding on the person previously entitled binds the person to whom the right passes in the same way as if the consent had been given by him.

194. Infringement actionable as breach of statutory duty

A1.33

An infringement of any of the rights conferred by this Part is actionable by the person entitled to the right as a breach of statutory duty.
An infringement of:

(a) **a performer's non-property rights, or**
(b) **any right conferred by this Part on a person having recording rights,**[14] **is actionable by the person entitled to the right as a breach of statutory duty.**

Delivery up or seizure of illicit recordings[15]

195. Order for delivery up

A1.34

(1) Where a person has in his possession, custody or control in the course of a business an illicit recording of a performance, a person having performer's rights or recording rights in relation to the performance under this Part may apply to the court for an order that the recording be delivered up to him or to such other person as the court may direct.

(2) An application shall not be made after the end of the period specified in section

---

[11] Substituted by C.R.R. 1996, Reg. 21(2). In force December 1, 1996.
[12] Inserted by C.R.R. 1996, Reg. 21(3)(a). In force December 1, 1996.
[13] Substituted by C.R.R. 1996, Reg. 21(3)(b). In force December 1, 1996.
[14] Substituted by C.R.R. 1996, Reg. 21(4). In force December 1, 1996.
[15] Inserted by C.R.R. 1996, Reg. 21(5). In force December 1, 1996.

203; and no order shall be made unless the court also makes, or it appears to the court that there are grounds for making, an order under section 204 (order as to disposal of illicit recording).

(3) A person to whom a recording is delivered up in pursuance of an order under the section shall, if an order under section 204 is not made, retain it pending the making of an order, or the decision not to make an order, under that section.

(4) Nothing in this section affects any other power of the court.

A1.35   **196. Right to seize illicit recordings**

(1) An illicit recording of a performance which is found exposed or otherwise immediately available for sale or hire, and in respect of which a person would be entitled to apply for an order under section 195, may be seized and detained by him or a person authorised by him.

The right to seize and detain is exercisable subject to the following conditions and is subject to any decision of the court under section 204 (order as to disposal of illicit recording).

(2) Before anything is seized under this section notice of the time and place of the proposed seizure must be given to a local police station.

(3) A person may for the purpose of exercising the right conferred by this section enter premises to which the public have access but may not seize anything in the possession, custody or control of a person at a permanent or regular place of business of his and may not use any force.

(4) At the time when anything is seized under this section there shall be left at the place where it was seized a notice in the prescribed form containing the prescribed particulars as to the person by whom or on whose authority the seizure is made and the grounds on which it is made.

(5) In this section:

— "premises" includes land, buildings, fixed or moveable structures, vehicles, vessels, aircraft and hovercraft; and
— "prescribed" means prescribed by order of the Secretary of State.

(6) An order of the Secretary of State under this section shall be made by statutory instrument which shall be subject to annulment in pursuance of a resolution of either House of Parliament.

A1.36   **197. Meaning of "illicit recording"**

(1) In this Part "illicit recording", in relation to a performance, shall be construed in accordance with this section.

(2) For the purpose of a performer's rights, a recording of the whole or any substantial part of a performance of his is an illicit recording if it is made, otherwise than for private purposes, without his consent.

(3) For the purposes of the rights of a person having recording rights, a recording of the whole or any substantial part of a performance subject to the exclusive recording contract is an illicit recording if it is made, otherwise than for private purposes, without his consent or that of the performer.

(4) For the purposes of sections 198 and 199 (offences and orders for delivery up in criminal proceedings), a recording is an illicit recording if it is an illicit recording for the purposes mentioned in subsection (2) or subsection (3).

(5) In this Part "illicit recording" includes a recording failing to be treated as an illicit recording by virtue of any of the following provisions of Schedule 2:

— paragraph 4(3) (recordings made for purposes of instruction or examination),
— paragraph 6(2) (recordings made by educational establishments for educational purposes),
— paragraph 12(2) (recordings of performance in electronic form retained on transfer of principal recording), or

— paragraph 16(3) (recordings made for purposes of broadcast or cable programme),

but otherwise does not include a recording made in accordance with any of the provisions of that Schedule.

(6) It is immaterial for the purposes of this section where the recording was made.

Offences

198. Criminal liability for making, dealing with or using illicit recordings

A1.37

(1) A person commits an offence who without sufficient consent:

   (a) makes for sale or hire, or

   (b) imports into the United Kingdom otherwise than for his private and domestic use, or

   (c) possesses in the course of a business with a veiw to committing any act infringing the rights conferred by this Part, or

   (d) in the course of a business:

      (i) sells or lets for hire, or

     (ii) offers or exposes for sale or hire, or

    (iii) distributes,

a recording which is, and which he knows or has reason to believe is, an illicit recording.

(2) A person commits an offence who causes a recording of a performance made without sufficient consent to be:

   (a) shown or played in public, or

   (b) broadcast or included in a cable programme service,

thereby infringing any of the rights conferred by this Part, if he knows or has reason to believe that those rights are thereby infringed.

(3) In subsections (1) and (2) "sufficient consent" means:

   (a) in the case of a qualifying performance, the consent of the performer, and

   (b) in the case of a non-qualifying performance subject to an exclusive recording contract:

      (i) for the purposes of subsection (1)(a) (making of recording), the consent of the performer or the person having recording rights, and

     (ii) for the purposes of subsection (1)(b), (c) and (d) and subsection (2) (dealing with or using recording), the consent of the person having recording rights.

The references in this subsection to the person having recording rights are to the person having those rights at the time the consent is given or, if there is more than one such person, to all of them.

(4) No offence is committed under subsection (1) or (2) by the commission of an act which by virtue of any provision of Schedule 2 may be done without infringing the rights conferred by this Part.

(5) A person guilty of an offence under subsection (1)(a), (b) or (d)(iii) is liable:

   (a) on summary conviction to imprisonment for a term not exceeding six months or a fine not exceeding the statutory maximum, or both;

   (b) on conviction on indictment to a fine or imprisonment for a term not exceeding two years, or both.

(6) A person guilty of any other offence under this section is liable on summary conviction to a fine not exceeding level 5 on the standard scale or imprisonment for a term not exceeding six months, or both.

A1.38   198A. Enforcement by local weights and measures authority

(1) It is the duty of every local weights and measures authority to enforce within their area the provisions of section 198.

(2) The following provisions of the Trade Descriptions Act 1968 apply in relation to the enforcement of that section by such an authority as in realtion to the enforcement of that Act:

— section 27 (power to make test purchases)
— section 28 (power to enter premises and inspect and seize goods and documents),
— section 29 (obstruction of authorised officers),and
— section 33 (compensation for loss, etc. of goods seized).

(3) Subsection (1) above does not apply in relation to the enforcement of section 198 in Northern Ireland, but it is the duty of the Department of Economic Development to enforce that section in Northern Ireland. For that purpose the provisions of the Trade Descriptions Act 1968 specified in subsection (2) apply as if for the references to a local weights and measures authority and any officer of such an authority there were substituted references to that Department and any of its officers.

(4) Any enactment which authorised the disclosure of information for the purpose of facilitating the enforcement of the Trade Descriptions Act 1968 shall apply as if section 198 were contained in that Act and as if the functions of any person in relation to the enforcement of that section were functions under that Act.

(5) Nothing in this section shall be construed as authorising a local weights and measures authority to bring proceedings in Scotland for an offence.[16]

A1.39   199. Order for delivery up in criminal proceedings

(1) The Court before which proceedings are brought against a person for an offence under section 198 may, if satisfied that at the time of his arrest or charge he had in his possession, custody or control in the course of a business an illicit recording of a performance, order that it be delivered up to a person having performers' rights or recording rights in relation to the performance or to such other person as the court may direct.

(2) For this purpose a person shall be treated as charged with an offence:

(a) in England, Wales and Northern Ireland, when he is orally charged or is served with a summons or indictment;
(b) in Scotland, when he is cautioned, charged or served with a complaint or indictment.

(3) An order may be made by the court of its own motion or on the application of the prosecutor (or, in Scotland, the Lord Advocate or procurator-fiscal), and may be made whether or not the person is convicted of the offence, but shall not be made:

(a) after the end of the period specified in section 203 (period after which remedy of delivery up not available), or
(b) if it appears to the court unlikely that any order will be made under section 204 (order as to disposal of illicit recording).

(4) An appeal lies from an order made under this section by a magistrates' court:

(a) in England and Wales, to the Crown Court, and
(b) in Northern Ireland, to the county court;

and in Scotland, where an order has been made under this section, the person from whose possession, custody or control the illicit recording has been removed may,

---

[16] Inserted by the Criminal Justice and Public Order Act 1994, s. 165(3). Not yet in force.

without prejudice to any other form of appeal under any rule of law, appeal against that order in the same manner as against sentence.

(5) A person to whom an illicit recording is delivered up in pursuance of an order under this section shall retain it pending the making of an order, or the decision not to make an order, under section 204.

(6) Nothing in this section affects the powers of the court under section 43 of the Powers of Criminal Courts Act 1973, section 223 or 436 of the Criminal Procedure (Scotland) Act 1975[17] or *Article 7 of the Criminal Justice (Northern Ireland) Order 1980* **or Article 11 of the Criminal Justice (Northern Ireland) Order 1994**[18] (general provisions as to forfeiture in criminal proceedings).

200. Search warrants

A1.40

(1)Where a justice of the peace (in Scotland, a sheriff or justice of the peace) is satisfied by information on oath given by a constable (in Scotland, by evidence on oath) that there are reasonable grounds for believing:

(a) that an offence under section 198(1)(a) (b) or (d)(iii) (offences of making, importing or distributing illicit recordings) has been or is about to be committed in any premises, and

(b) that evidence that such an offence has been or is about to be committed is in those premises,

he may issue a warrant authorising a constable to enter and search the premises, using such reasonable force as is necessary.

(2) The power conferred by subsection (1) does not, in England and Wales, extend to authorising a search for material of the kinds mentioned in section 9(2) of the Police and Criminal Evidence Act 1984 (certain classes of personal or confidential material).

(3) A warrant under subsection (1):

(a) may authorise persons to accompany any constable executing the warrant, and

(b) remains in force for 28 days from the date of its issue.

(4) In this section "premises" includes land, buildings, fixed or moveable structures, vehicles, vessels, aircraft and hovercraft.

201. False representation of authority to give consent

A1.41

(1) It is an offence for a person to represent falsely that he is authorised by any person to give consent for the purposes of this Part in relation to a performance, unless he believes on reasonable grounds that he is so authorised.

(2) A person guilty of an offence under this section is liable on summary conviction to imprisonment for a term not exceeding six months or a fine not exceeding level 5 on the standard scale or both.

202. Offence by body corporate: liability of officers

A1.42

(1) Where an offence under this Part committed by a body corporate is proved to have been committed with the consent or connivance of a director, manager, secretary or other similar officer of the body, or a person purporting to act in any such capacity, he as well as the body corporate is guilty of the offence and liable to be proceeded against and punished accordingly.

(2) In relation to a body corporate whose affairs are managed by its members "director" means a member of the body corporate.

---

[17] For special provisions see Criminal Procedure (Consequential Provisions) (Scotland) Act 1995, ss. 4, 5, Sched. 3.

[18] Substituted by the Criminal Justice (Northern Ireland) Order 1994, Art. 26(1), Sched. 2. Not yet in force.

Supplementary provisions with respect to delivery up and seizure

A1.43   **203. Period after which remedy of delivery up not available**

(1) An application for an order under section 195 (order for delivery up in civil proceedings) may not be made after the end of the period of six years from the date on which the illicit recording in question was made, subject to the following provisions.

(2) If during the whole or any part of that period a person entitled to apply for an order:

  (a) is under a disability, or
  (b) is prevented by fraud or concealment from discovering the facts entitling him to apply,

an application may be made by him at any time before the end of the period of six years from the date on which he ceased to be under a disability or, as the case may be, could with reasonable diligence have discovered those facts.

(3) In subsection (2) "disability":

  (a) in England and Wales, has the same meaning as in the Limitation Act 1980;
  (b) in Scotland, means legal disability within the meaning of the Prescription and Limitations (Scotland) Act 1973;
  (c) in Northern Ireland, has the same meaning as in the Statute of Limitation (Northern Ireland) 1958.

(4) An order under section 199 (order for delivery up in criminal proceedings) shall not, in any case, be made after the end of the period of six years from the date on which the illicit recording in question was made.

A1.44   **204. Order as to disposal of illicit recording**

(1) An application may be made to the court for an order that an illicit recording of a performance delivered up in pursuance of an order under section 195 or 199, or seized and detained in pursuance of the right conferred by section 196, shall be:

  (a) forfeited to such person having performer's rights or recording rights in relation to the performance as the court may direct, or
  (b) destroyed or otherwise dealt with as the court may think fit,

or for a decision that no such order should be made.

(2) In considering what order (if any) should be made, the court shall consider whether other remedies available in an action for infringement of the rights conferred by this Part would be adequate to compensate the person or persons entitled to the rights and to protect their interests.

(3) Provision shall be made by rules of court as to the service of notice on persons having an interest in the recording, and any such person is entitled:

  (a) to appear in proceedings for an order under this section, whether or not he was served with notice, and
  (b) to appeal against any order made, whether or not he appeared;

and an order shall not take effect until the end of the period within which notice of an appeal may be given or, if before the end of that period notice of appeal is duly given, until the final determination or abandonment of the proceedings on the appeal.

(4) Where there is more than one person interested in a recording, the court shall make such order as it thinks just and may (in particular) direct that the recording be sold, or otherwise dealt with, and the proceeds divided.

(5) If the court decides that no order should be made under this section, the person in whose possession, custody or control the recording was before being delivered up or seized is entitled to its return.

(6) References in this section to a person having an interest in a recording include any person in whose favour an order could be made in respect of the recording under this section or under section 114 or 231 of this Act or *section 58C of the Trade Marks Act 1938* **section 19 of the Trade Marks Act 1994**[19] (which make similar provision in relation to infringement of copyright, design right and trade marks).

205. Jurisdiction of county court and sheriff court   A1.45

(1) In England, Wales and Northern Ireland a county court may entertain proceedings under:

— section 195 (order for delivery up of illicit recording), or
— section 204 (order as to disposal of illicit recording),

save that, in Northern Ireland, a county court may entertain proceedings only[20] where the value of the illicit recordings in question does not exceed the county court limit for actions in tort.
(2) In Scotland proceedings for an order under either of those provisions may be brought in the sheriff court.
(3) Nothing in this section shall be construed as affecting the jurisdiction of the High Court or, in Scotland, the Court of Session.

205A. Licensing of performers' property rights   A1.46

The provisions of Schedule 2A have effect with respect to the licensing of performers' property rights.[21]

205B. Jurisdiction of Copyright Tribunal   A1.47

(1) The Copyright Tribunal has jurisidiction under this Part to hear and determine proceedings under:
   (a) section 182D (amount of equitable remuneration for exploitation of commercial sound recording);
   (b) section 190 (application to give consent on behalf of owner of reproduction right);
   (c) section 191H (amount of equitable remuneration on transfer of rental right);
   (cc) Paragraph 19 of Schedule 2 (determination of royalty or other remuneration to be paid with respect to re-transmission of broadcast including performance or recording);[22]
   (d) paragraph 3, 4 or 5 of Schedule 2A (reference to licensing scheme);
   (e) paragraph 6 or 7 of that Schedule (reference or application with respect to licence under licensing scheme);
   (f) paragraph 10, 11 or 12 of that Schedule (reference or application with respect to licensing by licensing body);
   (g) paragraph 15 of that Schedule (application to settle royalty for certain lending);
   (h) paragraph 17 of that Schedule (application to settle terms of licence available as of right).

(2) The provisions of Chapter VIII of Part I (general provisions relating to the Copyright Tribunal) apply in relation to the Tribunal when exercising any jurisdiction under this Part.
(3) Provision shall be made by rules under section 150 prohibiting the Tribunal from entertaining a reference under paragraph 3, 4 or 5 of Schedule 2A (reference of licensing scheme) by a representative organisation unless the Tribunal is satisfied that

---

[19] Substituted by the Trade Marks Act 1994, s. 106(1). In force October 31, 1994.
[20] Inserted by High Court and County Courts Jurisdiction Order 1991, S.I. 1991 No. 724.
[21] Inserted by C.R.R. 1996, Reg. 22(1). In force December 1, 1996.
[22] Inserted by Broadcasting Act 1996, Sched. 9. In force October 1, 1996.

the organisation is reasonably representative of the class of persons which it claims to represent.[23]

Qualification for protection and extent

A1.48   206. Qualifying countries, individuals and persons

(1) In this Part:

— "qualifying country" means:

    (a) the United Kingdom,
    (b) another member State of the European Economic Community, or
    (c) to the extent that an Order under section 208 so provides, a country designated under that section as enjoying reciprocal protection;

— "qualifying individual" means a citizen or subject of, or an individual resident in, a qualifying country; and
— "qualifying person" means a qualifying individual or a body corporate or other body having legal personality which:

    (a) is formed under the law of a part of the United Kingdom or another qualifying country, and
    (b) has in any qualifying country a place of business at which substantial business activity is carried on.

(2) The reference in the definition of "qualifying individual" to a person's being a citizen or subject of a qualifying country shall be construed:

    (a) in relation to the United Kingdom, as a reference to his being a British citizen, and
    (b) in relation to a colony of the United Kingdom, as a reference to his being a British Dependent Territories' citizen by connection with that colony.

(3) In determining for the purpose of the definition of "qualifying person" whether substantial business activity is carried on at a place of business in any country, no account shall be taken of dealings in goods which are at all material times outside that country.

A1.49   207. Countries to which this Part extends

This Part extends to England and Wales, Scotland and Northern Ireland.

A1.50   208. Countries enjoying reciprocal protection

(1) Her Majesty may by Order in Council designate as enjoying reciprocal protection under this Part:

    (a) a Convention country, or
    (b) a country as to which Her Majesty is satisfied that provision has been or will be made under its law giving adequate protection for British performances.

(2) A "Convention country" means a country which is a party to a Convention relating to performer's rights to which the United Kingdom is also a party.
(3) A "British performance" means a performance:

    (a) given by an individual who is a British citizen or resident in the United Kingdom, or
    (b) taking place in the United Kingdom.

(4) If the law of that country provides adequate protection only for certain descriptions of performance, an Order under subsection (1)(b) designating that

---

[23] Inserted by C.R.R. 1996, Reg. 24(1). In force December 1, 1996.

country shall contain provision limiting to a corresponding extent the protection afforded by this Part in relation to performances connected with that country.

(5) The power conferred by subsection (1)(b) is exercisable in relation to any of the Channel Islands, the Isle of Man or any colony of the United Kingdom, as in relation to a foreign country.

(6) A statutory instrument containing an Order in Council under this section shall be subject to annulment in pursuance of a resolution of either House of Parliament.

209. Territorial waters and the continential shelf

A1.51

(1) For the purposes of this Part the territorial waters of the United Kingdom shall be treated as part of the United Kingdom.

(2) This Part applies to things done in the United Kingdom sector of the continental shelf on a structure or vessel which is present there for purposes directly connected with the exploration of the sea bed or subsoil or the exploitation of their natural resources as it applies to things done in the United Kingdom.

(3) The United Kingdom sector of the continential shelf means the areas designated by order under section (17) of the Continental Shelf Act 1964.

210. British ships, aircraft and hovercraft

A1.52

(1) This Part applies to things done on a British ship, aircraft or hovercraft as it applies to things done in the United Kingdom.

(2) In this section:

— "British ship" means a ship which is a British ship for the purposes of the *Merchant Shipping Acts (see section 2 of the Merchant Shipping Act 1988)*, **Merchant Shipping Act 1995**[24] otherwise than by virtue of registration in a country outside the United Kingdom; and

— "British aircraft" and "British hovercraft" mean an aircraft or hovercraft registered in the United Kingdom.

Interpretation

211. Expressions having same meaning as in copyright provisions

A1.53

(1) The following expressions have the same meaning in this Part as in Part I (copyright):

— broadcast,
— business,
— cable programme,
— cable programme service,
— country,
— defendant (in Scotland),
— delivery up (in Scotland),
— **EEA national**[25]
— film,
— literary work,
— published, and
— sound recording.

(2) The provisions of section 6(3) to (5), section 7(5) and 19(4) (supplementary provisions relating to broadcasting and cable programme services) apply for the purposes of this Part, and in relation to an infringement of the rights conferred by this

---

[24] Substituted by the Merchant Shipping Act 1995, s. 314(2). In force January 1, 1996.
[25] Inserted by D.C.R.P. 1995, Reg. 11(3). In force January 1, 1996.

Part, as they apply for the purposes of Part I and in relation to an infringement of copyright.

A1.54   **212. Index of defined expressions**

The following Table shows provisions defining or otherwise explaining expressions used in this Part (other than provisions defining or explaining an expression used only in the same section):

broadcast (and related expressions)	section 211 (and section 6)
business	section 211(1) (and section 178)
cable programme, cable programme service (and related expressions)	section 211(1) (and section 7)
consent of performer (in relation to performer's property rights)	**section 191A(2)**[26]
country	section 211(1) (and section 178)
defendant (in Scotland)	section 211(1) (and section 177)
delivery up (in Scotland)	section 211(1) (and section 177)
distribution right	**section 182B(5)**[27]
EEA national	**section 211(1) (and section 172A**[28]
exclusive recording contract	section 185(1)
film	section 211(1) (and *section 5* **section 5B)**[29]
illicit recording	section 197
lending right	**section 182C(7)**[30]
literary work	section 211(1) (and section 3(1))
performance	section 180(2)
performer's non-property rights	**section 192A(1)**[31]
performer's property rights	**section 191A(1)**[32]
published	section 211(1) (and section 175)
qualifying country	section 206(1)
qualifying individual	section 206(1) and (2)
qualifying performance	section 181
qualifying person	section 206(1) and (3)
recording (of a performance)	section 180(2)
recording rights (person having)	section 185(2) and (3)
rental right	**section 182C(7)**[33]
reproduction right	**section 182A(3)**[34]
rights owner (in relation to performer's property rights)	**section 191A(3) and (4)**[35]
sound recording	section 211(1) (and *section 5* **section 5A)**[36]

---

[26] Inserted by C.R.R. 1996, Reg. 21(6). In force December 1, 1996.
[27] Inserted by C.R.R. 1996, Reg. 20(4). In force December 1, 1996.
[28] Inserted by D.C.R.P. 1996, Reg. 11(4). In force January 1, 1996.
[29] Substituted by D.C.R.P. 1995, Reg. 9(6). In force January 1, 1996.
[30] Inserted by C.R.R. 1996, Reg. 20(4). In force December 1, 1996.
[31] Inserted by C.R.R. 1996, Reg. 21(6). In force December 1, 1996.
[32] Inserted by C.R.R. 1996, Reg. 21(6). In force December 1, 1996.
[33] Inserted by C.R.R. 1996, Reg. 20(4). In force December 1, 1996.
[34] Inserted by C.R.R. 1996, Reg. 20(4). In force December 1, 1996.
[35] Inserted by C.R.R. 1996, Reg. 21(6). In force December 1, 1996.
[36] Substituted by D.C.R.P. 1995, Reg. 9(6). In force January 1, 1996.

SCHEDULE 2

RIGHTS IN PERFORMANCES: PERMITTED ACTS
Introductory

1. (1) The provisions of this Schedule specify acts which may be done in relation to a performance or recording notwithstanding the rights conferred by Part II; they relate only to the question of infringement of those rights and do not affect any other right or obligation restricting the doing of any of the specified acts.   A1.55

(2) No inference shall be drawn from the description of any act which may by virtue of this Schedule be done without infringing the rights conferred by Part II as to the scope of those rights.

(3) The provisions of this Schedule are to be construed independently of each other, so that the fact that an act does not fall within one provision does not mean that it is not covered by another provision.

Criticism, reviews and news reporting

2. (1) Fair dealing with a performance or recording: A1.56

   (a) for the purpose of criticism or review, of that or another performance or recording, or of a work, or

   (b) for the purpose of reporting current events,

does not infringe any of the rights conferred by Part II.

(2) Expressions used in this paragraph have the same meaning as in section 30.

Incidental inclusion of performance or recording

3. (1) The rights conferred by Part II are not infringed by the incidental inclusion of a performance or recording in a sound recording, film, broadcast or cable programme.   A1.57

(2) Nor are those rights infringed by anything done in relation to copies of, or the playing, showing, broadcasting or inclusion in a cable programme service of, anything whose making was, by virtue of sub-paragraph (1), not an infringement of those rights.

(3) A performance or recording so far as it consists of music, or words spoken or sung with music, shall not be regarded as incidentally included in a sound recording, broadcast or cable programme if it is deliberately included.

(4) Expressions used in this paragraph have the same meaning as in section 31.

Things done for purposes of instruction or examination

4. (1) The rights conferred by Part II are not infringed by the copying of a recording of a performance in the course of instruction, or of preparation for instruction, in the making of films or film sound-tracks, provided the copying is done by a person giving or receiving instruction.   A1.58

(2) The rights conferred by Part II are not infringed:

   (a) by the copying of a recording of a performance for the purposes of setting or answering the questions in an examination, or

   (b) by anything done for the purposes of an examination by way of communicating the questions to the candidates.

(3) Where a recording which would otherwise be an illicit recording is made in accordance with this paragraph but subsequently dealt with, it shall be treated as an illicit recording for the purposes of that dealing, and if that dealing infringes any right conferred by Part II for all subsequent purposes.

For this purpose "dealt with" means sold or let for hire, or offered or exposed for sale or hire.

(4) Expressions used in this paragraph have the same meaning as in section 32.

Playing or showing sound recording, film, broadcast or cable programme at educational establishment

A1.59   5. (1) The playing or showing of a sound recording, film, broadcast or cable programme at an educational establishment for the purposes of instruction before an audience consisting of teachers and pupils at the establishment and other persons directly connected with the activities of the establishment is not a playing or showing of a performance in public for the purposes of infringement of the rights conferred by Part II.

(2) A person is not for this purpose directly connected with the activities of the educational establishment simply because he is the parent of a pupil at the establishment.

(3) Expressions used in this paragraph have the same meaning as in section 34 and any provision made under section 174(2) with respect to the application of that section also applies for the purposes of this paragraph.

Recording of broadcasts and cable programmes by educational establishments

A1.60   6. (1) A recording of a broadcast or cable programme, or a copy of such a recording, may be made by or on behalf of an educational establishment for the educational purposes of that establishment without thereby infringing any of the rights conferred by Part II in relation to any performance or recording included in it.

(2) Where a recording which would otherwise be an illicit recording is made in accordance with this paragraph but is subsequently dealt with, it shall be treated as an illicit recording for the purposes of that dealing, and if that dealing infringes any right conferred by Part II for all subsequent purposes.

For this purpose "dealt with" means sold or let for hire, or offered or exposed for sale or hire.

(3) Expressions used in this paragraph have the same meaning as in section 35 and any provision made under section 174(2) with respect to the application of that section also applies for the purposes of this paragraph.

Lending of copies by educational establishments

A1.61   6A.(1) The rights conferred by Part II are not infringed by the lending of copies of a recording of a performance by an educational establishment.

(2) Expressions used in this paragraph have the same meaning as in section 36A; and any provision with respect to the application of that section made under section 174(2) (instruction given elsewhere than an educational establishment) applies also for the purposes of this paragraph.

Lending of copies by libraries or archives

A1.62   6B.(1) The rights conferred by Part II are not infringed by the lending of copies of a recording of a performance by a prescribed library or archive (other than a public library) which is not conducted for profit.

(2) Expressions used in this paragraph have the same meaning as in section 40A(2); and any provision under section 37 prescribing libraries or archives for the purposes of that section applies also for the purposes of this paragraph.[37]

---

[37] Inserted by C.R.R. 1996, Reg. 20(3). In force December 1, 1996.

Copy of work required to be made as condition of export

7. (1) If an article of cultural or historical importance or interest cannot lawfully be exported from the United Kingdom unless a copy of it is made and deposited in an appropriate library or archive, it is not an infringement of any right conferred by Part II to make that copy.

    (2) Expressions used in this paragraph have the same meaning as in section 44.

A1.63

Parliamentary and judicial proceedings

8. (1) The rights conferred by Part II are not infringed by anything done for the purposes of parliamentary or judicial proceedings or for the purpose of reporting such proceedings.

    (2) Expressions used in this paragraph have the same meaning as in section 45.

A1.64

Royal Commissions and statutory inquiries

9. (1) The rights conferred by Part II are not infringed by anything done for the purposes of the proceedings of a Royal Commission or statutory inquiry or for the purpose of reporting any such proceedings held in public.

    (2) Expressions used in this paragraph have the same meaning as in section 46.

A1.65

Public records

10. (1) Material which is comprised in public records within the meaning of the Public Records Act 1958, the Public Records (Scotland) Act 1937 or the Public Records Act (Northern Ireland) 1923 which are open to public inspection in pursuance of that Act, may be copied, and a copy may be supplied to any person, by or with the authority of any officer appointed under that Act, without infringing any right conferred by Part II.

    (2) Expressions used in this paragraph have the same meaning as in section 49.

A1.66

Acts done under statutory authority

11. (1) Where the doing of a particular act is specifically authorised by an Act of Parliament, whenever passed, then, unless the Act provides otherwise, the doing of that act does not infringe the rights conferred by Part II.

    (2) Sub-paragraph (1) applies in relation to an enactment contained in Northern Ireland legislation as it applies to an Act of Parliament.

    (3) Nothing in this paragraph shall be construed as excluding any defence of statutory authority otherwise available under or by virtue of any enactment.

    (4) Expressions used in this paragraph have the same meaning as in section 50.

A1.67

Transfer of copies of works in electronic form

12. (1) This paragraph applies where a recording of a performance in electronic form has been purchased on terms which, expressly or impliedly or by virtue of any rule of law, allow the purchaser to make further recordings in connection with his use of the recording.

    (2) If there are no express terms:

    (a) prohibiting the transfer of the recording by the purchaser, imposing obligations which continue after a transfer, prohibiting the assignment of any consent or terminating any consent on a transfer, or

    (b) providing for the terms on which a transferee may do the things which the purchaser was permitted to do,

anything which the purchaser was allowed to do may also be done by a transferee without infringement of the rights conferred by this Part, but any recording made by

A1.68

the purchaser which is not also transferred shall be treated as an illicit recording for all purposes after the transfer.

(3) The same applies where the original purchased recording is no longer usable and what is transferred is a further copy used in its place.

(4) The above provisions also apply on a subsequent transfer, with the substitution for references in sub-paragraph (2) to the purchaser of references to the subsequent transferor.

(5) This paragraph does not apply in relation to a recording purchased before the commencement of Part II.

(6) Expressions used in this paragraph have the same meaning as in section 56.

Use of recordings of spoken works in certain cases

A1.69   13. (1) Where a recording of the reading or recitation of a literary work is made for the purpose:

   (a) of reporting current events, or
   (b) of broadcasting or including in a cable programme service the whole or part of the reading or recitation,

it is not an infringement of the rights conferred by Part II to use the recording (or to copy the recording and use the copy) for that purpose, provided the following conditions are met.

(2) The conditions are that:

   (a) the recording is a direct recording of the reading or recitation and is not taken from a previous recording or from a broadcast or cable programme;
   (b) the making of the recording was not prohibited by or on behalf of the person giving the reading or recitation;
   (c) the use made of the recording is not of a kind prohibited by or on behalf of that person before the recording was made; and
   (d) the use is by or with the authority of a person who is lawfully in possession of the recording.

(3) Expressions used in this paragraph have the same meaning as in section 58.

Recordings of folksongs

A1.70   14. (1) A recording of a performance of a song may be made for the purpose of including it in an archive maintained by a designated body without infringing any of the rights conferred by Part II, provided the conditions in sub-paragraph (2) below are met.

(2) The conditions are that:

   (a) the words are unpublished and of unknown authorship at the time the recording is made,
   (b) the making of the recording does not infringe any copyright, and
   (c) its making is not prohibited by any performer.

(3) Copies of a recording made in reliance on sub-paragraph (1) and included in an archive maintained by a designated body may, if the prescribed conditions are met, be made and supplied by the archivist without infringing any of the rights conferred by Part II.

(4) In this paragraph:

   — "designated body" means a body designated for the purposes of section 61, and
   — "the prescribed conditions" means the conditions prescribed for the purposes of subsection (3) of that section;

and other expressions used in this paragraph have the same meaning as in that section.

Lending of certain recordings

14A.(1) The Secretary of State may by order provide that in such cases as may be specified in the order the lending to the public of copies of films or sound recordings shall be treated as licensed by the performer subject only to the payment of such reasonable royalty or other payment as may be agreed or determined in default of agreement by the Copyright Tribunal.
    (2) No such order shall apply if, or to the extent that, there is a licensing scheme certified for the purposes of this paragraph under paragraph 16 of Schedule 2A providing for the grant of licences.
    (3) An order may make different provision for different cases and may specify cases by reference to any factor relating to the work, the copies lent, the lender or the circumstances of the lending.
    (4) An order shall be made by statutory instrument; and no order shall be made unless a draft of it has been laid before and approved by a resolution of each House of Parliament.
    (5) Nothing in this section affects any liability under section 184(1)(b) (secondary infringement: possessing or dealing with illicit recording) in respect of the lending of illicit recordings.
    (6) Expressions used in this paragraph have the same meaning as in section 66.[38]

A1.71

Playing of sound recordings for purposes of club, society, etc.

15. (1) It is not an infringement of any right conferred by Part II to play a sound recording as part of the activities of, or for the benefit of, a club, society or other organisation if the following conditions are met.
    (2) The conditions are:

  (a) that the organisation is not established or conducted for profit and its main objects are charitable or are otherwise concerned with the advancement of religion, education or social welfare, and
  (b) that the proceeds of any charge for admission to the place where the recording is to be heard are applied solely for the purposes of the organisation.

    (3) Expressions used in this paragraph have the same meaning as in section 67.

A1.72

Incidental recording for purposes of broadcast or cable programme

16. (1) A person who proposes to broadcast a recording of a performance, or include a recording of a performance in a cable programme service, in circumstances not infringing the rights conferred by Part II shall be treated as having consent for the purposes of that Part for the making of a further recording for the purposes of the broadcast or cable programme.
    (2) That consent is subject to the condition that the further recording:

  (a) shall not be used for any other purpose, and
  (b) shall be destroyed within 28 days of being first used for broadcasting the performance or including it in a cable programme service.

    (3) A recording made in accordance with this paragraph shall be treated as an illicit recording:

  (a) for the purposes of any use in breach of the condition mentioned in sub-paragraph (2)(a), and
  (b) for all purposes after that condition or the condition mentioned in sub-paragraph (2)(b) is broken.

    (4) Expressions used in this paragraph have the same meaning as in section 68.

A1.73

---

[38] Inserted by C.R.R. 1992, Reg. 20(3). In force December 1, 1996.

Recordings for purposes of supervision and control of broadcasts and cable programmes

A1.74 17. (1) The rights conferred by Part II are not infringed by the making or use by the British Broadcasting Corporation, for the purpose of maintaining supervision and control over programmes broadcast by them, of recordings of those programmes.

(2) The rights conferred by Part II are not infringed by:

(a) the making or use of recordings by the Independent Broadcasting Authority for the purposes mentioned in section 4(7) of the Broadcasting Act 1981 (maintenance of supervision and control over programmes and advertisements); or

(b) anything done under or in pursuance of provision included in a contract between a programme contractor and the Authority in accordance with section 21 of that Act.

(3) The rights conferred by Part II are not infringed by:

(a) the making by or with the authority of the Cable Authority, or the use by that Authority, for the purpose of maintaining supervision and control over programmes included in services listed under Part I of the Cable and Broadcasting Act 1984, of recordings of those programmes; or

(b) anything done under or in pursuance of:

(i) a notice or direction given under section 16 of the Cable and Broadcasting Act 1984 (power of Cable Authority to require production of recordings); or

(ii) a condition included in a licence by virtue of section 35 of that Act (duty of Authority to secure that recordings are available for certain purposes).

A1.75 (2) The rights conferred by Part II are not infringed by anything done in pursuance of:

(a) section 11(1), 95(1) or 167(1) of the Broadcasting Act 1990 or section 115(4) or (6), 116(5) or 117 of the Broadcasting Act 1996;

(b) a condition which, by virtue of section 11(2) or 95(2) of the Broadcasting Act 1990, is included in a licence granted under Part I or III of that Act or Part I or II of the Broadcasting Act 1996; or

(c) a direction given under section 109(2) of the Broadcasting Act 1990 (power of Radio Authority to require production of recordings etc).

(3) The rights conferred by Part II are not infringed by:

(a) the use by the Independent Television Commission or the Radio Authority, in connection with the performance of any of their functions under the Broadcasting Act 1990 or the Broadcasting Act 1996, of any recording, script or transcript which is provided to them under or by virtue of any provision of those Acts; or

(b) the use by the Broadcasting Standards Commission, in connection with any complaint made to them under the Broadcasting Act 1996, of any recording or transcript requested or required to be provided to them, and so provided, under section 115(4) or (6) or 116(5) of that Act.[39]

(4) Expressions used in this paragraph have the same meaning as in section 69.

Free public showing or playing of broadcast or cable programme

A1.76 18. (1) The showing or playing in public of a broadcast or cable programme to an audience who have not paid for admission to the place where the broadcast or programme is to be seen or heard does not infringe any right conferred by Part II in relation to a performance or recording included in:

---

[39] Substituted by B.A. 1996, Sched. 10. In force October 1, 1996.

(a) the broadcast or cable programme, or
(b) any sound recording or film which is played or shown in public by reception of the broadcast or cable programme.

(2) The audience shall be treated as having paid for admission to a place:

(a) if they have paid for admission to a place of which that place forms part; or
(b) if goods or services are supplied at that place (or a place of which it forms part):

   (i) at prices which are substantially attributable to the facilities afforded for seeing or hearing the broadcast or programme, or
   (ii) at prices exceeding those usually charged there and which are partly attributable to those facilities.

(3) The following shall not be regarded as having paid for admission to a place:

(a) persons admitted as residents or inmates of the place;
(b) persons admitted as members of a club or society where the payment is only for membership of the club or society and the provision of facilities for seeing or hearing broadcasts or programmes is only incidental to the main purposes of the club or society.

(4) Where the making of the broadcast or inclusion of the programme in a cable programme service was an infringement of the rights conferred by Part II in relation to a performance or recording, the fact that it was heard or seen in public by the reception of the broadcast or programme shall be taken into account in assessing the damages for that infringement.

(5) Expressions used in this paragraph have the same meaning as in section 72.

Reception and re-transmission of broadcast in cable programme service

19. (1) This paragraph applies where a broadcast made from a place in the United Kingdom is, by reception and immediate re-transmission, included in a cable programme service.   **A1.77**

(2) The rights conferred by Part II in relation to a performance or recording included in the broadcast are not infringed:

(a) if the inclusion of the broadcast in the cable programme service is in pursuance of a requirement imposed under section 13(1) of the Cable and Broadcasting Act 1984 (duty of Cable Authority to secure inclusion in cable service of certain programmes), or
(b) if and to the extent that the broadcast is made for reception in the area in which the cable programme service is provided;

but where the making of the broadcast was an infringement of those rights, the fact that the broadcast was re-transmitted as a programme in a cable programme service shall be taken into account in assessing the damages for that infringement.

(3) Expressions used in this paragraph have the same meaning as in section 73.   **A1.78**

(2) The rights conferred by Part II in relation to a performance or recording included in the broadcast are not infringed if and to the extent that the broadcast is made for reception in the area in which the cable programme service is provided; but where the making of the broadcast was an infringement of those rights, the fact that the broadcast was re-transmitted as a programme in a cable programme service shall be taken into account in asessing the damages for that infringement.

(3) Where:

(a) the inclusion is in pursuance of a relevant requirement, but
(b) to any extent, the area in which the cable programme service is provided ("the cable area") falls outside the area for reception in which the broadcast is made ("the broadcast area"),

the inclusion in the cable programme service (to the extent that it is provided for so much of the cable area as falls outside the broadcast area) of any performance or recording included in the broadcast shall, subject to sub-paragraph (4), be treated as licensed by the owner of the rights conferred by Part II in relation to the performance or recording, subject only to the payment to him by the person making the broadcast of such reasonable royalty or other payment in respect of inclusion of the broadcast in the cable programme service as may be agreed or determined in default of agreement by the Copyright Tribunal.

(4) Sub-paragraph (3) does not apply if, or to the extent that, the inclusion of the work in the cable programme service is (apart from that sub-paragraph) licensed by the owner of the rights conferred by Part II in relation to the performance or recording.

(5) The Secretary of State may by order:

(a) provide that in specified cases sub-paragraph (2) is to apply in relation to broadcasts of a specified description which are not made as mentioned in that sub-paragraph, or

(b) exclude the application of that sub-paragraph in relation to broadcasts of a specified description made as mentioned in that sub-paragraph.

(6) Where the Secretary of State exercises the power conferred by sub-paragraph (5)(b) in relation to broadcasts of any description, the order may also provide for sub-paragraph (3) to apply, subject to such modifications as may be specified in the order, in relation to broadcasts of that description.

(7) An order under this paragraph may contain such transitional provision as appears to the Secretary of State to be appropriate.

(8) An order under this paragraph shall be made by statutory instrument which shall be subject to annulment in pursuance of a resolution of either House of Parliament.

(9) Expressions used in this paragraph have the same meaning as in section 73.[40]

A1.79   19A. (1) An application to settle the royalty or other sum payable in pursuance of sub-paragraph (3) of paragraph 19 may be made to the Copyright Tribunal by the owner of the rights conferred by Part II or the person making the broadcast.

(2) The Tribunal shall consider the matter and made such order as it may determine to be reasonable in the circumstances.

(3) Either party may subsequently apply to the Tribunal to vary the order, and the Tribunal shall consider the matter and make such order confirming or varying the original order as it may determine to be reasonable in the circumstances.

(4) An application under sub-paragraph (3) shall not, except with the special leave of the Tribunal, be made within twelve months from the date of the original order or of the order on a previous application under that sub-paragraph.

(5) An order under sub-paragraph (3) has effect from the date on which it is made or such later date as may be specified by the Tribunal.[41]

Provision of sub-titled copies of broadcast or cable programme

A1.80   20. (1) A designated body may, for the purpose of providing people who are deaf or hard of hearing, or physically or mentally handicapped in other ways, with copies which are sub-titled or otherwise modified for their special needs, make recordings of television broadcasts or cable programmes without infringing any right conferred by Part II in relation to a performance or recording included in the broadcast or cable programme.

(2) In this paragraph "designated body" means a body designated for the purposes of section 74 and other expressions used in this paragraph have the same meaning as in that section.

---

[40] Substituted by B.A. 1996, Sched. 9. In force November 1, 1996.
[41] Inserted by B.A. 1996, Sched. 9. In force November 1, 1996.

Recording of broadcast or cable programme for archival purposes

21. (1) A recording of a broadcast or cable programme of a designated class, or a copy   A1.81
of such a recording, may be made for the purpose of being placed in an archive
maintained by a designated body without thereby infringing any right conferred by
Part II in relation to a performance or recording included in the broadcast or cable
programme.

(2) In this paragraph "designated class" and "designated body" means a class or
body designated for the purposes of section 75 and other expressions used in this
paragraph have the same meaning as in that section.

SCHEDULE 2A

LICENSING OF PERFORMERS' PROPERTY RIGHTS

Licensing schemes and licensing bodies

1. (1) In Part II a "licensing scheme" means a scheme setting out: A1.82

  (a) the classes of case in which the operator of the scheme, or the person on whose
       behalf he acts, is willing to grant performers' property right licences, and
  (b) the terms on which licences would be granted in those classes of case;

and for this purpose a "scheme" includes anything in the nature of a scheme, whether
described as a scheme or as a tariff or by any other name.

(2) In Part II a "licensing body" means a society or other organisation which has as
its main object, or one of its main objects, the negotiating or granting, whether as
owner or prospective owner of a performer's property rights or as agent for him of
performers' property right licences, and whose objects include the granting of licences
covering the performances of more than one performer.

(3) In this paragraph "performers' property right licences" means licences to do, or
authorise the doing of, any of the things for which consent is required under section
182A, 182B or 182C.

(4) References in this Part to licences or licensing schemes covering the performances of more than one performer do not include licences or schemes covering only:

  (a) performances recorded in a single recording,
  (b) performances recorded in more than one recording where:
     (i)   the performers giving the performances are the same, or
     (ii) the recordings are made by, or by employees of or commissioned by, a single
           individual, firm, company or group of companies.

For purpose a group of companies means a holding company and its subsidiaries
within the meaning of section 736 of the Companies Act 1985.

References and applications with respect to licensing schemes

2. Paragraphs 3 to 8 (references and applications with respect to licensing schemes)   A1.83
apply to licensing schemes operated by licensing bodies in relation to a performer's
property rights which cover the performances of more than one performer, so far as
they relate to licences for:

  (a) copying a recording of the whole or any substantial part of a qualifying
       performance, or
  (b) renting or lending copies of a recording to the public;

and in those paragraphs "licensing scheme" means a licensing scheme of any of those
descriptions.

Reference of proposed licensing scheme to tribunal

A1.84 3. (1) The terms of a licensing scheme proposed to be operated by a licensing body may be referred to the Copyright Tribunal by an organisation claiming to be representative of persons claiming that they require licences in cases of a description to which the scheme would apply, either generally or in relation to any description of case.

(2) The Tribunal shall first decide whether to entertain the reference, and may decline to do so on the ground that the reference is premature.

(3) If the Tribunal decides to entertain the reference it shall consider the matter referred and make such order, either confirming or varying the proposed scheme, either generally or so far as it relates to cases of the description to which the reference relates, as the Tribunal may determine to be reasonable in the circumstances.

(4) The order may be made so as to be in force indefinitely or for such period as the Tribunal may determine.

Reference of licensing scheme to tribunal

A1.85 4. (1) If while a licensing scheme is in operation a dispute arises between the operator of the scheme and:

(a) a person claiming that he requires a licence in a case of a description to which the scheme applies, or

(b) an organisation claiming to be a representative of such persons,

that person or organisation may refer the scheme to the Copyright Tribunal in so far as it relates to cases of that description.

(2) A scheme which has been referred to the Tribunal under this paragraph shall remain in operation until proceedings on the reference are concluded.

(3) The Tribunal shall consider the matter in dispute and make such order, either confirming or varying the scheme so far as it relates to cases of the description to which the reference relates, as the Tribunal may determine to be reasonable in the circumstances.

(4) The order may by made so as to be in force indefinitely or for such period as the Tribunal may determine.

Further reference of scheme to tribunal

A1.86 5. (1) Where the Copyright Tribunal has on a previous reference of a licensing scheme under paragraph 3 or 4, or under this paragraph, made an order with respect to the scheme, then, while the order remains in force:

(a) the operator of the scheme,

(b) a person claiming that he requires a licence in a case of the description to which the order applies, or

(c) an organisation claiming to be representative of such persons,

may refer the scheme again to the Tribunal so far as it relates to cases of that description.

(2) A licensing scheme shall not, except with the special leave of the Tribunal, be referred again to the Tribunal in respect of the same description of cases:

(a) within twelve months from the date of the order on the previous reference, or

(b) if the order was made so as to be in force for 15 months or less, until the last three months before the expiry of the order.

(3) A scheme which has been referred to the Tribunal under this paragraph shall remain in operation until proceedings on the reference are concluded.

(4) The Tribunal shall consider the matter in dispute and make such order, either confirming, varying or further varying the scheme so far as it relates to cases of the

description to which the reference relates, as the Tribunal may determine to be reasonable in the circumstances.

(5) The order may be made so as to be in force indefinitely or for such period as the Tribunal may determine.

Application for grant of licence in connection with licensing scheme

6. (1) A person who claims, in a case covered by a licensing scheme, that the operator of the scheme has refused to grant him or procure the grant to him of a licence in accordance with the scheme, or has failed to do so within a reasonable time after being asked, may apply to the Copyright Tribunal.

(2) A person who claims, in a case excluded from a licensing scheme, that the operator of the scheme either:

   (a) has refused to grant him a licence or procure the grant to him of a licence, or has failed to do so within a reasonable time of being asked, and that in the circumstances it is unreasonable that a licence should not be granted, or

   (b) proposes terms for a licence which are unreasonable,

may apply to the Copyright Tribunal.

(3) A case shall be regarded as excluded from a licensing scheme for the purposes of sub-paragraph (2) if:

   (a) the scheme provides for the grant of licences subject to terms excepting matters from the licence and the case falls within such an exception, or

   (b) the case is so similar to those in which licences are granted under the scheme that it is unreasonable that it should not be dealt with in the same way.

(4) If the Tribunal is satisfied that the claim is well-founded, it shall make an order declaring that, in respect of the matters specified in the order, the applicant is entitled to a licence on such terms as the Tribunal may determine to be applicable in accordance with the scheme or, as the case may be, to be reasonable in the circumstances.

(5) The order may be made so as to be in force indefinitely or for such period as the Tribunal may determine.

Application for review of order as to entitlement to licence

7. (1) Where the Copyright Tribunal has made an order under paragraph 6 that a person is entitled to a licence under a licensing scheme, the operator of the scheme or the original applicant may apply to the Tribunal to review its order.

(2) An application shall not be made, except with the special leave of the Tribunal:

   (a) within twelve months from the date of the order, or of the decision on a previous application under this paragraph, or

   (b) if the order was made so as to be in force for 15 months or less, or as a result of the decision on a previous application under this paragraph is due to expire within 15 months of that decision, until the last three months before the expiry date.

(3) The Tribunal shall on an application for review confirm or vary its order as the Tribunal may determine to be reasonable having regard to the terms applicable in accordance with the licensing scheme or, as the case may be, the circumstances of the case.

Effect of order of tribunal as to licensing scheme

8. (1) A licensing scheme which has been confirmed or varied by the Copyright Tribunal:

   (a) under paragraph 3 (reference of terms of proposed scheme), or

A1.87

A1.88

A1.89

(b) under paragraph 4 or 5 (reference of existing scheme to Tribunal),

shall be in force or, as the case may be, remain in operation, so far as it relates to the description of case in respect of which the order was made, so long as the order remains in force.

(2) While the order is in force a person who in a case of a class to which the order applies:

(a) pays to the operator of the scheme any charges payable under the scheme in respect of a licence covering the case in question or, if the amount cannot be ascertained, gives an undertaking to the operator to pay them when ascertained, and

(b) complies with the other terms applicable to such a licence under the scheme,

shall be in the same position as regards infringement of performers' property rights as if he had at all material times been the holder of a licence granted by the rights owner in question in accordance with the scheme.

(3) The Tribunal may direct that the order, so far as it varies the amount of charges payable, has effect from a date before that on which it is made, but not earlier than the date on which the reference was made or, if later, on which the scheme came into operation.

If such a direction is made:

(a) any necessary repayments, or further payments, shall be made in respect of charges already paid, and

(b) the reference in sub-paragraph (2)(a) to the charges payable under the scheme shall be construed as a reference to the charges so payable by virtue of the order.

No such direction may be made where sub-paragraph (4) below applies.

(4) An order of the Tribunal under paragraph 4 or 5 made with respect to a scheme which is certified for any purpose under paragraph 16 has effect, so far as it varies the scheme by reducing the charges payable for licences, from the date on which the reference was made to the Tribunal.

(5) Where the Tribunal has made an order under paragraph 6 (order as to entitlement to licence under licensing scheme) and the order remains in force, the person in whose favour the order is made shall if he:

(a) pays to the operator of the scheme any charges payable in accordance with the order or, if the amount cannot be ascertained, gives an undertaking to pay the charges when ascertained, and

(b) complies with the other terms specified in the order,

be in the same position as regards infringement of the performers' property rights as if he had at all material times been the holder of a licence granted by the rights owner in question on the terms specified in the order.

References and applications with respect to licensing by licensing bodies

A1.90   9. Paragraphs 10 to 13 (references and applications with respect to licensing by licensing bodies) apply to licences relating to a performer's property rights which cover the performance of more than one performer granted by a licensing body otherwise than in pursuance of a licensing scheme, so far as the licences authorise:

(a) copying a recording of the whole or any substantial part of a qualifying performance, or

(b) renting or lending copies of a recording to the public;

and references in those paragraphs to a licence shall be construed accordingly.

Reference to tribunal of proposed licence

10. (1) The terms on which a licensing body proposes to grant a licence may be referred to the Copyright Tribunal by the prospective licensee.

(2) The Tribunal shall first decide whether to entertain the reference, and may decline to do so on the ground that the reference is premature.

(3) If the Tribunal decides to entertain the reference it shall consider the terms of the proposed licence and make such order, either confirming or varying the terms as it may determine to be reasonable in the circumstances.

(4) The order may be made so as to be in force indefinitely or for such period as the Tribunal may determine.

A1.91

Reference to tribunal of expiring licence

11. (1) A licensee under a licence which is due to expire, by effluxion of time or as a result of notice given by the licensing body, may apply to the Copyright Tribunal on the ground that it is unreasonable in the circumstances that the licence should cease to be in force.

(2) Such an application may not be made until the last three months before the licence is due to expire.

(3) A licence in respect of which a reference has been made to the Tribunal shall remain in operation until proceedings on the reference are concluded.

(4) If the Tribunal finds the application well-founded, it shall make an order declaring that the licensee shall continue to be entitled to the benefit of the licence on such terms as the Tribunal may determine to be reasonable in the circumstances.

(5) An order of the Tribunal under this paragraph may be made so as to be in force indefinitely or for such period as the Tribunal may determine.

A1.92

Application for review of order as to licence

12. (1) Where the Copyright Tribunal has made an order under paragraph 10 or 11, the licensing body or the person entitled to the benefit of the order may apply to the Tribunal to review its order.

(2) An application shall not be made, except with the special leave of the Tribunal:

(a) within twelve months from the date of the order or of the decision on a previous application under this paragraph, or

(b) if the order was made so as to be in force for 15 months or less, or as a result of the decision on a previous application under this paragraph is due to expire within 15 months of that decision, until the last three months before the expiry date.

(3) The Tribunal shall on an application for review confirm or vary its order as the Tribunal may determine to be reasonable in the circumstances.

A1.93

Effect of order of tribunal as to licence

13. (1) Where the Copyright Tribunal has made an order under paragraph 10 or 11 and the order remains in force, the person entitled to the benefit of the order shall if he:

(a) pays the licensing body any charges payable in accordance with the order or, if the amount cannot be ascertained, gives an undertaking to pay the charges when ascertained, and

(b) complies with the other terms specified in the order,

be in the same position as regards infringement of the performers' property rights as if he had at all material times been the holder of a licence granted by the rights owner in question on the terms specified in the order.

(2) The benefit of the order may be assigned:

A1.94

(a) in the case of an order under paragraph 10, if assignment is not prohibited under the terms of the Tribunal's order; and

(b) in the case of an order under paragraph 11, if assignment was not prohibited under the terms of the original licence.

(3) The Tribunal may direct that an order under paragraph 10 or 11, or an order under paragraph 12 varying such an order, so far as it varies the amount of charges payable, has effect from a date before that on which it is made, but not earlier than the date on which the reference or application was made or, if later, on which the licence was granted or, as the case may be, was due to expire.

If such a direction is made:

(a) any necessary repayments, or further payments, shall be made in respect of charges already paid, and

(b) the reference in sub-paragraph(1)(a) to the charges payable in accordance with the order shall be construed, where the order is varied by a later order, as a reference to the charges so payable by virtue of the later order.

General considerations: unreasonable discrimination

A1.95   14. (1) In determining what is reasonable on a reference or application under this Schedule relating to a licensing scheme or licence, the Copyright Tribunal shall have regard to:

(a) the availability of other schemes, or the granting of other licences, to other persons in similar circumstances, and

(b) the terms of those schemes or licences,

and shall exercise its powers so as to secure that there is no unreasonable discrimination between licensees, or prospective licensees, under the scheme or licence to which the reference or application relates and licensees under other schemes operated by, or other licences granted by, the same person.

(2) This does not affect the Tribunal's general obligation in any case to have regard to all relevant circumstances.

Application to settle royalty or other sum payable for lending

A1.96   15. (1) An application to settle the royalty or other sum payable in pursuance of paragraph 14A of Schedule 2 (lending of certain recordings) may be made to the Copyright Tribunal by the owner of a performer's property rights or the person claiming to be treated as licensed by him.

(2) The Tribunal shall consider the matter and make such order as it may determine to be reasonable in the circumstances.

(3) Either party may subsequently apply to the Tribunal to vary the order, and the Tribunal shall consider the matter and make such order confirming or varying the original order as it may determine to be reasonable in the circumstances.

(4) An application under sub-paragraph (3) shall not, except with the special leave of the Tribunal, be made within twelve months from the date of the original order or of the order on a previous application under that sub-paragraph.

(5) An order under sub-paragraph (3) has effect from the date on which it is made or such later date as may be specified by the Tribunal.

Certification of licensing schemes

A1.97   16. (1) A person operating or proposing to operate a licensing scheme may apply to the Secretary of State to certify the scheme for the purposes of paragraph 14A of Schedule 2 (lending of certain recordings).

(2) The Secretary of State shall by order made by statutory instrument certify the scheme if he is satisfied that it:

(a) enables the works to which it relates to be identified with sufficient certainty by persons likely to require licences, and

(b) sets out clearly the charges (if any) payable and the other terms on which licences will be granted.

(3) The scheme shall be scheduled to the order and the certification shall come into operation for the purposes of paragraph 14A of Schedule 2:

(a) on such date, not less than eight weeks after the order is made, as may be specified in the order, or

(b) if the scheme is the subject of a reference under paragraph 3 (reference of proposed scheme), any later date on which the order of the Copyright Tribunal under that paragraph comes into force or the reference is withdrawn.

(4) A variation of the scheme is not effective unless a corresponding amendment of the order is made; and the Secretary of State shall make such an amendment in the case of a variation ordered by the Copyright Tribunal on a reference under paragraph 3, 4 or 5, and may do so in any other case if he thinks fit.

(5) The order shall be revoked if the scheme ceases to be operated and may be revoked if it appears to the Secretary of State that it is no longer being operated according to its terms.

Powers exercisable in consequences of competition report

17. (1) Where the matters specified in a report of the Monopolies and Mergers Commission as being those which in the Commission's opinion operate, may be expected to operate or have operated against the public interest include:

A1.98

(a) conditions in licences granted by the owner of a performer's property rights restricting the use to which a recording may be put by the licensee or the right of the owner to grant other licences, or

(b) a refusal of an owner of a performer's property rights to grant licences on reasonable terms,

the powers conferred by Part I of Schedule 8 to the Fair Trading Act 1973 (powers exercisable for purpose of remedying or preventing adverse effects specified in report of Commission) include power to cancel or modify those conditions and, instead or in addition, to provide that licences in respect of the performer's property rights shall be available as of right.

(2) The references in sections 56(2) and 73(2) of that Act, and sections 10(2)(b) and 12(5) of the Competition Act 1980, to the powers specified in that Part of that Schedule shall be construed accordingly.

(3) A Minister shall only exercise the powers available by virtue of this paragraph if he is satisfied that to do so does not contravene any Convention relating to the performers' rights to which the United Kingdom is a party.

(4) The terms of a licence available by virtue of this paragraph shall, in default of agreement, be settled by the Copyright Tribunal on an application by the person requiring the licence; and terms so settled shall authorise the licensee to do everything in respect of which a licence is so available.

(5) Where the terms of a licence are settled by the Tribunal, the licence has effect from the date on which the application to the Tribunal was made.[42]

---

[42] Inserted by C.R.R. 1996, Reg. 22(2). In force December 1, 1996.

APPENDIX 2A

Dramatic and Musical Performers' Protection Act 1925 (15 & 16 Geo. 5, c. 46)

An Act to prevent unauthorised reproductions of dramatic and musical performances
[31 July 1925]

Be it enacted by the King's most Excellent Majesty, by and with the advice and consent of the Lords Spiritual and Temporal, and Commons, in this present Parliament assembled, and by the authority of the same, as follows:

A2.01 **1. Penalties for making, etc., records without consent of performers**

If any person knowingly:

    (a) makes any record, directly or indirectly, from or by any means of the performance of any dramatic or musical work without the consent in writing of the performers; or

    (b) sells or lets for hire, or distributes for the purposes of trade, or by way of trade exposes or offers for sale or hire, any record made in contravention of this Act; or

    (c) uses for the purpose of a public performance any record made in contravention of this Act,

he shall be guilty of an offence under this Act, and shall be liable, on summary conviction, to a fine not exceeding forty shillings for each record in respect of which an offence is proved, but not exceeding fifty pounds in respect of any one transaction: Provided that it shall be a defence to any proceedings in respect of an alleged offence under the foregoing paragraph (a) if the defendant proves that the record in respect of which the offence is alleged was not made for purposes of trade.

A2.02 **2. Penalties for making or having plates, etc., for making records in contravention of Act**

If any person makes, or has in his possession, any plate or similar contrivance for the purpose of making records in contravention of this Act, he shall be guilty of an offence under this Act, and shall be liable, on summary conviction, to a fine not exceeding fifty pounds for each plate or similar contrivance in respect of which an offence is proved.

A2.03 **3. Power to order destruction of records, etc., contravening Act**

The Court before which any proceedings are taken under this Act may, on conviction of the offender, order that all records or plates or similar contrivances in the possession of the offender which appear to the Court to have been made in contravention of this Act, and in respect of which the offender has been convicted, be destroyed, or otherwise dealt with as the Court may think fit.

A2.04 **4. Interpretation**

In this Act, unless the context otherwise requires,

    — The expression "record" means any record or similar contrivance for reproducing sound;

    — The expression "performance of any dramatic or musical work" includes any

274

performance, mechanical or otherwise, of any such work which performance is rendered or intended to be rendered audible by mechanical or electrical means;
— The expression "performers" in the case of a mechanical performance means the persons whose performance is mechanically reproduced.

5. Short title

A2.05

(1) This Act may be cited as the Dramatic and Musical Performers' Protection Act, 1925.
(2) This Act shall extend to Northern Ireland.

APPENDIX 2B

Dramatic and Musical Performers' Protection Act 1958 (as amended) (6 & 7 Eliz. 2, c. 44)

1. Penalization of making, etc., records without consent of performers
2. Penalization of making, etc., cinematograph films without consent of performers
3. Penalization of broadcasting without consent of performers
4. Penalization of making or having plates, etc., for making records in contravention of Act
5. Power of Court to order destruction of records, etc., contravening Act
6. Special defences
7. Consent on behalf of performers
8. Interpretation
9. Short title, extent, repeal and commencement

An Act to consolidate the Dramatic and Musical Performers' Protection Act 1925 and the provisions of the Copyright Act 1956 amending it [23 July 1958]

A2.06   **1. Penalization of making, etc., records without consent of performers**

Subject to the provisions of this Act, if a person knowingly:

(a) makes a record, directly or indirectly from or by means of the performance of a dramatic or musical work without the consent in writing of the performers, or
(b) sells or lets for hire, or distributes for the purposes of trade, or by way of trade exposes or offers for sale or hire, a record made in contravention of this Act, or
(c) uses for the purposes of a public performance a record so made,

he shall be guilty of an offence under this Act, and shall be liable, on summary conviction, to a fine not exceeding *forty shillings* [£20] *for each record in respect of which an offence is proved, but not exceeding fifty pounds* [£400] *in respect of any one transaction* [the prescribed sum] **or, on conviction on indictment, to imprisonment for a term not exceeding two years, or to a fine, or to both:**

Provided that, where a person is charged with an offence under paragraph (a) of this section, it shall be a defence to prove that the record was made for his private and domestic use only.

Note
As amended, firstly by substitution of the figures in bold square brackets by the Performers' Protection Act 1972, section 1 and Schedule and by addition of the words in bold by the Performers' Protection Act 1972, section 2; and secondly by substitution of the words in square brackets by the Magistrates' Courts Act 1980, section 32(2).

A2.07   **2. Penalization of making, etc., cinematograph films without consent of performers**

Subject to the provisions of this Act, if a person knowingly:

(a) makes a cinematograph film, directly or indirectly from or by means of the performance of a dramatic or musical work without the consent in writing of the performers, or
(b) sells or lets for hire, or distributes for the purposes of trade, or by way of trade exposes or offers for sale or hire, a cinematograph film made in contravention of this Act, or
(c) uses for the purposes of exhibition to the public a cinematograph film so made,

he shall be guilty of an offence under this Act, and shall be liable, on summary conviction, to a fine not exceeding *fifty pounds* **£400** [level 5 on the standard scale]:

Provided that, where a person is charged with an offence under paragraph (a) of this section, it shall be a defence to prove that the cinematograph film was made for his private and domestic use only.

Note
As amended, firstly by substitution of the figure in bold by the Performers' Protection Act 1972, section 1 and Schedule; and secondly by substitution of the words in square brackets by the Criminal Justice Act 1981, sections 38 and 46.

3. Penalization of broadcasting without consent of performers

A2.08

Subject to the provisions of this Act, a person who, otherwise than by the use of a record or cinematograph film, knowingly broadcasts a performance of a dramatic or musical work, or any part of such a performance, without the consent in writing of the performers, shall be guilty of an offence under this Act, and shall be liable, on summary conviction, to a fine not exceeding *fifty pounds* **£400** [level 5 on the standard scale].

Note
As amended, firstly by substitution of the figure in bold by the Performers' Protection Act 1972, section 1 and Schedule; and secondly by substitution of the words in square brackets by the Criminal Justice Act 1981, sections 38 and 46.

4. Penalization of making or having plates, etc., for making records in contravention of Act

A2.09

If a person makes, or has in his possession, a plate or similar contrivance for the purpose of making records in contravention of this Act, he shall be guilty of an offence under this Act, and shall be liable, on summary conviction, to a fine not exceeding *fifty pounds* **£400** [level 5 on the standard scale] for each plate or similar contrivance in respect of which an offence is proved.

Note
As amended, firstly by substitution of the figure in bold by the Performers' Protection Act 1972, section 1 and Schedule; and secondly by substitution of the words in square brackets by the Criminal Justice Act 1981, sections 38 and 46.

5. Power of Court to order destruction of records, etc., contravening Act

A2.10

The court before which any proceedings are taken under this Act may, on conviction of the offender, order that all records, cinematograph films, plates or similar contrivances in the possession of the offender which appear to the court to have been made in contravention of this Act, or to be adapted for the making of records in contravention of this Act, and in respect of which the offender has been convicted, be destroyed, or otherwise dealt with as the court may think fit.

6. Special defences

A2.11

Notwithstanding anything in the preceding provisions of this Act, it shall be a defence to any proceedings under this Act to prove:

(a) that the record, cinematograph film *or broadcast* **broadcast or *transmission*** [cable programme] to which the proceedings relate was made **or included** only for the purpose of reporting current events, or
(b) that the inclusion of the performance in question in the record, cinematograph film *or broadcast* **broadcast or *transmission*** [cable programme] to which the proceedings relate was only by way of background or was otherwise only

incidental to the principal matters comprised or represented in the record, film *or broadcast* **broadcast or** *transmission* [cable programme].

Note
As amended firstly by substitution of the words "broadcast or transmision" for the words "or broadcast" by the Performers Protection Act 1963, section 3(3); and secondly by substitution of the words "cable programme" for the word "transmission" and addition of the words "or included" by the Cable and Broadcasting Act 1984, section 57(1) and Schedule 5, para. 7(1).

A2.12 **7. Consent on behalf of performers**

Where in any proceedings under this Act it is proved:

   (a) that the record, cinematograph film *or broadcast* **broadcast or** *transmission* [cable programme] to which the proceedings relate was made **or included** with the consent in writing of a person who, at the time of giving the consent, represented that he was authorised by the performers to give it on their behalf, and
   (b) that the person making **or including** the record, film *or broadcast* **broadcast or** *transmission* [cable programme] had no reasonable grounds for believing that the person giving the consent was not so authorised,

the provisions of this Act shall apply as if it had been proved that the performers had themselves consented in writing to the making [or including] of the record, film *or broadcast* **broadcast or** *transmission* [cable programme].

Note
As amended firstly by substitution of the words "broadcast or transmission" for the words "or broadcast" by the Performers Protection Act 1963, section 3(3); and secondly by substitution of the words "cable programme" for the word "transmission" and addition of the words "or included" by the Cable and Broadcasting Act 1984, section 57(1) and Schedule 5, para. 7(2).

A2.13 **8. Interpretation**

(1) In this Act, unless the context otherwise requires, the following expressions have the meanings hereby respectively assigned to them, that is to say:

   — "broadcast" means broadcast by wireless telegraphy (within the meaning of the Wireless Telegraphy Act 1949), whether by way of sound broadcasting or of television;
   — "cable programme" means a programme included in a cable programme service, and references to the inclusion of a cable programme shall be construed accordingly;
   — "cable programme service" means a cable programme service within the meaning of the Cable and Broadcasting Act 1984 or a service provided outside the United Kingdom which would be such a service if subsection (7) of section 2 of that Act and references in subsection (1) of that section to the United Kingdom were omitted;
   — "cinematograph film" means any print, negative, tape or other article on which a performance of a dramatic or musical work or part thereof is recorded for the purposes of visual reproduction;
   — "performance of a dramatic or musical work" includes any performance, mechanical or otherwise, of any such work, being a performance rendered or intended to be rendered audible by mechanical or electrical means;
   — "performers", in the case of a mechanical performance, means the persons whose performance is mechanically reproduced;
   — "programme", in relation to a cable programme service, includes any item included in that service;
   — "record" means any record or similar contrivance for reproducing sound, including the sound-track of a cinematograph film.

(2) Any reference in this Act to the making of a cinematograph film is a reference to the carrying out of any process whereby the performance of a dramatic or musical work or part thereof is recorded for the purposes of visual reproduction.

[(3) Section 48(3) of the Copyright Act 1956 (which explains the meaning of references in that Act to the inclusion of a programme in a cable programme service) shall apply for the purposes of this Act as it applies for the purposes of that Act.]

Note
As amended, by addition of the words in bold by the Cable and Broadcasting Act 1984, section 57(1) and Schedule 5, para. 7(3)–(5).

9. Short title, extent, repeal and commencement   A2.14

(1) This Act may be cited as the Dramatic and Musical Performers' Protection Act 1958.

(2) It is hereby declared that this Act extends to Northern Ireland.

(3) The Dramatic and Musical Performers' Protection Act 1925, and section 45 of, and the Sixth Schedule to, the Copyright Act 1956, are hereby repealed.

(4) This Act shall come into operation at the expiration of one month beginning with the date of its passing.

Note
Subsection (3) was repealed by the Statute Law (Repeals) Act 1974.

APPENDIX 2C

Performers' Protection Act 1963 (as amended) (c. 53)

1. Performances to which Principal Act applies
2. Sales etc. of records made abroad
3. Relaying of performances
4. Giving of consent without authority
4A. Offences by bodies corporate
5. Citation, construction, commencement and extent

An Act to amend the law relating to the protection of performers so as to enable effect to be given to a Convention entered into at Rome on 26th October 1961[31 July 1963]

Whereas, with a view to the ratification by Her Majesty of the International Convention for the Protection of Performers, Producers of Phonograms and Broadcasting Organisations entered into at Rome on 26th October 1961, it is expedient to amend and supplement the Dramatic and Musical Performers' Protection Act 1958 (in this Act referred to as "the principal Act"):

A2.15   **1. Performances to which Principal Act applies**

(1) The principal Act shall have effect as if for references therein to the performance of a dramatic or musical work there were substituted references to the performance of any actors, singers, musicians, dancers or other persons who act, sing, deliver, declaim, play in or otherwise perform literary, dramatic, musical or artistic works, and the definition contained in section 8(1) of that Act of the expression "performance of a dramatic or musical work" (by which that expression is made to include a performance rendered or intended to be rendered audible by mechanical or electrical means) shall be construed accordingly.
(2) For the avoidance of doubt it is hereby declared that the principal Act applies as respects anything done in relation to a performance notwithstanding that the performance took place outside the United Kingdom, but this shall not cause anything done out of the United Kingdom to be treated as an offence.

A2.16   **2. Sales etc. of records made abroad**

For the purposes of paragraphs (b) and (c) of section 1 of the principal Act (by which sales of, and other dealing with, records made in contravention of the Act are rendered punishable) a record made in a country outside the United Kingdom directly or indirectly from or by means of a performance to which the principal Act applies shall, where the civil or criminal law of that country contains a provision for the protection of performers under which the consent of any person to the making of the record was required, be deemed to have been made in contravention of the principal Act if, whether knowingly or not, it was made without the consent in writing of the performers.

A2.17   **3. Relaying of performances**

(1) A person who, otherwise that by the use of a record or cinematograph film or the reception **and immediate re-transmission** of a broadcast, knowingly *causes a performance to which the principal Act applies, or any part of such a performance, to be transmitted without the consent in writing of the performers*:

(a) to subscribers to a diffusion service; or

(b) over wires or other paths provided by a material substance so as to be seen or heard in public,

includes a performance to which the principal Act applies, or any part of such performance, in a cable programme without the consent in writing of the performers shall be guilty of an offence, and shall be liable, on summary conviction, to a fine not exceeding *fifty pounds* **£400** [level 5 on the standard scale].

(2) Section 48(3) of the Copyright Act 1956 (which explains the meaning of references in that Act to the transmission of a work or other subject-matter to subscribers to a diffusion service) shall apply for the purposes of the preceding subsection as it applies for the purposes of that Act.

(3) Section 6 of the principal Act (which provides for special defences) shall have effect as if the preceding subsections were inserted immediately before that section, and that section and section 7 of the principal Act (which provides for the giving of consent on behalf of performers) shall have effect as if for the words "or broadcast" in each place where they occur there were substituted the words "broadcast or transmission".

Note

As amended, firstly by substitution of the figure in bold by the Performers' Protection Act 1972, section 1 and Schedule; secondly by substitution of the words in square brackets by the Criminal Justice Act 1982, sections 38 and 46; and thirdly by addition of the first set of bold words and substitution of the words in the second set of bold words by the Cable and Broadcasting Act 1984, section 57(1) and Schedule 5, para. 13(1). Subsection (2) was repealed by the Cable and Broadcasting Act 1984, section 57(2) and Schedule 6.

4. Giving of consent without authority   A2.18

(1) Where:

(a) a record, cinematograph film, *broadcast or transmission is made* **or broadcast is made or cable programme is included** with the consent in writing of a person who, at the time of giving the consent, represented that he was authorised by the performers to give it on their behalf when to his knowledge he was not so authorised, and

(b) if proceedings were brought against the person to whom the consent was given, the consent would by virtue of section 7 of the principal Act afford a defence to those proceedings,

the person giving the consent shall be guilty of an offence, and shall be liable, on summary conviction, to a fine not exceeding *fifty pounds* **£400** [level 5 on the standard scale].

(2) The said section 7 shall not apply to proceedings under this section.

Note

As amended, firstly by substitution of the figure in bold by the Performers' Protection Act 1972, section 1 and Schedule; secondly by substitution of the words in square brackets by the Criminal Justice Act 1982, sections 38 and 46; and thirdly by substitution of the bold wording by the Cable and Broadcasting Act 1984, section 57(1) and Schedule 5, para 13(2).

4A. Offences by bodies corporate   A2.19

Where an offence under the principal Act or this Act committed by a body corporate is proved to have been committed with the consent or connivance of, or to be attributable to any neglect on the part of, any director, manager, secretary or other similar officer of the body corporate or any person who was purporting to act in any such capacity, he, as well as the body corporate, shall be guilty of that offence and shall be liable to be proceeded against and punished accordingly.

Note
This section was added by the Performers' Protection Act 1972, section 3.

A2.20   **5. Citation, construction, commencement and extent**

(1) This Act may be cited as the Performers' Protection Act 1963, and the principal Act and this Act may be cited together as the Peformers' Protection Acts 1958 and 1963.
(2) This Act shall be construed as one with the principal Act.
(3) This Act shall come into operation at the expiration of the period of one month beginning with the date of its passing, and shall apply only in relation to performances taking place after its commencement.
(4) It is hereby declared that this Act extends to Northern Ireland.

APPENDIX 2D

Performers' Protection Act 1972 (c. 32)

1. Increase of fines under Performers' Protection Acts 1958 and 1963
2. Amendment of section 1 of Dramatic and Musical Performers' Protection Act 1958
3. Amendment of Performers' Protection Act 1963
4. Citation, construction, commencement and extent

SCHEDULE: INCREASE IN FINES

An Act to amend the Perfomers' Protection Acts 1958 and 1963 [29 June 1972]

1. Increase of fines under Performers' Protection Acts 1958 and 1963   A2.21

The enactments specified in column 1 of the Schedule to this Act (being enactments creating the offences under the Performers' Protection Acts 1958 and 1963 broadly described in column 2 of that Schedule) shall each have effect as if the maximum fine which may be imposed on summary conviction of any offence specified in that enactment were a fine not exceeding the amount specified in column 4 of that Schedule instead of a fine not exceeding the amount specified in column 3 of that Schedule.

Note
This has been superseded. See *ante*.

2. Amendment of Section 1 of Dramatic and Musical Performers' Protection Act 1958   A2.22

Section 1 of the Dramatic and Musical Performers' Protection Act 1958 (by which the making of records without the consent of the performers and sales of, and other dealings with, such records are rendered punishable) shall have effect as if after the word "transaction" there were inserted the words "or, on conviction on indictment, to imprisonment for a term not exceeding two years, or to a fine, or to both".

3. Amendment of Performers' Protection Act 1963   A2.23

In the Performers' Protection Act 1963 there shall be inserted after section 4 the following section:

4A. Offences by bodies corporate
Where an offence under the principal Act or this Act committed by a body corporate is proved to have been committed with the consent or connivance of, or to be attributable to any neglect on the part of, any director, manager, secretary or other similar officer of the body corporate or any person who was purporting to act in any such capacity, he, as well as the body corporate, shall be guilty of that offence and shall be liable to be proceeded against and punished accordingly.

4. Citation, construction, commencement and extent   A2.24

(1) This Act may be cited as the Performers' Protection Act 1972, and the Peformers' Protection Acts 1958 and 1963 and this Act may be cited together as the Performers' Protection Acts 1958 to 1972.
(2) This Act shall come into operation at the expiration of the period of one month beginning with the date of its passing, but nothing in this Act shall affect the punishment for an offence committed before the commencement of this Act.

(3) It is hereby declared that this Act extends to Northern Ireland.

SCHEDULE

A2.25

Section 1: Increase of fines

(1) Enactment	(2) Description of Offence	(3) Old Maximum Fine	(4) New Maximum Fine
The Dramatic and Musical Performers' Protection Act 1958			
Section 1	Making, etc., records without consent of performers	£2 for each record in respect of which an offence is proved subject to a limit of £50 in respect of any one transaction	£20 for each record in respect of which an offence is proved subject to a limit of £400 in respect of any one transaction
Section 2	Making, etc., cinematograph films without consent of performers	£50	£400
Section 3	Broadcasting without consent of performers	£50	£400
Section 4	Making or having plates, etc., for making records in contravention of Act	£50	£400
The Performers' Protection Act 1963			
Section 3(1)	Relaying performances without consent of performers	£50	£400
Section 4(1)	Giving consent without authority	£50	£400

APPENDIX 3A

The Copyright Tribunal Rules 1989

(S.I. 1989 No. 1129)

Made ....*4th July 1989*

Laid before Parliament ....*10th July 1989*

Coming into force ....*1st August 1989*

SCHEDULES

Schedule 1: Table of Fees
Schedule 2: Provisions of Arbitration Acts
Schedule 3: Forms

References and applications with respect to licensing schemes

A3.01 **10. Amendment of statement of case and answer**

(1) Subject to paragraph (3) of this rule, a party may at any time amend his statement of case or answer by serving on the Secretary the amended statement or answer.
(2) On being served with an amended statement of case or answer, the Secretary shall as soon as practicable serve a copy thereof on every other party.
(3) No amended statement of case or answer shall, without the leave of the Chairman, be served after such date as the Chairman may direct under rule 11(2)(iii).

A3.02 **11. Chairman's directions**

(1) Upon the expiration of the time specified by rule 9(2) for the service on the Secretary of a statement of case or answer, the Chairman shall appoint a date and place for the attendance of the parties for the purpose of his giving directions as to the further conduct of the proceedings, and the Secretary shall serve on every party and every person whose application under rule 7(1) has not been determined not less than 21 days' notice of such date and place.
(2) On the appointed day, the Chairman shall afford every party attending the appointment an opportunity of being heard and, after considering any representations made orally or in writing, give such directions as he thinks fit with a view to the just, expeditious and economical disposal of the proceedings and, without prejudice to the generality of the foregoing, may give directions as to:

(i) the date and place of any oral hearing requested by any party or which the Chairman for any reason considers necesary, and the procedure (including the number of representatives each party may appoint for the purpose of such hearing) and the timetable (including the allocation of time for the making of representations by each party) to be followed at such a hearing;
(ii) the procedure to be followed with regard to the submission and exchange of written arguments;
(iii) the date after which no amended statement of case or answer may be served without leave;
(iv) the preparation and service by each party, or any one party if all other parties agree, of a schedule setting out the issues to be determined by the Tribunal and brief particulars of the contentions of each party in relation thereto;
(v) the admission of any facts or documents, and the discovery and inspection of documents;
(vi) the giving of evidence on affidavit; and
(vii) the consideration by the Tribunal of whether any objection made to an intervener's credentials under rule 8 shall operate as a stay of the proceedings.

(3) The Chairman may postpone or adjourn to a later date to be apppointed by him the giving of any directions under this rule and, at any time after directions have been given under this rule the Chairman may, whether or not any application on that behalf has been made under rule 12, give such further directions as he may think fit.
(4) If any party fails to comply with any direction given or order made under this rule or rule 12, the Chairman may, without prejudice to the making of any order under rule 53, give such consequential directions as may be necessary and may order such a party to pay any costs occasioned by his default.

12. Application for directions   A3.03

(1) A party may, at any stage of the proceedings, apply to the Tribunal for directions with respect to any issue or other matter in the proceedings and, except where the Tribunal (whether generally or in any particular case) otherwise directs or these Rules otherwise provide, every such application shall be disposed of by the Chairman.
(2) The application shall be made by the service of a notice on the Secretary (stating the grounds upon which it is made) and, unless the notice is accompanied by the written consent of all parties to the proceedings, the party making the application shall serve a copy of the application on every other party to the proceedings and inform the Secretary of the date of such service.
(3) Any party who objects to the application may, within 7 days after being served with the copy thereof, serve a notice of objection (stating the grounds of objection) on the Secretary and he shall serve a copy of the same on the applicant and any other party to the proceedings and inform the Secretary of the date of such service.
(4) After considering the application and any objection thereto and, if he considers necessary, after having given all parties concerned an opportunity of being heard, the Chairman may make such order in the matter as he thinks fit and give such consequential directions as may be necessary.

13. Consolidation of proceedings   A3.04

Where there is pending before the Tribunal more than one reference under section 118, 119, or 120 of the Act, or more than one application under section 121 or 122 of the Act relating to the same licensing scheme, the Chairman may if he thinks fit, either of his own motion or on an application made under rule 12, order that some or all of the references or applications, as the case may be, shall be considered together, and may give such consequential directions as may be necessary:
    Provided that the Chairman shall not make an order under this rule of his own motion without giving all parties concerned a reasonable opportunity of objecting to the proposed order.

14. Procedure and evidence at hearing   A3.05

(1) Every party to a reference or application which is considered at an oral hearing before the Tribunal shall be entitled to attend the hearing, to address the Tribunal, to give evidence and call witnesses.
(2) Except where the Tribunal or the Chairman otherwise orders in the case of an application for directions under rule 12, the hearing shall be in public.
(3) Evidence before the Tribunal shall be given orally or, if the parties so agree or the Tribunal or the Chairman so orders, by affidavit, but the Tribunal may at any stage of the proceedings require the personal attendance of any deponent for examination and cross-examination.

15. Representation and rights of audience   A3.06

(1) Subject to paragraph (5) of this rule, a party may at any stage of the proceedings appoint some other person to act as agent for him in the proceedings.
(2) The appointment of an agent shall be made in writing and shall not be effective until notice thereof has been served on the Secretary, and a copy of the same has been served on every other party and the Secretary informed of the date of such service.
(3) Only one agent shall be appointed to act for a party at any one time.
(4) For the purpose of service on a party of any document, or the taking of any step required or authorised by these Rules, an agent appointed by a party shall be deemed to continue to have authority to act for such a party until the Secretary and every other party has received notice of the termination of his appointment.
(5) A party or an agent appointed by him under paragraph (1) of this rule by be

represented at any hearing, whether before the Tribunal or the Chairman, by a barrister, or in Scotland an advocate, or a solicitor, or by any other person allowed by the Tribunal or the Chairman to appear on his behalf or may, save in the case of a corporation or unincorporated body, appear in person.

A3.07 **16. Withdrawal of reference or application**

(1) The applicant may withdraw his reference or application made under rule 3 at any time before it has been finally disposed of by serving a notice thereof on the Secretary, but such withdrawal shall be without prejudice to the Tribunal's power to make an order as to the payment of costs incurred up to the time of service of the notice. The applicant shall serve a copy of the notice on every other party to the proceedings and inform the Secetary of the date of such service.

(2) Any party to the proceedings upon whom a copy of the notice of withdrawal is served under this rule may, within 14 days of such service, apply to the Tribunal for an order that, notwithstanding such withdrawal, such reference or application should proceed to be determined by the Tribunal, and if the Tribunal decides, at its discretion, to proceed with such reference or application it may for that purpose substitute such party as the applicant to the proceedings and give such consequential directions as may be necessary.

A3.08 **17. Decision of Tribunal**

The final decision of the Tribunal on a reference or an application made under rule 3 shall be given in writing and shall include a statement of the Tribunal's reasons and, where on any further reference or application for review of the Tribunal's order under section 120 or 122 of the Act the Tribunal has varied the licensing scheme, there shall be annexed to the decision a copy of the scheme as so varied, and the Secretary shall as soon as practicable serve on every party to the proceedings a copy of the Tribunal's decision.

A3.09 **18. Publication of decision**

The Secretary shall cause a copy of the Tribunal's decision to be made available at the office for public inspection during office hours and, if the Chairman so directs, shall cause to be advertised, in such manner as the Chairman thinks fit, short particulars of the decision.

A3.10 **19. Effective date of order**

Except where the operation of the order is suspected under rule 42 or 43, the order of the Tribunal shall take effect from such date, and shall remain in force for such period, as shall be specified in the order.

References and applications with respect to licensing by licensing bodies

A3.11 **23. Intervener's application (Forms 5 & 6)**

(1) A person or organisation who claims to have a substantial interest in proceedings in respect of a reference or an application under rule 20 may apply to the Tribunal to be made a party to that reference or application by serving on the Secretary a notice of intervention in Form 5, together with a statement of his interest.

(2) As soon as practicable after receipt of a notice under this rule the Secretary shall:

(a) serve a copy of the notice on every other party to the proceedings, and

(b) serve on the intervener a copy of the applicant's reference or application and statement of case, together with any other notice of intervention which has been served on him.

(3) Within 14 days of the service upon him of the notice, a party intending to object to an intervener's credentials shall serve on the Secretary a notice of objection in Form 6 and shall serve a copy of the same on the intervener and inform the Secretary of the date of such service.

(4) The Tribunal, after considering the intervener's application and any objection to his credentials and, if it considers necessary, after having given the intervener and any party who has served a notice of objection an opportunity of being heard, shall, if satisfied of the substantial interest of the intervener, grant the application and may thereupon give such directions or further directions as to the taking of any steps required or authorised under these Rules or as to any further matter as may be necessary to enable the intervener to participate in the proceedings as a party.

(5) Subject to any direction to the contrary that the Chairman may give under rule 11(2)(vii) an objection to an intervener's credentials shall not operate as a stay of proceedings and shall be considered by the Tribunal at the same time as the reference or application in question.

Application for Tribunal's consent on behalf of performer

34. Commencement of proceedings (Form 14)   A3.12

Proceedings under section 190 of the Act for the Tribunal's consent on behalf of the performer to the making of a recording from a previous recording of a performance shall be commenced by the service by the applicant on the Secretary of a notice in Form 14 together with a statement:

(a) where the identity or whereabouts of the performer cannot be ascertained, of the inquiries made by him in that respect and the result of those inquiries, or

(b) where the identity or whereabouts of the performer are known, of the grounds on which the applicant considers that the performer's withholding of consent is unreasonable, and by serving a copy thereof on the performer.

35. Inquiries by Tribunal   A3.13

(1) Where a notice has been served in accordance with rule 34(a), the Tribunal shall, after requiring of the applicant such further particulars as it may consider necessary, cause to be served on such persons as it considers are likely to have relevant information with regard to the identity or the whereabouts of the performer a notice seeking such information, and at the same time cause to be published, in such publications as it considers appropriate and at such intervals as it may determine, a notice setting out brief particulars of the application and requesting information on the identity or whereabouts of the performer.

(2) On the expiration of 28 days from the date of the publication of the notice, or the date of publication of the last such notice, the Tribunal may, on being satisfied that the identity or whereabouts of the performer cannot be ascertained, make an order giving its consent on such terms as it thinks fit.

36. Procedure, and decision of Tribunal   A3.14

(1) Within 21 days of the service of the notice under rule 34(b), the performer may serve on the Secretary his answer setting out his case and of the grounds for his withholding of consent, and shall serve a copy of the same on the applicant and inform the Secretary of the date of such service.

(2) Rules 10 to 16 shall apply to proceedings in respect of an application under rule 34(b) as they apply to proceedings in respect of an application under rule 3.

(3) The final decision of the Tribunal on an application under rule 34 shall be given in writing and shall include a statement of the Tribunal's reasons and where the Tribunal has, in default of an agreement between the applicant and the performer, made an order as to the payment to be made to the performer in consideration of the consent

given on his behalf by the Tribunal, there shall be annexed to the decision a copy of that order; and the Secretary shall as soon as practicable serve on every party to the proceedings a copy of the Tribunal's decision. Rules 18 and 19 shall apply with regard to the publication and the effective date of the decision.

A3.15   **37. Intervener's application (Forms 5 & 6)**

A person or organisation who claims to have substantial interest in proceedings in respect of an application under rule 34 may, in accordance with rule 23, apply to the Tribunal to be made a party, and that rule shall apply to proceedings in respect of such an application as it applies to proceedings in respect of an application under rule 20.

Appeal to the Court from decision of Tribunal and suspension of Tribunal's orders

A3.16   **42. Notice of appeal (Form 17)**

(1) An appeal to the High Court or, in the case of proceedings of the Tribunal in Scotland, to the Court of Session under section 152 of the Act on a point of law arising from a decision of the Tribunal shall be brought within 28 days of the date of the decision of the Tribunal or within such further period as the court may, on an application to it, allow.
(2) A party so appealing to the court on a point of law shall as soon as may be practicable serve on the Secretary a notice in Form 17 of such an appeal, and shall serve a copy thereof on every person who was a party to the proceedings giving rise to that decision.
(3) Where an appeal has been lodged with the court, the Tribunal shall not make any further order on the reference or application which is the subject of the appeal until the court has given its decision thereon.
(4) On receipt of the notice of appeal by the Secretary the Tribunal may of its own motion suspend the operation of any order contained in its decision, and shall, if an order is so suspended, cause notice of the same to be served on every person affected by the suspension and may, if it thinks fit, cause notice of the suspension to be published in such manner as it may direct.

A3.17   **43. Application for suspension of order (Form 18)**

(1) A party to the proceedings may, pending the determination of an appeal under rule 42, apply to the Tribunal to suspend the operation of an order made by it by serving on the Secretary a notice in Form 18 within 7 days of the receipt of the decision of the Tribunal together with a statement of the grounds for suspension, and he shall serve a copy of the same on every person who was a party to the proceedings giving rise to that decision and inform the Secretary of the date of such service.
(2) Within 14 days of the service of the notice under paragraph (1) above a party may serve on the Secretary a statement setting out the grounds of his objection to the applicant's case, and shall serve a copy of the same on every person who was a party to the proceedings giving rise to the decision and inform the Secretary of the date of such service.
(3) Rules 10 to 16 shall apply to proceedings in respect of an application under this rule as they apply to proceedings in respect of an application under rule 3.
(4) Where the Tribunal, after consideration of the application and any representations, refuses an application to suspend the operation of its order, the Secretary shall as soon as practicable serve on every party to the proceedings a copy of the Tribunal's decision together with a statement of the Tribunal's reasons for refusal.
(5) Where any order of the Tribunal has been suspended upon the application of a party to the proceedings or by the court the Secretary shall serve notice of the suspension on all parties to the proceedings, and if particulars of the order have been advertised shall cause notice of the suspension to be advertised in the same manner, and rule 18 shall apply with regard to the publication of the decision.

44. Intervener's application (Forms 5 & 6) A3.18

A person or organisation who claims to have a substantial interest in proceedings in respect of an application under rule 43 may, in accordance with rule 23, apply to the Tribunal to be made a party, and that rule shall apply to proceedings in respect of such an application as it applies to proceedings in respect of an application under rule 20.

45. Effect of suspension of order A3.19

If the operation of any order is suspended under rule 42 or 43, then, while the order remains suspended, sections 123 and 128 of the Act shall not have effect in relation to the order.

Miscellaneous and general

46. Application of Arbitration Acts A3.20

The provisions of sections 12, 14, 17 and 26 of the Arbitration Act 1950[1] (which are set out in Part 1 of Schedule 2), shall apply in the case of proceedings before the Tribunal in England and Wales, and the provisions of sections 13, 14, 16, 21 and 24 of, and paragraphs 4, 5 and 8 of Schedule 1 to, the Arbitration Act (Northern Ireland) 1937[2] (which are set out in Part 2 of Schedule 2), shall apply in the case of proceedings before the Tribunal in Northern Ireland, as those provisions respectively apply to an arbitration where no contrary intention is expressed in the arbitration agreement.

47. Enforcement of Tribunal's orders in Scotland A3.21

Any decision of the Tribunal may be enforced in Scotland in like manner as a recorded decree arbitral.

48. Costs A3.22

(1) The Tribunal may, at its discretion, at any stage of the proceedings make any order it thinks fit in relation to the payment of costs by one party to another in respect of the whole or part of the proceedings.
(2) Any party against whom an order for costs is made shall, if the Tribunal so directs, pay to any other party a lump sum by way of costs, or such proportion of the costs as may be just, and in the last mentioned case the Tribunal may assess the sum to be paid or may direct that it be assessed by the Chairman, or taxed by a taxing officer of the Supreme Court or the Supreme Court of Northern Ireland or by the Auditor of the Court of Session.

49. Fees A3.23

The fees specified in Schedule 1 shall be payable in respect of the matters therein mentioned.

50. Service of documents A3.24

(1) Any notice or other document required by these Rules to be served on any person may be sent to him by pre-paid post at his address for service, or, where no address for service has been given, at his registered office, principal place of business or last known address, and every notice or other document required to be served on the Secretary may be sent by pre-paid post to the Secretary at the office.
(2) Service of any notice or document on a successor in title or successor in interest of a

---

[1] 1950, c. 27.
[2] 1937, c. 8 (N.I.).

party to any proceedings shall be effective if served or sent to him in accordance with this rule.

(3) Any notice or other document required to be served on a licensing body or organisation which is not a body corporate may be sent to the secretary, manager or other similar officer.

(4) The Tribunal or the Chairman may direct that service of any notice or other document be dispensed with or effected otherwise than in the manner provided by these Rules.

(5) Service of any notice or document on a party's solicitor or agent shall be deemed to be service on such party, and service on a solicitor or agent acting for more than one party shall be deemed to be service on every party for whom such a solicitor or agent acts.

A3.25   **51. Time**

(1) Except in the case of the time limit imposed under rule 42(1), the time for doing any act may (whether it has already expired or not) be extended:

  (a) with the leave of the Tribunal or the Chairman, or
  (b) by the consent in writing of all parties, except where the Tribunal or Chairman has fixed the time by order or, if the time is prescribed by these Rules, has directed that it may not be extended or further extended without leave.

(2) A party in whose favour time is extended by consent under paragraph (1)(b) above shall, as soon as may be practicable after the necessary consents have been obtained, serve notice thereof on the Secretary.

(3) Where the last day for the doing of any act falls on a day on which the office is closed and by reason thereof the act cannot be done on that day, it may be done on the next day on which the office is open.

A3.26   **52. Office hours**

The office shall be open between 10.00am and 4.00pm Monday to Friday, excluding Good Friday, Christmas Day and any day specified or proclaimed to be a bank holiday under section 1 of the Banking and Financial Dealings Act 1971.[3]

A3.27   **53. Failure to comply with directions**

If any party fails to comply with any direction given, in accordance with these Rules, by the Tribunal or the Chairman, the Tribunal may, if it considers that the justice of the case so requires, order that such party be debarred from taking any further part in the proceedings without leave of the Tribunal.

A3.28   **54. Power of Tribunal to regulate procedure**

Subject to the provisions of the Act and these Rules, the Tribunal shall have power to regulate its own procedure.

A3.29   **55. Transitional provisions and revocation of previous Rules**

(1) In relation to any proceedings which are pending under Part IV of the Copyright Act 1956[4] when these Rules come into force, these Rules shall apply subject to such modifications as the Tribunal or the Chairman may, in the circumstances, consider appropriate.

(2) The Performing Right Tribunal Rules 1965[5] and the Performing Right Tribunal

---

[3] 1971, c. 80.
[4] 1956, c. 74.
[5] S.I. 1965 No. 1506.

(Amendment) Rules 1971[6] are hereby revoked, but without prejudice to anything done thereunder.

SCHEDULE 1 (RULE 49)

TABLE OF FEES
A3.30

(1) On serving notice in Forms 1, 2, 7, 8, 12, 14, 15 or 16	£30
(2) On serving notice in Forms 3, 4, 5, 6, 9, 10, 11, 13, 17 or 18	£15
(3) On every application for directions under rule 12	£10

(1) On serving notice in Forms 1, 2, 7, 8, 10A, 10B, 12, 14, 15, 16 or 16A	£30
(2) On serving notice in Forms 3, 4, 5, 6, 9, 10, 10C, 11, 13, 16B, 17 or 18	£15
(3) On every application for directions under rule 12	£10

Note
This Schedule was amended by the Copyright Tribunal (Amendment) Rules 1991, S.I. 1991 No. 201.

SCHEDULE 2 (RULE 46)

PROVISIONS OF ARBITRATION ACTS

PART 1

Provisions of the Arbitration Act 1950 which apply in the case of proceedings before the Tribunal in England and Wales.

12. Conduct of proceedings, witnesses, etc.
A3.31

(1) Unless a contrary intention is expressed therein, every arbitration agreement shall, where such a provision is applicable to the reference, be deemed to contain a provision that the parties to the reference, and all persons claiming through them respectively, shall, subject to any legal objection, submit to be examined by the arbitrator or umpire, on oath or affirmation, in relation to the matters in dispute, and shall, subject as aforesaid, produce before the arbitrator or umpire all documents within their possession or power respectively which may be required or called for, and do all other things which during the proceedings on the reference the arbitrator or umpire may require.
(2) Unless a contrary intention is expressed therein, every arbitration agreement shall, where such a provison is applicable to the reference, be deemed to contain a provision that the witnesses on the reference shall, if the arbitrator or umpire thinks fit, be examined on oath or affirmation.
(3) An aribitrator or umpire shall, unless a contrary intention is expressed in the

---

[6] S.I. 1971 No. 636.

arbitration agreement, have power to administer oaths to, or take the affirmations of, the parties to and witnesses on a reference under the agreement.

(4) Any party to a reference under an arbitration agreement may sue out a writ of subpoena ad testificandum or a writ of subpoena duces tecum, but no person shall be compelled under any such writ to produce any document which he could not be compelled to produce on the trial of an action, and the High Court or a judge thereof may order that a writ of subpoena ad testificandum or of subpoena duces tecum shall issue to compel the attendance before an arbitrator or umpire of a witness wherever he may be within the United Kingdom.

(5) The High Court or a judge thereof may also order that a writ of habeas corpus ad testificandum shall issue to bring up a prisoner for examination before an arbitrator or umpire.

(6) The High Court shall have, for the purpose of and in relation to a reference, the same power of making orders in respect of:

(a) security for costs;
(b) discovery of documents and interrogatories;
(c) the giving of evidence by affidavit;
(d) examination on oath of any witness before an officer of the High Court or any other person, and the issue of a commission or request for the examination of a witness out of the jurisdiction;
(e) the preservation, interim custody or sale of any goods which are the subject matter of the reference;
(f) securing the amount in dispute in the reference;
(g) the detention, preservation or inspection of any property or thing which is the subject of the reference or as to which any question may arise therein, and authorising for any of the purposes aforesaid any persons to enter upon or into any land or building in the possession of any party to the reference, or authorising any samples to be taken or any observation to be made or experiment to be tried which may be necessary or expedient for the purpose of obtaining full information or evidence; and
(h) interim injunctions or the appointment of a receiver;

as it has for the purpose of and in relation to an action or matter in the High Court:

Provided that nothing in this subsection shall be taken to prejudice any power which may be vested in an arbitrator or umpire of making orders with respect to any of the matters aforesaid.

A3.32   **14. Interim awards**

Unless a contrary intention is expressed therein, every arbitration agreement shall, where such a provision is applicable to the reference, be deemed to contain a provision that the arbitrator or umpire may, if he thinks fit, make an interim award, and any reference in this Part of this Act to an award includes a reference to an interim award.

A3.33   **17. Power to correct slips**

Unless a contrary intention is expressed in the arbitration agreement, the arbitrator or umpire shall have power to correct in an award any clerical mistake or error arising from any accidental slip or omission.

A3.34   **26. Enforcement of award**

(1) An award on an arbitration agreement may, by leave of the High Court or a judge thereof, be enforced in the same manner as a judgment or order to the same effect, and where leave is so given, judgment may be entered in terms of the award.

(2) If:

(a) the amount sought to be recovered does not exceed the county court limit, and

(b) a county court so orders,

it shall be recoverable (by execution issued from the county court or otherwise) as if payable under an order of that court and shall not be enforceable under subsection (1) above.

(3) An application to the High Court under this section shall preclude an application to a county court and an application to a county court under this section shall preclude an application to the High Court.

(4) In subsection (2)(a) above "the county court limit" means the amount which for the time being is the county court limit for the purposes of section 16 of the County Courts Act 1984 (money recoverable by statute).[*]

PART 2

Provisions of the Arbitration Act (Northern Ireland) 1937 which apply in the case of proceedings before the Tribunal in Northern Ireland.

13. Powers of arbitrators   A3.35

The arbitrators or umpire acting under a reference in an arbitration agreement shall, unless the arbitration agreement or the reference thereunder expresses a contrary intention, have power to administer oaths to or take the affirmations of the parties and witnesses appearing, and to correct in an award any clerical mistake or error arising from any accidental slip or omission.

14. Attendance of witnesses   A3.36

Any party to a reference under an arbitration agreement may sue out a writ of subpoena ad testificandum, or a writ of subpoena duces tecum, but no person shall be compelled under any such writ to produce any document which he could not be compelled to produce on the trial of an action:

Provided that no writ shall issue under this section unless the arbitrator has entered on the reference or has been called on to act by notice in writing from a party to the reference and has agreed to do so.

16. Entry of judgment in terms of award   A3.37

An award on a reference under an arbitration agreement may, by leave of the court, be entered as a judgment in terms of the award, and shall thereupon have the same force and effect as a judgment or order of the court.

21. Additional powers of court   A3.38

(1) The court shall have, for the purpose of and in relation to a reference, the same power of making orders in respect of any of the matters set out in the Second Schedule to this Act as it has for the purpose of and in relation to an action or matter in the court:

Provided that nothing in the foregoing provision shall be taken to prejudice any power which may be vested in an arbitrator or umpire of making orders with respect to any of the matters aforesaid.

(2) Where relief by way of interpleader is granted and it appears to the court that the claims in question are matters to which an arbitration agreement, to which the

---

[*] s. 26 was amended by s. 17(2) of the Administration of Justice Act 1977 (c. 38) and s. 148(1) of, and para. 22 of Schedule 2 to, the County Courts Act 1984 (c. 28).

claimants are parties, applies, the court may direct the issue between the claimants to be determined in accordance with the agreement.

(3) Where an application is made to set aside an award the court may order that any money made payable by the award shall be brought into court or otherwise secured pending the determination of the application.

A3.39 **24. Additional powers to compel attendance of witnesses**

(1) The court may order that a writ of subpoena ad testificandum or of subpoena duces tecum shall issue to compel the attendance of a witness before any referee, arbitrator or umpire.

(2) The court may also order that a writ of habeas corpus ad testificandum shall issue to bring up a prisoner for examination before any referee, arbitrator or umpire.

A3.40 **First Schedule (provisions to be implied in arbitration agreements):**

4. The parties to the reference and all persons claiming through them respectively shall, subject to any legal objection, submit to be examined by the arbitrators or umpire on oath or affirmation in relation to the matters in dispute and shall, subject as aforesaid, produce before the arbitrators or umpire all books, deeds, papers, accounts, writings and documents within their possession or power respectively which may be required or called for, and do all other things which during the proceedings on the reference the arbitrators or umpire may require.

5. The witnesses on the reference shall, if the arbitrators or umpire think fit, be examined on oath or affirmation.

8. The arbitrators or umpire may, if they think fit, make an interim award.

A3.41 **Second Schedule (matters in respect of which court may make orders):**

1. Security for costs.
2. Discovery of documents and interrogatories.
3. The giving of evidence by affidavit.
4. Examination on oath of any witnesses before an officer of the court or any other person, and the issue of a commission or request for the examination of a witness out of the jurisdiction.
5. The preservation, interim custody, or sale, of any goods which are the subject matter of the reference.
6. Securing the amount in dispute in the reference.
7. The detention, preservation or inspection of any property or thing which is the subject of the reference or as to which any question may arise therein, and authorising for any of the purposes aforesaid any persons to enter upon or into any land or building in the possession of any party to the reference, or authorising any samples to be taken or any observation to be made or experiment to be tried which may be necessary or expedient for the purpose of obtaining full information or evidence.
8. Interim injunctions or the appointment of a receiver.

SCHEDULE 3

FORM 14 (RULE 34)   A3.42

COPYRIGHT, DESIGNS AND PATENTS ACT 1988 COPYRIGHT TRIBUNAL

Notice of Application for Tribunal's Consent on behalf of Performer under Section 190

To,
   The Secretary to the Tribunal

   1. TAKE NOTICE that [name and address of applicant] ("the Applicant") wishes to make a recording from a previous recording of [specify performance]

*   [the identity or whereabouts of the performer(s) of which cannot be ascertained by reasonable inquiry]
*   [the performer(s) of which unreasonably withhold his/their consent]

hereby applies to the Tribunal for its consent to the recording.
   2. There is delivered herewith a statement setting out:

*   [the inquiries made by the Applicant as to the identity or whereabouts of the performer(s) and the result of those inquiries]
*   [the grounds on which the Applicant considers that the withholding of consent is unreasonable].

*3. [A copy of the Applicant's statement *has been/will be served on [date of service] on the performer(s) [state name(s) and address(es) of performer(s)]].
   4. All communciations about this reference should be addressed to

*   [the Applicant at the address shown above]
*   [name and address of Applicant's solicitor/agent].

Signed ....

Status of signatory .... [Applicant,
                                    an officer of Applicant, solicitor or agent]

Date ....

*Delete whichever is inappropriate

APPENDIX 3B

The Copyright and Rights in Performances (Notice of Seizure) Order 1989

(S.I. 1989 No. 1006)

Made ....*13th June 1989*

Laid before Parliament ....*26th June 1989*

Coming into force ....*1st August 1989*

The Secretary of State, in exercise of the powers conferred upon him by section 100(4) and (5) and section 196(4) and (5) of the Copyright, Designs and Patents Act 1988(a) ("the Act"), hereby makes the following Order:

A3.43

1. This Order may be cited as the Copyright and Rights in Performances (Notice of Seizure) Order 1989 and shall come into force on 1st August 1989.

2. The form set out in the Schedule to this Order is hereby prescribed for the notice required under section 100(4) and section 196(4), respectively, of the Act.

SCHEDULE (ARTICLE 2)

THE COPYRIGHT AND RIGHTS IN PERFORMANCES (NOTICE OF SEIZURE) ORDER 1989

A3.44 NOTICE OF SEIZURE

To Whom it May Concern

1. Goods in which you were trading have been seized. This notice tells you who carried out the seizure, the legal grounds on which this has been done and the goods which have been seized and detained. As required by the Copyright, Designs and Patents Act 1988, notice of the proposed seizure was given to the police station at (state address).

Person carrying out seizure

2. (State name and address)
   *acting on the authority of (state name and address).

Legal grounds for seizure and detention

3. This action has been taken under *section 100/section 196 of the Act which (subject to certain conditions) permit a copyright owner, or a person having performing rights or recording rights, to seize and detain infringing copies or illicit recordings found exposed or immediately available for sale or hire, or to authorise such seizure. The right to seize and detain is subject to a decision of the court under *section 114/section 204 of the Act (order as to disposal of goods seized and detained).

Nature of the goods seized and detained

*4. Infringing copies of works (within the meaning of section 27 of the Act)—(specify all articles seized)

Illicit recordings (within the meaning of section 197 of the Act)—(specify all articles seized)

Signed .... Date ....

---

* Delete as necessary

APPENDIX 3C

The Performances (Reciprocal Protection) (Convention Countries) Order 1995

(S.I. 1995 No. 2990)

Made ....*23rd November 1995*

Laid before Parliament ....*24th November 1995*

Coming into force
Articles 1, 2(a) and 4...*15th December 1995*
Articles 2(b) and 3 ....*1st January 1996*

At the Court at Buckingham Palace, the 23rd day of November 1995

Present,

The Queen's Most Excellent Majesty in Council

Her Majesty, by virtue of the authority conferred upon Her by section 208(1)(a) of the Copyright, Designs and Patents Act 1988,[1] is pleased, by and with the advice of Her Privy Council, to order, and it is hereby ordered as follows:

A3.45 1.(1) This Order may be cited as the Performances (Reciprocal Protection) (Convention Countries) Order 1995 and articles 1, 2(a) and 4 shall come into force on 15th December 1995 and articles 2(b) and 3 shall come into force on 1st January 1996.
(2) In this Order:

— "the Act" means the Copyright, Designs and Patents Act 1988.

A3.46 2. The countries specified in:

(a) Part 1, and
(b) subject to article 3 below, Part 2,

of the Schedule to this Order are designated as enjoying reciprocal protection under Part II of the Copyright, Designs and Patents Act 1988 (rights in performances).

A3.47 3. In the application of Part II of the Act by virtue of article 2(b) above in relation to those countries specified in Part 2 of the Schedule to this Order, that Part shall apply only to the extent that it confers rights on a performer in respect of:

(a) the making of:

(i)   a sound recording directly from a live performance of his;
(ii) a copy of that sound recording; and

---

[1] 1988, c. 48.

300

(b) the broadcast live, or the inclusion live in a cable programme service, of a performance of his.

4. The Performances (Reciprocal Protection) (Convention Countries) Order 1994[2] is hereby revoked.　　　　A3.48

SCHEDULE (ARTICLE 2)

PART 1

(Article 2(a))

A3.49

Argentina	Hungary
Australia	Iceland
Austria	Ireland, Republic of
Barbados	Italy
Bolivia	Jamaica
Brazil	Japan
Bulgaria	Lesotho
Burkina Faso	Luxembourg
Chile	Mexico
Colombia	Moldova
Congo	Monaco
Costa Rica	Netherlands
Czech Republic	Niger
Denmark (including Greenland and	
the Faeroe Islands)	Nigeria
Dominican Republic	Norway
Ecuador	Panama
El Salvador	Paraguay
Fiji	Peru
Finland	Philippines
France (including all Overseas	
Departments and Territories)	Slovak Republic
Germany	Spain
Greece	Sweden
Guatemala	Switzerland
Honduras	Uruguay

PART 2

(Articles 2(b) and 3)

A3.50

Antigua and Barbuda	Malta
Bahrain	Mauritania
Bangladesh	Mauritius
Belgium	Morocco
Belize	Mozambique
Botswana	Myanmar
Brunei Darussalam	Namibia
Burundi	New Zealand
Canada	Nicaragua

---

[2] S.I. 1994 No. 264.

Central African Republic
Côte D'Ivoire
Cuba
Cyprus
Djibouti
Dominica
Egypt
Gabon
Ghana
Guinea
Guinea-Bissau
Guyana
Hong Kong
India
Indonesia
Israel
Kenya
Korea, Republic of
Kuwait
Liechtenstein
Macau
Malawi
Malaysia
Maldives
Mali

Pakistan
Poland
Portugal
Romania
Saint Lucia
Saint Vincent and the Grenadines
Senegal
Sierra Leone
Singapore
Slovenia
South Africa
Sri Lanka
Suriname
Swaziland
Tanzania
Thailand
Togo
Trinidad and Tobago
Tunisia
Turkey
Uganda
United States
Venezuela
Zambia
Zimbabwe

APPENDIX 3D

The Duration of Copyright and Rights in Performances Regulations 1995

(S.I. 1995 No. 3297)

Made ....*19th December 1995*

Coming into force ....*1st January 1996*

PART I: INTRODUCTORY PROVISIONS

1. Citation, commencement and extent
2. Interpretation
3. Implementation of Directive, etc.
4. Scheme of the regulations

PART II: AMENDMENTS OF THE COPYRIGHT, DESIGNS AND PATENTS ACT 1988

Rights in performances

10. Duration of rights in performances

Supplementary

11. Meaning of EEA national and EEA state

PART III: SAVINGS AND TRANSITIONAL PROVISIONS

Introductory

12. Introductory

Rights in performances

27. Rights in performances: interpretation
28. Duration of rights in performances: general saving
29. Duration of rights in performances: application of new provisions
30. Extended and revived performance rights
31. Entitlement to extended or revived performance rights
32. Extended performance rights: existing consents, agreement, etc.
33. Revived performance rights: saving for acts of exploitation when performance in public domain, etc.
34. Revived performance rights: use as of right subject to reasonable remuneration
35. Revived performance rights: application to Copyright Tribunal

Supplementary

36. Construction of references to EEA states

PART I: INTRODUCTORY PROVISIONS

Citation, commencement and extent

A3.51   1.(1) These Regulations may be cited at the Duration of Copyright and Rights in Performances Regulations 1995.
(2) These Regulations come into force on 1st January 1996.
(3) These Regulations extend to the whole of the United Kingdom.

Interpretation

A3.52   2. In these Regulations:

— "EEA Agreement" means the Agreement on the European Economic Area signed at Oporto on 2nd May 1992,[1] as adjusted by the Protocol signed at Brussels on 17th March 1993[2]; and
— "EEA state" means a state which is a contracting party to the EEA Agreement.

Implementation of Directive, etc.

A3.53   3. These Regulations make provision for the purpose of implementing:

(a) the main provisions of Council Directive No. 93/98/EEC of 29th October 1993[3] harmonizing the term of protection of copyright and certain related rights; and
(b) certain obligations of the United Kingdom created by or arising under the EEA Agreement so far as relevant to the implementation of that Directive.

Scheme of the regulations

A3.54   4. The Copyright, Designs and Patents Act 1988[4] is amended in accordance with the provisions of Part II of these Regulations, subject to the savings and transitional provisions in Part III of these Regulations.

PART II: AMENDMENTS OF THE COPYRIGHT, DESIGNS AND PATENTS ACT 1988

Rights in performances

Duration of rights in performances

A3.55   10. In Part II (rights in performances), for section 191 (duration of rights) substitute:

"Duration of rights

191.(1) The following provisions have effect with respect to the duration of the rights conferred by this Part.
(2) The rights conferred by this Part in relation to a performance expire:

(a) at the end of the period of 50 years from the end of the calendar year in which the performance takes place, or
(b) if during that period a recording of the performance is released, 50 years from the end of the calendar year in which it is released,

subject as follows.

---

[1] Cm. 2073.
[2] Cm. 2183.
[3] [1993] O.J. L290/9.
[4] 1988, c. 48.

(3) For the purposes of subsection (2) a recording is "released" when it is first published, played or shown in public, broadcast or included in a cable programme service; but in determining whether a recording has been released no account shall be taken of any unauthorised act.

(4) Where a performer is not a national of an EEA state, the duration of the rights conferred by this Part in relation to his performance is that to which the performance is entitled in the country of which he is a national, provided that does not exceed the period which would apply under subsections (2) and (3).

(5) If or to the extent that the application of subsection (4) would be at variance with an international obligation to which the United Kingdom became subject prior to 29th October 1993, the duration of the rights conferred by this Part shall be as specified in subsections (2) and (3).".

Supplementary

Meaning of EEA national and EEA state

11.(1) In Chapter X of Part I (miscellaneous and general provisions), after section 172 insert: A3.56

"Meaning of EEA national and EEA state

172A.(1) In this Part:

— "EEA national" means a national of an EEA state; and
— "EEA state" means a state which is a contracting party to the EEA Agreement.

(2) References in this Part to a person being an EEA national shall be construed in relation to a body corporate as references to its being incorporated under the law of an EEA state.

(3) The "EEA Agreement" means the Agreement on the European Economic Area signed at Oporto on 2nd May 1992, as adjusted by the Protocol signed at Brussels on 17th March 1993.".

(2) In section 179 (index of defined expressions: Part I), at the appropriate place insert:

"EEA national and EEA state   section 172A".

(3) In section 211(1) (expressions in Part II having same meaning as in Part I), at the appropriate place insert:

"EEA national".

(4) In section 212 (index of defined expressions: Part II), at the appropriate place insert:

"EEA national   section 211(1) (and section 172A)".

PART III: SAVINGS AND TRANSITIONAL PROVISIONS

Introductory

Introductory

12.(1) References in this Part to "commencement", without more, are to the date on which these Regulations come into force.   A3.57

(2) In this Part:

— "the 1988 Act" means the Copyright, Designs and Patents Act 1988[5];
— "the 1988 provisions" means the provisions of that Act as they stood

---

[5] 1988, c. 48.

immediately before commencement (including the provisions of Schedule 1 to that Act continuing the effect of earlier enactments); and
— "the new provisions" means the provisions of that Act as amended by these Regulations.

(3) Expressions used in this Part which are defined for the purposes of Part I or II of the 1988 Act, in particular references to the copyright owner, have the same meaning as in that Part.

Rights in performances

Rights in performances: interpretation

A3.58   27.(1) In the provisions of this Part relating to rights in performances:

(a) "existing", in relation to a performance, means given before commencement; and
(b) "existing protected performance" means a performance in relation to which rights under Part II of the 1988 act (rights in performances) subsisted immediately before commencement.

(2) References in this Part to performers' rights are to the rights given by section 180(1)(a) of the 1988 Act and references to recording rights are to the rights given by section 180(1)(b) of that Act.

Duration of rights in performances: general saving

A3.59   28. Any rights under Part II of the 1988 Act in an existing protected performance shall continue to subsist until the date on which they would have expired under the 1988 provisions if that date is later than the date on which the rights would expire under the new provisions.

Duration of rights in performances: application of new provisions

A3.60   29. The new provisions relating to the duration of rights under Part II of the 1988 Act apply:

(a) to performances taking place after commencement;
(b) to existing performances which first qualify for protection under Part II of the 1988 Act after commencement;
(c) to existing protected performances, subject to Regulation 28 (general saving for any longer period applicable under 1988 provisions); and
(d) to existing performances:

    (i)   in which rights under Part II of the 1988 Act expired after the commencement of that Part and before 31st December 1995, or
    (ii)   which were protected by earlier enactments relating to the protection of performers and in which rights under that Part did not arise by reason only that the performance was given at a date such that the rights would have ceased to subsist before the commencement of that Part,

but which were on 1st July 1995 protected in another EEA state under legislation relating to copyright or related rights.

Extended and revived performance rights

A3.61   30. In the following provisions of this Part:

— "extended performance rights" means rights under Part II of the 1988 Act which subsist by virtue of the new provisions after the date on which they would have expired under the 1988 provisions; and

— "revived performance rights" means rights under Part II of the 1988 Act which subsist by virtue of the new provisions:

(a) after having expired under the 1988 provisions, or
(b) in relation to a performance which was protected by earlier enactments relating to the protection of performers and in which rights under that Part did not arise by reason only that the performance was given at a date such that the rights would have ceased to subsist before the commencement of that Part.

References in the following provisions of this Part to "revived pre-1988 rights" are to revived performance rights within paragraph (b) of the above definition.

Entitlement to extended or revived performance rights

31.(1) Any extended performance rights are exercisable as from commencement by the person who was entitled to exercise those rights immediately before commencement, that is: **A3.62**

(a) in the case of performers' rights, the performer or (if he has died) the person entitled by virtue of section 192(2) of the 1988 Act to exercise those rights:
(b) in the case of recording rights, the person who was within the meaning of section 185 of the 1988 Act the person having those rights.

(2) Any revived performance rights are exercisable as from commencement:

(a) in the case of rights which expired after the commencement of the 1988 Act, by the person who was entitled to exercise those rights immediately before they expired;
(b) in the case of revived pre-1988 performers' rights, by the performer or his personal representatives;
(c) in the case of revived pre-1988 recording rights, by the person who would have been the person having those rights immediately before the commencement of the 1988 Act or, if earlier, immediately before the death of the performer, applying the provisions of section 185 of that Act to the circumstances then obtaining.

(3) Any remuneration or damages received by a person's personal representatives by virtue of a right conferred on them by paragraph (1) or (2) shall devolve as part of that person's estate as if the right had subsisted and been vested in him immediately before his death.

Extended performance rights: existing consents, agreement, etc.

32. Any consent, or any term or condition of an agreement, relating to the exploitation of an existing protected performance which: **A3.63**

(a) subsists immediately before commencement, and
(b) is not to expire before the end of the period for which rights under Part II of the 1988 Act subsist in relation to that performance,

shall continue to subsist during the period of any extended performance rights, subject to any agreement to the contrary.

Revived performance rights: saving for acts of exploitation when performance in public domain, etc.

33.(1) No act done before commencement shall be regarded as infringing revived performance rights in a performance. **A3.64**
(2) It is not an infringement of revived performance rights in a performance:

(a) to do anything after commencement in pursuance of arrangements made before 1st January 1995 at a time when the performance was not protected, or

(b) to issue to the public after commencement a recording of a performance made before 1st July 1995 at a time when the performance was not protected.

(3) It is not an infringement of revived performance rights in a performance to do anything after commencement in relation to a sound recording or film made before commencement, or made in pursuance of arrangements made before commencement, which contains a recording of the performance if:

(a) the recording of the performance was made before 1st July 1995 at a time when the performance was not protected, or

(b) the recording of the performance was made in pursuance of arrangements made before 1st July 1995 at a time when the performance was not protected.

(4) It is not an infringement of revived performance rights in a performance to do after commencement anything at a time when, or in pursuance of arrangements made at a time when, the name and address of a person entitled to authorise the act cannot by reasonable inquiry be ascertained.

(5) In this Regulation "arrangements" means arrangements for the exploitation of the performance in question.

(6) References in this Regulation to a performance being protected are:

(a) in relation to the period after the commencement of the 1988 Act, to rights under Part II of that Act subsisting in relation to the performance, and

(b) in relation to earlier periods, to the consent of the performer being required under earlier enactments relating to the protection of performers.

Revived performance rights: use as of right subject to reasonable remuneration

A3.65   34.(1) In the case of a performance in which revived performance rights subsist any acts which require the consent of any person under Part II of the 1988 Act (the "rights owner") shall be treated as having that consent, subject only to the payment of such reasonable remuneration as may be agreed or determined in default of agreement by the Copyright Tribunal.

(2) A person intending to avail himself of the right conferred by this Regulation must give reasonable notice of his intention to the rights owner, stating when he intends to begin to do the acts.

(3) If he does not give such notice, his acts shall not be treated as having consent.

(4) If he does give such notice, his acts shall be treated as having consent and reasonable remuneration shall be payable in respect of them despite the fact that its amount is not agreed or determined until later.

Revived performance rights: application to Copyright Tribunal

A3.66   35.(1) An application to settle the remuneration payable in pursuance of Regulation 34 may be made to the Copyright Tribunal by the rights owner or the person claiming to be treated as having his consent.

(2) The Tribunal shall consider the matter and make such order as it may determine to be reasonable in the circumstances.

(3) Either party may subsequently apply to the Tribunal to vary the order, and the Tribunal shall consider the matter and make such order confirming or varying the original order as it may determine to be reasonable in the circumstances.

(4) An application under paragraph (3) shall not, except with the special leave of the Tribunal, be made within twelve months from the date of the original order or of the order on a previous application under that paragraph.

(5) An order under paragraph (3) has effect from the date on which it is made or such later date as may be specified by the Tribunal.

Supplementary

Construction of references to EEA states

36.(1) For the purpose of the new provisions relating to the term of copyright protection applicable to a work of which the country of origin is not an EEA state and of which the author is not a naitonal of an EEA state:

A3.67

(a) a work first published before 1st July 1995 shall be treated as published in an EEA state if it was on that date regarded under the law of the United Kingdom or another EEA state as having been published in that state;

(b) an unpublished film made before 1st July 1995 shall be treated as originating in an EEA state if it was on that date regarded under the law of the United Kingdom or another EEA state as a film whose maker had his headquarters in, or was domiciled or resident in, that state; and

(c) the author of a work made before 1st July 1995 shall be treated as an EEA national if he was on that date regarded under the law of the United Kingdom or another EEA state as a national of that state.

The references above to the law of another EEA state are to the law of that state having effect for the purposes of rights corresponding to those provided for in Part I of the 1988 Act.

(2) For the purposes of the new provisions relating to the term of protection applicable to a performance where the performer is not a national of an EEA state, the performer of a performance given before 1st July 1995 shall be treated as an EEA national if he was on that date regarded under the law of the United Kingdom or another EEA state as a national of that state.

The reference above to the law of another EEA state is to the law of that state having effect for the purposes of rights corresponding to those provided for in Part II of the 1988 Act.

(3) In this Regulation "another EEA state" means an EEA state other than the United Kingdom.

APPENDIX 3E

The Copyright and Related Rights Regulations 1996

(S.I. 1996 No. 2967)

Made...*26th November 1996*

Coming into force ....*1st December 1996*

PART I: INTRODUCTORY PROVISIONS

PART II: AMENDMENTS OF THE COPYRIGHT, DESIGNS AND PATENTS ACT 1988

Satellite broadcasts and cable re-transmission

Distribution right

Rental and lending right

Publication right

Authorship of films and certain photographs

Performers' rights

Whereas a draft of the following Regulations has been approved by resolution of each House of Parliament:

Now, therefore, the Secretary of State, being a Minister designated[1] for the purposes of section 2(2) of the European Communities Act 1972[2] in relation to measures relating to the protection of copyright and rights in performances, in exercise of powers conferred by section 2(2) and (4) of the said Act of 1972, hereby makes the following Regulations:

PART I: INTRODUCTORY PROVISIONS

Citation, commencement and extent

1.(1) These Regulations may be cited as the Copyright and Related Rights Regulations 1996.   **A3.68**

(2) These Regulations come into force on 1st December 1996.

(3) These Regulations extend to the whole of the United Kingdom.

---

[1] S.I. 1993 No. 595.

[2] 1972, c. 68; by virtue of the amendement of section 1(2) of that Act by section 1 of the European Economic Area Act 1993 (c. 51) regulations may be made under section 2(2) to implement obligations of the United Kingdom arising under the EEA Agreement.

Interpretation

A3.69 2. In these Regulations:

— "EEA Agreement" means the Agreement on the European Economic Area signed at Oporto on 2nd May 1992,[3] as adjusted by the Protocol signed at Brussels on 17th March 1993[4]; and
— "EEA state" means a state which is a contracting party to the EEA Agreement.

Implementation of Directives, etc.

A3.70 3. These Regulations make provision for the purpose of implementing:

(a) Council Directive No. 92/100/EEC of 19 November 1992[5] on rental right and lending right and on certain rights related to copyright in the field of intellectual property;
(b) Council Directive No. 93/83/EEC of 27 September 1993[6] on the coordination of certain rules concerning copyright and rights related to copyright applicable to satellite broadcasting and cable retransmission;
(c) the provisions of Council Directive No. 93/98/EEC of 29 October 1993[7] harmonizing the term of protection of copyright and certain related rights, so far as not implemented by the Duration of Copyright and Rights in Performances Regulations 1995[8]; and
(d) certain obligations of the United Kingdom created by or arising under the EEA Agreement so far as relevant to the implementation of those Directives.

Scheme of the regulations

A3.71 4. The Copyright, Designs, and Patents Act 1988[9] is amended in accordance with the provisions of Part II of these Regulations, subject to the savings and transitional provisions in Part III of these Regulations.

PART II: AMENDMENTS OF THE COPYRIGHT, DESIGNS AND PATENTS ACT 1988

Satellite broadcasts and cable re-transmission

Place where broadcast treated as made

A3.72 5. For section 6(4) (broadcasts: place where regarded as made) substitute:

"(4) For the purposes of this Part, the place from which a broadcast is made is the place where, under the control and responsibility of the person making the broadcast, the programme-carrying signals are introduced into an uninterrupted chain of communication (including, in the case of a satellite transmission, the chain leading to the satellite and down towards the earth).".

---

[3] Cm. 2073.
[4] Cm. 2183.
[5] [1992] O.J. L346/61.
[6] [1993] O.J. L248/15.
[7] [1993] O.J. L290/9.
[8] S.I. 1995 No. 3297.
[9] 1988, c. 48.

Safeguards in relation to certain satellite broadcasts

6.(1) In section 6 (broadcasts), after subsection (4) insert: A3.73

"(4A) Subsections (3) and (4) have effect subject to section 6A (safeguards in case of certain satellite broadcasts)."

(2) After that section insert:

"Safeguards in case of certain satellite broadcasts

6A.(1) This section applies where the place from which a broadcast by way of satellite transmission is made is located in a country rather than an EEA state and the law of that country fails to provide at least the following level of protection:

 (a) exclusive rights in relation to broadcasting equivalent to those conferred by section 20 (infringement by broadcasting) on the authors of literary, dramatic, musical and artistic works, films and broadcasts;
 (b) a right in relation to live broadcasting equivalent to that conferred on a performer by section 182(1)(b) (consent required for live broadcast of performance); and
 (c) a right for authors of sound recordings and performers to share in a single equitable remuneration in respect of the broadcasting of sound recordings.

(2) Where the place from which the programme-carrying signals are transmitted to the satellite ("the uplink station") is located in an EEA state:

 (a) that place shall be treated as the place from which the broadcast is made, and
 (b) the person operating the uplink station shall be treated as the person making the broadcast.

(3) Where the uplink station is not located in an EEA state but a person who is established in an EEA state has commissioned the making of the broadcast:

 (a) that person shall be treated as the person making the broadcast, and
 (b) the place in which he has his principal establishment in the European Economic Area shall be treated as the place from which the broadcast is made.".

Exercise of rights in relation to cable re-transmission

7. In Chapter VII of Part I (provisions as to copyright licensing), after section 144   A3.74
insert:

"Compulsory collective administration of certain rights

Collective exercise of certain rights in relation to cable re-transmission

144A.(1) This section applies to the right of the owner of copyright in a literary, dramatic, musical or artistic work, sound recording or film to grant or refuse authorisation for cable re-transmission of a broadcast from another EEA member state in which the work is included.
 That right is referred to below as "cable re-transmission right".
 (2) Cable re-transmission right may be exercised against a cable operator only through a licensing body.
 (3) Where a copyright owner has not transferred management of his cable re-transmission right to a licensing body, the licensing body which manages rights of the same category shall be deemed to be mandated to manage his right.
 Where more than one licensing body manages rights of that category, he may choose which of them is deemed to be mandated to manage his right.
 (4) A copyright owner to whom subsection (3) applies has the same rights and

obligations resulting from any relevant agreement between the cable operator and the licensing body as have copyright owners who have transferred management of their cable re-transmission right to that licensing body.

(5) Any rights to which a copyright owner may be entitled by virtue of subsection (4) must be claimed within the period of three years beginning with the date of the cable re-transmission concerned.

(6) This section does not affect any rights exercisable by the maker of the broadcast, whether in relation to the broadcast or a work included in it.

(7) In this section:

— "cable operator" means a person providing a cable programme service; and
— "cable re-transmission" means the reception and immediate re-transmission by way of a cable programme service of a broadcast.".

Meaning of wireless telegraphy

A3.75   8. In section 178 (minor definitions), in the definition of "wireless telegraphy" at the end insert, "but does not include the transmission of microwave energy between terrestrial fixed points".

Distribution right

Issue of copies of work to the public: extension of right

A3.76   9.(1) Section 18 (infringement of copyright by issue of copies of work to public) is amended as follows.

(2) For subsections (2) and (3) (meaning of issue of copies to the public) substitute:

"(2) References in this Part to the issue to the public of copies of a work are to:

(a) the act of putting into circulation in the EEA copies not previously put into circulation in the EEA by or with the consent of the copyright owner, or
(b) the act of putting into circulation outside the EEA copies not previously put into circulation in the EEA or elsewhere.

(3) References in this Part to the issue to the public of copies of a work do not include:

(a) any subsequent distribution, sale, hiring or loan of copies previously put into circulation (but see section 18A: infringement by rental or lending), or
(b) any subsequent importation of such copies into the United Kingdom or another EEA state,

except so far as paragraph (a) of subsection (2) applies to putting into circulation in the EEA copies previously put into circulation outside the EEA.".

(3) After subsection (3) add:

"(4) References in this Part to the issue of copies of a work include the issue of the original.".

(4) In consequence of the above amendments, in section 27 (meaning of "infringing copy") omit subsection (3A) and the words "Subject to subsection (3A)," in subsection (3).

(5) In section 172A (meaning of EEA national and EEA state), for the side-note and subsection (1) substitute:

"Meaning of EEA and related expressions

172A.(1) In this Part:

— "the EEA" means the European Economic Area;
— "EEA national" means a national of an EEA state; and

314

— "EEA state" means a state which is a contracting party to the EEA Agreement.".

(6) In section 179 (index of defined expressions):

(a) in the first column of the entry relating to the expressions "EEA national" and "EEA state", at the beginning insert "EEA,", and

(b) in the second column of the entry relating to the expression "issue of copies to the public" for "section 18(2)" substitute "section 18".

Rental and lending right

Rental or lending of copyright work

10.(1) In section 16 (the acts restricted by copyright in a work), in subsection (1), after paragraph (b) insert: **A3.77**

"(ba) to rent or lend the work to the public (see section 18A);".

(2) After section 18 (infringement of copyright by issue of copies of work), insert:

"Infringement by rental or lending of work to the public

18A.(1) The rental or lending of copies of the work to the public is an act restricted by the copyright in:

(a) a literary, dramatic or musical work,

(b) an artistic work, other than:

  (i)   a work of architecture in the form of a building or a model for a building, or

  (ii) a work of applied art, or

(c) a film or a sound recording.

(2) In this Part, subject to the following provisions of this section:

(a) "rental" means making a copy of the work available for use, on terms that it will or may be returned, for direct or indirect economic or commercial advantage, and

(b) "lending" means making a copy of the work available for use, on terms that it will or may be returned, otherwise than for direct or indirect economic or commercial advantage, through an establishment which is accessible to the public.

(3) The expressions "rental" and "lending" do not include:

(a) making available for the purpose of public performance, playing or showing in public, broadcasting or inclusion in a cable programme service;

(b) making available for the purpose of exhibition in public; or

(c) making available for on-the-spot reference use.

(4) The expression "lending" does not include making available between establishments which are accessible to the public.

(5) Where lending by an establishment accessible to the public gives rise to a payment the amount of which does not go beyond what is necessary to cover the operating costs of the establishment, there is no direct or indirect economic or commercial advantage for the purposes of this section.

(6) References in this Part to the rental or lending of copies of a work include the rental or lending of the original.".

(3) In section 178 (minor definitions), at the appropriate place insert:

" "rental right" means the right of a copyright owner to authorise or prohibit the rental of copies of the work (see section 18A);", and omit the definition of "rental".

(4) In section 179 (index of defined expressions), in the entry relating to the expression "rental" for "section 178" substitute "section 18A(2) to (6)", and at the appropriate places insert:

"lending   section 18A(2) to (6)"

"rental right   section 178".

Permitted lending of copyright works

A3.78   **11.**(1) In Chapter III of Part I (acts permitted in relation to copyright works), in the sections relating to education, after section 36 insert:

"Lending of copies by educational establishments

36A. Copyright in a work is not infringed by the lending of copies of the work by an educational establishment.".

(2) In the same Chapter, in the sections relating to libraries and archives, after section 40 insert:

"Lending of copies by libraries or archives.

40A.(1) Copyright in a work of any description is not infringed by the lending of a book by a public library if the book is within the public lending right scheme.
     For this purpose:

(a) "the public lending right scheme" means the scheme in force under section 1 of the Public Lending Right Act 1979, and

(b) a book is within the public lending right scheme if it is a book within the meaning of the provisions of the scheme relating to eligibility, whether or not it is in fact eligible.

(2) Copyright in a work is not infringed by the lending of copies of the work by a prescribed library or archive (other than a public library) which is not conducted for profit."

(3) In the same Chapter for section 66 (rental of sound recordings, films and computer programs), and the heading preceding it, substitute:

"Miscellaneous: lending of works and playing of sound recordings

Lending to public of copies of certain works

66.(1) The Secretary of State may by order provide that in such cases as may be specified in the order the lending to the public of copies of literary, dramatic, musical or artistic works, sound recordings or films shall be treated as licensed by the copyright owner subject only to the payment of such reasonable royalty or other payment as may be agreed or determined in default of agreement by the Copyright Tribunal.

(2) No such order shall apply if, or to the extent that, there is a licensing scheme certified for the purposes of this section under section 143 providing for the grant of licences.

(3) An order may make different provision for different cases and may specify cases by reference to any factor relating to the work, the copies lent, the lender or the circumstances of the lending.

(4) An order shall be made by statutory instrument; and no order shall be made unless a draft of it has been laid before and approved by a resolution of each House of Parliament.

(5) Nothing in this section affects any liability under section 23 (secondary

infringement: possessing or dealing with infringing copy) in respect of the lending of infringing copies.".

(4) In section 143(1) (certification of licensing schemes: relevant provisions), for paragraph (c) substitute:

"(c) section 66 (lending to public of copies of certain works),".

(5) In section 178 (minor definitions), insert at the appropriate place:

" "public library" means a library administered by or on behalf of:

(a) in England and Wales, a library authority within the meaning of the Public Libraries and Museums Act 1964;
(b) in Scotland, a statutory library authority within the meaning of the Public Libraries (Scotland) Act 1955;
(c) in Northern Ireland, an Education and Library Board within the meaning of the Education and Libraries (Northern Ireland) Order 1986;".

(6) In section 179 (index of defined expressions), at the appropriate place insert:

"public library   section 178".

(7) The following provisions (which relate to lending by public libraries) are repealed:
— section 4(2) of the Public Libraries (Scotland) Act 1955[10],
— section 8(6) of the Public Libraries and Museums Act 1964[11],
— Article 77(3) of the Education and Libraries (Northern Ireland) Order 1986[12]
— paragraphs 6, 8 and 34 of Schedule 7 to the Copyright, Designs and Patents Act 1988[13] (which insert the above provisions).

Presumption of transfer of rental right in case of film production agreement

12. In Chapter V of Part I (dealings with rights in copyright works), after section 93 insert: A3.79

"Presumption of transfer of rental right in case of film production agreement

93A.(1) Where an agreement concerning film production is concluded between an author and a film producer, the author shall be presumed, unless the agreement provides to the contrary, to have transferred to the film producer any rental right in relation to the film arising by virtue of the inclusion of a copy of the author's work in the film.

(2) In this section "author" means an author, or prospective author, of a literary, dramatic, musical or artistic work.

(3) Subsection (1) does not apply to any rental right in relation to the film arising by virtue of the inclusion in the film of the screenplay, the dialogue or music specifically created for and used in the film.

(4) Where this section applies, the absence of signature by or on behalf of the author does not exclude the operation of section 91(1) (effect of purported assignment of future copyright).

(5) The reference in subsection (1) to an agreement concluded between an author and a film producer includes any agreement having effect between those persons, whether made by them directly or through intermediaries.

(6) Section 93B (right to equitable remuneration on transfer of rental right) applies where there is a presumed transfer by virtue of this section as in the case of an actual transfer.".

---

[10] 1955, c. 27.
[11] 1964, c. 75.
[12] S.I. 1986 No. 594 (N.I. 3).
[13] 1988, c. 48.

Rental and lending: applications to Copyright Tribunal

A3.80　13.(1) In section 133 (licences to reflect payments in respect of underlying rights), for subsection (1) (considerations relevant to rental of certain works) substitute:

　　"(1) In considering what charges should be paid for a licence:

　　(a) on a reference or application under this Chapter relating to licences for the rental or lending of copies of a work, or

　　(b) on an application under section 142 (royalty or other sum payable for lending of certain works),

the Copyright Tribunal shall take into account any reasonable payments which the owner of the copyright in the work is liable to make in consequence of the granting of the licence, or of the acts authorised by the licence, to owners of copyright in works included in that work.".

(2) For section 142 (royalty or other sum payable for rental of sound recording, film or computer program), and the heading preceding it, substitute:

"Royalty or other sum payable for lending of certain works

Royalty or other sum payable for lending of certain works

142.(1) An application to settle the royalty or other sum payable in pursuance of section 66 (lending of copies of certain copyright works) may be made to the Copyright Tribunal by the copyright owner or the person claiming to be treated as licensed by him.

(2) The Tribunal shall consider the matter and make such order as it may determine to be reasonable in the circumstances.

(3) Either party may subsequently apply to the Tribunal to vary the order, and the Tribunal shall consider the matter and make such order confirming or varying the original order as it may determine to be reasonable in the circumstances.

(4) An application under subsection (3) shall not, except with the special leave of the Tribunal, be made within twelve months from the date of the original order or of the order on a previous application under that subsection.

(5) An order under subsection (3) has effect from the date on which it is made or such later date as may be specified by the Tribunal.".

(3) In section 149 (jurisdiction of the Copyright Tribunal), in paragraph (e) for "rental of sound recording, film or computer program" substitute "lending of certain works".

Right to equitable remuneration where rental right transferred

A3.81　14.(1) In Chapter V of Part I (dealings with rights in copyright works), after section 93A (inserted by regulation 12) insert:

"Right to equitable remuneration where rental right transferred

"Right to equitable remuneration where rental right transferred

93B.(1) Where an author to whom this section applies has transferred his rental right concerning a sound recording or a film to the producer of the sound recording or film, he retains the right to equitable remuneration for the rental.

The authors to whom this section applies are:

　　(a) the author of a literary, dramatic, musical or artistic work, and

　　(b) the principal director of a film.

(2) The right to equitable remuneration under this section may not be assigned by

the author except to a collecting society for the purpose of enabling it to enforce the right on his behalf.

The right is, however, transmissible by testamentary disposition or by operation of law as personal or moveable property; and it may be assigned or further transmitted by any person into whose hands it passes.

(3) Equitable remuneration under this section is payable by the person for the time being entitled to the rental right, that is, the person to whom the right was transferred or any successor in title of his.

(4) The amount payable by way of equitable remuneration is as agreed by or on behalf of the persons by and to whom it is payable, subject to section 93C (reference of amount to Copyright Tribunal).

(5) An agreement is of no effect in so far as it purports to exclude or restrict the right to equitable remuneration under this section.

(6) References in this section to the transfer of rental right by one person to another include any arrangement having that effect, whether made by them directly or through intermediaries.

(7) In this section a "collecting society" means a society or other organisation which has as its main object, or one of its main objects, the exercise of the right to equitable remuneration under this section on behalf of more than one author.

Equitable remuneration: reference of amount to Copyright Tribunal

93C.(1) In default of agreement as to the amount payable by way of equitable remuneration under section 93B, the person by or to whom it is payable may apply to the Copyright Tribunal to determine the amount payable.

(2) A person to or by whom equitable remuneration is payable under that section may also apply to the Copyright Tribunal:

(a) to vary any agreement as to the amount payable, or
(b) to vary any previous determination of the Tribunal as to that matter;

but except with the special leave of the Tribunal no such application may be made within twelve months from the date of a previous determination.

An order made on an application under this subsection has effect from the date on which it is made or such later date as may be specified by the Tribunal.

(3) On an application under this section the Tribunal shall consider the matter and make such order as to the method of calculating and paying equitable remuneration as it may determine to be reasonable in the circumstances, taking into account the importance of the contribution of the author to the film or sound recording.

(4) Remuneration shall not be considered inequitable merely because it was paid by way of a single payment or at the time of the transfer of the rental right.

(5) An agreement is of no effect in so far as it purports to prevent a person questioning the amount of equitable remuneration or to restrict the powers of the Copyright Tribunal under this section.".

(2) In section 149 (jurisdiction of the Copyright Tribunal), before paragraph (a) insert:

"(zb) section 93C (application to determine amount of equitable remuneration under section 93B);".

Consequential modification of provisions relating to licensing

15.(1) Chapter VII of Part I (copyright licensing) is amended as follows.   A3.82

(2) For section 117 (licensing schemes about which references and applications may be made) substitute:

"Licensing schemes to which following sections apply

117. Sections 118 to 123 (references and applications with respect to licensing schemes) apply to licensing schemes which are operated by licensing bodies and cover works of more than one author, so far as they relate to licences for:

(a) copying the work,
(b) rental or lending of copies of the work to the public,
(c) performing, showing or playing the work in public, or
(d) broadcasting the work or including it in a cable programme service;

and references in those sections to a licensing scheme shall be construed accordingly.".

(3) For section 124 (licences about which references and applications may be made) substitute:

"Licences to which following sections apply

124. Sections 125 to 128 (references and applications with respect to licensing by licensing bodies) apply to licences which are granted by a licensing body otherwise than in pursuance of a licensing scheme and cover works of more than one author, so far as they authorise:

(a) copying the work,
(b) rental or lending of copies of the work to the public,
(c) performing, showing or playing the work in public, or
(d) broadcasting the work or including it in a cable programme service;

and references in those sections to a licence shall be construed accordingly.".

Publication right

Publication right

A3.83   **16.**(1) A person who after the expiry of copyright protection, publishes for the first time a previously unpublished work has, in accordance with the following provisions, a property right ("publication right") equivalent to copyright.
(2) For this purpose publication includes any communication to the public, in particular:

(a) the issue of copies to the public;
(b) making the work available by means of an electronic retrieval system;
(c) the rental or lending of copies of the work to the public;
(d) the performance, exhibition or showing of the work in public; or
(e) broadcasting the work or including it in a cable programme service.

(3) No account shall be taken for this purpose of any unauthorised act.
In relation to a time when there is no copyright in the work, an unauthorised act means an act done without the consent of the owner of the physical medium in which the work is embodied or on which it is recorded.
(4) A work qualifies for publication right protection only if:

(a) first publication is in the European Economic Area, and
(b) the publisher of the work is at the time of first publication a national of an EEA state.

Where two or more persons jointly publish the work, it is sufficient for the purposes of paragraph (b) if any of them is a national of an EEA state.
(5) No publication right arises from the publication of a work in which Crown copyright or Parliamentary copyright subsisted.

(6) Publication right expires at the end of the period of 25 years from the end of the calendar year in which the work was first published.

(7) In this regulation a "work" means a literary, dramatic, musical or artistic work or a film.

(8) Expressions used in this regulation (other than "publication") have the same meaning as in Part I.

Application of copyright provisions to publication right

17.(1) The substantive provisions of Part I relating to copyright (but not moral rights in copyright works), that is, the relevant provisions of: A3.84

— Chapter II (rights of copyright owner),
— Chapter III (acts permitted in relation to copyright works),
— Chapter V (dealings with rights in copyright works),
— Chapter VI (remedies for infringement), and
— Chapter VII (copyright licensing),

apply in relation to publication right as in relation to copyright, subject to the following exceptions and modifications.

(2) The following provisions do not apply:

(a) in Chapter III (acts permitted in relation to copyright works), sections 57, 64, 66A and 67;
(b) in Chapter VI (remedies for infringement), sections 104 to 106;
(c) in Chapter VII (copyright licensing), section 116(4).

(3) The following provisions have effect with the modifications indicated:

(a) in section 107(4) and (5) (offences of making or dealing in infringing articles, etc.), the maximum punishment on summary conviction is imprisonment for a term not exceeding three months or a fine not exceeding level 5 on the standard scale, or both;
(b) in sections 116(2), 117 and 124 for "works of more than one author" substitute "works of more than one publisher".

(4) The other relevant provisions of Part I, that is:

— in Chapter I, provisions defining expressions used generally in Part I,
— Chapter VIII (the Copyright Tribunal),
— in Chapter IX:

    section 161 (territorial waters and the continental shelf), and
    section 162 (British ships, aircraft and hovercraft), and

— in Chapter X:

    section 171(1) and (3) (savings for other rules of law, etc.), and
    sections 172 to 179 (general interpretation provisions),

apply, with any necessary adaptations, for the purposes of supplementing the substantive provisions of that Part as applied by this regulation.

(5) Except where the context otherwise requires, any other enactment relating to copyright (whether passed or made before or after these regulations) applies in relation to publication right as in relation to copyright.

In this paragraph "enactment" includes an enactment contained in subordinate legislation within the meaning of the Interpretation Act 1978[14].

---

[14] 1978, c. 30.

Authorship of films and certain photographs

Authorship of films

A3.85   18.(1) In section 9(2) (person to be taken to be author of work), for paragraph (a) (sound recordings and films) substitute:

"(aa) in the case of a sound recording, the producer;
 (ab) in the case of a film, the producer and the principal director;".

(2) In section 10 (works of joint authorship), after subsection (1) insert:

"(1A) A film shall be treated as a work of joint authorship unless the producer and the principal director are the same person.".

(3) In section 11 (first ownership of copyright), in subsection (2) (work made by employee in course of employment) after "literary, dramatic, musical or artistic work" insert ", or a film,".

(4) In section 105 (presumptions relevant to sound recordings and films):

(a) in subsections (2)(a) and (5)(a) for "author or director" substitute "director or producer",
(b) in subsection (5), after paragraph (a) insert:

"(aa) that a named person was the principal director of the film, the author of the screenplay, the author of the dialogue or the composer of music specifically created for and used in the film, or,".

and

(c) after subsection (5) add:

"(6) For the purposes of this section, a statement that a person was the director of a film shall be taken, unless a contrary indication appears, as meaning that he was the principal dirctor of the film.".

(5) In section 178 (minor definitions), at the appropriate place insert:

" "producer", in relation to a sound recording or a film, means the person by whom the arrangements necessary for the making of the sound recording or film are undertaken;".

(6) In section 179 (index of defined expressions), at the appropriate place insert:

"producer (in relation to a sound recording or film) section 178".

Clarification of transitional provisions relating to pre-1989 photographs

A3.86   19. Any question arising, in relation to photographs which were existing works within the meaning of Schedule 1, as to who is to be regarded as the author for the purposes of:

(a) regulations 15 and 16 of the Duration of Copyright and Rights in Performances Regulations 1995[15] (duration of copyright: application of new provisions subject to general saving), or
(b) regulation 19(2)(b) of those regulations (ownership of revived copyright),

is to be determined in accordance with section 9 as in force on the commencement of those regulations (and not, by virtue of paragraph 10 of Schedule 1, in accordance with the law in force at the time when the work was made).

---

[15] S.I. 1995 No. 3297.

Performers' rights

Extension of performers' rights

20.(1) For section 182 (perfomers' rights: consent required for recording or live   **A3.87**
transmission of performance) substitute:

"Consent required for recording, etc. of live performance

182.(1) A performer's rights are infringed by a person who, without his consent:

- (a) makes a recording of the whole or any substantial part of a qualifying performance directly from the live performance,
- (b) broadcasts live, or includes live in a cable programme service, the whole or any substantial part of a qualifying performance,
- (c) makes a recording of the whole or any substantial part of a qualifying performance directly from a broadcast of, or cable programme including, the live performance.

(2) A performer's rights are not infringed by the making of any such recording by a person for his private and domestic use.

(3) In an action for infringement of a performer's rights brought by virtue of this section damages shall not be awarded against a defendant who shows that at the time of the infringement he believed on reasonable grounds that consent had been given.".

(2) After that section insert:

"Consent required for copying of recording

182A.(1) A performer's rights are infringed by a person who, without his consent, makes, otherwise than for his private and domestic use, a copy of a recording of the whole or any substantial part of a qualifying performance.

(2) It is immaterial whether the copy is made directly or indirectly.

(3) The right of a performer under this section to authorise or prohibit the making of such copies is referred to in this Part as "reproduction right"."

Consent required for issue of copies to public

182B.(1) A performer's rights are infringed by a person who, without his consent, issues to the public copies of a recording of the whole or any substantial part of a qualifying performance.

(2) References in this Part to the issue to the public of copies of a recording are to:

- (a) the act of putting into circulation in the EEA copies not previously put into circulation in the EEA by or with the consent of the performer, or
- (b) the act of putting into circulation outside the EEA copies not previously put into circulation in the EEA or elsewhere.

(3) References in this Part to the issue to the public of copies of a recording do not include:

- (a) any subsequent distribution, sale, hiring or loan of copies previously put into circulation (but see section 182C: consent required for rental or lending), or
- (b) any subsequent importation of such copies into the United Kingdom or another EEA state,

except so far as paragraph (a) of subsection (2) applies to putting into circulation in the EEA copies previously put into circulation outside the EEA.

(4) References in this Part to the issue of copies of a recording of a performance include the issue of the original recording of the live performance.

(5) The right of a performer under this section to authorise or prohibit the issue of copies to the public is referred to in this Part as "distribution right".

Consent required for rental or lending of copies to public

182C.(1) A performer's rights are infringed by a person who, without his consent, rents or lends to the public copies of a recording of the whole or any substantial part of a qualifying performance.

(2) In this Part, subject to the following provisions of this section:

(a) "rental" means making a copy of a recording available for use, on terms that it will or may be returned, for direct or indirect economic or commercial advantage, and

(b) "lending" means making a copy of a recording available for use, on terms that it will or may be returned, otherwise than for direct or indirect economic or commercial advantage, through an establishment which is accessible to the public.

(3) The expressions "rental" and "lending" do not include:

(a) making available for the purpose of public performance, playing or showing in public, broadcasting or inclusion in a cable programme service;

(b) making available for the purpose of exhibition in public; or

(c) making available for on-the-spot reference use.

(4) The expression "lending" does not include making available between establishment which are accessible to the public.

(5) Where lending by an establishment accessible to the public gives rise to a payment the amount of which does not go beyond what is necesary to cover the operating costs of the establishment, there is no direct or indirect economic or commercial advantage for the purposes of this section.

(6) References in this Part to the rental or lending of copies of a recording of a performance include the rental or lending of the original recording of the live performance.

(7) In this Part:

— "rental right" means the right of a performer under this section to authorise or prohibit the rental of copies to the public, and

— "lending right" means the right of a performer under this section to authorise or prohibit the lending of copies to the public.

Right to equitable remuneration for exploitation of sound recording

182D.(1) Where a commercially published sound recording of the whole or any substantial part of a qualifying performance:

(a) is played in public, or

(b) is included in a broadcast or cable programme service,

the performer is entitled to equitable remuneration from the owner of the copyright in the sound recording.

(2) The right to equitable remuneration under this section may not be assigned by the performer except to a collecting society for the purpose of enabling it to enforce the right on his behalf.

The right is, however, transmissible by testamentary disposition or by operation of law as personal or moveable property; and it may be assigned or further transmitted by any person into whose hands it passes.

(3) The amount payable by way of equitable remuneration is as agreed by or on behalf of the persons by and to whom it is payable, subject to the following provisions.

(4) In default of agreement as to the amount payable by way of equitable

remuneration, the person by or to whom it is payable may apply to the Copyright Tribunal to determine the amount payable.

(5) A person to or by whom equitable remuneration is payable may also apply to the Copyright Tribunal:

(a) to vary any agreement as to the amount payable, or

(b) to vary any previous determination of the Tribunal as to that matter;

but except with the special leave of the Tribunal no such application may be made within twelve months from the date of a previous determination.

An order made on an application under this subsection has effect from the date on which it is made or such later date as may be specified by the Tribunal.

(6) On an application under this section the Tribunal shall consider the matter and make such order as to the method of calculating and paying equitable remuneration as it may determine to be reasonable in the circumstances, taking into account the importance of the contribution of the performer to the sound recording.

(7) An agreement is of no effect in so far as it purports:

(a) to exclude or restrict the right to equitable remuneration under this section, or

(b) to prevent a person questioning the amount of equitable remuneration or to restrict the powers of the Copyright Tribunal under this section.".

(3) In Schedule 2 (rights in performances: permitted acts), after paragraph 6 insert:

"Lending of copies by educational establishments

6A.(1) The rights conferred by Part II are not infringed by the lending of copies of a recording of a performance by an educational establishment.

(2) Expressions used in this paragraph have the same meaning as in section 36A; and any provision with respect to the applciation of that section made under section 174(2) (instruction given elsewhere then an educational establishment) applies also for the purposes of this paragraph.

Lending of copies by libraries or archives

6B.(1) The rights conferred by Part II are not infringed by the lending of copies of a recording of a performance by a prescribed library or archive (other than a public library) which is not conducted for profit.

(2) Expressions used in this paragraph have the same meaning as in section 40A(2); and any provision under section 37 prescribing libraries or archives for the purposes of that section applies also for the purposes of this paragraph.";

and after paragraph 14 insert:

"Lending of certain recordings

14A.(1) The Secretary of State may by order provide that in such cases as may be specified in the order the lending to the public of copies of films or sound recordings shall be treated as licensed by the performer subject only to the payment of such reasonable royalty or other payment as may be agreed or determined in default of agreement by the Copyright Tribunal.

(2) No such order shall apply if, or to the extent that, there is a licensing scheme certified for the purposes of this paragraph under paragraph 16 of Schedule 2A providing for the grant of licences.

(3) An order may make different provision for different cases and may specify cases by refernce to any factor relating to the work, the copies lent, the lender or the circumstances of the lending.

(4) An order shall be made by statutory instrument; and no order shall be made

unless a draft of it has been laid before and approved by a resolution of each House of Parliament.

(5) Nothing in this section affects any liability under section 184(1)(b) (secondary infringement: possessing or dealing with illicit recording) in respect of the lending of illicit recordings.

(6) Expressions used in this paragraph have the same meaning as in section 66.".

(4) In section 212 (index of defined expressions: Part II), at the appropriate places insert:

"distribution right	section 182B(5)"
"lending right	section 182C(7)"
"rental right	section 182C(7)"
"reproduction right	section 182A(3)".

Performers' property rights

A3.88 **21.**(1) After section 191 insert:

"Performers' property rights

Performers' property rights

191A.(1) The following rights conferred by this Part on a performer:

— reproduction right (section 182A),
— distribution right (section 182B),
— rental right and lending right (section 182C),

are property rights ("a performer's property rights").

(2) References in this Part to the consent of the performer shall be construed in relation to a performer's property rights as references to the consent of the rights owner.

(3) Where different persons are (whether in consequence of a partial assignment or otherwise) entitled to different aspects of a performer's property rights in relation to a performance, the rights owner for any purpose of this Part is the person who is entitled to the aspect of those rights relevant for that purpose.

(4) Where a performer's property rights (or any aspect of them) is owned by more than one person jointly, references in this Part to the rights owner are to all the owners, so that, in particular, any requirement of the licence of the rights owner requires the licence of all of them.

Assignment and licences

191B.(1) A performer's property rights are transmissible by assignment, by testamentary disposition or by operation of law, as personal or moveable property.

(2) An assignment or other transmission of a performer's property rights may be partial, that is, limited so as to apply:

(a) to one or more, but not all, of the things requiring the consent of the rights owner;
(b) to part, but not the whole, of the period for which the rights are to subsist.

(3) An assignment of a performer's property rights is not effective unless it is in writing signed by or on behalf of the assignor.

(4) A licence granted by the owner of a performer's property rights is binding on every successor in title to his interest in the rights, except a purchaser in good faith for valuable consideration and without notice (actual or constructive) of the licence or a person deriving title from such a purchaser; and references in this Part to doing

anything with, or without, the licence of the rights owner shall be construed accordingly.

Prospective ownership of a performer's property rights

191C.(1) This section applies where by an agreement made in relation to a future recording of a performance, and signed by or on behalf of the performer, the performer purports to assign his performer's property rights (wholly or partially) to another person.

(2) If on the rights coming into existence the assignee or another person claiming under him would be entitled as against all other persons to require the rights to be vested in him, they shall vest in the assignee or his successor in title by virtue of this subsection.

(3) A licence granted by a prospective owner of a performer's property rights is binding on every successor in title to his interest (or prospective interest) in the rights, except a purchaser in good faith for valuable consideration and without notice (actual or constructive) of the licence or a person deriving title from such a purchaser.

References in this Part to doing anything with, or without, the licence of the rights owner shall be construed accordingly.

(4) In subsection (3) "prospective owner" in relation to a performer's property rights means a person who is prospectively entitled to those rights by virtue of such an agreement as is mentioned in subsection (1).

Exclusive licences

191D.(1) In this Part an "exclusive licence" means a licence in writing signed by or on behalf of the owner of a performer's property rights authorising the licensee to the exclusion of all other persons, including the person granting the licence, to do anything requiring the consent of the rights owner.

(2) The licensee under an exclusive licence has the same rights against a successor in title who is bound by the licence as he has against the person granting the licence.

Performer's property right to pass under will with unpublished original recording

191E. Where under a bequest (whether general or specific) a person is entitled beneficially or otherwise to any material thing containing an original recording of a performance which was not published before the death of the testator, the bequest shall, unless a contrary intention is indicated in the testator's will or a codicil to it, be construed as including any performer's rights in relation to the recording to which the testator was entitled immediately before his death.

Presumption of transfer of rental right in case of film production agreement

191F.(1) Where an agreement concerning film production is concluded between a performer and a film producer, the performer shall be presumed, unless the agreement provides to the contrary, to have transferred to the film producer any rental right in relation to the film arising from the inclusion of a recording of his performance in the film.

(2) Where this section applies, the absence of signature by or on behalf of the performer does not exclude the operation of section 191C (effect of purported assignment of future rights).

(3) The reference in subsection (1) to an agreement concluded between a performer and a film producer includes any agreement having effect between those persons, whether made by them directly or through intermediaries.

(4) Section 191G (right to equitable remuneration on transfer of rental right)

applies where there is a presumed transfer by virtue of this section as in the case of an actual transfer.

Right to equitable remuneration where rental right transferred

191G.(1) Where a performer has transferred his rental right concerning a sound recording or a film to the producer of the sound recording or film he retains the right to equitable remuneration for the rental.

The reference above to the transfer of rental right by one person to another includes any arrangement having that effect, whether made by them directly or through intermediaries.

(2) The right to equitable remuneration under this section may not be assigned by the performer except to a collecting society for the purpose of enabling it to enforce the right on his behalf.

The right is, however, transmissible by testamentary disposition or by operation of law as personal or moveable property; and it may be assigned or further transmitted by any person into whose hands it passes.

(3) Equitable remuneration under this section is payable by the person for the time being entitled to the rental right, that is, the person to whom the right was transferred or any successor in title of his.

(4) The amount payable by way of equitable remuneration is as agreed by or on behalf of the persons by and to whom it is payable, subject to section 191H (reference of amount to Copyright Tribunal).

(5) An agreement is of no effect in so far as it purports to exclude or restrict the right to equitable remuneration under this section.

(6) In this section a "collecting society" means a society or other organisation which has as its main object, or one of its main objects, the exercise of the right to equitable remuneration on behalf of more than one performer.

Equitable remuneration: reference of amount to Copyright Tribunal

191H.(1) In default of agreement as to the amount payable by way of equitable remuneration under section 191G, the person by or to whom it is payable may apply to the Copyright Tribunal to determine the amount payable.

(2) A person to or by whom equitable remuneration is payable may also apply to the Copyright Tribunal:

(a) to vary any agreement as to the amount payable, or
(b) to vary any previous determination of the Tribunal as to that matter;

but except with the special leave of the Tribunal no such application may be made within twelve months from the date of a previous determination.

An order made on an application under this subsection has effect from the date on which it is made or such later date as may be specified by the Tribunal.

(3) On an application under this section the Tribunal shall consider the matter and make such order as to the method of calculating and paying equitable remuneration as it may determine to be reasonable in the circumstances, taking into account the importance of the contribution of the performer to the film or sound recording.

(4) Remuneration shall not be considered inequitable merely because it was paid by way of a single payment or at the time of the transfer of the rental right.

(5) An agreement is of no effect in so far as it purports to prevent a person questioning the amount of equitable remuneration or to restrict the powers of the Copyright Tribunal under this section.

Infringement actionable by rights owner

191I.(1) An infringement of a performer's property rights is actionable by the rights owner.

(2) In an action for infringement of a performer's property rights all such relief by way of damages, injunctions, accounts or otherwise is available to the plaintiff as is available in respect of the infringement of any other property right.

(3) This section has effect subject to the following provisions of this Part.

Provisions as to damages in infringement action

191J.(1) Where in an action for infringement of a performer's property rights it is shown that at the time of the infringement the defendant did not know, and had no reason to believe, that the rights subsisted in the recording to which the action relates, the plaintiff is not entitled to damages against him, but without prejudice to any other remedy.

(2) The court may in an action for infringement of a performer's property rights having regard to all the circumstances, and in particular to:

(a) the flagrancy of the infringement, and
(b) any benefit accruing to the defendant by reason of the infringement,

award such additional damages as the justice of the case may require.

Undertaking to take licence of right in infringement proceedings

191K.(1) If in proceedings for infringement of a performer's property rights in respect of which a licence is available as of right under paragraph 17 of Schedule 2A (powers exercisable in consequence of competition report) the defendant undertakes to take a licence on such terms as may be agreed or, in default of agreement, settled by the Copyright Tribunal under that paragraph:

(a) no injunction shall be granted against him,
(b) no order for delivery up shall be made under section 195, and
(c) the amount recoverable against him by way of damages or on an account of profits shall not exceed double the amount which would have been payable by him as licensee if such a licence on those terms had been granted before the earliest infringement.

(2) An undertaking may be given at any time before final order in the proceedings, without any admission of liability.

(3) Nothing in this section affects the remedies available in respect of an infringement committed before licences of right were available.

Rights and remedies for exclusive licensee

191L.(1) An exclusive licensee has, except against the owner of a performer's property rights, the same rights and remedies in respect of matters occurring after the grant of the licence as if the licence had been an assignment.

(2) His rights and remedies are concurrent with those of the rights owner; and references in the relevant provisions of this Part to the rights owner shall be construed accordingly.

(3) In an action brought by an exclusive licensee by virtue of this section a defendant may avail himself of any defence which would have been available to him if the action had been brought by the rights owner.

Exercise of concurrent rights

191M.(1) Where an action for infringement of a performer's property rights brought by the rights owner or an exclusive licensee relates (wholly or partly) to an infringement in respect of which they have concurrent rights of action, the rights owner or, as the case may be, the exclusive licensee may not, without the leave of the court, proceed with the action unless the other is either joined as plaintiff or added as a defendant.

(2) A rights owner or exclusive licensee who is added as a defendant in pursuance of subsection (1) is not liable for any costs in the action unless he takes part in the proceedings.

(3) The above provisions do not affect the granting of interlocutory relief on an application by the rights owner or exclusive licensee alone.

(4) Where an action for infringement of a performer's property rights is brought which relates (wholly or partly) to an infringement in respect of which the rights owner and an exclusive licensee have or had concurrent rights of action:

(a) the court shall in assessing damages take into account:

(i) the terms of the licence, and
(ii) any pecuniary remedy already awarded or available to either of them in respect of the infringement;

(b) no account of profits shall be directed if an award of damages has been made, or an account of profits has been directed, in favour of the other of them in respect of the infringement; and

(c) the court shall if an account of profits is directed apportion the profits between them as the court considers just, subject to any agreement between them;

and these provisions apply whether or not the rights owner and the exclusive licensee are both parties to the action.

(5) The owner of a performer's property rights shall notify any exclusive licensee having concurrent rights before applying for an order under section 195 (order for delivery up) or exercising the right conferred by section 196 (right of seizure); and the court may on the application of the licensee make such order under section 195 or, as the case may be, prohibiting or permitting the exercise by the rights owner of the right conferred by section 196, as it thinks fit having regard to the terms of the licence.".

(2) For section 192 (transmission of rights) substitute:

"Non-property rights

Performers' non-property rights

192A.(1) the rights conferred on a performer by:

— section 182 (consent required for recording, etc. of live performance),
— section 183 (infringement of performer's rights by use of recording made without consent), and
— section 184 (infringement of performer's rights importing, possessing or dealing with illicit recording),

are not assignable or transmissible, except to the following extent.
They are referred to in this Part as "a performer's non-property rights".

(2) On the death of a person entitled to any such right:

(a) the right passes to such person a he may by testamentary disposition specifically direct, and
(b) if or to the extent that there is no such direction, the right is exercisable by his personal representatives.

(3) References in this Part to the performer, in the context of the person having any such right, shall be construed as references to the person for the time being entitled to exercise those rights.

(4) Where by virtue of subsection (2)(a) a right becomes exercisable by more than one person, it is exercisable by each of them independently of the other or others.

(5) Any damages recovered by personal representatives by virtue of this section in respect of an infringement after a person's death shall devolve as part of his estate as if the right of action had subsisted and been vested in him immediately before his death.

Transmissibility of rights of person having recording rights

192B.(1) The rights conferred by this Part on a person having recording rights are not assignable or transmissible.

(2) This does not affect section 185(2)(b) or (3)(b), so far as those provisions confer rights under this Part on a person to whom the benefit of a contract or licence is assigned.".

(3) In section 193 (consent):

(a) in subsection (1), after "Consent for the purposes of this Part" insert "by a person having a performer's non-property rights, or by a person having recording rights,"; and

(b) in subsection (3), for "a right conferred by this Part" substitute "a performer's non-property right".

(4) In section 194 (infringement actionable as breach of statutory duty), for "any of the rights conferred by this Part" substitute:"

(a) a performer's non-property rights, or

(b) any right conferred by this Part on a person having recording rights,".

(5) The headings in Part II falsified by the above amendments are amended as follows:

(a) for the heading before section 191 substitute:

"Duration of rights";

(b) omit the heading before section 194;

(c) before section 195 insert the heading:

"Delivery up or seizure of illicit recordings".

(6) In section 212 (index of defined expressions: Part II), at the appropriate places insert:

— "consent of performer (in relation to performer's property rights) section 191A(2)"

— "performer's non-property rights section 192A(1)"

— "performer's property rights section 191A(1)"

— "rights owner (in relation to performer's property rights) section 191A(3) and (4)".

Licensing of performers' property rights

22.(1) In Part II (performers' rights), after section 205 insert: A3.89

"Licensing of performers' property rights

Licensing of performers' property rights

205A. The provisions of Schedule 2A have effect with respect to the licensing of performers' property rights.".

(2) After Schedule 2 insert:

"SCHEDULE 2A

LICENSING OF PERFORMERS' PROPERTY RIGHTS

Licensing schemes and licensing bodies

1.(1) In Part II a "licensing scheme" means a scheme setting out:

(a) the classes of case in which the operator of the scheme, or the person on whose behalf he acts, is willing to grant performers' property right licences, and

(b) the terms on which licences would be granted in those classes of case;

and for this purpose a "scheme" includes anything in the nature of a scheme, whether described as a scheme or as a tariff or by any other name.

(2) In Part II a "licensing body" means a society or other organisation which has as its main object, or one of its main objects, the negotiating or granting, whether as owner or prospective owner of a performer's property rights or as agent for him, of performers' property right licences, and whose objects include the granting of licences covering the performances of more than one performer.

(3) In this paragraph "performers' property right licences" means licences to do, or authorise the doing of, any of the things for which consent is required under section 182A, 182B or 182C.

(4) References in this Part to licences or licensing schemes covering the performances of more than one performer do not include licences or schemes covering only:

(a) performances recorded in a single recording,

(b) performances recorded in more than one recording where:

(i) the performers giving the performances are the same, or

(ii) the recordings are made by, or by employees of or commissioned by, a single individual, firm, company or group of companies.

For purpose a group of companies means a holding company and its subsidiaries within the meaning of section 736 of the Companies Act 1985.

References and applications with respect to licensing schemes

2. Paragraphs 3 to 8 (references and applications with respect to licensing schemes) apply to licensing schemes operated by licensing bodies in relation to a performer' property rights which cover the performances of more than one performer, so far as they relate to licences for:

(a) copying a recording of the whole or any substantial part of a qualifying performance, or

(b) renting or lending copies of a recording to the public;

and in those paragraphs "licensing scheme" means a licensing scheme of any of those descriptions.

Reference of proposed licensing scheme to tribunal

3.(1) The terms of a licensing scheme proposed to be operated by a licensing body may be referred to the Copyright Tribunal by an organisation claiming to be representative of persons claiming that they require licences in cases of a description to which the scheme would apply, either generally or in relation to any description of case.

(2) The Tribunal shall first decide whether to entertain the reference, and may decline to do so on the ground that the reference is premature.

(3) If the Tribunal decides to entertain the reference it shall consider the matter referred and make such order, either confirming or varying the proposed scheme, either generally or so far as it relates to cases of the description to which the reference relates, as the Tribunal may determine to be reasonable in the circumstances.

(4) Theorder may be made so as to be in force indefinitely or for such period as the Tribunal may determine.

Reference of licensing scheme to tribunal

4.(1) If while a licensing scheme is in operation a dispute arises between the operator of the scheme and:

(a) a person claiming that he requires a licence in a case of a description to which the scheme applies, or
(b) an organisation claiming to be representative of such persons,

that person or organisation may refer the scheme to the Copyright Tribunal in so far as it relates to cases of that description.

(2) A scheme which has been referred to the Tribunal under this paragraph shall remain in operation until proceedings on the reference are concluded.

(3) The Tribunal shall consider the matter in dispute and make such order, either confirming or varying the scheme so far as it relates to cases of the description to which the reference relates, as the Tribunal may determine to be reasonable in the circumstances.

(4) The order may be made so as to be in force indefinitely or for such period as the Tribunal may determine.

Further reference of scheme to tribunal

5.(1) Where the Copyright Tribunal has on a previous reference of a licensing scheme under paragraph 3 or 4, or under this paragraph, made an order with respect to the scheme, then, while the order remains in force:

(a) the operator of the scheme,
(b) a person claiming that he requires a licence in a case of the description to which the order applies, or
(c) an organisation claiming to be representative of such persons,

may refer the scheme again to the Tribunal so far as it relates to cases of that description.

(2) A licensing scheme shall not, except with the special leave of the Tribunal, be referred again to the Tribunal in respect of the same description of cases:

(a) within twelve months from the date of the order on the previous reference, or
(b) if the order was made so as to be in force for 15 months or less, until the last three months before the expiry of the order.

(3) A scheme which has been referred to the Tribunal under this paragraph shall remain in operation until proceedings on the reference are concluded.

(4) The Tribunal shall consider the matter in dispute and make such order, either confirming, varying or further varying the scheme so far as it relates to cases of the description to which the reference relates, as the Tribunal may determine to be reasonable in the circumstances.

(5) The order may be made so as to be in force indefinitely or for such period as the Tribunal may determine.

Application for grant of licence in connection with licensing scheme

6.(1) A person who claims, in a case covered by a licensing scheme, that the operator of the scheme has refused to grant him or procure the grant to him of a licence in accordance with the scheme, or has failed to do so within a reasonable time after being asked, may apply to the Copyright Tribunal.

(2) A person who claims, in a case excluded from a licensing scheme, that the operator of the scheme either:

(a) has refused to grant him a licence or procure the grant to him of a licence, or has failed to do so within a reasonable time of being asked, and that in the circumstances it is unreasonable that a licence should not be granted, or

(b) proposes terms for a licence which are unreasonable,

may apply to the Copyright Tribunal.

(3) A case shall be regarded as excluded from a licensing scheme for the purposes of sub-paragraph (2) if:

(a) the scheme provides for the grant of licences subject to terms excepting matters from the licence and the case falls within an exception, or

(b) the case is so similar to those in which licences are granted under the scheme that it is unreasonable that it should not be dealt with in the same way.

(4) If the Tribunal is satisfied that the claim is well-founded, it shall make an order declaring that, in respect of the matters specified in the order, the applicant is entitled to a licence on such terms as the Tribunal may determine to be applicable in accordance with the scheme or, as the case may be, to be reasonable in the circumstances.

(5) The order may be made so as to be in force indefinitely or for such period as the Tribunal may determine.

Application for review of order as to entitlement to licence

7.(1) Where the Copyright Tribunal has made an order under paragraph 6 that a person is entitled to a licence under a licensing scheme, the operator of the scheme or the original applicant may apply to the Tribunal to review its order.

(2) An application shall not be made, except with the special leave of the Tribunal:

(a) within twelve months from the date of the order, or of the decision on a previous application under this paragraph, or

(b) if the order was made so as to be in force for 15 months or less, or as a result of the decision on a previous application under this paragraph is due to expire within 15 months of that decision, until the last three months before the expiry date.

(3) The Tribunal shall on an application for review confirm or vary its order as the Tribunal may determine to be reasonable having regard to the terms applicable in accordance with the licensing scheme or, as the case may be, the circumstances of the case.

Effect of order of tribunal as to licensing scheme

8.(1) A licensing scheme which has been confirmed or varied by the Copyright Tribunal:

(a) under paragraph 3 (reference of terms of proposed scheme), or

(b) under paragraph 4 or 5 (reference of existing scheme to Tribunal),

shall be in force or, as the case may be, remain in operation, so far as it relates to the description of case in respect of which the order was made, so long as the order remains in force.

(2) While the order is in force a person who in a case of a class to which the order applies:

(a) pays to the operator of the scheme any charges payable under the scheme in respect of a licence covering the case in question or, if the amount cannot be ascertained, gives an undertaking to the operator to pay them when ascertained, and

(b) complies with the other terms applicable to such a licence under the scheme,

shall be in the same position as regards infringement of performers' property rights as if he had at all material times been the holder of a licence granted by the rights owner in question in accordance with the scheme.

(3) The Tribunal may direct that the order, so far as it varies the amount of charges payable, has effect from a date before that on which it is made, but not earlier than the date on which the reference was made or, if later, on which the scheme came into operation.

If such a direction is made:

(a) any necessary repayments, or further payments, shall be made in respect of charges already paid, and

(b) the reference in sub-paragraph (2)(a) to the charges payable under the scheme shall be construed as a reference to the charges so payable by virtue of the order.

No such direction may be made where sub-paragraph (4) below applies.

(4) An order of the Tribunal under paragraph 4 or 5 made with respect to a scheme which is certified for any purpose under paragraph 16 has effect, so far as it varies the scheme by reducing the charges payable for licences, from the date on which the reference was made to the Tribunal.

(5) Where the Tribunal has made an order under paragraph 6 (order as to entitlement to licence under licensing scheme) and the order remains in force, the person in whose favour the order is made shall if he:

(a) pays to the operator of the scheme any charges payable in accordance with the order or, if the amount cannot be ascertained, gives an undertaking to pay the charges when ascertained, and

(b) complies with the other terms specified in the order,

be in the same position as regards infringement of performers' property rights as if he had at all material times been the holder of a licence granted by the rights owner in question on the terms specified in the order.

References and applications with respect to licensing by licensing bodies

9. Paragraphs 10 to 13 (references and applications with respect to licensing by licensing bodies) apply to licences relating to a performer's property rights which cover the performance of more than one performer granted by a licensing body otherwise than in pursuance of a licensing scheme, so far as the licences authorise:

(a) copying a recording of the whole or any substantial part of a qualifying performance, or

(b) renting or lending copies of a recording to the public;

and references in those paragraphs to a licence shall be construed accordingly.

Reference to tribunal of proposed licence

10.(1) The terms on which a licensing body proposes to grant a licence may be referred to the Copyright Tribunal by the prospective licensee.

(2) The Tribunal shall first decide whether to entertain the reference, and may decline to do so on the ground that the reference is premature.

(3) If the Tribunal decides to entertain the reference it shall consider the terms of

the proposed licence and make such order, either confirming or varying the terms as it may determine to be reasonable in the circumstances.

(4) The order may be made so as to be in force indefinitely or for such period as the Tribunal may determine.

Reference to tribunal of expiring licence

11.(1) A licensee under a licence which is due to expire, by effluxion of time or as a result of notice given by the licensing body, may apply to the Copyright Tribunal on the ground that it is unreasonable in the circumstances that the licence should cease to be in force.

(2) Such an application may not be made until the last three months before the licence is due to expire.

(3) A licence in respect of which a reference has been made to the Tribunal shall remain in operation until proceedings on the reference are concluded.

(4) If the Tribunal finds the application well-founded, it shall make an order declaring that the licensee shall continue to be entitled to the benefit of the licence on such terms as the Tribunal may determine to be reasonable in the circumstances.

(5) An order of the Tribunal under this paragraph may be made so as to be in force indefinitely or for such period as the Tribunal may determine.

Application for review of order as to licence

12.(1) Where the Copyright Tribunal has made an order under paragraph 10 or 11, the licensing body or the person entitled to the benefit of the order may apply to the Tribunal to review its order.

(2) An application shall not be made, except with the special leave of the Tribunal:

(a) within twelve months from the date of the order or of the decision on a previous application under this paragraph, or

(b) if the order was made so as to be in force for 15 months or less, or as a result of the decision on a previous application under this paragraph is due to expire within 15 months of that decision, until the last three months before the expiry date.

(3) The Tribunal shall on an application for review confirm or vary its order as the Tribunal may determine to be reasonable in the circumstances.

Effect of order of tribunal as to licence

13.(1) Where the Copyright Tribunal has made an order under paragraph 10 or 11 and the order remains in force, the person entitled to the benefit of the order shall if he:

(a) pays to the licensing body any charges payable in accordance with the order or, if the amount cannot be ascertained, gives an undertaking to pay the charges when ascertained, and

(b) complies with the other terms specified in the order,

be in the same position as regards infringement of performers' property rights as if he had at all material times been the holder of a licence granted by the rights owner in question on the terms specified in the order.

(2) The benefit of the order may be assigned:

(a) in the case of an order under paragraph 10, if assignment is not prohibited under the terms of the Tribunal's order; and

(b) in the case of an order under paragraph 11, if assignment was not prohibited under the terms of the original licence.

(3) The Tribunal may direct that an order under paragraph 10 or 11, or an order

under paragraph 12 varying such an order, so far as it varies the amount of charges payable, has effect from a date before that on which it is made, but not earlier than the date on which the reference or application was made or, if later, on which the licence was granted or, as the case may be, was due to expire.

If such a direction is made:

(a) any necessary repayments, or further payments, shall be made in respect of charges already paid, and
(b) the reference in sub-paragraph (1)(a) to the charges payable in accordance with the order shall be construed, where the order is varied by a later order, as a reference to the charges so payable by virtue of the later order.

General considerations: unreasonable discrimination

14.(1) In determining what is reasonable on a reference or application under this Schedule relating to a licensing scheme or licence, the Copyright Tribunal shall have regard to:

(a) the availability of other schemes, or the granting of other licences, to other persons in similar circumstances, and
(b) the terms of those schemes or licences,

and shall exercise its powers so as to secure that there is no unreasonable discrimination between licensees, or prospective licensees, under the scheme or licence to which the reference or application relates and licensees under other schemes operated by, or other licences granted by, the same person.

(2) This does not affect the Tribunal's general obligation in any case to have regard to all relevant circumstances.

Application to settle royalty or other sum payable for lending

15.(1) An application to settle the royalty or other sum payable in pursuance of paragraph 14A of Schedule 2 (lending of certain recordings) may be made to the Copyright Tribunal by the owner of a performer's property rights or the person claiming to be treated as licensed by him.

(2) The Tribunal shall consider the matter and make such order as it may determine to be reasonable in the circumstances.

(3) Either party may subsequently apply to the Tribunal to vary the order, and the Tribunal shall consider the matter and make such order confirming or varying the original order as it may determine to be reasonable in the circumstances.

(4) An application under sub-paragraph (3) shall not, except with the special leave of the Tribunal, be made within twelve months from the date of the original order or of the order on a previous application under that sub-paragraph.

(5) An order under sub-paragraph (3) has effect from the date on which it is made or such later date as may be specified by the Tribunal.

Certification of licensing schemes

16.(1) A person operating or proposing to operate a licensing scheme may apply to the Secretary of State to certify the scheme for the purposes of paragraph 14A of Schedule 2 (lending of certain recordings).

(2) The Secretary of State shall by order made by statutory instrument certify the scheme if he is satisfied that it:

(a) enables the works to which it relates to be identified with sufficient certainty by persons likely to require licences, and
(b) sets out clearly the charges (if any) payable and the other terms on which licences will be granted.

(3) The scheme shall be scheduled to the order and the certification shall come into operation for the purposes of paragraph 14A of Schedule 2:

(a) on such date, not less than eight weeks after the order is made, as may be specified in the order, or

(b) if the scheme is the subject of a reference under paragraph 3 (reference of proposed scheme), any later date on which the order of the Copyright Tribunal under that paragraph comes into force or the reference is withdrawn.

(4) A variation of the scheme is not effective unless a corresponding amendment of the order is made; and the Secretary of State shall make such an amendment in the case of a variation ordered by the Copyright Tribunal on a reference under paragraph 3, 4 or 5, and may do so in any other case if he thinks fit.

(5) The order shall be revoked if the scheme ceases to be operated and may be revoked if it appears to the Secretary of State that it is no longer being operated according to its terms.

Powers exercisable in consequence of competition report

17.(1) Where the matters specified in a report of the Monopolies and Mergers Commission as being those which in the Commission's opinion operate, may be expected to operate or have operated against the public interest include:

(a) conditions in licences granted by the owner of a performer's property rights restricting the use to which a recording may be put by the licensee or the right of the owner to grant other licences, or

(b) a refusal of an owner of a performer's property rights to grant licences on reasonable terms,

the powers conferred by Part I of Schedule 8 to the Fair Trading Act 1973 (powers exercisable for purpose of remedying or preventing adverse effects specified in report of Commission) include power to cancel or modify those conditions and, instead or in addition, to provide that licences in respect of the performer's property rights shall be available as of right.

(2) The references in sections 56(2) and 73(2) of that Act, and sections 10(2)(b) and 12(5) of the Competition Act 1980, to the powers specified in that Part of that Schedule shall be construed accordingly.

(3) A Minister shall only exercise the powers availble by virtue of this paragraph if he is satisfied that to do so does not contravene any Convention relating to performers' rights to which the United Kingdom is a party.

(4) The terms of a licence available by virtue of this paragraph shall, in default of agreement, be settled by the Copyright Tribunal on an application by the person requiring the licence; and terms so settled shall authorise the licensee to do everything in respect of which a licence is so available.

(5) Where the terms of a licence are settled by the Tribunal, the licence has effect from the date on which the application to the Tribunal was made.".

Performers' rights: power of Copyright Tribunal to give consent

A3.90   23.(1) Section 190 (power of tribunal to give consent on behalf of performer in certain cases) is amended as follows.

(2) For subsection (1) substitute:

"(1) The Copyright Tribunal may, on the application of a person wishing to make a copy of a recording of a performance, give consent in a case where the identity or whereabouts of the person entitled to the reproduction right cannot be ascertained by reasonable inquiry.".

(3) In subsection (2) for "the performer" substitute "the person entitled to the reproduction right".

(4) Omit subsection (4).

(5) In subsection (6):

(a) for "the performer" in the first place where it occurs substitute "the person entitled to the reproduction right", and

(b) for "the performer" in the second place where it occurs substitute "that person".

Performers' rights: jurisdiction of Copyright Tribunal

24.(1) After section 205A (inserted by regulation 22(1)) insert: **A3.91**

"Jurisdiction of Copyright Tribunal

Jurisdiction of Copyright Tribunal

205B.(1) The Copyright Tribunal has jurisdiction under this Part to hear and determine proceedings under:

(a) section 182D (amount of equitable remuneration for exploitation of commercial sound recording);

(b) section 190 (application to give consent on behalf of owner of reproduction right);

(c) section 191H (amount of equitable remuneration on transfer of rental right);

(d) paragraph 3, 4 or 5 of Schedule 2A (reference of licensing scheme);

(e) paragraph 6 or 7 of that Schedule (application with respect to licence under licensing scheme);

(f) paragraph 10, 11 or 12 of that Schedule (reference or application with respect to licensing by licensing body);

(g) paragraph 15 of that Schedule (application to settle royalty for certain lending);

(h) paragraph 17 of that Schedule (application to settle terms of licence available as of right).

(2) The provisions of Chapter VIII of Part I (general provisions relating to the Copyright Tribunal) apply in relation to the Tribunal when exercising any jurisdiction under this Part.

(3) Provision shall be made by rules under section 150 prohibiting the Tribunal from entertaining a reference under paragraph 3, 4 or 5 of Schedule 2A (reference of licensing scheme) by a representative organisation unless the Tribunal is satisfied that the organisation is reasonably representative of the class of persons which it claims to represent.".

(2) In section 149 (jurisdiction of the Tribunal):

(a) in the opening words for "The function of the Copyright Tribunal is" substitute "The Copyright Tribunal has jurisdication under this Part";

(b) omit paragraphs (g) and (h).

(3) In paragraph 5 of Schedule 6 (determination by Tribunal of royalty or other remuneration to be paid), after sub-paragraph (4) add:

"(5) The provisions of Chapter VIII of Part I (general provisions relating to the Copyright Tribunal) apply in relation to the Tribunal when exercising any jurisdiction under this paragraph.".

PART III: TRANSITIONAL PROVISIONS AND SAVINGS

General provisions

Introductory

A3.92 25.(1) In this Part:

— "commencement" means the commencement of these Regulations; and
— "existing", in relation to a work or performance, means made or given before commencement.

(2) For the purposes of this Part a work of which the making extended over a period shall be taken to have been made when its making was completed.

(3) In this Part a "new right" means a right arising by virtue of these Regulations, in relation to a copyright work or a qualifying performance, to authorise or prohibit an act.

The expression does not include:

(a) a right corresponding to a right which existed immediately before commencement, or
(b) a right to remuneration arising by virtue of these Regulations.

(4) Expressions used in this Part have the same meaning in relation to copyright as they have in Part I of the Copyright, Designs and Patents Act 1988,[16] and in relation to performances as in Part II of that Act.

General rules

A3.93 26.(1) Subject to anything in regulations 28 to 36 (special transitional provisions and savings), these regulations apply to copyright works made, and to performances given, before or after commencement.

(2) No act done before commencement shall be regarded as an infringement of any new right, or as giving rise to any right to remuneration arising by virtue of these Regulations.

Saving for certain existing agreements

A3.94 27.(1) Except as otherwise expressly provided, nothing in these Regulations affects an agreement made before 19th November 1992.

(2) No act done in pursuance of any such agreement after commencement shall be regarded as an infringement of any new right.

Special provisions

Broadcasts

A3.95 28. The provisions of:

— regulation 5 (place where broadcast treated as made) and
— regulation 6 (safeguards in relation to certain satellite broadcasts),

have effect in relation to broadcasts made after commencement.

Satellite broadcasting: international co-production agreements

A3.96 29.(1) This regulation applies to an agreement concluded before 1st January 1995:

(a) between two or more co-producers of a film, one of whom is a national of an EEA state, and

---

[16] 1988, c. 48.

(b) the provisions of which grant to the parties exclusive rights to exploit all communciation to the public of the film in separate geographical areas.

(2) Where such an agreement giving such exclusive exploitation rights in relation to the United Kingdom does not expressly or by implication address satellite broadcasting from the United Kingdom, the person to whom those exclusive rights have been granted shall not make any such broadcast without the consent of any other party to the agreement whose language-related exploitation rights would be adversely affected by that broadcast.

New rights: exercise of rights in relation to peformances

30.(1) Any new right conferred by these Regulations in relation to a qualifying performance is exercisable as from commencement by the performer or (if he has died) by the person who immediately before commencement was entitled by virtue of section 192(2) to exercise the rights conferred on the performer by Part II in relation to that performance. **A3.97**

(2) Any remuneration or damages received by a person's personal representatives by virtue of a right conferred on them by paragraph (1) shall devolve as part of that person's estate as if the right had subsisted and been vested in him immediately before his death.

New rights: effect of pre-commencement authorisation of copying

31. Where before commencement: **A3.98**

(a) the owner or prospective owner of copyright in a literary, dramatic, musical or artistic work has authorised a person to make a copy of the work, or
(b) the owner or prospective owner of performers' rights in a performance has authorised a person to make a copy of a recording of the performance,

any new right in relation to that copy shall vest on commencement in the person so authorised, subject to any agreement to the contrary.

New rights: effect of pre-commencement film production agreement

32.(1) Sections 93A and 191F (presumption of transfer of rental right in case of production agreement) apply in relation to an agreement concluded before commencement. **A3.99**

As section 93A so applies, the restriction in subsection (3) of that section shall be omitted (exclusion of presumption in relation to screenplay, dialogue or music specifically created for the film).

(2) Sections 93B and 191G (right to equitable remuneration where rental right transferred) have effect accordingly, but subject to regulation 33 (right to equitable remuneration applicable to rental after 1st April 1997).

Right to equitable remuneration applicable to rental after 1st April 1997

33. No right to equitable remuneration under section 93B or 191G (right to equitable remuneration where rental right transferred) arises: **A3.100**

(a) in respect of any rental of a sound recording or film before 1st April 1997, or
(b) in respect of any rental after that date of a sound recording or film made in pursuance of an agreement entered into before 1st July 1994, unless the author or performer (or a successor in title of his) has before 1st January 1997 notified

the person by whom the remuneration would be payable that he intends to exercise that right.

Savings for existing stocks

A3.101 34.(1) Any new right in relation to a copyright work does not apply to a copy of the work acquired by a person before commencement for the purpose of renting or lending it to the public.

(2) Any new right in relation to a qualifying performance does not apply to a copy of a recording of the performance acquired by a person before commencement for the purpose of renting or lending it to the public.

Lending of copies by libraries or archives

A3.102 35. Until the making of regulations under section 37 of the Copyright, Designs and Patents Act 1988[17] for the purposes of section 40A(2) of that Act (lending of copies by libraries or archives), the reference in section 40A(2) (and in paragraph 6B of Schedule 2) to a prescribed library or archive shall be construed as a reference to any library or archive in the United Kingdom prescribed by paragraphs 2 to 6 of Part A of Schedule 1 to the Copyright (Librarians and Archivists) (Copying of Copyright Material) Regulations 1989.[18]

Authorship of films

A3.103 36.(1) Regulation 18 (authorship of films) applies as from commencement in relation to films made on or after 1st July 1994.

(2) It is not an infringement of any right which the principal director has by virtue of these Regulations to do anything after commencement in pursuance of arrangements for the exploitation of the film made before 19th November 1992.

This does not affect any right of his to equitable remuneration under section 93B.

---

[17] 1988, c. 48.
[18] S.I. 1989 No. 1212.

APPENDIX 4A

COUNCIL DIRECTIVE 92/100

of November 19, 1992
on rental right and lending right and on certain rights related to copyright in the field
of intellectual property

([1992] O.J. L346/61)

THE COUNCIL OF THE EUROPEAN COMMUNITIES

Having regard to the Treaty establishing the European Economic Community, and in particular Articles 57(2), 66 and 100a thereof,

A4.01

Having regard to the proposal from the Commission

In cooperation with the European Parliament

Having regard to the opinion of the Economic and Social Committee

(1) Whereas differences exist in the legal protection provided by the laws and practices of the Member States for copyright works and subject matter of related rights protection as regards rental and lending; whereas such differences are sources of barriers to trade and distortions of competition which impede the achievement and proper functioning of the internal market;

(2) Whereas such differences in legal protection could well become greater as Member States adopt new and different legislation or as national case-law interpreting such legislation develops differently;

(3) Whereas such differences should therefore be eliminated in accordance with the objective of introducing an area without internal frontiers as set out in Article 8a of the Treaty so as to institute, pursuant to Article 3(f) of the Treaty, a system ensuring that competition in the common market is not distorted;

(4) Whereas rental and lending of copyright works and the subject matter of related rights protection is playing an increasingly important role in particular for authors, performers and producers of phonograms and films; whereas piracy is becoming an increasing threat;

(5) Whereas the adequate protection of copyright works and subject matter of related rights protection by rental and lending rights as well as the protection of the subject matter of related rights protection by the fixation right, reproduction right, distribution right, right to broadcast and communication to the public can accordingly be considered as being of fundamental importance for the Community's economic and cultural development;

(6) Whereas copyright and related rights protection must adapt to new economic developments such as new forms of exploitation;

(7) Whereas the creative and artistic work of authors and performers necessitates an adequate income as a basis for further creative and artistic work, and the investments required particularly for the production of phonograms and films are especially high and risky; whereas the possibility for securing that income and recouping that investment can only effectively be guaranteed through adequate legal protection of the rightholders concerned;

(8) Whereas these creative, artistic and entrepreneurial activities are, to a large extent, activities of self-employed persons; whereas the pursuit of such activities must be made easier by providing a harmonized legal protection within the Community;

(9) Whereas, to the extent that these activities principally constitute services, their

343

provision must equally be facilitated by the establishment in the Community of a harmonized legal framework;

(10) Whereas the legislation of the Member States should be approximated in such a way so as not to conflict with the international conventions on which many Member States' copyright and related rights laws are based;

(11) Whereas the Community's legal framework on the rental right and lending right and on certain rights related to copyright can be limited to establishing that Member States provide rights with respect to rental and lending for certain groups of rightholders and further to establishing the rights of fixation, reproduction, distribution, broadcasting and communication to the public for certain groups of rightholders in the field of related rights protection;

(12) Whereas it is necessary to define the concepts of rental and lending for the purposes of this Directive;

(13) Whereas it is desirable, with a view to clarity, to exclude from rental and lending within the meaning of this Directive certain forms of making available, as for instance making available phonogram or films (cinematographic or audiovisual works or moving images, whether or not accompanied by sound) for the purpose of public performance or braodcasting, making available for the purpose of exhibition, or making available for on-the-spot reference use; whereas lending within the meaning of this Directive does not include making available between establishments which are accessible to the public;

(14) Whereas, where lending by an establishment accessible to the public gives rise to a payment the amount of which does not go beyond what is necessary to cover the operating costs of the establishment, there is no direct or indirect economic or commercial advantage within the meaning of this Directive;

(15) Whereas it is necessary to introduce arrangements ensuring that an unwaivable equitable remuneration is obtained by authors and performers who must retain the possibility to entrust the administration of this right to collecting societies representing them;

(16) Whereas the equitable remuneration may be paid on the basis of one or several payments at[1] any time on or after the conclusion of the contract;

(17) Whereas the equitable remuneration must take account of the importance of the contribution of the authors and performers concerned to the phonogram or film;

(18) Whereas it is also necessary to protect the rights at least of authors as regards public lending by providing for specific arrangements; whereas, however, any measures based on Article 5 of this Directive have to comply with Community law, in particular with Article 7 of the Treaty;

(19) Whereas the provisions of Chapter II do not prevent Member States from extending the presumption set out in Article 2(5) to the exclusive rights included in that chapter; whereas furthermore the provisions of Chapter II do not prevent Member States from providing for a rebuttable presumption of the authorization of exploitation in respect of the exclusive rights of performers provided for in those articles, in so far as such presumption is compatible with the International Convention for the Protection of Performers, Producers of Phonograms and Broadcasting Organizations (hereinafter referred to as the Rome Convention);

(20) Whereas Member States may provide for more far-reaching protection for owners of rights related to copyright than that required by Article 8 of this Directive;

(21) Whereas the harmonized rental and lending rights and the harmonized protection in the field of rights related to copyright should not be exercised in a way which constitutes a disguised restriction on trade between Member States or in a way which is contrary to the rule of media exploitation chronology, as recognized in the Judgment handed down in *Société Cinéthèque v. FNCF*,[2]

HAS ADOPTED THIS DIRECTIVE

---

[1] O.J. text has "an".
[2] Cases 60/84 and 61/84, [1985] E.C.R. 2605.

CHAPTER I

RENTAL AND LENDING RIGHT

Article 1

Object of harmonization   A4.02

1. In accordance with the provisions of this Chapter, Member States shall provide, subject to Article 5, a right to authorize or prohibit the rental and lending of originals and copies of copyright works, and other subject matter as set out in Article 2(1).
2. For the purposes of this Directive, "rental" means making available for use, for a limited period of time and for direct economic or commercial advantage.
3. For the purposes of this Directive, "lending" means making available for use, for a limited period of time and not for direct or indirect economic or commercial advantage, when it is made through establishments which are accessible to the public.
4. The rights referred to in paragraph 1 shall not be exhausted by any sale or other act of distribution of originals and copies of copyright works and other subject matter as set out in article 2(1).

Article 2

Rightholders and subject matter of rental and lending right   A4.03

1. The exclusive right to authorize or prohibit rental and lending shall belong:

— to the author in respect of the original and copies of his work,
— to the performer in respect of fixations of his performance,
— to the phonogram producer in respect of his phonograms, and
— to the producer of the first fixation of a film in respect of the original and copies of his film. For the purposes of this Directive, the term "film" shall designate a cinematographic or audiovisual work or moving images, whether or not accompanied by sound.

2. For the purposes of this Directive the principal director of a cinematographic or audiovisual work shall be considered as its author or one of its authors. Member States may provide for others to be considered as its co-authors.
3. This Directive does not cover rental and lending rights in relation to buildings and to works of applied art.
4. The rights referred to in paragraph 1 may be transferred, assigned or subject to the granting of contractual licences.
5. Without prejudice to paragraph 7, when a contract concerning film production is concluded, individually or collectively, by performers with a film producer, the performer covered by this contract shall be presumed, subject to contractual clauses to the contrary, to have transferred his rental right, subject to Article 4.
6. Member States may provide for a similar presumption as set out in paragraph 5 with respect to authors.
7. Member States may provide that the signing of a contract concluded between a performer and a film producer concerning the production of a film has the effect of authorizing rental, provided that such contract provides for an equitable remuneration within the meaning of Article 4. Member States may also provide that this paragraph shall apply *mutatis mutandis* to the rights included in Chapter II.

Article 3

A4.04   Rental of computer programs

This Directive shall be without prejudice to Article 4(c) of Council Directive 91/250/EEC of May 14, 1991 on the legal protection of computer programs.

Article 4

A4.05   Unwaivable right to equitable remuneration

1. Where an author or performer has transferred or assigned his rental right concerning a phonogram or an original or copy of a film to a phonogram or film producer, that author or performer shall retain the right to obtain an equitable remuneration for the rental.
2. The right to obtain an equitable remuneration for rental cannot be waived by authors or performers.
3. The administration of this right to obtain an equitable remuneration may be entrusted to collecting societies representing authors or performers.
4. Member States may regulate whether and to what extent administration by collecting societies of the right to obtain an equitable remuneration may be imposed, as well as the question from whom this remuneration may be claimed or collected.

Article 5

A4.06   Derogation from the exclusive public lending right

1. Member States may derogate from the exclusive right provided for in Article 1 in respect of public lending, provided that at least authors obtain a remuneration for such lending. Member States shall be free to determine this remuneration taking account of their cultural promotion objectives.
2. When Member States do not apply the exclusive lending right provided for in Article 1 as regards phonograms, films and computer programs, they shall introduce, at least for authors, a remuneration.
3. Member States may exempt certain categories of establishments from the payment of the remuneration referred to in paragraphs 1 and 2.
4. The Commission in cooperation with the Member States, shall draw up before July 1, 1997 a report on public lending in the Community. It shall forward this report to the European Parliament and to the Council.

CHAPTER II

RIGHTS RELATED TO COPYRIGHT

Article 6

A4.07   Fixation right

1. Member States shall provide for performers the exclusive right to authorize or prohibit the fixation of their performances.
2. Member States shall provide for broadcasting organizations the exclusive right to authorize or prohibit the fixation of their broadcasts, whether these broadcasts are transmitted by wire or over the air, including by cable or satellite.
3. A cable distributor shall not have the right provided for in paragraph 2 where it merely retransmits by cable the broadcasts of broadcasting organizations.

Article 7

Reproduction right   A4.08

1. Member States shall provide the exclusive right to authorize or prohibit the direct or indirect reproduction:

— for performers, of fixations of their performances,
— for phonogram producers, of their phonograms,
— for producers of the first fixations of films, in respect of the original and copies of their films, and
— for broadcasting organizations, of fixations of their broadcasts, as set out in Article 6(2).

2. The reproduction right referred to in paragraph 1 may be transferred, assigned or subject to granting of contractual licences.

Article 8

Broadcasting and communication to the public   A4.09

1. Member States shall provide for performers the exclusive right to authorize or prohibit the broadcasting by wireless means and the communication to the public of their performances, except where the performance is itself already a broadcast performance or is made from a fixation.
2. Member States shall provide a right in order to ensure that a single equitable remuneration is paid by the user, if a phonogram published for commercial purposes, or a reproduction of such phonogram, is used for broadcasting by wireless means or for any communciation to the public, and to ensure that this remuneration is shared between the relevant performers and phonogram producers. Member States may, in the absence of agreement between the performers and phonogram producers, lay down the conditions as to the sharing of this remuneration between them.
3. Member States shall provide for broadcasting organizations the exclusive right to authorize or prohibit the rebroadcasting of their broadcasts by wireless means, as well as the communication to the public of their broadcasts if such communciation is made in places accessible to the public against payment of an entrance fee.

Article 9

Distribution right   A4.10

1. Member States shall provide

— for performers, in respect of fixations of their performances,
— for phonogram producers, in respect of their phonograms,
— for producers of the first fixations of films, in respect of the original and copies of their films,
— for broadcasting organizations, in respect of fixations of their braodcast as set out in Article 6(2),

the exclusive right to make available these objects, including copies thereof, to the public by sale or otherwise hereafter referred to as the "distribution right".
2. The distribution right shall not be exhausted within the Community in respect of an object as referred to in paragraph 1, except where the first sale in the Community of that object is made by the rightholder or with his consent.
3. The distribution right shall be without prejudice to the specific provisions of Chapter I, in particular Article 1(4).
4. The distribution right may be transferred, assigned or subject to the granting of contractual licences.

Article 10

A4.11   Limitations to rights

1. Member States may provide for limitations to the rights referred to in Chapter II in respect of:

(a) private use;
(b) use of short excerpts in connection with the reporting of current events;
(c) ephemeral fixation by a broadcasting organization by means of its own facilities and for its own broadcasts;
(d) use solely for the purposes of teaching or scientific research.

2. Irrespective of paragraph 1, any Member State may provide for the same kinds of limitations with regard to the protection of performers, producers of phonograms, broadcasting organizations and of producers of the first fixations of films, as it provides for in connection with the protection of copyright in literary and artistic works. However, compulsory licences may be provided for only to the extent to which they are compatible with the Rome Convention.

3. Paragraph 1(a) shall be without prejudice to any existing or future legislation on remuneration for reproduction for private use.

CHAPTER III

DURATION

Article 11

A4.12   *Duration of authors' rights*

Without prejudice to further harmonization, the authors' rights referred to in this Directive shall not expire before the end of the term provided by the Berne Convention for the Protection of Literary and Artistic Works.

Article 12

A4.13   *Duration of related rights*

Without prejudice to further harmonization, the rights referred to in this Directive of performers, phonogram producers and broadcasting organizations shall not expire before the end of the respective terms provided by the Rome Convention. The rights referred to in this Directive for producers of the first fixations of films shall not expire before the end of a period of 20 years computed from the end of the year in which the fixation was made.

Note: Articles 11 and 12 have been repealed by Article 11(2) of Directive 93/98: see *post*, para. A4.45.

CHAPTER IV

COMMON PROVISIONS

Article 13

A4.14   Application in time

1. This Directive shall apply in respect of all copyright works, performances, phonograms, broadcasts and first fixations of films referred to in this Directive which

are, on 1 July 1994, still protected by the legislation of the Member States in the field of copyright and related rights or meet the criteria for protection under the provisions of this Directive on that date.

2. This Directive shall apply without prejudice to any acts of exploitation performed before 1 July 1994.

3. Member States may provide that the rightholders are deemed to have given their authorization to the rental or lending of an object referred to in Article 2(1) which is proven to have been made available to third parties for this purpose or to have been acquired before 1 July 1994. However, in particular where such an object is a digital recording, Member States may provide that rightholders shall have a right to obtain an adequate remuneration for the rental or lending of that object.

4. Member States need not apply to provisions of Article 2(2) to cinematographic or audiovisual works created before 1 July 1994.

5. Member States may determine the date as from which the Article 2(2) shall apply, provided that that date is not later than 1 July 1997.

6. This Directive shall, without prejudice to paragraph 3 and subject to paragraphs 8 and 9, not affect any contracts concluded before the date of its adoption.

7. Member States may provide, subject to the provisions of paragraphs 8 and 9, that when rightholders who acquire new rights under the national provisions adopted in implementation of this Directive have, before 1 July 1994, given their consent for exploitation, they shall be presumed to have transferred the new exclusive rights.

8. Member States may determine the date as from which the unwaivable right to an equitable remuneration referred to in Article 4 exists, provided that that date is not later than 1 July 1997.

9. For contracts concluded before 1 July 1994, the unwaivable right to an equitable remuneration provided for in Article 4 shall apply only where authors or performers or those representing them have submitted a request to that effect before 1 January 1997. In the absence of agreement between rightholders concerning the level of remuneration, Member States may fix the level of equitable remuneration.

Article 14

Relation between copyright and related rights   A4.15

Protection of copyright-related rights under this Directive shall leave intact and shall in no way affect the protection of copyright.

Article 15

Final provisions   A4.16

1. Member States shall bring into force the laws, regulations and administrative provisions necessary to comply with this Directive not later than 1 July 1994. They shall forthwith inform the Commission thereof.

When Member States adopt these measures, they shall contain a reference to this Directive or shall be accompanied by such reference at the time of their official publication. The methods of making such a reference shall be laid down by the Member States.

2. Member States shall communicate to the Commission the main provisions of domestic law which they adopt in the field covered by this Directive.

Article 16

This Directive is addressed to the Member States.   A4.17

Done at Brussels, 19 November 1992.

APPENDIX 4B

COUNCIL DIRECTIVE 93/83

of September 27, 1993
on the coordination of certain rules concerning copyright and rights related to copyright applicable to satellite broadcasting and cable retransmission

([1993] O.J. L248/15)

THE COUNCIL OF THE EUROPEAN COMMUNITIES

A4.18   Having regard to the Treaty establishing the European Economic Community, and in particular Articles 57(2) and 66 thereof,

Having regard to the proposal from the Commission,

In cooperation with the European Parliament,

Having regard to the opinion of the Economic and Social Committee.

(1) Whereas the objectives of the Community as laid down in the Treaty include establishing an ever closer union among the peoples of Europe, fostering closer relations between the States belonging to the Community and ensuring the economic and social progress of the Community countries by common action to eliminate the barriers which divide Europe;

(2) Whereas, to that end, the Treaty provides for the establishment of a common market and an area without internal frontiers; whereas measures to achieve this include the abolition of obstacles to the free movement of services and the institution of a system ensuring that competition in the common market is not distorted; whereas, to that end, the Council may adopt directives for the coordination of the provisions laid down by law, regulation or administrative action in Member States concerning the taking up and pursuit of activities as self-employed persons;

(3) Whereas broadcasts transmitted across frontiers within the Community, in particular by satellite and cable, are one of the most important ways of pursuing these Community objectives, which are at the same time political, economic, social, cultural and legal;

(4) Whereas the Council has already adopted Directive 89/552/EEC of 3 October 1989 on the coordination of certain provisions laid down by law, regulation or administrative action in Member States concerning the pursuit of television broadcasting activities, which makes provision for the promotion of the distribution and production of European television programmes and for advertising and sponsorship, the protection of minors and the right of reply;

(5) Whereas, however, the achievement of these objectives in respect of cross-border satellite broadcasting and the cable retransmission of programmes from other Member States is currently still obstructed by a series of differences between national rules of copyright and some degree of legal uncertainty; whereas this means that holders of rights are exposed to the threat of seeing their works exploited without payment of remuneration or that the individual holders of exclusive rights in various Member States block the exploitation of their rights; whereas the legal uncertainty in particular constitutes a direct obstacle in the free circulation of programmes within the Community;

(6) Whereas a distinction is currently drawn for copyright purposes between communication to the public by direct satellite and communication to the public by communications satellite; whereas, since individual reception is possible and

affordable nowadays with both types of satellite, there is no longer any justification for this differing legal treatment;

(7) Whereas the free broadcasting of programmes is further impeded by the current legal uncertainty over whether broadcasting by a satellite whose signals can be received directly affects the rights in the country of transmission only or in all countries of reception together; whereas, since communications satellites and direct satellites are treated alike for copyright purposes, this legal uncertainty now affects almost all programmes broadcast in the Community by satellite;

(8) Whereas, furthermore, legal certainty, which is a prerequisite for the free movement of broadcasts within the Community, is missing where programmes transmitted across frontiers are fed into and retransmitted through cable networks;

(9) Whereas the development of the acquisition of rights on a contractual basis by authorization is already making a vigorous contribution to the creation of the desired European audiovisual area; whereas the continuation of such contractual agreements should be ensured and their smooth application in practice should be promoted wherever possible;

(10) Whereas at present cable operators in particular cannot be sure that they have actually acquired all the programme rights covered by such an agreement;

(11) Whereas, lastly, parties in different Member States are not all similarly bound by obligations which prevent them from refusing without valid reason to negotiate on the acquisition of the rights necessary for cable distribution or allowing such negotiations to fail;

(12) Whereas the legal framework for the creation of a single audiovisual area laid down in Directive 89/552/EEC must, therefore, be supplemented with reference to copyright;

(13) Whereas, therefore, an end should be put to the differences of treatment of the transmission of programmes by communications satellite which exist in the Member States, so that the vital distinction throughout the Community becomes whether works and other protected subject matter are communicated to the public; whereas this will also ensure equal treatment of the supplies of cross-border broadcasts, regardless of whether they use a direct broadcasting or a communications satellite;

(14) Whereas the legal uncertainty regarding the rights to be acquired which impedes cross-border satellite broadcasting should be overcome by defining the notion of communication to the public by satellite at a Community level; whereas this definition should at the same time specify where the act of communication takes place; whereas such a definition is necessary to avoid the cumulative application of several national laws to one single act of broadcasting; whereas communication to the public by satellite occurs only when, and in the Member State where, the programme-carrying signals are introduced under the control and responsibility of the broad-casting organization into an uninterrupted chain of communication leading to the satellite and down towards the earth; whereas normal technical procedures relating to the programme-carrying signals should not be considered as interruptions to the chain of broadcasting;

(15) Whereas the acquisition on a contractual basis of exclusive broadcasting rights should comply with any legislation on copyright and rights related to copyright in the Member State in which communication to the public by satellite occurs;

(16) Whereas the principle of contractual freedom on which this Directive is based will make it possible to continue limiting the exploitation of these rights, especially as far as certain technical means of transmission or certain language versions are concerned;

(17) Whereas, in arriving at the amount of the payment to be made for the rights acquired, the parties should take account of all aspects of the broadcast such as the actual audience, the potential audience and the language version;

(18) Whereas the application of the country-of-origin principle contained in this Directive could pose a problem with regard to existing contracts; whereas this Directive should provide for a period of five years for existing contracts to be adapted, where necessary, in the light of the Directive; whereas the said country-of-origin

principle should not, therefore, apply to existing contracts which expire before 1 January 2000; whereas if by that date parties still have an interest in the contract, the same parties should be entitled to renegotiate the conditions of the contract;

(19) Whereas existing international co-production agreements must be interpreted in the light of the economic purpose and scope envisaged by the parties upon signature; whereas in the past international co-production agreements have often not expressly and specifically addressed communication to the public by satellite within the meaning of this Directive a particular form of exploitation; whereas the underlying philosophy of many existing international co-production agreements is that the rights in the co-production are exercised separately and independently by each co-producer, by dividing the exploitation rights between them along territorial lines; whereas, as a general rule, in the situation where a communication to the public by satellite athorized by one co-producer would prejudice the value of the exploitation rights of another co-producer, the interpretation of such an existing agreement would normally suggest that the latter co-producer, would have to give his consent to the authorization, by the former co-producer, of the communication to the public by satellite; whereas the language exclusivity of the latter co-producer will be prejudiced where the language version or versions of the communication to the public, including where the version is dubbed or subtitled, coincide(s) with the language or the languages widely understood in the territory allotted by the agreement to the latter co-producer; whereas the notion of exclusivity should be understood in a wider sense where the communication to the public by satellite concerns a work which consists merely of images and contains no dialogue or subtitles; whereas a clear rule is necessary in cases where the international co-production agreement does not expressly regulate the division of rights in the specific case of communication to the public by satellite within the meaning of this Directive;

(20) Whereas communications to the public by satellite from non-member countries will under certain conditions be deemed to occur within a Member State of the Community;

(21) Whereas it is necessary to ensure that protection for authors, performers, producers of phonograms and broadcasting organizations is accorded in all Member States and that this protection is not subject to a statutory licence system; whereas only in this way is it possible to ensure that any difference in the level of protection within the common market will not create distortions of competition;

(22) Whereas the advent of new technologies is likely to have an impact on both the quality and the quantity of the exploitation of works and other subject matter;

(23) Whereas in the light of these developments the level of protection granted pursuant to this Directive to all rightholders in the areas covered by this Directive should remain under consideration;

(24) Whereas the harmonization of legislation envisaged in this Directive entails the harmonization of the provisions ensuring a high level of protection of authors, performers, phonogram producers and broadcasting organizations; whereas this harmonization should not allow a broadcasting organization to take advantage of differences in levels of protection by relocating activities, to the detriment of audiovisual productions;

(25) Whereas the protection provided for rights related to copyright should be aligned on that contained in Council Directive 92/100/EEC of 19 November 1992 on rental right and lending right and on certain rights related to copyright in the field of intellectual property for the purposes of communication to the public by satellite; whereas, in particular, this will ensure that performers and phonogram producers are guaranteed an appropriate remuneration for the communication to the public by satellite of their performances or phonograms;

(26) Whereas the provisions of Article 4 do not prevent Member States from extending the presumption set out in Article 2(5) of Directive 92/100/EEC to the exclusive rights referred to in Article 4; whereas, furthermore, the provisions of Article 4 do not prevent Member States from providing for a rebuttable presumption of the authorization of exploitation in respect of the exclusive rights of performers referred

to in that Article, in so far as such presumption is compatible with the International Convention for the Protection of Performers, Producers of Phonograms and Broadcasting Organizations;

(27) Whereas the cable retransmission of programmes from other Member States is an act subject to copyright and, as the case may be, rights related to copyright; whereas the cable operator must, therefore, obtain the authorization from every holder of rights in each part of the programme retransmitted; whereas, pursuant to this Directive, the authorizations should be granted contractually unless a temporary exception is provided for in the case of existing legal licence schemes;

(28) Whereas, in order to ensure that the smooth operation of contractual arrangements is not called into question by the intervention of outsiders holding rights in individual parts of the programme, provision should be made, through the obligation to have recourse to a collecting society, for the exclusive collective exercise of the authoriztion right to the extent that this is required by the special features of cable retransmission; whereas the authorization right as such remains intact and only the exercise of this right is regulated to some extent, so that the right to authorize a cable retransmision can still be assigned; whereas this Directive does not affect the exercise of moral rights;

(29) Whereas the exemption provided for in Article 10 should not limit the choice of holders of rights to transfer their rights to a collecting society and thereby have a direct share in the remuneration paid by the cable distributor for cable retransmission;

(30) Whereas contractual arrangements regarding the authorization of cable retransmission should be promoted by additional measures; whereas a party seeking the conclusion of a general contract should, for its part, be obliged to submit collective proposals for an agreement; whereas furthermore, any party shall be entitled, at any moment, to call upon the assistance of impartial mediators whose task is to assist negotiations and who may submit proposals; whereas any such proposals and any opposition thereto should be served on the parties concerned in accordance with the applicable rules concerning the service of legal documents, in particular as set out in existing international conventions; whereas, finally, it is necesary to ensure that the negotiations are not blocked without valid justification or that individual holders are not prevented without valid justification from taking part in the negotiations; whereas none of these measures for the promotion of the acquisition of rights calls into question the contractual nature of the acquisition of cable retransmission rights;

(31) Whereas for a transitional period Member States should be allowed to retain existing bodies with jurisdiction in their territory over cases where the right to retransmit a programme by cable to the public has been unreasonably refused or offered on unreasonable terms by a broadcasting organization; whereas it is understood that the right of parties concerned to be heard by the body should be guaranteed and that the existence of the body should not prevent the parties concerned from having normal access to the courts;

(32) Whereas, however, Community rules are not needed to deal with all of those matters, the effects of which perhaps with some commercially insignificant exceptions, are felt only inside the borders of a single Member State;

(33) Whereas minimum rules should be laid down in order to establish and guarantee free and uninterrupted cross-border broadcasting by satellite and simultaneous, unaltered cable retransmission of programmes broadcast from other Member States, on an essentially contractual basis;

(34) Whereas this Directive should not prejudice further harmonization in the field of copyright and rights related to copyright and the collective administration of such rights; whereas the possibility for Member States to regulate the activities of collecting societies should not prejudice the freedom of contractual negotiation of the rights provided for in this Directive, on the understanding that such negotiation takes place within the framework of general or specific national rules with regard to competition law or the prevention of abuse of monopolies;

(35) Whereas it should, therefore, be for the Member States to supplement the general provisions needed to achieve the objectives of this Directive by taking

legislative and administrative measures in their domestic law, provided that these do not run counter to the objectives of this Directive and are compatible with Community law;

(36) Whereas this Directive does not affect the applicability of the competition rules in Articles 85 and 86 of the Treaty,

HAS ADOPTED THIS DIRECTIVE:

CHAPTER I

DEFINITIONS

Article 1

A4.19 **Definitions**

1. For the purpose of this Directive, "satellite" means any satellite operating on frequency bands which, under telecommunications law, are reserved for the broadcast of signals for reception by the public or which are reserved for closed, point-to-point communication. In the latter case, however, the circumstances in which individual reception of the signals takes place must be comparable to those which apply in the first case.

2. (a) For the purpose of this Directive, "communication to the public by satellite" means the act of introducing, under the control and responsibility of the broadcasting organization, the programme-carrying signals intended for reception by the public into an uninterrupted chain of communication leading to the satellite and down towards the earth.

   (b) The act of communication to the public by satellite occurs solely in the Member State where, under the control and responsibility of the broadcasting organization, the programme-carrying signals are introduced into an uninterrupted chain of communication leading to the satellite and down toward the earth.

   (c) If the programme-carrying signals are encrypted, then there is communication to the public by staellite on condition that the means for decrypting the broadcast are provided to the public by the broadcasting organization or with its consent.

   (d) Where an act of communication to the public by satellite occurs in a non-Community State which does not provide the level of protection provided for under Chapter II,

   (i) if the programme-carrying signals are transmitted to the satellite from an uplink station[1] situated in a Member State, that act of communication to the public by satellite shall be deemed to have occurred in that Member State and the rights provided for under Chapter II shall be exercisable against the person operating the uplink station; or

   (ii) if there is no use of an uplink station situated in a Member State but a broadcasting organization established in a Member State has commissioned the act of communication to the public by satellite, that act shall be deemed to have occurred in the Member State in which the broadcasting organization has its principal establishment in the Community and the rights provided for under Chapter II shall be exercisable against the broadcasting organization.

3. For the purposes of this Directive, "cable retransmission" means the simultaneous, unaltered and unabridged retransmission by a cable or microwave system for reception by the public of an initial transmission from another Member State, by wire

---

[1] O.J. text has "situation".

or over the air, including that by satellite, of television or radio programmes intended for reception by the public.

4. For the purposes of this Directive "collecting society" means any organization which manages or administers copyright or rights related to copyright as its sole purpose or as one of its main purposes.

5. For the purposes of this Directive, the principal director of a cinematographic or audiovisual work shall be considered as its author or one of its authors. Member States may provide for others to be considered as its co-authors.

CHAPTER II

BROADCASTING OF PROGRAMMES BY SATELLITE

Article 2

Broadcasting right   A4.20

Member States shall provide an exclusive right for the author to authorize the communication to the public by satellite of copyright works, subject to the provisions set out in this chapter.

Article 3

Acquisition of broadcasting rights   A4.21

1. Member States shall ensure that the authorization referred to in Article 2 may be acquired only by agreement.
2. A Member State may provide that a collective agreement between a collecting society and a broadcasting organization concerning a given category of works may be extended to rightholders of the same category who are not represented by the collecting society, provided that:

— the communication to the public by satellite simulcasts a terrestrial broadcast by the same broadcaster, and
— the unrepresented rightholder shall, at any time, have the possibility of excluding the extension of the collective agreement to his works and of exercising his rights either individually or collectively.

3. Paragraph 2 shall not apply to cinematographic works, including works created by a process analogous to cinematography.
4. Where the law of a Member State provides for the extension of a collective agreement in accordance with the provisions of paragraph 2, that Member State[2] shall inform the Commission which broadcasting organizations are entitled to avail themselves of that law. The Commission shall publish this information in the *Official Journal of the European Communities* (C series).

Article 4

Rights of performers, phonogram producers and broadcasting organizations   A4.22

1. For the purposes of communication to the public by satellite, the rights of performers, phonogram producers and broadcasting organizations shall be protected in accordance with the provisions of Articles 6, 7, 8 and 10 of Directive 92/100/EEC.
2. For the purposes of paragraph 1, "broadcasting by wireless means" in Directive 92/100/EEC shall be understood as including communication to the public by satellite.

---

[2] O.J. text has "States".

3. With regard to the exercise of the rights referred to in paragraph 1, Articles 2(7) and 12 of Directive 92/100/EEC shall apply.

Article 5

A4.23 **Relation between copyright and related rights**

Protection of copyright-related rights under this Directive shall leave intact and shall in no way affect the protection of copyright.

Article 6

A4.24 **Minimum protection**

1. Member States may provide for more far-reaching protection for holders of rights related to copyright than that required by Article 8 of Directive 92/100/EEC.
2. In applying paragraph 1 Member States shall observe the definitions contained in Article 1(1) and (2).

Article 7

A4.25 **Transitional provisions**

1. With regard to the application in time of the rights referred to in Article 4(1) of this Directive, Article 13(1), (2), (6) and (7) of Directive 92/100/EEC shall apply. Article 13(4) and (5) of Directive 92/100/EEC shall apply *mutatis mutandis*.
2. Agreements concerning the exploitation of works and other protected subject matter which are in force on the date mentioned in Article 14(1) shall be subject to the provisions of Articles 1(2), 2 and 3 as from 1 January 2000 if they expire after that date.
3. When an international co-production agreement concluded before the date mentioned in Article 14(1) between a co-producer from a Member State and one or more co-producers from other Member States or third countries expressly provides for a system of division of exploitation rights between the co-producers by geographical areas for all means of communication to the public, without distinguishing the arrangements applicable to communication to the public by satellite from the provisions applicable to the other means of communication, and where communication to the public by satellite of the co-production would prejudice the exclusivity, in particular the language exclusivity, of one of the co-producers or his assignees in a given territory, the authorization by one of the co-producers or his assignees for a communication to the public by satellite shall require the prior consent of the holder of that exclusivity, whether co-producer or assignee.

CHAPTER III

CABLE RETRANSMISSION

Article 8

A4.26 **Cable retransmision right**

1. Member States shall ensure that when programmes from other Member States are retransmitted by cable in their territory the applicable copyright and related rights are observed and that such retransmission takes place on the basis of individual or collective contractual agreements between copyright owners, holders of releated rights and cable operators.
2. Notwithstanding paragraph 1, Member States may retain until 31 December 1997

such statutory licence systems which are in operation or expressly provided for by national law on 31 July 1991.

Article 9

Exercise of the cable retransmission right   A4.27

1. Member States shall ensure that the right of copyright owners and holders of related rights to grant or refuse authorization to a cable operator for a cable retransmission may be exercised only through a collecting society.
2. Where a rightholder had not transferred the management of his rights to a collecting society, the collecting society which manages rights of the same category shall be deemed to be mandated to manage his rights. Where more than one collecting society manages rights of that category, the rightholder shall be free to choose which of these collecting societies is deemed to be mandated to manage his rights. A rightholder referred to in this paragraph shall have the same rights and obligations resulting from the agreement between the cable operator and the collecting society which is deemed to be mandated to manage his rights as the rightholders who have mandated that collecting society and he shall be able to claim those rights within a period, to be fixed by the Member State concerned, which shall not be shorter than three years from the date of the cable retransmission which includes his work or other protected subject matter.
3. A Member State may provide that, when a rightholder authorizes the initial transmission within its territory of a work or other protected subject matter, he shall be deemed to have agreed not to exercise his cable retransmission rights on an individual basis but to exercise them in accordance with the provisions of this Directive.

Article 10

Exercise of the cable retransmission right by broadcasting organizations   A4.28

Member States shall ensure that Article 9 does not apply to the rights exercised by a broadcasting organization in respect of its own transmission, irrespective of whether the rights concerned are its own or have been transferred to it by other copyright owners and/or holders of related rights.

Article 11

Mediators   A4.29

1. Where no agreement is concluded regarding authorization of the cable retransmission of a broadcast, Member States shall ensure that either party may call upon the assistance of one or more mediators.
2. The task of the mediators shall be to provide assistance with negotiation. They may also submit proposals to the parties.
3. It shall be assumed that all the parties accept a proposal as referred to in paragraph 2 if none of them expresses its opposition within a period of three months. Notice of the proposal and of any opposition thereto shall be served on the parties concerned in accordance with the applicable rules concerning the service of legal documents.
4. The mediators shall be so selected that their independence and impartiality are beyond reasonable doubt.

Article 12

Prevention of the abuse of negotiating positions   A4.30

1. Member States shall ensure by means of civil or administrative law, as appropriate, that the parties enter and conduct negotiations regarding authorization for cable retransmission in good faith and do not prevent or hinder negotiation without valid justification.

2. A Member State which, on the date mentioned in Article 14(1), has a body with jurisdiction in its territory over cases where the right to retransmit a programme by cable to the public in that Member State has been unreasonably refused or offered on unreasonable terms by a broadcasting organization may retain that body.

3. Paragraph 2 shall apply for a transitional period of eight years from the date mentioned in Article 14(1).

CHAPTER IV

GENERAL PROVISIONS

Article 13

A4.31   **Collective administration of rights**

This Directive shall be without prejudice to the regulation of the activities of collecting societies by the Member States.

Article 14

A4.32   **Final provisions**

1. Member States shall bring into force the laws, regulations and administrative provisions necessary to comply with this Directive before 1 January 1995. They shall immediately inform the Commission thereof.

When Member States adopt these measures, the latter shall contain a reference to this Directive or shall be accompanied by such reference at the time of their official publication. The methods of making such a reference shall be laid down by the Member States.

2. Member States shall communicate to the Commission the provisions of national law which they adopt in the field covered by this Directive.

3. Not later than 1 January 2000, the Commission shall submit to the European Parliament, the Council and the Economic and Social Committee a report on the application of this Directive and, if necessary, make further proposals to adapt it to developments in the audio and audiovisual sector.

Article 15

A4.33   This Directive is addressed to the Member States.

Done at Brussels, 27 September 1993.

APPENDIX 4C

COUNCIL DIRECTIVE 93/98

of October 29, 1993
harmonizing the term of protection of copyright and certain related rights
([1993] O.J. L290/9)

THE COUNCIL OF THE EUROPEAN COMMUNITIES

Having regard to the Treaty establishing the European Economic Community, and in particular Articles 57(2), 66 and 100a thereof,

A4.34

Having regard to the proposal from the Commission,

In cooperation with the European Parliament,

Having regard to the opinion of the Economic and Social Committee,

(1) Whereas the Berne Convention for the protection of literary and artistic works and the International Convention for the protection of performers, producers of phonograms and broadcasting organizations (Rome Convention) lay down only minimum terms of protection of the rights they refer to, leaving the Contracting States free to grant longer terms; whereas certain Member States have exercised this entitlement; whereas in addition certain Member States have not become party to the Rome Convention;

(2) Whereas there are consequently differences between the national laws governing the terms of protection of copyright and related rights, which are liable to impede the free movement of goods and freedom to provide services, and to distort competition in the common market; whereas therefore with a view to the smooth operation of the internal market, the laws of the Member States should be harmonized so as to make terms of protection identical throughout the Community;

(3) Whereas harmonization must cover not only the terms of protection as such, but also certain implementing arrangements such as the date from which each term of protection is calculated;

(4) Whereas the provisions of this Directive do not affect the application by the Member States of the provisions of Article 14a(2)(b), (c) and (d) and (3) of the Berne Convention;

(5) Whereas the minimum term of protection laid down by the Berne Convention, namely the life of the author and 50 years after his death, was intended to provide protection for the author and the first two generations of his descendants; whereas the average lifespan in the Community has grown longer, to the point where this term is no longer sufficient to cover two generations;

(6) Whereas certain Member States have granted a term longer than 50 years after the death of the author in order to offset the effects of the world wars on the exploitation of authors' works;

(7) Whereas for the protection of related rights certain Member States have introduced a term of 50 years after lawful publication or lawful communication to the public;

(8) Whereas under the Community position adopted for the Uruguay Round negotiations under the General Agreement on Tariffs and Trade (GATT) the term of protection for producers of phonograms should be 50 years after first publication;

(9) Whereas due regard for established rights is one of the general principles of law protected by the Community legal order; whereas, therefore, a harmonization of the terms of protection of copyright and related rights cannot have the effect of reducing the protection currently enjoyed by rightholders in the Community; whereas in order

to keep the effects of transitional measures to a minimum and to allow the internal market to operate in practice, the harmonization of the term of protection should take place on a long term basis;

(10) Whereas in its communication of 17 January 1991 "Follow-up to the Green Paper—Working programme of the Commission in the field of copyright and neighbouring rights" the Commission stresses the need to harmonize copyright and neighbouring rights at a high level of protection since these rights are fundamental to intellectual creation and stresses that their protection ensures the maintenance and development of creativity in the interest of authors, cultural industries, consumers and society as a whole;

(11) Whereas in order to establish a high level of protection which at the same time meets the requirements of the internal market and the need to establish a legal environment conducive to the harmonious development of literary and artistic creation in the Community, the term of protection for copyright should be harmonized at 70 years after the death of the author or 70 years after the work is lawfully made available to the public, and for related rights at 50 years after the event which sets the term running;

(12) Whereas collections are protected according to Article 2(5) of the Berne Convention when, by reason of the selection and arrangment of their content, they constitute intellectual creations; whereas those works are protected as such, without prejudice to the copyright in each of the works forming part of such collections, whereas in consequence specific terms of protection may apply to works included in collections;

(13) Whereas in all cases where one or more physical persons are identified as authors the term of protection should be calculated after their death; whereas the question of authorship in the whole or a part of a work is a question of fact which the national courts may have to decide;

(14) Whereas terms of protection should be calculated from the first day of January of the year following the relevant event, as they are in the Berne and Rome Conventions;

(15) Whereas Article 1 of Council Directive 91/250/EEC of May 14, 1991 on the legal protection of computer programs provides that Member States are to protect computer programs, by copyright, as literary works within the meaning of the Berne Convention; whereas this Directive harmonizes the term of protection of literary works in the Community; whereas Article 8 of Directive 91/250/EEC, which merely makes provisional arrangements governing the term of protection of computer programs, should accordingly be repealed;

(16) Whereas Articles 11 and 12 of Council Directive 92/100/EEC of November 19, 1992 on rental right and lending right and on certain rights related to copyright in the field of intellectual property make provision for minimum terms of protection only, subject to any further harmonization; whereas this Directive provides such further harmonization; whereas these Articles should accordingly be repealed;

(17) Whereas the protection of photographs in the Member States is the subject of varying regimes; whereas in order to achieve a sufficient harmonization of the term of protection of photographic works, in particular of those which, due to their artistic or professional character, are of importance within the internal market, it is necessary to define the level of originality required in this Directive; whereas a photographic work within the meaning of the Berne Convention is to be considered original if it is the author's own intellectual creation reflecting his personality, no other criteria such as merit or purpose being taken into account; whereas the protection of other photographs should be left to national law;

(18) Whereas, in order to avoid differences in the term of protection as regards related rights it is necessary to provide the same starting point for the calculation of the term throughout the Community; whereas the performance, fixation, trans-mission, lawful publication, and lawful communication to the public, that is to say the means of making a subject of a related right perceptible in all appropriate ways to persons in general, should be taken into account for the calculation of the term of

protection regardless of the country where this performance, fixation, transmission, lawful publication, or lawful communication to the public takes place;

(19) Whereas the rights of broadcasting organizations in their broadcasts, whether these broadcasts are transmitted by wire or over the air, including by cable or satellite, should not be perpetual; whereas it is therefore necessary to have the term of protection running from the first transmission of a particular broadcast only; whereas this provision is understood to avoid a new term running in cases where a broadcast is identical to a previous one;

(20) Whereas the Member States should remain free to maintain or introduce other rights related to copyright in particular in relation to the protection of critical and scientific publications; whereas, in order to ensure transparency at Community level, it is however necessary for Member States which introduce new related rights to notify the Commission;

(21) Whereas it is useful to make clear that the harmonization brought about by this Directive does not apply to moral rights;

(22) Whereas, for works whose country of origin within the meaning of the Berne Convention is a third country and whose author is not a Community national, comparison of terms of protection should be applied, provided that the term accorded in the Community does not exceed the term laid down in this Directive;

(23) Whereas where a rightholder who is not a Community national qualifies for protection under an international agreement the term of protection of related rights should be the same as that laid down in this Directive, except that it should not exceed that fixed in the country of which the rightholder is a national;

(24) Whereas comparison of terms should not result in Member States being brought into conflict with their international obligations;

(25) Whereas, for the smooth functioning of the internal market this Directive should be applied as from 1 July 1995;

(26) Whereas Member States should remain free to adopt provisions on the interpretation, adaptation and further execution of contracts on the exploitation of protected works and other subject matter which were concluded before the extension of the term of protection resulting from this Directive;

(27) Whereas respect of acquired rights and legitimate expectations is part of the Community legal order; whereas Member States may provide in particular that in certain circumstances the copyright and related rights which are revived pursuant to this Directive may not give rise to payments by persons who undertook in good faith the exploitation of the works at the time when such works lay within the public domain,

HAS ADOPTED THIS DIRECTIVE:

Article 1

Duration of author's rights A4.35

1. The rights of an author of a literary or artistic work within the meaning of Article 2 of the Berne Convention shall run for the life of the author and for 70 years after his death, irrespective of the date when the work is lawfully made available to the public.

2. In the case of a work of joint authorship the term referred to in paragraph 1 shall be calculated from the death of the last surviving author.

3. In the case of anonymous or pseudonymous works, the term of protection shall run for seventy years after the work is lawfully made available to the public. However, when the pseudonym adopted by the author leaves no doubt as to his identity, or if the author discloses his identity during the period referred to in the first sentence, the term of protection applicable shall be that laid down in paragraph 1.

4. Where a Member State provides for particular provisions on copyright in respect of collective works or for a legal person to be designated as the rightholder, the term of protection shall be calculated according to the provisions of paragraph 3, except if the natural persons who have created the work as such are identified as such in the versions of the work which are made available to the public. This paragraph is without prejudice to the rights of identified authors whos identifiable contributions are included in such works, to which contributions paragraph 1 or 2 shall apply.

5. Where a work is published in volumes, parts, instalments, issues or episodes and the term of protection runs from the time when the work was lawfully made available to the public, the term of protection shall run for each such item separately.

6. In the case of works for which the term of protection is not calculated from the death of the author or authors and which have not been lawfully made available to the public within seventy years from their creation, the protection shall terminate.

Article 2

A4.36 Cinematographic or audiovisual works

1. The principal director of a cinematographic or audiovisual work shall be considered as its author or one of its authors. Member States shall be free to designate other co-authors.

2. The term of protection of cinematographic or audiovisual works shall expire 70 years after the death of the last of the following persons to survive, whether or not these persons are designated as co-authors: the principal director, the author of the screenplay, the author of the dialogue and the composer of music specifically created for use in the cinematographic or audiovisual work.

Article 3

A4.37 Duration of related rights

1. The rights of performers shall expire 50 years after the date of the performance. However, if a fixation of the performance is lawfully published or lawfully communicated to the public within this period, the rights shall expire 50 years from the date of the first such publication or the first such communciation to the public, whichever is the earlier.

2. The rights of producers of phonograms shall expire 50 years after the fixation is made. However, if the phonogram is lawfully published or lawfully communicated to the public during this period, the rights shall expire 50 years from the date of the first such publication or the first such communication to the public, whichever is the earlier.

3. The rights of producers of the first fixation of a film shall expire 50 years after the fixation is made. However, if the film is lawfully published or lawfully communicated to the public during this period, the rights shall expire 50 years from the date of the first such publication or the first such communication to the public, whichever is the earlier. The term "film" shall designate a cinematographic or audiovisual work or moving images, whether or not accompanied by sound.

4. The rights of broadcasting organizations shall expire 50 years after the first transmission of a broadcast, whether this broadcast is transmitted by wire or over the air, including by cable or satellite.

Article 4

A4.38 Protection of previously unpublished works

Any person who, after the expiry of copyright protection, for the first time lawfully publishes or lawfully communicates to the public a previously unpublished work, shall benefit from a protection equivalent to the economic rights of the author. The term of protection of such rights shall be 25 years from the time when the work was first lawfully published or lawfully communicated to the public.

Article 5

Critical and scientific publication   A4.39

Member States may protect critical and scientific publications of works which have come into the public domain. The maximum term of protection of such rights shall be 30 years from the time when the publication was first lawfully published.

Article 6

Protection of photographs   A4.40

Photographs which are original in the sense that they are the author's own intellectual creation shall be protected in accordance with Article 1. No other criteria shall be applied to determine their eligibility for protection. Member States may provide for the protection of other photographs.

Article 7

Protection *vis-à-vis* third countries   A4.41

1. Where the country of origin of a work, within the meaning of the Berne Convention, is a third country, and the author of the work is not a Community national, the term of protection granted by the Member States shall expire on the date of expiry of the protection granted in the country of origin of the work, but may not exceed the term laid down in Article 1.
2. The terms of protection laid down in Article 3 shall also apply in the case of rightholders who are not Community nationals, provided Member States grant them protection. However, without prejudice to the international obligations of the Member States, the term of protection granted by Member States shall expire no later than the date of expiry of the protection granted in the country of which the rightholder is a national and may not exceed the term laid down in Article 3.
3. Member States which, at the date of adoption of this Directive, in particular pursuant to their international obligations, granted a longer term of protection than that which would result from the provisions, referred to in paragraphs 1 and 2 may maintain this protection until the conclusion of international agreements on the term of protection by copyright or related rights.

Article 8

Calculation of terms   A4.42

The terms laid down in this Directive are calculated from the first day of January in the year following the event which gives rise to them.

Article 9

Moral rights   A4.43

This Directive shall be without prejudice to the provisions of the Member States regulating moral rights.

Article 10

Application in time   A4.44

1. Where a term of protection, which is longer than the corresponding term provided for by this Directive, is already running in a Member State on the date referred to in

Article 13(1), this Directive shall not have the effect of shortening that term of protection in that Member State.

2. The terms of protection provided for in this Directive shall apply to all works and subject matter which are protected in at least one Member State, on the date referred to in Article 13(1), pursuant to national provisions on copyright or related rights or which meet the criteria for protection under Directive 92/100/EEC.

3. This Directive shall be without prejudice to any acts of exploitation performed before the date referred to in Article 13(1). Member States shall adopt the necessary provisions to protect in particular acquired rights of third parties.

4. Member States need not apply the provisions of Article 2(1) to cinematographic or audiovisual works created before 1 July 1994.

5. Member States may determine the date as from which Article 2(1) shall apply, provided that date is not later than 1 July, 1997.

Article 11

A4.45 **Technical adaptation**

1. Article 8 of Directive 91/250/EEC is hereby repealed.
2. Articles 11 and 12 of Directive 92/100/EEC are hereby repealed.

Article 12

A4.46 **Notification procedure**

Member States shall immediately notify the Commission of any governmental plan to grant new related rights, including the basic reasons for their introduction and the term of protection envisaged.

Article 13

A4.47 **General provisions**

1. Member States shall bring into force the laws, regulations and administrative provisions necessary to comply with Articles 1 to 11 of this Directive before 1 July 1995.

When Member States adopt these provisions, they shall contain a reference to this Directive or shall be accompanied by such reference at the time of their official publication. The methods of making such a reference shall be laid down by the Member States.

Member States shall communicate to the Commission the texts of the provisions of national law which they adopt in the field governed by this Directive.

2. Member States shall apply Article 12 from the date of notification of this Directive.

Article 14

A4.48 This Directive is addressed to the Member States.

Done at Brussels, 29 October 1993.

APPENDIX 5A

ROME CONVENTION 1961

International Convention for the Protection of Performers, Producers of Phonograms and Broadcasting Organisations[1]

Rome, October 26, 1961

The Contracting States, moved by the desire to protect the rights of performers, producers of phonograms, and broadcasting organisations,
Have agreed as follows:

Article 1   A5.01

Protection granted under this Convention shall leave intact and shall in no way affect the protection of copyright in literary and artistic works. Consequently, no provision of this Convention may be interpreted as prejudicing such protection.

Article 2   A5.02

1. For the purposes of this Convention, national treatment shall mean the treatment accorded by the domestic law of the Contracting State in which protection is claimed:

(a) to performers who are its nationals, as regards performances taking place, broadcast, or first fixed, on its territory;
(b) to producers of phonograms who are its nationals, as regards phonograms first fixed or first published on its territory;
(c) to braodcasting organisations which have their headquarters on its territory, as regards broadcasts transmitted from transmitters situated on its territory.

2. National treatment shall be subject to the protection specifically guaranteed, and the limitations specifically provided for, in this Convention.

Article 3   A5.03

For the purposes of this Convention:

(a) "Performers" means actors, singers, musicians, dancers, and other persons who act, sing, deliver, declaim, play in, or otherwise perform literary or artistic works;
(b) "Phonogram" means any exclusively aural fixation of sounds of a performance or of other sounds;
(c) "Producer of phonograms" means the person who, or the legal entity which, first fixes the sounds of a performance or other sounds;
(d) "Publication" means the offering of copies of a phonogram to the public in reasonable quantity;
(e) "Reproduction" means the making of a copy or copies of a fixation;
(f) "Broadcasting" means the transmission by wireless means for public reception of sounds or of images and sounds;

---

[1] Cmnd. 2425. Ratified by the United Kingdom on October 30, 1963, and entered into force on May 18, 1964.

(g) "Rebroadcasting" means the simultaneous broadcasting by one broadcasting organisation of the broadcast of another broadcasting organisation.

A5.04   *Article 4*

Each Contracting State shall grant national treatment to performers if any of the following conditions is met:

(a) the performance takes place in another Contracting State;
(b) the performance is incorporated in a phonogram which is protected under Article 5 of this Convention;
(c) the performance, not being fixed on a phonogram, is carried by a broadcast which is protected by Article 6 of this Convention.

A5.05   *Article 5*

1. Each Contracting State shall grant national treatment to producers of phonograms if any of the following conditions is met:

(a) the producer of the phonogram is a national of another Contracting State (criterion of nationality);
(b) the first fixation of the sound was made in another Contracting State (criterion of fixation);
(c) the phonogram was first published in another Contracting State (criterion of publication).

2. If a phonogram was first published in a non-contracting State but if it was also published, within thirty days of its first publication, in a Contracting State (simultaneous publication), it shall be considered as first published in the Contracting State.
3. By means of a notification deposited with the Secretary-General of the United Nations, any Contracting State may declare that it will not apply the criterion of publication or, alternatively, the criterion of fixation. Such notification may be deposited at the time of ratification, acceptance or accession, or at any time thereafter; in the last case, it shall become effective six months after it has been deposited.

A5.06   *Article 6*

1. Each Contracting State shall grant national treatment to broadcasting organis-ations if either of the following conditions is met:

(a) the headquarters of the broadcasting organisation is situated in another Contracting State;
(b) the broadcast was transmitted from a transmitter situated in another Contract-ing State.

2. By means of a notification deposited with the Secretary-General of the United Nations, any Contracting State may declare that it will protect broadcasts only if the headquarters of the broadcasting organisation is situated in another Contracting State and the broadcast was transmitted from a transmitter situated in the same Contracting State. Such notification may be deposited at the time of ratification, acceptance or accession, or at any time thereafter; in the last case, it shall become effective six months after it has been deposited.

A5.07   *Article 7*

1. The protection provided for performers by this Convention shall include the possibility of preventing:

    (a) the broadcasting and the communication to the public, without their consent, of their performance, except where the performance used in the broadcasting or the public communication is itself already a broadcast performance or is made from a fixation;

    (b) the fixation, without their consent, of their unfixed performance;

    (c) the reproduction, without their consent, of a fixation of their performance:

        (i)   if the original fixation itself was made without their consent;

        (ii) if the reproduction is made for purposes different from those for which the performers gave their consent;

        (iii) if the original fixation was made in accordance with the provisions of Article 15, and the reproduction is made for purposes different from those referred to in those provisions.

2.(1) If broadcasting was consented to by the performers, it shall be a matter for the domestic law of the Contracting State where protection is claimed to regulate the protection against rebroadcasting, fixation for braodcasting purposes, and the reproduction of such fixation for broadcasting purposes.

(2) The terms and conditions governing the use by broadcasting organisations of fixations made for broadcasting purposes shall be determined in accordance with the domestic law of the Contracting State where protection is claimed.

(3) However, the domestic law referred to in sub-paragraphs (1) and (2) of this paragraph shall not operate to deprive performers of the ability to control, by contract, their relations with broadcasting organisations.

Article 8

                                                                            A5.08

Any Contracting State may, by its domestic laws and regulations, specify the manner in which performers will be represented in connexion with the exercise of their rights if several of them participate in the same performance.

Article 9

                                                                            A5.09

Any Contracting State may, by its domestic laws and regulations, extend the protection provided for in this Convention to artistes who do not perform literary or artistic works.

Article 10

                                                                              A5.10

Producers of phonograms shall enjoy the right to authorise or prohibit the direct or indirect reproduction of their phonograms.

Article 11

                                                                              A5.11

If, as a condition of protecting the rights of producers of phonograms, or of performers, or both, in relation to phonograms, a Contracting State, under its domestic law, requires compliance with formalities, these shall be considered as fulfilled if all the copies in commerce of the published phonogram or their containers bear a notice consisting of the symbol ℗, accompanied by the year date of the first publication, placed in such a manner as to give reasonable notice of claim of protection; and if the copies or their containers do not identify the producer or the licensee of the producer (by carrying his name, trademark or other appropriate designation), the notice shall also include the name of the owner of the rights of the producer; and, furthermore, if the copies or their containers do not identify the principal performers, the notice shall also include the name of the person who, in the country in which the fixation was effected, owns the rights of such performers.

A5.12

Article 12

If a phonogram published for commercial purposes, or a reproduction of such phonogram, is used directly for broadcasting or for any communication to the public, a single equitable remuneration shall be paid by the user to the performers, or to the producers of the phonograms, or to both. Domestic law may, in the absence of agreement between these parties, lay down the conditions as to the sharing of this remuneration.

A5.13

Article 13

Broadcasting organisations shall enjoy the right to authorise or prohibit:

(a) the rebroadcasting of their broadcasts;
(b) the fixation of their broadcasts;
(c) the reproduction:

   (i) of fixations, made without their consent, of their broadcasts;
   (ii) of fixations, made in accordance with the provisions of Article 15, of their broadcasts, if the reproduction is made for purposes different from those referred to in those provisions;

(d) the communication to the public of their television broadcasts if such communication is made in places accessible to the public against payment of an entrance fee; it shall be a matter for the domestic law of the State where protection of this right is claimed to determine the conditions under which it may be exercised.

A5.14

Article 14

The term of protection to be granted under this Convention shall last at least until the end of a period of twenty years computed from the end of the year in which:

(a) the fixation was made—for phonograms and for performers incorporated therein;
(b) the performance took place—for performances not incorporated in phonograms;
(c) the broadcast took place—for broadcasts.

A5.15

Article 15

1. Any Contracting State may, in its domestic laws and regulations, provide for exceptions to the protection guaranteed by this Convention as regards:

(a) private use;
(b) use of short excerpts in connexion with the reporting of current events;
(c) ephemeral fixation by a broadcasting organisation by means of its own facilities and for its own broadcasts;
(d) use solely for the purposes of teaching or scientific research.

2. Irrespective of paragraph 1 of this Article, any Contracting State may, in its domestic laws and regulations, provide for the same kinds of limitations with regard to the protection of performers, producers and phonograms and broadcasting organisations, as it provides for, in its domestic laws and regulations, in connexion with the protection of copyright in literary and artistic works. However, compulsory licences may be provided for only to the extent to which they are compatible with this Convention.

Article 16   A5.16

1. Any State, upon becoming party to this Convention, shall be bound by all the obligations and shall enjoy all the benefits thereof. However, a State may at any time, in a notification deposited with the Secretary-General of the United Nations, declare that:

(a) as regards Article 12:

(i)   it will not apply the provisions of that Article;
(ii) it will not apply the provisions of that Article in respect of certain uses;
(iii) as regards phonograms the producer of which is not a national of another Contracting State, it will not apply that Article;
(iv) as regards phonograms the producer of which is a national of another Contracting State, it will limit the protection provided for by that Article to the extent to which, and to the term for which, the latter State grants protection to phonograms first fixed by a national of the State making the declaration; however, the fact that the Contracting State of which the producer is a national does not grant the protection to the same beneficiary or beneficiaries as the State making the declaration shall not be considered as a difference in the extent of the protection;

(b) as regards Article 13, it will not apply item (d) of that Article; if a Contracting State makes such a declaration, the other Contracting States shall not be obliged to grant the right referred to in Article 13, item (d), to broadcasting organisations whose headquarters are in that State.

2. If the notification referred to in paragraph 1 of this Article is made after the date of the deposit of the instrument of ratification, acceptance or accession, the declaration will become effective six months after it has been deposited.

Article 17   A5.17

Any State which, on 26 October 1961, grants protection to producers of phonograms soley on the basis of the criterion of fixation may, by a notification deposited with the Secretary-General of the United Nations at the time of ratification, acceptance or accession, declare that it will apply, for the purposes of Article 5, the criterion of fixation alone and, for the purposes of paragraph 1(a)(iii) and (iv) of Article 16, the criterion of fixation instead of the criterion of nationality.

Article 18   A5.18

Any State which has deposited a notification under paragraph 3 of Article 5, paragraph 2 of Article 6, paragraph 1 of Article 16 or Article 17, may, by a further notification deposited with the Secretary-General of the United Nations, reduce its scope or withdraw it.

Article 19   A5.19

Notwithstanding anything in this Convention, once a performer has consented to the incorporation of his performance in a visual or audio-visual fixation, Article 7 shall have no further application.

Article 20   A5.20

1. This Convention shall not prejudice rights acquired in any Contracting State before the date of coming into force of this Convention for that State.
2. No Contracting State shall be bound to apply the provisions of this Convention to

performances or broadcasts which took place, or to phonograms which were fixed, before the date of coming into force of this Convention for that State.

A5.21   *Article 21*

The protection provided for in this Convention shall not prejudice any protection otherwise secured to performers, producers of phonograms and broadcasting organisations.

A5.22   *Article 22*

Contracting States reserve the right to enter into special agreements among themselves in so far as such agreements grant to performers, producers of phonograms or broadcasting organisations more extensive rights than those granted by this Convention or contain other provisions not contrary to this Convention.

A5.23   *Article 23*

This Convention shall be deposited with the Secretary-General of the United Nations. It shall be open until 30 June 1962 for signature by any State invited to the Diplomatic Conference on the International Protection of Performers, Producers of Phonograms and Broadcasting Organisations which is a party to the Universal Copyright Convention or a member of the International Union for the Protection of Literary and Artistic Works.

A5.24   *Article 24*

1. This Convention shall be subject to ratification or acceptance by the signatory States.
2. This Convention shall be open for accession by any State invited to the Conference referred to in Article 23, and by any State Member of the United Nations, provided that in either case such State is a party to the Universal Copyright Convention or a member of the International Union for the Protection of Literary and Artistic Works.
3. Ratification, acceptance or accession shall be effected by the deposit of an instrument to that effect with the Secretary-General of the United Nations.

A5.25   *Article 25*

1. This Convention shall come into force three months after the date of deposit of the sixth instrument of ratification, acceptance or accession.
2. Subsequently, this Convention shall come into force in respect of each State three months after the date of deposit of its instrument of ratification, acceptance or accession.

A5.26   *Article 26*

1. Each Contracting State undertakes to adopt, in accordance with its Constitution, the measures necessary to ensure the application of this Convention.
2. At the time of deposit of its instrument of ratification, acceptance or accession, each State must be in a position under its domestic law to give effect to the terms of this Convention.

A5.27   *Article 27*

1. Any State may, at the time of ratification, acceptance or accession, or at any time thereafter, declare by notification addressed to the Secretary-General of the United Nations that this Convention shall extend to all or any of the territories for whose international relations it is responsible, provied that the Universal Copyright

Convention or the International Convention for the Protection of Literary and Artistic Works applies to the territory or territories concerned. This notification shall take effect three months after the date of its receipt.

2. The notifications referred to in paragraph 3 of Article 5, paragraph 2 of Article 6, paragraph 2 of Article 16 and Articles 17 and 18, may be extended to cover all or any of the territories referred to in paragraph 1 of this Article.

Article 28

A5.28

1. Any Contracting State may denounce this Convention, on its own behalf, or on behalf of all or any of the territories referred to in Article 27.

2. The denunciation shall be effected by a notification addressed to the Secretary-General of the United Nations and shall take effect twelve months after the date of receipt of the notification.

3. The right of denunciation shall be not exercised by a Contracting State before the expiry of a period of five years from the date on which the Convention came into force with respect to that State.

4. A Contracting State shall cease to be a party to this Convention from that time when it is neither a party to the Universal Copyright Convention nor a member of the International Union for the Protection of Literary and Artistic Works.

5. This Convention shall cease to apply to any territory referred to in Article 27 from that time when neither the Universal Copyright Convention nor the International Convention for the Protection of Literary and Artistic Works applies to that territory.

Article 29

A5.29

1. After this Convention has been in force for five years, any Contracting States may, by notification addressed to the Secretary-General of the United Nations, request that a conference be convened for the purpose of revising the Convention. The Secretary-General shall notify all Contracting States of this request. If, within a period of six months following the date of notification by the Secretary-General of the United Nations, not less than one half of the Contracting States notify him of their concurrence with the request, the Secretary-General shall inform the Director-General of the International Labour Office, the Director General of the United Nations Educational, Scientific and Cultural Organization and the Director of the Bureau of the International Union for the Protection of Literary and Artistic Works, who shall convene a revision conference in co-operation with the Intergovernmental Committee provided for in Article 32.

2. The adoption of any revision of this Convention shall require an affirmative vote by two-thirds of the States attending the revision conference, provided that this majority includes two-thirds of the States which, at the time of the revision conference, are parties to the Convention.

3. In the event of adoption of a Convention revising this Convention in whole or in part, and unless the revising Convention provides otherwise:

    (a) this Convention shall cease to be open to ratification, acceptance or accession as from the date of entry into force of the revising Convention;

    (b) this Convention shall remain in force as regards relations between or with Contracting States which have not become parties to the revising Convention.

Article 30

A5.30

Any dispute which may arise between two or more Contracting States concerning the interpretation or application of this Convention and which is not settled by negotiation shall, at the request of any one of the parties to the dispute, be referred to the International Court of Justice for decision, unless they agree to another mode of settlement.

A5.31

Article 31

Without prejudice to the provisions of paragraph 3 of Article 5, paragraph 2 of Article 6, paragraph 1 of Article 16 and Article 17, no reservation may be made to this Convention.

A5.32

Article 32

1. An Intergovernmental Committee is hereby established with the following duties:

(a) to study questions concerning the application and operation of this Convention; and
(b) to collect proposals and to prepare documentation for possible revision of this Convention.

2. The Committee shall consist of representatives of the Contracting States, chosen with due regard to equitable geographical distribution. The number of members shall be six if there are twelve Contracting States or less, nine if there are thirteen to eighteen Contracting States and twelve if there are more than eighteen Contracting States.

3. The Committee shall be constituted twelve months after the Convention comes into force by an election organised among the Contracting States, each of which shall have one vote, by the Director-General of the International Labour Office, the Director-General of the United Nations Educational, Scientific and Cultural Organization and the Director of the Bureau of the International Union for the Protection of Literary and Artistic Works, in accordance with rules previously approved by a majority of all Contracting States.

4. The Committee shall elect its Chairman and officers. It shall establish its own rules of procedure. These rules shall in particular provide for the future operation of the Committee and for a method of selecting its members for the future in such a way as to ensure rotation among the various Contracting States.

5. Officials of the International Labour Office, the United Nations Educational, Scientific and Cultural Organization and the Bureau of the International Union for the Protection of Literary and Artistic Works, designated by the Directors-General and the Director thereof, shall constitute the Secretariat of the Committee.

6. Meetings of the Committee, which shall be convened whenever a majority of its members deems it necesary, shall be held successively at the headquarters of the International Labour Office, the United Nations Educational, Scientific and Cultural Organization and the Bureau of the International Union for the Protection of Literary and Artistic Works.

7. Expenses of members of the Committee shall be borne by their respective Governments.

A5.33

Article 33

1. The present Convention is drawn up in English, French and Spanish, the three texts being equally authentic.
2. In addition, official texts of the present Convention shall be drawn up in German, Italian and Portuguese.

A5.34

Article 34

1. The Secretary-General of the United Nations shall notify the States invited to the Conference referred to in Article 23 and every State Member of the United Nations, as well as the Director-General of the International Labour Office, the Director-General of the Unitied Nations Educational, Scientific and Cultural Organization and the Director of the Bureau of the International Union for the Protection of Literary and Artistic Works:

(a) of the deposit of each instrument of ratification, acceptance or accession;

(b) of the date of entry into force of the Convention;

(c) of all notifications, declarations[2] or communications provided for in this Convention;

(d) if any of the situations referred to in paragraphs 4 and 5 of Article 28 arise.

2. The Secretary-General of the United Nations shall also notify the Director-General of the International Labour Office, the Director-General of the United Nations Educational, Scientific and Cultural Organization and the Director of the Bureau of the International Union for the Protection of Literary and Artistic Works of the requests communicated to him in accordance with Article 29, as well as of any communication received from the Contracting States concerning the revision of the Convention.

IN FAITH WHEREOF, the undersigned, being duly authorised thereto, have signed this Convention.

DONE at Rome, this twenty-sixth day of October 1961, in a single copy in the English, French and Spanish languages. Certified true copies shall be delivered by the Secretary-General of the United Nations to all the States invited to the Conference referred to in Article 23 and to every State Member of the United Nations, as well as to the Director-General of the International Labour Office, the Director-General of the United Nations Educational, Scientific and Cultural Organization and the Director of the Bureau of the International Union for the Protection of Literary and Artistic Works.

---

[2] The United Kingdom ratification was accompanied by the following declaration:

(1) in respect of Article 5(1)(b) and in accordance with Article 5(3) of the Convention, the United Kingdom will not apply, in respect of phonograms, the criterion of fixation;

(2) in respect of Article 6(1) and in accordance with Article 6(2) of the Convention, the United Kingdom will protect broadcasts only if the headquarters of the broadcasting organisation is situated in another Contracting State and the broadcast was transmitted from a transmitter situated in the same Contracting State;

(3) in respect of Article 12 and in accordance with Article 16(1) of the Convention,

  (a) the United Kingdom will not apply the provisions of Article 12 in respect of the following uses:

    (i) the causing of a phonogram to be heard in public at any premises where persons reside or sleep, as part of the amenities provided exclusively or mainly for residents or inmates therein except where a special charge is made for admission to the part of the premises where the phonogram is to be heard,

    (ii) the causing of a phonogram to be heard in public as part of the activities of, or for the benefit of, a club, society or other organisation which is not established or conducted for profit and whose main objects are charitable or are otherwise concerned with the advancement of religion, education or social welfare, except where a charge is made for admission to the place where the phonogram is to be heard, and any of the proceeds of the charge are applied otherwise than for the purpose of the organisation;

  (b) as regards phonograms the producer of which is not a national of another Contracting State or as regards phonograms the producer of which is a national of a Contracting State which has made a declaration under Article 16(1)(a)(i) stating that it will not apply the provisions of Article 12, the United Kingdom will not grant the protection provided for by Article 12, unless, in either event, the phonogram has been first published in a Contracting State which has made no such declaration.

APPENDIX 5B

AGREEMENT ON TRADE-RELATED ASPECTS OF INTELLECTUAL PROPERTY RIGHTS, INCLUDING TRADE IN COUNTERFEIT GOODS[*]

PART I: GENERAL PROVISIONS AND BASIC PRINCIPLES

PART II: STANDARDS CONCERNING THE AVAILABILITY, SCOPE AND USE OF INTELLECTUAL PROPERTY RIGHTS

1. Copyright and Related Rights

PART III: ENFORCEMENT OF INTELLECTUAL PROPERTY RIGHTS

1. General Obligations
2. Civil and Administrative Procedures and Remedies
3. Provisional Measures
4. Special Requirements Related to Border Measures
5. Criminal Procedures

PART IV: ACQUISITION AND MAINTENANCE OF INTELLECTUAL PROPERTY RIGHTS AND RELATED *INTER-PARTES* PROCEDURES

PART VI: TRANSITIONAL ARRANGEMENTS

PART VII: INSTITUTIONAL ARRANGEMENTS; FINAL PROVISIONS

Members

A5.35   *Desiring* to reduce distortions and impediments to international trade, and taking into account the need to promote effective and adequate protection of intellectual property rights, and to ensure that measures and procedures to enforce intellectual property rights do not themselves become barriers to legitimate trade:
Recognizing, to this end, the need for new rules and disciplines concerning:

  (a) the applicability of the basic principles of the GATT 1994 and of relevant international intellectual property agreements or conventions;
  (b) the provision of adequate standards and principles concerning the availability, scope and use of trade-related intellectual property rights;
  (c) the provision of effective and appropriate means for the enforcement of trade-related intellectual property rights, taking into account differences in national legal systems;
  (d) the provision of effective and expeditious procedures for the multilateral prevention and settlement of disputes between governments; and

[*] Concluded at Geneva on December 15, 1993, GATT document MTN/FA II-AIC.

374

(e) transitional arrangements aiming at the fullest participation in the results of the negotiations;

Recognizing the need for a multilaterial framework of principles, rules and disciplines dealing with international trade in counterfeit goods;
Recognizing that intellectual property rights are private rights;
Recognizing the underlying public policy objectives of national systems for the protection of intellectual property, including development and technological objectives;
Recognizing also the special needs of the least-developed country Members in respect of maximum flexibility in the domestic implementation of laws and regulations in order to enable them to create a sound and viable technological base;
Emphasizing the importance of reducing tensions by reaching strengthened commitments to resolve disputes on trade-related intellectual property issues through multilateral procedures;
Desiring to establish a mutually supportive relationship between the MTO and the World Intellectual Property Organization (WIPO) as well as other relevant international organisations;
Hereby agree as follows:

PART I: GENERAL PROVISIONS AND BASIC PRINCIPLES

Article 1: Nature and scope of obligations   A5.36

1. Members shall give effect to the provisions of this Agreement. Members may, but shall not be obliged to, implement in their domestic law more extensive protection than is required by this Agreement, provided that such protection does not contravene the provisions of this Agreement. Members shall be free to determine the appropriate method of implementing the provisions of this Agreement within their own legal system and practice.
2. For the purposes of this Agreement, the term "intellectual property" refers to all categories of intellectual property that are the subject of Sections 1 to 7 of Part II.
3. Members shall accord the treatment provided for in this Agreement to the nationals of other Members.[1] In respect of the relevant intellectual property right, the nationals of other Members shall be understood as those natural or legal persons that would meet the criteria for eligibility for protection provided for in the Paris Convention (1967), the Berne Convention (1971), the Rome Convention and the Treaty on Intellectual Property in Respect of Integrated Circuits, were all Members of the MTO members of those conventions.[2] Any Member availing itself of the possibilities provided in paragraph 3 of Article 5 of paragraph 2 of Article 6 of the Rome Convention shall make a notification as foreseen in those provisions to the Council for Trade-Related Aspects of Intellectual Property Rights.

---

[1] When "nationals" are referred to in this Agreement, they shall be deemed, in the case of a separate customs territory Member of the MTO, to mean persons, natural or legal, who are domiciled or who have a real and effective industrial or commercial establishment in that customs territory.
[2] In this Agreement, "Paris Convention" refers to the Paris Convention for the Protection of Industrial Property: "Paris Convention (1967)" refers to the Stockholm Act of this Convention of 14 July 1967. "Berne Convention" refers to the Berne Convention for the Protection of Literary and Artistic Works: "Berne Convention (1971)" refers to the Paris Act of this Convention of 24 July 1971. "Rome Convention" refers to the International Convention for the Protection of Performers, Producers of Phonograms and Broadcasting Organisations, adopted at Rome on 26 October 1961. "Treaty on Intellectual Property in Respect of Integrated Circuits" (IPIC Treaty) refers to the Treaty on Intellectual Property in Respect of Integrated Circuits, adopted at Washington on 26 May 1989.

A5.37   *Article 2: Intellectual property conventions*

1. In respect of Parts II, III and IV of this Agreement, Members shall comply with Articles 1–12 and 19 of the Paris Convention (1967).
2. Nothing in Parts I to IV of this Agreement shall derogate from existing obligations that Members may have to each other under the Paris Convention, the Berne Convention, the Rome Convention and the Treaty on Intellectual Property in Respect of Integrated Circuits.

A5.38   *Article 3: National treatment*

1. Each Member shall accord to the nationals of other Members treatment no less favourable than that it accords to its own nationals with regard to the protection[3] of intellectual property, subject to the exceptions already provided in, respectively, the Paris Convention (1967), the Berne Convention (1971), the Rome Convention and the Treaty on Intellectual Property in Respect of Integrated Circuits. In respect of performers, producers of phonograms and broadcasting organizations, this obligation only applies in respect of the rights provided under this Agreement. Any Member availing itself of the possibilities provided in Article 6 of the Berne Convention and paragraph 1(b) of Article 16 of the Rome Convention shall make a notification as foreseen in those provisions to the Council for Trade-Related Aspects of Intellectual Property Rights.
2. Members may avail themselves of the exceptions permitted under paragraph 1 above in relation to judicial and administrative procedures, including the designation of an address for service or the appointment of an agent within the jurisdiction of a Member, only where such exceptions are necessary to secure compliance with laws and regulations which are not inconsistent with the provisions of this Agreement and where such practices are not applied in a manner which would constitute a disguised restriction on trade.

A5.39   *Article 4: Most-favoured-nation treatment*

With regard to the protection of intellectual property, any advantage, favour, privilege or immunity granted by a Member to the nationals of any other country shall be accorded immediately and unconditionally to the nationals of all other Members. Exempted from this obligation are any advantage, favour, privilege or immunity accorded by a Member:

    (a) deriving from international agreements on judicial assistance and law enforcement of a general nature and not particularly confined to the protection of intellectual property;
    (b) granted in accordance with the provisions of the Berne Convention (1971) or the Rome Convention authorizing that the treatment accorded be a function not of national treatment but of the treatment accorded in another country;
    (c) in respect of the rights of performers, producers of phonograms and broadcasting organizations not provided under this Agreement;
    (d) deriving from international agreements related to the protection of intellectual property which entered into force prior to the entry into force of the Agreement Establishing the MTO, provided that such agreements are notified to the Council for Trade-Related Aspects of Intellectual Property Rights and do not constitute an arbitrary or unjustifiable discrimination against nationals of other Members.

---

[3] For the purposes of Articles 3 and 4 of this Agreement, protection shall include matters affecting the availability, acquisition, scope, maintenance and enforcement of intellectual property rights as well as those matters affecting the use of intellectual property rights specifically addressed in this Agreement.

Article 5: Multilateral agreements on acquisition or maintenance of protection   A5.40

The obligations under Articles 3 and 4 above do not apply to procedures provided in multilateral agreements concluded under the auspices of the World Intellectual Organization relating to the acquisition or maintenance of intellectual property rights.

Article 6: Exhaustion   A5.41

For the purposes of dispute settlement under this Agreement, subject to the provisions of Articles 3 and 4 above nothing in this Agreement shall be used to address the issue of the exhaustion of intellectual property rights.

Article 7: Objectives   A5.42

The protection and enforcement of intellectual property rights should contribute to the promotion of technological innovation and to the transfer and dissemination of technology, to the mutual advantage of producers and users of technological knowledge and in a manner conducive to social and economic welfare, and to a balance of rights and obligations.

Article 8: Principles   A5.43

1. Members may, in formulating or amending their national laws and regulations, adopt measures necessary to protect public health and nutrition, and to promote the public interest in sectors of vital importance to their socio-economic and technological development, provided that such measures are consistent with the provisions of this Agreement.
2. Appropriate measures, provided that they are consistent with the provisions of this Agreement, may be needed to prevent the abuse of intellectual property rights by rightholders or the resort to practices which unreasonably restrain trade or adversely affect the international transfer of technology.

PART II: STANDARDS CONCERNING THE AVAILABILITY, SCOPE AND USE OF INTELLECTUAL PROPERTY RIGHTS

SECTION 1: COPYRIGHT AND RELATED RIGHTS

Article 14: Protection of performers, producers of phonograms (sound recordings)   A5.44
and broadcasting organizations

1. In respect of a fixation of their performance on a phonogram, performers shall have the possibility of preventing the following acts when undertaken without their authorization: the fixation of their unfixed performance and the reproduction of such fixation. Performers shall also have the possibility of preventing the following acts when undertaken without their authorization: the broadcasting by wireless means and the communication to the public of their live performance.
2. Producers of phonograms shall enjoy the right to authorize or prohibit the direct or indirect reproduction of their phonograms.
3. Broadcasting organizations shall have the right to prohibit the following acts when undertaken without their authorization: the fixation, the reproduction of fixations, and the rebroadcasting by wireless means of broadcasts, as well as the communication to the public of television broadcasts of the same. Where Members do not grant such rights to broadcasting organizations, they shall provide owners of copyright in the subject matter of broadcasts with the possibility of preventing the above acts, subject to the provisions of the Berne Convention (1971).

4. The provisions of Article 11 in respect of computer programs shall apply *mutatis mutandis* to producers of phonograms and any other rightholders in phonograms as determined in domestic law. If, on the date of the Ministerial Meeting concluding the Uruguay Round of Multilateral Trade Negotiations, a Member has in force a system of equitable remuneration of rightholders in respect of the rental of phonograms, it may maintain such system provided that the commercial rental of phonograms is not giving rise to the material impairment of the exclusive rights of reproduction of rightholders.

5. The term of the protection available under this Agreement to performers and producers of phonograms shall last at least until the end of a period of fifty years computed from the end of the calendar year in which the fixation was made or the performance took place. The term of protection granted pursuant to paragraph 3 above shall last for at least twenty years from the end of the calendar year in which the broadcast took place.

6. Any Member may, in relation to the rights conferred under paragraphs 1–3 above, provide for conditions, limitations, exceptions and reservations to the extent permitted by the Rome Convention (1971) shall also apply, *mutatis mutandis*, to the rights of performers and producers of phonograms in phonograms.

PART III: ENFORCEMENT OF INTELLECTUAL PROPERTY RIGHTS

SECTION 1: GENERAL OBLIGATIONS

A5.45   *Article 41*

1. Members shall ensure that enforcement procedures as specified in this Part are available under their national laws so as to permit effective action against any act of infringement of intellectual property rights covered by this Agreement, including expeditious remedies to prevent infringements and remedies which constitute a deterrent to further infringements. These procedures shall be applied in such a manner as to avoid the creation of barriers to legitimate trade and to provide for safeguards against their abuse.

2. Procedures concerning the enforcement of intellectual property rights shall be fair and equitable. They shall not be unnecessarily complicated or costly, or entail unreasonable time-limits or unwarranted delays.

3. Decisions on the merits of a case shall preferably be in writing and reasoned. They shall be made available at least to the parties to the proceeding without undue delay. Decisions on the merits of a case shall be based only on evidence in respect of which parties were offered the opportunity to be heard.

4. Parties to a proceeding shall have an opportunity for review by a judicial authority of final administrative decisions and, subject to jurisdictional provisions in national laws concerning the importance of a case, of at least the legal aspects of initial judicial decisions on the merits of a case. However, there shall be no obligation to provide an opportunity for review of acquittals in criminal cases.

5. It is understood that this Part does not create any obligation to put in place a judicial system for the enforcement of intellectual property rights distinct from that for the enforcement of laws in general, nor does it affect the capacity of Members to enforce their laws in general. Nothing in this Part creates any obligation with respect to the distribution of resources as between enforcement of intellectual property rights and the enforcement of laws in general.

SECTION 2: CIVIL AND ADMINISTRATIVE PROCEDURES AND REMEDIES

Article 42: Fair and equitable procedures   A5.46

Members shall make available to rightholders[4] civil judicial procedures concerning the enforcement of any intellectual property right covered by this Agreement. Defendants shall have the right to written notice which is timely and contains sufficient detail, including the basis of the claims. Parties shall be allowed to be represented by independent legal counsel, and procedures shall not impose overly burdensome requirements concerning mandatory personal appearances. All parties to such procedures shall be duly entitled to substantiate their claims and to present all relevant evidence. The procedure shall provide a means to identify and protect confidential information, unless this would be contrary to existing constitutional requirements.

Article 43: Evidence of proof   A5.47

1. The judicial authorities shall have the authority, where a party has presented reasonably available evidence sufficient to support its claims and has specified evidence relevant to substantiation of its claims which lies in the control of the opposing party, to order that this evidence by produced by the opposing party, subject in appropriate cases to conditions which ensure the protection of confidential information.

2. In cases in which a party to a proceeding voluntarily and without good reason refuses access to, or otherwise does not provide necessary information within a reasonable period, or significantly impedes a procedure relating to an enforcement action, a Member may accord judicial authorities the authority to make preliminary and final determinations, affirmative or negative, on the basis of the information presented to them, including the complaint or the allegation presented by the party adversely affected by the denial of access to information, subject to providing the parties an opportunity to be heard on the allegations or evidence.

Article 44: Injunctions   A5.48

1. The judicial authorities shall have the authority to order a party to desist from an infringement, *inter alia* to prevent the entry into the channels of commerce in their jurisdiction of imported goods that involve the infringement of an intellectual property right, immediately after customs clearance of such goods. Members are not obliged to accord such authority in respect of protected subject-matter acquired or ordered by a person prior to knowing or having reasonable grounds to know that dealing in such subject-matter would entail the infringement of an intellectual property right.

2. Notwithstanding the other provisions of this Part and provided that the provisions of Part II specifically addressing use by governments, or by third parties authorized by a government, without the authorization of the rightholder are complied with, Members may limit the remedies available against such use to payment of remuneration in accordance with sub-paragraph (h) of Article 31 above. In other cases, the remedies under this Part shall apply or, where these remedies are inconsistent with national law, declaratory judgments and adequate compensation shall be available.

Article 45: Damages   A5.49

1. The judicial authorities shall have the authority to order the infringer to pay the rightholder damages adequate to compensate for the injury the rightholder has

---

[4] For the purpose of this Part, the term "right holder" includes federations and associations having legal standing to assert such rights.

suffered because of an infringement of his intellectual property right by an infringer who knew or had reasonable grounds to know that he was engaged in infringing activity.

2. The judicial authorities shall also have the authority to order the infringer to pay the rightholder expenses, which may include appropriate attorney's fees. In appropriate cases, Members may authorize the judicial authorities to order recovery of profits and/or payment of pre-established damages even where the infringer did not know or had no reasonable grounds to know that he was engaged in infringing activity.

A5.50

Article 46: Other remedies

In order to create an effective deterrent to infringement, the judicial authorities shall have the authority to order that goods that they have found to be infringing be, without compensation of any sort, disposed of outside the channels of commerce in such a manner as to avoid any harm caused to the rightholder, or, unless this would be contrary to existing constitutional requirements, destroyed. The judicial authorities shall also have the authority to order that materials and implements the predominant use of which has been in the creation of the infringing goods be, without compensation of any sort, disposed of outside the channels of commerce in such a manner as to minimize the risks of further infringements. In considering such requests, the need for proportionality between the seriousness of the infringement and the remedies ordered as well as the interests of third parties shall be taken into account. In regard to counterfeit trademark goods, the simple removal of the trademark unlawfully affixed shall not be sufficient, other than in exceptional cases, to permit release of the goods into the channels of commerce.

A5.51

Article 47: Right of information

Members may provide that the judicial authorities shall have the authority, unless this would be out of proportion to the seriousness of the infringement, to order the infringer to inform the rightholder of the identity of third persons involved in the production and distribution of the infringing goods or services and of their channels of distribution.

A5.52

Article 48: Indemnification of the defendant

1. The judicial authorities shall have the authority to order a party at whose request measures were taken and who has abused enforcement procedures to provide to a party wrongfully enjoined or restrained adequate compensation for the injury suffered because of such abuse. The judicial authorities shall also have the authority to order the applicant to pay the defendant expenses, which may include appropriate attorney's fees.

2. In respect of the administation of any law pertaining to the protection or enforcement of intellectual property rights, Members shall only exempt both public authorities and officials from liability to appropriate remedial measures where actions are taken or intended in good faith in the course of the administration of such laws.

A5.53

Article 49: Administrative procedures

To the extent that any civil remedy can be ordered as a result of administrative procedures on the merits of a case, such procedures shall conform to principles equivalent in substance to those set forth in this Section.

SECTION 3: PROVISIONAL MEASURES

Article 50 A5.54

1. The judicial authorities shall have the authority to order prompt and effective provisional measures:

(a) to prevent an infringement of any intellectual property right from occurring, and in particular to prevent the entry into the channels of commerce in their jurisdiction of goods, including imported goods immediately after customs clearance;

(b) to preserve relevant evidence in regard to the alleged infringement.

2. The judicial authorities shall have the authority to adopt provisional measures *inaudita altera parte* where appropriate, in particular where any delay is likely to cause irreparable harm to the rightholder, or where there is a demonstrable risk of evidence being destroyed.

3. The judicial authorities shall have the authority to require the applicant to provide any reasonably available evidence in order to satisfy themselves with a sufficient degree of certainty that the applicant is the rightholder and that his right is being infringed or that such infringement is imminent, and to order the applicant to provide a security or equivalent assurance sufficient to protect the defendant and to prevent abuse.

4. Where provisional measures have been adopted *inaudita altera parte*, the parties affected shall be given notice, without delay after the execution of the measures at the latest. A review, including a right to be heard, shall take place upon request of the defendant with a view to deciding, within a reasonable period after the notification of the measures, whether these measures shall be modified, revoked or confirmed.

5. The applicant may be required to supply other information necessary for the identification of the goods concerned by the authority that will execute the provisional measures.

6. Without prejudice to paragraph 4 above, provisional measures taken on the basis of paragraphs 1 and 2 above shall, upon request by the defendant, be revoked or otherwise cease to have effect, if proceedings leadings to a decision on the merits of the case are not initiated within a reasonable period, to be determined by the judicial authority ordering the measures where national law so permits or, in the absence of such a determination, not to exceed twenty working days or thirty-one calendar days, whichever is the longer.

7. Where the provisional measures are revoked or where they lapse due to any act or omission by the applicant, or where it is subsequently found that there has been no infringement or threat of infringement of an intellectual property right, the judicial authorities shall have the authority to order the applicant, upon request of the defendant, to provide the defendant appropriate compensation for any injury caused by these measures.

8. To the extent that any provisional measure can be ordered as a result of administrative procedures, such procedures shall conform to principles equivalent in substance to those set forth in this Section.

SECTION 4: SPECIAL REQUIREMENTS RELATED TO BORDER MEASURES[5]

A5.55 *Article 51: Suspension of release by customs authorities*

Members shall, in conformity with the provisions set out below, adopt procedures[6] to enable a rightholder, who has valid grounds for suspecting that the importation of counterfeit trademark or pirated copyright goods[7] may take place, to lodge an application in writing with competent authorities, administrative or judicial, for the suspension by the customs authorities of the release into free circulation of such goods. Members may enable such an application to be made in respect of goods which involve other infringements of intellectual property rights, provided that the requirements of this Section are met. Members may also provide for corresponding procedures concerning the suspension by the customs authorities of the release of infringing goods destined for exportation from their territories.

A5.56 *Article 52: Application*

Any rightholder initiating the procedures under Article 51 above shall be required to provide adequate evidence to satisfy the competent authorities that, under the laws of the country of importation, there is *prima facie* an infringement of his intellectual property right and to supply a sufficiently detailed description of the goods to make them readily recognizable by the customs authorities. The competent authorities shall inform the applicant within a reasonable period whether they have accepted the application and, where determined by the competent authorities, the period for which the customs authorities will take action.

A5.57 *Article 53: Security or equivalent assurance*

1. The competent authorities shall have the authority to require an applicant to provide a security or equivalent assurance sufficient to protect the defendant and the competent authorities and to prevent abuse. Such security or equivalent assurance shall not unreasonably deter recourse to these procedures.
2. Where pursuant to an application under this Section the release of goods involving industrial designs, patents, layout-designs or undisclosed information into free circulation has been suspended by customs authorities on the basis of a decision other than by a judicial or other independent authority, and the period provided for in Article 55 has expired without the granting of provisional relief by the duly empowered authority, and provided that all other conditions for importation have been complied with, the owner, importer, or consignee of such goods shall be entitled to their release on the posting of a security in an amount sufficient to protect the rightholder for any infringement. Payment of such security shall not prejudice any

---

[5] Where a Member has dismantled substantially all controls over movement of goods across its border with another member with which it forms part of a customs union, it shall not be required to apply the provisions of this Section at that border.

[6] It is understood that there shall be no obligation to apply such procedures to imports of goods put on the market in another country by or with the consent of the rightholder, or to goods in transit.

[7] For the purposes of this Agreement:

counterfeit trademark goods shall mean any goods, including packaging, bearing without authorization a trademark which is identical to the trademark validly registered in respect of such goods, or which cannot be distinguished in its essential aspects from such a trademark, and which thereby infringes the rights of the owner of the trademark in question under the law of the country of importation;

pirated copyright goods shall mean any goods which are copies made without the consent of the rightholder or person duly authorized by him in the country of production and which are made directly or indirectly from an article where the making of that copy would have constituted an infringement of a copyright or a related right under the law of the country of importation.

other remedy available to the rightholder, it being understood that the security shall be released if the rightholder fails to pursue his right of action within a reasonable period of time.

Article 54: Notice of suspension
A5.58

The importer and the applicant shall be promptly notified of the suspension of the release of goods according to Article 51 above.

Article 55: Duration of suspension
A5.59

If, within a period not exceeding ten working days after the applicant has been served notice of the suspension, the customs authorities have not been informed that proceedings leading to a decision on the merits of the case have been initiated by a party other than the defendant, or that the duly empowered authority has taken provisional measures prolonging the suspension of the release of the goods, the goods shall be released, provided that all other conditions for importation or exportation have been complied with; in appropriate cases, this time-limit may be extended by another ten working days. If proceedings leading to a decision on the merits of the case have been initiated, a review, including a right to be heard, shall take place upon request of the defendant with a view to deciding, within a reasonable period, whether these measures shall be modified, revoked or confirmed. Notwithstanding the above, where the suspension of the release of goods is carried out or continued in accordance with a provisional judicial measure, the provisions of Article 50, paragraph 6 above shall apply.

Article 56: Indemnification of the importer and of the owner of the goods
A5.60

Relevant authorities shall have the authority to order the applicant to pay the importer, the consignee and the owner of the goods appropriate compensation for any injury caused to them through the wrongful detention of goods or through the detention of goods released pursuant to Article 55 above.

Article 57: Right of inspection and information
A5.61

Without prejudice to the protection of confidential information, Members shall provide the competent authorities the authority to give the rightholder sufficient opportunity to have any product detained by the customs authorities inspected in order to substantiate his claims. The competent authorities shall also have authority to give the importer an equivalent opportunity to have any such product inspected. Where a positive determination has been made on the merits of a case, Members may provide the competent authorities the authority to inform the rightholder of the names and addresses of the consignor, the importer and the consignee and of the quantity of the goods in question.

Article 58: Ex officio action
A5.62

Where Members require competent authorities to act upon their own initiative and to suspend the release of goods in respect of which they have acquired *prima facie* evidence that an intellectual property right is being infringed:

(a) the competent authorities may at any time seek from the rightholder any information that may assist them to exercise these powers:
(b) the importer and the rightholder shall be promptly notified of the suspension. Where the importer has lodged an appeal against the suspension with the competent authorities, the suspension shall be subject to the conditions, *mutatis mutandis*, set out at Article 55 above;

(c) Members shall only exempt both public authorities and officials from liability to appropriate remedial measures where actions are taken or intended in good faith.

A5.63   *Article 59: Remedies*

Without prejudice to other rights of action open to the rightholder and subject to the right of the defendant to seek review by a judicial authority, competent authorities shall have the authority to order the destruction or disposal of infringing goods in accordance with the principles set out in Article 46 above. In regard to counterfeit trademark goods, the authorities shall not allow the re-exportation of the infringing goods in an unaltered state or subject to a different customs procedure, other than in exceptional circumstances.

A5.64   *Article 60: De minimis imports*

Members may exclude from the application of the above provisions small quantities of goods of a non-commercial nature contained in travellers' personal luggage or sent in small consignments.

SECTION 5: CRIMINAL PROCEDURES

A5.65   *Article 61*

Members shall provide for criminal procedures and penalties to be applied at least in cases of wilful trademark counterfeiting or copyright piracy on a commercial scale. Remedies available shall include imprisonment and/or monetary fines sufficient to provide a deterrent, consistently with the level of penalties applied for crimes of a corresponding gravity. In appropriate cases, remedies available shall also include the seizure, forfeiture and destruction of the infringing goods and of any materials and implements the predominant use of which has been in the commission of the offence. Members may provide for criminal procedures and penalties to be applied in other cases of infringement of intellectual property rights, in particular where they are committed wilfully and on a commercial scale.

PART IV: ACQUISITION AND MAINTENANCE OF INTELLECTUAL PROPERTY RIGHTS AND RELATED *INTER-PARTES* PROCEDURES

A5.66   *Article 62*

1. Members may require, as a condition of the acquisition or maintenance of the intellectual property rights provided for under Sections 2–6 of Part II of this Agreement, compliance with reasonable procedures and formalities. Such procedures and formalities shall be consistent with the provisions of this Agreement.
2. Where the acquisition of an intellectual property right is subject to the right being granted or registered, Members shall ensure that the procedures for grant or registration, subject to compliance with the substantive conditions for acquisition of the right, permit the granting or registration of the right within a reasonable period of time so as to avoid unwarranted curtailment of the period of protection.
3. Article 4 of the Paris Convention (1967) shall apply *mutatis mutandis* to service marks.
4. Procedures concerning the acquisition or maintenance of intellectual property rights and, where the national law provides for such procedures, administrative revocation and *inter partes* procedures such as opposition, revocation and cancellation, shall be governed by the general principles set out in paragraphs 2 and 3 of Article 41.
5. Final administrative decisions in any of the procedures referred to under paragraph

4 above shall be subject to review by a judicial or quasi-judicial authority. However, there shall be no obligation to provide an opportunity for such review of decisions in cases of unsuccessful opposition or administrative revocation, provided that the grounds for such procedures can be the subject of invalidation procedures.

PART VI: TRANSITIONAL ARRANGEMENTS

Article 65: Transitional arrangements **A5.67**

1. Subject to the provisions of paragraphs 2, 3 and 4 below, no Member shall be obliged to apply the provisions of this Agreement before the expiry of a general period of one year following the date of entry into force of the Agreement Establishing the MTO.
2. Any developing country Member is entitled to delay for a further period of four years the date of application, as defined in paragraph 1 above, of the provisions of this Agreement other than Articles 3, 4 and 5 of Part I.
3. Any other Member which is in the process of transformation from a centrally-planned into a market, free-enterprise economy and which is undertaking structural reform of its intellectual property system and facing special problems in the preparation and implementation of intellectual property laws, may also benefit from a period of delay as foreseen in paragraph 2 above.
4. To the extent that a developing country Member is obliged by this Agreement to extend product patent protection to areas of technology not so protectable in its territory on the general date of application of this Agreement for that member, as defined in paragraph 2 above, it may delay the application of the provisions on product patents of Section 5 of Part II of this Agreement to such areas of technology for an additional period of five years.
5. Any Member availing itself of a transitional period under paragraphs 1, 2, 3 or 4 above shall ensure that any changes in its domestic laws, regulations and practice made during that period do not result in a lesser degree of consistency with the provisions of this Agreement.

Article 66: Least-developed country Members **A5.68**

1. In view of their special needs and requirements, their economic, financial and administrative constraints, and their need for flexibility to create a viable technological base, least-developed country Members shall not be required to apply the provisions of this Agreement, other than Articles 3, 4 and 5, for a period of 10 years from the date of application as defined under paragraph 1 of Article 65 above. The Council shall, upon duly motivated request by a least-developed country Member, accord extensions of this period.
2. Developed country Members shall provide incentives to enterprises and institutions in their territories for the purpose of promoting and encouraging technology transfer to least-developed country Members in order to enable them to create a sound and viable technological base.

PART VII: INSTITUTIONAL ARRANGEMENTS; FINAL PROVISIONS

Article 70: Protection of existing subject-matter **A5.69**

1. This Agreement does not give rise to obligations in respect of acts which occurred before the date of application of the Agreement for the Member in question.
2. Except as otherwise provided for in this Agreement, this Agreement gives rise to obligations in respect of all subject matter existing at the date of application of this Agreement for the Member in question, and which is protected in that Member on the said date, or which meets or comes subsequently to meet the criteria for protection under the terms of this Agreement. In respect of this paragraph and paragraphs 3 and

4 below, copyright obligations with respect to existing works shall be solely determined under Article 18 of the Berne Convention (1971), and obligations with respect to the rights of producers of phonograms and performers in existing phonograms shall be determined solely under Article 18 of the Berne Convention (1971) as made applicable under paragraph 6 of Article 14 of this Agreement.

3. There shall be no obligation to restore protection to subject matter which on the date of application of this Agreement for the member in question has fallen into the public domain.

4. In respect of any acts in respect of specific objects embodying protected subject matter which become infringing under the terms of legislation in conformity with this Agreement, and which were commenced, or in respect of which a significant investment was made, before the date of acceptance of the Agreement Establishing the MTO by that Member, any member may provide for a limitation of the remedies available to the rightholder as to the continued performance of such acts after the date of application of the Agreement for that Member. In such cases the Member shall, however, at least provide for the payment of equitable remuneration.

5. A Member is not obliged to apply the provisions of Article 11 and of paragraph 4 of Article 14 with respect to originals or copies purchased prior to the date of application of this Agreement for that Member.

6. Members shall not be required to apply Article 31, or the requirement in paragraph 1 of Article 27 that patent rights shall be enjoyable without discrimination as to the field of technology, to use without the authorization of the rightholder where authorization for such use was granted by the government before the date this Agreement became known.

7. In the case of intellectual property rights for which protection is conditional upon registration, applications for protection which are pending on the date of applciation of this Agreement for the Member in question shall be permitted to be amended to claim any enhanced protection provided under the provisions of this Agreement. Such amendments shall not include new matter.

8. Where a Member does not make available as of the date of entry into force of the Agreement Establishing the MTO patent protection for pharmaceutical and agricultural chemical products commensurate with its obligations under Article 27, that Member shall:

(i) notwithstanding the provisions of Part VI above, provide as from the date of entry into force of the Agreement Establishing the MTO a means by which applications for patents for such inventions can be filed;

(ii) apply to these applications, as of the date of application of this Agreement, the criteria for patentability as laid down in this Agreement as if those criteria were being applied on the date of filing in that Member or, where priority is available and claimed, the priority date of the application;

(iii) provide patent protection in accordance with this Agreement as from the grant of the patent and for the remainder of the patent term, counted from the filing date in accordance with Article 33 of this Agreement, for those of these applications that meet the criteria for protection referred to in sub-paragraph (ii) above.

9. Where a product is the subject of a patent application in a Member in accordance with paragraph 8(i) above, exclusive marketing rights shall be granted, notwithstanding the provisions of Part VI above, for a period of five years after obtaining market approval in that Member or until a product patent is granted or rejected in that Member, whichever period is shorter, provided that, subsequent to the entry into force of the Agreement Establishing the MTO, a patent application has been filed and a patent granted for that product in another Member and marketing approval obtained in such other Member.

APPENDIX 5C

WIPO PERFORMANCES AND PHONOGRAMS TREATY

Preamble

A5.71 *The Contracting Parties,*

Desiring to develop and maintain the protection of the rights of performers and producers of phonograms in a manner as effective and uniform as possible,
Recognizing the need to introduce new international rules in order to provide adequate solutions to the questions raised by economic, social, cultural and technological developments,
Recognizing the profound impact of the development and convergence of information and communication technologies on the production and use of performances and phonograms,
Recognizing the need to maintain a balance between the rights of performers and producers of phonograms and the larger public interest, particularly education, research and access to information,

Have agreed as follows:

CHAPTER I: GENERAL PROVISIONS

A5.72 *Article 1: Relation to other Conventions*

(1) Nothing in this Treaty shall derogate from existing obligations that Contracting Parties have to each other under the International Convention for the Protection of Performers, Producers of Phonograms and Broadcasting Organizations done in Rome, October 26, 1961 (hereinafter the "Rome Convention").
(2) Protection granted under this Treaty shall leave intact and shall in no way affect the protection of copyright in literary and artistic works. Consequently, no provision of this Treaty may be interpreted as prejudicing such protection.
(3) This Treaty shall not have any connection with, nor shall it prejudice any rights and obligations under, any other treaties.

A5.73 *Article 2: Definitions*

For the purposes of this Treaty:

- (a) "performers" are actors, singers, musicians, dancers, and other persons who act, sing, deliver, declaim, play in, interpret, or otherwise perform literary or artistic works or expressions of folklore;
- (b) "phonogram" means the fixation of the sounds of a performance or of other sounds, or of a representation of sounds, other than in the form of a fixation incorporated in a cinematographic or other audiovisual work;
- (c) "fixation" means the embodiment of sounds, or of the representations thereof, from which they can be perceived, reproduced or communicated through a device;
- (d) "producer of a phonogram" means the person, or the legal entity, who or which takes the initiative and has the responsibility for the first fixation of the sounds of a performance or other sounds, or the representations of sounds;
- (e) "publication" of a fixed performance or a phonogram means the offering of copies of the fixed performance or the phonogram to the public, with the consent of the rightholder, and provided that copies are offered to the public in reasonable quantity;
- (f) "broadcasting" means the transmission by wireless means for public reception of sounds or of images and sounds or of the representations thereof; such transmission by satellite is also "broadcasting"; transmission of encrypted signals is "broadcasting" where the means for decrypting are provided to the public by the broadcasting organization or with its consent;

(g) "communication to the public" of a performance or a phonogram means the transmission to the public by any medium, otherwise than by broadcasting, of sounds of a performance or the sounds or the representations of sounds fixed in a phonogram. For the purposes of Article 15, "communication to the public" includes making the sounds or representations of sounds fixed in a phonogram audible to the public.

Article 3: Beneficiaries of protection under this Treaty   A5.74

(1) Contracting Parties shall accord the protection provided under this Treaty to the performers and producers of phonograms who are nationals of other Contracting Parties.
(2) The nationals of other Contracting Parties shall be understood to be those performers or producers of phonograms who would meet the criteria for eligibility for protection provided under the Rome Convention, were all the Contracting Parties to this Treaty Contracting States of that Convention. In respect of these criteria of eligibility, Contracting Parties shall apply the relevant definitions in Article 2 of this Treaty.
(3) Any Contracting Party availing itself of the possibilities provided in Article 5(3) of the Rome Convention or, for the purposes of Article 5 of the same Convention, Article 17 thereof shall make a notification as foreseen in those provisions to the Director General of the World Intellectual Property Organization (WIPO).

Article 4: National treatment   A5.75

(1) Each Contracting Party shall accord to nationals of other Contracting Parties, as defined in Article 3(2), the treatment it accords to its own nationals with regard to the exclusive rights specifically granted in this Treaty, and to the right to equitable remuneration provided for in Article 15 of this Treaty.
(2) The obligation provided for in paragraph (1) does not apply to the extent that another Contracting Party makes use of the reservations permitted by Article 15(3) of this Treaty.

CHAPTER II: RIGHTS OF PERFORMERS

Article 5: Moral rights of performers   A5.76

(1) Independently of a performer's economic rights, and even after the transfer of those rights, the performer shall, as regards his live aural performances or performances fixed in phonograms, have the right to claim to be identified as the performer of his performances, except where omission is dictated by the manner of the use of the performance, and to object to any distortion, mutilation or other modification of his performances that would be prejudicial to his reputation.
(2) The rights granted to a performer in accordance with paragraph (1) shall, after his death, be maintained, at least until the expiry of the economic rights, and shall be exercisable by the persons or institutions authorized by the legislation of the Contracting Party where protection is claimed. However, those Contracting Parties whose legislation, at the moment of their ratification of or accession to this Treaty, does not provide for protection after the death of the performer of all rights set out in the preceding paragraph may provide that some of these rights will, after his death, cease to be maintained.
(3) The means of redress for safeguarding the rights granted under this Article shall be governed by the legislation of the Contracting Party where protection is claimed.

A5.77   *Article 6: Economic rights of performers in their unfixed performances*

Performers shall enjoy the exclusive right of authorizing, as regards their perform-ances:

  (i)   the broadcasting and communication to the public of their unfixed perform-ances except where the performance is already a broadcast performance; and
  (ii) the fixation of their unfixed performances.

A5.78   *Article 7: Right of reproduction*

Performers shall enjoy the exclusive right of authorizing the direct or indirect reproduction of their performances fixed in phonograms, in any manner or form.

A5.79   *Article 8: Right of distribution*

(1) Performers shall enjoy the exclusive right of authorizing the making available to the public of the original and copies of their performances fixed in phonograms through sale or other transfer of ownership.
(2) Nothing in this Treaty shall affect the freedom of Contracting Parties to determine the conditions, if any, under which the exhaustion of the right in paragraph (1) applies after the first sale or other transfer of ownership of the original or a copy of the fixed performance with the authorization of the performer.

A5.80   *Article 9: Right of rental*

(1) Performers shall enjoy the exclusive right of authorizing the commercial rental to the public of the original and copies of their performances fixed in phonograms as determined in the national law of Contracting Parties, even after distribution of them by, or pursuant to, authorization by the performer.
(2) Notwithstanding the provisions of paragraph (1), a Contracting Party that, on April 15, 1994, had and continues to have in force a system of equitable remuneration of performers for the rental of copies of their performances fixed in phonograms, may maintain that system provided that the commercial rental of phonograms is not giving rise to the material impairment of the exclusive right of reproduction of performers.

A5.81   *Article 10: Right of making available of fixed performances*

Performers shall enjoy the exclusive right of authorizing the making available to the public of their performances fixed in phonograms, by wire or wireless means, in such a way that members of the public may access them from a place and at a time individually chosen by them.

CHAPTER III: RIGHTS OF PRODUCERS OF PHONOGRAMS

A5.82   *Article 11: Right of reproduction*

Producers of phonograms shall enjoy the exclusive right of authorizing the direct or indirect reproduction of their phonograms, in any matter or form.

A5.83   *Article 12: Right of distribution*

(1) Producers of phonograms shall enjoy the exclusive right of authorizing the making available to the public of the original and copies of their phonograms through sale or other transfer of ownership.
(2) Nothing in this Treaty shall affect the freedom of Contracting Parties to determine the conditions, if any, under which the exhaustion of the right in paragraph (1) applies

after the first sale or other transfer of ownership of the original or a copy of the phonogram with the authorization of the producer of the phonogram.

Article 13: Right of rental   A5.84

(1) Producers of phonograms shall enjoy the exclusive right of authorizing the commercial rental to the public of the original and copies of their phonograms, even after distribution of them by or pursuant to authorization by the producer.
(2) Notwithstanding the provisions of paragraph (1), a Contracting Party that, on April 15, 1994, had and continues to have in force a system of equitable remuneration of producers of phonograms for the rental of copies of their phonograms, may maintain that system provided that the commercial rental of phonograms is not giving rise to the material impairment of the exclusive rights of reproduction of producers of phonograms.

Article 14: Right of making available of phonograms   A5.85

Producers of phonograms shall enjoy the exclusive right of authorizing the making available to the public of their phonograms, by wire or wireless means, in such a way that members of the public may access them from a place and at a time individually chosen by them.

CHAPTER IV: COMMON PROVISIONS

Article 15: Right to remuneration for broadcasting and communication to the public   A5.86

(1) Performers and producers of phonograms shall enjoy the right to a single equitable remuneration for the direct or indirect use of phonograms published for commercial purposes for broadcasting or for any communication to the public.
(2) Contracting Parties may establish in their national legislation that the single equitable remuneration shall be claimed from the user by the performer or by the producer of a phonogram or by both. Contracting Parties may enact national legislation that, in the absence of an agreement between the performer and the producer of a phonogram, sets the terms according to which performers and producers of phonograms shall share the single equitable remuneration.
(3) Any Contracting Party may in a notification deposited with the Director General of WIPO, declare that it will apply the provisions of paragraph (1) only in respect of certain uses, or that it will limit their application in some other way, or that it will not apply these provisions at all.
(4) For the purposes of this Article, phonograms made available to the public by wire or wireless means in such a way that members of the public may access them from a place and at a time individually chosen by them shall be considered as if they had been published for commercial purposes.

Article 16: Limitations and exceptions   A5.87

(1) Contracting Parties may, in their national legislation, provide for the same kinds of limitations or exceptions with regard to the protection of performers and producers of phonograms as they provide for, in their national legislation, in connection with the protection of copyright in literary and artistic works.
(2) Contracting Parties shall confine any limitations of or exceptions to rights provided for in this Treaty to certain special cases which do not conflict with a normal exploitation of the performance or phonogram and do not unreasonably prejudice the legitimate interests of the performer or of the producer of the phonogram.

A5.88   *Article 17: Term of protection*

(1) The term of protection to be granted to perfomers under this Treaty shall last, as least, until the end of a period of 50 years computed from the end of the year in which the performance was fixed in a phonogram.

(2) The term of protection to be granted to producers of phonograms under this Treaty shall last, at least, until the end of a period of 50 years computed from the end of the year in which the phonogram was published, or failing such publication within 50 years from fixation of the phonogram, 50 years from the end of the year in which the fixation was made.

A5.89   *Article 18: Obligations concerning technological measures*

Contracting Parties shall provide adequate legal protection and effective legal remedies against the circumvention of effective technological measures that are used by performers or producers of phonograms in connection with the exercise of their rights under this Treaty and that restrict acts, in respect of their performances or phonograms, which are not authorized by the performers or the producers of phonograms concerned or permitted by law.

A5.90   *Article 19: Obligations concerning rights management information*

(1) Contracting Parties shall provide adequate and effective legal remedies against any person knowingly performing any of the following acts knowing, or with respect to civil remedies having reasonable grounds to know, that it will induce, enable, facilitate or conceal an infringement of any right covered by this Treaty:

    (i)   to remove or alter any electronic rights management information without authority;

    (ii) to distribute, import for distribution, broadcast, communicate or make available to the public, without authority, performances, copies of fixed performances or phonograms knowing that electronic rights management information has been removed or altered without authority.

(2) As used in this Article, "rights management information" means information which identifies the performer, the performance of the performer, the producer of the phonogram, the phonogram, the owner of any right in the performance or phonogram, or information about the terms and conditions of use of the performance or phonogram, and any numbers or codes that represent such information, when any of these items of information is attached to a copy of a fixed performance or a phonogram or appears in connection with the communciation or making available of a fixed performance or a phonogram to the public.

A5.91   *Article 20: Formalities*

The enjoyment and exercise of the rights provided for in this Treaty shall not be subject to any formality.

A5.92   *Article 21: Reservations*

Subject to the provisions of Article 15(3), no reservations to this Treaty shall be permitted.

A5.93   *Article 22: Application in time*

(1) Contracting Parties shall apply the provisions of Article 18 of the Berne Convention, *mutatis mutandis*, to the rights of performers and producers of phonograms provided for in this Treaty.

(2) Notwithstanding paragraph (1), a Contracting Party may limit the application

of Article 5 of this Treaty to performances which occurred after the entry into force of this Treaty for that Party.

Article 23: Provisions on enforcement of rights

A5.94

(1) Contracting Parties undertake to adopt, in accordance with their legal systems, the measures necessary to ensure the application of this Treaty.

(2) Contracting Parties shall ensure that enforcement procedures are available under their law so as to permit effective action against any act of infringement of rights covered by this Treaty, including expeditious remedies to prevent infringements and remedies which constitute a deterrent to further infringements.

CHAPTER V: ADMINISTRATIVE AND FINAL CLAUSES

Article 24: Assembly

A5.95

(1)(a) The Contracting Parties shall have an Assembly.

(b) Each Contracting Party shall be represented by one delegate who may be assisted by alternate delegates, advisors and experts.

(c) The expenses of each delegation shall be borne by the Contracting Party that has appointed the delegation. The Assembly may ask WIPO to grant financial assistance to facilitate the participation of delegations of Contracting Parties that are regarded as developing countries in conformity with the established practice of the General Assembly of the United Nations or that are countries in transition to a market economy.

(2)(a) The Assembly shall deal with matters concerning the maintenance and development of this Treaty and the application and operation of this Treaty.

(b) The Assembly shall perform the function allocated to it under Article 26(2) in respect of the admission of certain intergovernmental organizations to become party to this Treaty.

(c) The Assembly shall decide the convocation of any diplomatic conference for the revision of this Treaty and give the necessary instructions to the Director General of WIPO for the preparation of such diplomatic conference.

(3)(a) Each Contracting Party that is a State shall have one vote and shall vote only in its own name.

(b) Any Contracting Party that is an intergovernmental organization may participate in the vote, in place of its Member States, with a number of votes equal to the number of its Member States which are party to this Treaty. No such intergovernmental organization shall participate in the vote if any one of its Member States exercises its right to vote and vice versa.

(4) The Assembly shall meet in ordinary session once every two years upon convocation by the Director General of WIPO.

(5) The Assembly shall establish its own rules of procedure, including the convocation of extraordinary sessions, the requirements of a quorum and, subject to the provisions of this Treaty, the required majority for various kinds of decisions.

Article 25: International Bureau

A5.96

The International Bureau of WIPO shall perform the administrative tasks concerning the Treaty.

Article 26: Eligibility for becoming party to the Treaty

A5.97

(1) Any Member State of WIPO may become party to this Treaty.

(2) The Assembly may decide to admit any intergovernmental organization to become party to this Treaty which declares that it is competent in respect of, and has its own

legislation binding on all its Member States on, matters covered by this Treaty and that it has been duly authorized, in accordance with its internal procedures, to become party to this Treaty.

(3) The European Community, having made the declaration referred to in the preceding paragraph in the Diplomatic Conference that has adopted this Treaty, may become party to this Treaty.

A5.98
Article 27: Rights and obligations under the Treaty

Subject to any specific provisions to the contrary in this Treaty, each Contracting Party shall enjoy all of the rights and assume all of the obligations under this Treaty.

A5.99
Article 28: Signature of the Treaty

This Treaty shall be open for signature until December 31, 1997, by any Member State of WIPO and by the European Community.

A5.100
Article 29: Entry into force of the Treaty

This Treaty shall enter into force three months after 30 instruments of ratification or accession by States have been deposited with the Director General of WIPO.

A5.101
Article 30: Effective date of becoming party to the Treaty

This Treaty shall bind

(i)   the 30 States referred to in Article 29, from the date on which this Treaty has entered into force;
(ii) each other State from the expiration of three months from the date on which the State has deposited its instrument with the Director General of WIPO;
(iii) the European Community, from the expiration of three months after the deposit of its instrument of ratification or accession if such instrument has been deposited after the entry into force of this Treaty according to Article 29, or, three months after the entry into force of this Treaty if such instrument has been deposited before the entry into force of this Treaty;
(iv) any other intergovernmental organization that is admitted to become party to this Treaty, from the expiration of three months after the deposit of its instrument of accession.

A5.102
Article 31: Denunciation of the Treaty

This Treaty may be denounced by any Contracting Party by notification addressed to the Director General of WIPO. Any denunciation shall take effect one year from the date on which the Director General of WIPO received the notification.

A5.103
Article 32: Languages of the Treaty

(1) This Treaty is signed in a single original in English, Arabic, Chinese, French, Russian and Spanish languages, the versions in all these languages being equally authentic.

(2) An official text in any language other than those referred to in paragraph (1) shall be established by the Director General of WIPO on the request of an interested party, after consultation with all the interested parties. For the purposes of this paragraph, "interested party" means any Member State of WIPO whose official language, or one of whose official languages, is involved and the European Community, and any other intergovernmental organization that may become party to this Treaty, if one of its official languages is involved.

Article 33: Depositary   A5.104

The Director General of WIPO is the depositary of this Treaty.

ADDENDUM 1: AGREED STATEMENTS CONCERNING THE WIPO PERFORMANCES AND PHONOGRAMS TREATY
ADOPTED BY THE DIPLOMATIC CONFERENCE ON DECEMBER 20, 1996

Concerning Article 1   A5.105

It is understood that Article 1(2) clarifies the relationship between rights in phonograms under this Treaty and copyright in works embodied in the phonograms. In cases where authorization is needed from both the author of a work embodied in the phonogram and a performer or producer owning rights in the phonogram, the need for the authorization of the author does not cease to exist because the authorization of the performer or producer is also required, and vice versa.

It is further understood that nothing in Article 1(2) precludes a Contracting Party from providing exclusive rights to a performer or producer of phonograms beyond those required to be provided under this Treaty.

Concerning Article 2(b)

It is understood that the definition of phonogram provided in Article 2(b) does not suggest that rights in the phonogram are in any way affected through their incorporation into a cinematographic or other audiovisual work.

Concerning Articles 2(e), 8, 9, 12 and 13

As used in these Articles, the expressions "copies" and "original and copies", being subject to the right of distribution and the right of rental under the said Articles, refer exclusively to fixed copies that can be put into circulation as tangible objects.

Concerning Article 3

It is understood that the reference in Articles 5(a) and 16(a)(iv) of the Rome Convention to "national of another Contracting State" will, when applied to this Treaty, mean, in regard to an intergovernmental organization that is a Contracting Party to this Treaty, a national of one of the countries that is a member of that organization.

Concerning Article 3(2)

For the application of Article 3(2), it is understood that fixation means the finalization of the master tape ("bandemère").

Concerning Articles 7, 11 and 16

The reproduction right, as set out in Articles 7 and 11, and the exceptions permitted thereunder through Article 16, fully apply in the digital environment, in particular to the use of performances and phonograms in digital form. It is udnerstood that the storage of a protected performance or phonogram in digital form in an electronic medium constitutes a reproduction within the meaning of these Articles.

Concerning Article 15

It is understood that Article 15 does not represent a complete resolution of the level of rights of broadcasting and communication to the public that should be enjoyed by performers and phonogram producers in the digital age. Delegations were unable to achieve consensus on differing proposals for aspects of exclusivity to be provided in certain circumstances or for rights to be provided without the possibility of reservations, and have therefore left the issue to future resolution.

Concerning Article 15

It is understood that Article 15 does not prevent the granting of the right conferred by this Article to performers of folklore and producers of phonograms recording folklore where such phonograms have been published for commercial gain.

Concerning Article 16

The agreed statement concerning Article 10 (on Limitations and Exceptions) of the WIPO Copyright Treaty is applicable *mutatis mutandis* also at Article 16 (on Limitations and Exceptions) of the WIPO Performances and Phonograms Treaty.

Concerning Article 19

The agreed statement concerning Article 12 (on Obligations Concerning Rights Management Information) of the WIPO Copyright Treaty is applicable *mutatis mutandis* also to Article 19 (on Obligations Concerning Rights Management Information) of the WIPO Performances and Phonograms Treaty.

ADDENDUM 2: RESOLUTION CONCERNING AUDIOVISUAL PERFORMANCES
ADOPTED BY THE DIPLOMATIC CONFERENCE ON DECEMBER 20, 1996

A5.106 The Delegations participating in the Diplomatic Conference on Certain Copyright and Neighboring Rights Questions in Geneva,

Noting that the development of technologies will allow for a rapid growth of audiovisual services and that this will increase the opportunities for performing artists to exploit their audiovisual performances that will be transmitted by these services;

Recognizing the great importance of ensuring an adequate level of protection for these performances, in particular when they are exploited in the new digital environment, and that sound and audiovisual performances are increasingly related;

Stressing the urgent need to agree on new norms for the adequate legal international protection of audiovisual performances;

Regretting that, in spite of the efforts of most Delegations, the WIPO Performances and Phonograms Treaty does not cover the rights of performers in the audiovisual fixations of their performance;

Call for the convocation of an extraordinary session of the competent WIPO Governing Bodies during the first quarter of 1997 to decide on the schedule of the preparatory work on a protocol to the WIPO Performances and Phonograms Treaty, concerning audiovisual performances, with a view to the adoption of such a protocol not later than in 1998.

APPENDIX 5D

TREATY OF ROME (EXTRACTS)

From Part Two ("Foundation of the Community"), Title 1 ("Free movement of goods"), Chapter 2 ("Elimination of Quantitative Restrictions between Member States")

Article 6

A5.107

Within the scope of application of this Treaty, and without prejudice to any special provisions contained therein, any discrimination on the grounds of nationality shall be prohibited.

The Council, acting in accordance with the procedure referred to in Article 189c, may adopt rules designed to prohibit such discrimination.

Article 30

A5.108

Quantitative restrictions on imports and all measures having equivalent effect shall, without prejudice to the following provisions, be prohibited between Member States.

Article 34

A5.109

1. Quantitative restrictions on exports, and all measures having equivalent effect, shall be prohibited between Member States.
2. Member States shall, by the end of the first stage at the latest, abolish all quantitative restrictions on exports and any measures having equivalent effect which are in existence when this Treaty enters into force.

Article 36

A5.110

The provisions of Articles 30 to 34 shall not preclude prohibitions or restrictions on imports, exports or goods in transit justified on grounds of public morality, public policy or public security; the protection of health and life of humans, animals or plants; the protection of national treasures possessing artistic, historic or archaeological value; or the protection of industrial and commercial property. Such prohibitions or restrictions shall not, however, constitute a means of arbitrary discrimination or a disguised restriction on trade between Member States.

From Part Three ("Policy of the Community"), Title 1 ("Common Rules"), Chapter 1 ("Rules on Competition")

Article 85

A5.111

1. The following shall be prohibited as incompatible with the common market: all agreements between undertakings, decision by associations of undertakings and concerted practices which may affect trade between Member States and which have as their object or effect the prevention, restriction or distortion of competition within the common market, and in particular those which:
   (a) directly or indirectly fix purchase or selling prices or any other trading conditions;
   (b) limit or control production, markets, technical development, or investment;

(c) share markets or sources of supply;
(d) apply dissimilar conditions to equivalent transactions with other trading parties, thereby placing them at a competitive disadvantage;
(e) make the conclusion of contracts subject to acceptance by the other parties of supplementary obligations which, by their nature or according to commercial usage, have no connection with the subject of such contracts.

2. Any agreements or decisions prohibited pursuant to this Article shall be automatically void.

3. The provision of paragraph 2 may, however, be declared inapplicable in the case of:

— any agreement or category of agreements between undertakings;
— any decision or category of decisions by associations of undertakings;
— any concerted practice or category of concerted practices;

which contributes to improving the production or distribution of goods or to promoting technical or economic progress, while allowing consumers a fair share of the resulting benefit, and which does not:

(a) impose on the undertakings concerned restrictions which are not indispensable to the attainment of these objectives;
(b) afford such undertakings the possibility of eliminating competition in respect of a substantial part of the products in question.

A5.112   *Article 86*

Any abuse by one or more undertakings of a dominant position within the common market or in a substantial part of it shall be prohibited as incompatible with the common market in so far as it may affect trade between Member States. Such abuse may, in particular, consist in:

(a) directly or indirectly imposing unfair purchase or selling prices or other unfair trading conditions;
(b) limiting production, markets or technical development to the prejudice of consumers;
(c) applying dissimilar conditions to equivalent transactions with other trading parties, thereby placing them at a competitive disadvantage;
(d) making the conclusion of contracts subject to acceptance by the other parties of supplementary obligations which, by their nature or according to commercial usage, have no connection with the subject of such contracts.

APPENDIX 5E

EUROPEAN ECONOMIC AREA AGREEMENT
(EXTRACTS)

PART ONE: OBJECTIVES AND PRINCIPLES

Article 1   A5.113

1. The aim of this Agreement of association is to promote a continuous and balanced strengthening of trade and economic relations between the Contracting Parties with equal conditions of competition, and the respect of the same rules, with a view to creating a homogeneous European Economic Area, hereinafter referred to as the EEA.
2. In order to attain the objectives set out in paragraph 1, the association shall entail in accordance with the provisions of this Agreement:

- (a) the free movement of goods;
- (b) the free movement of persons;
- (c) the free movement of services;
- (d) the free movement of capital;
- (e) the setting up of a system ensuring that competition is not distorted and that the rules thereon are equally respected; as well as
- (f) closer co-operation in other fields, such as research and development, the environment, education and social policy.

PROTOCOL 28: ON INTELLECTUAL PROPERTY

Article 1: Substance of protection   A5.114

1. For the purposes of this Protocol, the term "intellectual property" shall include the protection of industrial and commercial property as covered by Article 13 of the Agreement.
2. Without prejudice to the provisions of this Protocol and of Annex XVII, the Contracting Parties shall upon the entry into force of the Agreement adjust their legislation on intellectual property so as to make it compatible with the principles of free circulation of goods and services and with the level of protection of intellectual property attained in Community law, including the level of enforcement of those rights.
3. Subject to the procedural provisions of the Agreement and without prejudice to the provisions of this Protocol and of Annex XVII, the EFTA States will adjust, upon request and after consultation between the Contracting Parties, their legislation on intellectual property in order to reach at least the level of protection of intellectual property prevailing in the Community upon signature of the Agreement.

Article 2: Exhaustion of rights   A5.115

1. To the extent that exhaustion is dealt with in Community measures or jurisprudence, the Contracting Parties shall provide for such exhaustion of intellectual property rights as laid down in Community law. Without prejudice to future developments of case law, this provision shall be interpreted in accordance with the meaning established in the relevant rulings of the Court of Justice of the European Communities given prior to the signature of the Agreement.

2. As regards patent rights, this provision shall take effect at the latest one year after the entry into force of the Agreement.

A5.116 *Article 5: International conventions*

1. The Contracting Parties shall undertake to obtain their adherence before January 1, 1995 to the following multilateral conventions on industrial, intellectual and commercial property:

  (a) Paris Convention for the Protection of Industrial Property (Stockholm Act, 1967);
  (b) Berne Convention for the Protection of Literary and Artistic Works (Paris Act, 1971);
  (c) International Convention for the Protection of Performers, Producers of Phonograms and Broadcasting Organizations (Rome 1961);
  (d) Protocol relating to the Madrid Agreement concerning the international Registration of Marks (Madrid 1989);
  (e) Nice Agreement concerning the International Classification of Goods and Services for the purpose of the Registration of Marks (Geneva 1977, amended 1979);
  (f) Budapest Treaty on the International Recognition of the Deposit of Micro-organisms for the purposes of Patent Procedure (1980);
  (g) Patent Co-operation Treaty (1984).

2. For the adherence of Finland, Ireland and Norway to the Protocol relating to the Madrid Agreement the date mentioned in paragraph 1 shall be replaced by January 1, 1996 and, for Iceland, January 1, 1997, respectively.

3. Upon entry into force of this Protocol, the Contracting Parties shall comply in their internal legislation with the substantive provisions of the Conventions listed in paragraph 1(a) to (c). However, Ireland shall comply in its internal legislation with the substantive provisions of the Berne Convention by January 1, 1995.

Index